MAGAZINE PUBLISHING

A RESEARCHERS OF THE

1930s who studied mass

ts saw the media audienc

less blob, a huge ma

d undifferentiated nob

n the 1970s said it was ti

at these people as indivi

hat motivated them and

nedia scholars have studie

n Americans use their m

cations they receive fro

MAGAZINE PUBLISHING

Sammye Johnson
Trinity University

Patricia Prijatel
Drake University

NTC College Division
NTC/Contemporary Publishing Group
Lincolnwood, Illinois USA

Sponsoring Editor: Marisa L. L'Heureux
Editor: Lisa A. De Mol
Art Director: Ophelia Chambliss
Production Coordinator: Denise Duffy Fieldman

ISBN (student text): 0-8442-3356-0
ISBN (instructor's manual): 0-8442-3357-9

Acknowledgements begin on page 347, which is to be considered an extension of this copyright page.

Published by NTC College Publishing,
a division of NTC/Contemporary Publishing Group, Inc.,
4255 West Touhy Avenue,
Lincolnwood (Chicago), Illinois 60646-1975 U.S.A.

Manufactured in the United States of America.

Library of Congress Cataloging-in-Publication Data

Johnson, Sammye, 1946–
Magazine publishing / Patricia Prijatel, Sammye Johnson.
p. cm.
Includes bibliographical reference and index.
ISBN 0-8442-3356-0
1. Periodicals, Publishing of—United States. I. Prijatel,
Patricia, 1945– . II. Title
Z479.J58 1999
070.5'72'0973—dc21 99-21757
CIP

90 VL 0 9 8 7 6 5 4 3 2 1

CONTENTS

CHAPTER 

The Magazine as a Historical Document: *Trends over Time* 43

CHAPTER 

The Magazine as a Social Barometer: *Political and Cultural Interaction* 75

PART TWO

The Magazine's Blueprint 105

CHAPTER 

Magazine Concepts: *Formulas for Success* 107

CHAPTER 

Magazine Designs: *Creating the Look* 213

CHAPTER 

Magazine Production: *Manufacturing Issues* 249

CHAPTER 11

Magazine Legalities: *Understanding the Law* 269

CHAPTER 

PREFACE

The relationship Americans enjoy with their magazines is one of the most intimate, yet least understood, aspects of our culture. Since the mid-1700s, the magazine has played a role in shaping what individuals think and how they respond to the world around them. Magazines help us understand ourselves, live more fully, and vicariously enjoy different lifestyles. The result: We are what we read.

We believe this book reflects the spirit and spunk of the American magazine—and the industry that supports it. For three centuries, the magazine has endured as the medium for thoughtful analysis, perspective, context, information, and sheer fun. The magazine was an established national medium before the nation itself was established. In the midst of war, peace, or apathy, the magazine has thrived. During depressed, recessed, and inflated economies, the magazine has endured. It has adapted to change in mores, morals, and the marketplace. Unlike many national trends, the magazine is not only here today, but it will be here tomorrow.

A comprehensive overview of the magazine industry, this book guides readers through the dynamic magazine world from concept to finished product, including the historical context and trends that affect the industry and the broad range of topics, issues, and personalities involved. The book focuses on how magazines use information to build relationships with specific audiences to meet emotional, social, economic, and intellectual needs. It helps readers understand, analyze, and appreciate new dimensions of the magazine, as well as plan and implement managerial and publishing strategies. Emphasizing a pragmatic approach to the theories and principles of magazine publishing, the book focuses on why we do what we do in the magazine field rather than how to do it. It uses vignettes and case histories of selected magazines and insights from publishers and editors to demonstrate in detail the extraordinary creativity and energy of the field.

Through the nearly three years it took us to finish the book, the industry has continued to evolve. Several of the editors we quoted in the text changed jobs; some of the magazines died. Nevertheless, we felt it important to include real people and real examples so this book not only reflects the vitality of the industry, but it also reads with the energy expected of magazine writing. It is a picture of a moment in time. Even though some of the names on the mastheads may now be different and the mastheads themselves no longer in existence, the message remains valuable and timely. We have, of course, made the information as up-to-date as possible, a tricky task in an industry that changes from second to second.

We used personal interviews when possible to get up-to-the-minute and on-the-spot information. In those cases, we did not use endnotes. In other instances, we have used the industry magazine, *Folio:*, as well as national and local newspapers, other trade magazines, industry seminars, and academic conferences as our sources; we have referenced these. Teachers and students alike can gain a great deal by searching through our original sources. We have been able to include only a taste of the wisdom that exists in the magazine field.

In this book, we define *magazine* to include consumer titles as well as the business press, organizational and association publications, public relations magazines, imprint and custom publishing, and the less sophisticated 'zines. We have defined the Internet as a valuable resource for magazines, especially in terms of their connection with their audiences, but have not attempted to analyze and explain publications created entirely on the Internet; we consider those a separate medium, worthy of their own book. In all instances, we have tried to explain the unique nature of magazines.

Organization

We have organized the book into three units and 12 chapters. In addition, we have included four essays from top magazine professionals—Robin Morgan, Jean LemMon, Jay Walljasper, and James Autry—describing specific industry issues within the context of their publications.

Part 1, "The Enduring Medium," provides an introduction to the field and gives a historical and social context. Chapter 1, "The Magazine as a Storehouse," defines the medium, explains magazine types, and offers a picture of the size and scope of the industry. Chapter 2, "The Magazine as a Marketplace," describes the role of advertising and marketing with a historical as well as contemporary perspective. Chapter 3, "The Magazine as a Historical Document," examines trends over time, tracing the development of the magazine through three centuries of American history. Chapter 4, "The Magazine as a Social Barometer," asks whether magazines lead or follow social change and focuses on their political and cultural impact.

Part 2, "The Magazine's Blueprint," takes a pragmatic approach to planning and organizing a magazine and its staff. Chapter 5, "Magazine Concepts," explores proven formulas for success as an answer to why some magazines fail and others thrive. Chapter 6, "Magazine Business Plans," takes a hands-on approach to how magazines make and lose money; it offers an outline for determining a magazine's budget and bottom line. Chapter 7, "Magazine Structures," introduces the business and creative staffs—the people who make the magazine work—and provides job descriptions and organizational charts.

Part 3, "The Magazine's Content," explores editorial, design, production, legal and ethical issues. Chapter 8, "Magazine Editorial," analyzes the variety of magazine articles written today as a way of recognizing quality magazine editorial content. Chapter 9, "Magazine Designs," looks at the package of words, graphics, and illustrations that entice and satisfy readers—turning the casual browser into the committed subscriber. Chapter 10, "Magazine Production," introduces methods of planning for and managing the manufacture of the printed product. Chapter 11, "Magazine Legalities," makes sense of the legal ramifications of creative and business decisions. Chapter 12, "Magazines for the Twenty-First Century," considers the ethical implications of the magazine's role in American culture and commerce.

Several features add to the breadth and depth of material presented in the text. Each chapter includes both sidebars and "Research in Briefs." The "Research in Briefs" are a synopsis of research by various scholars in the field and illustrate the broad reach of magazines and their influence. The sidebars highlight a particular aspect of magazine publishing. And in the appendix, "Magazine Voices," top professionals give us food for thought on such topics as ad-free magazines, the magazine's influence on the American family, alternative publications, and celebrity journalism.

Acknowledgments

Finally, we want to thank all those who offered us information, guidance, and support: Silvey Barge and Ginger Bassett, *Better Homes and Gardens*; Mary Kay Baumann and Will Hopkins, Hopkins/Baumann; James Butler, *Fly Rod & Reel*; Karen Chiovaro, Meredith Corporation; Camerin Courtney, *Today's Christian Woman*; Jim English, *Adweek*; Vicki Feinmel, Hachette Filipacchi Magazines; Will Guilliams, *Poz*; Nigel Holmes, Information Graphic Designer; Gordon T. Hughes, American Business Press; Debbie Humphreys, American Business Press; Marlene Kahan, American Society of Magazine Editors; Phyllis Pollak Katz, *Archaeology*; Larry Kaufman, Magazine Publishers of America; William T. Kerr, Meredith Corporation; Charles Lake, Hachette Filipacchi Magazines; Jean LemMon, *Better Homes and Gardens*; Christopher Little, Meredith Corporation; Jesse Loving, *Poz*; Lany W. McDonald, Time Inc.; Michael Mettler, *Car Stereo Review*; Mark Miller, Hearst Magazines; Peter Mitchel, Diversified Publications; Elizabeth Muhler, Walgreens; Phyllis Reed, Business Press Educational Foundation; Andrew Rhodes, American Society of Magazine Editors; Jim Roberts, Miller-Freeman; Richard Sasso, *Scientific American*; Norbert Schumacher, McGraw-Hill; Amy Seirer, Rodale Press; David Speer, Meredith Corporation; Gail Stilwill, Meredith Corporation; Laura Sutcliffe, Hachette Filipacchi Magazines; Jill Waage, Better Homes and Gardens *Window and Wall Ideas*; and Brad Waggoner, R. R. Donnelley.

Because we felt we did not have the detailed grasp of the law needed to write a definitive chapter on the subject, we enlisted the aid of our colleague and friend, Michael Perkins, to write Chapter 11, "Magazine Legalities." Perkins, associate dean of the School of Journalism and Mass Communication at Drake University, is a journalism professor as well as a lawyer. His perspective offers both insight and authority.

We offer a huge thanks to all the students who read this manuscript in its various incarnations. We also offer many thanks to the reviewers from throughout the country who gave us advice and direction: David Abrahamson, Northwestern University; Sharon M. W. Bass, University of Kansas; Nancy Brendlinger, Bowling Green State University; Margaret Davidson, University of Wisconsin–Oshkosh; Scott Fosdick, Columbia College; Harvey Gotliffe, San Jose State University; Gerald Grow, Florida A&M University; Cathy Johnson, Evangel College; Don Ranly, University of Missouri; Barbara Straus Reed, Rutgers University; David Sumner, Ball State University; Jay Walljasper, *Utne Reader*; and Thomas H. Wheeler, University of Oregon. Our thanks as well to Marcia Prior-Miller, Iowa State University, for her help at the beginning of this project.

Our colleagues at Drake University and at Trinity University have been supportive and helpful in a variety of ways. Our thanks to the following people from Drake University: Barry Foskit, Nicholas Fonseca, Lee Jolliffe, Janet Hill Keefer, Henry Milam, Michael Perkins, David Wright, and Anu Varma. And thanks to the following people from Trinity University: Robert O. Blanchard, James Bynum, Ronald K. Calgaard, William G. Christ, Delia Rios, Michael Hoefges, Edward C. Roy, Scott Sowards, and William O. Walker Jr.

We thank our editors, Lisa A. De Mol and Marisa L. L'Heureux, for their commitment to this book and for their time and attention in shepherding it along.

And, finally, to our family and friends without whom we could not have made this journey, our deepest thanks: Nancy Jay; Joe, Ellen, and Joshua Kucera; Sam and Poppy Malosky; Ed and Gwyn Prijatel; John and Dana Prijatel; Phyllis Smith; Gail Stilwill; Kathleen Wilhite; Katherine West; and last, but never least, Marty West.

Sammye Johnson
Patricia Prijatel

FOREWORD

When I was asked to write the foreword to this book, I was pleased and honored. It is, to my knowledge, the first and only time such a comprehensive overview of magazine publishing has been compiled. While it is written for graduate and undergraduate magazine students, I believe it will have strong appeal for professionals in the field as well. In fact, it will serve as a valuable resource for anyone wanting to learn about magazine publishing.

The book is right on target. Magazine professors Patricia Prijatel and Sammye Johnson have conducted considerable research and interviewed a broad spectrum of industry professionals to put together this solid analysis of how magazines are published. Their overview of the complex, complicated, and fascinating magazine publishing industry covers all components, from the editorial to the business side. Their book is an important contribution and will be a valuable resource for current and future magazine students—those who will design, edit, and manage magazines in the future.

The book is timely. The future for magazines is strong and viable. Despite the fact that some Cassandras continue to predict the death of print in an "Internet Age," more and more magazines continue to be introduced to an enthusiastic public. And a good many, though certainly not all, are successful.

The hard lesson is that if a magazine is to succeed it must be continuously focused on the needs and interests of its readers. It must be well written, creatively designed, carefully managed, and thoroughly prepared to compete in an increasingly tough marketplace.

A truly successful magazine must have one thing more—a heart. Its makers must have a real passion for their subject matter and the intellectual energy to convey their knowledge and passion to readers. Good magazines have the ability—as no other medium does—to create a sense of intimacy and friendliness. If there is a disconnect between a magazine and its readers, the magazine is to blame for losing touch, for not listening to its readers.

I am very enthused about the future of magazines, about the industry that produces them, and about the contributions that they make to our society. Our industry has undergone substantial change. Clearly, more changes are on the way. Those changes will have a significant impact but will, for the most part, make magazines and the companies that publish them stronger. Here are a few of the major challenges and opportunities I believe are in store for our industry:

- **Demographic Change.** The magazine industry will have to determine how to deal with the challenges and opportunities presented by changing demographics, particularly the aging of the baby boomers and greatly increased Hispanic and Asian-American populations. In the next 20 years, baby boomers and teenagers will rule the marketplace. Generation X will have relatively less influence as consumers.
- **Increased Power of Branding.** The most successful magazines will be those who have—and build on—their strong brand name. Dramatic growth can come from spin-off magazines, books, television programming, licensing, and the Internet. But these brand extensions must be appropriate for the brand and be able to add to its strength. Magazines that just peddle their name to the highest bidders will lose the strength and credibility of their brands.
- **Continued Evolution of Visuals.** The heart of any good magazine is in its editorial content, but there is a strong and growing emphasis on design, on how the magazine looks. Television and the whole world of new media have strongly influenced this trend. The result: almost all mass magazines will be packaged

to feature shorter material and more and stronger visuals.

Today's magazine editors are packagers of information, not just "writers" or "editors." With an audience that measures time in nanoseconds, journalists must be at ease using both words and graphics with impact.

- **Niches and More Niches.** "Conspicuous cultivation," to borrow a phrase from trend researcher Madelyn Hochstein, is the desire to feel special by knowing a great deal about a fairly arcane subject. We will see more magazines offer this conspicuous cultivation by focusing on subjects that are of interest to specialized groups of readers. Entrepreneurial individuals still want to start their own magazine and magazine companies still want to start additional magazines because they believe there is a subject waiting to be explored or an attitude waiting to be reflected in a new publication.
- **Marketing in Addition to Advertising.** The magazine industry will have to manage the advertising business cycle. But since magazines, by their nature, provide targeted marketing for advertisers and targeted content delivery for consumers, the industry will remain strong.

  The relationships magazines have with their advertisers will continue to change as they work together to create cross-marketing promotions and programs. Editors will continue to see themselves as key to marketing the brand as well as editing the magazine.
- **New Media Opportunities.** Magazines will benefit from, rather than be threatened by, the proliferation of video options such as cable networks, and by the greatly increased use of the Internet. In fact, the Internet may well prove to be one of the best things that has ever happened to magazines. It provides a means of easy, direct personal contact between the magazine and the reader—an ideal two-way "conversation."

  The Internet also provides an additional service to magazine advertisers, bringing with it additional revenue opportunities. And it offers a very inexpensive source of potential new subscribers, and may, in time, offer an inexpensive means of billing and renewing a large number of subscribers.

Magazines continue to flex their muscles, even in this age of high tech. They have a place in our future; a leadership role in the ever-expanding communications arena; a world to describe; generations to educate and entertain. This book will help prepare magazine makers of the future for the challenging world of magazine publishing.

William T. Kerr
Chairman and CEO
Meredith Corporation

PART ONE

The Enduring Medium

CHAPTER 1

The Magazine as a Storehouse

The Scope of the Medium

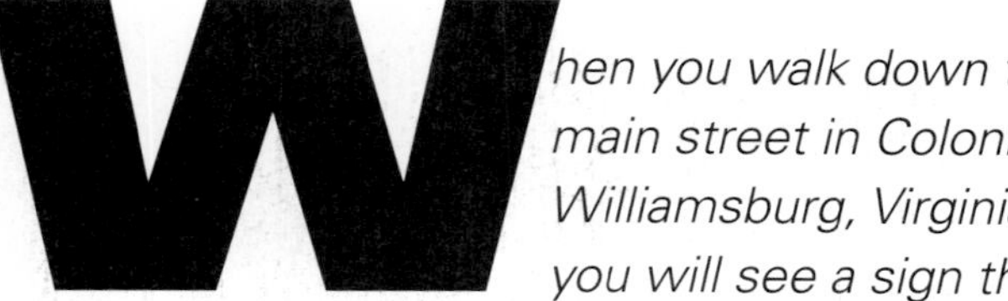

hen you walk down the main street in Colonial Williamsburg, Virginia, you will see a sign that points the way to a "Magazine." Follow the directions on the sign and you will end up at a brick building that once housed ammunition. Today, we would call that building a storehouse. 📖 In the 1800s, almost two centuries after Williamsburg was founded, American children read a magazine named Merry's Museum. *Started in 1841, the publication was later edited by Louisa May Alcott, author of* Little Women. *Even though it resembles what we would today call a magazine, it—like some other publications of the time—was called a museum. What is one definition of museum? Storehouse. 📖 Magazines in America have taken a variety of shapes and have been given a variety of names. In the 1800s, some were even called caskets, a name now limited to a less pleasant and more permanent form of storage. 📖 All the names and all the forms had one thing in common: the concept of storage. The word* magazine, *in fact, comes from the Arabic* makhazin, *which means warehouse or storehouse. Today, magazines no longer house gunshot and cannonballs; instead they house ideas, opinions, and information. 📖 Magazines have been the medium of our country's brightest minds and have provided a forum for some of our most important political, social, and cultural discussions. In recent years, however, magazine professionals as well as critics outside the industry have bemoaned some magazines' tendencies toward tabloidization, celebrity journalism, and an overall appeal to our basest instincts.*

Poets, novelists, essayists, and journalists have used magazines to reach the heart and soul of America. Our best American writers have been published in magazines: Annie Dillard, William Faulkner, Ernest Hemingway, Toni Morrison, Edgar Allan Poe, and scores of others who have penned our classics and have won Pulitzer and Nobel Prizes.

Photographers have used magazines to engage and enlarge the American consciousness by showing us images of ourselves that are both raw and wonderful. Mathew Brady photographed the Civil War for *Harper's Weekly*, Margaret Bourke-White captured World War II on film for *Life*, and Annie Leibovitz gave us a lasting Vietnam Era icon: Yoko Ono and John Lennon nude on the cover of *Rolling Stone*.

Artists have used magazines to experiment with techniques and styles and to show us their vision of the world. Winslow Homer created stark black-and-white engravings of life in New York City in the 1870s for *Harper's Weekly;* six decades later, Salvador Dali colorfully illustrated *Vogue* covers of the 1930s. Magazines helped refine cartoons as a medium of expression, with Charles Addams giving birth to his delightfully ghoulish creation, the Addams Family, on the pages of *The New Yorker*. Designers, from the legendary *Harper's Bazaar* art director Alexey Brodovitch to the contemporary creators of *Wired* and *Bikini*, also have used magazines to blend words and pictures to catch the eye and capture the spirit.

On a less impressive note, magazines have given us *Playboy* Playmates and made Demi Moore a household name for modeling nude and pregnant on the cover of *Vanity Fair*. Magazines have even been sued for matching hit men with husbands who want to kill their wives, as happened in the classified ad section of *Soldier of Fortune*.[1] William T. Kerr, chief executive officer of Meredith Corporation, one of the world's largest magazine publishers, sees a troubling trend toward "tabloidization" in some contemporary magazines. This, he says, may be a "broader societal trend" characterized by "trashy talk shows on television, the success of the supermarket tabloids, the rise of *People*—a 'soft-tabloid'—and the creeping tabloid-like content into many magazines." This trend emphasizes sensationalism and caters to the lowest levels of readers' intelligence.

Magazines, however, remain a vibrant and healthy medium, serving the rabble, the rebel, and the responsible citizen. Magazines, in a way, are a voice of the country. They are published by huge media conglomerates and tiny publishing houses, by trade and religious groups, by professional associations, and by academics. They are created for thinkers, laborers, activists, and couch potatoes. Some are huge financial machines; others don't make a dime. Some need two city blocks to staff their offices; others need nothing more than a kitchen table. No other medium is as diverse; nor does any other medium have such a rich past and limitless future.

"It's the children, darling—back from camp."

AUGUST 30, 1947: Cartoonist Charles Addams found fertile ground in *The New Yorker* for his family of ghouls.

MAGAZINES AND THE MEDIA MIX

Developing an operational definition of the word *magazine* has kept scholars twitching and arguing, looking for commonality in a medium that's as individualistic as the Americans it serves. We can work toward a definition of magazines by comparing them with other media. Magazines exist in both print and broadcast format. The broadcast programs "60 Minutes," "20/20," and "Dateline" all call themselves magazines. There's good reason for this name: These shows follow basic magazine guidelines. If we look at how these programs differ from their televised news counterparts, we get an idea why broadcasters have usurped the term *magazine.*

Depth and Timelessness

A magazine has more in-depth coverage than its news counterpart, and it deals with less timely information, often on trends and issues. It takes what we generally call a feature, rather than a hard news, approach. That is, its articles go beyond the news. If an earthquake hits Los Angeles, the news media will give the current information on the size and effect of the quake. The magazine—or the broadcast magazine show—will give background information and analysis on, perhaps, the history of quakes in California, the geological formations that cause them, and architectural developments that might make them less deadly. *The Los Angeles Times* will be on top of the day-to-day story of the quake; *Los Angeles Magazine* will profile families who live on the fault line.

In 1743, Alexander Pope described magazines as "upstart collections in prose and verse . . . where Dulness assumes all the various shapes of Folly to draw in and cajole the rabble."

Specialization of Content and Audience

Magazines are highly specialized in content and in audience. Want sports information? Try a sports magazine. There are general titles (*Sports Illustrated* and *The Sporting News*), but the field narrows according to types of sport (*Golf Illustrated* and *Quarter Horse Journal*), then narrows further by gender (*Golf for Women*) and region (*North Texas Golfer*).

By comparison, network television has both a broad audience and broad content. Cable television competes with its network counterpart in much the same way magazines do: It is more specialized, and this specialization helps cable TV compete head-on with magazines in many ways. Cable television viewers, like magazine readers, appreciate information that seems aimed directly at their needs and interests.

RESEARCH IN BRIEF

Magazine Uses and Gratifications

The American media consumer at the turn of the twenty-first century is a savvy individual. She knows what she expects from the various media, and she heads for a specific medium to fill a specific need.

Researchers of the 1920s and 1930s who studied mass media effects saw the media audience as a faceless blob, a huge mass of unnamed and undifferentiated nobodies. Researchers in the 1970s said it was time to stop and look at these people as individuals, to question what motivated them and why. In response, media scholars have studied the way in which Americans use their media and the gratifications they receive from this use. Called, not surprisingly, uses and gratifications theory, this approach encourages researchers to focus not on the medium, but on the user of that medium. Researchers have suggested that contemporary consumers use media for five needs: cognitive, affective, personal, social, and tension release.[1]

COGNITIVE

Magazines help us acquire information, knowledge, and understanding. They inform us on issues and events that might affect us; they tell us what's going on in our world and what that means to us. *Newsweek* and *Time* give us the background on methods of cloning animals and analyze the possibilities and problems of human cloning. *RN* magazine helps nurses assess changes in health care. *Tricycle* explains how Buddhism is influencing mainstream America.

AFFECTIVE

We use magazines to seek emotional, pleasurable, or aesthetic experiences. Will we ever be able to afford that house in *Architectural Digest*? Maybe not, but we can dream. Magazines are great dream machines, and readers know that, using magazines for vicarious experiences. We scan fashion magazines for trends we may never adopt, but which are fun to imagine. We read *Print* to see the beauty that graphic designers are creating, and to aspire to that level of creativity ourselves. We look at *Gourmet* and think that, someday, we might make that kiwi torte on the cover. We read *Travel & Leisure* and lose ourselves in a mythical vacation to the Greek isles.

PERSONAL

Magazines can help us live our lives as sane individuals, strengthening our credibility, confidence, stability, and status. They reinforce our values, provide us with psychological reassurance and self-understanding, and give us a chance to explore reality. *Glamour* tells us it's okay to hate those fashionable shoes; *Self* gives us healthy ways to look and feel better; *Esquire* provides us with fashion rules and the courage to break them; *Essence* reminds us we are not alone in our world view.

SOCIAL

We use the media to help us fit in with our society. Researchers call this function the "social utility of information." You, too, can be a brilliant conversationalist, if you read enough. You can use that article on insomnia in *Health* to offer advice to the boss's wife with whom you thought you had nothing in common. That article you read in *The Atlantic Monthly* on the cause of middle America's cynicism might even help you through that political science test.

TENSION RELEASE

Readers often head for magazines for escape and diversion. We read *Entertainment Weekly, People,* and *Soap Opera Digest* to get away from our own mundane world and live for a while in the world of the stars, to peek for a moment into the bedrooms and boardrooms of the glamorous and the powerful. Sure, you're up to your ears in student loans and your shortsighted girlfriend just dumped you. But the cast of "Baywatch" is featured in *TV Guide*. That will take your mind off your problems for a while. 📖

[1] Several researchers were responsible for developing a list of media uses, including Elihu Katz, Jack McLeod, Denis McQuail, Jay G. Blumler, Michael Gurevitch, and H. Haas. The list used was taken from Katz, Gurevitch and Haas, "On the Use of the Mass Media for Important Things," *American Sociological Review*, 38 (1973): 164–81.

A newspaper covers topics of general interest for a specific geographic area. Many newspapers have strong features sections, which increasingly contain specialized information on, for example, wedding planning, home remodeling, and parenting. These, however, are a supplement to the newspaper's primary goal of presenting timely information. Readers depend on the newspaper for day-to-day news, not for the specialized information in these sections. If you want to build a house, you will head to the newsstand for home building magazines; you won't wait for the Friday feature in the newspaper, although you will enjoy reading it when it comes. In 1982, the Magazine Publishers of America (MPA) offered an expansion of this point:

A magazine is like no other medium for the simple reason that it isn't a daily routine. Depending on its scope and its point of view, it may be published once every week, once every two weeks, or once every three months. Its subject matter may be the world at large, but more often, it's a study in depth of a vital part of someone's world—an art, a science, a sport, or a certain way of looking at the world for a certain man, a certain woman, a certain child.[2]

Audience and content work in tandem: All content must be geared to the magazine's specific audience. Articles or photos that miss the mark in terms of audience are ineffective, no matter how brilliantly composed and technically elegant they might be. An article on menopause has no place in *Mademoiselle*, even if the information is ground-breaking. Likewise, articles on great bars to visit during spring break won't cut it in *Mature Outlook*.

Magazine editors see their readers as part of a community; readers of a successful publication have a sense of ownership of *their* magazine. Any editor who changes a popular feature has to steel herself for the inevitable letters asking, "What have you done to *my* magazine?"

Many editors run ideas by a panel of readers before an article is even written. *Wood* magazine, for example, has instituted a policy of asking a few hundred readers what they think of article titles. *Better Homes and Gardens* staff members call 200 of the magazine's subscribers, ask them to bring the magazine to the telephone, and respond to questions about certain aspects of the publication. Have they read a particular article? Did they use that article in some way? *Better Homes and Gardens* editor-in-chief Jean LemMon strives to present articles and photography that engage the audience emotionally. Researchers call readers to find out when and how the magazine succeeds in this goal and often talk to subscribers one-on-one to avoid the problem of group dynamics influencing results. When *Country Home* began considering a repositioning—redefining the magazine's look and focus—in 1996, staff members met with subscribers individually; in preparation, the magazine sent readers a disposable camera and asked them to take pictures of what "country" meant to them.

In other cases, the readers are already enthusiastic about the content—they have written it. *A Taste of Home* contains recipes and cooking ideas submitted by readers. The magazine's tagline: "The Magazine Edited by a Thousand Country Cooks."

A magazine's audience is well-defined and can be national, international, regional, or local.

WELL-DEFINED. Magazines do not try to be all things to all people. Magazine editors target a precise niche—a narrowly defined focus—and study the characteristics of the individuals in that niche. They then aim the magazine directly at those individuals. These characteristics concern both demographics—easily quantified elements such as age, income, geographic location—and psychographics—harder-to-measure issues such as values, attitudes, and beliefs. Advertisers look at demographics and psychographics and match them with the characteristics of the target audience for their products.

The readers of *American HomeStyle & Gardening* magazine illustrate the detail with which magazines define their audience:

DEMOGRAPHICS

Age: Median age is 42.6 years

Employment: 52.8 percent of readers are employed women

Gender: 80.9 percent of readers are women

Family: 49.8 percent of readers live in households with children

PSYCHOGRAPHICS

Readers want practical advice about architecture, remodeling, decorating, gardening, and entertaining that is geared toward an upscale, cutting-edge home.[3]

Many publishers offer special editions aimed at segments of their audience. *Modern Plastics* has special sections with editorial content and advertising designed and edited for readers in particular fields, such as medical, automotive, and packaging. The reader who, for example, manages a packaging plant will get articles about packaging regulations and ads for packaging machinery and materials. *Child* magazine has inserts geared to parents of children of certain ages: babies, toddlers, preschoolers, and so on. These inserts, titled "Your Child Now," are matched to the demographics of the audience, so parents who have one preschooler and one baby get two inserts aimed precisely at their needs and the needs of their children. The section goes only

The Global Magazine: Not Always a Direct Translation

On the Boulevard St. Germain in Paris, the Telerama newsstand offers an array of French-language newspapers and magazines. If you had visited there in April 1997, you would have found some American staples: *Elle, Premiere, Cosmopolitan, Business Week,* even *Muscle and Fitness.* Plus, you would have seen *Pour La Science,* the French edition of *Scientific American.*

These magazines have varying degrees of similarity to their American counterparts. Some are joint ventures between American and foreign publishers, with content that is highly targeted to international readers. Others are merely foreign translations of American publications.

The May 1997 French edition of *Muscle and Fitness* was a direct reflection of its American cousin. The cover photos were identical: two sinewy models with huge muscles and tiny bathing suits. The cover lines translated directly from French to English. "Une Meilleure Sexualité: Grace à un Seul Exercice," announced the French edition. The American version read: "Better Sex: Just One Exercise Away." The main difference inside was the advertising. The majority of the articles, illustrations, and designs were identical. "Spin Cycle: The Fun, Fast and Furious Way to Reduce Your Waistline" translated to "Le Spinning: Affinez Votre Taille Agreablement, Rapidement et Avec Acharnement." The illustration for both was a full-bleed time-lapse photo of four healthy bodies cycling furiously.

The covers of the French and American *Business Week* also looked identical, even to the language—English in both. The French edition was the same version available elsewhere in Europe. On the heels of Tiger Woods's success on the golf course, the April 29, 1997, issue of both American and European *Business Week* editions ran a photo of the young golfer with the coverline, "Tiger, Inc." Inside, both ran articles on Woods's value as a spokesman for brands such as Nike and Titleist/Cobra golf supplies. Other content, however, showed a continental-American split. The European version had separate departments on European, Asian, Latin American, and American business. The American version dumped all the continents into one "International Business" department. It also added departments on "The Government" (meaning the one based in Washington, D.C.) and an all-American consumerist look at "Personal Business," which that week covered "Hot Wheels: Great New Excuses to Take the Top Down."

It was a different story with the French editions of the May 1997 *Cosmopolitan, Premiere,* and *Scientific American*, which had completely

to subscribers. In newsstand copies, the section appears in the table of contents; turn to the page listed and you will find an ad for the insert.

NATIONAL. Until the advent of television, magazines were America's only national medium. Magazines now combine their national reach with an appeal to specialized audiences, providing a package available with no other medium. If you're a gourmet cook living in a small town where fried chicken is considered a delicacy, you can reach for *Gourmet* magazine and immediately be among friends. If you are an advertiser of quality food products with national franchises, *Gourmet* will deliver an audience that newspapers, radio, and television can't touch. Why advertise in the local newspaper and reach only a small percentage of customers when you can advertise in a magazine where *all* the readers are possible customers?

INTERNATIONAL. Visit a newsstand in London, and there's your faithful *Esquire.* The British edition, however, has John Cleese on the cover, with a subtitle under his name: "Britain's funniest man gets indiscreet." Other cover lines are obviously geared to British readers: "The Ruling Class: The 25 men who really run Britain (and the ones who only think they do)" and a teaser on a Scottish murder. Ads are for British products and services.

The newsweeklies span the globe, with *Time* and *Newsweek* editions available throughout Europe, South America, Africa, Asia, and Australia. With the fall of the Soviet Union, Russia became a hot market for American magazines; titles such as *Men's Health, Cosmopolitan,* and *Harper's Bazaar* began hitting Russian newsstands in the 1990s.

Modern Plastics International, a sister publication of *Modern Plastics,* has a full-time staff of different cover images and articles from the American versions. *Pour La Science* (literally, *"For Science"*) even has a different name, showing its American roots with the subtitle "édition française de *Scientific American*." The cover of the American version carried a close-up of a lion for a story on "The King of Beasts Masters the Politics of Survival." The French edition cover offered a nose-to-nose view of a rat for a series on "L'expérimentation Animale." Inside the two were completely different: no articles on rodents in the American edition and no lion details in the French.

The May 1997 French *Premiere* highlighted the 50th anniversary of the Cannes Film Festival with a photo of actress Isabelle Adjani; the American edition had a photo of Steven Spielberg surrounded by Jurassic beasts for an article on *The Lost World*.

Cosmopolitan's American cover girl for May 1997 was Elsa Benitez; in the French edition it was Claudia Schiffer. "J'adore la Vie Conjugale (Tellement que J'en Ai Deux)," suggested the French edition, which translated to an enigmatic "I Love Married Life (Especially Since I Have Two)." The American cover took a tad more direct approach: "Lovers for Life: Success Secrets about Mad-About-You Relationships." The American cover also went out on a sexual limb with "More Foreplay, Please," highlighting an article that appeared in the "Sex and Love" department. The French edition has no such department, but has a focus on fashion, food, and decorating that is absent from the American edition.

The French *Elle* also had a cover story and cover photo on Isabelle Adjani, with a cover story on "Clonage: Au Secours, les Males Sont en Peril," which translated to "Cloning: Help, Males Are in Danger!" The American cover focused on model Stella Tennant and offered "The Season's Must Haves: Sandals for Summer, Diamonds Forever."

MAY 1997: Like many American magazines, *Premiere* publishes international editions; in this case, the French and the American issues for the same month have different cover images and topics.

editors around the world—in Europe, Asia, and the Americas. It reaches more than 177,000 readers in more than 110 countries. Most readers are corporate managers, engineers, and marketing staff members. Circulation ranges from one subscriber in Algeria, one in Libya, and one in Tunisia to 4,489 in the People's Republic of China.[4] Advertisers include producers of plastic-related machinery, materials, and services from organizations with addresses in Germany, Spain, Canada, Chile, Brazil, and Belgium.

REGIONAL. Conversely, some magazines succeed by aiming at a narrow geographic target. Some have a regional appeal as part of their editorial focus; others have a national reach but offer regional editions. *Midwest Living* was one of the success stories of the 1980s because it spoke enthusiastically about an area of the country too long ignored, and this message resonated with those living in America's heartland. It followed other regional successes, such as *Southern Living*, *Texas Monthly*, and *Arizona Highways*.

National magazines recognize the importance of targeting regional readers. Initially this was done for advertising, to give regional advertisers the chance to advertise in a national magazine, thereby targeting their narrow audience while at the same time enjoying the credibility and reputation of the national publication. That is why you see your local bank's ads in *Time* and *Newsweek*. In recent years, regional editions have also included specialized editorial content. Likewise, publishers have combined geographic characteristics with other demographic traits that have narrowed and specialized the audience dramatically.

Technology has made it increasingly easy for magazines to create multiple editions for specific

City Magazines: Catering to Instant Status and Ego Gratification

City magazines—published for a local, urban market—have been a significant development in niche magazine publishing since 1968 when *New York* magazine burst on the scene with an exciting new look that was soon emulated in city after city. Designed for upscale, sophisticated, status-conscious readers, city magazines primarily compete against local newspapers for their audience and their advertisers. Because national advertisers also want to reach the desirable demographic package of the affluent urbanite, city magazines often carry the same liquor and cigarette ads found in national publications.

City magazines can trace their history back to 1888 when *Honolulu* began life as *Paradise of the Pacific*. Boston has had various city titles since 1900, while *Philadelphia* has been published since 1909. However, the period of greatest growth for city magazines was 1962 to 1974, with the heyday for the genre occurring during the late 1970s and early 1980s when virtually every large and medium-sized city had its own magazine. By 1980, as many as 250 cities had magazines of their own.

City magazines have a breezy, sassy style of writing and a definite local orientation. Because they publish strictly local stories, they usually do not make interesting reading for people in other cities. In topic and tone, city magazines are less formal and more eclectic than national magazines, tending to concentrate on three kinds of articles: informational or service features, personality profiles, and investigative pieces. As early as 1976, David Shaw of *The Los Angeles Times* offered an assessment of the city magazine genre: "City magazines have tapped not just an audience but a neurosis—an audience increasingly anxious (if not, indeed, desperate) about the challenges, complexities and frustrations of the contemporary urban environment . . . . Most people, it seems, read city magazines either to learn how to cope with their environment, or to enjoy, vicariously, the success that others more wealthy and fortunate than themselves have had in doing so."[1]

Under publisher Clay Felker and his merry band of writers (Tom Wolfe, Gloria Steinem, Gail Sheehy, and Jimmy Breslin), *New York* offered New Journalism—outrageous, bold, and stylistically innovative writing that allowed readers to vicariously participate in an event. *New York* set the tone for most city magazines with upbeat, consumer-oriented pieces, such as "A Smart-Ass Guide to Designer Jeans" which ran in the July 23, 1979, issue. This is an approach still found in successful city magazines. For many, however, the quintessential city magazine article appeared in the June 8, 1970, issue of *New York* under Tom Wolfe's byline. With his usual irreverent Wolfean wit, he skewered "limousine liberals" who threw elaborate parties and invited the less fortunate as social pets, in "Radical Chic: That Party at Lenny's." According to Felker, the article "killed radical chic."[2]

City magazines have produced cutting-edge journalism, top-flight graphics, and literary gems. But they have also served as content-weak promotional vehicles for local governments or civic boosters of chambers of commerce. Most have tended to locate

regions. *TV Guide* has 119 regional editions. All have a common full-color cover and features section but different black-and-white features and listing sections. *Successful Farming* has more than 140 regional editions that are further narrowed into demographic categories—size of farm, type of production, income—for a whopping 3,500 special editions, some so highly targeted they consist of only six subscribers.

Field & Stream includes regional inserts that focus on outdoor activities such as hunting and fishing within specific areas of the country. The Midwest Edition has articles on Missouri's wild trout and the rabbit season in Ohio, while the South Edition offers pieces on North Carolina wolves and their effects on the state's game population.

LOCAL. The success of city magazines throughout this century has proven that magazines need not have a large geographic reach to be successful. In fact, many top magazines in reputation, readership, advertising volume, and circulation income are city magazines. *The New Yorker,* hailed at various times in recent history as America's premier magazine, also has a national audience, although its attitude and emphasis are strictly Big Apple.

themselves in the middle of these extremes, with lists citing the best the city has to offer running side by side with trenchant features on the uses and abuses of power designed to rattle the town's movers and shakers.

One of the authors of this text was a city magazine editor in the late 1970s, and she still can recite by heart her magazine's editorial philosophy: "*San Antonio Magazine* offers an urban survival manual consisting of entertaining human interest stories and specific service guides in a lively, conversational tone not found in local newspapers. Like all magazines, we offer readers vicarious experiences as well as information that can be used. What distinguishes us is that our readers know they, too, *really* can experience what we write about because they live in this city. The topics we cover—where to dine, where to shop, and what to see—are right here, waiting for the reader to participate along with us."

In retrospect, the former city magazine editor realizes that *San Antonio*, and every other city magazine, perfectly fulfills all five needs of the uses and gratification theory. But she admits that such fulfillment was intuitive rather than conscious at the time and, therefore, a lot more fun than fuss.

As for the status of city magazines today, Ernest C. Hynds, a professor of journalism at the University of Georgia, reports that all sections of the country have city magazines, with the largest number in the South.[3] Circulation figures range from the large, such as *New York* with 435,000 readers, to the small, such as *Greenwich* (Connecticut) with 6,500 and *Columbia* (South Carolina) with 5,000. In a 1993 replication of his 1979 survey of city magazines, Hynds found that 89 percent of city magazines today are privately owned, a reversal from the 1960s and 1970s when many were operated by chambers of commerce.

More important, city magazines continue to emphasize information about living in the city, in terms of lifestyles and entertainment options, as well as community needs and problems. City magazines still provide an alternative point of view to local newspapers, with many taking thoughtful stands on critical issues of the day.

[1] David Shaw, "List Grows: Magazines of the Cities, A Success Story," *The Los Angeles Times* (April 5, 1976): 3, 16.

[2] Ibid., 18.

[3] Ernest C. Hynds, "Today's Diverse City Magazines Have Many Roles, Much Potential" (paper presented at the annual meeting of the Association for Education in Journalism and Mass Communication, Kansas City, MO, August 1993).

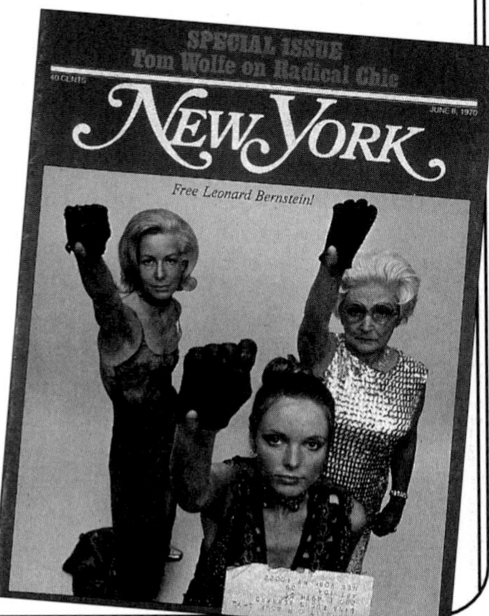

JUNE 8, 1970: Tom Wolfe's *New York* article, "Radical Chic: That Party at Lenny's," mocked the late-1960s tendency for rich liberals to flaunt their friendships with the less fortunate at elegant—and, some say, inappropriate—parties.

Most large cities have at least one city magazine: *Chicago, Atlanta, Baltimore, Phoenix.* City magazine readers look to these publications to supplement their daily newspapers and to improve the experience of living in their communities. Today, like all other magazines, city magazines are finding increasingly narrower niches, as illustrated by such local bridal magazines as *Mountain High Weddings* and *Minnesota Bride.* And yet, Northwestern University magazine professor Abe Peck argues that some niches may be too narrow. Peck asks, "How thin can you slice it before it is all baloney? We have to look for authentic niches."[5]

Opinion, Interpretation, and Advocacy

Because their communities of readers are so well defined and close-knit, magazines are far more comfortable than any other medium in providing opinion and interpretation and in advocating for the causes of their audiences. Journals of opinion, such as *The Nation* and *The Atlantic Monthly*, have been magazine standard-bearers throughout American history and have traditionally provided interpretation and analysis. In recent years, much of the growth in magazines has been related to the growth and influence of special interest groups with an advocacy function.

Historian Arthur Schlesinger Jr. called magazines "the means of expression for the more reflective interpretation so vital to the educational process."[6] Magazine scholar Theodore Peterson called them the "medium of instruction and interpretation for the leisurely, critical reader."[7] The MPA says, "A magazine is a tangible enduring companion, a friend that you can enjoy at home, work, traveling, anywhere at all."[8]

Magazines, in short, take the time to help us make sense of our world and our lives. They require that we sit down, read, and reflect. To use a magazine, we have to pay close attention to it, and we have to invest a bit of ourselves in that use. In the process, we become more thoughtful and critical.

In 1979, former *Esquire* publisher Sam Ferber penned one of the most eloquent statements on magazines. In it he said, "Magazines must probe, analyze, and offer background material. They must provide a broader perspective, they must synthesize and define complex issues." What's more, Ferber noted, "A magazine today must stand for something or it represents nothing."[9]

According to the MPA, "The art of editing a magazine is to look beneath and beyond the surface of daily events. And whenever a magazine does its job particularly well, it is not only capable of opening the eyes of its readers, the truth is, it can often open the eyes of the very journalists whose job it is to deliver the news day and night."[10]

SEPTEMBER 1984: ***Catholic Rural Life,*** **the magazine of the National Catholic Rural Life Conference, was at the forefront of the farm crisis of the 1980s.**

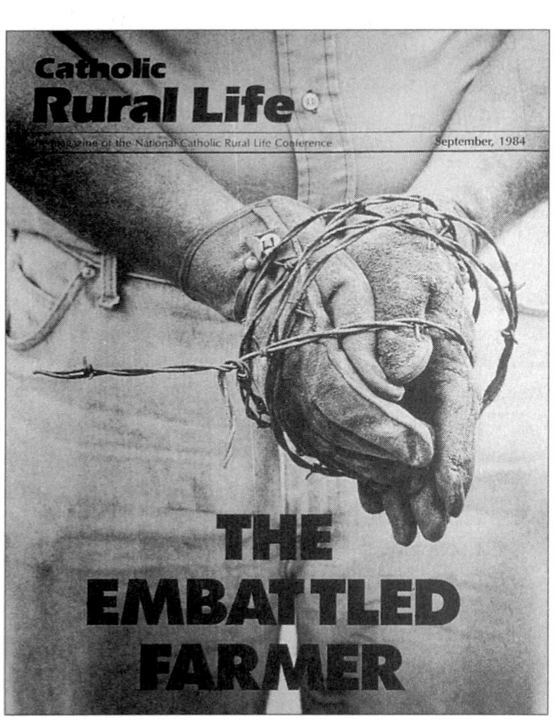

Many trade and organization magazines were built on advocacy. The growth and decline of certain businesses and industries, in fact, have historically been marked by these magazines. *The American Railroad Journal* was first published in 1832, a year before a railroad was built; *Quill*, the magazine of the Society of Professional Journalists, was founded in 1912, when journalism itself was first recognized as a legitimate profession.

Religion magazines have long been advocates as well, many being published by religious organizations. *Youth Alive!* is produced as a "ministry tool of Youth Encounter, which seeks to provide events and resources to most effectively reach youth with the life-changing message of knowing Jesus Christ in a personal way," says Youth Encounter President Larry Dean Johnson.[11] *Tricycle: The Buddhist Review,* published by The Buddhist Ray, advocates meditation and Zen in the workplace.

Catholic Rural Life magazine, published by the National Catholic Rural Life Conference, is an ecumenical voice and has long been an advocate of the family farm. In 1985, the magazine won top awards from the Catholic Press Association for its November 1984 issue on violence in rural America, spotlighting the activities of militias and separatist groups that were recruiting members among farmers who were losing their land during the farm crisis of the 1980s.

Within the past 30 years, several consumer magazines have been launched to advocate specific causes, including *Ms.*, for feminism; *The American Spectator,* for conservative politics; and *The Advocate,* for gay and lesbian issues. *American Rifleman,* published by the National Rifle Association, is also available on the newsstand. As the association's voice, it has been a solid advocate of the rights of gun owners.

Permanence

The pages of a magazine are stapled, glued, or sewn together—that is, they are bound—to create what often looks like a small book. And because magazines are printed and bound, they are the most permanent of all media. We shut off the television, leave the room, and forget about it, but we keep our magazines, stockpiling old issues of *National Geographic* in the spare room until we're forced to sell them to make room for the baby.

The broadcast media are ephemeral by nature. The sitcom comes and goes within 30 minutes. Broadcast news stories last, at most, three to five minutes. More and more, television is aimed at a moving target, geared to a short attention span. Newspapers take more time with the information but focus on day-to-day issues. Magazines, however, are created to last.

This permanence means that we can use and reuse magazines. We pass along the article in *Mother Earth News* on new roofing material to our brother who is building a cabin or the story on a real-life murder mystery in *Ladies' Home Journal* to our mystery-loving friends. The average issue of an American magazine has 5.2 readers. Consequently, a magazine with a circulation of 100,000 actually has 520,000 readers. Publishers call this pass-along readership.

Even in Japan, goofy trends can lead to magazines. The popularity of "low riders"—1960s and 1970s American gas-guzzlers fitted with hydraulic shocks and highlighted with rap music played on huge speakers—was the impetus behind the launch of a new Japanese magazine in 1997. The rider audience is now served by the 100,000 circulation *Roraida Magajin*, or *Low-Rider Magazine.*

Consistency

Each issue of *Wood* magazine, launched in 1985, profiles one kind of wood, such as ebony, tiger wood, or cherry. In the first years of the magazine, these profiles appeared on the same page in each issue. As the magazine grew and content changed, editors decided to put this feature on a different page. Readers complained. They were accustomed to finding their favorite feature in a specific place; they didn't like it when they turned to that page and found a different article.

Not all magazine readers are as precise as the woodworkers who subscribe to *Wood,* but they do demand a certain amount of consistency from their publications. They open the magazine each month with expectations; the successful magazine meets these expectations. Consistency comes in the magazine's format: its writing, design, and graphic style, and its regular departments, columns, and features.

Consistency, however, does not mean sameness. Readers challenge editors to make the magazine different with each issue, but within a coherent and harmonious structure. The proper balance of consistency and the element of surprise is one hallmark of a quality publication.

Wood's editor Larry Clayton says that, while magazines need to modify their approach over time, he and his staff try to implement those changes slowly and explain them to the readers. His readers, he says, "will comment on anything we change." The success of this approach is reflected in the success of the magazine: *Wood* is the country's largest woodworking magazine, with a 630,000 circulation, and is now enjoying all-time record advertising sales and profits.[12]

Frequency

Consistency is also attained in the form of regular publication. Magazines may be published weekly, biweekly, monthly, bimonthly, quarterly, or at predetermined, but irregular intervals throughout the year. Some special editions are published annually.

Wood is published nine times a year—every month except May, July, and September. Woodworking, Clayton says, is a school-year activity, and *Wood* readers are do-it-yourselfers who may be involved in other projects in the summer. *The New Yorker* is published weekly, a frequency that may operate against the magazine by building reader guilt. Who can read that much magazine every week?

Definition

When we take all these elements into consideration, we end up with the definition of magazines that will guide us throughout this book:

> *Magazines are printed and bound publications offering in-depth coverage of stories often of a timeless nature. Their content may provide opinion and interpretation as well as advocacy. They are geared to a well-defined, specialized audience, and they are published regularly, with a consistent format.*

THE SCOPE OF THE MEDIUM

You have been job hunting and told your dad you want to work for a magazine. A look of panic clouds his face. He's thinking, "She'll never work again!" He worries that the field is limited and your prospects correspondingly dim, no matter your brilliance. Don't blame dad. Like so many members of the general public, he is thinking of only the smallest number of magazines: those we see on the newsstands or those we subscribe to and receive in the mail.

This is merely the tip of the magazine iceberg. To get a picture of the scope of the magazine medium, we will briefly look at the different types of magazines being published today and at the size of the contemporary magazine industry.

The magazine reading capital of the U.S. is Boston, where adults spend an average of 29 minutes a day reading magazines, according to a survey by Young and Rubicam in 1990. Boston beat out the U.S. average of 20 minutes a day by 42 percent. What do they read? The top-selling magazine in Boston is *TV Guide.* At the bottom: Laredo, Texas, with an average of 10 minutes per adult.

Magazine Types

Have you read *Adventure Road, Modern Baker, Comment, Association Management, Crayola Kids,* or *Journal of Soil and Water Conservation*? These all fit the definition of a magazine. The staffs of these publications all put pages together in much the same way; their goals, however, are quite different. Magazine professionals classify magazines into three types: consumer, trade, and organization. Understanding these categories gives us a clear and encouraging picture of the breadth of the magazine field.

CONSUMER. Consumer magazines are created primarily for popular consumption. They are sold on the newsstand or by subscriptions and are marketed like any other consumer product. They usually contain advertising; readers are important to advertisers because of their potential as consumers. Most of the largest circulation magazines are consumer publications, such as *Reader's Digest* with 15 million circulation and *TV Guide* with 13 million circulation. There are fewer consumer magazines than any other type, but individual consumer magazines generally have the largest audiences of all types.

Consumer magazines can be further narrowed into general interest and special interest. General interest titles contain material of interest to a broad audience, such as *Reader's Digest* and *The Atlantic Monthly.* Special interest magazines focus on a narrow issue, which may be a hobby, issue of concern, or activity, such as *American Patchwork and Quilting, Extra,* and *Internet* magazine.

TRADE. Trade magazines are also called specialized business magazines or business-to-business magazines. Their content is job-related and their audience consists of readers in specific occupations or professions. *Baking Management,* for example, goes to high-volume bakers, such as Mrs. Smith Bakeries. Some trade

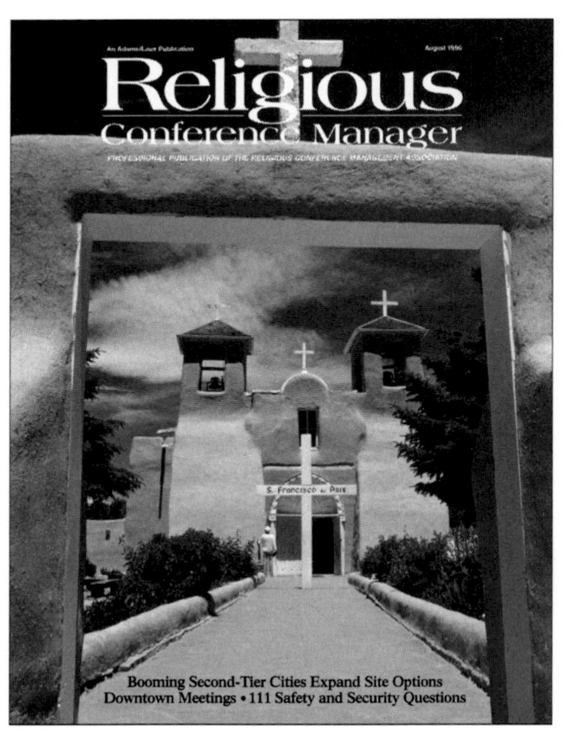

AUGUST 1996: Professional meeting planners don't have to go it alone; at least seven trade—or business-to-business—magazines such as *Religious Conference Manager* offer advice, ideas, and inspiration.

magazines, such as *PC World*, are sold on the newsstand, but most are sold only through subscriptions, which usually go to readers at their workplaces.

The American Business Press (ABP) says these publications "provide a select group of readers with the in-depth reporting and clear analysis that they need to get ahead professionally and to make their businesses a success."[13] Occasionally publishers of these magazines offer controlled circulation, whereby readers who possess specific occupational characteristics receive the magazine free, because these readers have high appeal to advertisers. The largest circulation trade magazines often have as sizable an audience as their consumer counterparts; the largest, *PC Magazine*, has a circulation of one million.

Many industries are served by multiple magazines. For example, professional meeting planners have a host of magazines to help them understand their industry and excel at their jobs. These include *Meeting Manager*, *Successful Meetings*, *Corporate & Incentive Travel*, *Religious Conference Manager*, *Medical Meetings*, *Insurance Conference Planner*, and *Convene*.

At one time, farm magazines were considered a distinct magazine type, reflective of the importance of agriculture to the American economy. In most cases today, farm magazines operate like trade publications.

ORGANIZATION. Organization magazines fall into three general categories: society and association, public relations, and custom. All are published by organizations for their internal and external constituencies.

Society and association magazines. These magazines usually come as one benefit of membership in the society or association. Examples here include some top names—*Sierra*, *National Geographic*, and *Smithsonian*—as well as the less well-known *Association Management* published by the American Society of Association Executives. Some association magazines look and act like consumer magazines, and many boast huge readerships.

The largest circulation magazine in the United States is an association publication: *Modern Maturity*, the magazine of the American Association of Retired Persons, with a 20.4 million circulation. *National Geographic*, the country's fourth largest title, has a circulation of 8.7 million and is one of our largest, oldest, most respected, and well-known magazines. As a publication of the National Geographic Society, its goal is to enhance the operation of that agency, and its format and organizational style are determined by the society. Beginning with the November 1998 issue, *National Geographic* became available on selected newsstands in 80 large cities across the United States. To get a subscription, you must join the organization. The organization, a $500-million-a-year enterprise, in turn supports the magazine.[14]

JULY/AUGUST 1998: America's largest circulation magazine, *Modern Maturity*, is an organization publication of the American Association of Retired Persons (AARP).

Magazines are essential components of an association. Elissa Matulis Myers, vice president and publisher of the American Society of Association Executives, says, "For many members, the periodical *is* the association—the monthly visit through the mailbox of colleagues with similar interests." The association magazine, she adds, can "unify an industry, profession or interest group. Tightly drawn, a periodical can have remarkable influence for the association and can be a powerful force in support of members."[15]

Why a Magazine: The Iowa Natural Heritage Foundation

The Iowa Natural Heritage Foundation considered changing its 16-page quarterly magazine, *Iowa Natural Heritage*, into a newsletter, hoping to cut costs and, perhaps, reach its 5,000 members more quickly and efficiently. The magazine format won out in the long run. Why? Anita O'Gara, director of communications, said the statewide foundation opted for the magazine because it offers more:

- Value to readers. The magazine has a pass-along readership of at least three people; a newsletter couldn't offer that benefit.
- Depth of content. A magazine allows the foundation to provide background information that may encourage members to act on the group's agenda: protecting the state's land.
- Emotion. A magazine helps the foundation show why it is important to serve as stewards of the land.
- Opportunity for commentary. A magazine offers a convenient and credible venue for the foundation's opinions.

What's more, the group found that they would save little money by switching to the newsletter format. Because they use the association magazine to build and maintain membership, the foundation staff decided the most effective format for this important communication was the format they had been using: a magazine.

Association magazines may carry advertising, and most are sold to readers through subscriptions; a few are available on the newsstands. Their general goal, however, is service to the association, rather than profit; whatever profit they earn is returned to the association. Dues for new members of the Sierra Club in 1998 were $15 a year; $7.50 of that was earmarked for the organization's magazine, *Sierra*.

Scholarly journals are also association publications and are used by scholars and researchers to share academic information. They differ from other association magazines because the content usually consists of scholarly papers selected by peer review, that is, by a board of scholars or academics. Content is valued because of its contribution to knowledge of the field. Most journals have little or no advertising and go to readers as part of membership in a scholarly or professional organization. Included here are the *ABA Journal*, with 385,000 circulation, and the *New England Journal of Medicine*, with 258,000 circulation. Less well known is *Word Ways: The Journal of Recreational Linguistics*, which offers erudite word games and analyses of the effects of popular culture—computers, MTV, professional sports—on language. *Wilson Quarterly*, published by the Woodrow Wilson International Center for Scholars, has the slogan, "Surveying the World of Ideas." Its content is an eclectic mix of poetry, historical analysis, and gleanings from other scholarly publications.

Journals are often the source of material for consumer magazine articles. Some even study magazines themselves. In 1992, the *New England Journal of Medicine* ran a study that showed a relationship between cigarette advertising and positive articles on smoking. Those magazines that had a great deal of cigarette advertising were also those magazines that tended either to downplay the dangers of smoking, or to even present positive side effects. The authors cited an article from *Cosmopolitan*, suggesting smoking might alleviate endometriosis, a conclusion, the medical writers noted, that had no basis in fact.[16]

Many association magazines, such as *National Geographic*, are also included in lists of consumer magazines; others, such as *Quill*, the magazine of the Society of Professional Journalists, show up in trade magazine lists.

Public relations magazines. Also called corporate communications magazines, these are probably the most ubiquitous of all magazine types. Most large organizations have at least one; some have several. These magazines tell employees what's happening in the organization, explain the organization to clients, and smooth the way for

The Magazine's Personality

Like people, successful magazines have personalities that reflect their philosophies, energy, wisdom, and wit. The cover is a magazine's statement of its identity, as the following examples demonstrate.

INSIDE: MORE THAN 300 SIERRA CLUB OUTINGS FOR 1996
SIERRA
ENDANGERED SPECIES
THE PEOPLE,
THE POLITICS,
AND THE LAW
PROTECTING
THE RAREST
ATURES
N EARTH
GONE IN A FLASH?
PHOTOS FROM THE EDGE

YEAR IN REVIEW: THE BEST, THE WORST...THE WACKIEST
JANUARY 1997
OUTDOOR LIFE
THE SPORTSMAN'S AUTHORITY SINCE 1898
Adventure Special
FOUND!
A LOST HUNTING SAGA
BY JACK O'CONNOR
GRIZZLY ATTACKS
SURVIVING
THE UNTHINKABLE
BUSH PILOTS
TALES FROM
THE LEFT SEAT
PLUS
•SPAWN TACTICS FOR HUGE BASS
•HIGH-TECH ICEFISHING
$2.95
CANADA $3.50
A TIMES MIRROR MAGAZINE

JANUARY/FEBRUARY 1996 /JANUARY 1997: Which bear would you want to protect? The cuddly fellow on the *Sierra* cover, of course. *The Outdoor Life* bear, meanwhile, sends you searching for your gun. It's all part of the magazines' plan. *Sierra,* the magazine of the Sierra Club, is aimed at individuals who advocate the importance of maintaining our natural environment. *Outdoor Life,* "The Sportsman's Authority," includes hunters in its audience.

TONS OF USEFUL STUFF
JULY/AUGUST 1997
Men's Health
Train for GREAT SEX
The Hard-Body Diet
SLEEP YOUR WAY TO SUCCESS (pg. 74)
Amazing Abs→
How This Guy Did It
10 FASTEST WORKOUTS
FREE EXERCISE POSTER INSIDE

JULY/AUGUST 1997: *Men's Health* filled a marketplace need by offering personal service information for men, a content area that had previously been limited to women's magazines.

PLAYBOY
ENTERTAINMENT FOR MEN
1990 • $4.00
"Nice magazine. Want to sell it?"
DONALD TRUMP INTERVIEW
ROCK AND RACISM
Has the dark side taken over pop music?
FAX 'N' FIGURES
Sex comes to the electronic office
CARS 1990
We pick the hottest, sharpest, sexiest
WORLD-CLASS PLAYMATES FROM OUR FAR-FLUNG EMPIRE

MARCH 1990: Only a handful of men have appeared on the cover of *Playboy,* which always includes the signature Playboy rabbit, shown here as a cuff link in Donald Trump's shirt. Other celebrities who have made the cover of this popular men's magazine are Peter Sellers, Burt Reynolds, Steve Martin, Dan Aykroyd, and Jerry Seinfeld.

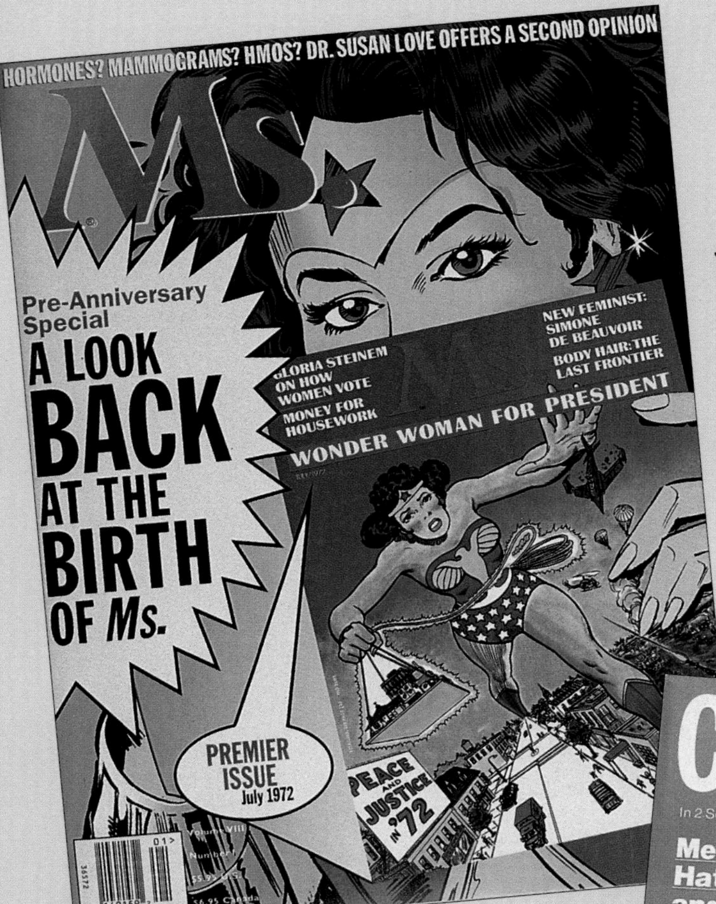

JULY/AUGUST 1997: *Ms.* celebrated its 25th anniversary by reprinting the cover of its July 1972 premiere issue. The Wonder Woman theme demonstrated the magazine's focus on feminist issues as well as its ability to be playful.

JANUARY 1987: *Cosmopolitan*'s "bedside astrologer" is always a big newsstand seller for the magazine. The cover model for this issue was a young Cindy Crawford.

Buddhism & Psychedelics
tricycle
THE BUDDHIST REVIEW
5th Anniversary
SPECIAL ISSUE

SEPTEMBER 1996: *Tricycle: The Buddhist Review* celebrates its fifth anniversary as a religion magazine that is an advocate for a spiritual life.

Today's Christian
Woman
January/February 1996
Abstinence Advocate
Patricia
Funderburk Ware
Teaches Teens the
Facts
of Life
page 26
7 Friendship
Myths Unmasked
Discover
the Gifts God's
Given YOU
"My Daughter
Was a Victim of
Domestic Violence"
$3.95

JANUARY/FEBRUARY 1996: *Today's Christian Woman* is aimed at contemporary women who seek to follow biblical values in their home, workplace, and community. Patricia Funderburk Ware's message of sexual abstinence sets the tone for this cover.

HI-YIELD, HI-TECH GROWING
HIGH TIMES
HIGH TIMES
25 YEARS
THE MOST NOTORIOUS MAGAZINE IN THE WORLD
25 TOP GROW TIPS
FROM NOVICE TO MASTER
STONER'S GUIDE TO
MILLENNIUM
FEVER
Escape from the
DEA
EX-AGENT TELLS ALL
Smokin' in the
White House with
PEARL JAM & MUDHONEY
www.hightimes.com

JANUARY 1999: As its name and cover treatment demonstrate, *High Times* is a magazine all about marijuana.

NOVEMBER 1997: *Latina* is a dual-language magazine for today's Hispanic woman, reaching one of the fastest-growing ethnic groups in the United States. Giselle Fernandez, who gave up a successful news-reporting career to cover entertainment as cohost of "Access Hollywood," is on the cover.

Latina
magazine
ilingüe
NOVEMBER 1997
$2.50 • FOREIGN $3.50
Amor Inter-Latino
Dating outside your group
Fiesta tips:
A Día de los Muertos party
Feeding a crowd
One-pot meals
Uncurl your rizos
PLUS:
Mark Consuelos
Gigi Fernández
Moda de la calle en Spanish Harlem
Why we don't Breastfeed
Get fit at any age
One Latina's story
Giselle Fernandez
How she got access to Hollywood

A Loose Canon: 150 Mind-Altering Masterpieces
UTNE READER
THE BEST OF THE ALTERNATIVE MEDIA
$4.99 USA $5.99 CAN
MAY-JUNE 98
Jammin' with the Giants
How to keep your mind alive for life
Adultery: The Upside
Taming the Gene Kings
Empty Oceans: The End of Free-Range Fish?

MAY/JUNE 1998: In this issue, *Utne Reader* introduced a list of artistic works that went "beyond the valley of the dead white male." This "revised canon" transcended literature to include movies, TV shows, plays, and music. Depicted on the cover, from left to right, are some of the artists whose works were featured: Marcus Aurelius, Thelonius Monk, Jane Austen, Mohandas Gandhi, Groucho Marx, Toni Morrison, William Shakespeare, and Hildegard of Bingen.

DECEMBER 1995: ***National Geographic*** **is, in many ways, America's premier nature magazine. This cover shows researcher Jane Goodall being groomed by a close friend—a chimpanzee. The magazine's yellow border is part of its distinctive personality.**

Better
http://www.bhglive.com
DECEMBER 1997 $2.49
Wishing you a
joyful
holiday
Watch
Better Homes
and Gardens
TV
on weekends
p.46
75
Helping
families live
better lives for
75 years
The first Better Homes and Gardens holiday cover

DECEMBER 1997: To celebrate its 75th year of serving America's families, *Better Homes and Gardens* reprinted its 1924 holiday cover, a charming image of a joyful child. Juxtaposed against the image is a jolt into the present: a reminder that the magazine is now on television.

the organization to deal with outside agencies. At one time, these magazines were called house organs to indicate their importance in the communication process of the organization. Included in this group are magazines for nonprofit groups, such as hospitals and universities, as well as magazines produced by and for the government.

Public relations magazines are either internal or external. Internal audiences include employees and retirees; external audiences include clients, governmental agencies, and other companies.

Comment is an internal magazine published by Principal Financial Group that includes regular departments on changes within the company and responses to employee questions. Feature articles help readers learn about the broad international markets with which they now deal, highlight employee successes, and provide general service information for members of a rapidly growing industry. It reaches 21,000 employees, retirees, and affiliates throughout the world.

Farm Bureau Insurance produces *Family Ties*, an internal magazine that explains company activities and changes and highlights top employees; it is sent to 2,000 employees and retirees in 15 midwestern states. The company also produces *Keeping In Touch*, a publication for agents to send to some 95,000 policyholders, offering them information on new products, seasonal reminders on issues such as tax preparation, and wellness tips. It is an imprint publication, produced by Farm Bureau but distributed later with individual agencies' names on the cover.

Public relations magazines traditionally do not have advertising and are distributed free to readers. They fulfill one of the major objectives of the Public Relations Society of America (PRSA): "To exchange ideas and experience, and to collect and disseminate information of value to public relations professionals and the public."[17]

Custom magazines. Also called sponsored publications, these magazines are a type of public relations magazine, but with a slightly different focus. They are sent to clients as a benefit of purchasing a particular product or service. Like public relations magazines, they seek to present that product or service in a positive light. Unlike public relations magazines, though, they seldom present direct information about the activities of the organization or the direct benefits of the product or service. Most have advertising—usually for the sponsoring organization, but often for other advertisers as well. Most are given to readers free, although some are sold on newsstands and through subscriptions.

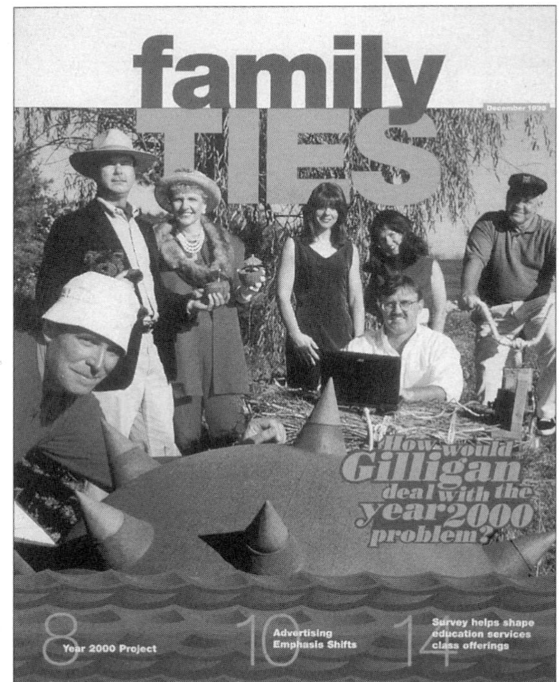

DECEMBER 1998: *Family Ties* is an internal public relations—or corporate communications—magazine for employees and retirees of Farm Bureau Insurance.

Amoco Oil Company produces *Adventure Road*, a magazine that provides information on car travel. The magazine contains few references to Amoco. Its goal is to encourage readers to take road trips and to use their Amoco credit cards. Publishers occasionally work with a corporation to publish a special edition of a consumer magazine for custom use. *McCall's*, for example, has published a special *McCall's Beauty;* this is given only to Mary Kay Cosmetics consultants, who then distribute it to their customers. A quick read of *McCall's Beauty* yields little evidence that it is supported by a cosmetics manufacturer. Editorial content does not mention Mary Kay but provides general reader service: tips on hair care, make-up, and skin care. These tips, however, suggest using products such as creams with alpha and beta hydroxy acids, which, of course, are offered by Mary Kay, as well as other beauty suppliers. A more attentive reader will see the letter from Mary Kay and the huge number of Mary Kay ads.

Sometimes the sponsoring organization is

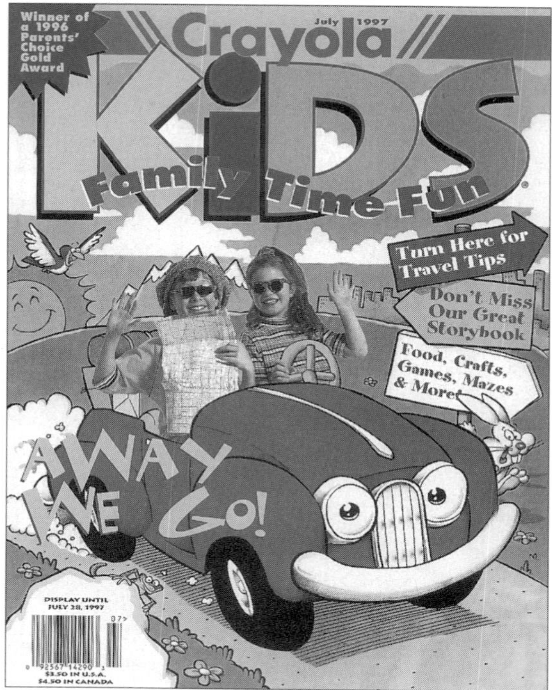

JULY 1997: *Crayola Kids* is a custom magazine that encourages kids to write, dream, and create—often using their crayons.

more obvious and may even be included in the title. In 1996, *Family Circle* launched *Mary Higgins Clark Mystery Magazine,* full of magazine-length whodunits accompanied by profiles of the writers. Interestingly, many of the cover stories were written by Clark's rivals—P. D. James, Edna Buchanan, Tony Hillerman, Sara Paretsky, and Elizabeth George. The bonus thriller, of course, was penned by Clark, who also wrote the editor's letter, titled "In Defense of Suspense." Advertising is sparse: the back cover is sold to General Foods International Coffees—for the mysteries of our lives—and other ads are for books by Clark and others.

Crayola Kids lists the sponsoring company in the title; the graphics and colors, likewise, are straight from the Crayola box. The magazine, which is sold through subscriptions, encourages children to develop their creativity by presenting them with problems to solve and games to play. Each issue encourages kids to write or draw a response to the magazine—they might, of course, use their Crayola crayons. The July 1997 issue included a profile of a truck driver. After the article, kids were given a page to cut out and return, with a drawing of "a place I have been to that I think everyone should see." Kids who reponded received a specially created postcard from the truck driver.

The most visible type of custom publication may be the in-flight magazines produced for major airlines, such as Northwest Airlines's *World Traveler,* and United Airlines's *Hemispheres.* These look like consumer magazines but are organized around the interests of airline passengers. Their goal is to keep airline customers happy and occupied while flying. Articles include travel, business profiles, and general features. Special departments include shopping guides and airport maps. These magazines seldom do investigative stories; if they did, one area they would not investigate would be airline crashes.

OTHER TYPES. The vitality of the magazine field is also evident in the various mutations of the magazine, including the following.

Literary magazines. Literary publications, such as *The North American Review,* publish a steady diet of quality poetry, fiction, literary nonfiction, and literary criticism. The magazine even critiques other magazines. The March/April 1996 issue took *The New Yorker* to task for using the television sitcom queen, Roseanne, as an editorial consultant for a special double issue devoted entirely to women.[18] Literary magazines are sometimes called "little" magazines because of their circulations and, occasionally, their page size.

'Zines. These low-budget publications are usually created on a home computer and have typically been on topics such as celebrities, science fiction, video games, television, and music. Increasingly, though, content has diversified to include broader topics such as parenting, travel, and culture. *Rozek's,* for example, offers its 3,000 subscribers in-depth profiles of "ordinary people doing extraordinary things."[19]

Randy Jones, founder of *Worth,* calls 'zines "magazines in their rawest form." He says they offer a look at the health of the whole industry and he sees their growth and energy as positive signs for magazines as a whole. "They're the canary in the cage for the future of our industry," Jones says.[20]

PERSPECTIVE: THE INTERNET VERSUS THE MAGAZINE

"The Internet is a great message medium," says information designer Nigel Holmes, "but it's not a potential competitor for magazines." The Internet makes it possible for Holmes to work out of his Connecticut home as a designer and consultant for magazines in New York City. Holmes, whose information graphics have appeared in most American magazines, was graphics director of *Time* until 1994. He is the author of *The Smallest Ever Guide to the Internet*, a 2.75-by-4.25-inch booklet that explains everything from ADSLs to URLs with ingenuous Holmes graphics.

Holmes says he relies on the Internet to send and receive information and for research. The Internet is "no threat" to magazines, he says, because "it's more comfortable, more rewarding, to see information in print than on the screen." Magazines, however, don't have completely smooth sailing ahead, he says. Some magazines will continue to fail for the same low-tech reason: "They are irrelevant."

Sunday supplements. Opinions differ on whether these are magazines or not. The largest, *Parade*, has a circulation of more than 37 million. Some newspaper supplements are bound, as is *The New York Times Magazine*. Because these publications, while often of high editorial quality, are simply an added feature of—and are distributed along with—the newspaper, most magazine professionals, including the Magazine Publishers of America, consider them newspaper supplements, rather than independent magazines.

Free urban magazines. These narrow niche publications compete with local newspapers for advertisers and succeed because they provide what the newspaper cannot: a well-defined target audience, a design style that allows a more creative and appealing presentation of their products and services, and, occasionally, better advertising rates. While they often take a magazine approach to design and content, they are usually printed on newsprint and are unbound, making them magapapers, that is, a combination newspaper and magazine. Many specialized city magazines are entirely supported by advertisers and given to readers free. Minneapolis has three such free local magazines: *Minneapolis Skywalk News, Twin Cities Reader,* and *Family Times.* All are printed on newsprint and cover issues the traditional local media may either ignore or give short shrift: a critical analysis of the growing victims' rights movement in the *Reader* and education tips for local parents in *Family Times.*

Internet magazines, or E-Zines. Are *Slate* and *Hot Wired* magazines? Is *Hot Wired* more of a magazine than the on-line version of *Mother Jones*—or is it less so—because it is created entirely for the Internet while the other is an Internet version of the print publication? The Internet format is closely tied to the magazine format and the two are similar in goals and relationship with their audience. This means that magazines translate easily to the Internet. However, the Internet is a separate medium, so magazines created there are different and distinct from printed magazines, just as TV magazines are.

Number of Magazines

How many magazines exist in America today? It depends on who is counting and what kinds of titles are being counted. Some agencies count only consumer magazines, others combine consumer and farm publications, some add newspapers and magazines together, and still others count only association publications. Some magazines aren't included in any list. It is also difficult to get current data, as many agencies wait until the end of the year to start counting; therefore, solid numbers for 1999 might not be available until 2001.

Nevertheless, a look at the reference books that count magazines reveals a huge inconsistency in the number of magazines being published, inconsistencies that continue from year to year. Look at how the following agencies counted magazines in 1999:

- *Gale Directory of Publications*: More than 12,000 periodicals, which include consumer, trade, religion, foreign language, and agricultural publications.
- *National Directory of Magazines*: 20,000 titles, including consumer, trade, and organization.
- *Working Press of the Nation*: 5,500 consumer, farm, service, trade, professional, and industrial publications; 2,500 internal publications.
- *Standard Rate and Data Service*: More than 2,700 consumer and farm magazines; more than 7,500 business publications.
- *Ulrich's International Periodical Directory*: 157,173 journals, trade, and consumer publications worldwide.
- *Standard Periodical Directory*: 85,000 U.S. and Canadian periodicals, including trade and consumer publications.
- *Policies and Procedures in Association Management*: Nearly 1,400 association periodicals.
- *Oxbridge Communicators MediaFinder Web Site*: More than 100,000 publications and catalogs.

Whole groups of magazines, however, fall through the cracks in these lists: most public relations magazines, many custom publications, magazines that do not accept advertising, many regional publications, and small or newly created magazines.

Allure, a beauty magazine for women, paid homage to three beauty icons in October 1994: Grace Kelly, Audrey Hepburn, and Jacqueline Kennedy Onassis. At the same time, *Esquire*, a magazine for men, featured "Women We Love" with a cover photo of Madonna clad in black leather underwear and a diamond dog collar and chain.

The Magazine Publishers of America has 197 domestic and 59 international members, publishing nearly 1,200 titles. The American Business Press serves 179 member companies with 1,100 member publications. The *Encyclopedia of Associations* lists 22,901 nonprofit associations in the United States. A 1996 survey by the American Society of Association Executives found that half of its members published a periodical.[21] No accounting has been done of public relations magazines; estimates by scholars and researchers have ranged from 10,000 to 100,000. The Public Relations Society of America has 17,000 members. Many of them have editorial duties; others don't. Although magazines are important public relations vehicles, they are usually part of a larger communications strategy, and many organizations do not separate them discretely enough for them to be enumerated.

Readership

The size and health of magazines is also determined by the number of people who buy magazines. Each particular magazine is measured by its circulation, which is the sum of the number of people who buy it on the newsstand and the number of people who buy it through a subscription. A magazine with newsstand sales of 60,000 per issue and with 40,000 subscribers has a circulation of 100,000. And this number, as we have already seen, is only the beginning of an analysis of readership. If that magazine has a pass-along readership of 3.2, it then has 320,000 readers. Table 1.1 offers a glimpse of the leaders in total circulation as well as in subscription and single copy sales.

The total paid circulation of American consumer magazines added up to 364.6 million in 1997, 66.6 million in single-copy, or newsstand, sales and 298 million in subscriptions. Trade, or business-to-business, magazines had a total circulation of 201.14 million. This was divided between paid circulation, at 119.57 million, and controlled circulation, at 81.57 million.[22]

MAGAZINES AND EMERGING MEDIA

Competition from television was probably the best thing that happened to the American magazine in the second half of the twentieth century; it forced magazines to define themselves and to act on their strengths. Each new communications technology not only brings competition, it also brings the doomsday prophets who declare the magazine all but dead. Television will kill magazines, they said in the 1950s. It didn't. Cable TV will kill magazines, they said in the 1980s. It didn't. The CD-ROM will kill magazines, they said in the early 1990s. It didn't. The Internet will kill magazines, they said in the late 1990s. It hasn't.

Emerging technology, in fact, brings new audiences. As the computer came along, with

TABLE 1.1 Circulation Leaders: Top Ten American Magazines[1]

TOTAL PAID CIRCULATION[2]		TOTAL SUBSCRIPTIONS[3]		TOTAL SINGLE COPIES[4]	
Modern Maturity	20,454,478	*Modern Maturity*	20,454,478	*TV Guide*	3,532,309
Reader's Digest	15,086,390	*Reader's Digest*	14,286,953	*National Enquirer*	2,225,533
TV Guide	13,171,025	*TV Guide*	9,638,716	*Family Circle*	1,972,111
National Geographic	9,013,113	*National Geographic*	8,856,838	*Woman's Day*	1,951,222
Better Homes and Gardens	7,614,737	*Better Homes and Gardens*	7,241,570	*Star*	1,829,353
Family Circle	5,054,263	*Time*	3,956,838	*Cosmopolitan*	1,711,936
Good Housekeeping	4,643,428	*Ladies' Home Journal*	3,933,129	*Woman's World*	1,486,668
Ladies' Home Journal	4,513,629	*McCall's*	3,868,117	*People*	1,405,627
McCall's	4,255,784	*Good Housekeeping*	3,408,778	*First for Women*	1,294,813
Woman's Day	4,163,248	*Car and Travel*	3,349,118	*Good Housekeeping*	1,234,649

[1] Figures from Magazine Publishers of America for first half of 1997.
[2] Leading Audit Bureau of Circulation (ABC) magazines by average total paid circulation.
[3] Leading ABC magazines by average subscriptions sold per issue.
[4] Leading ABC magazines by average single copies sold per issue.

bells and whistles to threaten magazines, what did the magazine industry do? Start more magazines about computers. The same thing is happening with the Internet, as demonstrated by such magazines as *Yahoo Internet Life,* a custom publication that previews and evaluates on-line sites available through the Yahoo search engine.

Magazines also use the new technology to improve their service to their audience. In 1996, *Better Homes and Gardens* introduced a CD-ROM, "Remodeling Your Home," that contains more than 100 examples of remodeled homes. Slip it into your computer and take a virtual tour of remodeled houses; you can even listen to the audio from homeowners on how they created their new room or added that bay window.[23]

In today's world chock full of media, with competition from television, CD-ROMs, the Internet, and other rapidly emerging technology, how can magazines compete? Very well. Those magazines that recognize the inherent strengths of the medium—and use those strengths to fill readers' needs—will be those that survive any onslaught of media competition.

Internet

Magazine publishers have created a comfortable presence on the Internet, recognizing in this technology some important similarities to the magazine format. In addition to being a new way to link with readers, the Internet also has enhanced the manner in which magazines do business. It has improved the way magazines communicate with one another and with their suppliers, staff members, and freelancers.

The concept of interactive communication, the mainstay of the Internet, is nothing new to magazines. Cullen Murphy, managing editor of one of the country's oldest titles, *The Atlantic Monthly*, said in 1996 that today's magazine professionals have the most solid understanding of what audiences want. He wrote on the magazine's Web site:

> *. . . aren't today's publishers the most qualified people to step up to the potential, and the challenge, of interactivity? Of creating new special interest communities and new relationships between reader and expert? Or between reader and reader? The new medium demands organized, vital, up-to-date content. It demands authoritative points of view. The relationship between user and provider requires the very trust that readers bestow on a magazine brand or brands of their choice.*[24]

The *Mother Jones* magazine on-line site—*The MoJo Wire: Mother Jones Interactive*—offers "News for the hell-raising citizen."[25] In launching the on-line version of *Country Living* magazine in 1995, editor Rachel Newman wrote that the magazine embraced the change "wholeheartedly

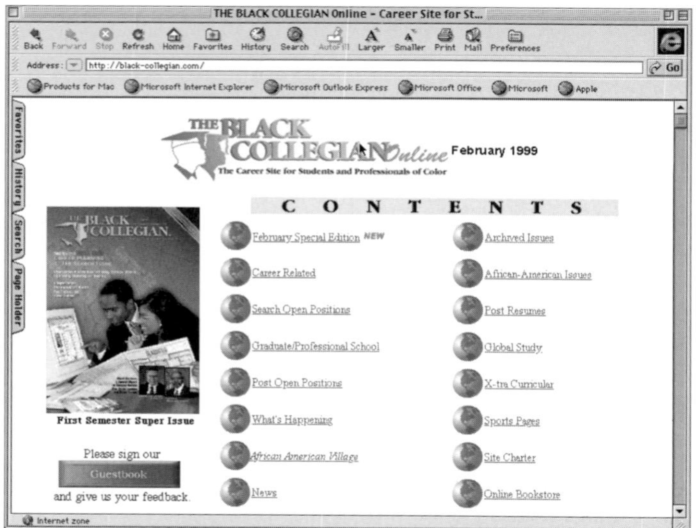

***Black Collegian*'s Web site helps students search for information about Historically Black Colleges and Universities.**

for the accessibility it affords our viewers, the unlimited expansion it offers us as editors, and the interactive potential it promises us both."[26] *Black Collegian* helps on-line readers, usually college-bound students, search Historically Black Colleges and Universities. Not only does this technology give readers an opportunity to communicate with one another directly, it does so internationally, creating a worldwide community of readers.

Doing Business on the Internet

The Internet has replaced or supplemented some of the traditional ways magazine staffs do business. Magazines use the Internet to check proofs, find clip art, search for staff members and freelancers, sell subscriptions, do research, and send and receive material. Magazine editors also run ideas past readers on the Internet, asking opinions on cover ideas, articles, redesigns, and magazine focus in general. Webb Howell, president of Journalistic, Inc., a Durham, North Carolina, publisher, says his group has used the Internet to find 85 percent of the writers it uses: "We routinely scan forums, newsgroups and mailing lists for interesting topics and new people qualified to write about them."[27]

In recent decades, many magazines have reduced their full-time staffs to rely more on freelancers than they have in the past. Today's typical magazine freelancer needs a computer and modem connected to the Internet. He can write in Billings, Montana, or Keokuk, Iowa, and find major library collections, government documents, and other research publications on the Internet. He can then sell his ideas, arrange a contract, and send his finished article to his editors electronically. If it snows in Billings or Keokuk and he's stuck in the house, he can continue to go about his business, connected electronically to his library, publisher, and editor. His editor in New York may be snowed in as well, but she will still receive the article electronically and can edit or check facts at home.

What can we expect from magazines in the third millennium? Magazine professionals say, for the short run, we can look for more of the same. The electronic magazine will not replace the printed form. We can soak in the tub with our magazines, take them hiking in the mountains with us, sit down with a cup of tea and relax with them. That's a relationship the computer cannot match. The Internet, like the magazine, has become a storehouse. And magazines have expanded into an electronic form. Their strength, however, continues to be in their printed and bound nature, in the comfort level a reader reaches when he settles down with his favorite magazine, puts his feet up, and reads. What Sam Ferber said of magazines in 1979 continues to be true:

> *Magazines define who we are and where we fit into society. They delineate the problems with which we are faced and, when they are functioning at their best, provide the range of solutions that are open to us. They remind us that news, or information, is not necessarily understanding. They help us search for meaning in a complex, often bewildering world. Above all, they force us to take the time to reflect when life is moving all around us at a breakneck pace.*[28]

Publishing a magazine overnight is not impossible, although it is demanding. At the 1996 summer Olympic Games in Atlanta, *Sports Illustrated* produced 18 daily issues, going to press every night. Titled *Sports Illustrated Olympics Daily*, the magazine had 12 advertisers, including Visa, Xerox, and Atlanta-based Coca-Cola.

FOR ADDITIONAL READING

Abrahamson, David, ed. *The American Magazine: Research Perspectives and Prospects.* Ames: Iowa State University, 1995.

Click, J. William, and Russell N. Baird. *Magazine Editing and Production,* 6th ed. Madison, WI: Brown & Benchmark, 1994.

Ford, James L. C. *Magazines for Millions.* Carbondale: Southern Illinois University Press, 1969.

Husni, Samir. *Samir Husni's Guide to New Consumer Magazines, 1997 edition.* New York: Oxbridge Communications, 1997.

Peterson, Theodore. *Magazines in the Twentieth Century.* Urbana: University of Illinois Press, 1964.

Riley, Sam G., and Gary W. Selnow, eds. *Regional Interest Magazines of the United States.* New York: Greenwood Press, 1991.

Taft, William H. *American Magazines for the 1980s.* New York: Hastings House, 1982.

Wolseley, Roland E. *Understanding Magazines.* Ames: Iowa State University Press, 1965.

ENDNOTES

[1] In 1990, a jury found *Soldier of Fortune* magazine liable for $12 million for publishing an ad: "GUN FOR HIRE: 37-year-old professional mercenary desires jobs. Vietnam veteran. Discreet and very private. Body guard, courier and other special skills. All jobs considered." A businessman used the ad to hire a person to kill his associate. The associate's sons sued successfully; the District Court judge noted that "the publisher could recognize the offer of criminal activity as readily as its readers obviously did." John D. Zelezny, *Communications Law, Liberties, Restraints and the Modern Media* (Belmont, CA: Wadsworth, 1993): 95.

[2] "The News That Isn't Delivered Day and Night," advertisement appearing in *The New Yorker* (January 24, 1983): 75.

[3] *American HomeStyle & Gardening* (Media Kit, Spring 1997).

[4] *Modern Plastics International 1996 Market and Media Guide* (Media Kit, Spring 1997).

[5] Marty Oetting, "Journalism as Commerce," *Service Journalism Dialogue* (November 1988): 5.

[6] Sam Ferber, "Magazines: The Medium of Enlightenment," *USA Today* (July 1979): 43–44.

[7] Theodore Peterson, *Magazines in the Twentieth Century* (Urbana: University of Illinois Press, 1964): 442.

[8] *The 1996/97 Magazine Handbook: A Comprehensive Guide for Advertisers, Ad Agencies and Magazine Marketers,* 68 (New York: Magazine Publishers of America, 1996): 43.

[9] Ferber, 44.

[10] "The News That Isn't Delivered Day and Night."

[11] "A Note from the President," *Youth Alive!* (Winter 1996): 5.

[12] Unless otherwise noted, circulation numbers are the most current audited figures available when this book went to print and reflect the first half of 1998.

[13] *The Business Side of Business Magazines* (New York: Business Press Educational Foundation, Inc., no date): 1.

[14] Constance L. Hays, "Seeing Green in a Yellow Border," *The New York Times* (August 3, 1997): 1F.

[15] Elissa Matulis Myers, "The Special Challenge of Association Periodicals Publishing," in *A Guide to Periodicals Publishing for Associations,* Frances Shuping, ed. (Washington, DC: The American Society of Association Executives, 1995), vii–ix.

[16] Kenneth E. Warner, Linda M. Goldenhar, and Catherine G. McLaughlin, "Cigarette Advertising and Magazine Coverage of the Hazards of Smoking," *The New England Journal of Medicine* (January 20, 1992): 305–9.

[17] *The Blue Book* (New York: Public Relations Society of America, 1996): 10.

[18] "About This Issue," *The North American Review* (March/April 1996): 2.

[19] Tom McNichol, "The Mini-Magazine Craze," *USA Weekend* (August 11–13, 1995): 10.

[20] Randy Jones, "What Drives Magazine Publishing Now," Stanford Professional Publishing Course, Palo Alto, CA (July 21, 1997).

[21] *Policies and Procedures in Association Management 1996.*

[22] *Veronis, Suhler & Associates Communications Industry Forecast,* "Magazine Publishing" Veronis, Suhler and Associates: 1998): 304, 322–33.

[23] Carol McGarvey, "Remodel with the Click of a Mouse," *The Des Moines Register* (September 13, 1996): 3T.

[24] http://www2.The Atlantic.com/Atlantic/home.htm.

[25] http://www.motherjones.com/info/bios.html. January 19, 1999.

[26] http://homearts.com/homepage.html. February 16, 1995.

[27] Jeff Laurie, "Web Offers Natural Resources for Publishers," *Folio:* (December 15, 1995): 55.

[28] Ferber, 43.

CHAPTER 2

The Magazine as a Marketplace

The Role of Advertising

Pete Shepley had a hobby he loved—designing archery equipment. In the late 1970s, he began mass-producing his high-tech bows and turned to magazines for promotion. He advertised in the highly targeted titles Bowhunting World *and* Archery Business. *By 1982, he had moved his production out of the barn behind his Tucson, Arizona, home into a 75,000-square-foot plant. By the late 1980s, he had added 100,000 square feet and entered the world of big business. Shepley's hobby had become Precision Shooting Equipment, a leader in the multimillion-dollar bowhunting and archery industry. "Innovation and magazines have been the backbone of our 20 years of continued success," Shepley said.*[1] 📖 *Shepley's success hinged on producing a quality product promoted directly to the people who wanted it and could afford it. He chose magazines to reach his consumers because of the effectiveness of special interest titles in reaching a highly defined audience.* 📖 *As advertising vehicles, magazines are part of our marketing system. Advertising sales people talk about magazines as "buys" and view magazine audiences not just as readers but as potential markets for their products. Publishers define a successful magazine as one that not only appeals to its audience of readers but also develops a loyal base of readership that appeals to advertisers.* 📖 *Advertisers spent $17.9 billion in magazines in 1997—$8.1 billion in trade magazines and $9.8 billion in consumer magazines. Advertising grew steadily through the 1990s, beginning with a $12.2 billion total in 1990.*[2]

Advertisers choose magazines because, simply, that's where they find consumers of their products, and advertising rates are determined by the specific characteristics of the magazine audience. Today's major advertisers are manufacturers and retailers of consumer goods such as automobiles and computers; media conglomerates and multiple-title publishing houses are the leaders in advertising revenue. Historically, magazines became major players in the ad game when publishers discovered that advertising could help pay the bills, allowing them to lower the cost of the magazine to readers. Some magazines, however, have chosen to avoid advertising because of concerns about advertiser influence on the editorial product as well as because of personal preference.

WHY ADVERTISERS CHOOSE MAGAZINES

Advertisers follow readers and, therefore, depend on magazines because of the credibility of the medium, the quality of the reader, and the quality of the product or brand.

Credibility

Advertisers are attracted to magazines because of their halo effect. Readers believe so strongly in their magazines and feel such a solid connection with them that they tend to trust the advertising they carry. Research done by the Opinion Research Corporation found that consumers consider magazines the most helpful and least confusing medium for product information. For example, 51 percent of those surveyed believed that magazines are the most helpful in making healthy or nutritious food choices, compared with just 22 percent who said the same of television. Conversely, 51 percent of the respondents consider TV food ads the most misleading of all media, compared with just 10 percent for magazines.[3]

Reader Quality

When advertisers buy space in magazines, they are buying the magazine's audience. In fact, you can usually determine the characteristics of a magazine's audience just by looking at the ads. Luxury cars are advertised in magazines that appeal to high-income consumers—*Saveur* or *Condé Nast Traveler*—while minivans are advertised in home and family titles—*Family Fun* or *Parenting*. Magazines appeal to advertisers

WHAT DO PEOPLE READ IN THE BATHROOM?

A study done in 1985 by Simmons Market Research found that one out of every three Americans reads in the bathroom. Based on a survey of 1,000 adults above the age of 18 years, Simmons found that women between the ages of 35 and 49 are "especially avid bathroom readers." Their magazine of choice was *True Story,* founded in 1919.

In order, here's what people said they preferred to read:

1. *True Story*
2. *Seventeen* (Simmons said that it "may be that a magazine is brought into the bathroom by a young woman or teenager and then read there by Mom or an older sister.")
3. *Time*
4. *Sport*
5. *Sports Illustrated*
6. *Money* (tied)
   Mother Earth News
8. *Sports Afield*
10. *Prevention* (tied)
    Cosmopolitan

Others listed: *Playboy, Popular Mechanics,* and *Reader's Digest.* 

because of their highly targeted audiences. In general, magazine readers have higher incomes and are better educated than users of other media, and magazine audiences show a higher level of commitment and response. Advertising rates are determined by audience characteristics.

HIGHLY TARGETED. When advertisers buy placement in a magazine, they carefully study the readers' demographics and psychographics. Demographics include a precise definition of characteristics such as age, education, income levels, and geographic location. Psychographics include lifestyle issues such as how readers feel about classical music, whether they vote, and if they like to travel.

When the Lexus automobile was introduced, the advertising for the new car ran in *AutoWeek* magazine. The Lexus was a new luxury car competing against established brands, and the advertising staff looked for the most efficient method of reaching those consumers who tend to buy cars often and who have the income to afford a high sticker price. *AutoWeek* readers fit the bill: They owned an average of 4.7 vehicles and, in 1990 when Lexus was launched, earned an average income of $89,300. Equally important is that *AutoWeek* readers are opinion leaders about automobiles, advising others on buying decisions. Richard Anderman, national advertising manager of Lexus, credited the magazine's weekly publication with spreading the news about the new car quickly, thus making it "an indispensable part of what has proven to be one of the most successful launches in history."[4]

HIGH INCOME AND EDUCATION. Magazine readers are, on average, more educated and affluent than the average adult. Research by Audits and Surveys, Inc., shows that educated adults "read magazines more thoroughly, are exposed to the average page more frequently, and also see the ads more frequently" than less-educated readers. Who are magazine readers? Look at the figures on the following page.

AUGUST 20, 1990: *AutoWeek* readers own an average of 4.7 vehicles and are opinion leaders about automobiles, advising others on buying decisions.

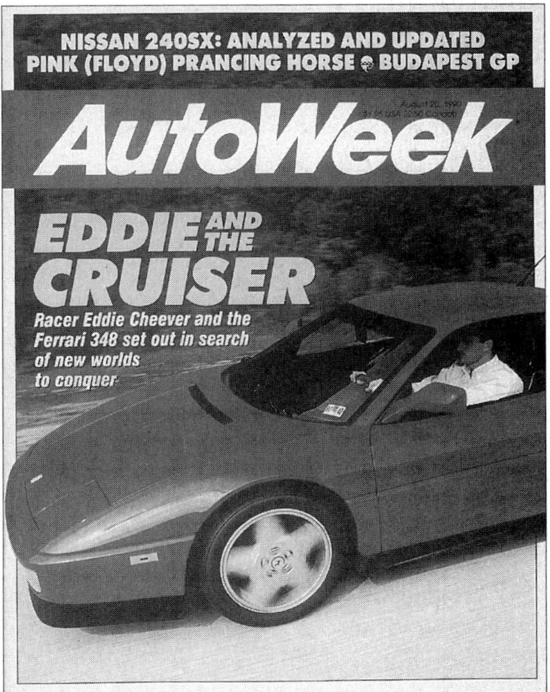

NISSAN 240SX: ANALYZED AND UPDATED
PINK (FLOYD) PRANCING HORSE BUDAPEST GP
AutoWeek
EDDIE AND THE CRUISER
Racer Eddie Cheever and the Ferrari 348 set out in search of new worlds to conquer

- Adults with college educations, those who have professional or managerial jobs, and those with household incomes over $60,000 read an average of 13.9 issues a month.
- 166 million adults—87 percent of the U.S. population 18 years or older—read one or more magazines a month. These readers read an average of 12.3 different issues per month.
- 84 percent of U.S. men and 89 percent of U.S. women read at least one issue a month. More than 90 percent of adults who have graduated from college read more than one magazine a month.[5]

American magazines distributed 8 billion pages of information on business and industry in 1996. Magazines are the medium of choice for information on money matters: According to research done in 1996, 45 percent of all U.S. adults chose magazines as the top source for knowledge and usable ideas on personal economic issues, compared to 11 percent who chose television, 31 percent who chose newspapers, and 2 percent who chose radio.

Harper's and *The Atlantic Monthly* appeal to an audience of avid readers interested in quality fiction and essays as well as analytical and in-depth nonfiction. Even though they are two of the country's oldest titles—both were started in the 1850s—in recent years their fortunes have been mixed because of a seemingly limited audience base. However, in 1994 both magazines began rebounding; it was the first time in decades that both were in the black. Both saw an increase in advertising and in subscription and newsstand sales. Analysts suggested that the magazines' editorial strength and emphasis on providing top-quality reading material were the keys to their newfound success. Both advertisers and readers rediscovered the magazines that had been around more than a century because both were creatively and effectively reaching the needs of their audience.[6]

COMMITTED AND RESPONSIVE. Magazine readers keep their magazines and reread them. The typical magazine hangs around the house or office for 29 days, and the typical adult reader spends nearly four hours reading each issue. Magazine readers remember what they read in their magazines—both ads and other specific information—better than newspaper readers remember what was in the newspaper or television viewers remember what they saw on television. Magazine readers are more likely to purchase products they read about in a magazine advertisement than products advertised on television. They also are more likely to make purchases or act on information found in magazines than on television. Research done for the Magazine Publishers of America by Beta Research found:

- 83 percent of adults consider magazine ads "usually appealing." Only 69 percent of television viewers made the same statement.
- 44 percent of magazine readers shopped for a product or service after seeing it advertised in magazines, compared with 36 percent who were motivated by television commercials.[7]

Product

Magazines are essentially luxury items: Nobody really *needs* a magazine. Imagine living without your favorite title for a year. Chances are pretty good you would survive. Yet, even when you're trying to save pennies, it is still hard to resist that copy of *Entertainment Weekly* with Brad Pitt on the cover.

"Magazines are the classic impulse item," says Mike Gummeson, president of Aramark, a magazine and book distributor.[8] Fewer than 40 percent of magazine buyers intend to buy a magazine when they enter a store.[9] Why do they leave with a copy of *Self* or *Motor Trend* tucked under their arm? Because of the appeal of the product. They see a cover line that interests them, and, while leafing through the magazine, find an article they want to read, a photo that intrigues them, or a recipe they want to clip.

Advertisers know that readers are loyal to those titles that serve them well. A magazine's economic health hinges on the product. A quality product—be it a magazine or a pair of running shoes—attracts buyers. Conversely, without a quality product, sales eventually drop. In the case of magazines, without product sales, advertising income eventually drops.

Busy Buyers

The busiest newsstand in the country, according to the Magazine Publishers of America, is in New York City's Metropolitan Life building, which is connected by escalator to Grand Central station. The newsstand carries nearly 4,000 magazine titles and serves an average 132,378 people a day. Its reach and diversity are demonstrated by this snippet of sales in a typical week:

15 copies of *West Africa;*

40 copies of *Broadcasting;*

60 to 80 copies of *Adweek* and *Advertising Age.*

The best-selling monthly is *Penthouse* at 550 copies. For weeklies, it's *Time* at 225 a week.

Brands

Marketers differentiate between products and brands. The product, they contend, is simply utilitarian, something the buyer values because of how usable it is. A brand, however, implies a specific product image and means that the consumer has some sort of relationship with that brand. For example, you might go to Sears for your car battery because that's where your parents bought their car batteries. Similarly, you trust *Good Housekeeping* because you grew up with it.

A well-positioned and well-produced brand builds consumer loyalty and allows the creative publisher to create product extensions, or ancillary products.

Ancillary Products

Magazines are increasing their profits by lending their names to related products, such as *Field & Stream* fishing lures, *Martha Stewart Living* house paint, *Playboy*'s Hugh Hefner signature cigars, *National Geographic* greeting cards, and *WorkBoat*'s annual International WorkBoat Show. According to the Magazine Publishers of America, magazines earned more than $60 million from such ancillary products or product extensions in 1994. Most of these products are marketing endeavors, created to expand the profitability and advertising reach of the original brand. These extensions are based on the belief that a magazine name, like other brand names, can be franchised, or leased, for use on related goods or services. The Magazine Publishers of America called the 1990s "The Decade of Franchise Development."[10]

On its May 1951 cover, *McCall's* introduced its Betsy McCall paper doll. For 40 years, the magazine carried stories about Betsy, accompanied by the cutout doll and new clothes. In 1996, the three-dimensional Betsy debuted. The newest incarnation, however, is for grown-up baby boomers—a $75 artist-designed collector's doll.

Magazines have traditionally published related books, with the *Better Homes and Gardens New Cook Book* being perhaps the most famous. Now, Meredith Corporation, *Better Homes and Gardens*'s publisher, has diversified that product name to include connections with Hallmark Cards and Wal-Mart gardening supplies, plus a syndicated television show. TWA even offers extra frequent flyer miles to those who do business with Better Homes and Gardens Real Estate. According to Meredith CEO William T. Kerr, for every dollar the company earns from *Better Homes and Gardens* magazine, it earns another dollar from products carrying the *Better Homes* name.

The president of Hearst Magazines, Cathleen Black, expects editors to consider product extension a part of their jobs. "Being a magazine editor," she says, "is more than just literally producing a magazine."[11] Hearst magazines offer a panoply of related products: a *Sports Afield* cookbook, plus hunting and fishing supplies; *House Beautiful* paint; and *Popular Mechanics* tools and plumbing supplies.

Trade shows and professional seminars are becoming an increasingly popular ancillary product offered by trade, or business-to-business, magazines. *Folio:*, the magazine for magazine management, sponsors the *Folio:* Show, a conference and exposition for the magazine industry, held yearly in New York, Chicago, and Los Angeles.

Forty percent of all readers start a magazine at the back, and 67 percent start from some place other than the front of the book.

CONFIDENCE IN THE *GOOD HOUSEKEEPING* SEAL OF APPROVAL

Since the early 1900s, *Good Housekeeping* has operated in a climate of confidence that benefits both readers and advertisers. For advertisers, the strength of a magazine is determined by the degree of confidence readers have in the editorial product. No magazine has been more successful in gaining readers' confidence than *Good Housekeeping*.

The magazine was an early champion of reliable products for its homemaker readers at the turn of the century, creating a *Good Housekeeping* Testing Institute in 1901 as a place to test foods and household products for purity. In 1909, the magazine went a step further with the *Good Housekeeping* Seal. This was a guarantee that products advertised in the magazine had been "tested and approved by the *Good Housekeeping* Institute" for quality assurance.

Dr. Harvey A. Wiley, a chemist for the Department of Agriculture, became the head of the *Good Housekeeping* Institute in 1912. Wiley quickly established the Seal's clout and integrity, making *Good Housekeeping* a trusted family friend to its readers. The Seal of Approval was explained to readers in a June 1919 issue:

> Good Housekeeping *guarantees its advertisements.* Good Housekeeping *maintains laboratories where all good products are tested and all household appliances are tried out before they are admitted to our advertising pages.* Good Housekeeping *will not accept the advertisement of any kind of a product in which it does not have full confidence.* Good Housekeeping *will not knowingly advertise a good product for a wrong purpose.*

Said Wiley upon his retirement in 1929, *"Good Housekeeping* has never advertised any articles unless approved by me. In 17 years more than a million dollars of advertising offered *Good Housekeeping* in my department has been rejected."[1]

The Seal has been modified or redesigned just three times. In 1941, a "Guaranty Seal" replaced the "Seal of Approval," stating that *Good Housekeeping* would give readers a replacement or a refund if a product was "not as advertised therein." By 1975, the Seal's guarantee conditions became "A Limited Warranty to Consumers" with *Good Housekeeping*'s promise of "replacement or refund if defective." This change reflected 1975 federal law

National Geographic has expanded into television documentaries on NBC and PBS, in addition to creating road maps, travel atlases, and national park guides to be sold in retail outlets. Former *National Geographic* publisher Gil Grosvenor, whose family held the reins at the National Geographic Society for five generations, says successful branding requires caution. Speaking in 1997, a year after retiring, he said, "Image takes a long time to develop, in our case, 108 years. But images can be destroyed overnight. They are very fragile."[12]

***Folio:* magazine's ancillary products include books, conferences, and expositions—even training materials on developing ancillary products.**

requirements regulating consumer warranties and guarantees.

The most recent modification for the Seal, in 1997, was an extension of the long-standing warranty on products to two years from one year. According to publisher Patricia Haegele, a two-year *Good Housekeeping* Seal warranty is advantageous for both consumers and advertisers. Pointing out that many companies already provide one-year warranties for their products, Haegele said the two-year *Good Housekeeping* Seal warranty "gives the consumer an advantage over what they are getting."[2] The Seal continues to provide for the replacement or refund of products that are defective. "No other magazine in the world offers this kind of service to its readers," stated *Good Housekeeping* in its 1997 advertising campaign about the warranty extension.

It is obvious that the *Good Housekeeping* Seal has become a potent advertising tool on several levels. Consumers feel good about buying products advertised in *Good Housekeeping,* while advertisers gain an image of enhanced reliability and security. The result for advertisers, according to *Good Housekeeping,* is that the Seal increases sales: "Periodic marketplace tests . . . conclusively prove that the Seal is a positive and powerful persuader that helps sell merchandise."[3] While an advertiser can't buy the use of the Seal, it must purchase at least a page of advertising a year to be tested. In 1998, a full-page color ad cost $174,385.

Good Housekeeping's advertising revenues have been enhanced rather than hurt by the Seal. From the start, *Good Housekeeping* refused the lucrative cigarette and alcohol advertising dollars accepted by other women's magazines. Consequently, it was free to publish such articles as "Can Your Husband's Cigarette Give You Cancer?" (as early as May 1981) without worrying about advertiser pressure. In an April 1983 letter to the editor, one reader praised *Good Housekeeping* for its refusal to publish cigarette ads, noting that as much as 12 percent of the ad pages in other women's magazines featured cigarettes. Yet in 1983, *Good Housekeeping* was number one among the Seven Sisters in both ad volume and revenue with 2,097 ad pages and $127.2 million in ad sales.[4]

Even now, *Good Housekeeping*'s ad pages are growing at more than twice the rate of its sister magazines. Publisher's Information Bureau figures put *Good Housekeeping*'s ad pages up 13 percent in the first half of 1997, with *Redbook* placing second at 5.9 percent. *Good Housekeeping* also continues to be one of the top 10 magazines in circulation year after year.

[1] Helen Woodward, *The Lady Persuaders* (New York: Ivan Obolensky, 1960): 128.
[2] "*Good Housekeeping* to Boost Warranty on Advertised Products to Two Years," *The Wall Street Journal* (August 1, 1997): 12B.
[3] Advertisement, *Advertising Age* (November 8, 1982): 7.
[4] *The Folio: 400/1984,* (October 1984): 329.

Advertising Rates

Advertising rates are based on the size of the magazine audience—its total circulation—and the specific demographics and psychographics of that audience. A magazine with a highly desirable audience that can't be reached easily by other magazines or other media can ask higher rates than a magazine that appeals to audiences easily reached by other media. Food advertisers can reach the American family through television, radio, newspapers, and a variety of magazines, so ad rates for family magazines have to reflect that competitive environment. Manufacturers of commercial boats, however, can reach professional fishermen through only a handful of trade publications, which can therefore ask premium ad rates. Advertisers determine the actual cost of a magazine ad based on costs per thousand, or CPMs.

Costs per thousand, or CPMs, help advertisers determine the relative value of a magazine ad. The CPM is the cost of the ad divided by the audience delivered, or circulation, divided by a thousand. Advertising professionals use the following formula:

$$\frac{\text{Total Ad Cost}}{\text{Gross Audience} \div 1{,}000} = \text{CPM}$$

If an ad costs $10,000 a page for a magazine with 100,000 circulation, the CPM is $100; an ad that costs $100,000 a page in a magazine with 1 million circulation also has a CPM of $100:

$$\frac{\$10{,}000}{1{,}000\ (100{,}000 \div 1{,}000)} = \$100$$

$$\frac{\$100{,}000}{10{,}000\ (1{,}000{,}000 \div 1{,}000)} = \$100$$

Table 2.1 demonstrates the relationship between audience, circulation, ad cost, CPMs, and advertisers.

TABLE 2.1 Magazines and Their Audiences

MAGAZINE	READER BRIEF	AD COST[1]	CIRCULATION[2]	CPM	MAJOR ADVERTISERS[3]
American HomeStyle & Gardening	Upscale homeowners who want practical advice about architecture, remodeling, decorating, gardening, and entertaining.	$39,240	930,155	$42	Chevy Astro KitchenAid Kohler
Gourmet	Affluent, middle-aged, educated professionals with an interest in fine food, travel, and entertaining.	$49,640	880,744	$56	Lexus Benson & Hedges Chanel
Guitar Player	Dedicated guitarists committed to their music and their equipment; 97 percent record their own music.	$8,320	133,163	$62	Fender Mackie Kaman Corporation
Poz	People who are HIV positive or have AIDS.	$11,050	70,382	$158	Crixivan Capsules Stadtlanders Pharmacy Sandoz Nutrition Laboratories
Window Fashions	Dealers, retailers, designers, and fabric consultants involved in selling or designing window furnishings.	$5,325	18,664	$280	Graber ADO Kirsch
WorkBoat	Captains, owners, managers, operators, and chief engineers of commercial marine vessels under 400 feet in length.	$3,170	16,065	$198	Simrad Karl Senner, Inc. Furuno

[1] Rates are for full-color, full-page ads inside the magazine, one-time insertion, for 1997.
[2] 1997 figures.
[3] Second, third, and fourth covers—or inside front cover, inside back cover, and back cover.

WHO ADVERTISES IN MAGAZINES

The biggest magazine advertisers are automotive manufacturers; they contributed $1.8 billion to the consumer magazine economy in 1997. They were followed by toiletries and cosmetics at $1.12 billion; direct response companies at $1.09 billion; computers, office equipment, and stationery at $1.08 billion; and business and consumer services at $1.02 billion.[13]

The top individual magazine advertisers are large, multinational corporations. The top advertiser, General Motors, dominates transportation on the highways, railways, and skyways by owning Buick, Cadillac, Chevrolet, Oldsmobile, Pontiac, and Saturn, and by producing aircraft engines as well as diesel locomotives and engines. The number two advertiser, Procter & Gamble, manufactures and distributes household, personal care, food, and coffee products such as Tide, Ivory Soap, Crisco, Pringle's, Duncan Hines, Charmin, Pampers, and Folgers. Philip Morris, number three, owns such cigarette brands as Marlboro, Virginia Slims, and Benson & Hedges, as well as Miller Brewing and Kraft Foods. The top advertisers and their spending for 1997, in millions, are shown in Table 2.2.

TABLE 2.2 Top Advertisers and Their Spending in 1997 (in Millions)[1]

General Motors Corporation	$ 588.4
Procter & Gamble	$ 363.4
Philip Morris Companies	$ 345.4
Chrysler Corporation	$ 327.9
Ford Motor Company	$ 284.8
Time Warner	$ 180.1
Toyota Motor Company	$ 149.1
Johnson & Johnson	$ 140.8
Unilever	$ 131.1
L'Oreal	$ 104.3

[1] "Top 25 Magazine Advertisers," *Advertising Age* (September 28, 1998): s26.

TABLE 2.3 Top Companies in Advertising Income[1]

PUBLISHER	REPRESENTATIVE TITLES	1997 AD INCOME
Time Warner	*Time, People, Sports Illustrated, Entertainment Weekly*	$1.8 billion
Condé Nast	*The New Yorker, Gourmet, Glamour, GQ, Vanity Fair*	$743 million
Hearst Magazines	*Cosmopolitan, Esquire, Harper's Bazaar, Sports Afield*	$704 million
Hachette Filipacchi	*Car Stereo Review, Elle, Metropolitan Home, Premiere*	$612 million
Meredith Corporation	*Better Homes and Gardens, Ladies' Home Journal, Successful Farming*	$494 million

[1] "1997 Ad Page Leaders," *Advertising Age* (October 27, 1997): 68.

WHERE THEY ADVERTISE

Today's magazine industry is also controlled by large corporations—media conglomerates or multiple-title publishing houses. Not surprisingly, these magazine corporations are the leaders in advertising income. At the top is Time Warner, a major publisher of weekly magazines—*People, Sports Illustrated, Entertainment Weekly,* and *Time.* Weeklies can earn more yearly advertising income than other titles because of the frequency with which they are published; they lead in the total number of pages published and, therefore, they lead in advertising pages and advertising income. The top companies in advertising income are shown in Table 2.3.

Advertising revenue translates into a tidy sum for individual titles. The top 10 U.S. magazines in total ad revenues in 1997 brought in a combined $4.1 billion, or an average of $400 million per magazine. The totals were, in millions:[14]

People	$588
Sports Illustrated	$548
Time	$533
TV Guide	$469
Newsweek	$408
Better Homes and Gardens	$377
PC Magazine	$333
Business Week	$329
Forbes	$243
U.S. News & World Report	$239

The "hottest" magazines are rated every year by *Adweek* in terms of advertising page increase, advertising revenue gain, and circulation gains in a year's time. Additionally, advertising media buyers are interviewed. Magazines must have a minimum ad revenue in order to be considered; that minimum has ranged from $8 million in 1985 to $10 million in 1990. It then jumped to $20 million for 1995. Table 2.4 shows the winners for 1985, 1990, and 1995.

An examination of these three years shows some interesting marketplace changes. In 1985, smaller magazines dominated the list of hot magazines. *American Health* took the top spot as Americans began to show more interest in fitness issues. *Parade* was a surprise to some because many magazine professionals consider it a newspaper supplement and not a magazine. *New Woman,* a new entry in the slick women's magazine field, seemed to appeal to women tired of the so-called "Seven Sisters" service-oriented magazines: *Good Housekeeping, Ladies' Home Journal, Redbook, McCall's, Family Circle, Woman's Day,* and *Better Homes and Gardens.* Not surprisingly, *Modern Maturity* did well as more people began nearing their fifties. *Rolling*

TABLE 2.4

Adweek's Hottest Magazines

1985	1990	1995
American Health	Parenting	Martha Stewart Living
Parade	Condé Nast Traveler	Men's Health
New Woman	Victoria	Better Homes and Gardens
Modern Maturity	The Economist	Allure
Country Living	Financial World	SmartMoney
Gourmet	Decorating Remodeling	Country Living
Rolling Stone	The Atlantic	Newsweek
Car and Driver	Entrepreneur	Condé Nast Traveler
Home	Parade	Entertainment Weekly
Motor Trend	Premiere	Prevention

Stone was helped by a "Perception vs. Reality" ad campaign that reminded a lot of media buyers that the rock 'n' rollers of the 1960s continued to be buyers of big-ticket items in the 1980s and were still reading the magazine. Advertisers and readers seemed to favor three quintessential American interests in 1985: home, car, and food (*Country Living, Home, Car and Driver, Motor Trend,* and *Gourmet*).

Although 1989 was one of the most prosperous years in magazine history, 1990 saw the bubble burst. Advertising pages fell short month after month, and publishers felt the sting of too many start-ups and acquisitions. The top magazine, *Parenting,* was successful because of its conceptual approach to child rearing, a method that found a lot of appeal among upscale, issues-oriented yuppies who were becoming parents. *Condé Nast Traveler* was favored because of its honest and strong editorial stance, while *Victoria* seemed to take the opposite end of the spectrum with its dreamy escapism and lace-filled elegance of times gone by. *The Economist* and *Financial World* both reflected the need for world views and business sense in a tough American economy. Most home and shelter books saw substantial page and ad revenue drops in 1990, but *Decorating Remodeling* did well with its practical, affordable approach to changing residential needs. *The Atlantic Monthly* received kudos for being an "egghead" magazine appealing to a solidly intellectual audience. *Entrepreneur* reflected the growth of small businesses and the number of American white-collar workers who decided to take control of their working lives by starting their own companies. This year also marked the start of massive corporate layoffs and downsizing; some people simply were forced to go into business for themselves. *Parade,* still on the list five years later, was a good buy for newspapers who cut their own Sunday magazines in a bid to save money. *Premiere,* the movie magazine with a movie-buff approach to the industry, caught the wave of a down economy that traditionally drives people to search for escape through entertainment.

The 1995 list highlighted magazine categories that baby boomers tend to devour—home, health, money, and leisure. Shelter magazines were triumphantly led by *Martha Stewart Living;* its circulation jumped 53 percent in just one year. The long-lived *Better Homes and Gardens* appeared on the hot list for the first time, while *Country Living* returned after a 10-year absence. Two magazines represented the burgeoning health market. The service-oriented *Men's Health* continued its run as a hot magazine, although it slipped from its number one place in 1994. The 46-year-old *Prevention,* riding high on its new mainstream editorial focus, joined the list for the first time. *SmartMoney,* also a repeat from 1994, reflected the ongoing interest in personal finance. Leisure interests were represented by two magazines. *Condé Nast Traveler* again surfaced to tell the truth about travel after last being seen in second place in 1990 and in sixth place in 1989. *Entertainment Weekly,* with its chatty coverage of film, theater, books, and popular culture, seemed to be a perennial favorite, becoming the only magazine to make the hot list for five consecutive years, starting in 1991. The women's fashion and beauty market was represented by *Allure,* a hot magazine since 1993, while *Newsweek* made news fashionably

> ***Soldier of Fortune*** magazine avoids cigarette ads but fills its ad pages with messages from the National Rifle Association, Military Book of the Month Club, and Wesson Firearms.

MAGAZINE NUMBERS: WHO'S COUNTING?

The accuracy of circulation numbers for magazines published before 1914 depended on the integrity of the publisher. There was no system to check the numbers, so a publisher could tell advertisers his magazine reached 100,000 readers and the advertiser would have no way to verify that claim. The Audit Bureau of Circulations (ABC) was created to remedy this. Founded by publishers, advertisers, wholesalers, and retailers in 1914, its goal is to issue and verify standardized statements of circulation. Data provided by ABC are now used by agencies that report on magazine statistics.

BPA International was founded in 1931 as Controlled Circulation Audit to audit magazines with less than 70 percent paid circulation. It changed its name to Business Publication Audit of Circulation in 1954 and now, as BPA International, audits consumer as well as specialized business magazines.

Standard Rate and Data Service (SRDS) publishes monthly guidebooks that list the consumer and business magazines that carry advertising: *SRDS Consumer Magazine Advertising Source* and *SRDS Business Publication Advertising Source.* Both books provide a magazine's editorial profile as well as statistics on magazine ad rates, circulation, discounts, and special editions.

Mediamark Research Inc. (MRI) offers a precise analysis of magazine readers, organizing them into categories such as age, income, time spent reading, and occupation. MRI publishes reports twice a year, based on thousands of personal interviews. Its primary focus is on magazines, although its scope is multimedia. MRI provides estimates of audiences of major consumer publications by demographics and product usage characteristics. MRI also publishes annual studies of business-purchase decision makers, the affluent market, and the top 10 local markets. These provide estimates of demography, magazine readership, audience usage of other media, and marketing behavior. Because MRI is a resource for advertisers, it studies only magazines that carry advertising.

Simmons Market Research Bureau publishes *Study of Media and Markets,* an annual report similar to MRI's. Simmons profiles magazine readership by demography and purchase behaviors through personal interviews.

The Publishers Information Bureau, a division of the Magazine Publishers of America, provides analyses of revenue and expenses of major American magazines.

interesting. *Newsweek* had last appeared as a hot magazine in 1979.

Over 17 years, has any publication on *Adweek*'s hottest magazine list ever failed or been shut down? *Signature,* on the list in 1986, was purchased from Citicorp Diners Club by Condé Nast and shut down, then relaunched as the very successful *Condé Nast Traveler* in 1987. *Connoisseur,* a Hearst magazine targeted to affluent readers, was laid to rest in 1992 despite raves as a hot magazine in 1986. *House & Garden,* a hot book for 1984, got the ax in 1993 but returned to the newsstands in 1996. *Decorating Remodeling* was bought by Gruner and Jahr in 1990; the name has since been changed to *American HomeStyle & Gardening.*

THE BIRTH OF ADVERTISING IN MAGAZINES

The first ad in an American magazine appeared the same year the magazine medium appeared in this country: 1741. On May 10 of that year, Richard Brett, deputy postmaster at the Potomac River, ran an ad in Benjamin Franklin's *The General Magazine, and Historical Chronicle, For All the British Plantations in America,* for a ferry across the Potomac from Annapolis to Williamsburg.[15] It was small and unobtrusive, typical of advertising at that time. The earliest American magazines had little or no advertising. What ads appeared were hidden in the back of the magazine. Most were for almanacs or books, and their design resembled that of contemporary classified advertising. Before 1860, the typical business-to-business magazine had only 25 percent advertising, compared with an average of 60 percent today.[16] All this changed during the industrial revolution at the turn of the twentieth century that brought mass production, mass distribution, and the potential for mass audiences.

Up to that time, Americans generally bought from people they knew—cheese from the farmer down the road and wool from the mill on the edge of town. When they did shop in retail stores,

TABLE 2.5

Advertising Income and Circulation for the *Saturday Evening Post*[1]

YEAR	AVERAGE CIRCULATION	AVERAGE ADVERTISING INCOME
1902	314,671	$360,125
1912	1,920,550	$7,114,581
1922	2,187,024	$28,278,755

[1] Theodore Peterson, *Magazines in the Twentieth Century* (Urbana: University of Illinois Press, 1964): 12.

the goods they purchased were usually locally made and fresh. They bought one pickle at a time from the pickle barrel and a hunk of cheese from the farm in the next county. Few prepackaged goods existed.

Mass production and the growth of the railroads changed all this, starting in the late 1880s. America became a national, rather than local, economy. The mill in Massachusetts could mass-produce and mail its woolens to customers in Wisconsin. The farmer in Wisconsin could send his cheese to Massachusetts. How, though, were producers to educate potential buyers about the quality of their products? How would the buyer be able to differentiate among different cheeses and woolens? Enter the concept of brand names. In 1900, only 1,721 trademarks were registered by the United States Patent Office.[17] Twenty years later that had increased to 10,282. No longer was cheese just cheese—it was a Kraft product. Those woolens were made into scarves sold at newly created retail chains such as F.W. Woolworth or JCPenney.

Mass production and distribution also made the mass circulation magazine possible. Beginning at the turn of the twentieth century and continuing until the 1960s, magazines were characterized by huge circulations going to general audiences. Larger circulations could be produced more cheaply and distributed farther than at any time in American magazine history. As the only national medium, magazines were the logical conduit for information on brand differences.

Trade magazines provide information on a $14 trillion institutional investing market. Readership of these magazines include more than 40,000 corporate treasury managers and 28,000 executives responsible for retirement plans.

Still, some publishers were reluctant to jump on the advertising bandwagon, preferring to keep their magazines unsullied by advertising. Occasionally the issue was more pragmatic than philosophical. At the turn of the twentieth century, *Harper's* refused $18,000 for an ad for Howe sewing machines on their back cover because they reserved that space to advertise their own books.[18]

Frank Munsey, though, jumped right in. In the 1890s Munsey, publisher and editor of *Munsey's* magazine, opened his pages to advertisers at the same time he boosted circulation and distribution. He reached a high volume of readers, which made his magazine appealing to a high volume of advertisers. The amount the advertisers paid for their ads allowed Munsey to reduce the price of his magazine from 35 cents to 10 cents. The low cost made the magazine more affordable to the less affluent reader, which increased circulation even more. The first 10-cent issue of *Munsey's*, in October 1893, had a 40,000 circulation. By 1895, it had reached 500,000.[19]

Contemporaries didn't look upon Munsey kindly, calling him a magazine "manufacturer" rather than a publisher. Munsey charged a flat CPM of $1. Other magazines printed a set rate but often gave advertisers a reduction for a variety of reasons. This practice, called rate dealing, had roots in the infancy of magazine advertising. The editor of *The Druggist*, writing in 1859, accused *Druggists' Circular* of accepting "half to two-thirds its published rates."[20] Rate dealing was the precursor to today's practice of "selling off the card," or offering rates lower than those published.

Once Munsey opened the door to advertising, however, other publishers moved right on in, and advertising in magazines has been a given ever since. In 1900 alone, *Harper's* carried more advertising than in its entire preceding 22 years combined.[21]

Magazine advertising income and circulation increased throughout the early years of the twentieth century, sometimes with awesome speed. Consider the examples for the *Saturday Evening Post* in Table 2.5.

The April 1929 issue of *Scribner's*, a literary monthly, included ads, all in either the front or the back of the book, for:

- Williams Ice-O-Matic Refrigeration: "Always Icy Cold, Never Merely Cool"
- Ciné-Kodak: "Simplest of Home Movie Cameras"
- Union Pacific, offering rail access to "Bryce Canyon, Our Newest National Park"
- Listerine antiseptic, advertised as a shampoo to rid the hair of dandruff
- Burleson Sanitarium, "An Ethical Institution Devoted Exclusively to the Treatment of All Rectal Diseases—EXCEPT CANCER"
- Lucky Strike cigarettes, illustrated with a young flapper with the ad copy reading: "I'm a 'Lucky Girl' because I've found a new way to keep my figure trim. Whenever the desire for a sweet tempts me, I light up a Lucky Strike."

Most advertising in *Scribner's* was for expensive products, illustrating the magazine's affluent target audience. The majority of magazines in the first half of the twentieth century, however, were less precisely targeted. Most were huge mass circulation vehicles, going to mass audiences. They were oversized—common cover dimensions were 10 by 12 inches—and fat with editorial content and advertising. The December 7, 1929, issue of the *Saturday Evening Post* was so ad-heavy it weighed nearly two pounds. Merchants bought copies of the magazine to use as wrapping paper because it was cheaper than a roll of paper. Many magazine publishers felt they had moved into something of an economic nirvana, with advertising providing a huge new source of income.

Most magazines kept roughly an average 60:40 advertising-to-editorial ratio, which translated into hundreds of ad pages a month for top sellers. For example:

- *Saturday Evening Post:* The October 9, 1954, issue sold for 15 cents, had 152 total pages, with 92 of those in ads, for a 60:40 advertising:editorial ratio.
- *Life*: The October 11, 1954, issue sold for 20 cents, had a total of 196 pages, with 114 of those in ads, for a 58:42 ratio.
- *Look*: The October 4, 1955, issue sold for 15 cents, had 122 total pages, with 66 of those being filled with ads, for a 54:46 ratio.

In 1954, the circulation leaders were general interest magazines with wide appeal. Table 2.6

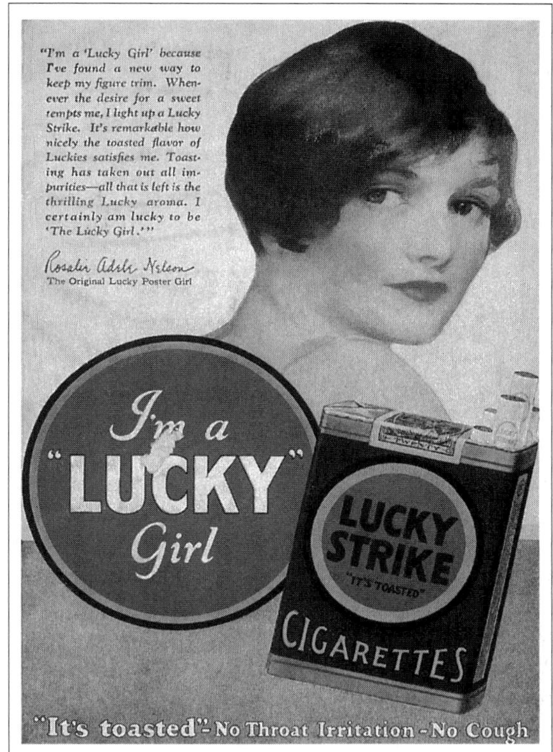

APRIL 1929: This Lucky Strike ad in *Scribner's* magazine advocated cigarette smoking as weight control.

illustrates how their 1954 and 1994 circulations compare.

Three titles showed an increase in the 40 years from 1954 to 1994—*Reader's Digest, Ladies' Home Journal,* and *McCall's*—but only *Reader's Digest* showed an increase above 5 percent. *Life* decreased by nearly 70 percent, and the current *Saturday Evening Post* is only one-tenth the size of its 1954 counterpart. Two 1954 top sellers, *Look* and *Woman's Home Companion,* no longer exist.

The fortunes of these magazines were tied to a startling change in the media marketplace beginning in the 1950s. With the advent of television, magazines lost their place as this country's only national medium. Advertisers flocked to television in the 1950s and 1960s because it reached more people than magazines and offered immediacy, drama, and emotion.

By the 1970s, magazines had re-created themselves into smaller, more efficient and more effective advertising vehicles by positioning themselves as the medium for the specialized audience. Gone were the two-pound ad-fat bullies. In their place were the streamlined and

TABLE 2.6

1954 and 1994 Circulation Figures for General Interest Magazines

MAGAZINE	1954 CIRCULATION[1]	1994 CIRCULATION[2]	PERCENT CHANGE
Reader's Digest	11,353,823	15,340,722	(+35%)
Life	5,311,747	1,610,329	(-69%)
Ladies' Home Journal	4,869,174	5,014,988	(+3%)
McCall's	4,446,146	4,603,692	(+4%)
Woman's Home Companion	4,315,147	no longer published	
Saturday Evening Post	4,216,017	460,044	(-89%)
Look	3,717,859	no longer published	

[1] Harry Hansen, ed., *The World Almanac Book of Facts 1954* (New York: World Telegram and Sun, 1954).
[2] *SRDS Consumer Magazine Advertising Source* (Des Plaines, Ill.: Standard Rate and Data Service, December 1995).

specialized titles that characterize the industry today.

Woman's Home Companion and *Look* were casualties of the television revolution, as was *Life*, which was killed in the 1970s, then restarted as a magazine better suited to the television age. *McCall's* and *Ladies' Home Journal* saw no benefit in growing significantly beyond 1950s numbers, choosing to offer the advertiser quality rather than quantity. *Reader's Digest*, a general interest mass market magazine just as it was in the 1950s, saw both a benefit and a need for a significant increase in numbers.

A study of *Life* provides an intriguing picture of magazines immediately before and after television. Like *Look*, it was a picture magazine, created to take advantage of the newly refined photographic technology. It predated television and did in print what television did in video—showed America pictures of itself.

The Absolut Vodka magazine ads have become so popular as art in college dorm rooms that some college and university libraries are placing a large black "X" over the entire ad to keep undergraduate interior designers from swiping the ad from the library's copy.

Life was America's first picture magazine and was published weekly at a cover price of 10 cents. The weekly magazine premiered on November 23, 1936, with a cover photo of Fort Peck Dam in Montana. The first editorial picture inside the magazine was symbolic: a full-page photo of an obstetrician slapping a baby to life, with the headline, "Life Begins." That issue sold out, and customers bought second-hand copies for as much as $1. Within weeks the magazine was selling a million copies an issue.

Life was founded in 1936 by Henry Luce, who bought the name from a humor magazine. Luce had been highly successful with the launch of *Time* and *Fortune*, and critics wondered why he would bother with a new start-up, instead of resting on his laurels. His excitement for the new magazine, however, was supported—some say initiated—by his wife Clare Booth Luce and was evident in a memo he sent to staffers four months after the first issue: "*Life* has a bias. *Life* is in favor of the human race, and is hopeful. *Life* is quicker to point with pride than to view with alarm."[22]

Life became one of America's most popular and best-read magazines by offering exclusive and timely coverage of the important moments in America's life, advertising itself as being "the showbook of the world." Its photographs often mesmerized a world not yet accustomed to breaking news, covered live. They remain some of the best photographic work ever published of World War II, the Vietnam conflict, and the civil rights movement, as well as the everyday lives of the impoverished and the powerful. In 1959, *Life* offered eyewitness stories of the first seven American astronauts; in 1961, it ran a special edition on the inauguration of the young president John F. Kennedy; and in 1963, it ran another special edition on his death. All were printed in the 10 1/2-by-13 1/2-inch format that gave photographs plenty of room.

Advertisers loved the magazine because Americans loved it. That relationship began to change in the late 1950s. *Life* continued publishing its impressive photography, but by this time

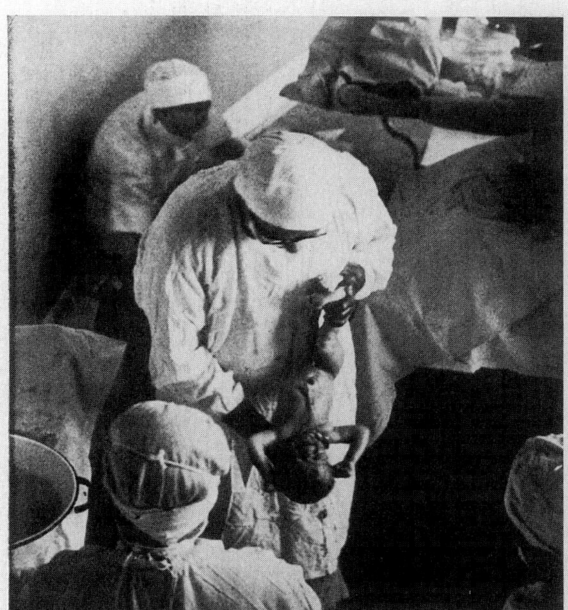

LIFE BEGINS

The camera records the most vital moment in any life: Its beginning. A few hours ago, the child lay restless in its mother's womb. A second ago, its foetal life was rudely ended when the surgeon snipped its umbilical cord—through which the unborn child had drawn all existence from its mother. Then, for a second or two, the child hung lank and unbreathing between two lives. Its blood circulated and its heart beat only on the impetus given by its mother. Suddenly the baby's new and independent life begins. He jerks up his arms, bends his knees and, with his first short breath, gives out a redfaced cry.

2 LIFE

Introduction to this first issue of

LIFE

Nov. 23rd 3

NOVEMBER 23, 1936 (PREMIERE ISSUE): *Life* magazine celebrated its own beginning with the photo of the birth of a baby, with the caption, "Life Begins."

other photographers were on the scene—those with television cameras. The photos *Life* ran were characteristically engaging, but the country had already seen many of the images on live television: John F. Kennedy Jr. saluting his father's coffin and the eternal flame being lit at Arlington National Cemetery. In 1969, *Life* published some of the first shots of the moon, but, once again, most Americans had stayed up late to watch the astronauts walk live on television. Television got to the consumer first.

The magazine continued to grow, however, continuing to believe in the prevalent pretelevision mentality that bigger was better. By 1969, *Life* had a circulation of 8.5 million, and a full-page color ad cost $64,000, which was more than the cost of a minute on prime-time television.[23]

In 1972, *Life* ceased publication, a victim not only of television but of high production and postal rates that punished large circulation magazines; the oversized format not only used more paper but was heavier and, therefore, more expensive to mail. Staff members also argued that the magazine was hurt by poor management and an unwillingness to change content to suit changing times. Whatever the cause of death, few advertisers mourned the magazine's passing; instead, they rode off into the sunset with the Cartwright family in "Bonanza," gambled on "Maverick," and took heavenly flight with "The Flying Nun." Food advertisers especially were lured to the new, more colorful and emotional medium that could reach consumers right before dinnertime, when their stomachs were the most susceptible to the television ads' messages.

The passing of *Life* magazine was like a death in the family to its staff. The last issue had one small word printed under the dateline and price: "Goodbye."

This emotion was behind the relaunching of the magazine six years later, in October 1978. The new *Life*, still published by Time/Life Inc., once again emphasized photography. This time, however, it was a monthly, with a cover price of $1.50, an initial run of only 700,000, and a target

RESEARCH IN BRIEF

Magazine-Made America

One of the most fascinating eras in magazine history came after World War II, when America's culture and economy were transformed by technology and social change. Professor David Abrahamson of Northwestern University charts this change in his book, *Magazine-Made America: The Cultural Transformation of the Postwar Periodical.*

Magazines published immediately after the war, Abrahamson writes, mirrored prewar publications aimed at general audiences and presenting general interest content. By the early 1970s, however, many of America's premier magazines had died: *Collier's, Liberty,* and *Woman's Home Companion.* Others faltered: *Life, Look,* and *Saturday Evening Post.*

According to Abrahamson, "Three principal causes led to these failures: television, mismanagement by publishing companies, and, as a less obvious but important undercurrent, an inability on the part of some of the publications to respond to fundamental sociocultural changes."[1]

Television lured many readers and advertisers away from magazines with its promise of more immediate and exciting news and entertainment. However, Abrahamson argues, management decisions made the situation worse. Publishers responded to television competition by trying to increase circulation, even to the extent of exaggerating pass-along readership. In addition, instead of selling advertisers on the quality of their readers, publishers promoted simple numbers, and increased ad rates to boot. So, while advertisers were hesitating about the appeal of magazines in comparison to television, publishers gave them added ammunition: They raised prices so that magazine advertising became increasingly less competitive than television advertising.

Abrahamson provides insight into advertisers' reaction to this dilemma. Wanting to help out magazines in the late 1960s, General Foods conducted a survey of reader reaction to television and to magazines. The results showed that readers were as likely to respond to magazine advertising as to television. As a result, General Foods, eventually joined by other advertisers, required that all ad buys include magazines. Abrahamson quotes General Foods' executive Archa Knowlton: "We wanted magazines to be able to compete against this monster that was devouring them."[2]

Many of the magazines that faltered or died, though, simply lost sight of their relationships with their audiences and with the changes in those audiences. Social researchers, notes Abrahamson, characterize the 1960s as a time of new attitudes and rules, and "the social and cultural values inherent in, for example, a Norman Rockwell *[Saturday Evening] Post* cover, *Liberty's* 'reading times,' or another starlet pictorial in *Life* seemed clearly out of step with the times."[3]

[1] David Abrahamson, *Magazine-Made America: The Cultural Transformation of the Postwar Periodical* (Cresskill, NJ: Hampton Press, 1996): 19.
[2] Ibid., 21.
[3] Ibid., 24.

DECEMBER 8, 1934: *Collier's,* a general interest magazine that didn't survive the advent of television, had a robust circulation of more than 2.4 million in the 1930s.

circulation of only 2 million—a fourth of its previous size. Ad rates also were quartered, with a full-color page selling for $13,900. The page size shrank several times through the years until it reached its present 9 by 10.87 inches.

Advertisers in that first "new" issue covered the economic gamut and included Mercedes-Benz, Lincoln-Mercury, Polaroid, Kmart, and McDonald's, indicating the broad range of the readers. Advertisers were eventually won over by a return of quality photography—this time matched with a smaller, more precise audience of avid readers with above-average education and income—and with significantly lower ad rates. Those rates only recently passed 1969 levels—a full-page color ad cost $67,575 in 1998, a scant $3,575 increase from 30 years before.

The new *Life,* while a slim version of its 1960s incarnation, remains a general interest publication, an anomaly in today's world of niche titles.

With its more affordable rates and more clearly defined audience, advertisers now view it as a good buy. Barbara Thompson, then vice president and associate media director of the advertising agency Lord, Dentsu and Partners in Los Angeles, said in 1994 that the magazine's appeal to advertisers was that it was "a very broad-based publication."[24]

Life continues publication, but it is neither a circulation nor advertising leader. Those places are now held by specialized titles. Look at the advertising leaders shown on page 33. All are specialized titles; the only one with broad appeal is the one with the closest tie to television: *TV Guide.*

AD-FREE MAGAZINES

Several contemporary magazines have made a conscious decision to avoid advertising. Some magazines, such as *Consumer Reports,* believe advertising would compromise their editorial integrity. *Consumer Reports* tests and evaluates consumer products; because the magazine does not depend on advertising, the staff can present an unflattering report on a product without risk of offending advertisers. The magazine often prints negative information about products—not a great environment for advertising.

Other magazines, like the on-again, off-again *Ms.*, believe advertising interferes with their advocacy function. *Ms.* accepted advertising for nearly 20 years, but ran head-first into advertiser opposition to the magazine's articles on such topics as battered women and abortion. In 1990, the editors and publishers launched an ad-free *Ms.* Robin Morgan, former editor of *Ms.*, chronicles the magazine's fight with advertisers in the "Magazine Voices" section at the back of this book. The magazine suspended publication twice in its short life—once in 1989 and once in 1998.

Most children's magazines, such as *Highlights for Children,* traditionally have been advertising-free because of a desire to keep commerce from competing with the magazine's educational function.

Some relatively recent magazine launches, though, have been advertising-free simply because of the publisher's preference. Reiman Publishing in Wisconsin and August Home Publishing in Iowa are multimillion-dollar enterprises built primarily on circulation, or income from readers. August's flagship magazine, *Woodsmith,* is ad-free, as are its newer starts *Cuisine* and *Garden Gate.* Founder Don Peschke says he simply didn't want to bother with advertising when he first started publishing. Advertising costs money to get, he notes, and he had very little of that at the beginning. He also had a staff of one and felt he would be better served by spending all his time creating and promoting the magazine to and for readers rather than advertisers. August's renewal rates are enviable—75 percent to 85 percent of *Woodsmith* readers typically renew.

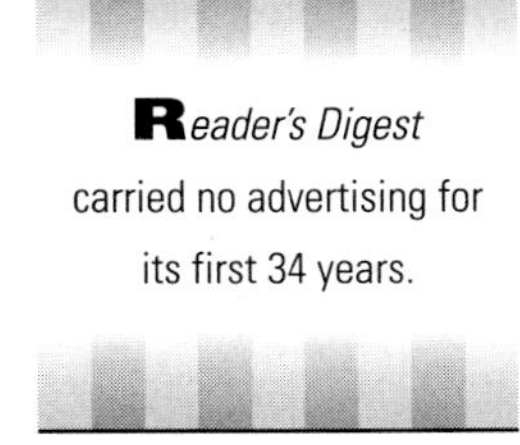

Reader's Digest carried no advertising for its first 34 years.

Reiman's titles, *Country, Country Woman, Farm & Ranch Living, Crafting Traditions, Reminisce, Taste of Home,* and *Birds & Blooms* are the brainchildren of Roy Reiman, founder and publisher, who says the ad-free decision has paid off in reader loyalty. *Folio:* magazine recently estimated total Reiman revenues at between $185 million and $300 million.[25]

Mad magazine is another story entirely—on just about all counts. Publisher William Gaines launched the magazine in 1952; by 1960 it was so financially successful he regularly took his staff and contributors on all-expenses-paid junkets around the world. Exact circulation numbers and audience characteristics are hard to find for the magazine, which does little market research because such research is geared to advertising sales. Alfred E. Neuman and his band of odd friends have parodied the American scene for nearly half a century, appealing to actual adolescents and the adolescent in all of us. If he accepted advertising, Gaines said in 1972, he would have to change the magazine, and he wasn't sure that would get him anywhere:

> *We'd have to improve our package. Most advertisers want to appear in a magazine that's loaded with color and has super-slick paper. So you find yourself being pushed into producing a more expensive package. You get bigger and fancier and attract more advertisers. Then you find you're losing some of your advertisers. Your readers still expect the fancy package, so you keep putting it out, but now you don't have your advertising income, which is why you got fancier in the first place—and now you're sunk.*[26]

Compare that with the enthusiasm, even cockiness, of an ebullient Henry Luce, speaking before the American Association of Advertising Agencies in April 1937, five months after the launching of *Life*:

> *It has been an enormous success. Evidently it is what the public wants more than it has wanted any product of ink and paper. . . . Should we publish* Life? *We have decided. . . . But it is also for you to decide. It is a question for each and every one of you to decide in your heart and in your mind because each of you is deciding it in the pocketbook of your client. . . . Here today I make application not for a few incidental pennies: I ask that you appropriate over the next ten critical years no less than one hundred million dollars for the publication of a magazine called* Life.[27]

FOR ADDITIONAL READING

Abrahamson, David. *Magazine-Made America: The Cultural Transformation of the Postwar Periodical.* Cresskill, NJ: Hampton Press, 1996.

James, Frank. *The Mad World of William M. Gaines.* Secaucus, NJ: Lyle Stuart, 1972.

Peterson, Theodore. *Magazines in the Twentieth Century.* Urbana: University of Illinois Press, 1964.

Wainwright, Loudon. *The Great American Magazine: An Inside History of* Life. New York: Alfred A. Knopf, 1986.

Woodward, Helen. *The Lady Persuaders.* New York: Ivan Obolensky, 1960.

ENDNOTES

1 *52 More Magazine Success Stories* (New York: Magazine Publishers of America, 1996): 75.

2 *Veronis, Suhler & Associates Communications Industry Forecast,* "Magazine Publishing" (Veronis, Suhler and Associates, 1998): 309, 336.

3 "The New Food Attitude and Brand Loyalty," *MPA Research Newsletter* 68 (New York: Magazine Publishers of America, 1996): 4

4 *52 More Marketing Success Stories:* 63.

5 *The 1996/97 Magazine Handbook: A Comprehensive Guide for Advertisers, Ad Agencies and Magazine Marketers,* 68 (New York: Magazine Publishers of America, 1996): 46–47.

6 Deirdre Carmody, "A Rebound for *Harper's* and *Atlantic,*" *The New York Times* (April 25, 1994): C9.

7 *The 1996/97 Magazine Handbook:* 38–39.

8 "Aramark's Gummeson Speaks to Retail Task Force," *MPA Consumer Marketing Newsletter* (July 1996): 1.

9 "Analyzing Covers That Sell," *Folio:* (November 1989): 139.

10 *The 1996/97 Magazine Handbook:* 59.

11 Constance L. Hays, "Magazine Chief Shakes Things Up at Hearst," *The New York Times* (June 2, 1997): 9.

12 Constance L. Hays, "Seeing Green in a Yellow Border," *The New York Times* (August 3, 1997): 13.

13 *Veronis, Suhler & Associates Communications Industry Forecast:* 296.

14 "Magazine Ad Page Leaders," *Advertising Age* (November 2, 1998): 18.

15 Frank Luther Mott, *A History of American Magazines 1744-1850,* Vol. 1 (Cambridge, MA: Harvard University Press, 1939): 34–35.

16 David Forsyth and Warren Berger, "Trading Places," *Folio:* (March 1991): 85.

17 Theodore Peterson, *Magazines in the Twentieth Century* (Urbana: University of Illinois Press, 1964): 5.

18 Ibid., 21.

19 Ibid., 9–10.

20 Forsyth and Berger, 88.

21 Peterson, 22.

22 Loudon Wainwright, *The Great American Magazine: An Inside History of* Life (New York: Knopf, 1986): 92–93.

23 Betsey Carter, "As Big as *Life,*" *Newsweek* (October 2, 1978): 83.

24 Deirdre Carmody, "A Rejuvenated *Life* Magazine Bounces Back," *The New York Times* (September 26, 1994): C6.

25 Chris Mean, "The Reiman Reason," *Folio:* (September 15, 1996): 30.

26 Vincent P. Norris, "*Mad* Economics: An Analysis of an Adless Magazine, *Journal of Communication,* Vol. 84, No.1 (Winter 1984): 45.

27 Wainwright, 94.

CHAPTER 3

The Magazine as a Historical Document

Trends over Time

Today's newsstands cradle the great-great-grandchildren of America's magazine pioneers. Harper's Magazine *is the offspring of* Harper's Monthly, *the country's oldest continuous consumer title,*[1] *first published in June 1850. The Harper brothers—Fletcher, James, John, and Joseph—were successful book publishers who decided a literary magazine would be a good way to keep their printing presses busy. They also started* Harper's Weekly, *which provided a rich illustration of American civilization through engravings, woodcuts, and cartoons from 1857 until 1916. Nearly 150 years later, the Harper name still graces the cover of one of America's most respected magazines.* 📖 The Atlantic Monthly, *our second oldest continuous consumer magazine title, saw its first press run in November 1857. It was started by writers with the age-old pursuit of an audience. The magazine succeeded and so did the writers, whose works today fill American literature classes: Ralph Waldo Emerson, Harriet Beecher Stowe, Oliver Wendell Holmes, and Henry Wadsworth Longfellow.* 📖 Cosmopolitan *dates back to 1886 and originally carried the tagline, "The world is my country and all mankind are my countrymen." Like* Harper's *and* The Atlantic, *it was one of the quality journals of opinion and the arts that characterized magazines started after the Civil War. Its contemporary incarnation is, likewise, representative of its era, encouraging sexual freedom and individual expression.*

These magazines are survivors in a media world that rewards creativity, tenacity, and adaptability. Unfortunately, numerous magazines stumble and fall because they cannot successfully refocus or reinvent themselves. Even magazine dinosaurs, however, provide insight into a particular time and place in society. The magazine's role in American history is secure. For more than 250 years, magazines have shown themselves to be an enduring medium.

THE BEGINNING

In 1741, the first American magazines were established within three days of each other, the result of intense rivalry between Benjamin Franklin and Andrew Bradford. That event in Philadelphia foreshadowed the future competitiveness and challenges of the magazine industry. Bradford's *The American Magazine, or A Monthly*

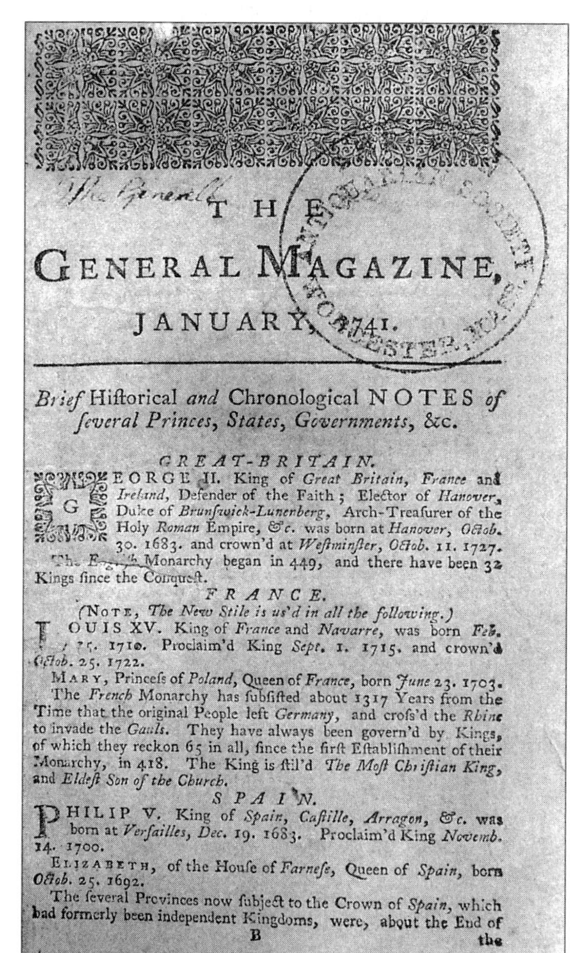

THE

GENERAL MAGAZINE,

JANUARY, 1741.

Brief Hiſtorical *and* Chronological NOTES *of ſeveral Princes, States, Governments,* &c.

GREAT-BRITAIN.

GEORGE II. King of *Great Britain, France* and *Ireland,* Defender of the Faith; Elector of *Hanover,* Duke of *Brunſwick-Lunenberg,* Arch-Treaſurer of the Holy *Roman* Empire, *&c.* was born at *Hanover, Octob.* 30. 1683. and crown'd at *Weſtminſter, Octob.* 11. 1727.

The E[illegible] Monarchy began in 449, and there have been 32 Kings ſince the Conqueſt.

FRANCE.

(NOTE, *The New Stile is us'd in all the following.*)

LOUIS XV. King of *France* and *Navarre,* was born *Feb.* [illegible]. 1710. Proclaim'd King *Sept.* 1. 1715. and crown'd *Octob.* 25. 1722.

MARY, Princeſs of *Poland,* Queen of *France,* born *June* 23. 1703.

The *French* Monarchy has ſubſiſted about 1317 Years from the Time that the original People left *Germany,* and croſs'd the *Rhine* to invade the *Gauls.* They have always been govern'd by Kings, of which they reckon 65 in all, ſince the firſt Eſtabliſhment of their Monarchy, in 418. The King is ſtil'd *The Moſt Chriſtian King,* and *Eldeſt Son of the Church.*

SPAIN.

PHILIP V. King of *Spain, Caſtille, Arragon, &c.* was born at *Verſailles, Dec.* 19. 1683. Proclaim'd King *Novemb.* 14. 1700.

ELIZABETH, of the Houſe of *Farneſe,* Queen of *Spain,* born *Octob.* 25. 1692.

The ſeveral Provinces now ſubject to the Crown of *Spain,* which had formerly been independent Kingdoms, were, about the End of

B the

JANUARY 1741: Like most eighteenth-century magazines, Benjamin Franklin's *The General Magazine, and Historical Chronicle, For All the British Plantations in America,* lasted only a few months.

TABLE 3.1 The Magazine Century Club

DATE ESTABLISHED	MAGAZINE
1812	*New England Journal of Medicine*
1821	*Saturday Evening Post* (died 1969; reborn 1971 as a quarterly)
1836	*American Banker*
1845	*Scientific American*
1846	*Town & Country*
1850	*Harper's*
1855	*Hardware Age* (now *Home Improvement Market*)
1857	*The Atlantic Monthly*
1865	*The Nation*
1865	*Protection*
1867	*The Locomotive*
1867	*Harper's Bazaar*
1871	*American Druggist*
1876	*McCall's*
1883	*Ladies' Home Journal*
1883	*Journal of the American Medical Association (JAMA)*
1884	*Editor & Publisher*
1884	*The Christian Century*
1885	*American Rifleman*
1885	*Good Housekeeping*
1886	*Cosmopolitan*
1886	*The Sporting News*
1886	*Progressive Farmer*
1887	*Sports Afield*
1888	*National Geographic*
1892	*Sierra*
1892	*Vogue*
1895	*Field & Stream*
1898	*Sunset*
1898	*Outdoor Life*
1899	*Audubon*

View of the Political State of the British Colonies preceded Franklin's equally wordy *The General Magazine, and Historical Chronicle, For All the British Plantations in America.* However, Franklin had the idea first. Bradford's magazine lasted just three months; Franklin's survived for six months. They were followed by other titles to satisfy an eighteenth-century audience enthralled by this new medium that differed significantly from books and newspapers.

No magazines published between 1741 and 1800 lasted more than 18 months, and 60 percent of the periodicals started between 1741 and 1794 did not survive even their first year. Noah Webster, who published several magazines before finding success with his dictionary, said in 1788, "The expectation of *failure* is connected with the very name of a Magazine."[2]

Today's magazines have more optimistic publishers and a lower mortality rate, with 30 percent of all start-ups lasting more than five years. Hundreds of magazines are now developed every year—852 new titles burst onto the newsstands in 1997 alone[3]—but only 98 magazines were published during the entire eighteenth century.[4] These early American magazines were victims of a variety of influences. As early as 1828, an article in the *New-York Mirror* stated: "These United States are fertile in most things, but in periodicals they are extremely luxuriant. They spring up as fast as mushrooms, in every corner, and like all rapid vegetation bear the seeds of early decay within them." The article continued its plant-like analogy of new magazines:

> *They put forth their young green leaves in the shape of promises and prospectuses—blossom through a few numbers—and then comes a "frost, a killing frost," in the form of bills due and debts unpaid. . . . This is the fate of hundreds; but hundreds more are found to supply their place, to tread in their steps, and share their destiny. The average age of periodicals in this country is found to be six months.*[5]

Even when magazines have longer life spans—*Scientific American* and *Town & Country* are more than 150 years old, while *The Nation*, established in 1865, is the oldest continuously published weekly—there will always be survivors and failures.

Five factors have had an ongoing impact on the magazine industry from 1741 to the present: (1) literacy and education, (2) content, (3) appearance, (4) transportation and delivery, and (5) production and technology. Within these categories, structural and cultural shifts appear that can be studied as trends over time. A chart demonstrating these factors can be found in Table 3.2.

For example, the audience of literate readers since 1741 moves from small, elite, and upper-class groups, to middle-class masses with leisure time, to well-educated, special interest niches. Magazine content reflects changing attitudes as

TABLE 3.2 Magazine Trends

	1741–1800	1801–1865	1866–1889
Longevity	Less than 18 months	Decades	
Numbers	Few titles	Thousands launched	Boom years
Audience	Few readers	Rising literacy	Compulsory education
	Mostly male Educated elite High income	Male & female readers Rising middle class	 Middle class
Content	Assorted miscellany Few bylines	Variety Bylined articles	Biographies
	Reproduce British articles	American literature Specialized business press	Serializations Short stories Long essays
Appearance	Plain Few illustrations Type heavy Small type size	Hand-tinted illustrations Wood cuts Copper engravings	Photography
Delivery and Transportation	Up to postmaster	More indulgent postal	Second-class mailing
	Reader pays postage Mostly northeast Philadelphia key city By foot, horse, carriage	Publisher pays postage To frontier's edge New York key city Improved roads	 West past Mississippi River Railroads
Production and Technology	Hand-set type	Machine-set type	
	Hand-operated press Handmade paper	Mechanical press	 Cheap wood pulp paper
	Costly to produce		
Circulation	Very low, about 500 By subscription	Higher, up to 40,000	Exceeds 100,000
Cost	Very expensive	Affordable	Affordable

1890–1920	1921–1959	1960–1979	1980–2000
	Death of some quality magazines	Many start-ups and some surprising failures	Continued growth
High school education	Literate		Readers as consumers
Mass audience More leisure	Demographically targeted High income	Discretionary income	Niche audience
General interest	Shorter articles Departments	Specialized departments	Custom publications
Muckraking Advice	Tighter writing More fiction	Specialized topics	More service topics Less fiction
Fine illustrations Increased photos Color Larger page sizes	Photo heavy	More color Smaller page size	Anything goes
Rural free delivery	Reduced rates	Postal reorganization Increased rates	Increased postal costs
Coast to coast			
			Experiments with alternative delivery systems
Improved machinery Halftones Four-color printing Faster, cheaper to produce	Slick, coated paper	Inflation and increased production costs	Computers cut costs Desktop publisher Slick and some recycled paper Digital production
Hits 1 million Newsstand single copies	In the millions Subscription and newsstand	Intentionally reduced	Variable
Cheap	Inexpensive	Inflationary	Affordable

BRITISH MAGAZINES TAKE PRECEDENCE BY A DECADE

When Edward Cave produced *The Gentleman's Magazine* in England in January 1731, it was the first publication to call itself a magazine. Periodicals featuring essays, journals, verse, and fiction had been around since the late 1690s. But Cave, departing from the popular periodical format of essays and journals used by Richard Steele's *Tatler* and Joseph Addison's *Spectator,* offered something different. Cave's publication featured useful news, miscellaneous extracts, and various articles—or "tydings"—taken from the leading publications of the day. In that sense, it was more like a *Reader's Digest* in its eclectic choice of content, which ran the gamut from the literary to the political, from the critical to the biographical. A new concept for British readers was Cave's "The Monthly Intelligencer," a regular department with short excerpts—vital statistics (births, deaths, marriages), book lists, foreign and domestic news, and current prices—taken from different newspapers.

Cave promised his new magazine would live up to its name before the first issue even appeared. His January 30, 1731, advertisement in the *Universal Spectator* announced the content of *The Gentleman's Magazine* as being:

> A Collection of all Matters
> of Information and Amusement:
> Compriz'd under the following Heads, viz.
> Publick Affairs, Foreign and Domestick,
> Births, Marriages, and Deaths of Eminent Persons,
> Preferments, Ecclesiastical and Civil.
> Prices of Goods, Grain and Stocks.
> Bankrupts declar'd and Books Publish'd
> Pieces of Humour and Poetry
> Disputes in Politicks and Learning.
> Remarkable Advertisements and Occurrences.
> Lists of the Civil and Military Establishment.
> And whatever is worth quoting from the
> Numerous Papers of News and Entertainment,
> British and Foreign; or shall be Communicated
> proper for Publication. With Instructions
> in Gardening, and the Fairs for February.[1]

Dr. Samuel Johnson, the leading literary scholar and critic of the period, wrote numerous articles, biographies, essays, and literary tidbits for *The Gentleman's Magazine.* By 1744, the

editorial copy segues from ponderous treatises about government and politics interspersed with sentimental musings by anonymous authors, to signed general interest articles with a muckraking agenda, to an emphasis on fiction, to the current domination of nonfiction and service journalism. The magazine's appearance reflects the impact of design innovations as the look of the book shifts from a type-heavy, plain document; to one with limited use of woodcuts, drawings, and varying typefaces; to a merger of design and type with photographs, color, and large page sizes; to a design-driven appearance reflective of fast-paced lifestyles. Transportation and delivery, influenced by geography and government postal regulations, dramatically affect circulation's pendulum from low to widely expanded to intentionally reduced. Finally, production and technological innovations lead magazines from provincialism to mass consumption as the first national communications medium and as a multimillion-dollar business.

LITERACY AND EDUCATION

One of the most consistent correlations reflected in American magazine readership over time is the literacy rate. Literacy and formal education are the cornerstones for an audience of readers. Class and income also influence magazine readership. However, the only statement that can be made about magazines and their readers with any certainty is that the number of readers is seldom static. Instead, magazine audiences evolve and shift as different societal influences and individual interests come into play.

Eighteenth Century: Educated Elite

Eighteenth-century magazines were few in number because there were few readers. In 1741, the British colonies in America had a population of about one million. Fifty years later, the population had increased to about 4.5 million. Although there was no universal education, it has circulation of the magazine had reached 10,000, and Johnson became Cave's assistant as well as his chief reporter, writer, and editor.

Soon other successful publications with the storehouse approach were started. *The London Magazine* and *The Monthly Review* were two rivals to *The Gentleman's Magazine* by the middle of the eighteenth century. Of course, these magazines were read in the American colonies. In fact, *The Gentleman's Magazine* was one of the primary sources for material published by both Benjamin Franklin and Andrew Bradford in their new magazines.

Historians have pointed out that Franklin and Bradford had no intention of publishing anything but a British magazine in America. Certainly, they took the majority of their editorial content from British periodicals and copied their profitable formats. Bradford acknowledged the profit motive in the January 1741 issue of his *American Magazine:* "The Success and Approbation which the MAGAZINES, published in *Great-Britain,* have met with for many Years past, among all Ranks and Degrees of People, *Encouraged* us to *Attempt* a Work of the like Nature in *America.*"[2]

Presenting a favorable picture of the American colonies to England and Europe was an equally strong reason for starting a magazine. Bradford wrote that he desired *"That the Parliament and People* of Great Britain, *may be* truly *and* clearly *informed of the Constitutions and Governments in the Colonies,* whose great Distance from their Mother-Country seems, in some sense, to have placed them out of her View."

[1] C. Lennart Carlson, *The First Magazine: A History of* The Gentleman's Magazine (Providence, RI: Brown University, 1938): 30.

[2] Andrew Bradford, "The Plan of the Undertaking," *The American Magazine, or A Monthly View of the Political State of the British Colonies* (January 1741): i.

The Gentleman's Magazine:

St JOHN'S GATE.

Or, MONTHLY INTELLIGENCER.

For JANUARY, 1731.

CONTAINING,

(more in Quantity, and greater Variety, than any Book of the Kind and Price.)

I. A VIEW of the WEEKLY ESSAYS, *viz.* Of Queen *Elizabeth*; Ministers; Treaties; Liberty of the Press; Riot Act; Armies; Traytors; Patriots; Reason; Criticism; Versifying; Ridicule; Humours; Love; Prostitutes; Musick; Pawn-brokers; Surgery; Law.

II. POETRY. The Ode for the New Year, by *Colly Cibber*, Esq; Remarks upon it; Imitations of it, by way of *Burlesque*; Verses on the same Subject; ingenious Epitaphs and Epigrams.

III. DOMESTICK OCCURRENCES; *viz.* Births, Deaths, Marriages, Preferments, Casualties, Burials and Christenings in *London.*

IV. Melancholy Effects of Credulity in *Witchcraft.*

V. Prices of Goods, Grain, Stocks, and a List of Bankrupts.

VI. A correct List of the Sheriffs for the current Year.

VII. Remarkable Advertisements.

VIII. FOREIGN Affairs, with an Introduction to this Year's History.

IX. REGISTER of Books.

X. Observations on Gardening.

XI. Table of CONTENTS.

By *SYLVANUS URBAN*, Gent.

The FIFTH EDITION.

LONDON: Printed for the AUTHOR, and sold at St *John's Gate*: By F. *Jefferies*, in *Ludgate-street*; all other Booksellers; and by the Persons who serve Gentlemen with the News-papers: *Of whom may be had* Compleat Sets, *or any* single Number.

A few are printed on ROYAL PAPER, *large Margin*, for the CURIOUS.

JANUARY 1731 (PREMIERE ISSUE): Publisher Edward Cave was the first to use the word *magazine*—referring to storehouse—in connection with *The Gentleman's Magazine* in London, England.

been estimated that approximately 60 percent of the male population in colonial America from 1650 to 1750 was literate, based on whether they could sign their wills.[6] Female literacy during the same period was considerably lower, around 30 percent.

There were differing attitudes toward literacy in the colonies. The southern colonies—Georgia, North Carolina, and South Carolina—were primarily agricultural and did not have compulsory education laws. Such laws had been enacted in New England, where many dissident religious groups migrated, to ensure that everyone could read the Bible. The middle colonies—Virginia, Maryland, New York, and Pennsylvania—with their mix of commerce and church, also appreciated educated readers. But it was Massachusetts, with its Puritan heritage that particularly valued male literacy, that had the highest literacy rates. Ninety percent of all men were literate by 1790 in Suffolk and Middlesex counties in Massachusetts.[7]

So it is not surprising that when magazines were established during the late eighteenth century, they were found in cities such as Boston, New York, and Philadelphia. In comparison, about 50 percent of the adult males in the other colonies could read and write. However, literacy was almost universal among wealthy males, wherever they lived.

During the eighteenth century, the average periodical's circulation was 500, and only about half of them were fully paid subscriptions. A high income was necessary for magazine readership, and barter, rather than cash, was the prevailing economic unit until after the American Revolution. Both Bradford's and Franklin's magazines sold for one shilling. The wage for a colonial artisan, such as a carpenter, was two shillings a day during this period. Few people wanted to pay half a day's wages for a magazine, and most laborers had to work four or five days to earn enough for a year's subscription to a magazine. Imagine paying what you would earn if you received $5 an hour for a 40-hour workweek ($200) in order to have a one-year subscription to a magazine—you can see why magazines were not widely purchased during the eighteenth century. Dockworkers and laborers weren't interested in the price of wheat or the latest essays about drawing-room manners. Clearly, early magazines were aimed at specific social and economic groups with some discretionary income—gentlemen and merchants, as opposed to farmers and laborers.

Because relatively few women were well educated, audiences for eighteenth-century American magazines were assumed to be male, which was reflected in the heavy dose of political, commercial, agricultural, scientific, and moral topics found within a publication's pages. Women were perceived as not being interested in those topics, a perception reinforced by the few female magazine subscribers. In a study of the readers of *New-York Magazine* in 1790, David Paul Nord, a journalism professor at Indiana University, discovered that 98 percent of the 370 subscribers were male; only seven women were subscribers in their own names.[8] Furthermore, nearly 50 percent of the readers were professionals, primarily lawyers and physicians, or merchants, bankers, and brokers. The subscription list included the names of old, moneyed families still familiar to New Yorkers today: Roosevelt, Van Rensselaer, Beekman, and Livingston. President George Washington, Vice President John Adams, and Chief Justice John Jay were subscribers, as was the mayor of New York, Richard Varick.

Shopkeepers and artisans made up the rest of the readers of *New-York Magazine* in 1790. Broadway was the main address for shopkeeper subscribers with their taverns, tobacco shops, bookstores, livery stables, and hardware stores. Artisans identified themselves as carpenters, printers, sea captains, barbers, shoemakers, bakers, tailors, and watchmakers. Most worked in the commercial district, and some headed craft organizations and committees.

Miriam Leslie took over her husband Frank Leslie's magazine empire following his death in 1880 and legally changed her name to Frank Leslie in order to retain control. *Frank Leslie's Illustrated Weekly* became a financial success in 1881 as a result of the magazine's coverage of the assassination of President James A. Garfield. Certain that Garfield would die, Miriam Leslie had a special edition printed in advance that was rushed to the streets within minutes after his death.

These subscribers, ranging from "gentlemen" to "glover" were the typical readers of late eighteenth-century American magazines, and, according to Nord, "they suggest the importance of reading as a form of participation in the new social order of post-revolutionary America." At this time, the heartbeat of New York City revolved around trade, and many shopkeepers and artisans clearly had aspirations for culture and a better life. They showed this by subscribing to *New-York Magazine,* priced at $2.25 per year, during a time when a typical New York working man made 50 cents a day. Nord states, however, that if the price was "somewhat aristocratic," the content was not elitist and ranged from the arcane to the earthy.

While *New-York Magazine* positioned itself as a publication designed to "contribute greatly to diffuse knowledge throughout a community and to create in that community a taste for literature," other publishers saw a need for magazines that would provide highly detailed and useful information to a concentrated group of readers. *The South-Carolina Price-Current,* established in 1774, marked the start of the specialized business press. This first magazine to reach a specialized business audience informed readers of price quotes for buying and shipping the staples of the day, such as wheat, hog's lard, ginseng, wax candles, and beer. Armed with that knowledge, readers could make business decisions that were timely and exclusive. This became the formula for success in the specialized business press, which would grow as more and more men became better educated.

As for women, those who lived in Boston were likely to have a 60 percent literacy rate by 1787, versus a 45 percent rate for women living in rural areas.[9] In 1784, *The Gentleman and Lady's Town and Country Magazine* became the first magazine to appeal to women readers with a stated editorial policy that featured "the elegant polish of the Female Pencil, where purity of sentiment, and impassioned Fancy, are happily blended together."[10] Published in

Boston, the magazine reached north to New Hampshire, southwest into Connecticut, and south toward Rhode Island. The female reader of *The Gentleman and Lady's Town and Country Magazine* was married and knew her place was at home, caring for husbands and children—or brothers and sisters if she was unmarried. As an educated woman, it was her responsibility to teach children "rationally and carefully, preferably by example" the proper republican values of a new nation.[11] Women were provided an editorial diet of etiquette, morality, instruction, and amusement, all designed around the notion that a woman's place was in the home.

Nineteenth Century: Rising Literacy

By 1800, with a more stable society in place and a larger population density concentrated in existing cities and newly formed towns, literacy rates across the fledgling United States rose to 75 percent.[12] In general, literacy was higher in the northern and eastern states than in the southern or western ones. Literacy was particularly low along the frontier, where individual settlers were concerned primarily with clearing forests and building log homes. They were unable to support schools, while residents of "older" states had both the resources and the time to offer educational opportunities.

By 1830, when the United States stretched from the Atlantic Ocean across the Mississippi River, followers of President Andrew Jackson began making a connection between education and citizenship. Recognizing that an industrialized America needed laborers who could think, read, write, and add, Jacksonian Democrats argued that literacy was a birthright. They supported numerous workingmen's associations that urged a public primary education for every child and the systematic establishment of common schools throughout the United States. Compulsory education laws were passed by a number of states following the Civil War, and by 1880, school attendance laws and their enforcement were on the books.[13]

After the Civil War, literacy was no longer the domain of the well-educated few; the majority now could be reached. Indeed, education became the foundation for the development of the great American middle class. Nowhere was this relationship stronger than in women's magazines.

GODEY'S

Lady's Book and Magazine.

PHILADELPHIA, OCTOBER, 1866.

RIZPAH'S IDOLS.

BY MARION HARLAND.

"To make you idols, and to find them clay."

[Entered, according to Act of Congress, in the year 1866, by Louis A. Godey, in the clerk's office of the District Court of the United States, in and for the Eastern District of Pennsylvania.]

(Concluded from page 211.)

CHAPTER X.

It is seldom, in this world of cross-purposes, that the same number and variety of motives contribute to the production of one result, as occurred in the choice made by the Hopeton and Lowrie families of Cape May as a watering-place for the summer succeeding Rizpah's *début* in the gay world of Gotham exclusiveness.

To begin with the household of the bridegroom expectant. The politic matron, who was still the nominal head thereof, having rallied from the severe indisposition that threatened, some months before, a premature cessation of all worldly scheming, was anxious to see, with her own visual organs—and they were of the sharpest—whether the reported transformation in the gawky school-girl she had erst tolerated, despite her eccentricities, because of her doating attachment to her winning daughter, were not, to a certain, and perhaps great, extent, the work of Gerald's brain. Furthermore, should this prove to be a radical and conspicuous change, she coveted the distinction of appearing in public as the mother-in-law elect of the belle and heiress. There was no certainty that she would ever live to see another summer, said her physicians, and the dominant passion of social ambition, the hankering after display and grand appearances, was in nowise enfeebled by enervated physical force.

Secondly, the lovely Ada was "positively dying" for a glimpse of the beloved intimate of her school-days; said fatal malady being a compound of curiosity, a sisterly disposition to advance her brother's cause, and a wish to confirm her own influence in a heart where she had once reigned supreme.

"And," said this incarnation of feminine virtues and graces, in a conference with "dear mamma," "since she has grown into a celebrity, we may as well avail ourselves of her reputation. I am not too proud to receive whatever share of reflected light falls to my portion from this 'bright particular.'"

Gerald's anxiety was redoubled, with each monthly pilgrimage to the home of his dulcinea, to bring her again within the sphere of attraction, the centre of which was to be found in the old country-house near the confluence of the lordly Potomac with the broad Chesapeake. More madly enamored of her than, at their earliest and eventful meeting after her return to America, he had supposed that he could ever become of her, or of any other woman, he could not close his eyes to the disheartening circumstance of her non-participation in his loverly impatience at the tardy approach of the day that was to unite them in the holy estate, the beatitude of which he never wearied in depicting to her and to himself. She listened patiently to his rhapsodies; submitted to his caresses; con-

295

OCTOBER 1866: *Godey's Lady's Book* was the most popular women's magazine of the mid-nineteenth century, affecting the manners, morals, fashions, and fads of middle-class "ladies."

Godey's Lady's Book, under the direction of Sarah Josepha Hale and Louis A. Godey, influenced women's manners, morals, and milieu in polite society for much of the mid-nineteenth century. Hale was a forceful advocate of education for women, child welfare, and national recognition of Thanksgiving. However, she avoided discussion of abolition, slavery, and women's suffrage; literate ladies, according to Hale, were not supposed to be concerned with such issues.

Nineteenth-century magazines addressed their reader with such flattering adjectives as "gentle," "genteel," and "moral." While this might be expected in the women's magazines being published, even publications with predominantly male subscribers, such as *The Atlantic Monthly, Harper's, Scribner's,* and *The Century,* assumed that literate, educated audiences wanted a genteel mixture of romantic and practical content in their magazines. Middle-class sensibilities were enshrined in material that tended to be sentimental, optimistic, and nationalistic. These

RESEARCH IN BRIEF

Portrayal of Women in Eighteenth-Century Magazines

Feminists argue that the media's backlash toward the women's rights movement began at the Seneca Falls convention in 1848; men saw the emergence of women into public life as a threat to male dominance in politics, business, society, and the family. Consequently, male editors started to depict women as unfit for public life and as being "unnatural" in their desire to define themselves in new ways. Author Susan Faludi says the message was no different during the 1970s and 1980s.[1]

Media historian Karen List, a professor of journalism at the University of Massachusetts, places the backlash date considerably earlier. List says the first media backlash against women's involvement and visibility in society occurred during the 1790s in the days of the new American republic.[2] She reached this conclusion after studying 15 magazines published in Philadelphia during the last decade of the eighteenth century.[3] List used the original magazines as windows on the past, to reveal what actually was written, as opposed to what historians suspect may have happened.

American women were actively involved in the revolutionary fight against England, taking on jobs as printers, blacksmiths, and undertakers while their husbands fought at Valley Forge and Yorktown. Women competently ran the farms and shops; some even practiced law and medicine. In short, many women, mainly upper- and middle-class white women, began to define themselves as individuals who had public lives. But after the war, they were told to go home and forget about their political progress and business participation; they were told to become once again dependent wives and loving mothers with private rather than public lives. They were given this message through the magazines being published during the last decade of the eighteenth century.

List writes that "the groundwork for the media's depiction of women was laid in the 1790s, almost 60 years before the women's movement began, and the media since that time have often conveyed the same thinking on women's place that appeared in these publications 200 years ago."[4] Although the new nation was founded in Enlightenment ideology, a free and equitable society belonged to white men only. Mary Wollstonecraft may have argued for the extension of democracy to women, but the men of the new republic and the magazines they published glorified marriage, worshipped motherhood, and supported domesticity.

Two main themes could be found in magazines of the 1790s, reports List: "First, women generally lacked the ability to get on in the public world because they were different from and inferior to men. Second, women could not find happiness through autonomy but only through affiliation with others, preferably husbands and children." Even *Ladies Magazine,* the first magazine directed exclusively to female readers, supported the superiority of men and the need for women to submit. The role of women in the new nation was to nurture their husbands and educate their sons in the virtues of republican government. In other words, the only power women had was through their relationships in the home.

List points out that while historians have suggested that early magazines merely held up a mirror to national life, the reality was that the magazines authoritatively told women to achieve a particular ideal. Her opinion is that the tone of eighteenth-century magazines was "one of paternalistic lecturing." The content arbitrarily and stridently stressed the status quo. List says women were stereotyped as "giddy nonentities" who were to blame if their husbands were

nineteenth-century magazines were merely matching the dominant educational values and traditions of the day.

As America's population dramatically increased in size and diversity, due to immigration, and in both agrarian and industrial income, due to productivity, so did the number of magazines. From 1825 to 1850, as many as 5,000 American magazines were launched. Their chances for survival were better than eighteenth-century start-ups because salaried jobs and a rising middle class went along with the country's great expansion westward. There was simply more money to spend throughout the nineteenth century. This eliminated the income problem faced by eighteenth-century publishers who often took eggs, corn, or butter as payment for their publications. Nineteenth-century magazines were solid entrepreneurial ventures grounded in cash paid by individuals who appreciated the publications' professional, personal, and patriotic value.

unfaithful. A sentence from the September 1792 issue of *Ladies Magazine* makes the point: "A husband may, possibly, in his daily excursions, see many women he thinks handsomer than his wife; but it is generally her fault if he meets with one that he thinks more amiable."

Women did not engage in conversation, but gossiped, tattled, and tittered. As for friendship, a woman's best friend was her husband; other women were viewed as rivals. Those women who were held up as role models in the magazines were either fictional, exotic, or long dead and political, such as Queen Elizabeth I and Lady Jane Grey. The lives and situations of real, contemporary women who might have deviated from the ideal were not depicted since almost all the essays, articles, and letters were written by men.

Why, List asks, did magazines harp so continuously on women's compliant domestic role if they did not fear some deviation from it? Although most women chose not to challenge convention, some did move outside the narrow boundaries of "republican motherhood" embodied in the magazines of the 1790s. Historians are still finding out about these exceptions, since the press of the day seldom wrote about them. Only occasionally was there an article in a late eighteenth-century magazine where women were portrayed as rational beings capable of finding the truth and acting on it.

Concludes List, "No matter what their effect may have been, the periodicals clearly attempted to influence the course of women's development, and in so doing, they provided a basis for thinking on women's progress that would recur for the next two centuries."

[1] Susan Faludi, *Backlash: The Undeclared War Against American Women* (New York: Crown Publishers): 1991.

[2] Karen List, "The Media and the Depiction of Women," in *The Significance of the Media in American History*, James D. Startt and Wm. David Sloan, eds. (Northport, Ala.: Vision Press, 1994): 106–128.

[3] List has done extensive research on late eighteenth-century magazines and newspapers. Among her numerous articles about the role of women as revealed in the publications of the new republic, these three are particularly relevant: Karen K. List, "Magazine Portrayals of Women's Role in the New Republic," *Journalism History*, 13: 2 (Summer 1986): 64–70; Karen K. List, "The Post-Revolutionary Woman Idealized: Philadelphia Media's 'Republican Mother,'" *Journalism Quarterly*, 66: 1 (Spring 1989): 65–75; and Karen K. List, "Reflections on Realities and Possibilities: Women's Lives in New Republic Periodicals" (paper presented at the annual meeting of the Association for Education in Journalism and Mass Communication, Boston, MA, August 1991).

[4] List, "The Media and the Depiction of Women," 110.

THE

Ladies Magazine;

For SEPTEMBER, 1792.

SEPTEMBER 1792: Women were told they were different from and inferior to men even in eighteenth-century magazines written exclusively for them, such as *Ladies Magazine*.

The specialized business press made strong contributions to the literate American's life during the middle of the nineteenth century. Matching the rise in education was a burst of technological improvements prior to the Civil War that demanded more informed managers and workers, with both turning to such publications as *American Mechanics Magazine*. Specialized agricultural magazines for farmers, law journals for attorneys, and scientific periodicals for physicians were developed. Magazines were devoted to covering specific industries—mining, metals, printing, pharmaceuticals, railroads, and banking. Many are still around, such as *American Banker*, established in 1836 as *Thompson's Bank Note Reporter*, and *American Druggist*, which began in 1871 as *New Remedies: A Quarterly Retrospect of Therapeutics, Pharmacy and Allied Subjects*. These early specialized business and trade magazines recorded the diversification and progress occurring in a variety of occupations and fields.

Although men were likely to be regular readers of the specialized trade magazines, well-to-do ladies devoured sentimental fiction and were prime targets for magazines such as *Godey's Lady's Book, Ladies' Repository,* and *Peterson's Magazine* that recognized women's homemaker interests and increasing amounts of leisure time. Reading clubs, literary societies, and lending libraries were established by women who read as much for entertainment as they did to expand the confines of their traditional roles as wife and mother. Turn-of-the-century magazines such as *Ladies' Home Journal, Woman's Home Companion,* and *McCall's* recognized the liberating needs of middle-class women. These magazines took the lead in the emergence of a national magazine industry because of their scope and range of readers. By 1903, *Ladies' Home Journal* became the first magazine to reach one million readers; others were not far behind.

For much of the nineteenth century, magazine readers tended to be concentrated in the northeast portion of the United States, as were most publishing headquarters. New York, the largest city in 1860, accounted for one-third of all magazines published at that time.[14] Although Boston had a smaller population than Philadelphia, where such popular magazines as *Saturday Evening Post* and *Peterson's Magazine* were headquartered, Boston was considered the rival to New York's publishing excellence because of *The Atlantic Monthly, North American Review, Youth's Companion,* and *Christian Examiner.*[15] New York continues to be the consumer magazine media capital today. However, second place in magazine headquarters now belongs to Los Angeles. New York also is home to the most magazines in the business and trade category today, with Chicago ranking second.

Twentieth Century: Niche Audiences

"The reading of magazines," wrote William B. Cairns in 1921 when he was associate professor of American literature at the University of Wisconsin, "has come to be far more common than the reading of books. Thousands of persons who would resent the imputation that they are lacking in culture read almost no books at all. . . . No home, however, in which there is pretence of intellectual interest is without magazines, which are usually read by all members of the family."[16]

If magazines were capable of reaching just about every American during the twentieth century, it was because of a greater appreciation for their content. Magazine reading, which depends on an educated audience, became ubiquitous during the twentieth century as increasing numbers of Americans attended and completed high school. In 1920, only 32 percent of young people ages 14 to 17 years were in school, but by 1950, more than 77 percent were attending high school.[17] College enrollments continued to rise, slowly from 1900 to 1920, spurting between 1920 and 1940, dropping a bit during World War II, and jumping after 1946. A study of readers in 1923 found that 97 percent of the respondents with a college degree read magazines; 83 percent of those with a high school education did so; and just 57 percent of those with less than an eighth grade education were magazine aficionados.[18] Almost 40 years later, a 1960 study found that regular magazine readers included 86 percent of all college-educated respondents, 68 percent of those with a high school education, and only 41 percent of those with a grade school education.[19]

Today's college educated adults continue to read more magazines than the average American adult. "You have more educated people today than at any other time in history," says Clay Felker, founder of *New York* magazine and director of the Felker Magazine Center at the University of California at Berkeley Graduate School of Journalism.[20] "People want and need historical perspective," he points out.

Magazines have been successful in providing that historical perspective to a literate audience. However, today's publishers consider audience psychographics and buying behavior to be as important as literacy. This has resulted in magazine niche marketing and fragmentation of various social attributes according to age, education, income, occupation, and geography. In the 1960s, audience specialization became the name of the magazine game, with four new magazines appearing for

Historian John Bainbridge, in his 1945 book about *Reader's Digest,* observed: "As a publishing phenomenon, the *Reader's Digest* compares favorably with the Holy Bible. Except for the Scriptures, nothing ever published has been circulated more widely than the *Digest.*"

every one that folded. Specialized magazine debuts increased in the 1970s to take advantage of every new constituency and micromarket interest group that appeared.

This concept of specialization began at the start of the twentieth century and coincided with a shift in how the literate reader was addressed. Gone were "gentle readers." An audience of hungry consumers had taken their place. During the early years of the twentieth century, Cyrus Curtis, publisher of *Saturday Evening Post* and *Ladies' Home Journal*, was among the first to understand the relationship between the audience as reader and the audience as consumer—and to link that concept to advertising. According to media historian Douglas B. Ward, Curtis, *Saturday Evening Post* editor George Horace Lorimer, and *Ladies' Home Journal* editor Edward Bok argued that their turn-of-the-century publications "reached the elite of American society—people with culture and, most important, people with money."[21] Through advertisements in the trade press intended to reach big-ticket companies such as Packard and Pierce-Arrow automobiles, they depicted a specific kind of reader: "the intelligent, the earnest and the progressive." *Saturday Evening Post*, while appealing to men and women, concentrated on male readers in its promotions during the 1910s and 1920s. Said Lorimer, the *Post* reaches "two classes of men: Men with income, and men who are going to have incomes, and the second is quite as important as the first to the advertiser."

Although *Ladies' Home Journal* was "designed for the home loving," Bok delineated readers by income during the first two decades of the twentieth century because he recognized the relationship between income and discretionary spending. From 1918 to 1919, for example, only 3 percent of the population earned more than $2,500 per year; 71 percent of them purchased magazines.[22] However, the majority of the population, 55 percent, had a yearly income between $1,200 and $1,800. Almost half of them, about 48 percent, bought magazines.[23] Bok positioned *Ladies' Home Journal* as primarily reaching those families with yearly incomes of $1,200 to $2,500.

Ward points out that income, education, and literacy had been the key factors in determining magazine development until the turn of the century. But now, in trying to tap the ever-expanding middle class, Curtis specified only "worth-while white families" in an advertising piece in 1922. Blacks and recent immigrants were excluded from consideration as regular readers of either *Saturday Evening Post* or *Ladies' Home Journal* because, in general, they had low literacy rates and even lower incomes. Even native-born white families were eliminated as a target audience unless they lived in "accessible" cities or affluent suburbs.[24]

According to Ward, even though the *Post*, *Journal*, and other similar large-circulation magazines were considered "mass" magazines because they reached a national audience, in many ways they "were closer to a niche market in that they represented only a fraction of the population—a fraction targeted and defined by income" and literacy.[25] That's why the concept of a specialized readership is only a derivative of a mass audience and why magazines have glided so smoothly from one approach to the other.

In 1850, the editors of *Scientific American* set up the Scientific American Patent Agency to give advice to novice inventors and assist them in registering new inventions with the U.S. Patent Office. While running for president of the United States, Abraham Lincoln sent in a patent proposal to the magazine for a device to buoy steamboats over bars and shoals. *Scientific American's* tactful rejection appeared shortly after the 1860 presidential election: "It is probable among our readers there are thousands of mechanics who would devise a better apparatus, but how many of them would be able to compete successfully in the race for President?"

CONTENT

A reader is drawn to a magazine's content and appearance for a variety of reasons: aesthetic, pragmatic, whimsical, sensational, or ideological. While the form of a magazine hasn't changed that much—a magazine published in 1775 or 1875 somewhat resembles today's publications—the content and the way it is presented have changed dramatically. Early magazines were little wrens, plain and content-heavy, with few artistic embellishments and little to no advertising. In comparison, most of today's magazines are screeching peacocks. Their colorfully written pages are filled with so many photographs and illustrations that the line between advertisement and editorial is not always distinguishable.

Eighteenth Century: Assorted Articles

Eighteenth-century magazines were literally storehouses of material, mostly gathered from British magazines, books, and pamphlets. About three-fourths of the content of eighteenth-century American magazines was lifted from English publications and reprinted in their entirety, generally without credit since there were no copyright laws. Yet there existed a strong nationalistic orientation because of the inclusion of colonial state and regional political documents. From the start, the content of a magazine was considerably broader than that of a local newspaper. About one-third of Franklin's *General Magazine* was devoted to proceedings of parliament and state assemblies. Essays about currency concerns, historical sketches, firearms manuals, current events, and "Extracts from New Books, Pamphlets, etc. Published in the Plantations" made up the rest.

Most Americans can recite the first stanza of "Mary's Lamb," but very few know that the 24-line poem beginning "Mary had a little lamb" was written in 1830 by Sarah Josepha Hale. Hale, a widow with five children, was best known as the editor of *Godey's Lady's Book,* the most successful women's magazine of the early nineteenth century.

The 1758 editorial profile of the *New England Magazine of Knowledge and Pleasure,* written in verse, is reflective of the varied and eclectic content of early publications:

Old-fashioned writings, and Select Essays,
Queer Notions, Useful Hints, Extracts from Plays,
Relations Wonderful, and Psalm and Song,
Good Sense, Wit, Humour, Morals, all ding dong;
Poems and Speeches, Politicks and News,
What Some *will like, and other* Some *refuse;*
Births, Deaths, and Dreams, and Apparitions too;
With some Thing suited to each different Geû [view]
To Humour Him, *and* Her, *and* Me, *and* You.[26]

Despite the miscellany, early editors primarily were interested in influencing opinion in the colonies and in England; the perception in Europe was that New World folks were raw, rude, and rambunctious. Colonial publishers wanted to depict American social and political life in a favorable light. For the most part, the publisher was also the editor, the primary author, and the printer. Consequently, articles tended to be lengthy and unsigned.

When revolutionary ideas began to ferment, magazines quickly reflected increasingly strong political and partisan views. During this period, magazines helped unify the colonies and fanned the patriotic fervor of the people, resulting in a much greater influence than their low circulation figures might indicate. Magazines were cherished; every page was read closely by many individuals.

Contributors to eighteenth-century magazines included every great thinker and statesman of early American history: George Washington, Alexander Hamilton, John Jay, John Hancock, Thomas Paine, Benjamin Franklin, John Quincy Adams, Noah Webster, Mathew Carey, and Isaiah Thomas. However, the majority of early magazine writers did not receive credit for their work because there were no professional writers. Writing for money was frowned upon as unbecoming to ladies and unsporting for gentlemen. This attitude probably had its roots in Puritan beliefs that modesty was its own reward, particularly when writing one's opinion about art or literature. When bylines were given, initials, Greco-Roman names such as Minerva and Romulus, and popular pseudonyms of the period such as Frank Amity or Jemima Loveleap often were used.

Nineteenth Century: Material Mania

Led by Joseph Dennie's *Port Folio,* considered the first significant and successful literary magazine to be published after 1800, magazines became broader in content, with sentimental fiction, plays, essays, and poetry added to expected articles about industry, education, agriculture, economics, science, and politics. Education, enlightenment, and entertainment were the legs of an increasingly successful industry. Popular publications of the magazine boom years from 1825 to 1850 included *North American Review, New-York Mirror,* and *Saturday Evening Post.* British authors, particularly Walter Scott, George Byron, Samuel Taylor Coleridge, and William Wordsworth, were widely read in America. However, a number of magazines, such as *Graham's* and *Knickerbocker,* preferred to support the American literature of Washington Irving, Edgar Allan Poe, Nathaniel Hawthorne, and John Greenleaf Whittier. Indeed, literature, both prose and poetry, dominated magazine content until the 1890s, and

You Read It in a Magazine First

The following were all published in *The Atlantic Monthly:*

1858 Henry David Thoreau, "Chesuncook"
1860 Walt Whitman, "Bardic Symbols"
1862 Julia Ward Howe, "Battle Hymn of the Republic"
1863 Henry Wadsworth Longfellow, "Paul Revere's Ride"
1866 Frederick Douglass, "Reconstruction"
1869 Harriet Beecher Stowe, "The True Story of Lady Byron's Life"
1875 Mark Twain, "Old Times on the Mississippi"
1897 Theodore Roosevelt, "Municipal Administration: The New York Police Force"
1900 Kate Douglas Wiggin, "Tuppenny Travels in London"
1901 John Muir, "Hunting Big Redwoods"
1902 Jack London, "Li Wan, the Fair"
1915 Robert Frost, "A Group of Poems"
1923 Woodrow Wilson, "The Road Away from Revolution"
1929 Emily Dickinson, "Poems"
1932 John Maynard Keynes, "The World's Economic Outlook"
1933 Edith Wharton, "Confessions of a Novelist"
1940 Gertrude Stein, "The Winner Loses; A Picture of Occupied France"
1947 Dylan Thomas, "In Country Sleep"
1948 E. B. White, "Death of a Pig"
1956 John Steinbeck, "How Mr. Hogan Robbed a Bank"
1957 Ernest Hemingway, "Two Tales of Darkness"
1959 James Thurber, "The Porcupines in the Artichokes"
1963 Martin Luther King Jr., "The Negro Is Your Brother"
1964 Sylvia Plath, "The Wishing Box"
1969 Margaret Atwood, "A Night in the Royal Ontario Museum"
1973 Annie Dillard, "The Force That Drives the Flower"
1973 Gabriel Garcia Marquez, "Death Constant Beyond Love"
1976 John Cheever, "The President of the Argentine"
1979 William Faulkner, "Evangeline"
1982 William Least Heat Moon, "Blue Highways"
1984 Benjamin Spock, "School Reform: Coercion in the Classroom Won't Work"
1989 Amy Tan, "Two Kinds"
1992 John Updike, "The Brown Chest"
1994 Art Levine, "Education: The Great Debate Revisited"
1995 William Zinsser, "Doin' the Chameleon"
1996 Garrison Keillor, "The Poetry Judge"
1997 Arthur Schlesinger Jr., "A Man from Mars"
1998 Garry Wills, "A Cinema of Private Lives"

even through the 1950s, many consumer publications carried several short stories and poems per issue.

By the 1830s and 1840s, paid editors and bylined contributors became the norm. A new class of writers developed; they called themselves "magazinists" because they made their living by editing or writing for magazines. Nathaniel Parker Willis was the most successful, praised during his lifetime as the preeminent magazine writer and editor in the United States and Europe. Ironically, though Willis became a wealthy man as a professional writer, he is not as well remembered for his achievements as his contemporary Edgar Allan Poe, who received much less money from the same magazines. For example, both Poe and Willis wrote for *Godey's Lady's Book, Graham's,* and *New-York Mirror.* However, Willis received as much as $11 per page for his prose from *Graham's,* while Poe's payment was only $4 per page. By 1842, Willis was earning $1,500 a year—which was more than the salary of the governor of Connecticut—from four monthly magazines for which he wrote clever, short sketches about picturesque places. In comparison, Poe earned just $300 in 1843.[27]

Following the Civil War, magazines that had fought for the abolition of slavery, such as *The Liberator,* died once they no longer had a cause to support. Other magazines rushed in to fill the gap. In 1867, the editors of *The Round Table* wrote about a "mania" of magazine start-ups, which they predicted would spend itself only "by every successful writer's becoming possessed of a magazine of his own, or by the exhaustion of names for new essays—a contingency which seems by no means remote when we find old titles revived."[28] *The Round Table*'s editors itemized some of the new magazines, which included "trash" such as *Kitchen Corners, Chambermaid's Delights, Prize Fighter's Joys,* and *Tattler's Teapots,* as well as "newcomers of a more than respectable character":

> *We have new quarterlies of Law, of Medicine, of Speculative Philosophy; new monthlies of Natural History, of Art, of Music, of Numismatics, of the Davis Family; a publication of some sort and of some merit from nearly every live college in the country; our first creditable fashion weekly; numberless admirable innovations in juvenile journalism; three presentable weeklies whose business is to wrangle with ability over the tariff—all these and more like unto them, coming from almost as many parts of the country.*

The number of religious publications doubled between 1865 and 1885, while the number of specialized business publications quadrupled in the three decades following the Civil War. The overall number of magazines available increased from 700 in 1865 to 3,300 in 1885, according to census figures. As many as 9,000 magazines, now with an average life span of four years, were published during the period. The number of magazines continued to accelerate. By 1890, there were more than 4,400; by 1895, more than 5,100. And 1900 rang in the new century with more than 5,500 magazines.

Specialized trade and business magazines in particular took advantage of the reader-as-consumer movement. Useful information was the focus of business publications, as stated by Rufus Porter, founder of *Scientific American:* "Our readers have already learned that instead of detailing stories and narratives to the full extent of words and phrases for the purpose of filling up our columns, our custom is to curtail and abbreviate, giving the pith and substance of a story in as few words as possible."[29]

By the end of the nineteenth century, it would have been difficult to find a trade, profession, or industry without at least one magazine devoted to it. Indeed, magazine historian Frank Luther Mott commented that only bootblacks, nursemaids, and janitors lacked individual publications by 1885.[30] By 1921, when Standard Rate and Data Service (SRDS) produced the first listing of trade and business magazines, there were 1,235 publications covering a variety of fields. Leading the list of categories was "Medical and Surgical" with 95 magazines, followed by "Automotive" with 60, "Export Trade" with 47, "Financial and Banking" with 46, and "Drugs, Pharmaceutics, etc." with 33.[31]

Companies began publishing their own sponsored magazines as public relations tools as early as 1847 when *Mechanic* was founded by the H. B. Smith Machine Company of Smithville, New Jersey. Two of the oldest corporate communications magazines still being published today were founded in Hartford, Connecticut, after the Civil War. *Protection,* in print since 1865, is the house organ for the Travelers Insurance Company, while *The Locomotive,* established in 1867, belongs to the Hartford Steam Boiler Inspection and Insurance Company.

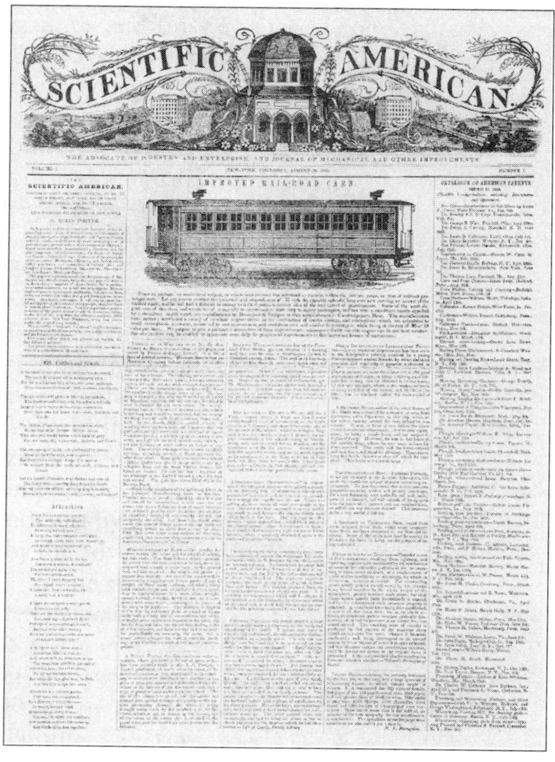
SCIENTIFIC AMERICAN.

AUGUST 28, 1845 (PREMIERE ISSUE): ***Scientific American,*** **which began as a weekly trade newspaper devoted to new inventions and patents, is now a monthly magazine where scientists and experts write about new discoveries and technological innovations for the general public.**

URBAN HUMOR IN NINETEENTH-CENTURY MAGAZINES

Magazine historian Frank Luther Mott was nothing if not thorough. Each of his five volumes about magazine history detailed the business of magazine publishing and the parade of leading magazines. Every volume also included voluminous information about the artistic, educational, political, social, literary, scientific, religious, philosophical, agricultural, and recreational content of magazines that flourished and failed over time.

So it's not surprising to find that Mott, when discussing humor as a literary device, compiled a list of the standard urban jokes to be found in nineteenth-century magazines. He called his list of 22 jokes "urban comedy" and said that while the material may have been worn, " most of them bloom perennially."[1] Unfortunately, he didn't include the content of any of the jokes. But the titles of these 10 jokes suggest that many of them have mutated only a little bit and now can be found on Internet joke Web sites.

The wedding night joke
The newly rich joke
The unwelcome suitor joke
The old maid joke
The drunkard's return joke
The bashful suitor joke
The sleeping policeman joke
The black eye joke
The peddler (salesman) joke
The love letter joke

[1] Frank Luther Mott, *A History of American Magazines, 1850–1865,* Vol. 2 (Cambridge, MA: Harvard University Press, 1957): 178–79.

Trade, professional, and corporate magazines took a businesslike approach to their editorial content, stressing application and utility in straightforward language. Consumer magazine content tended to be high in tone, stressing quality fiction and biographies, although there seemed to be an abundance of religious and sentimental points of view in women's magazines. Biographies were popular because Americans wanted to be reassured that their past was glorious, despite the vicissitudes of the recently fought Civil War. Various magazines also maneuvered to take advantage of readers' interest in fiction, which still was influenced by such English writers as Thomas Hardy, Charles Dickens, Wilkie Collins, and George Eliot. Their novels were run serially and offered as "serious" reading, while the short story was considered entertainment designed to be read aloud in a family circle in the parlor. In the period after the Civil War, the short story was sentimental and romantic, recounting suffering, exploitation, poverty, and even abuse in terms of moral fortitude and eventual triumph. Humor frequently was found in magazines as fillers, departments, and entire stories. Urban humor parodied social and cultural fads, follies, and functions, while frontier humor, especially in dialect, was popularized by Mark Twain, who knew just how far to go with his exaggerations. Twain's "The Celebrated Jumping Frog of Calaveras County" was first published in *Saturday Press,* which was established in 1857 as a humor magazine.

During the 1890s, when industrial turmoil and crowded cities became social problems, muckraking and service articles dominated many magazines' tables of contents. Edward Bok offered advice and information to the women's market, stating that *Ladies' Home Journal* was edited for "the intelligent American woman rather than to the intellectual type."[32] Women who read *Ladies' Home Journal* could find material about everyday concerns both in and out of the home, as well as advertisements that offered labor-saving products and practical housekeeping remedies. Other women's magazines soon followed Bok's mix of information, advice, fiction, and advertising—a content base that continues to be successful today.

Magazines for children and young people flourished, with *Youth's Companion,* founded in 1827, leading the field for many years. *Youth's Companion,* designed to amuse and instruct children, featured the works of Rudyard Kipling, Jack London, Jules Verne, and Alfred Tennyson. The emphasis was on action and adventure, with a strong moral tone that shut out anything related to sex, crime, or violence. The writing was of such high quality that many adults also read the magazine.

Youth's Companion effectively reached young readers through a special circulation device; it was one of the first magazines to give premiums for annual subscriptions. Children could receive toys ranging from dolls to miniature printing presses if they obtained two, three, or a certain number of new or renewed subscriptions. The list of available premiums was so extensive that it filled 36 pages of each October's issue. Circulation soared, from 385,000 in 1885 to more than 500,000 in 1898. Yet *Youth's Companion* failed in 1929, a victim of the uninhibited amusements of the 1920s. The editors were unable to meet the new interests of youth, who found radio more exciting and the fledgling motion picture industry more entertaining.

MARCH 1876: Many historians consider *St. Nicholas* to be the best magazine for children ever published, yet it failed to evolve with the needs of its readers and died in 1943.

St. Nicholas, with its lavish illustrations and stories by Mark Twain, Robert Louis Stevenson, Louisa May Alcott, and Theodore Roosevelt, is considered by many historians to be the best magazine for children ever published in America. Established in 1873, *St. Nicholas* defined a child's magazine as a playground, rather than a restrictive playpen, and avoided the moralistic tone of most children's magazines. Despite its beautiful printing and numerous pictures, *St. Nicholas* died in 1943, unable to keep up with children's changing tastes. Both *Youth's Companion* and *St. Nicholas* died because they did not evolve with the needs of their readers.

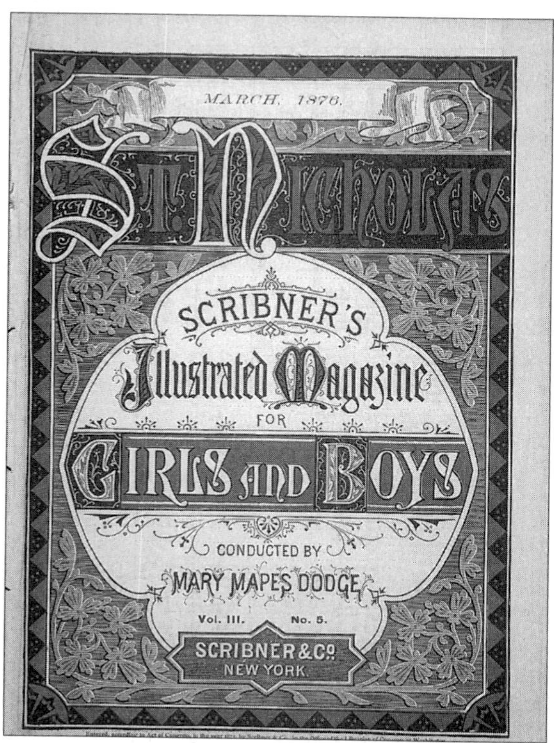

Twentieth Century: Subtle Specialization

Probably the most dramatic change in content came in the 1920s. Three magazines—*Time, Reader's Digest,* and *The New Yorker*—were created in response to shifts in attitudes toward work and leisure time following World War I. Each periodical offered new approaches to reading in a fast-paced society. While other magazines were publishing long pieces about immigration or labor strife, along with serialized romances, westerns, and mysteries, *Time* and *Reader's Digest* chose to focus on brevity and the need to know. *The New Yorker,* on the other hand, created an urban magazine product that oozed brilliance and critical style.

Henry Luce and Briton Hadden founded *Time* in 1923 because they believed busy Americans were poorly informed. Newspapers, they said, were unorganized and random in their content, making it difficult for people to understand what was happening in the world around them. *Time*'s content was driven by four key concepts, which continue to be followed today: (1) The week's news would be organized logically in short departments; (2) while both sides of a story would be told, *Time* would be evaluative and interpret what the news meant; (3) writing would be crisp, curt, and complete; and (4) emphasis would be on the personalities who made the news. The weekly news magazine was a new animal, grounded in a group journalism approach where field correspondents gathered data that would be organized and rewritten by editors in New York. Articles in *Time* seldom had bylines, but they did have perspective—Luce's particular ideas on politics, government, economics, and philosophy shaped each issue for many years.

A different kind of editorial shaping was done by DeWitt Wallace and his wife Lila Acheson Wallace, who created *Reader's Digest* in 1922.

Magazine digests were not new—magazines during the eighteenth century and well into the nineteenth century frequently reprinted articles from other publications, sometimes with, but mostly without, attribution or payment. The Wallaces got written permission to reprint articles and later paid both the publisher and the author for the option. That in itself was groundbreaking. But what really made *Reader's Digest* different was that the Wallaces condensed material only if it contained three characteristics: (1) applicability and value for readers; (2) lasting interest to the extent that it was worth reading a year later; and (3) optimistic constructiveness. Finding the right mix of perennially optimistic articles was easy for DeWitt Wallace, who stated, "I simply hunt for things that interest me, and if they do, I print them."[33]

DeWitt Wallace claimed he could eliminate as much as 75 percent of an article and still publish a piece of substance, style, and authority. That brevity was a great service to busy readers who could read 31 articles each month selected from a myriad of leading magazine sources. The first *Reader's Digest,* dated February 1922, set the tone for all that followed, with articles from such popular magazines as *The Atlantic, Ladies' Home Journal, Scientific American, Popular Science, Delineator, Theatre Magazine, Scribner's, House Beautiful, Good Housekeeping, The Nation's Business, McClure's,* and *Physical Culture.* Adding to the distinctiveness of the content was the appearance of *Reader's Digest*: It was small enough to fit in a jacket pocket or handbag at a time when most magazines were a considerably larger 9-by-12 inches.

In their intentional brevity of content, both *Time* and *Reader's Digest* capitalized on a trend that had started around 1900. While nineteenth-century magazines featured very long essays and rambling short stories, early twentieth-century editors began running shorter articles to match the busier urban lives of their readers. David Graham Phillips, author of "The Treason of the Senate" (*Cosmopolitan,* March 1906), one of the most famous muckraking articles of the early twentieth century, wrote about the demise of long essays in a 1903 article in *Success*: "The wise editors won't have them any more, because the people won't read them and won't even take magazines that get the reputation of harboring them." Phillips cited impatience on the part of the "present generation" whose only interests were the "here and now."[34]

Phillips' observation was prescient: only two of the four general interest literary magazines popular at the turn of the century have survived. *The Century,* an elegant magazine that demanded a long, focused attention span, and *Scribner's Magazine,* which competed as a less costly literary option that was strong in biography and autobiography, died during the 1930s.[35] *The Atlantic Monthly* and *Harper's* have managed to survive to this day as thoughtful literary magazines but with considerably fewer readers and clout than they once had.

The third twentieth-century magazine start-up to have a long lasting effect on content was *The New Yorker,* established by Harold Ross in 1925. While the Wallaces were folksy and inspirational, Ross was witty and acerbic. Ross's distinctive approach to content in a metropolitan magazine is forever immortalized in *The New Yorker*'s prospectus:

> The New Yorker *will be a reflection in word and pictures of metropolitan life. It will be human. Its general tenor will be one of gaiety, wit and satire, but it will be more than a jester. It will not be what is commonly called sophisticated, in that it will assume a reasonable degree of enlightenment on the part of its readers. It will hate bunk. . . . Its integrity will be above suspicion. It hopes to be so entertaining and informative as to be a necessity for the person who knows his way about or wants to.*
>
> The New Yorker *will be the magazine which is not edited for the old lady in Dubuque. It will not be concerned in what she is thinking about. This is not meant in disrespect, but* The New Yorker *is a magazine avowedly published for a metropolitan audience and thereby will escape an influence which hampers most national publications. It expects a considerable national circulation, but this will come from persons who have a metropolitan interest.*

Ross demanded perfection from his writers, and *The New Yorker* revolutionized editorial content through its individualistic essays, droll cartoons, biting criticism, plotless short stories, wry humor, ironic fragments used as fillers, and interpretive profiles. Then and now, *The New Yorker, Time,* and *Reader's Digest* lead the way

RESEARCH IN BRIEF

The Historical Legacy of *Reader's Digest*

Reader's Digest can be studied as a reflection of the political and social climate of the 1920s, says Carolyn L. Kitch of Northwestern University, allowing us to see why a particular type of journalism began at a particular time and place. Since it still successfully attracts millions of readers today, *Reader's Digest* also can be scrutinized as a key player in current mass culture.[1]

On the heels of World War I, the 1920s ushered in flaming flappers, jazz-age speakeasies, and disillusioned youth. A pro-business economy supported mass production in factories, leading to uniformity and conformity on and off the job. For the first time, more people lived in cities than in rural areas; look-alike housing developments flourished, and even furniture and accessories were similar, thanks to Sears, Roebuck & Company. "America and Americans First" was the motto of the day. This was accompanied by an increase in nativism and racism, as exemplified by the 1924 National Origins Act that severely restricted immigration from non-English-speaking countries.

The time was ripe for a magazine that matched how people were thinking. Kitch cites historian Paul Boyer's explanation for founder DeWitt Wallace's roaring success with *Reader's Digest:* "What Ford [did] in automobile manufacturing, Wallace [did] in publishing. Ford gave Everyman a car he could drive, [and] Wallace gave Everyman some literature he could read; both turned the trick with mass production." By adapting assembly-line techniques to the production of a magazine, Wallace made *Reader's Digest* emblematic of America during the 1920s.

The prototype *Reader's Digest,* with 31 articles filling 64 pages of copy, was rejected by publishers all over the country. So Wallace and his wife, Lila Acheson Wallace, decided to produce the new magazine themselves. Kitch studied the first issue to determine its appeal to a 1922 reader. She found articles that clearly matched the prevailing attitudes and assumptions of the time:

- Lots of lists (24 articles took this form).
- Articles touting America's scientific progress (aerial photography to promote property sales) and science trivia (how fireflies light up).
- Emphasis on self-improvement ("Be More Popular and Make More Money" and a guide to effective complaining).
- Reliance on expert advice (from Thomas Edison about the qualities of a good business executive).
- Scientific arguments to justify nativism: One article said broad-hipped, short-legged, immigrant women with "necks like prize fighters" were producing three babies for every one borne by "the beautiful women of old American stock." The racist result: "The moment we lose beauty we lose intelligence."
- Articles disapproving of women who were childless or who kept "the apron strings" tied to teenage sons ready to go out in the world and become men.

as successful, long-term survivors by giving readers precisely the kind of concentrated content they want.

APPEARANCE

Most of today's magazines are visual entities filled with colors, photos, illustrations, varied typefaces, and assorted graphic tricks. The words are so closely intertwined with the designs that it is hard to imagine that a magazine was ever anything but slick, vibrant, and glossy. However, the appearance of the magazine has changed significantly over the past two centuries, from a dull all-type document to one that is design driven to reflect the expectations of readers who want to be dazzled visually by images as well as by content.

Eighteenth Century: Deficient Design

Although the content of early American magazines was engaging and diverse, the look was merely serviceable. Indeed, reading magazines published prior to 1825 took a great deal of concentration and determination. Capitalization, punctuation, and spelling were capricious. The type size for articles was a minuscule six or seven points (about the size of today's classified advertisements), and type was densely set by hand. Most eighteenth-century printers used Caslon Old Style as their typeface, which is the font used in the Declaration of Independence. While patriotic, it is a difficult typeface for today's reader to comprehend: the "long s," which resembles a lowercase italic "f" was frequently used; for example, "blessings" looked like "ble*ff*ings."

Also in the first issue were human interest fillers, a personality profile, and a round-up department. Along with self-help, scientific progress, and relationship pieces, these would set the tone for future issues. The prose was straightforward and conversational and the editorial voice was optimistic, two welcome changes of pace from the grim realism of many magazine articles of the Roaring Twenties. *Reader's Digest* offered subscribers editorial consistency in a world of increasing turmoil, and, with its compact size, instant recognition.

Kitch's reading of the September 1995 through December 1995 issues shows ongoing similarities to themes discussed in that first issue. Also enduring is the magazine's constructiveness—no matter what the problem, an answer can be found. Kitch points out that innovative editorial devices found in the first *Reader's Digest,* such as the list format and expert bylines, are now standard fare in modern consumer magazines.

Reader's Digest has been attacked as being shallow and insulting to the American public, yet the magazine's reduction of information and ideas obviously met a need for its readers in the 1920s, 1930s, and 1940s, through to the present day. Kitch says this is because "the social and cultural phenomena that made the *Digest* a welcome new idea in 1922—the forces of urbanization, mass production, information explosion, and the busyness of daily life—are still with us in 1996."

Originally a product of a specific time and place, *Reader's Digest* continues to thrive. The 1922 formula established by *Reader's Digest* remains popular at home and around the world. Today the magazine reaches 15 million readers in 19 languages.

[1] Carolyn L. Kitch, "'Of Enduring Interest': The First Issue of the *Reader's Digest* as a 'Snapshot' of America in 1922—and Its Legacy in a Mass-Market Culture" (paper presented at the annual meeting of the Association for Education in Journalism and Mass Communication, Anaheim, CA, August 1996).

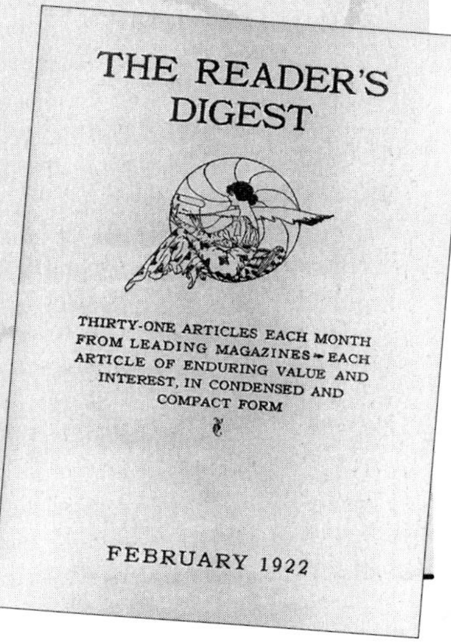

THE READER'S DIGEST

THIRTY-ONE ARTICLES EACH MONTH FROM LEADING MAGAZINES—EACH ARTICLE OF ENDURING VALUE AND INTEREST, IN CONDENSED AND COMPACT FORM

FEBRUARY 1922

FEBRUARY 1922 (PREMIERE ISSUE): This first issue of *Reader's Digest* had 31 articles—one for each day of the month—and no advertising.

The concept of basing design on a two-page spread was unknown. A thin rule typically separated the end of one article and the beginning of the next. Placement of headlines and bylines was inconsistent. Even serialized articles ended arbitrarily rather than at an exciting moment to be continued. Graphic design was nonexistent until the 1830s; there were few type embellishments and limited type variation of size or family. A 1784 issue of *The Gentleman and Lady's Town and Country Magazine* reveals the standard look of late eighteenth-century magazines: gray and boring because just two narrow columns of type filled the 5 3/4-by-8 3/4-inch page.

Most eighteenth-century magazines measured about 5 to 6 inches by 8 to 9 inches per full page. Franklin's early magazine had one of the smallest type pages of the day, measuring a mere 3 1/8 by 6 1/4 inches on a full page measuring 4 by 6 5/8 inches. Bradford's magazine was larger in size, measuring a full 5 by 8 inches. However, Bradford's first issue ran 34 pages, while Franklin published 76 pages.

Stiff, rough, rag paper was used. The paper stock of these early magazines has turned out to be surprisingly durable. Most are still intact, though yellowed and crumbling a bit around the edges. You can find many of the earliest magazines in the American Antiquarian Society Library in Worcester, Massachusetts.

The quality of printing varied from copy to copy because magazines were printed from hand-set type on hand-operated wooden presses. The title page or cover generally was illustrated with a crude woodcut, although some magazine publishers of the eighteenth century could afford

The Temple of Pleaſure. 89

Meſſir's Printers,

I ſend you the following, entitled The Temple of Pleaſure : *If you think it worthy a place in your Magazine, it is at your ſervice.*

The TEMPLE *of* PLEASURE;

——A Vision.——

'TIS juſtly obſerved by Milton, that it is the bent of human nature to admit delight; and pleaſure, rightly underſtood, muſt be allowed to be that *ſummum bonum* concerning which the ancients loſt themſelves in vain diſputes. Pleaſure, however, ſeems to be confined to one ſtage of life; when youth, which the French emphatically call *la belle age*, is over, pleaſure ſeems to expire at the ſame time. The enjoyments of manhood are more cloſely connected with reaſon, and dull tranquility is the utmoſt old age can hope for. Theſe reflections were raiſed in my mind by a viſion I beheld a few nights ago, which I apprehend to have been occaſioned by the impreſſion made on me by Virgil's beautiful deſcription of the Elyſian Fields, which I had peruſed with attention juſt before I went to bed. I imagined myſelf in a plain of vaſt extent, the livelineſs of whoſe verdure ſurpaſſed any thing I had ever ſeen; through the midſt of it rolled a river of a conſiderable breadth, the banks of which ſeemed to reſemble the Heſperian gardens; they were beautifully variegated with vineyards, groves of pomegranate and orange, and orchards loaden with all ſorts of the moſt delicious fruits. The azure canopy was of a colour not to be matched in the fineſt climate upon earth, nor repreſented by the pencil of a Lorraine. Methought I advanced to the banks of the river, where I ſaw a bark which was upon the point of ſetting ſail, and crowds of perſons of both ſexes, ſtood upon the ſhore waiting for a paſſage.

The bark reſembled that in which Cleopatra ſailed down the river Cydnus to meet Mark Antony. I preſſed forward with a croud of young men, elate with hope, and fluſhed with joy. When we were upon the point of entering, a group of venerable old men approached the pilot, and deſired to be admitted in preference to us, on account of their age. "The very plea you urge (anſwered the pilot) excludes you, the rule which obtains elſewhere is here inverted; the bark is bound to the iſland of Pleaſure, and in that voyage young men have always the precedence." As ſoon as there was a ſufficient nnmber on board we ſet off, and were wafted by a proſperous gale to the iſland of Pleaſure, ſoft muſic playing to entertain us during the paſſage. As we approached this iſland, the fragrance exhaled from thence, filled all our ſenſes with delight; and when we landed, a band of young perſons of both ſexes approached us, with eyes which ſwam with joy, and welcomed us to the iſland of Pleaſure. They were all of them of the moſt exquiſite beauty, and dreſſed in the gayeſt and moſt becoming manner imaginable. Their treſſes were adorned with wreaths of finer flowers, than thoſe gathered by Proſerpine on Sicilian plains, and in their hands

M

JULY 1784: *The Gentleman and Lady's Town and Country Magazine,* like most eighteenth-century magazines, looks gray and dull by today's standards, with two narrow columns of type set in Caslon Old Style and no illustrations.

to print the more detailed copperplate engravings laboriously done by hand.

The Royal American Magazine, established in Boston in 1774 by Isaiah Thomas, was the first one to use illustrations on a regular basis. Over a 15-issue run, a total of 22 engravings were published in *The Royal American,* with Paul Revere's political cartoons appearing regularly. One of Revere's most popular engravings was "The Able Doctor, or America Swallowing the Bitter Draught" in the June 1774 *Royal American.* That engraving showed a half-naked "America" held down by a bewigged and robed judge while "Parliament" forcibly poured tea from the spout of a teapot into her mouth—a clear reference to the British taxation of tea.

But most publishers felt the use of woodcuts or copperplate engravings to break up long pages of text was simply too expensive and time-consuming to produce. In the first issue of *The Gentleman and Lady's Town and Country Magazine,* publishers Job Weeden and William Barrett apologized for the lack of a "frontispiece and other plates," which they "could not obtain."[36]

Nineteenth Century: Engraved Embellishments

By the early 1800s, magazines were using at least an inch of white space around the type page and a larger type size of at least 8 points for the body copy. Headlines, clearly delineating copy, tended to be in 10 or 12 point boldface with all capital letters. In format, magazines of the period from 1825 to 1855 tended to look like books, with a one-column width.

The migration of English engravers to America during the early nineteenth century greatly improved the look of magazines. The use of sketches, drawings, and engravings became more prevalent, resulting in more attractive pages than had been found in eighteenth-century magazines. By 1809, *Port Folio* began publishing one copperplate engraving with each monthly issue, usually miniature scenes from the novels of Sir Walter Scott. Other magazines such as *Graham's* and *Peterson's* used numerous steel and copperplate engravings in each issue.

Fashion and flower copperplate engravings often were highlighted with watercolors individually applied by hand. *Godey's Lady's Book* led the way here beginning in 1830, with publisher Louis A. Godey eventually hiring 150 women to color pages by hand. *Godey's Lady's Book*'s published plates were so lovely that many readers cut them out, framed them, and hung them in parlors and bedrooms. You still can find framed pages from *Godey's Lady's Book* in antique stores throughout the country, selling for upwards of $50 each. Hand-etched copper and steel engravings were very expensive; editors at *New-York Mirror* wrote that large plates cost a thousand dollars apiece.[37] That meant a publisher sometimes paid more for an illustration than he did for all the literary content in a single issue. An advertisement in *Godey's Lady's Book* in 1831 stated that "the publishers have expended for Embellishments alone upwards of SEVEN THOUSAND DOLLARS" during the first 18 months of publication.[38]

Woodcuts were cheaper to use, but for many years they were crude in detail and utilitarian in design. They also didn't last as long as steel plates, which were more durable than copper ones. By 1835, engraving on wood blocks had improved considerably in detail, delicacy, and durability. Wood engravings became more frequent because they were more cost efficient, at about $30 each, compared to the several hundred dollars required for each average-sized steel plate.

During the Civil War, a variety of illustrations depicted life and death on the battlefield. Mathew Brady's photographs of war scenes and national leaders during the Civil War could be found in some magazines as wood engravings of the original photographs. Artists had to carefully etch out the relief image of each scene, a task that took considerably more time than it did for Brady to set up his camera and snap. Most Civil War illustrations in the magazines of the day were grim battlefield sketches by artists who were called "picture correspondents." *Harper's Weekly* offered a variety of Civil War images, with artist Winslow Homer specializing in camp life while cartoonist Thomas Nast drew sentimental works such as "Santa Claus in Camp" for the magazine's Christmas 1862 issue. Nast's later political cartoons for *Harper's Weekly* were dark and satirical, focusing on corrupt politicians and urban social ills in the 1870s.

During the 1880s, fine illustrations of beautiful young women became a popular form of pictorial content in magazines. Charles Dana Gibson was famous for his "Gibson Girl" who appeared in magazines as wide ranging as *Collier's, Cosmopolitan,* and *Saturday Evening Post* from 1887 until prior to World War I. Harrison Fisher and James Montgomery Flagg were other artists who drew lovely, all-American girls for women's magazines. The works of all three often were framed and hung in homes; many of their portraits were made into posters. Clearly, magazines were contributing to both the artistic and decorative instincts of their readers.

TABLE 3.3 Gone But Not Forgotten: Some Significant Magazines of the Eighteenth and Nineteenth Centuries

MAGAZINE	DATES PUBLISHED
The American Magazine, or A Monthly View of the Political State of the British Colonies	1741–1741
The General Magazine, and Historical Chronicle, For All the British Plantations in America	1741–1741
South-Carolina Price-Current	1774–1774
The Royal American Magazine	1774–1775
Pennsylvania Magazine	1775–1776
United States Magazine	1779–1779
The Gentleman and Lady's Town and Country Magazine	1784–1784
The Columbian Magazine	1786–1792
The American Museum	1787–1792
New-York Magazine	1790–1797
Ladies Magazine (also published as *Lady's Magazine*)	1792–1793
Port Folio	1801–1827
New-York Mirror	1823–1842
American Mechanics Magazine	1825–1826
Youth's Companion	1827–1929
Godey's Lady's Book	1830–1898
The Liberator	1831–1865
The American Railroad Journal	1832–1837
Southern Literary Messenger	1834–1864
Graham's	1840–1858
Merry's Museum	1841–1872
Peterson's Magazine	1842–1898
Frank Leslie's Illustrated Weekly	1855–1922
Harper's Weekly	1857–1916
The Century (initially *Scribner's Monthly*)	1870–1930
St. Nicholas	1873–1943
Woman's Home Companion	1873–1957
Scribner's Magazine	1887–1939
Collier's	1888–1957
Munsey's	1889–1929
McClure's	1892–1929

Twentieth Century: Popular Photography

Photography didn't revolutionize the appearance of magazines until the 1890s when improved printing presses and the invention of the halftone brought the costs of production down. With photography, both the artist and the engraver were eliminated since the print could be rephotographed onto a sensitized plate and an acid bath could create the contrasting points needed in the final plate. Wood engravings became a dinosaur art form.

More and more magazines began using halftones to embellish articles. *McClure's,* for example, included photographs from the lives of famous men in its "Human Document" series, while *Munsey's* used the nude female to illustrate a department titled "Artists and Their Work." These

JANUARY 1905: Readers stopped editor Gilbert Hovey Grosvenor on the street to tell him how much they enjoyed the *National Geographic* article with its extensive use of photos of Lhasa, Tibet.

photos were not as colorful or bright as they are today. Photography was still black and white, yet the images were certainly dramatic. *Collier's* news photographs of the 1898 Spanish-American War established the publication as the premier picture magazine of the time. *Collier's* also led the way in color illustration with the publication of Maxfield Parrish's imaginative series of Arabian Nights drawings from 1906 to 1907. Women's magazines such as *Ladies' Home Journal* also featured Parrish's ethereal and dreamlike images and landscapes on their covers.

Better paper quality, improved printing capabilities, and lowered costs all resulted in a vastly improved physical product. Soon after the turn of the century, the photographic halftone cost just $20 to produce while a full page fine-line wood engraving cost up to $300. Magazines featured more photography, more color, more attention to the layout of pages, and more design tricks. Two publications are responsible for critical turning points in the visual appearance of magazines.

Gilbert Hovey Grosvenor was editor of *National Geographic* in December 1904 when he learned from the printer that he was short on copy for the next issue. Lacking any manuscripts to fill the space, Grosvenor told the story of his eventual good fortune in his seventy-fifth anniversary salute to the magazine, appropriately titled "The Romance of the *Geographic*." Wrote Grosvenor:

> *By sheer chance I received in the mail 50 beautiful photographs of Lhasa, the mysterious capital of Tibet, on the very day that I urgently needed 11 pages of material for the January 1905 issue. The Russian explorers who took the pictures offered them free. So I filled the entire 11 pages with the photographs, raiding the Society's slim treasury to make the plates.*[39]

Grosvenor said he expected to be fired by the magazine's board of directors for filling so much space with just photos. But when the magazine appeared, people stopped Grosvenor on the street to congratulate him on the Lhasa photo spread. That incident led him to run more and more photos in *National Geographic.* In the April 1905 issue, Grosvenor published 138 photos depicting the Philippines, which had been sent to him by his cousin William Howard Taft, who was governor general of the islands. Readers were so enamored of the issue that a second printing was ordered. Membership in the National Geographic Society soared from 3,662 in January 1905 to 11,479 by the end of the year.

Equally significant were the photos in the July 1906 issue: the first "flashlight pictures" of wild animals in their natural habitats. Grosvenor published 74 animal photos on 50 pages, with just four pages of text. It is not surprising that *National Geographic* was the first to run hand-tinted photographs of Korea and China in November 1910 and the first true color photograph in 1914.

With each new photographic delight, the circulation of *National Geographic* grew. This was noticed by other magazines, which began increasing the number of photos issue by issue. During the 1920s, fashion and high society magazines, particularly *Vogue* and *Vanity Fair,* enthusiastically embraced photography, as did *Harper's Bazaar* and *Town & Country.*

But it wasn't until November 1936 that a full-fledged modern picture magazine appeared on the newsstands: Henry Luce's *Life.* Unlike earlier magazines that had photos to illustrate copy (such as *Collier's* and *Frank Leslie's Illustrated Weekly*), *Life* used pictures to tell the story. Through the camera lenses of staff photographers Margaret Bourke-White, Alfred Eisenstaedt, Peter Stackpole, and Thomas McAvoy, *Life* introduced a whole new genre in content and form to the magazine industry: photojournalism.

Life wouldn't be the only picture magazine game in town for long. *Look* appeared in January 1937, and although it also was a picture magazine, there were fundamental differences in content. *Life* used photos that highlighted news and information; *Look* opted for shots that were sensational and entertaining.

Adding photos and more color to editorial pages not only contributed to the physical improvement of magazines, they also affected the visual literacy of readers, who became more demanding. During the 1930s and 1940s, art direction became a factor in magazine design. Art directors were added to a staff that had long been top-heavy with editors and writers, and this contributed to a significant evolution in the visual component of magazines.

Under the creative eyes of such art directors as Alexey Brodovitch at *Harper's Bazaar* and Mehemed Fehmy Agha at *Vogue* and *Vanity Fair,* magazine pages finally had a sense of unity, continuity, and most important, style. For Brodovitch, magazine design was "a musical feeling, a rhythm resulting from the interaction of space and time—he wanted the magazine to read like a sheet of music. He and [editor] Carmel Snow would dance around the pages spread before them on the floor, trying to pick up the rhythm."[40] In general, magazines became bolder in their design and more dramatic in their appearance through the use of large blocks of white space. This continues today.

A special exhibit about magazines is part of the Newseum, a 72,000-square-foot multimedia space in Arlington, Virginia. The Newseum is the brainchild of the Freedom Forum, an independent nonprofit foundation dedicated to freedom of speech and the press. The history section includes the first issues of *The Nation, Cosmopolitan, The New Yorker,* and *George,* among others. Groundbreaking magazine covers include the first Norman Rockwell illustration for a 1916 *Saturday Evening Post.* Visitors can even put their own faces on covers of *Sports Illustrated* or *Newsweek* in the interactive section.

TRANSPORTATION AND DELIVERY

Transportation is dependent upon geography, terrain, and location, while delivery is influenced by postal regulations. Both factors affect a magazine's range and reach in terms of circulation and impact. While transportation facilities showed continual improvement, mail delivery was hampered by costly and capricious laws that did not always favor the early magazine industry.

Eighteenth Century: Limited Restraints

When Bradford and Franklin established the first magazines in 1741, the American colonies stretched about 1,200 miles from northeast to southwest along the Atlantic Ocean. Although the colonies went inland as far west as 1,000 miles, most of the development was concentrated along the Atlantic seaboard. The population of the colonies was about one million people, with Philadelphia as the midpoint between New England and the Carolinas. By 1783, when the United States was recognized as a nation, 13 states extended north to Canada, west to the Mississippi River, and south to Florida. But during all of the eighteenth century and well into the nineteenth century, magazine readership was centered in a narrow strip from Boston to Baltimore.

Transportation was either by foot, by horse, or by carriage during the eighteenth century. Roads were poor, and the stagecoach averaged only two miles an hour. The journey from Boston to New York, a distance of 208 miles, took a stagecoach eight to ten days. As late as 1789, postal roads, where post offices were located and used by mail carriers, were few, numbering only 75 and scattered over a thousand miles of terrain. Through the late 1780s most post roads ran along a north-south axis near the Atlantic seaboard.

The colonies had enjoyed a postal system since Queen Anne's Act of 1710, but no specific provisions had been made for carrying magazines in the mails. Each postmaster had considerable discretion over what could and could not be sent. Ben Franklin was the postmaster for Philadelphia in 1741, which explains why his magazine lasted three months longer than Bradford's. Franklin allowed post riders to carry his magazine, but not his rival's.

Magazines were bulkier and heavier than newspapers and letters and were often rejected because of space since mail was delivered on horseback. Even when stagecoaches carried mail, space and weight were at a premium. When allowed to use the mails, magazines were charged more than newspapers for the same service. The cost of postage was paid by the reader directly to the post riders or postmasters. For the first 50 years of American magazine publishing, individual postmasters determined whether periodicals would be delivered, although some magazine publishers used independent "newscarriers" for distribution.

Although postmasters may have been capricious, their approach was more favorable for magazine delivery than the Postal Act of 1792. This act allowed newspapers to be mailed for 1 cent postage for a distance of up to 100 miles, and 1.5 cents for more than 100 miles. This was a fraction of the cost of letters, which cost 6 cents per sheet for delivery up to 30 miles. Yet a typical newspaper was four times larger than the one sheet of paper used for letters.[41] Nothing was said about magazines, and this was interpreted by postmasters as meaning they now could charge magazines the much higher letter rates.

Two popular magazines were hurt by the Postal Act of 1792. Both *The Columbian Magazine,* established in 1786, and *The American Museum,* started in 1787, had exceeded the typical magazine's life span because they were original and ambitious: new magazines for a new nation. Both publications collected and published Revolutionary War documents, letters, and essays so everyone could become familiar with the great thinkers of the war years. Some historians consider *The American Museum* to be the most important American magazine of the eighteenth century because it reached a circulation of more than 1,200, which was enormous for the time period. Yet, despite the insight and obvious appeal of the two magazines, both died in 1792, victims of the postal system. Neither magazine could afford the new prohibitive and unequal postal rates.

A more indulgent postal law was passed by Congress in 1794 that recognized the importance of magazines and lowered their costs significantly. This resulted in an increasing number of magazine start-ups and was a factor in the magazine boom that occurred during the nineteenth

World-famous artists have created variations of their trademark landscapes and images for magazine covers. Salvador Dali's June 1939 bridal cover for *Vogue* is eerily similar to his renowned "Persistence of Memory," while Roy Lichtenstein's May 24, 1968, *Time* cover of Robert Kennedy reeks of the artist's colorful Pop Art comic book style. Erté's June 1936 cover for *Harper's Bazaar* is Art Deco at its most elegant with his use of a slinky, sinuous tie to suggest a speeding automobile for the "Travel and Resort Fashions" issue.

TABLE 3.4 Early Magazine Postage Costs

YEAR	MAGAZINE SIZE	DISTANCE	COST TO MAIL
1794	64 pages Weight not a factor	Up to 100 miles More than 100 miles	6 cents 8 cents
1825	96 pages Weight not a factor	Up to 100 miles More than 100 miles	18 cents 30 cents
1845	96 pages 5 ounces in weight	Any distance	6.5 cents
1852	96 pages 5 ounces in weight	Any distance	1.5 cents
1885	Any size Second-class privileges	Any distance	1 cent a pound (16 ounces)

century. However, it did not alleviate the expenses associated with magazines for readers. A 64-page magazine delivered more than 100 miles cost 8 cents postage. Eight cents in 1794 would buy a chair or pay the wages of a cleaning woman for a day. The postage fee was in addition to the subscription cost of a magazine. Many readers simply refused to pay for their magazines upon delivery, which affected the fortunes of magazine publishers. Consequently, some editors even printed the names of debtors in each issue in an attempt to shame delinquent readers into paying for the magazine.

Nineteeth Century: Postal Improvements

By 1800 the United States had a much improved road system linking many communities. Postal roads were extended inland, and the government began to build federal highways. The famous Erie Canal across New York State from Buffalo to Albany, completed in 1825, established the destiny of New York City as the biggest city and the center of American communications. Railroads began to be laid westward by the Baltimore and Ohio Railroad, offering another way for mail to reach readers. Unfortunately, postal rates did not decline as roads improved or as other transportation modes developed.

In 1825, Congress connected magazine postage to size and distance, at 1.5 cents per octavo sheet (per eight pages printed on a single sheet of paper) for up to 100 miles, and 2.5 cents for greater distances. This meant that a 96-page magazine paid 18 cents per issue for postage up to 100 miles and 30 cents for greater distances—or rather, subscribers paid. Yet newspapers, regardless of size, still paid a maximum of 1.5 cents for delivery anywhere in the country. Because of the extra cost of mailing a magazine more than 100 miles, circulation tended to remain concentrated in the northeast portion of the United States.

Newspapers sent fewer than 30 miles were mailed free. Some magazines tried to get newspaper classification, even calling themselves newspapers. Finally, in 1845, Congress abolished the distance factor and fixed the rate by weight at 2.5 cents for the first ounce of weight and 1 cent for each additional ounce. Most monthlies weighed between 5 ounces and 6 ounces, so this meant a reduction in postal costs. That typical 96-page magazine now cost between 6.5 and 7.5 cents to mail.

Magazine circulations continued to be low, ranging from a few hundred up to the 40,000 claimed by *Godey's Lady's Book* in 1849. Readership tended to be concentrated east of the Mississippi River. Circulation figures are hard to determine, but it's estimated that the average during the 1850s was about 7,500.

Magazine publishers continued to lobby for reduced rates, and a significant turning point occurred in 1852 when postal rates dropped again. The average 96-page magazine that weighed 5 ounces had cost 6.5 cents to receive under the 1845 Post Office Act; now it would cost 1.5 cents to send. More fundamental was that the 1852 Post Office Act allowed postal fees to be paid at the mailing office, and publishers decided it would be better policy to absorb the cost of postage at that point. No longer would subscribers have to prepay the postage sum on a quarterly basis at their post offices.

Following the Civil War, another round of magazine expansion began, with as many as 9,000 periodicals established. These now had an average life of four years. Transportation channels for distribution were greatly improved when the East and West Coasts were connected by rail in 1869; tracks laid from the east by the Union Pacific joined those from the west laid by the Central Pacific at Promontory Point, Utah. Magazines became more national in approach, and circulations regularly began to exceed 100,000. Between 1865 and 1885, more than 30 magazines boasted having circulations of 100,000 or more. Among them were *Youth's Companion, Harper's Monthly, Godey's Lady's Book,* and *Peterson's.*

The most important postal date in conjunction with the modern magazine is 1879, when special second-class mailing privileges were given to magazines. Delivery had long been a major, if not the major, problem facing publishers. For the first time, the federal government in effect subsidized magazine delivery. The Postal Act of 1879 meant that magazines could be mailed from coast to coast at the same low cost newspapers had long enjoyed. Scores of magazines were then developed and designed for the average working man and woman, as opposed to the more prosperous urban professional who previously had been the primary audience.

Postage rates for second-class mail dropped again in 1885, to 1 cent a pound, and in 1897 the rural free delivery system was instituted. Both developments helped farm, agriculture, and women's periodicals. Magazines now could reach every corner of the nation, and circulations soared to the millions. Delivery and transportation costs were more than covered by advertising revenue. Most magazines were sold by subscription, although newsstand single copy sales became a more important factor after publishers begin distributing their magazines to dealers through independent wholesalers during the 1890s.

Twentieth Century: Complex Costs

Transportation and delivery systems became linked to production and technological improvements that grew out of the Industrial Revolution's impact on the United States after 1900. Postal regulations grew more complex; starting in 1917, editorial matter was charged a flat rate, while advertising pages were zoned and cost accordingly. Since the 1950s, one of the concerns in magazine budgets has been to allow for rising second class postage rates. Consequently, after years of increasingly higher circulations, many publishers found it prudent to deliberately cut back or reduce circulation numbers after the 1960s.

The Postal Reorganization Act of 1970 took away the power to set rates and classifications from Congress and made the post office an independent regulatory agency. This quasi-government agency, the United States Postal Service (USPS) with its Postal Rate Commission, now sets rates, reviews mail service, and investigates complaints. Greatly increased second-class rates were established in 1970, but these were phased in over a 10-year period. By 1980, after a decade of runaway inflation, postal rates had increased more than 400 percent. Some publishers began experimenting with alternative delivery systems, such as private carriers, in an attempt to meet the essential goal of getting magazines to subscribers.

PRODUCTION AND TECHNOLOGY

Increases in the amount of leisure time, shorter workweeks, appliances that lightened household chores, transportation improvements, and significant changes in technology and production all had an impact on American magazines.

Eighteenth Century: Intensive Hand Labors

An enormous amount of labor was needed to produce a magazine during the eighteenth century. Printing a magazine was slow, hard work done by hand. Printing presses were virtually the same in the eighteenth century as they had been in 1448 when Johannes Gutenberg created moveable type. The cumbersome wooden press used by Franklin and Bradford in 1741 was still based on the screw-operated press devised by Gutenberg when he printed the Bible in the mid-fifteenth century. More than a dozen distinct operations—all done by hand—were needed to turn out a single page.

Type was set by hand, one letter, one line, one page at a time. Then the page form would be broken up so the type could be used again—and again. Paper also was made by hand from rags and scraps of linen cloth. Ink, too, tended to be produced by the printer using lampblack and boiled linseed oil, with each printer having his own "secret" formula. Although the first ink factory was established in America in 1742, its output was limited and costly.

In order to have consistent quality and quantity of paper and ink as well as the best type and presses, those American printers who could afford it imported their printing necessities from England. With the Revolutionary War, however, England embargoed all paper and printing equipment. Consequently, magazine publication came to a standstill during the American Revolution.

Nineteenth Century: Mass Production Procedures

Mass production methods were introduced to printing during the last 10 years of the nineteenth century: timed production scheduling, conveyor systems, and assembly lines. The slow flatbed press that printed merely one sheet at a time gave way to the steam-powered press in 1822, then to the swifter rotary press in 1847, and finally, by 1871, to the web perfecting press capable of simultaneously printing both sides of a continuous roll of paper. Color printing was part of the production process by the 1860s.

Magazines no longer had to depend on sketches that were laboriously copied, expensively engraved on copper or wood, and then colored by hand, for illustrations. With new photoengraving techniques, photographs became common. In 1886, the Mergenthaler Linotype machine revolutionized publishing by eliminating the need to set type by hand. The Linotype could do the work of seven or eight hand typesetters faster and more efficiently.

Papermaking techniques also improved as publishers moved from the costly handmade linen pulp of the eighteenth century to cheap wood pulp during the mid-nineteenth century to elegant, yet affordable, slick and coated sheets in the twentieth century. The result was that technology allowed for attractive magazines to be turned out at a low unit cost, again leading to lower prices for the magazine reader. Today, some environmentally conscious publishers are turning to recycled paper, although it is not always an economical decision.

Twentieth Century: Technological Techniques

The twentieth century brought more technological improvements to the magazine industry. Computer and satellite technology narrowed the amount of time needed to accept advertising as well as to print fast-breaking stories. That same technology, along with demographic information, encouraged publishers to target narrowly defined, niche audiences through selective binding as early as 1982. Where technology has had its biggest impact, however, is in the production process.

Scientific American offers an excellent example of the steps a magazine takes in adapting to technology. According to Richard Sasso, associate publisher and vice president of production, the first desktop, or computer-assisted, issue of *Scientific American* was published in 1978. By 1989, the art and production departments were using Macintosh computers to their fullest capacity, with editors switching to Macintosh in 1991. All departments were networked by 1993.

In October 1994, the first computer-to-plate (CTP) test took place: 16 pages were produced using all digital information. No film was shot and no negatives were made for those pages. According to Sasso, the quality of CTP technology was excellent, and editors agreed to try it with an entire issue. The convincing argument for editors was that three to five days could be cut from the editorial schedule using CTP. Advertisers could also send in material later than normal.

The January 1995 issue of *Scientific American*, touting "The Computer in the 21st Century" on the cover, became the first true digital web offset magazine. All ads and editorial in the 200-page magazine were produced without film. Apple Computer supplied the ads, 22 full-color pages in digital form. Says Sasso, "It was a first for the web offset magazine industry."[42]

By the end of 1995, 70 million copy pages had been produced for the magazine using CTP. *Scientific American* announced it would begin accepting digital advertising, but Sasso said there were no takers at first. By the March 1996 issue, however, half of the ads were supplied as digital data. Currently, all editorial material is being produced without film.

Sasso says he wants to encourage the use of CTP because it means better quality, lower costs, and faster editorial turnaround time. As with any technological innovation, there's a need for a common format and standards in the industry. Sasso observes, "Education, communication, and a lot of cooperation are needed."

Those words are almost a mantra for the magazine field. Throughout history, the constantly evolving magazine remains a vehicle for communication and a marketplace of ideas. Or, as Art Cooper, *GQ*'s editor-in-chief, explains it: "A magazine is a living thing, not a museum. The magazine that doesn't continue to change is going to perish."[43]

FOR ADDITIONAL READING

Bainbridge, John. *Little Wonder or, the* Reader's Digest and *How It Grew.* New York: Reynal & Hitchcock, 1945.

Bok, Edward. *The Americanization of Edward Bok.* New York: Scribner's Sons, 1920.

Canning, Peter. *American Dreamers: The Wallaces and* Reader's Digest: *An Insider's Story.* New York: Simon and Schuster, 1996.

Cohn, Jan. *Creating America: George Horace Lorimer and the* Saturday Evening Post. Pittsburgh: University of Pittsburgh Press, 1989.

Edgar, Neal L. *A History and Bibliography of American Magazines, 1810–1820.* Metuchen, NJ: Scarecrow Press, 1975.

Elson, Robert T. *Time Inc.: The Intimate History of a Publishing Enterprise 1923–1941.* New York: Atheneum, 1968.

———. *The World of Time Inc.: The Intimate History of a Publishing Enterprise 1941–1960.* New York: Atheneum, 1973.

Ford, James L. C. *Magazines for Millions: The Story of Specialized Publications.* Carbondale, IL: Southern Illinois University Press, 1969.

Forsyth, David P. *The Business Press in America 1750–1865.* Philadelphia: Chilton Books, 1964.

Harper, J. Henry. *The House of Harper: A Century of Publishing in Franklin Square.* New York: Harper and Brothers Publishing, 1912.

Janello, Amy and Brennon Jones. *The American Magazine.* New York: Harry N. Abrams, Inc., 1991.

Mott, Frank Luther. *A History of American Magazines, 1741–1850,* Vol. 1. Cambridge, MA: Harvard University Press, 1939.

———. *A History of American Magazines, 1850–1865,* Vol. 2. Cambridge, MA: Harvard University Press, 1957.

———. *A History of American Magazines, 1865–1885,* Vol. 3. Cambridge, MA: Harvard University Press, 1957.

———. *A History of American Magazines, 1885–1905,* Vol. 4. Cambridge, MA: Harvard University Press, 1957.

———. *A History of American Magazines, 1905–1930,* Vol. 5. Cambridge, MA: Harvard University Press, 1968.

Nourie, Alan and Barbara Nourie, eds. *American Mass-Market Magazines.* Westport, CT: Greenwood Press, 1990.

Peterson, Theodore. *Magazines in the Twentieth Century.* Urbana: University of Illinois Press, 1964.

Prendergast, Curtis with Geoffrey Colvin. *The World of Time Inc.: The Intimate History of a Changing Enterprise 1960-1980.* New York: Atheneum, 1986.

Richardson, Lyon N. *A History of Early American Magazines 1741–1789.* New York: Octagon Books, 1978.

Schneirov, Matthew. *The Dream of a New Social Order: Popular Magazines in America 1893–1914.* New York: Columbia University Press, 1994.

Swanberg, W. A. *Luce and His Empire.* New York: Charles Scribner's Sons, 1972.

Tassin, Algernon. *The Magazine in America.* New York: Dodd, Mead, 1916.

Tebbel, John. *The American Magazine: A Compact History.* New York: Hawthorn Books, 1969.

Tebbel, John and Mary Ellen Zuckerman. *The Magazine in America 1741–1990.* New York: Oxford University Press, 1991.

Thurber, James. *The Years with Ross.* Boston: Little, Brown, 1957.

Weber, Ronald. *Hired Pens: Professional Writers in America's Golden Age of Print.* Athens, OH: Ohio University Press, 1997.

Wood, James Playsted. *Magazines in the United States,* 2nd ed. New York: Ronald Press, 1956.

———. *Of Lasting Interest: The Story of the* Reader's Digest. New York: Doubleday, 1958.

Zuckerman, Mary Ellen. *A History of Poplar Women's Magazines in the United States, 1792-1995.* Westport, CT: Greenwood Press, 1998.

ENDNOTES

[1] Some historians cite *Town & Country* and *Scientific American* as the oldest magazine titles. However, both started as newspapers. *Town & Country,* which celebrated its 150th anniversary in October 1996, began in 1846 as a weekly newspaper titled *National Press,* then changed its name to *Home Journal* nine months later. *Town & Country* did not receive its current name until 1901. *Scientific American* was established as a weekly newspaper in 1845, and didn't evolve into a monthly magazine until 1921.
[2] "Acknowledgements," *The American Magazine* (February 1788) 130.
[3] Samir Husni, "What's New?" in "Magazines: The Medium of the Moment" Special Supplement, *The New York Times* (October 8, 1998): 18.
[4] William Beer, *Checklist of American Magazines, 1741–1800* (Worcester, MA: American Antiquarian Society, 1923).
[5] "American Periodicals," *New-York Mirror* (November 15, 1828): 151.
[6] Lee Soltow and Edward Stevens, *The Rise of Literacy and the Common School in the United States: A Socioeconomic Analysis to 1870* (Chicago: University of Chicago Press, 1981): 34–51.
[7] Kenneth A. Lockridge, *Literacy in Colonial New England* (New York: W. W. Norton, 1974): 13.
[8] David Paul Nord, "A Republican Literature: A Study of Magazine Reading and Readers in Late-Eighteenth-Century New York" (paper presented at the annual meeting of the Association for Education in Journalism and Mass Communication, Norman, OK, August 1986).
[9] Lockridge, 38–42.
[10] Job Weeden and William Barrett, "To the Public," *The Gentleman and Lady's Town and Country Magazine* (May 1784): 4.
[11] Sara M. Evans, *Born for Liberty: A History of Women in America* (New York: Free Press, 1989), 65.
[12] Soltow and Stevens: 51.
[13] Ibid., 51.
[14] Frank Luther Mott, *A History of American Magazines, 1850-1865,* vol. 2 (Cambridge, MA: Harvard University Press, 1957): 103.
[15] Ibid., 106–107.
[16] William B. Cairns, "Later Magazines," in *Cambridge History of American Literature,* vol. 3, William Peterfield Trent, John Erskine, Stuart P. Sherman, and Carl Van Doren, eds. (New York: G. P. Putnam's Sons, 1921): 299.
[17] Carl F. Kaestle, Helen Damon-Moore, Lawrence C. Stedman, Katherine Tinsley, and William Vance Trollinger Jr., *Literacy in the United States: Readers and Reading Since 1880* (New Haven: Yale University Press, 1991): 283.
[18] Ibid., 193.
[19] Paul F. Lazarsfeld and Patricia Kendall, "The Communications Behavior of the Average American," in *Mass Communications,* Wilbur Schramm, ed. (Urbana: University of Illinois Press, 1960): 432.
[20] Stephen G. Smith, "From the Editor: The Bond Between a Magazine and Its Readers," *Civilization* (May/June 1995): 6.
[21] Douglas B. Ward, "The Reader as Consumer: Curtis Publishing Company and Its Audience, 1910-1930," *Journalism History* (Summer 1996): 47.
[22] Kaestle, 172.
[23] Ibid., 172.
[24] Ward, 52.
[25] Ibid., 53.
[26] Isaiah Thomas, *The History of Printing in America* (New York: Weathervane Books, 1970, from the second edition printed by the American Antiquarian Society Library, 1824): 284.
[27] Frank Luther Mott, *A History of American Magazines, 1741-1850,* vol. 1 (Cambridge, MA: Harvard University Press, 1939): 494–513.
[28] "The Magazine Galore," *The Round Table* (November 23, 1867): 337.
[29] David Forsyth and Warren Berger, "Trading Places," *Folio:* (March 1991): 82.
[30] Frank Luther Mott, *A History of American Magazines, 1865–1885,* vol. 3 (Cambridge, MA: Harvard University Press, 1957): 133.
[31] American Business Press website (June 16, 1998), http://www.americanbusinesspress.com.
[32] Edward Bok, *The Americanization of Edward Bok* (New York: Scribner's Sons, 1920): 374–375.
[33] "The Common Touch," *Time* (December 10, 1951): 64.
[34] Wm. David Sloan and James D. Startt, *The Media in America: A History,* 3rd ed. (Northport, AL: Vision Press, 1996): 472–73.
[35] *Scribner's Monthly* was founded in 1870 and published as a literary magazine until 1881 when it was sold because of a difference of opinions between the book publishing Scribners (Charles Scribner's Sons) and the magazine publishing Scribners (Scribner and Company). The magazine's name was changed to *The Century* under a new publisher and editor; *The Century* died in 1930. The book publishing Scribners promised not to start another magazine within five years. Their *Scribner's Magazine* was established in 1887 and died in 1939.
[36] Weeden and Barrett, 4.
[37] "American Periodical Literature," *New-York Mirror* (January 4, 1834): 215.
[38] *Godey's Lady's Book* (July 1831), back cover.
[39] Gilbert Hovey Grosvenor, "The Romance of the *Geographic*," *National Geographic* (October 1963): 565.
[40] "*Harper's Bazaar* at 100," *Print* (September/October 1967): 46.
[41] Kielbowicz, Richard B. *News in the Mail: The Press, Post Office, and Public Information, 1700–1860s* (New York: Greenwood Press, 1989): 33–36.
[42] Richard Sasso, "The Art of Magazine Production," Stanford Professional Publishing Course, Palo Alto, CA (July 27, 1997).
[43] Keith J. Kelly, "Magazines Put on New Face," *Advertising Age* (November 28, 1994), 8.

CHAPTER 4

The Magazine as a Social Barometer

Political and Cultural Interaction

When Thomas Edison fine-tuned his phonograph and was ready to show it to somebody outside his shop, whom did he choose? The editor of Scientific American. *When you were a child, you may have used your phonograph to play the* Free To Be . . . You And Me *album produced as an offshoot of the television special by the same name. The sponsor of that special?* Ms. *magazine. Depending on their generation, young men have used* National Geographic, Playboy, *or* Hustler *as their introduction to the female form. Young women have read* Seventeen, Sassy, *or* Cosmopolitan *for advice on how to deal with those young men. Their parents read* Parents *or* Psychology Today *to try and figure it all out.* 📖 *Magazines are lively and engaging societal resources, affecting the world around them and, in turn, being affected themselves by that world. The social influence of magazines is as diverse as the magazines themselves. Magazines such as* The New Yorker, Ebony, Glamour, *and* Utne Reader *have influenced their worlds by the nature of the information they present as well as by the way they present that information. The world is different in a variety of ways because magazines exist.* 📖 *That world is far from static, though. Just as magazines influence society, they are influenced by it. Magazines are born, die, shrink, grow, and change their appearances and audiences because of a host of developments within society. As society changes, so do magazines.*

THE INTERACTION OF MAGAZINES AND SOCIETY

Do magazines mirror society or does society mirror magazines? An easy answer would be "both." A more complete explanation, however, would recognize magazines as active members of a complex society, leading the discussion in many cases, but allowing others in society to take the action that will cause change. Change only happens when the messages magazines present find a receptive ear in society. Conversely, those messages may not be heard without the help of magazines.

Your family, education, religious background, job, geographic location, political beliefs, gender, cultural history, and a host of other factors cause you to react differently from your neighbor and similarly to your best friend when faced with information from a magazine. For example, you may base all your stereo purchases on ratings from *Consumer Reports*, while your neighbor swears by *Car Stereo Review*. Your sister trusts *The Nation;* you trust *National Review*. You get your sports information from *Sports Illustrated;* your brother turns to *Sport*. We all live our lives differently—we're all surrounded by different phenomena—so we react differently to the media and they affect us differently.

The phenomenalistic approach to the study of magazines takes all these differences into account and recognizes that magazines are but one influence in a whole universe of influences. Named by mass communications researcher Joseph Klapper,[1] this theory grew out of scholars' frustration with their attempts to prove specific, absolute media effects. Those effects, Klapper suggested, were difficult to isolate because the media aren't isolated entities. They are, instead, phenomena operating within a system of other phenomena.

In 1987, *Hustler* magazine was sued for publishing an article titled "Orgasm of Death," which explained autoerotic asphyxia, the practice of masturbating while hanging oneself, supposedly to increase pleasure. It began with examples of deaths caused by the practice and included a warning against trying the act. It also, however, included information on how to do it. At least one young man tried the act after reading the article, and died. The issue of *Hustler* with the "Orgasm" article was found at his feet. The boy's mother and his close friend sued the magazine and were awarded $200,000 in damages. The judgment was reversed, however, by the federal court of appeals, which noted the lack of evidence that the article by itself could have caused the death.[2] What was the effect of that article? The magazine did provide the information, but it was just one phenomenon. It, alone, was not responsible for the reader's actions, but it did have an influence.

To study the interaction between magazines and society, it is necessary to break society into smaller segments and analyze those segments. We can study the political and cultural nature of magazines through four perspectives: magazines as political influences; political influences on magazines; magazines as cultural influences; and cultural influences on magazines.

The "most obnoxious" fad of the decade? According to *Spy*'s October 1996 edition, it's cigar smoking. The magazine fingers *Cigar Aficionado* as one leader of the trend that, they contend, started when the magazine did. Interestingly, *Cigar Aficionado* is still smoking, while *Spy* took its last puff in 1998.

MAGAZINES AS POLITICAL INFLUENCES

The voice magazines give to political causes—mainstream and alternative, popular and unpopular—may be one of the medium's most important influences. The diversity of magazines makes them, in total, a balanced voice that speaks for liberal as well as conservative viewpoints, for groups who seek to change society as well as those who advocate maintaining the status quo. While *National Review* focuses on the shortcomings of liberal Democrats, *The Nation* looks at errors in the ways of conservative Republicans.

As political influences, magazines are agenda setters and advocates. Agenda setters influence change, often unintentionally, simply by calling public attention to an issue. The term *agenda setting* began to be used by 1960s media scholars who were still searching for a way to isolate and analyze media effects, and it represented an important change in approach.[3] Until that time, theorists had been looking at the ways in which the media made us think, with brainwashing being an early concern. The focus in **agenda setting** theory is on the belief that the media do not tell us *how* to think, they tell us what to think *about.*

Magazines act as agenda setters when they identify and frame the issues on which society focuses. They tell the public, in essence, that something is important and should be discussed. Magazine journalists, agenda setting theorists believe, do not directly cause social change. They provide information that may motivate others to enact change.

Changes influenced by agenda setters may be direct or indirect, for good or for ill. Magazines were setting the public agenda long before the term was coined. In the past, agenda setters have been called muckrakers; today they are likely to be called investigative reporters.

In other cases, magazine staffers can be advocates for a cause affecting their audience. Advocates can also be agenda setters. In fact, in most cases, agenda setting is an advocate's goal.

Agenda Setters

Magazines set the public agenda by their emphasis on the major as well as the minor. When *Education Week* magazine runs a state-by-state critique of the nation's schools, it sends school boards across the country scurrying, some heading for the press room to crow about their accomplishments, others to the back room to figure out an excuse for their poor rating. When *Money* magazine ranks the tax burdens of individual states, legislators throughout the nation huddle in strategy sessions, often discussing ways to change the tax structure that led to a low evaluation.

You will see examples of agenda setting throughout this book, ranging from *Playboy*'s creation of Playmates to *Glamour*'s fashion "Don'ts." The very existence of titles such as *Latina* and *Yolk* set the nation's agenda by stressing the importance of groups within society, in these cases Hispanics and Asian-Americans.

Seldom was the case for agenda setting so clear and so strong, however, as it was with Rachel Carson's environmental writing. In 1960, Carson, a journalist and biologist, wrote a series of articles for *The New Yorker* about the dangers of pesticides, specifically DDT. Carson's work, titled "Silent Spring," also was published in a book of the same name. Based on meticulous research and

FEBRUARY 3, 1986: Aerospace insiders and outsiders around the world looked to *Aviation Week & Space Technology* for expert, technical coverage of the *Challenger* explosion.

SHUTTLE 51-L LOSS

Shuttle Destroyed, Killing Crew; Manned Space Flights Halted

Shuttle Challenger clears Pad 39B at Kennedy Space Center (above) in what appeared to be a routine launch of the twenty-fifth shuttle on Jan. 28. Mission 51-L was the first shuttle launched from this facility, which is a refurbished and modified pad from the Apollo, Spacelab and Apollo-Soyuz Test Project missions ending in the mid-1970s. Mission 51-L astronauts are shown (opposite page) during orbiter training. In photo at top, opposite page, mission commander Francis R. Scobee is at front right and mission pilot Navy Cdr. Michael J. Smith is at front left. Mission specialist Judith A. Resnik is in the center seat flight engineer position, while USAF Lt. Col. Ellison S. Onizuka is at aft left. Seated in the orbiter middeck in the lower photo are mission specialist Ronald E. McNair, at aft right near the orbiter hatch, Hughes payload specialist Gregory B. Jarvis is at center right, and teacher Christa McAuliffe is at center left. Aiding in this preflight simulation at aft left was backup teacher payload specialist Barbara Morgan, who was not on board Challenger for the flight.

Johnson Space Center—Destruction of the shuttle orbiter Challenger Jan. 28 has halted the U.S. manned space program for the foreseeable future, threatening cancellation or postponement of key near-term science missions and placing future commercial, military and space research projects into competition for reduced shuttle launch capacity.

The worst accident in U.S. space program history also will affect planning for the U.S./International Space Station, the pace of space commercialization and confidence in the space shuttle as the nation's operational launch system.

Mission 51-L astronauts Francis R. Scobee, Navy Cdr. Michael J. Smith, Judith A. Resnik, USAF Lt. Col. Ellison Onizuka, Ronald E. McNair, Hughes payload specialist Gregory B. Jarvis and teacher observer Christa McAuliffe became the first U.S. space crew to die in flight when their vehicle exploded 72 sec. following liftoff from Kennedy Space Center at 11:38 a.m. EST.

Detailed failure analysis is beginning this week on data transmitted from Challenger. Emphasis is being placed on assessing the potential for failure within a joint between the segments of the Morton Thiokol/United Space Booster solid propellant rockets. It has always been known that any joint failure or motor burn-through would result in an unsurvivable accident. Emphasis also is being given to the Martin Marietta external tank and the two large oxygen/hydrogen umbilicals that enter the orbiter from the tank on the spacecraft's aft belly.

Kennedy Space Center personnel have on at least two previous prelaunch checkouts needed to reassess the integrity of the seals between the tank's umbilicals and the orbiter when tests showed that integrity was in question.

The National Aeronautics and Space Administration is beginning a broad replanning effort to recover from the loss of Challenger and its seven-member crew.

"The future schedule of the space program and our shuttle activities cannot be determined at this time," William R. Graham, Jr., NASA acting administrator, said.

"We certainly intend to go forward with the program. The timing under which we can do all that depends to a great extent on what we find out [about the accident], and that is still to be determined," he said.

Challenger was valued at about $1.5 billion and its primary Tracking and Data Relay Satellite/Inertial Upper Stage payload at over $117 million.

No malfunction or unusual conditions were detected in the S-band real-time data received at the mission control center here in the moments before the explosion. "It just stopped," Lead Ascent Flight Director Jay Greene said about data from the orbiter. More detailed FM telemetry data

16 AVIATION WEEK & SPACE TECHNOLOGY/February 3, 1986

AVIATION WEEK & SPACE TECHNOLOGY/February 3, 1986 17

articulated with grace and detail, *Silent Spring* is credited with causing the ban on DDT use and production in this country and is seen by many as the seed that eventually grew into the Environmental Protection Agency. *The New Yorker* in this case was an agenda setter. It brought forth a topic to discuss and let society as a whole make its own decision on how to deal with the issue.

Carson's *Silent Spring* demonstrated how chemicals were contaminating the food chain, leading to health dangers such as cancer and to possible genetic effects that might not be known for generations. It led the nation into a debate on the issue, with articles in *Time*, *Consumer Bulletin*, and *Saturday Evening Post* broadening the discussion.[4] By 1970, state and federal legislation severely restricted the use of DDT. By 1980, the use of DDT was eliminated in the United States and limited in Third World countries. In addition, chemical companies reacted to Carson's criticisms by producing less dangerous chemical pesticides and by directing agrochemical research toward the creation of pesticides that are used in smaller doses and with less frequent application.[5]

Carson was not universally supported, however. *Time* called her work "oversimplified" and suggested she might do more harm than good with "her emotional and inaccurate outburst." Edwin Diamond, writing in *Saturday Evening Post,* also called Carson "emotional" and said that, thanks to her, "a big fuss has been stirred up to scare the American public out of its wits." Likewise, this discussion of Carson's ideas became part of the public agenda, although final action was left to politicians. Carson's role was to get the country talking, and she did: The discussion of chemical pesticides continues, nearly 40 years after Carson sat down at her typewriter.

Trade magazines, likewise, can be effective agenda setters. *Aviation Week & Space Technology* has long been acknowledged as the leader in aerospace information. Dating back to pre-World War I daredevil days of flight, the magazine devotes page after page to all facets of aircraft production, the airline industry, and both defense and civil aerospace concerns.

Whenever a new aircraft is developed at home or abroad, when an airline reconfigures its seat pitch, or when an airplane crashes, *Aviation Week & Space Technology* authoritatively tells readers what it means from a technical point of view. Its coverage of the 1986 *Challenger* explosion, with photos of the spaceship's solid booster spraying stray fire at the external tank, was studied closely by aerospace insiders and by outside experts.

The publication maintains a staunch independence from the industry it covers and is regularly quoted by newspapers and television network news programs. Military coverage has long been dominant in the magazine's pages. The Persian Gulf War in 1991, however, was the first time *Aviation Week & Space Technology* covered a military conflict as a breaking news story, while also relating technical and operational air aspects.[6]

Possibly the best-known agenda setters were the muckrakers, the early investigative reporters who wrote in magazines at the turn of the century: journalists such as Ida M. Tarbell, Lincoln Steffens, and Ray Stannard Baker. The term *muckrakers* was coined in 1906 by President Theodore Roosevelt, who compared such writers to "the Man with the Muckrake" who dug through the filth without seeing the positive side of life in John Bunyan's *Pilgrim's Progress.*[7] Generally supportive of the reforms encouraged by muckrakers, Roosevelt nevertheless became frustrated with the intensity of the movement. His frustration no doubt grew out of the tempestuous mood of social change fostered by the articles.

Tarbell's series on "The History of the Standard Oil Company" chronicled John D. Rockefeller's often ruthless treatment of employees and competitors; it took her five years to research. Steffens outlined local political corruption in New York, Minneapolis, and St. Louis in "Shame of the Cities." Baker wrote a treatise on employment practices and working conditions titled "The Right to Work." All three had segments of their work published in the January 1903 issue of *McClure's*; that issue is generally regarded as the first breath of the muckraking movement. Magazines such as *Collier's, Cosmopolitan,* and *Hampton's* also jumped on the muckraking bandwagon, which rolled along until roughly 1912.

Even the top women's magazines at the start of the twentieth century engaged in muckraking. *Good Housekeeping, Woman's Home Companion, McCall's,* and *Ladies' Home Journal* took the position that a woman's sphere—her influence or place in society—could go beyond the traditional home environment. With women's magazines forging a link between the narrow confines of the home and the larger "national household," a proper Victorian lady could address housekeeping issues facing the whole community. The women's sphere argument allowed middle-class women and their magazines to respond to and participate in the muckraking movement.

Professor Kathleen L. Endres of the University of Akron has argued that writers for the top four women's magazines of this period did not just illustrate scandalous situations. They also were expected to offer solutions to the ills they reported, while continuing to support the prevalent conservative view of women as homemakers and nurturers.[8] The homemaker who would not tolerate adulterated food in her own kitchen—rotten apples used in commercial jellies, milk with formaldehyde as a preservative, or vanilla extract laced with wood alcohol—could protect her family through intelligent shopping. And because, as the "perfect" wife and mother, she was the primary consumer of the period, she waged war against corrupted food at the national level through her purchases. The women's magazines, by telling readers how to shop, elevated domestic concerns to national consciousness.

Fall and Redemption of Minneapolis
McCLURE'S MAGAZINE
FOR JANUARY 1903
PUBLISHED MONTHLY BY THE S.S. McCLURE CO., 141-155 E. 25th ST., NEW YORK CITY

JANUARY 1903: This issue of *McClure's* included investigative articles by muckrakers Ida M. Tarbell, Lincoln Steffens, and Ray Stannard Baker.

Good Housekeeping was the first to enter the fight against the misrepresentation of products, setting up a Good Housekeeping Testing Institute in 1901 as a place to test foods and household products for purity. By 1906, the magazine was providing monthly reports of brand-name foods that met its standards for purity, as well as annual summaries to be used as guides to safe shopping. Similarly, *Ladies' Home Journal* crusaded against the patent medicines used by women to doctor themselves and their families. Unknown to users, many patent medicines with reassuring names like "Carney's Common Sense Cure" or "Children's Comfort" contained high percentages of alcohol or addictive narcotics

RESEARCH IN BRIEF

Agenda Setting

In July 1962, *The Journal of the American Medical Association (JAMA)* published an article by Dr. C. Henry Kempe on "The Battered Child Syndrome." In the decade before the article, mass circulation magazines carried only three articles on child abuse. In the decade following the article, these same magazines published 28 such articles, a 900 percent increase. What's most important, however, is that Kempe gave a phenomenon a catchy name: battered child syndrome. Ultimately, through significant media use, this name became part of our language.

In *Making an Issue of Child Abuse,* media scholar Barbara Nelson studied this phenomenon.[1] Nelson noted that the news magazines—*Time* and *Newsweek*—were the first to run articles on Kempe's research, and *Saturday Evening Post* and *Life* followed with articles within months. Kempe was always listed as a source. All articles took Kempe's slant, emphasizing the medical rather than the criminal aspects of the "syndrome." What had been seen as an activity was now seen as a disease—treatable and preventable. The Battered Child Syndrome, a phrase invented in 1962 and introduced to the public through *JAMA,* had become the defining term.

One magazine—*JAMA,* the organizational magazine for the medical industry—led the way as the source for other magazines. It also led the way for newspapers and TV. The syndrome appeared on "Dragnet" as well as on "Dr. Kildare" and "Ben Casey, M.D."—the 1960s forerunners of "Chicago Hope" and "ER"—and was the subject of 16 stories in *The New York Times* in 1964 alone.

The child abuse issue reached consideration in state legislatures and in Congress, Nelson maintains, due in part to "sustained coverage in professional journals, popular magazines and newspapers."

[1] Barbara Nelson, *Making an Issue of Child Abuse: Political Agenda Setting for Social Problems* (Chicago: University of Chicago Press, 1984).

(opium, morphine, codeine, laudanum). Medical surveys revealed that by 1900 as many as two-thirds of American opiate addicts were women.

Both magazines urged existing women's clubs and leagues to show support for a national pure foods act by contacting their legislators. Magazines also offered free "kits" to women to help them mobilize public opinion. In 1906, the federal Pure Food and Drug Act was enacted.

Yet turn-of-the-century readers did not always endorse women's magazines in their muckraking approach. *Ladies' Home Journal* lost 75,000 subscribers in 1906 after printing an editorial about the dangers of venereal disease, a topic that was seldom discussed.[9]

Scholars have credited muckrakers as a whole with the passage of child labor laws, workmen's compensation, the pure food and drug act, and the development of congressional investigations. Tarbell, though, thought the muckraker title unfair. She argued with Roosevelt that *McClure's* writers "were concerned only with the facts, not with stirring up revolt."[10] Muckraking magazines, Tarbell wrote in her autobiography, "sought to present things as they were, not as somebody thought they ought to be. We were journalists, not propagandists; and as journalists we sought new angles on old subjects."[11]

Advocacy

The ability to expose dangerous or unhealthy situations continues to be a powerful aspect of magazines' editorial mix. Many of today's writers and editors are likely to practice **advocacy journalism:** taking an editorial stand that enables readers to become more aware of social concerns, empowers them, and urges them to act.

Following America's involvement in the Vietnam War during the late 1960s and early 1970s, magazine editors began to react to major societal concerns—about the environment, the homeless, drugs, and gun control—by choosing to go beyond covering an issue to advocating specific support for a cause. This was a break with the traditional journalistic mandate that editors must offer objective analysis and verifiable opinions if they were to maintain editorial perspective, balanced coverage, and their readers' trust.

Although some popular historians identify advocacy journalism as a product of the post-Vietnam War period, the advocacy role has long been a key part of American magazines. *Editor & Publisher,* founded in 1884 as a national trade magazine, offers an early illustration. The period from 1870 through the 1920s was one of unprecedented growth for newspapers as well as magazines. It was also a time when journalists

OUTSIDE IN THREE DIFFERENT MEDIA

A blizzard on Mount Everest that killed eight climbers in 1996 became an award-winning story for *Outside*. The story then avalanched into a television movie as well as a *New York Times* best-seller. *Outside* won a 1997 National Magazine Award for "Into Thin Air," a September 1996 article about a tragic climb up Mount Everest. Judges for the National Magazine Award reporting category praised the article, with one saying it had "riveted me to my chair," while another dubbed it "the best first-person reporting I've ever seen."

Writer Jon Krakauer was hired by *Outside* to make the trek up the highest mountain in the world as part of a guided group. Eight people died on the mountain, and Krakauer turned the hike into a compellingly personal 17,000-word magazine story.

In November 1997, ABC made the article into a television movie of the same name, with Krakauer as the main character. Krakauer also expanded his article into a book, also called *Into Thin Air,* which became a *New York Times* hardback bestseller. The book also topped the charts as a nonfiction paperback.

Ostensibly aimed at hard-core sports enthusiasts, *Outside* reaches a much broader audience than such competitors as *Outdoor Life* or *Field & Stream* in the outdoors category. Indeed, *Men's Journal, Life, Vanity Fair, Newsweek,* and *Vogue* all featured the Everest tragedy, with *Outside*'s article praised as the definitive account.

Krakauer's article is typical of *Outside*'s commitment to meaningful pieces about the outdoors, as opposed to adventurous, over-the-top, man-conquers-nature themes. The editors sent Krakauer to Nepal in search of a story about "the widening death trap created by guides whose financial incentives were in bringing increasing numbers of amateurs to the top and climbers from nations untrained in the rigors of high-ice climbing." The result was more than cautionary; it was a tale of death that would be told in more than one medium.

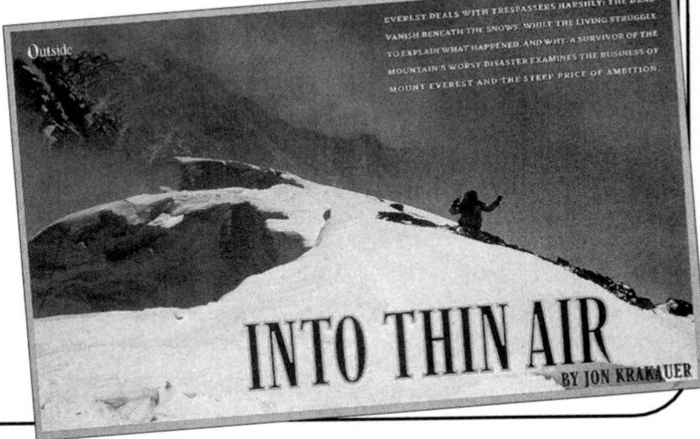

Outside

EVEREST DEALS WITH TRESPASSERS HARSHLY: THE DEAD VANISH BENEATH THE SNOWS, WHILE THE LIVING STRUGGLE TO EXPLAIN WHAT HAPPENED, AND WHY. A SURVIVOR OF THE MOUNTAIN'S WORST DISASTER EXAMINES THE BUSINESS OF MOUNT EVEREST AND THE STEEP PRICE OF AMBITION.

INTO THIN AIR

BY JON KRAKAUER

SEPTEMBER 1996: Jon Krakauer's 17,000-word article for *Outside* about a tragic climb up Mount Everest won a 1997 National Magazine Award for reporting.

began viewing their job as a profession with ethical standards and educational requirements rather than as a trade.

Editor & Publisher's pages were filled with articles and editorials encouraging professionalism and calling on the press to become accountable for its actions. Professor Mary M. Cronin of Washington State University has studied the trade press's role in promoting early professional values and ethics among journalists. She points out that *Editor & Publisher* regularly used the term "profession" in articles and frequently praised politically independent newspapers during its first 15 years of publication.[12] According to Cronin, the first major crusade by *Editor & Publisher* occurred in 1902 and was aimed at stamping out fake news stories. Journalists supported that crusade, as well as others led by *Editor & Publisher,* including campaigns for higher salaries needed to attract loyal, reliable, and intelligent workers. Today's *Editor & Publisher* continues to advocate such professional standards as honesty, accuracy, political independence, and morality while urging readers to honor their watchdog function.

Magazines occasionally go beyond their pages to promote specific causes of importance to their field or their audience. Editors and staff members of these magazines may choose to take a leadership role in societal concerns. In 1988, for example, *Metropolitan Home* pushed beyond editorial objectivity and lent its name to a project to raise both money for and awareness of AIDS. After much discussion about the ethics of advocacy, the editors agreed that the design community had been greatly affected by AIDS and to ignore it was unconscionable.

The project originally involved charging the public $10 each to view showcase rooms designed by some of the world's best interior decorators and artists in a five-story house on Manhattan's Upper East Side. The money raised would go to the Design Industries Foundation for AIDS (DIFFA). But the editor at the time, Dorothy Kalins, soon realized that "we could never raise enough just by putting people through the house, so we decided to hold a gala charity ball for 1,000 people to celebrate the opening."[13] Editors found themselves planning an auction, gathering items, publishing catalogues, seeking corporate sponsors, and asking for donations in addition to producing three of the largest issues in *Metropolitan Home*'s history.

What was the result of all their hard work as advocates for AIDS awareness? Including *Metropolitan Home*'s donation of 5 percent of its ad revenues from a special show house issue, more than $1 million was raised. DIFFA netted $800,000 from the project.

"I believe magazines are very potent communications tools and they should take a leadership role," Kalins said, adding that the issue being tackled should relate to legitimate concerns of the readers and be within the editorial scope of the magazine.[14] "In our case, readers could get interested in the issue because it showed rooms by David Hockney and Michael Graves and people they never would have seen. We were serving the basic reasons that readers came to *Met Home,* which is that we were showing them great designs."[15]

Kalins summarized the advocacy experience: "Beating people over the head with an issue would be very inappropriate. When magazines work best, there is a sacred bond between the reader and the thing that is held in the hand. You have to treat that relationship with great care. Otherwise you're just using the magazine as a platform, and I feel this is a terrible misuse."

But the advocacy role is troubling to many editors. At what point does a magazine become a social force simply by presenting ideas? *Texas Monthly* editor Gregory Curtis argues, "There is a boundary between good coverage and advocacy. When you cross that line, people will begin to think that you have an ax to grind."[16] For Curtis, magazines should not step beyond covering issues of concern to readers, nor should magazines lead the charge.

Robert Kincaid, heart-throb hero of *The Bridges of Madison County,* was described in the novel as a *National Geographic* photographer. Readers, however, didn't quite understand that the book was fiction. Hundreds of fans wrote to the magazine asking which issues contained Kincaid's work. The magazine responded in detail in an article, "Reel to Real," in August 1995: *National Geographic* photographers spend decades preparing an acceptable portfolio before they get an assignment and spend months shooting one story. Calendar photographers like Kincaid, they noted, need not apply.

POLITICAL INFLUENCES ON MAGAZINES

The political realm, in war and in peace, has driven editorial coverage since the earliest magazines began publication. At important periods in American history, wartime issues drove editorial coverage; at other times, peacetime political shenanigans kept magazines buzzing. America's political climate changed as the country moved from conservative to liberal and then back to conservative again and as political activism forced a focus on minority rights and redefined the roles of women and men.

Among the major political movements to push their way onto magazines' pages were colonial concerns of independence; slavery and abolition surrounding the Civil War; the 1950s Cold War anti-Communism hysteria; the Civil Rights movement; the counterculture of the Vietnam era that challenged government authority; the constitutional crisis of Watergate; and the feminist activism that changed the way women saw their lives and their magazines.

Not all magazines embraced all these issues; some embraced none of them. Some of these movements spawned their own magazines, often alternative in structure and content. In other cases, mainstream magazines took a position that might have seemed to run counter to their traditional editorial stance.

Independence

During the colonial period, the vital political questions of the day—King George's War, the

French and Indian War, treaties with Indian tribes, territorial expansion, shipping routes, taxation, and the relationship with England—filled page upon page of magazines published in Philadelphia, Boston, and New York. Of particular concern to many colonists was their role within the British Empire, especially when they had to follow laws made thousands of miles away. Although most early editors tried to steer clear of independence issues and party connections, by 1770 political essays and articles were clearly either Whig (reflecting American grievances and questioning the crown's domination of colonial affairs) or Tory (pro-England). By 1772, growing discontent among American colonists led by John Adams, Thomas Paine, and Isaiah Thomas precluded any but anti-British political views in the few magazines being published. Indeed, between 1772 and 1783, only three magazines were published in America: *The Royal American Magazine,* with engravings by Paul Revere, January 1774–March 1775; *Pennsylvania Magazine,* January 1775–July 1776, with the last issue including the text of the Declaration of Independence; and *United States Magazine,* the first to refer to the colonies as united states, January 1779–December 1779.[17] For all practical purposes, magazine printing halted as colonists fought for their independence from England.

The new republic ushered in more mature, varied, and insightful magazines as Americans turned their thoughts from war to peace after 1800. This led to what many historians have dubbed a Golden Age of Magazines, from 1825 to 1850, when as many as 5,000 magazines were launched.

Abolition

The next major political event to affect magazines occurred during the Civil War period. Anti-slavery magazines such as *The Liberator* spoke out as early as 1831. Once war appeared imminent, magazines responded to prevailing political attitudes as Yankees and Confederates clashed on American soil. Magazines published in the South, such as the *Southern Literary Messenger,* lined up squarely for secession and lost their Northern subscribers. Yet magazines published in the North did not fare much better, as they lost Southern subscribers and faced soaring printing costs.

The outstanding magazine for eyewitness accounts of the Civil War was *Harper's Weekly,* which hired a team of correspondents, artists, and photographers to cover the conflict. Their reports immediately placed the images of war into the hands of a reading public far away from the front lines. However, *Harper's Weekly* soon found itself in a political quandary as a result of its photography. Federal Secretary of War Edwin Stanton thought the horrific images gave aid and comfort to the enemy and ordered the publication to cease. But editor Fletcher Harper convinced Stanton that *Harper's Weekly* was actually a powerful political tool for the Union, showing the military strength and economic resolve of the North. The ban was lifted. *Harper's Weekly*'s Civil War coverage is so important that an interactive electronic database, "HarpWeek: The Civil War Era 1857–1865," was created in 1997 specifically to study the magazine's stories of that era. The CD-ROM is available only to libraries for $16,900. Three additional databases, covering *Harper's Weekly* from 1866 to 1900, are planned.

The Cold War

The Cold War, a metaphor that reflected a battle between democracy and communism, also affected magazine coverage, particularly in terms of how the specialized business press covered military and aviation developments. In its December 22, 1947, issue, *Aviation Week* (the title was expanded to include space technology in 1958) scooped the national and world media with the revelation that the U.S. Air Force had broken the sound barrier in a rocket-powered experimental plane. The magazine was accused of revealing top secret information to the Soviet military and was the focus of an investigation by the FBI and the Justice Department. Subscription records revealed Russian names, undoubtedly Soviet intelligence officers who assiduously read the magazine for its detailed data.

Although *Aviation Week* was not prosecuted because no federal laws had been violated, the Truman Administration tightened secrecy codes and information access. Yet the magazine continued to irritate the U.S. government with articles pointing out that the Soviet-built MiG-15 could outmaneuver America's first jet fighter.

The Cold War found Americans worrying about the threat of Communism in their own backyards. Red Scare paranoia culminated in the House Un-American Activities Committee investigations led by Senator Joseph R. McCarthy

Reactions to Race and Rights

In 1966, *Look* won the first annual National Magazine Award for "skillful editing, imagination and integrity, all of which were reflected particularly in its treatment of the racial issue during 1965."[1]

The magazine's audience, however, was not always receptive. Letters to the editor after the April 30, 1957, publication of a story about the Ku Klux Klan revealed a mixture of revulsion for the Klan and anger at *Look* for "brainwashing." One reader asked if *Look*'s editors wanted to have mulatto descendants, another said the magazine was biased and vindictive, and still another wrote, "All people are not equal and white people have a right to pick their friends." Nevertheless, many readers wrote to praise the piece, calling the Klansmen hypocrites and expressing shock at the Klan's activities, especially at the number of ministers who were active members.[2]

Publisher and *Look* founder Gardner Cowles wrote in his autobiography that publication of articles about civil rights issues brought hundreds of "the most violent letters calling us 'nigger lovers' and everything else you can think of." Cowles also maintained that certain advertisers "steadfastly refused to use *Look* solely on the basis of its human rights coverage."[3]

Although the picture magazines were offering portraits of the country during change, their approach sometimes missed the mark. Historian Loudon Wainwright noted that *Life*'s October 1938 essay on the country's "minority problem," while unusual and impressive for the time, was replete with stereotypes and occasionally racist cutlines. One photo of men picking cotton was captioned, "Tote dat barge. Lift dat bale." Nevertheless, it was well received because it was one of the first times such topics were discussed in the mainstream press. Jazz great Duke Ellington wrote, "I believe this is one of the fairest and most comprehensive articles ever to appear in a national publication."[4]

[1] "Coverage of Racial Troubles Earned New National Journalistic Honors," *The Look Years* (Cowles Communications, 1972): 78.
[2] "Letters to the Editor," *Look* (June 11, 1957): 26.
[3] Gardner Cowles, *Mike Looks Back* (New York: Gardner Cowles, 1985): 204.
[4] Loudon Wainwrght, *The Great American Magazine: An Inside History of* Life (New York: Alfred A. Knopf, 1986): 100.

JANUARY 14, 1964: One of the most enduring magazine images from the Civil Rights movement is this Norman Rockwell illustration for a *Look* article about desegregation in Little Rock, Arkansas.

of Wisconsin during the 1950s. McCarthy's Communist witch-hunt dragged many authors, actors, and directors into the congressional limelight. In 1956, playwright Arthur Miller was among those cited for contempt of Congress for refusing to name past associates who might have been members of the Communist Party.

Author John Steinbeck eloquently questioned the morality of the investigations in a June 1957 *Esquire* essay: "If I were in Arthur Miller's shoes, I do not know what I would do, but I could wish, for myself and for my children, that I would be brave enough to fortify and defend my private morality as he has." However, it would not be until after the death of McCarthy in 1957 that assessments of "the most dangerous man in America" began appearing. Richard H. Rovere's "The Frivolous Demagogue," in the August 1958 issue of *Esquire*, was one of the most thoughtful, revealing, and longest, at six pages of dense copy with no photos.

Civil Rights

Mainstream magazines such as *Look* and *Life* took on the fight against racism, offering pictorial representation of the real world of segregation, the day-to-day lives of American blacks, and the Civil Rights movement in its infancy.

In 1938, the country was still reeling from the effects of the Great Depression, and astute observers were looking with worried eyes at growing unrest in Europe. *Life*, meanwhile, was looking at the heart of the country with a 14-page photo essay titled "Negroes: The U.S. Also Has a Minority Problem." Featuring the work of premier photographer Alfred Eisenstaedt, the feature included photos of 20 distinguished black Americans and offered comments on their contributions to American culture. It also acknowledged the social structure that kept these achievements from the public eye.[18]

> ***F**olio:* magazine gave its 1995 "Bad Timing Award" to *Elle* for its "Bring Me the Head of Jerry Garcia" headline in its 10th anniversary September issue. Garcia, of the Grateful Dead, had died in August.

In 1956, *Life* covered a bus boycott in Montgomery, Alabama. Under a photo of the man who had yet to reach national prominence ran the line, "Boycott Director, Rev. Martin King, head of association which guides it, is mugged after arrest."[19]

Look, likewise, covered the Civil Rights movement in the 1950s. The April 30, 1957, issue included an eight-page article on "Eight Klans Bring New Terror to the South," written by Fletcher Knebel and Pulitzer Prize-winner Clark Mollenhoff. Chronicling a resurgence of Ku Klux Klan activity—100,000 new members had joined since the Supreme Court outlawed school segregation in 1954—the article described clandestine Klan meetings and local sheriffs who looked the other way. Cross burnings, Klansmen dressed in hoods, and the angry face of the Reverend Alvin Horn, Alabama grand dragon of the Klan, were depicted. A month earlier, in the March 19 issue, *Look* had taken a more positive approach. "Los Angeles: A Race Relations Success Story" profiled Willard Johnson, a young black man who was elected president of the UCLA student body. When school desegregation was enforced in Little Rock, Arkansas, Knebel was again on the scene with "The Real Little Rock Story" in the November 12, 1957, issue. Probably the magazine's most famous Civil Rights statement was also about Little Rock desegregation: a poignant illustration by Norman Rockwell, showing a young black girl, dressed primly in white, carrying her school supplies, walking solemnly but proudly into school, flanked by U.S. Marshals.[20]

Perhaps it was time for blacks to present their own picture of the world. In 1942, while black people were still prohibited from trying on hats in Atlanta department stores or staying in hotels in downtown Chicago, the time came for a magazine devoted to black readers. Using his mother's furniture as collateral for a $500 loan, John H. Johnson founded *Negro Digest*. Soon it had a circulation of 50,000 readers a month, although at first distributors told him they didn't "handle colored books because colored books didn't sell," as Johnson wrote in his 1989 autobiography.[21]

Johnson showed his political savvy in 1943 when he convinced Eleanor Roosevelt to contribute to an ongoing series, "If I Were a Negro." White authors, including Orson Welles, Pearl Buck, and Marshall Field, had already answered difficult questions such as whether they would want their children to wait another generation for quality education. But Johnson craved a bigger editorial attraction—an exclusive from the wife of the president of the United States. Mrs. Roosevelt wrote in the October 1943 cover story that if she were a Negro, she would "have great patience and great bitterness." Circulation leaped to more than 100,000 with that single issue.

Johnson's *Ebony*, a picture magazine established in 1945 with the stated goal "to emphasize the positive aspects of black life," placed the day's political realities in tandem with what readers wanted.[22] Said Johnson, "Black people wanted to see themselves in photographs. We were dressing up for society balls, and we wanted to see that. We were going places we had never been before and doing things we'd never done before, and we wanted to see that. . . . We intended to highlight black breakthroughs and pockets of progress. But we didn't intend to ignore difficulties and harsh realities." An examination of *Ebony*'s 50-plus years of publication reveals that Johnson consistently has chosen to take the political high road by emphasizing the brighter side of black life rather than by publishing articles critical of black problems.

Vietnam Era

A new kind of political consciousness and literary dissent developed during the 1960s and 1970s that resulted in a degree of criticism not often seen in the mainstream American press. The harsh realities of the Vietnam War caused numerous underground and alternative magazines to spring up in response to governmental and military actions at home and abroad.

From roughly 1964 to 1973, the underground press reacted to changes occurring in society that were, for the most part, politically driven. The period from 1967 to 1969 was particularly dramatic:

> *Demonstrations grew from 100,000 one year to 1 million two years later. Students went from peaceful petitioning to seizing university buildings all in the same period. Black nationalists overtook the civil rights movement, and strident radical declarations were met with systematic police violence. In Vietnam, the United States went from rosy predictions of "the light at the end of the tunnel" to the devastating Tet offensive that forced Lyndon Johnson from office.*[23]

Such magazines as *Ramparts, Counter-Spy,* and *High Times* served the counterculture generation through an editorial milieu that challenged authority, particularly the CIA, and supported readers who inhaled, swallowed, or snorted drugs other than alcohol.

Of course, established alternative magazines such as *The Progressive* and *Mother Jones* and liberal publications such as *The Nation* and *The New Republic* also criticized the war and the government, but in less strident terms. Even religious magazines responded to the growing ideological split in society over the Vietnam War. Researcher David E. Settje recently compared how two prominent Protestant periodicals, *Christianity Today* and *The Christian Century,* reacted to the Vietnam War.[24] According to Settje, the conservative, evangelical *Christianity Today* presented pro-war opinions in support of the various presidential administrations, while the liberal *The Christian Century* argued for an end to American involvement and supported most types of war resistance. Yet both magazines cautioned about total trust of Communists and vilified the Soviet Union. The two magazines reflected American worries about the Cold War while debating U.S. involvement in Southeast Asia.

Similarly, *Aviation Week & Space Technology* was skeptical of American involvement in the Vietnam War, objecting to President Lyndon Johnson's air war. The magazine urged an all-out, uninterrupted air campaign rather than Johnson's stop-and-start approach after breaking the news that the Soviet Union was shipping surface-to-surface missiles to North Vietnam. Yet for the most part, the magazine supported the war effort and the military personnel in combat.

Women's magazines took a different approach to the Vietnam War. *Ladies' Home Journal* recognized its "unique position as representative of millions of American women" by offering its readers a forum for expressing concern about the 1,500 American military personnel who were prisoners of war and missing in action. In the December 1970 issue, *Ladies' Home Journal* published a petition in cooperation with the National League of Families of American Prisoners and Missing in Southeast Asia, and asked for reader signatures. More than 60,000 readers signed the petition and sent it to the magazine. Among the signers were Joyce Carol Oates, Katherine Anne Porter, Senator Margaret Chase Smith, and Martha Mitchell. The response "was among the greatest in our publishing history," wrote the editors in an April 1971 open letter. Addressed to North and South Vietnamese officials, the letter proposed a meeting in Paris between "a small group of *Journal* editors and reader representatives" with representatives of the North Vietnamese and Provisional Revolutionary Governments.[25]

The petitions were delivered to the Paris peace talks by *Ladies' Home Journal* editor John Mack Carter and co-managing editor Lenore Hershey. "Did we make a step toward peace? Time will tell," wrote the editors in the July 1971 issue, adding:

> *We had a commitment. We honored it. We do not know if we changed anybody's mind. But we do know that as the only magazine to speak in a nonpolitical, humanitarian way in behalf of our readers, we were continuing a long history of public service. If we have not brought peace closer, and brought home our men from Southeast Asia, let the record show that at least we tried.*[26]

Watergate

The period following the June 1972 discovery that burglars hired by the Republican Committee for the Re-Election of the President had been caught breaking into the Democratic National Committee offices at the Watergate apartment-hotel complex came to be known as Watergate. During 1973 and 1974, *Time* magazine put Richard M. Nixon on the cover 14 times during the unraveling of the Watergate plot. More than 20 other *Time* covers were devoted to the Watergate personalities, hearings, trials, and aftermath. Indeed, the first editorial published by *Time,* in November 1973, called for Nixon to resign for the good of the country.[27]

The two other weekly news magazines, *Newsweek* and *U.S. News & World Report,* also hammered home that this was one of the gravest constitutional crises in the nation's history. Opinion publications such as *The Atlantic Monthly* and *Harper's* and political journals such as *The Nation* and *National Review* also commented extensively on the scandal.

Even magazines written for women responded to the heightened interest in Watergate by interviewing the spouses of indicted White House aides, such as Maureen "Mo" Dean. Never before had so many magazines devoted so much space for so long to a single topic.

Feminism

During the same period, feminist magazines also developed in response to changes in society. Many feminist magazines had their roots in the women's political movement of the 1970s and stretched from scholarly to popular in tone, content, and audience. Only a few had a significant national distribution, but their grassroots impact was impressive at a time when women were beginning to seek and achieve equality in the workplace.

Feminist magazines eschewed advertising that depicted women as sex objects and turned away from the argument that women have only one goal: to find a man. Titles of note included *Aphra, Chrysalis, Lesbian Tide, Lilith,* and, of course, the most successful feminist magazine of all time, *Ms.*

Feminist magazines were not always as radical or as bitter as the underground periodicals, but they still had an uncompromising approach to an enormous range of issues of importance to women. To reread these publications is like taking an immersion course in feminist activism. The breadth and depth of coverage is striking, including information about women's studies courses, health issues, economic solutions, legal strategies, and programs to assist women outside the mainstream of society, as well as fiction and poetry. Although underpaid secretaries, overworked waitresses, women in poverty, women in prison, Native American women, black women, and Third World women tended to receive more attention than white female executives, all were embraced by this niche.

MAGAZINES AS CULTURAL INFLUENCES

Magazines help us choose our kitchen colors and Christmas trees, raise our children and our standards, save our marriages and our money. Open the pages of a magazine and it can open the world to us and help us build our foundation, our beliefs. From the homespun humor of "Life in These United States" in *Reader's Digest* to the ribald raciness of *Playboy*'s "Advisor," magazines reflect and transmit our cultural standards.

When social conditions reach a certain fever, or mass, you can be certain that a magazine will come along to either tell you about it or persuade you to follow its moral or ideological stance. Magazines are cultural artifacts and, as such, are as complex as our society. They are natural community builders, they create the symbolic meaning that we use to interpret our world, and they present pseudoworlds and pseudoevents we often mistake for reality.

Community Builders

Throughout history, magazines have connected people with common interests and concerns, and they have forged a solid bond through shared knowledge. As magazines target increasingly narrow audience segments, they can address increasingly special needs and interests.

Time's inventive use of language has resulted in new words being added to the American vernacular. *Socialite, guesstimate, televangelist, male chauvinist,* and *op art* are all words coined by *Time.* Words used by *Time* that didn't make it include *cinemoppet, cinemactor, Broadwayfarer, nudancer, sexational, politricks,* and *newshawk.*

The communities magazines help build run the cultural gamut, but their vitality is well demonstrated by titles that give voice to groups previously unheard, such as gays, lesbians, and the disabled. Community building, however, is not limited to narrow social groups. Businesses, trades, and organizations use magazines to rally colleagues and members around causes and issues.

Perhaps most importantly, magazines help readers relate to one another, building reader-to-reader relationships. The ways in which magazines help readers build communities are as common as letters to the editors, as unusual as the creation of actual face-to-face groups, and as high-tech as the development of on-line relationships.

GIVING VOICE TO GROUPS. *The Advocate* and *Gay Times* speak the language of and focus on the issues faced by their gay and lesbian readers, in addition to dealing with real-world issues everybody faces. Magazines reaching this group have been around for decades—*The Advocate* was started in 1967—but the number of titles mushroomed in the 1990s and, like magazines for all other groups, became more specialized. Advertisers' acceptance of these magazines may herald a larger social acceptance. It may, also, simply be good economic sense: The gay and lesbian audience has the income and purchasing patterns that appeal to Madison Avenue. Gay and lesbian titles had a 36 percent increase in ad growth between 1996 and 1997. That made it the fastest growing print market for the third year in a row, according to the Gay Annual Report by Manhattan advertising agency Mulryan/Nash.[28]

JUNE 11, 1996: ***The Advocate,*** **which focuses on issues facing gay and lesbian readers, came out of the closet in 1967.**

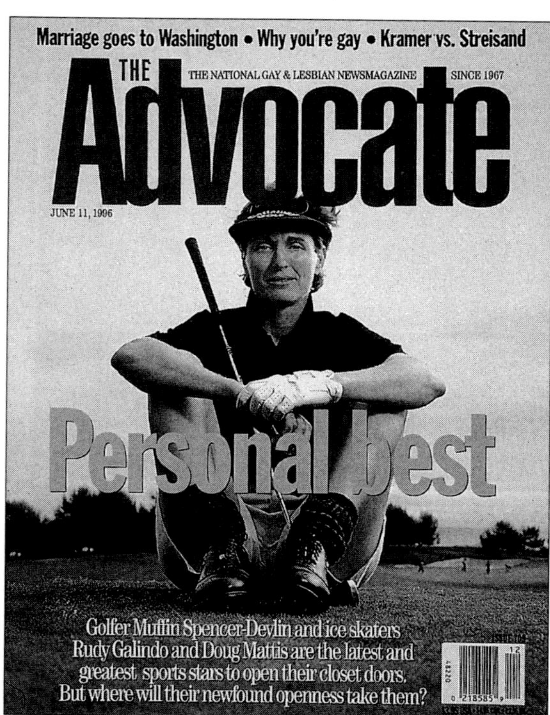

Some analysts say the gay and lesbian market is 20 million strong, others say it is less than half that size. Whatever the size, it is increasingly visible and is now served by a spectrum of magazines. *Out*, a gay lifestyle magazine, was launched in 1993, and within two years reached a circulation of 120,000 and advertising revenues of $3.5 million.[29] It taps an audience with high appeal to advertisers: The average reader is 35, with a household income of $65,000. Other gay and lesbian titles are more specialized, such as *Genre* and *Men's Style,* which focus on male readers, and *Curve* and *Girlfriends,* which target women. Even more specialized titles, *Next News* and *Victory,* reach the gay business community. *Plus Voice* narrows the focus even more, providing articles on people, politics, health, and lifestyle issues for those living with the HIV virus.

Likewise, the disabled are increasingly recognized as a viable audience. Brigham Young University professor Jack A. Nelson has identified the period following World War II when a large number of war wounded returned home to try to live normal lives as a turning point.[30] The oldest and largest magazine, *Paraplegia News,* was founded in 1945 to meet the informational needs of veterans with spinal injuries. Today the magazine serves anyone with a mobility impairment. Another magazine in the field is *Accent on Living,* established in 1956 as a source for products that offer disabled people more independence in their day-to-day lives.

According to Nelson, publications targeting the disabled build a sense of identity and community, provide information, and advance an activist agenda. The 1998 SRDS *Consumer Magazine Advertising Source* lists only eight magazines in its disabilities classification, although Nelson points to a directory published in late 1995 that identified 70 disability magazines.

Certainly, the passage of the Americans with Disabilities Act (ADA) in 1990 contributed to many start-ups, including *Ability* (1992) and *Disability International* (1995). *Disability International* is the first commercial magazine dealing strictly with disability issues to be distributed worldwide. The first issue, in May 1995, reached 10,000 readers in 120 countries.[31] The magazine was launched with the help of Disabled Peoples' International, a nonprofit worldwide group that enjoys United Nations status and supports the advancement of disability rights.

BUSINESSES, TRADES, AND ORGANIZATIONS. Specialized business magazines, because they are aimed at readers as members of a clearly defined trade or occupation, exist, in many cases, specifically to build relationships. In February 1988, *Hardware Age* provided a valuable service to its readers, largely independent hardware retailers, who were facing a common enemy: Wal-Mart. The large chain was offering prices so low that Main Street retailers couldn't match them; the result was the failure of many local businesses. *Hardware Age* issued a call to competitive action, suggesting that independent stores owners regularly advertise and promote the fact that they provide better and more varied service from knowledgeable clerks. The magazine also suggested local retailers change their hours to be open the same hours as Wal-Mart. Editor-in-chief Jim Cory, who wrote the story, says the result was wiser and more competitive local stores owners who were equipped to compete. The magazine won a 1989 Neal Award from the American Business Press for the article.

Six years later, *Hardware Age* went to Spokane, Washington—considered an economic microcosm of the country as a whole—to study the potential battle between the independents and the fast-growing Home Depot chain. Editors commissioned a study of hardware consumers to determine their shopping preferences. Because Home Depot had not yet entered the Spokane market, local retailers were the shoppers' favorites, although many consumers were aware of Home Depot from other cities. The magazine studied why consumers were loyal to the independents—in most cases, because of service—and again suggested the local stores promote that difference. The 1995 Neal Award winning series, written by Jim Cory and Liz Smutko, was the first step the magazine—now called *Home Improvement Market*—took in a continuing plan to study Home Depot's influence.[32]

Organization magazines exist largely to build communities. The National Audubon Society hopes its magazine, *Audubon,* will help differentiate itself from the Sierra Club and the National Wildlife Federation. These two other groups have the same hopes for *Sierra* and *Wildlife* magazines. Public relations magazines are information sources as well as advocacy vehicles for readers both within the organization and outside of it. Their audiences include employees, customers, clients, and others within the field and in related agencies. *Adobe* magazine talks to users of that company's software, helps them with problems, shows that the company cares, piques their interest in new programs, and helps them connect with one another on-line.

READER-TO-READER RELATIONSHIPS. Some magazines take community building a step further by establishing reading groups, study circles, and, most recently, salons, to bring like-minded people together. As early as the 1960s, study circles were formed by readers of *Commentary,* a Jewish opinion magazine. In the 1980s, *Tikkun,* a magazine of liberal Jewish thought, sponsored more than 40 reader discussion groups throughout the United States.[33] Concurrently, *Utne Reader,* featuring articles from the alternative press, formed groups it called salons. *Utne Reader* advertised the salons in its pages and in mailings to readers, who were asked to write to the magazine expressing interest. More than 8,000 readers responded. Groups were formed by location, and then the magazine bowed out, leaving the readers to bond on their own. By 1994, more than 500 salons had grown throughout the country. In an era of disappearing communities, national magazines give neighbors a chance to meet one another, creating a printed and bound replacement for the front porch.

In the letters to the editor sections of many magazines, readers sometimes share more with one another than they do with their families. In its early years, *Ms.* showed readers that women throughout the country were experiencing similar frustrations. The letters were such important documents that editor Mary Thom collected them in a book, *Letters to* Ms. Readers of *The Mother Earth News,* likewise, connected through the letters columns. Letters were answered in the magazine by "Mother" and readers were referred to as Mother's "children." One reader, writing in the May 1970 third issue, suggested a readers' convention. Several others asked for information on communes. Another, writing in the fourth issue, July 1970, said "Hey, we're a movement? I thought I was the only one."

Other relationships bloom on-line, where *Better Homes and Gardens* readers share recipes, *Wired* readers share philosophies, and *Utne Reader* continues its salons electronically. The community bond can be created through humor as well. In 1995, two users of the *Better Homes and Gardens* Web site were sharing recipes for muffins. One reader got waylaid because of her pets and sent this message, which made the magazine's food staff chuckle:

> *Sorry I took so long to reply back but my dog had pups so I've been very busy. They turned out really good. The only thing I'm going to change is instead of putting them in the muffin pans I'm going to put them in a pie plate or cookie sheet so the outside will be softer. Mine came out kind of hard on the outside but they were much softer on the inside.*

For an alternative approach to community building, see Jay Walljasper's discussion in the "Magazine Voices" section at the back of this book.

Symbolic Meaning

Magazines give symbolic meaning to our world through the images they present in pictures and words. *Gourmet* pictures the perfect apple pie, *Sports Illustrated* the ideal athlete, *Architectural Digest* the exquisitely decorated vacation cottage. Who would want to make the pie if *Gourmet* showed a burned crust and drooping center? How could we aspire to sports success if we had before us an image of a couch potato? Who would want to mimic the look of a cottage decorated with pictures of dogs playing poker?

The study of these symbolic messages, or semiotics, is as old as western civilization, with origins in Plato and St. Augustine and more recent popularization by Sigmund Freud and Claude Levi-Strauss. The premise of semiotic theory is that all communication is symbolic and these symbols are brimming with cultural meaning. Semioticians believe any culture can be defined and understood by studying its symbols.[34] A study of magazines is a study of our culture. Look at an *Esquire* from 1950 and you will not only read the news of that year, but you will also wade into the social mores, trends, and styles of the time.

In magazines, symbolic messages are created in words as well as in pictures. The cover lines tempt us: "Lose 10 Pounds by Christmas," "Great Pecs in a Month," "What Your Lover *Really* Wants." The assumption is that we are flawed—overweight, dumpy, and sexually deficient—and that by reading the articles we can improve ourselves. Photographs illustrate the perfection we try to achieve.

Psychologists say we would be healthier mentally if the images in magazines were more attainable—if the bodies pictured were rounder, the homes were less perfect, the sexual standards saner and safer. Many magazine editors agree and have sought to present realism rather than fantasy in their pages. In the mid-1980s, *Better Homes and Gardens* began experimenting with photography of food that looked as if it had actually been tasted—for example, pies showing crumbs and missing pieces. Food editor Nancy Byal says this approach was successful and is now the magazine's photographic standard: "We want our images to be approachable, doable, realistic, but not picture perfect. We want people to get a sense that 'Yeah, I could sit down and eat this right now.' We're hoping to project a sense that something has happened to this food. A sense of humanity."

Editors realize, though, that readers often look for the fantasy that magazines present. By presenting the ideals to which we aspire—a great pie, a fantastic body—magazines provide us with a world that motivates us. We often buy magazines to enter that world and use those images to improve ourselves. This fantasy world is created not just by the editorial content of magazines but by the advertising as well.

Some magazines present contradictory written messages from page to page. For example, the November 1, 1996, issue of *Woman's Day* contained two weight-related cover lines: "10 Diet Rules to Break and Lose Weight" and "Dress Thinner." Pictured on the cover is an "Easy to

Mixed Messages on Women

Of special concern to magazine researchers are images of women in editorial content as well as advertising. Are these images negative or positive? Researchers' assessments are mixed, as are the images themselves.

As in all areas of magazines, editorial goals and audiences determine the type of images presented. In a study done in 1985, researchers divided women's magazines into two types: traditional—such as *McCall's* and *Family Circle*—and nontraditional—such as *Working Woman* and *New Woman*. The traditional magazines more frequently presented women in conventional occupations such as homemakers or nurses.[1]

Northwestern University professor Carolyn Kitch notes that in the "golden age of illustration," the first three decades of the twentieth century, women were either depicted as "girls"—most notably, the Gibson Girl drawn by Charles Dana Gibson for *Collier's* magazine—or as mothers.[2] The girls, she notes, were drawn by men—Gibson, Howard Chandler Christy, and John Held Jr. The mothers were drawn by women, the most prolific being Jessie Willcox Smith who drew nearly 200 covers for *Good Housekeeping* between 1917 and 1933. Moreover, Kitch says, the girls "bore little relationship at all to flesh-and-blood females." Some were bathing beauties; others, like Held's flapper, were caricatures—"skinny, flat-chested and hipless." The female illustrators, in contrast, drew realistic images of women as mature adults. Smith and other women illustrators, Kitch maintains, offered readers an "alternative view of womanhood" that was "consistently respectful."

Much current research on portrayal of women in magazines has dealt with the content of the advertising. Researchers at Texas Tech University studied magazine advertisements from late 1994 to early 1995 and found that women were most often portrayed as decorative objects or entertainers.[3] They duplicated research done in 1971 and found that images of women were even less representative of reality in 1995 than they were in 1971. The researchers studied *Cosmopolitan, Redbook, Glamour, Self, Shape, Gentleman's Quarterly, Esquire, Men's Journal, Men's Fitness, Business Week, Vanity Fair, Better Homes and Gardens, People,* and *Time*. These were chosen because of their wide appeal to both male and female audiences. The researchers found that women were still portrayed in stereotypical homemaker roles or as decoration, holding a bag of potato chips, for example, even though they had no direct connection to the product. Men continued to be pictured as professionals, managers, or administrators, while the women were shown predominantly as homemakers and parents.

But the story isn't that simple. In *The Beauty Myth,* author Naomi Wolf paints a seemingly contradictory picture of women's magazines as keepers of the flame of women's rights as well as dangerous stereotypers of women's lives. She pinpoints substantial differences between advertising and editorial content, and takes these magazines to task for creating an unrealistic image of women in photos, beauty articles, and advertising. However, she emphasizes that these messages are often offset by other editorial decisions. In fact, she praises the editorial content of women's magazines and considers these publications as a whole "the only products of popular culture that change with women's reality, are mostly written by women for women about women's issues, and take women's concerns seriously." She calls them "potent agents of social change" and says they "have popularized feminist ideas more widely than any other medium—certainly more widely than explicitly feminist journals."[4]

[1] J. A. Ruggerio, and L. C. Weston, "Work Options for Men and Women in Women's Magazines: The Medium and the Message," *Sex Roles* (12 , 1985): 535–47.

[2] Carolyn Kitch, "Maternal Images in the Age of the Girl: The Work of Jessie Willcox Smith and Other Women Artists in Early-Twentieth Century Magazine Illustration" (paper presented at the annual meeting of the Association for Education in Journalism and Mass Communication, Anaheim, CA, August 1996): 20.

[3] Diana Cornelius, Christine Thompson, Wayne Melanson, and Christen Zelaya, "The Portrayal of Women in Magazine Advertising: A Content Analytical and Comparative Study" (paper presented at the annual convention of the Association for Education in Journalism and Mass Communication, Anaheim, CA, August 1996).

[4] Naomi Wolf, *The Beauty Myth* (New York: William Morris and Company, 1991): 70–72.

AUGUST 1968: With this issue, *Glamour* became the first major women's magazine to place a black woman on the cover.

SEX AND THE SINGLE MAGAZINE

The sexual revolution of the 1960s would have been a mere skirmish without magazines. More explicit language appeared in magazines in response to a loosening of morality. Treatment of sexual topics, once ignored or draped with euphemisms, became the norm in magazines. Articles about orgasms and erections appeared alongside pumpkin pie recipes and shopping tips. By far, the magazine leaders of the revolution were *Playboy* and *Cosmopolitan.*

Begun in 1953 by a young *Esquire* staffer who asked for a raise and was rejected, *Playboy* was not only a magazine but also a social phenomenon. That young man, Hugh Hefner, became renowned for parties at his Playboy Mansion, and for his womanizing. He also made a fortune by expanding the magazine to national *Playboy* clubs, with entry by keys and service by women barely dressed as *Playboy* bunnies. The women who starred in his magazine were the young, buxom Playmates of the Month, a cottage industry of their own, with calendars and television specials. Along the way, Hefner mainstreamed barroom humor and made modeling nude into a socially accepted activity to which college women throughout the country aspired.

Playboy clashed with social and economic reality in the 1980s, however, when a conservative mood hit the country politically, and when other, brasher magazines such as *Penthouse* outdid it in the soft pornography category. A boom in men's health and lifestyle magazines made some of the articles in *Playboy* somewhat passé. Hefner's daughter Christie now runs the company, a phenomenon in itself: a woman who lives the feminist ideal of the successful professional edits a magazine that is the bane of feminists' existence. The magazine's strong circulation of 3.2 million makes it one of the top reads among men.

A close second in the category of sex and the single copy is *Cosmopolitan,* which did an about-face in 1965, from a staid general interest magazine to the guidebook for the *Cosmo* Girl. The force behind the

Make Sunflower Cake." The cake, a delicious combination of pound cake and cookies, packs a hefty 744 calories into each piece. Where does that fit into a healthy diet?

Do these images affect us? Consider this: This book is being written in a house that one of the authors first saw on the pages of *Better Homes and Gardens Home Plan Ideas.* She saved the magazine, looking at the house regularly and imagining it as her own. A year later, she called a builder and signed a contract to build the house. The house has been standing for five years now, and the author has written two articles about it so far for *Better Homes and Gardens* Special Interest Publications. Now other readers are looking at the images in those articles and calling the author to talk about the house they saw in words and pictures. They, too, are planning to build it.

Pseudoworlds

Closely related to these images is the concept of the pseudoworld. Journalist Walter Lippmann coined the term to refer to a world of the media's creation, which has little, if any, connection to reality.[35] In today's magazines, it is a world where Madonna changes personae five times a year, where the Kennedys reign from generation to generation, where men and women are healthy, well dressed and, usually, middle class and white. It is a world where all this matters. The world portrayed in many magazines, however, is not the world in which most people live.

The pseudoworld created by magazines is largely populated by celebrities. *George* magazine's covers initially featured celebrities dressed in garb related to George Washington's life. Contemporary celebrities posed as political legends, such as Barbra Streisand as Martha. The line between journalists and celebrities has become so blurred that journalists compete for celebrities to sit at their tables at galas sponsored by Washington, D.C., journalists. Kevin Costner, Anthony Hopkins, and Streisand have to sit somewhere, and it is a feather in the cap of whichever journalist perches next to them. *Vanity Fair, National Review, Newsweek, Time,* and *The New Republic* all play the game, but the game may not be fair to readers.

Charles Peters, editor-in-chief of *Washington Monthly,* says this practice of focusing on celebrities dilutes the real purpose of journalism:

metamorphosis, Helen Gurley Brown, modeled the magazine after her successful book, *Sex and the Single Girl.* Her advice to readers: "If you're not flirting daily, I want you to start."

Cosmo cover girls are notable for necklines that either plunge to the waist or tickle the chin in see-through filmy fabric. Another *Cosmo* standard is the sex quiz, with explicit questions, followed by advice on improving your sex life and your appeal to men. The *Cosmo* girl doesn't wait for a man to make the first move, no matter what that move might be. In the first decade of the magazine, readers hoped to make themselves into the women who would marry the chairman of the board. As the feminist movement gained momentum, *Cosmo* girls not only angled to marry the chairman—but to be one, too.

Cosmopolitan was a huge success under Brown. Promoting itself as "the largest selling young women's magazine in the world," it boasts a paid circulation of 2.6 million, with Spanish and Australian editions, plus a yearly spin-off, *Life After College.* After 32 years as editor-in-chief, however, Brown was officially replaced in March 1997 by Bonnie Fuller, who had been editor of *Marie Claire.* Brown remains at *Cosmopolitan* as editor-in-chief of international editions.

Surprisingly, though, one magazine that challenged many of our sexual assumptions did so with quiet deliberation rather than fanfare: *Glamour,* launched in 1939. Ruth Whitney, who enjoyed one of the longest tenures of American magazine executives, became editor of the magazine in 1967 and led it through more than three decades of social change. Whitney retired in August 1998. In a much-talked-about maneuver, Bonnie Fuller left *Cosmopolitan* after 18 months to replace Whitney at *Glamour.* The editorial shift put Kate White, formerly *Redbook*'s editor, as the latest editor-in-chief of *Cosmopolitan.*

Under Whitney, *Glamour* published more articles about abortion than any other women's magazine. In 1968, it was the first major women's magazine to place a black woman on the cover. *Glamour* ran a controversial yet moving article on two young lesbians going to the prom together in 1992. *Glamour* is the only women's magazine to twice win the National Magazine Award for general excellence. In the bargain, it reaches 2.3 million readers. Whitney's philosophy was presented at a lecture at Drake University in 1993: "I truly believe that if six months go by and you have offended neither your readers nor your advertisers, chances are you're not doing your job as an editor."

"The terrible thing is what the reporters do in order to get big shots for their table, particularly those with out-of-town bosses. The reporters get desperate to get stars to impress their bosses. Nobody who has any intelligence can doubt the reporter is compromised in that desperation. He makes an implied promise to be nice in print to the guy he gets to come."[36]

Perhaps the most dangerous aspect of the pseudoworld created by consumer-based media is that it is a world in which the proper use of the proper product buys prestige and social acceptance. *Mountain Bike* offers advice on which bike to buy, *Outside* shows us where we need to ride that bike, *Shape* tells us to avoid last year's biking shorts styles, and *Health* advises us to build our biking muscles with the right vitamins. The biking fashions and fitness regimens, however, change from month to month.

Perhaps this consumerism is most obvious in fashion. The October 1995 issue of *Harper's Bazaar* demonstrated a many-faceted media pseudoworld. An article on shoes starts with a quote, "The more shoes I get the more I want," from Amy Fine Collins, contributing editor of *Vanity Fair.*[37] Collins, then, is a celebrity of note, not only for her consumption of shoes, but because of her position in the magazine world. In the same issue, a reader talks of her own consumption patterns: "I sometimes think designers stay up nights thinking of new things for me to want. The 'Mod Times' Trunkshow of watches (August) was a prime example. More is never enough."[38]

Media critic Michael Parenti offers an explanation for the pseudoworld phenomenon. The American media, he says, tend to "favor personality over issue, event over content, official positions over popular grievances, the atypical over the systemic."[39]

Pseudoevents

A corollary to the pseudoworld is the pseudoevent, named by historian Daniel Boorstin[40] to refer to the super-hyped events the media create and then cover as though they had evolved on their own. A magazine cover can be viewed as an event: Put a model on that cover and she starts dating rock stars; put a rock star on the cover and his career takes off.

Magazines select our best and worst cities, celebrities, schools, investments, cars, stereos, and people, and these selections become fodder for other media stories. A city chosen as one of *Money* magazine's most livable becomes the headline of newspaper stories across the country, and the selection becomes the chamber of commerce's biggest asset. Likewise, colleges and universities recommended by *U.S. News & World Report* are then perceived as the top schools because the magazine made them so. It is even better if *Barron's* also names them a "Best Buy."

Celebrities, again, are the highlight of pseudoevents. Who reads *People*'s list of the most intriguing people other than celebrity-watchers? Writer Martha Sherrill got so frustrated with writing celebrity profiles that she decided to create her own celebrity and see what happened. She went beyond the pseudoevent and created a pseudoperson. The result was a mythical starlet, Allegra Coleman. Coleman was *Esquire*'s November 1996 cover model, seducing readers with the cover line: "Forget Gwyneth . . . Forget Mira . . . Here's Hollywood's Next Dream Girl. The Allegra Coleman Nobody Knows." Nobody knew Allegra because she didn't exist. The cover model was actually Ali Larter, an actress who, the magazine said, "is the perfect expression of the movie industry today and its cult of instant celebrity." The model's role in the pseudoworld became oddly real, though, when she began getting calls from modeling and theatrical agents. "I think she's going to get a little career," *Esquire*'s then editor-in-chief Edward Kosner said. "Isn't that the ultimate irony?"[41] Maybe. Or maybe the irony was the realistic self-involved tone of the article, which started like so many "I'm-amazing-because-I-was-right-there-with-her" profiles:

NOVEMBER 1996: This *Esquire* cover story on Allegra Coleman was supposedly about a hot new movie starlet; in reality, she didn't exist.

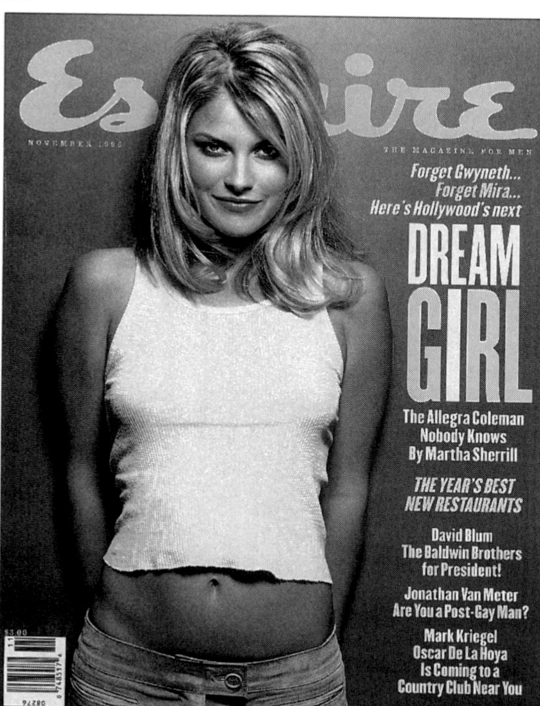

> *She is laughing, and in my head she is smiling, and she's thinking, holding a notion, the whole thought of her life and her stardom in her laugh. Allegra Coleman is sitting in her old white bathtub of a car, her old Porsche, older than she is, even older than I am. She is speeding. The road is winding . . . .*

Kosner called the piece "a brilliant parody of the brainless celebrity fluff that fills the media these days, and her article—a work of fiction from beginning to end—provides an occasion for all of us in the media to cast a fresh eye on celebrity mania."[42] How fresh that eye actually is might be open to discussion. In justifying Sherrill's piece, the magazine's public relations newsletter stated, "One of the roles of *Esquire* ever since the magazine's founding more than sixty years ago is to identify and examine what's happening in the culture."[43] That's all well and good, but should any cultural examination be based on fiction?

CULTURAL INFLUENCES ON MAGAZINES

The twentieth century has been a time of intense cultural change. After World War II, the population boomed, the economy blasted off, leisure activities mushroomed, and affluence spread more than ever before throughout society. As the century moved on, ethnic groups increasingly left their mark on the culture and demanded their voices be heard.

The 40-hour workweek, a product of labor unions' political activism during the 1920s and 1930s, became standard in the 1970s, leading to more leisure time, though not necessarily more time reading magazines. A 1938 Gallup Poll

MAGAZINES ON TELEVISION

As part of the convergence of the mass media that has dominated the 1990s, magazines began telling their stories and sharing their particular brand of service journalism with television viewers. In 1993, *Reader's Digest* produced adaptations of their popular magazine articles for a national television audience. The TV table of contents for "*Reader's Digest:* On Television" included a dramatized version of the rescue of a driver from his burning truck; a report on a campaign for mandatory life sentences for repeat sex offenders; an interview with a dog expert on how to keep from being bitten; and "All God's Angels," a mother's first-person account of how her daughter's death changed her life.

Like the print version, these *Reader's Digest* television re-enactments were patriotic and uplifting, looking on the bright side even in tragedy. The ABC broadcast, hosted by Hal Linden and Robin Young, had no violence, no sex, and no smutty language. Founders DeWitt and Lila Acheson Wallace would have approved of the message that hope springs eternal and can be condensed into an hour-long television special.

Magazines as varied in audience and tone as *People, Ebony, Town & Country,* and *Ladies' Home Journal* showcased themselves on television in recent years. Gossipy *People* revealed what went on "Behind the Scenes at *People* Magazine" on the Turner Broadcasting System (TBS), while *Ebony* marked its golden anniversary with "Celebrate the Dream: 50 Years of *Ebony* Magazine" on ABC. Through interviews with various editors and designers at the magazine's headquarters in New York City, *People* highlighted how cover decisions and story assignments are made. *Ebony* took the more formal route, taping a black-tie gathering at the Shrine Auditorium in Los Angeles in a two-hour special. Live performances by leading entertainment personalities were intercut with appearances by black community leaders. Film clips also accentuated contributions by blacks to film, television, music, sports, and social issues.

Town & Country also celebrated an anniversary and looked at different social issues on the Arts and Entertainment channel. Narrated by actress and socialite Dina Merrill, *Town & Country*'s two-hour special covered "The Rich in America: 150 Years of *Town & Country* Magazine." Using early film clips and photos, *Town & Country* unfolded the opulence and ostentation of upper-crust American society prior to the more approachable "rich and famous" lives uncovered by Robin Leach. *Town & Country*'s October 1996 sesquicentennial issue paralleled the television special with a whopping 356 pages about the wit, sophistication, and glamour associated with the privileged lives covered by the magazine.

Both *Ladies' Home Journal* and *Time* have depicted their most fascinating people picks on CBS. Since 1996 *Ladies' Home Journal* has showcased "The Most Fascinating Women" of the year as a one-hour TV special, along with accompanying magazine cover stories every January. *Time* produced a series of six special issues and six television shows with CBS News in 1998 and 1999 that highlighted the 100 most influential men and women of the last 100 years in the categories of "Leaders and Revolutionaries," "Artists and Entertainers," "Builders and Titans," "Scientists and Thinkers," and "Heroes and Inspiration."

This incursion into television simply reflects the magazine medium's ability to adapt successfully to changing roles in society. Regardless of what new forms or shapes are imposed on information and entertainment, magazines historically have had the strength and the ability to continue to reach new audiences.

found Americans' favorite way to spend an evening was reading, followed by going to the movies/theater, and dancing.[44] By 1974 the answers to the same question put watching television as first choice, followed by reading, and then dining out.[45] In 1986 respondents told Gallup their first choice was watching television, followed by a tie between resting and reading. Our world and our magazines have been influenced by the birth of and power wielded by the baby boomers and by racial and ethnic shifts.

Baby Boomers

The baby boom produced about four million babies a year between 1946 and 1964, adding more than 76 million people to America's population. Today's first baby boomers have hit 50 years of age, and this fact alone represents a shift from a youth culture to a middle-aged culture. Magazines that established themselves as the voices of youth, such as *Rolling Stone*, have had to decide whether to shift their focus to match their older, but still loyal, readers, or to stay with the age group they know—and cater to a smaller audience. Unfortunately, advertisers historically have been reluctant to tap into the mature market, preferring to concentrate on the 18- to 34-year-old group. Yet the Generation X baby busters, who followed the boomers, simply don't have the volume of buying power that their predecessors had at their age and continue to have a generation later.

From the time they graduated from college in record numbers, boomer readers have been touted as being more educated, more affluent, and more interested in pursuing the good life than the previous World War II generation, many of whom came of age during the Depression of the 1930s. Most revealing is the fact, however, that 50-year-old baby boomers don't act like their parents did at that age. Magazine publishers who can correctly predict the desires, needs, and behaviors of aging boomers (who are resistant to the mature market label) will do well, say futurists.

What are some of the potential magazine topics likely to interest and excite baby boomers over the next decade? Health, shelter, personal finance, and leisure are the four horsemen of the boomer apocalypse, as evidenced by a growing number of successful launches and ongoing prosperity of established consumer and trade titles in those areas.

HEALTH. Women traditionally have kept on top of health concerns through the various service departments in the slew of women's beauty, fashion, and service magazines being published. Special health titles for women, such as *Shape, Fit,* and *Fitness,* are a slice of the niche, which is no longer the exclusive domain of female readers. Men's magazines such as *Men's Journal, Men's Health, Men's Fitness,* and *Details* also have jumped on the service journalism bandwagon and are dispensing advice ranging from hiking to hair care. *Men's Health* and *Men's Journal,* in particular, have been stressing health and fitness themes, and even a traditional men's book like *Esquire* recently added sections on staying fit and trim.

Long-time top circulation titles in the health and fitness market include *Prevention* (a boomer itself with a birth year of 1950), at more than 3.25 million, and *American Health,* at more than 679,000. *Prevention* editor Mark Bricklin pointed out in 1996 that the magazine is perfectly positioned to reach baby boomers. "We're standing at the door, ready to receive them," said Bricklin, who added that the average reader of *Prevention* is 48 years old.[46] Hard-core and gloomy in tone with a "health nut" image during the 1950s and 1960s, today's *Prevention* takes a "can-do" approach. Along with mainstream articles such as "Walk Off 10, 25 or Even 50+ Pounds," the magazine practices what it preaches. At the annual rally and walking club event sponsored by *Prevention,* editors walk with readers.

Health also dominates the business and trade magazine category, with healthcare and pharmaceutical publications having a separate advertising book devoted to them (*SRDS Business Publication Advertising Source*). There you will find more than 900 medical, surgical, dental, nursing, hospital administration, drugs, pharmaceutical, and health-care titles, including *New England Journal of Medicine, Surgical Rounds, Dental Products Report, RN, Medical Economics, American Druggist,* and *Contemporary Long Term Care.*

SHELTER. Home has long been where the heart is, and the shelter magazines show no signs of slowing down. Futurists predict that as more and more boomers enter their forties and fifties, they will want to spend more time at home. The home service magazine category has been extremely active in the last several years.

Typical of the strength in the shelter category was *Apartment Life*'s title change in 1981 to *Metropolitan Home.* The change, which included a complete makeover, reflected the fact that the magazine's baby boomer readers were beginning to disdain the apartment renter nomenclature and were purchasing co-ops, condos, lofts, and townhouses in cities across the nation. Editors wanted to reflect the boomer audience's desire for a more upscale, refined, mature look in their more spacious abodes. After all, by 1986 their median household income was $81,900 and their median home value was $184,200.[47] These readers were no longer 1970s radicals. They had settled down to comfortable affluence.

Likewise, the September 1996 return of *House & Garden,* which had folded in July 1993 after 92 years of publication, spotlighted the ongoing interest in the home and shelter category. Even "This Old House," the highest-rated series on public television, has been translated into a magazine offering. *This Old House* was launched in 1995 as a joint venture between Time Inc. and WGBH of Boston, the producer of the program.

The tone of the magazine perfectly matches that of the PBS show, while successfully filling the fixer-upper niche in the shelter market. Most shelter books deal with finished space, but *This Old House* is walking more than 300,000 readers through the entire process. It joins the already-established *Old House Journal,* with a 142,000 circulation, in a niche position between traditional home service publications such as *House Beautiful* and *Home* and magazines providing professional level, in-depth information about residential building and remodeling, such as *Fine Homebuilding.*

Gardens and outdoor patios are a natural extension of the homebody lifestyle. After baby boomers put finishing touches on the inside of their homes (how many times can you reupholster that chair or repaint that wall?), it is logical to turn to the adjacent outdoor areas. In 1996, according to the National Gardening Association, gardening was a $22.5 billion a year business. More than 65 million households in the United States spent money on plants and tools, with the bulk of purchases—45 percent of all sales—made by 30- to 49-year-old baby boomers.[48]

It is not surprising that gardening magazines are a growth category. *Country Gardens* recently raised its frequency from quarterly to bimonthly. According to Meredith group publisher Chris Little, "People in publishing said for a long time that you couldn't have a large-circulation gardening magazine with strong advertising because the gardening advertising market was so limited. But now we're seeing more and more advertisers who like the demographic and also see a market for the environment of a garden magazine because it can be so beautiful."[49]

Paralleling the consumer interest in shelter are trade magazines focusing on architecture, construction, air conditioning, plumbing, hardware, interior design, floriculture, and landscape and garden supplies. The more than 300 titles listed in the 1998 *SRDS Business Publication Advertising Source* range from *Builder* and *Construction Specifier* to *Nursery Retailer* and *Landscape and Irrigation.*

PERSONAL FINANCE. Another burgeoning area for magazines has been in the consumer business and finance sector, long dominated by *Forbes, Fortune,* and *Business Week.* More recent business titles of note include *Venture, Entrepreneur, Black Enterprise,* and *Inc.,* which all tend to stress business-to-business advertisements and feature articles focusing on corporate image and management issues for an audience of businesspeople.

Playboy's rabbit, symbolizing the magazine, is so well known that in 1959, a New York reader sent a letter to *Playboy* in Chicago with "Rabbit Head" as the only address.

However, the most intriguing aspect of this category has been its movement into the lifestyle and service-oriented personal finance niche. Baby boomers are moving from being spenders to savers as they age and worry about financing their children's college education and having enough money for their own retirement. This shift in focus has affected the magazines they want to purchase and read. *Worth, SmartMoney, Money,* and *Kiplinger's Personal Finance* have taken advantage of the boomers' new attitude and emphasize financial planning in terms of better savings and wiser investments.

But not all baby boomers are worried about their current financial status or their future. Providing an interesting wrinkle in the personal finance market is *American Benefactor,* focusing entirely on philanthropy. A sibling of *Worth, American Benefactor* is based on the belief that successful boomers want to share their financial prosperity with others but need insight and information about philanthropy and philanthropists. The biannual magazine, which debuted in March 1997, is distributed by nonprofit organizations to their donors, present and potential.

Business and finance ranks just behind health as a mega-classification in the trade magazine category, with more than 500 titles in the 1998 *SRDS Business Publication Advertising Source.* This is where you will find magazines devoted to business concerns *(Industry Week),* banking (*American Banker*), finance, (*Institutional Investor*), insurance (*Business Insurance*), and legal issues (*ABA Journal*).

LEISURE. Leisure, desired by all and consumed most avidly and sumptuously by the well-to-do baby boomer, is the wild card in the deck. Pinpointing leisure magazines is a matter of determining prevailing trends and interests.

Leisure-oriented magazines take the attitude that the general lifestyle magazine is dead. Consequently, leisure titles—all competing for variations in the same educated, affluent niche—

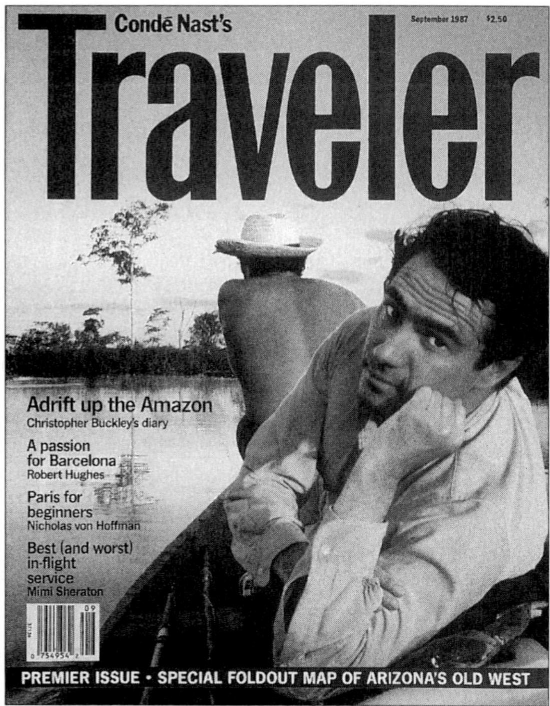

Condé Nast's
Traveler
September 1987 $2.50
Adrift up the Amazon
Christopher Buckley's diary
A passion for Barcelona
Robert Hughes
Paris for beginners
Nicholas von Hoffman
Best (and worst) in-flight service
Mimi Sheraton
PREMIER ISSUE • SPECIAL FOLDOUT MAP OF ARIZONA'S OLD WEST

SEPTEMBER 1987 (PREMIERE ISSUE): *Condé Nast Traveler* is a popular choice for baby boomers interested in travel and leisure.

range from *Cigar Aficionado* for stogie stokers to *Fine Woodworking* for crafty carvers to *Robb Report* for materialistic millionaires. Leisure magazines tend to be expensive. *Fine Woodworking* and *Robb Report* both sport a hefty cover price, of $6.95 and $6.99 respectively, while *Cigar Aficionado* puffs a price of $4.95. The average cover price of a magazine on the newsstands in 1997 was $2.41.[50]

Of course, there are less opulent and less outrageous leisure and lifestyle offerings for the middle-class reader, baby boomer or not. Leisure magazines account for the myriad growth of special interest magazines each year, but the standard categories in the leisure market continue to prosper. For example, the big three travel magazines, *Condé Nast Traveler, Travel Holiday,* and *Travel & Leisure,* have maintained their high circulations even with the advent of more focused titles like *Islands* and *Historic Traveler.* Association magazines also fill the leisure niche, particularly in the travel field where state, regional, and national automobile associations cover American destinations and resorts.

For every new sport or hobby that becomes popular, you can be sure that a magazine won't be far behind. *Snowboarder* is one magazine that developed only after snowboards had found acceptance on popular ski slopes, while soccer magazines are growing along with the sport. Magazines serve every conceivable craft or hobby, and thrive despite competition for a narrow slice of the reader pie. For example, Teddy bear collectors can choose between *Teddy Bear Review* and *Teddy Bear and Friends,* while numismatists have a wider currency to pick from, with *World Coin News, Coins, Coinage, Coin World,* and *Coin Prices.* Guitarists can strum through *Acoustic Guitar, Guitar, Guitar Player, Guitar Shop, Guitar World, Guitar Techniques, Just Jazz Guitar, Freestyle Guitar, Maximum Guitar,* and more. The circulation of narrowly focused magazines can range from a few thousand to more than 250,000.

In the business and trade magazine area, technology magazines have both leisure and personal/finance overtones, due to the computer, telecommunications, and electronic engineering explosion. There are more than 500 titles listed in this category in the 1998 *SRDS Business Publication Advertising Source.* The top three circulation leaders in the specialized trade genre are *PC Magazine, PC World,* and *PC Computing.*

Racial and Ethnic Shifts

The aging of the baby boomer generation is one of the two significant forces shaping U.S. society for the next 40 years; the other involves the shifting balance of racial and ethnic groups. Population Reference Bureau researcher Carol J. De Vita points out that minorities remained a relatively small percentage of the U.S. population until the 1960s.[51] In 1996, De Vita predicted, "Within the next 25 years, about one in three Americans will come from a minority background, and by the middle of the twenty-first century, the size of the 'minority' population should just about equal the size of the non-Hispanic white population."

What does this mean for the magazine industry? More magazines will be launched that specifically target blacks, Asians, and Hispanics. All three population groups are growing, but Hispanics are adding the most to their numbers. By 2020, the Hispanic population is expected to exceed 50 million, while the Asian population should more than double in size between 1995 and 2020 to 21 million. Blacks will reach 42 million by 2020, but the pace of growth will be slower than for the other two.

HISPANIC TITLES. For many years there have been Spanish-language versions of *Reader's Digest, Cosmopolitan, Harper's Bazaar, Good Housekeeping,* and *Popular Mechanics* distributed throughout Latin America and the Caribbean, as well as Spanish-language publishers like Editorial América, S.A. These magazines see their readership as Spanish-speaking and largely foreign. Now publishers are specifically targeting Americans of Hispanic background through magazines written in English or a mix of English and Spanish. Four new national magazines appeared during 1995 and 1996 to reach those Hispanics in the United States with incomes of $35,000 to $120,000—the affluent middle class. This group tends to use Spanish as a second language; English is their first. *Latina Style* and *Sí* use English, while *Latina* and *Moderna* are dual-language. All four aim for upscale advertisers such as Estée Lauder and Nordstrom department store who want to reach affluent, educated Hispanic women living in the United States.

Previously, the most successful mass market Hispanic title was the Spanish-language publication *Mas.* During the late 1980s and early 1990s *Mas* had a newsstand circulation of 680,000, and a full-page ad cost $20,000.[52] "We were the *Time* magazine, the *Vanity Fair,* the *Vogue* of the American Hispanic," said former publisher Roger Toll. Started by Univision, the popular Spanish-language television network, *Mas* was shut down in 1993 when Mexican media giant Televisa purchased Univision.

The Washington Post Company and Time Warner seem to be betting that the Spanish-language market is the way to go. *Newsweek en Español* hit the newsstands in May 1996 under a licensing agreement between the Washington Post Company's *Newsweek* and Miami-based Ideas & Capital.[53] *Newsweek en Español* is aimed primarily at Latin readers south of the American border, although an estimated 25,000 copies are being distributed in the United States.

People en Español is targeting American Hispanics rather than just the market in Mexico, primarily because of *People*'s success with an April 17, 1995, cover story about popular Mexican-American singer Selena who had been murdered in Texas. That issue sold 442,000 copies in a single day, and a later special Selena "tribute" memorial issue sold a million copies.[54]

Now other magazines are getting into this ethnic niche. The December 7, 1996, issue of *TV*

COUNTING ON THE BABY BOOMERS

The numbers alone between 1963 and 1990 show the explosive baby boomer influence on America's magazine culture, particularly in the areas of health and fitness, shelter, and personal finance.[1] These categories thrive in both advertising and circulation, showing continued growth in 1998.[2]

YEAR	NUMBER OF HEALTH AND FITNESS	CONSUMER MAGAZINE EXAMPLES
1963	9	*Prevention, American Health, Healthy Living, Fitness, Health,* Vim & *Vigor, Yoga Journal , Flex, Self, Shape, Fit, Men's Health*
1990	26	
1998	62	

YEAR	NUMBER OF HOME SERVICE & HOMES (SHELTER) AND GARDENING (HOME)	CONSUMER MAGAZINES EXAMPLES
1963	9	*Elle Decor, House Beautiful, Better Homes and Gardens, Metropolitan Home, Martha Stewart Living, Garden Design, Country Living, This Old House, Organic Gardening*
1990	83	
1998	164	

YEAR	NUMBER OF BUSINESS & FINANCE (PERSONAL FINANCE)	CONSUMER MAGAZINES EXAMPLES
1963	17	*Business Week, Fortune, Forbes, Entrepreneur, Venture, Worth, Money, Kiplinger's Personal Finance, Black Enterprise, Inc.*
1990	33	
1998	47	

1 James B. Kobak, "25 Years of Change," *Folio:* (March 1990): 87.
2 *SRDS Consumer Magazine Advertising Source* (Des Plaines, IL: Standard Rate and Data Service, May 1998).

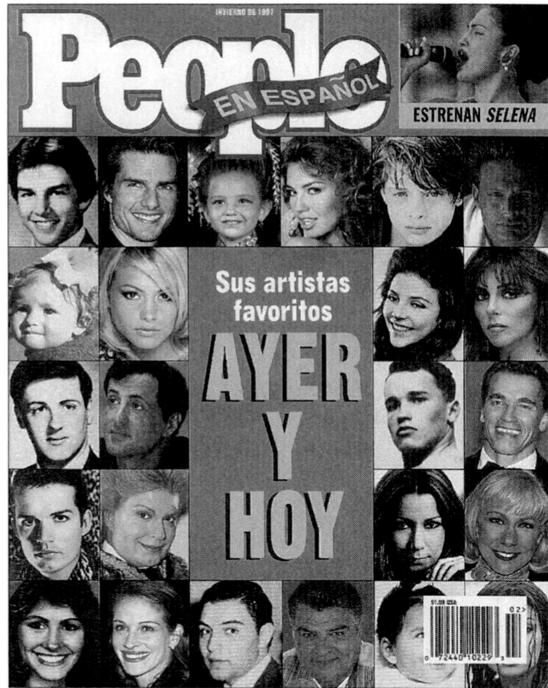

WINTER 1997 (PREMIERE ISSUE): ***People en Español,*** **one of several Spanish-language magazines to target the fast-growing Hispanic population in the United States, has been very successful as a brand extension that follows *People*'s editorial format.**

Guide, containing a long story about Selena's life, featured a smiling picture of the singer on the cover for certain markets across the United States. Selena was the cover photo for *TV Guide* in Texas, the West Coast, and Colorado, while Drew Carey and his ABC show co-star Kathy Kinney were on the cover for the New York issue. Tailoring different covers to various areas of the country is part of a marketing strategy now being used by magazines.

BLACK TITLES. Titles for black readers grew in the 1990s while, at the same time, advertising pages in established black magazines—*Ebony, Essence, Jet,* and *Black Enterprise*—increased. Editors of both new and established magazines for the black audience say the market can hold still more titles and point to the lack of images of blacks in mainstream magazines as a reason for introducing new publications. The appeal of the black audience is strong enough to lure mainstream publishers into the ring. Rodale Press started *Heart & Soul,* a black women's health magazine, in 1993; it now has a circulation of 309,000 and solid advertising support. In 1998, Rodale sold *Heart & Soul* to BET Holdings, Inc., the parent of Black Entertainment Television.

Heart & Soul's former editor, Stephanie Stokes Oliver, said the positive response to the magazine is due to its merging of health issues and black readers. Pointing to women's health magazines such as *Self* and *Shape,* and black women's magazines such as *Essence,* Oliver said only *Heart & Soul* is devoted to encouraging a healthy lifestyle for black women: "My mission is to not only make *Heart & Soul* a household name, but to position the magazine as a resource for information on fitness, weight loss, exercise, parenting and love relationships edited specifically for the black community."[55]

Vibe carved a special niche among black men and women in their twenties when it hit the newsstands in 1993 as the cultural purveyor of the hip-hop music scene. *Vibe* is one of the fastest-growing magazines in America, increasing its rate base, its ad pages, and its newsstand sales every year. Its dramatic covers featuring Whitney Houston, Tupac Shakur, Death Row, and Juice reach "a generation of young men and women whose lives defy categorizing along conventional lines of race, class or gender."[56] Twenty-eight percent of *Vibe*'s audience is "white or other," reflecting the publication's passionate commitment to an inclusive, multicultural perspective on urban music, fashion, and culture.

ASIAN TITLES. Almost 10 million Asian Americans now live in the United States. This well-educated, high-earning ethnic group commands $110 billion in spending power, according to a study by the University of Georgia and Market Research & Consulting. Yet the market is underserved, with only 17 percent of marketers targeting Asian Americans, compared to 78 percent who target blacks and 65 percent who target Hispanics.[57]

So far, only a handful of magazines are targeted specifically to Asian Americans. Although there are numerous Asian languages and dialects, English is the unifying language among Asian Americans and their magazines. The top circulation magazine for the market, *A. Magazine,* was started in 1989 as a lifestyle book covering news, politics, and culture; it reaches 100,000 readers. Unlike older publications, such as *Transpacific,* that profile Asian Americans, *A. Magazine* goes "inside Asian America" for its stories.

DECEMBER 1998/JANUARY 1999: *A. Magazine,* the top circulation publication in the growing Asian-American market, covers news, politics, and lifestyles.

Said *A. Magazine*'s former editor-in-chief, Angelo Ragaza, "We want to show that Asians are sexy and beautiful. Asian women read the beauty books, which are dominated by images of white beauty. We want to promote images of Asian-attractive. And we work hard at it."[58] Asian-American women also turn to the fashion magazine *Face*, established in 1992 for women in their twenties and thirties. It was joined by *Niko* in 1995.

There's also *Yolk*, an entertainment magazine aimed at the "NewGenerAsian," as editor Larry Tazuma likes to call his audience. Launched in 1994, *Yolk* already has reached a circulation of 45,000. Tazuma argues that as the numbers of Asian Americans grow, more specialized magazines—for Chinese Americans or Korean Americans—will emerge.

For now, though, media analysts seem cautious about this market. Says one media buyer, "I think the Asian market is a sleeping giant. There's a great potential for the upscale segment of the Asian population that advertisers will find desirable, but nobody's paying attention to it yet."[59]

Specialization, whether of content or audience, is nothing new for magazines. In their role as both shapers and reflectors of American society, magazines have made a critical impact on each century's readers and writers. In December 1846, Edgar Allan Poe, himself an influential magazine editor and freelance writer, wrote in *Graham's American Monthly Magazine of Literature and Art:*

> *Whatever may be the merits or demerits, generally of the Magazine Literature of America, there can be no question as to its extent or influence. The topic—Magazine Literature—is therefore an important one. In a few years its importance will be found to have increased in geometrical ratio. The whole tendency of the age is Magazine-ward.*[60]

FOR ADDITIONAL READING

Carson, Rachel. *Silent Spring.* Boston: Houghton Mifflin, 1962.

Damon-Moore, Helen. *Magazines for the Millions: Gender and Commerce in the* Ladies' Home Journal *and the* Saturday Evening Post, *1880–1910.* Albany: State University of New York, 1994.

Endres, Kathleen L., ed. *Trade, Industrial, and Professional Periodicals of the United States.* Westport, CT: Greenwood Press, 1994.

Endres, Kathleen L. and Therese L. Lueck, eds. *Women's Periodicals in the United States: Consumer Magazines.* Westport, CT: Greenwood Press, 1995.

———. *Women's Periodicals in the United States: Social and Political Issues.* Westport, CT: Greenwood Press, 1996.

Garcia, John. *The Success of* Hispanic Magazine: *A Publishing Success Story.* New York: Walker & Co., 1995.

Johnson, John H. *Succeeding Against the Odds.* New York: Warner Books, 1989.

Marco, Gino, Robert M. Hollingworth, and William Durham. *Silent Spring Revisited.* Washington, DC: American Chemical Society, 1987.

Pearman, Phil, ed. *Dear Editor: Letters to* Time *Magazine, 1923–1984.* Salem, NH: Salem House, 1985.

Regier, C. C. *The Era of the Muckrakers.* Chapel Hill: The University of North Carolina Press, 1932.

Rennie, Susan and Kirsten Grimstad. *The New Woman's Survival Sourcebook.* New York: Alfred A. Knopf, 1975.

Sandra, Jaida N'Ha and the editors of *Utne Reader. The Joy of Conversation: The Complete Guide to Salons.* Minneapolis: Utne Reader Books, 1997.

Scanlon, Jennifer. *Inarticulate Longings: The* Ladies' Home Journal, *Gender and the Promises of Consumer Culture.* New York: Routledge, 1995.

Solomon, Martha A., ed. *A Voice of Their Own: The Woman Suffrage Press, 1840–1920.* Tuscaloosa: University of Alabama Press, 1991.

Tarbell, Ida M. *All in the Day's Work: An Autobiography.* New York: Macmillan, 1939.

Thom, Mary. *Letters to* Ms. *1972–1987.* New York: Holt, 1987.

———. *Inside* Ms.: *25 Years of the Magazine and the Feminist Movement.* New York: Holt, 1997.

Wachsberger, Ken, ed. *Voices from the Underground: Volume I, Insider Histories of the Vietnam Era Underground Press.* Tempe, AZ: Mica Press, 1993.

———. *Voices from the Underground: Volume II, A Directory of Sources and Resources on the Vietnam Era Underground Press.* Tempe, AZ: Mica Press, 1993.

Weinberg, Arthur and Lila Weinberg. *The Muckrakers: The Era of Journalism That Moved America to Reform—The Most Significant Magazine Articles of 1902–1912.* New York: Simon and Schuster, 1961.

Wilson, Harold S. McClure's *Magazine and the Muckrakers.* Princeton: Princeton, NJ: Princeton University Press, 1970.

Wolf, Naomi. *The Beauty Myth.* New York: William Morrow, 1991.

Wood, James Playsted. *Magazines in the United States,* 2d ed. New York: Ronald Press, 1956.

ENDNOTES

1 Joseph Klapper, *The Effects of Mass Communication*, 2nd ed. (Glencoe, IL: The Free Press, 1961).

2 John D. Zelezny, *Communications Law, Liberties, Restraints and the Modern Media* (Belmont, CA: Wadsworth, 1993): 95.

3 Maxwell McCombs and Donald Shaw, "The Agenda-Setting Function of Mass Media," *Public Opinion Quarterly,* 36 (Summer 1972): 176–85.

4 Edwin Diamond, "The Myth of the 'Pesticide Menace,'" *Saturday Evening Post* (September 28, 1963): 16–18; "Pesticides: The Price for Progress," *Time* (September 28, 1962): 45–48; "Can Human Beings Withstand the Barrage of Economic Poisons?" *Consumer Bulletin* (October 1962): 36–37.

5 Gino Marco, Robert M. Hollingworth, and William Hollingworth, *Silent Spring Revisited* (Washington, DC: American Chemical Society, 1987).

6 Kathleen L. Endres, ed. *Trade, Industrial, and Professional Periodicals of the United States* (Westport, CT: Greenwood Press, 1994): 72–84.

7 Arthur Weinberg and Lila Weinberg, *The Muckrakers: The Era of Journalism That Moved America to Reform—The Most Significant Magazine Articles of 1902-1912.* (New York: Simon and Schuster, 1961): 58.

8 Kathleen L. Endres, "Women and the 'Larger Household': An Examination of Muckraking in Women's Magazines" (paper presented at the annual meeting of the Association for Education in Journalism and Mass Communication, Atlanta, GA, August 1994). Later published as "Women and the 'Larger Household': The 'Big Six' and Muckraking," *American Journalism*, 14: 3-4 (Summer-Fall 1997): 262–82.

9 James Playsted Wood, *Magazines in the United States,* 2nd ed. (New York: Ronald Press, 1956): 119–20.

10 Ida M. Tarbell, *All in the Day's Work: An Autobiography* (New York: Macmillan, 1939): 242.

11 Ibid., 281.

12 Mary M. Cronin, "A Master for the Watchdog: The Progressive Era Trade Press' Role in Promoting Professional Values and Ethics Among Journalists" (paper presented at the annual meeting of the Association for Education in Journalism and Mass Communication, Boston, MA, August 1991).

13 Richard Edel, "How 'Passionate Commitment' Raised $1 Million for AIDS," *Advertising Age* (May 24, 1989): 34.

14 Richard Edel, "Advocacy Picks Up Steam," *Advertising Age* (May 24, 1989): 34.

15 Edel, "How 'Passionate Commitment,'" 74.

16 Edel, "Advocacy," 40.

17 Lyon N. Richardson, *A History of Early American Magazines 1741-1789* (New York: Octagon Books, 1978): 163–210.

18 Loudon Wainwright, *The Great American Magazine: An Inside History of* Life (New York: Alfred A. Knopf, 1986): 100–1.

19 Ibid., 235.

20 Gardner Cowles, *Mike Looks Back* (New York: Gardner Cowles, 1985): 151; and "The Fifties," *The Look Years* (Cowles Communications, 1972): 22–23.

21 John H. Johnson, *Succeeding Against the Odds* (New York: Warner Books, 1989): 125.

22 Ibid., 156–57.

23 Bob Hippler, "Fast Times in the Motor City—The First Ten Years of the Fifth Estate: 1965–1975," in *Voices from the Underground: Volume 1, Insider Histories of the Vietnam Era Underground Press,* ed. Ken Wachsberger (Tempe, AZ: Mica Press, 1993): 18.

24 David E. Settje, "The Vietnam War, the Cold War, and Protestants: How *The Christian Century* and *Christianity Today* Reflected American Society in the 1960s" (paper presented at the annual meeting of the American Journalism History Association, London, Ontario, Canada, October 1996).

25 "An Open Letter to," *Ladies' Home Journal* (April 1971): 50.

26 "The Power of a Woman," *Ladies' Home Journal* (July 1971): 46 and 152.

27 Elizabeth Valk Long, "To Our Readers," *Time* (May 2, 1994): 4.

28 Neil Cassidy, "Gay Titles Enjoy 36 Percent Ad Growth," *Folio:* (November 15, 1997): 14.

29 Susan Hovey, "They're Here, They're Queer, They're on a Roll," *Folio:* (June 1, 1995): 70–71.

30 Jack A. Nelson, "Disability Magazines: The Search for Identity and Empowerment" (paper presented at the annual meeting of the Association for Education in Journalism and Mass Communication, Anaheim, CA, August 1996).

[31] Mary Ann Farrell, "New Magazine Explores Global Disability Issues," *San Antonio Express-News* (July 9, 1995): 1H.
[32] Jim Cory, "The Spokane Story," *Hardware Age* (October 1994): 30–52.
[33] Jonathan Rabinovitz, "Attempted Comeback for the Literary Salon," *The New York Times* (April 13, 1992): B2.
[34] Kaja Silverman, *The Subject of Semiotics* (New York: Oxford University Press, 1983).
[35] Walter Lippmann, *Public Opinion* (New York: Macmillan Publishing, 1922).
[36] Alicia C. Shepard, "Schmoozing with the Stars," *American Journalism Review* (July-August 1996): 23.
[37] Jennifer Jackson, "Sole Devotion," *Harper's Bazaar* (October 1995): 82.
[38] Ibid., 60.
[39] Michael Parenti, *Inventing Reality: The Politics of News Media,* 2nd ed. (New York: St. Martin's Press, 1993): 191.
[40] Daniel Boorstin, *The Image or What Happened to the American Dream* (New York: Atheneum, 1962).
[41] "Unlike Madonna, She's Fake, But Not Icky," *Des Moines Register* (October 28, 1996): 2.
[42] "*Esquire* Spoofs Celebrity Journalism," *Esquire News* (October 23, 1996): 1.
[43] Ibid., 2.
[44] Edward W. Barrett, "Sex, Death and Other Trends in Magazines," in *Mass Media & Society,* 2nd ed., Alan Wells, ed. (Palo Alto, CA: Mayfield Publishing, 1975): 35–37.
[45] Ibid., 37.
[46] Judith Pollack, "*Prevention* Prepares for Managed Care," *Advertising Age* (March 11, 1996): S4.
[47] Kathleen L. Endres and Theresa L. Lueck, ed. *Women's Periodicals of the United States: Consumer Magazines* (Westport, CT: Greenwood Press, 1995): 225–29.
[48] Tony Case, "Where's the Dirt? Garden Books Sell a Lifestyle," *Folio:* (March 15, 1998): 15.
[49] Ibid., 15.
[50] *Veronis, Suhler and Associates Communications Industry Forecast,* "Consumer Magazine Publishing" (Veronis, Suhler and Associates, 1998):305.
[51] Carol J. De Vita, "The United States at Mid-Decade," *Population Bulletin* (Vol. 50, No. 4): 17.
[52] Marie Arana-Wood, "Magazines, Latinos Find Themselves on the Same Page," *Washington Post* (December 5, 1996): A24.
[53] Keith J. Kelly and Jeffrey D. Zbar, "Spanish Magazines Capture Attention with 3 New Entries," *Advertising Age* (June 3, 1996): 44.
[54] Arana-Wood, A23.
[55] *DM News*, "Wholehearted Commitment" in *What's Next in Mass Communication: Readings on Media and Culture,* ed. by Christopher Harper (New York: St. Martin's Press, 1998): 120.
[56] *Vibe* (Fifth Anniversary Media Kit, #7, 1998).
[57] Gilbert Cheah, "Fulfillment's Neglected Niche," *Folio:* (March 15, 1998): 37.
[58] Courtenay Martin, "The Chic Chronicles," *San Antonio Express-News* (June 4, 1998): 1F.
[59] Chris Beam, "Asian-American Titles Take Off," *Folio:* (June 1, 1995): 27.
[60] Edgar Allan Poe, *Marginalia* (Charlottesville, Va.: University Press of Virginia, 1981): 139.

PART TWO

The Magazine's Blueprint

CHAPTER 5

Magazine Concepts

Formulas for Success

In 1983, Harper's Magazine *seemed to be at the end of its 133-year life. It was losing nearly $1 million a year and circulation was dwindling. Subscriptions were sold at discount rates to buyers who felt little loyalty to the finished product; advertisers saw small appeal in a title that seemed to have outlived its usefulness.* Harper's *was on life support, and magazine experts waited for the inevitable: The venerable old title would soon follow* The Century *and* Scribner's *to the magazine cemetery.* 📖 *It didn't happen.* 📖 Harper's *editors responded to the crisis by refashioning an innovative magazine that is now as representative of its time as the original publication was when it was launched in 1850. It was the magazine's fifth revision. The editors retooled the editorial philosophy, or mission statement, and redrew the formula of the magazine. They introduced elements, such as the* Harper's *Index and Annotation, that tapped the national mood so well they were eventually emulated by other magazines.* 📖 *This is a process all successful editors follow, in one way or another, to create a package that every reader wants: consistency with an element of surprise. The magazine field is a highly competitive and harsh market; only those publications with clear philosophies and formulas succeed. Often the title is the strongest indication of the magazine's focus. Magazines with long lives, like* Harper's, *reformulate themselves regularly, following life cycles built around audience growth and change.*

MAGAZINE SUCCESS AND FAILURE

Bob Anderson was a high-school student in 1966 when he personally stapled together a 28-page magazine about his favorite sport. He spent $100 on that first *Runner's World* and started a whole new field of magazines. He lured 350 subscribers that first year; the magazine, now owned by Rodale Press, has a circulation of 480,000. In 1978, Anderson explained his success: "I had an idea I believed in—I'm a dedicated runner myself, and I knew there were a lot of others like me—and I started small."[1]

Compare that with *You,* a magazine started in 1977 with the enigmatic philosophy:

> ***We're definitely not about celebrities, not about bionic people, not about fantasy lifestyles that aren't available. . . . We're about people taking responsibility for their own lives, people taking part in the personal revolution going on coast to coast. And we're saying, 'That's great, get some happiness in your own life and maybe you'll bring it to others, too.'***[2]

Disco music outlived *You,* which lasted less than a year. Editor Rick Bard talked about investors

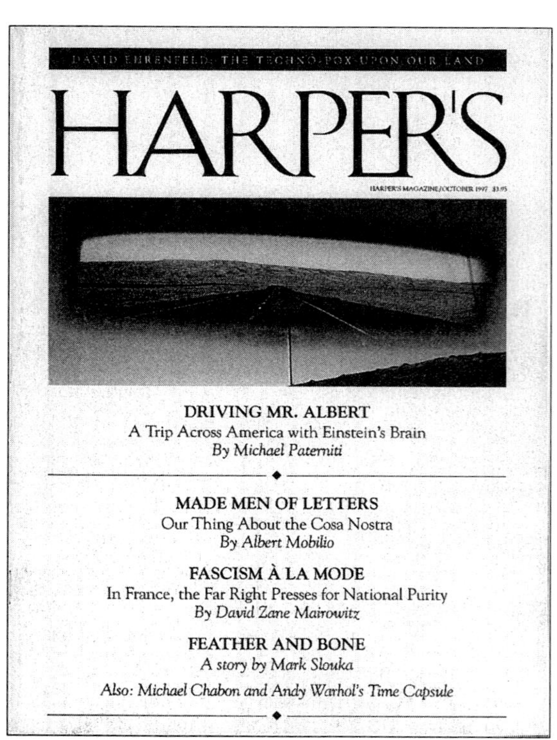
DAVID EHRENFELD: THE TECHNO-POX UPON OUR LAND

HARPER'S

HARPER'S MAGAZINE/OCTOBER 1997 $3.95

DRIVING MR. ALBERT
A Trip Across America with Einstein's Brain
By *Michael Paterniti*

MADE MEN OF LETTERS
Our Thing About the Cosa Nostra
By *Albert Mobilio*

FASCISM À LA MODE
In France, the Far Right Presses for National Purity
By *David Zane Mairowitz*

FEATHER AND BONE
A story by Mark Slouka

Also: Michael Chabon and Andy Warhol's Time Capsule

OCTOBER 1997: "Driving Mr. Albert," an article about transporting Albert Einstein's brain cross-country, won *Harper's* a 1998 National Magazine Award for feature writing.

who never materialized, and said his problem was not "readjusting my budget accordingly." Unenthusiastic supporters, however, were probably a symptom of a magazine with a vague direction.

Have you read *Politicks and Other Human Interests*? Few others have, either. The magazine started in 1977 and was gone in 1978. According to editor Thomas Morgan, "A magazine for the community of political activists in the country was necessary in a period when there was so much political apathy." Started with $900,000 private money, the magazine lost more than $1 million. Why did it fold? Morgan talked about the magazine's "cash-flow concept" and said, "We didn't develop circulation fast enough to attract advertisers."[3] The base problem, however, was in the concept. You can't make kids love broccoli and you can't make people who do not care about politics read a political magazine, especially one with archaic spelling in the title.

Sometimes, though, magazines with illustrious careers and award-winning histories fail. *High Fidelity*, launched in 1950, published its last issue in 1989; readers with remaining subscriptions received copies of *Stereo Review*. The titles tell all. We no longer talk about high fidelity, but about stereo.

Magazine consultant James Kobak said the primary reason for the failure of most magazines is lack of reader interest and a loss of editorial focus, which can kill previously successful magazines as times and audience interests change.[4] A major error in publishing new magazines, he said, is in creating titles nobody wants, titles that are of interest to the staff but that hold little appeal to a larger group of readers.[5] The editor may be a member of the audience, but he may be the only one in the audience.

Harlan Logan, publishing consultant for *Scribner's*, looked at the problem in the 1940s, during the era of large, general interest magazines and, not surprisingly, emphasized audience less than analysts studying contemporary special interest magazines. Nevertheless, his conclusions often mirror those of modern scholars. Magazines failed, he said, because they lacked an "editorial reason for existence," a "clearly defined editorial pattern," and a solid advertising base.[6]

Researcher Milton Hollstein surveyed magazine publishers in the 1960s in search of the reasons for magazine success. His respondents said magazines failed because of "managerial inexperience or incompetence."[7] Writer Christopher Byron provided perhaps one of the best examples of the influence of management on a magazine's success or failure in a study of *TV-Cable Week*. That magazine suffered, he said, from the "business school orientation" that created a product geared not to the reader's needs but, rather, to the needs of the MBAs who started it. These needs included making use of analytical skills taught at Harvard and making a mark on the corporate environment. Instead of relying on editorial talent, skills, and connections with the audience, the managers relied only on the numbers.[8]

Advertisers choose magazines based on: an identifiable target audience (72 percent), the quality of the editorial product (41 percent), circulation stability (40 percent), and pricing flexibility (14 percent).

The perspectives of these scholars create a picture of the reasons for a magazine's success. In order, they are:

1. A highly focused editorial philosophy;
2. A clearly defined formula;
3. A thorough understanding of and connection with the audience.

These elements exist within a supportive structure that includes adequate financial support; a well-planned marketing and distribution system; and solid management. All the money in the world, however, cannot save an ill-conceived magazine.

EDITORIAL PHILOSOPHY

Editors differ on what they call their statement of goals. Some call it an editorial philosophy, some call it a mission statement, some call it nothing at all but know intuitively what it is.

An **editorial philosophy** is a magazine's focus. Just as we develop our own personal philosophies, which differentiate us from our friends and serve as the basis for our personalities, a magazine has a driving philosophy that, if strongly defined, gives the publication its identity and personality. An editorial philosophy explains what the magazine is intended to do, what areas of interest it covers, how it will approach those interests, and the voice it will use to express itself. It is highly specific.

Harper's current philosophy, developed in 1984, still guides the magazine today. That philosophy was reiterated in a 1992 essay by editor Lewis Lapham:

> *The magazine set itself the task of asking questions. Instead of attempting to provide approved answers, the magazine said, in effect, look at this or imagine that—see how much more beautiful and strange and full of possibility is the world than has been dreamed of by the philosophers at* Time *or NBC. The proposition assumed the complicity of a reader willing to concede that for the time being it was enough to assemble the pieces of the puzzle and to try to figure out what goes with what.*
>
> *The revised text of the magazine introduced an anthology of new forms . . . intended to convey a sense of the world's ambiguity and surprise.*[9]

The 1966 cover of the ninth annual edition of *The Worst of* Mad sold for $19,550 at a Sotheby's auction in 1995. Although it sounds like a *Mad* parody (Alfred E. Neuman's portrait being peddled next to Van Goghs and Renoirs), don't expect the late staff artist Norman Mingo's toothy renditions to be hanging anytime soon in a museum.

The magazine was redefined as "an interpretative instead of an investigative instrument" that would help readers place information into "some sort of plausible context or intelligible sequence." Lapham acknowledged that readers had information coming at them from all directions—cable and network television, radio, newspapers, magazines—and needed help making sense of it all. The editors at *Harper's* also recognized that helping readers conquer the information glut could not only be educational, it could also be fun. The result: an organized hodgepodge of essays, excerpts, discussions, and fiction. Circulation has rebounded, from 140,000 in 1983, to 218,000 in 1998. Advertisers include BMW, Absolut, Remy Martin, and Allstate. And readers are engaged, carrying on their own energetic dialogue on the magazine's letters pages. Some lambaste Lapham for his liberal views, others for his selling out to conservatives. Having offended both sides, the magazine is promoting national discussion of the significant issues of the day: technology, the media, and politics.

Harper's clearly redefined its nature and its scope, and that redefinition serves as the staff's organizing force. It provides direction for editorial planning as well as for advertising sales.

Dorothy Kalins, editor of *Saveur* and *Garden Design*, suggests editors write down their philosophy, or mission statement, and then convince everyone on staff of its value. She finds the philosophy especially important with the advertising staff and says that she explains magazine content to advertisers in the context of the magazine's philosophy, noting why an article was written or designed a particular way. This helps advertisers understand the magazine and keeps potential complaints to a minimum. "Nothing that happens on a magazine," she says, "should happen by accident."[10]

Anne Graham, former editor of *Internal Auditor*, published by the Institute of Internal Auditors, says a cogent editorial philosophy is especially important for an association magazine, in that it "heightens awareness of the magazine's role, contributes to organizational success, and inspires support for magazine initiatives."[11]

The statement of philosophy serves as the guide in developing a new magazine and keeps an existing magazine on track. It defines the purpose of the magazine, the type of content that will serve that purpose, and the voice the magazine will use. Essential to the philosophy is an understanding of the magazine's target audience. All this is built on a title that embodies the magazine's image and identity.

Title

A good title positions the magazine, and it does so with as few words as possible. It is short, direct, and clear. It also should be timeless, able to grow old with the magazine. Titles can position the magazine vertically, indicating that it gives in-depth coverage of a narrow topic, such as *Detroit Cigar Lifestyles.* Or it can position the magazine horizontally, indicating that it covers a wide range of topics, such as United Airlines's in-flight magazine *Hemispheres.*

Many magazines can make their point quickly and succinctly, such as *Money, Southern Lumberman*, and *Student Lawyer.* Some trade and organization magazines often require longer, more detailed names, such as *The Skin Care Foundation Journal* and *Pharmaceutical and Medical Packaging News*. Some local magazines go for the deliciously quirky, such as *The Improper Bostonian*.

Editorial drector Mike Lafavore says *Men's Health* is one of the few titles in the men's field that position the magazine. When you pick up his *Men's Health*, you know exactly what you're getting. This is less true of *Esquire*. What is an *esquire*, and what can you expect from one? An esquire is a courtesy title often used by lawyers, and the name for the magazine came about serendipitously when *Esquire*'s founding editors were searching for a title and received a letter from their lawyer. After the lawyer's name was the word *esquire*. That summed up the attitude the editors were seeking, and a title was born. It came just in time: The editors had toyed with the names *Beau* and *Stag*, and had even completed a prototype with the name *Town and Gown*.

Facts was the planned title for the new weekly magazine being created by Henry Luce and Briton Hadden. But neither was crazy about the name. One night, Luce was riding the subway home, reading ads that shouted "time to change" and "time to retire." He knew then it was time to retitle his magazine: *Time*.

Garden Design was a trade magazine title when Dorothy Kalins and her partners at Meigher Communications bought it in 1994 and repositioned it to become an upscale consumer publication. The title does just what Kalins wants it to do: focus on the design elements, not the growing, of the garden. *Entertainment Weekly* takes two words to spell out the magazine's focus as well as its frequency. *Glamour* uses only one word to demonstrate content as well as attitude. Several trade magazines include the year in their titles. *RN '97* becomes *RN '98*, and *RN '99*; *Pork '98* becomes *Pork '99*.

In 1967, Jann Wenner considered calling his new magazine *The Electric Newspaper*. Instead, he wisely chose the name *Rolling Stone*, which has weathered the passage of time. *Icon* and *Vibe* are both titles with attitude that will probably travel well through time.

Magazine Purpose

Whether working with an established magazine or a new launch, the essential question to ask is: Why does this magazine exist? Magazines may inform, interpret, entertain, advocate, and provide service.

INFORM. Magazines whose function is primarily to inform include the news magazines and many trade titles that provide basic day-to-day industry information to professionals. *Time* and *Newsweek* writers follow the same news stories as newspaper and television reporters. *Folio:* magazine is a must-read for those in the magazine industry who need to know what new magazines have been launched, how circulation and distribution are changing, and who has moved from one publishing house to another. *National Geographic* informs us about the world and its people, *Aramco World* informs us about the history and culture of the Arab nations.

INTERPRET. Many journalists are still uncertain about the place of interpretation in a field heralded for its objectivity. Interpretation, however, helps readers make sense of a complex world. Readers head to *Money*, *Worth*, and *Family Money* because they want those magazines to help them make some sense of their finances. In its award-winning series "The Plague Years," published in the March 28 and April 25, 1985, issues, *Rolling Stone* helped make some sense of a relatively new disease: AIDS.

ENTERTAIN. Content that entertains makes readers laugh, smile, or simply relax. *Reader's Digest* has long provided readers with "Humor in Uniform," "Campus Comedy," and "Life in These United States." The goal of these departments is purely entertainment. *Mad* exists primarily to entertain although, as is the case with most humor, it offers pointed social commentary.

ADVOCATE. Advocacy goes beyond interpretation into taking a position on not only what *is* but what *should be*. Advocacy examples include *Sierra* for the environment and *Modern Maturity* for the rights of older Americans.

PROVIDE SERVICE. Service articles help readers take action to better their lives. How-to articles are included here, but service goes beyond simply telling us how to firm our abs or file our taxes. Service pieces provide the information and incentive to build a model airplane, bake a cake, travel to Budapest, sleep better, get along with our parents, and find the loves of our lives. *Mamm* steers readers through the medical and legal rights of women with cancer, and *Smart Computing* helps readers overcome Windows 98 chaos.

Better Homes and Gardens implants service in its editorial philosophy:

> *To serve husbands and wives who have a serious interest in home and family as the focal point of their lives, and to provide this service in the form of ideas, help, information and inspiration to achieve a better home and family. Inherent in this philosophy is the editorial responsibility to move these husbands and wives to action.*

Most magazines provide a combination of these five functions. Individual magazines, however, develop their unique identity by determining which purposes take precedence and which will be secondary. *Harper's* primary purpose is to interpret, but it also informs and entertains. *The Web* informs, but it also has a strong service function. *Emerge* is an advocate, while it also provides service. *Modern Baking* and *Home Improvement Market* inform and advocate. *The American Spectator* informs and interprets. *Crayola Kids* informs and entertains.

The more explicit the statement of purpose, the better the philosophy and, therefore, the better the magazine's direction. The purpose, of course, has to be logically tied to a need or interest in the broader society. Kalins, of *Garden Design* and *Saveur*, says the successful magazine "catches a wave in the culture. Something big has to be happening out there that your magazine relates to."

Garden Design, for example, is about how gardening "informs our lives," Kalins says. When she began planning the magazine in 1994, she says, "Baby boomers were beginning to garden, to look for the substance beneath the style. They knew nothing about the garden except that they wanted to be there." *Garden Design* was "the first magazine to treat the garden as a state of mind as well as a place to be."

The magazine's philosophy is also clearly defined by what it is not. Kalins says *Garden Design* is not a "root ball" magazine—it's not about *how* to garden. Kalins advises new editors not to be so arrogant as to think they can do something better than the competition. "Do something different," she says.[12]

Type of Content

How is a magazine's purpose to be achieved? What is its character and overall slant? What special mood or tone does it capture? The answers to these questions help determine the type of editorial, design, and advertising content that will characterize that magazine.

EDITORIAL. If it is an entertainment publication, is that entertainment straightforward and practical, as in *Games*? Or satirical, as in *Mad*? Does the magazine inform people on how to do things of a practical nature, as does *Wood*? Does it inform about general weekly events, as do *Time* and *Newsweek*, or does it cover only business news, as does *Business Week*? Is the advocacy going to be forthright, as in *The Advocate* or does the magazine have an understated political point of view, as is the case now with *Mother Earth News*, or even *George*?

Kalins notes that successful magazines have a "compelling editorial strength." The reader expects a specific kind of content served in a specific style. The successful magazine does not disappoint.

Mike Lafavore says *Men's Health* succeeds because it provides readers with personal service. Before the magazine's start in 1988, he says, "men had never been treated to service journalism." He regularly read his wife's copy of *Glamour* and asked why men couldn't have a magazine like that. The personal service emphasis, he says, makes *Men's Health* stand out in a field that previously offered men information only on "cars, tools, science." *Men's Health* provides tips on keeping in shape, building relationships, and creating a fulfilling life. Lafavore calls this a "benefit-oriented approach." Today's men, he says, "feel their lives are out of control. Service journalism gives them a sense of private control." And it works: The magazine doubled its circulation every year for its first five years and now has five international editions and five on-line editions.[13]

DESIGN. A magazine's look is essential to its concept. Just as the way you dress represents who you are, so too does the way a magazine dresses define what it is. Although not all editors include

MAMM AND *POZ*: HELPING READERS SURVIVE

Poz magazine was launched in April 1994 as a response to the growing AIDS threat. As a health magazine for people with a life-threatening disease, its philosophy is two-fold:

- *To improve and extend the lives of people facing long-term or life-threatening illnesses by providing the first-rate treatment information needed for survival.*
- *To bridge the gap between the mainstream media's coverage of AIDS and HIV health issues and the technical, professional and medical media (newsletters and journals) which cater to select audiences.*[1]

Advertising manager Will Guilliams says the magazine has successfully appealed to medical advertisers and pharmaceutical companies who have only recently begun advertising in consumer magazines. He is now trying to appeal to advertisers such as manufacturers of natural foods, vitamins, and alternative remedies.

Mamm is *Poz*'s sister publication, launched in 1997, and serving readers who have been diagnosed with breast cancer. Its philosophy:

Mamm *is a bimonthly women's health and features magazine focusing on cancer prevention, treatment and survival.* Mamm *gives its readers the essential tools and emotional support they need before, during and after diagnosis of breast, ovarian and other women's cancers. Offering a mix of survivor profiles, the latest treatment information, investigative features, alternative treatments and cutting-edge news,* Mamm *informs, inspires and entertains.* Mamm*'s editorial demonstrates first-hand that life goes on after diagnosis—with strength, elegance and humor.*[2]

Guilliams says *Mamm* is an easier sell than *Poz,* because breast cancer is random, while AIDS is sexually transmitted. He also can target mainstream advertisers in *Mamm,* for companies whose products "make women look good and feel better," such as Avon, Revlon, and Estée Lauder.

Poz en Español has an innovative distribution system underwritten by Hitachi that provides the magazine free to community clinic managers. Guilliams is working with companies such as PepsiCo and General Motors for similar sponsorships, as well as for advertising. Corporations are interested in the magazine because of their "diversity efforts," he says. The Latino audience is especially in need of the magazine's information, he says, with AIDS/HIV cases in Latino women increasing, while cases in white urban males are dropping.

Poz has a circulation of 91,000, *Mamm* is at 75,000, and *Poz en Español* has more than 100,000.

1 *Poz* (Media Kit, 1997).
2 *Mamm* (Media Kit, 1997).

APRIL 1994 (PREMIERE ISSUE): *Poz*—an abbreviated reference to "HIV positive"—is a health magazine for people with life-threatening diseases.

design concepts in their editorial philosophy, they have a strong sense of what look will best achieve their purposes. How does the magazine look, and why does it look that way?

Does the magazine make generous use of white space? Is it type-heavy? Are photographs used for information or illustration or both? Does it always use large photos? Sometimes? Never? How much color does the magazine have? Does it use spot colors? Where? How? Why?

Wired, Harper's, and *Men's Health* have such distinctive looks that a reader would recognize the magazines even if their names were hidden. *Wired*'s look is bold and experimental, trying new tricks. It is a format that offers few constraints and is built around bright colors, sometimes neon tints, in type as well as illustrations. The dull-coated paper stock sets it apart from the crowd of traditional magazines with glossy pages. The logo, which resembles a movie marquee, looks electrical. The magazine and its readers are similarly plugged in. At the same time, *Wired* provides reader service with explanatory photographs clarifying the text and articles organized logically for an audience that has grown up with MTV and computers. Reading the magazine is like using the computer.

Reading *Harper's* is more like reading a book or listening to an engaging speaker. Every month, the magazine cover features a small horizontally cropped photo surrounded by a sea of white space. The rest of the cover is type-heavy, giving article titles, subtitles, and bylines. The message: This is a magazine for people who like to read and are open to new ways of viewing the world. Inside, the magazine has a highly formulaic design. The emphasis on text allows the occasional illustration to shine and encourages the reader to think and make up her own mind about what all this means.

Men's Health demonstrates its service approach in a lively but straightforward design with photographs of men whose physiques the reader hopes to emulate. Lafavore says the magazine uses no celebrities on the cover because that would give the impression that the magazine is about that person, rather than about the reader. In fact, the type of cover model the magazine uses is a reaction to a reader who criticized the man on one cover. "I could beat him up," the reader said. Lafavore says he now makes sure the model could beat the reader up.

ADVERTISING. Readers assess the identity of a magazine through both its editorial and advertising content. What's more, readers hold the editors responsible for that ad content. Advertising should do more than simply match a magazine's audience demographics and psychographics. It should match the philosophy. A magazine that doesn't want cigarette ads, waif-thin models, red meat, or liquor should say so up front. The advertising and editorial staffs should be singing the same song.

The editorial philosophy is also the best defense against advertisers who expect special treatment of their products, or who cringe at a magazine's coverage of topical events or issues. Often, an ill-defined advertising philosophy will cause the editorial staff to self-censor material. In other cases, it causes advertisers to pull out because their perception of the magazine is different from the editors' vision.

Arthritis Today rejects advertisements for products with unproven claims. "The best interest of our members and readers always come first," says William M. Otto, group vice president, publications, of the Arthritis Foundation, publisher of the magazine.[14]

Good Housekeeping has turned down ads for handguns designed for women, editor-in-chief Ellen Levine says, because they did not suit the magazine's philosophy. The magazine was also one of many to refuse a Shake 'n Bake ad that would have placed a chicken leg in the middle of a page, wrapped by copy; the resulting design would have served the advertiser but not the reader. The reader would have to try to navigate around an odd invasion of the page, while the advertiser would benefit because the reader's eye would have to keep going back to the product. The magazine even lost the Campbell's soup account in 1997 because food editors used too little creamed soup in the recipes they published. "It's an on-going dance," Levine says.[15]

Harper's has also battled friction between the magazine's editorial and advertising interests. In 1992, former section editor Alexandra Ringe criticized a system in which, she said, the editorial staff tiptoed around advertiser interests: "I found that we were censoring ourselves before advertisers were even shown something that might be objectionable."[16] Writer Allan Gurganus, who has won a National Magazine Award for work published in *Harper's*, alleged in 1997 that Lapham refused to print his story, "30 Dildos," because of concerns the title would offend advertisers. Lapham said advertisers were not the issue. "I thought it would put readers off the story," he said of the title. "It was offensive."

Lapham acknowledged that the magazine has had dissatisfied advertisers. "But," he said, "it's after the fact, not beforehand."[17]

In 1913, The *Merchants' and Manufacturers' Journal* of Baltimore published an essay by Condé Nast, founder of the publishing house

If she were stuck
on a desert island and
could choose only one
magazine to read,
Fleur Cowles, founding
editor of *Flair*, said,
"I'd start one."

that bears his name and publishes magazines such as *Vogue, Glamour, Vanity Fair,* and *Gourmet.* Nast clearly articulated the appeal to advertisers of what he called "Class Publications":

> *The exact value of any particular class publication to any given advertiser depends entirely on the accuracy with which it performs its duty of selecting possible buyers in his line, which, in turn, depends upon the degree of authority accorded the editorial side of the publication within its own class, and on the methods by which circulation is obtained. And in the judgment of this, each publication must, of course, rest entirely on its own merits.*[18]

ADVERTISING HYBRIDS. Advertising hybrids have complicated advertising-editorial dynamics, at the same time adding a boost to the magazine economy. One reason for the healthy growth in magazine advertising is the creative use of hybrid advertising forms such as advertorials, inserts, and outserts.

Advertorials. An **advertorial** combines articles and advertising in a magazine supplement sponsored entirely by the advertiser. Advertorials began regularly appearing in magazines in the 1970s, and have stirred up their own storm of controversy. At the outset, many were written and designed by magazine staff members, so readers could not tell where the magazine editorial ended and where the advertising began. In response, the American Society of Magazine Editors developed guidelines that require that advertorials be clearly labeled as advertising supplements and that their design be noticeably different from the design of the magazine. Advertorials can be as short as four pages and as long as 32. They are produced separately from the magazine, then bound in. Many look like miniature magazines; some even have covers.

Advertorials can be an important income stream, but how well do they serve the reader? Advertorials are neither inherently evil nor inherently good, but their use does require forethought. When dropped right in the middle of an article, they are intrusive. When placed between articles, they can blend with other editorial. More than one advertorial in an issue can seriously hurt the magazine's flow, no matter the location.

Advertorial content can actually serve the reader. Health advertorials can provide important supplementary information in a women's magazine; travel advertorials can offer service information for the readers of a general interest title.

Inserts. An **insert** is an ad created and produced by the advertiser; it comes to the magazine already printed and is then bound into the magazine. An insert is noticeable because it is often printed on different paper from the rest of the magazine: Nautica used a heavy card stock for an insert on its bicycling products that appeared in magazines such as *George.* An insert might even be a different shape: Marlboro used cutout images of products in its inserts for Marlboro Gear in a variety of magazines. Premiere Technologies offered readers of United Airlines's *Hemispheres* magazine a temporary telephone card—just tear it out at the perforations.

The omnipresent cologne ads with scented samples are usually inserts. Other inserts advertisers have used include computer CDs, holograms, pop-ups, and stand-alone booklets. In 1998, *Allure* and *Glamour* began including actual cosmetic samples with its ads—lipsticks, creams, and blushes from advertisers such as Estée Lauder and Revlon.

Outserts. An **outsert** is a preprinted publication that contains advertising and may also include editorial material. An outsert differs from an insert in that it is not bound into the magazine. It is mailed to subscribers with the magazine, the two being contained inside a shrink-wrap. Some outserts are also included in shrink-wrap in newsstand copies, but that causes an obvious problem: Readers cannot then browse through the magazine.

Trade magazines use outserts to mail readers information on trade shows sponsored by the magazine, travel titles use them for special tours, and women's magazines use them for beauty or health material.

Voice

A magazine's identity is most easily defined by its voice, that is, the tone and tenor of articles and graphics. A magazine with a well-defined voice not only offers the reader consistency and imagination, it also gives advertisers the opportunity to develop unique ads to match the magazine's voice.

THIN MAY STILL BE "IN," BUT SIZES 12, 14, 16, AND 18 ARE IN THE *MODE*

When *Mode* premiered in March 1997, the millions of American women who wear size 12 and up clothes finally had a magazine just for them. Finally, the full-figured woman with generous cleavage and curving hips could open a slick, glossy fashion magazine and find clothes in her size that would look good on her body. Finally, a fashion magazine with no diet tips and no exercise sermons.

Founders Nancy Nadler LeWinter and Julie Lewit-Nirenberg said they listened to focus groups, held meetings, and had "between us girls" conversations across the country to see if the timing was right for *Mode.* Obviously it was.

According to *Women's Wear Daily,* the average woman is a size 14, and approximately half of all American women, some 65 million, wear a size 12 or larger. Clothing size 14 and up represents $20 billion in yearly fashion sales.[1] Once relegated to fashion's back room, the large-size clothes market is no longer dowdy or drab. According to *Mode*'s research, only 200 retail outlets catered exclusively to the large-size market in 1990; today more than 2,000 do.[2] Plus, high-fashion designers—such as Liz Claiborne, Carole Little, Emanuel Ungaro, Jones New York, Halston, Harve Bernard, and Givenchy—are now making clothes for full figures as well as skinny sizes 4, 6, and 8.

"What inspired us to do this was there were 60 million women out there without a fashion magazine to serve their needs," said Lewit-Nirenberg, who was founding publisher of *Mirabella* and most recently publisher of *Mademoiselle.* "We wanted to literally do a fashion and beauty magazine that was not size-specific," added LeWinter, who directed the launch of the American *Marie Claire* and was former publishing director of *Esquire.*[3]

Focus groups "told us they wanted to see gorgeous clothes on gorgeous models that inspire them, motivate them, and make them feel good about themselves," said LeWinter. "What makes them feel good is finding themselves

Lafavore says the voice of *Men's Health* is of the "wise guy buddy who knows everything." The August 1997 issue features a man with washboard abs and a cover line offering the reader "Amazing Abs: How This Guy Did It," with a red arrow pointing to the model. Inside, the article starts with an off-the-cuff conversation: "Hey, pal, how'd you get those abdominal muscles?" It gives an easy-to-follow plan for how the cover model—whose last name was actually Guy—built his body.

Don Peschke of *Woodsmith* invented a "little old woodworker named Don" as the voice of his magazine. All articles in *Woodsmith* are in first person and are from the point of view of this idealized Don. When readers visit the magazine, as they often do, they come asking for Don. When the magazine was in its infancy in the 1980s, visitors were met by the thirty-something Peschke and were a tad bewildered. Where was that old man who spoke so convincingly about woodworking?

Jay Walljasper, editor-at-large of *Utne Reader,* says the magazine speaks with a "contrarian voice" and has a "set of values as well as a gadfly role," which means it challenges authority but within responsible bounds. In 1996, the magazine was redesigned and the tone was changed to what Walljasper saw as being "gadfly for gadfly's sake." The Summer 1996 issue ran a cover line on "The Familiar Face of Fascism" with a foil insert for the reader to see his own reflection. "That wasn't us," Walljasper says. Readers hated the redesign and the magazine has since returned to its original contrarian tone.

EDITORIAL FORMULA

The **editorial formula** ties all the elements of a magazine together, logically and coherently, in a readable, usable package. It is the practical application of the editorial philosophy, and it offers a blueprint for each issue of the magazine. It defines the type of content staff members will use in implementing the editorial philosophy. The editorial formula also details the specific subjects with which the magazine will deal and defines how much emphasis will be given to each subject. Like the philosophy, the formula should be written down and should be highly detailed and specific.

reflected on the newsstand as fashion-savvy, not size-obsessed."[4]

As stated on the debut cover, "Style Beyond Size" is the driving force behind *Mode.* Editorial copy is upbeat and, as promised, all articles and advertisements eschew the thin, the teensy, and the taut of body. Bette Midler, Rosie O'Donnell, Aretha Franklin, Whoopi Goldberg, and Kathy Bates are a few of the celebrities highlighted. Even the models in the ads and editorial copy affirm the magazine's fuller-is-in foundation. All clothing featured and all models are size 12 and up.

Mode carried 75 ad pages in its 168-page premiere issue, a rousing show of support from a Madison Avenue that long has been hung up on the young, the beautiful, and the emaciated. Yet *Mode*'s circulation leaped from 250,000 to more than 1 million in a single year, according to editor Michele Weston when she appeared on NBC's "Today" show on April 15, 1998 with sleek, yet full-figured, clothing styles.

Such enthusiastic acceptance was not the experience of *Big Beautiful Woman,* which folded in 1998 after 19 years in the market. *Radiance: The Magazine for Large Women* has published since 1984, but has a circulation of just 16,000. Neither magazine convinced big-name advertisers of the market's viability or made much of a splash in the fashion magazine pool. *Mode,* however, is going along just swimmingly.

[1] Robin Givhan, "Magazine Living Large," *San Antonio Express-News* (April 3, 1997): 1F.

[2] "Delta Burke Proud to Be a Weighty Role Model," *San Antonio Express-News* (March 30, 1997): 8G.

[3] Givhan, 10F.

[4] Lorraine Calvacca, "Living Large à la *Mode,*" *Folio:* (May 1, 1997): 27–28.

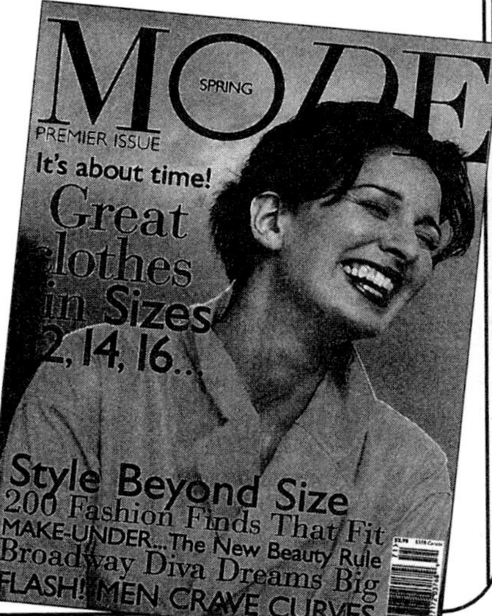

MARCH 1997 (PREMIERE ISSUE): *Mode* celebrates—in editorial as well as in advertising—the fact that many American women wear clothes larger than a size 10.

Questions editors ask when planning a formula are: How many pages will the magazine typically be? What is the advertising-to-editorial ratio? How many continuing departments will the magazine have? What will they be? How long will department stories be? How many feature-length articles will the magazine have? What types of articles will they be? How long will they be? Will the magazine include fiction? Poetry? Photo essays? Any other special content? How will this content be organized?

Developing an editorial formula is as simple as it is vital. A worksheet for an editorial formula typically contains the following information:

- Number of total pages;
- Number of pages of advertising;
- Number of pages of editorial, including cover, masthead, and table of contents;
- Number, if any, of pages of continuing departments;
- Number of feature pages;
- Breakdown of feature material, including types of articles, the number of each type, and their length;
- Names of continuing departments, plus a description of what each department will cover, how many articles may be included and their length;
- Placement of content.

Advertising and Editorial Pages

The successful magazine staff determines in advance how many pages it will target for advertising and how many for editorial. This is stated in terms of the advertising-editorial ratio as well as the total number of pages. An advertising-editorial ratio of 60:40 means a magazine has 60 pages of advertising for every 40 pages of editorial. If that magazine has 100 pages, 60 contain advertising and 40 contain editorial. If it has 120 pages, 72 are advertising and 48 are editorial.

The magazine staff must determine how many pages it can reasonably sell to advertisers and how many pages it needs for the level of content it has planned. The ideal ratio and number of pages usually is the result of trial and error and reaches a balance after a magazine has been published for several years.

Details was a trendy Manhattan nightlife magazine for both sexes when it was repositioned by Condé Nast Publications in 1990 as a young men's (under 35) fashion periodical.

The best advice when starting a new magazine is to study the competition. What is the audience size of the closest possible competitor? How similar is the new magazine to that competitor? How different? What are the competition's ad and circulation rates, number of ads run, number of pages, and advertising-editorial ratio?

Competition includes magazines, newspapers, and broadcast programs that reach the new magazine's target audience as well as other media that cover the same type of content. The television show "Entertainment Tonight" preceded *Entertainment Weekly* and demonstrated that regular coverage of TV, music, and film news would appeal to advertisers. Personal finance columns ran in newspapers nationwide before the launches of *Worth* and *Family Money*, and advertisers sought placement on those pages because of their appeal to a select audience.

What advertisers are missing from the competition that could be lured to a new magazine? Could this new magazine reach a larger audience? Or a smaller audience with more targeted information? *Time* and *Newsweek* have long covered financial issues for a middle-class audience but not with the detail provided by *Family Money*.

Media that successfully serve the target audience will also appeal to the same advertisers, whether or not the content is at all similar. Kellogg's traditionally advertised heavily on family-oriented television programming, so it was no surprise that they would be drawn to *Family Life* as well.

Look at what is already being done and compare this to what a new magazine could do. More important, look at what is not being done and imagine what gaps a new magazine could fill. *Spin* was launched to compete against *Rolling Stone*; *Vibe* was launched to compete against *Details* and *Rolling Stone* and to provide a unique black focus.

Editors often start magazines because they are frustrated readers: No existing magazine serves a specific need they have. Gloria Steinem and Patricia Carbine saw no magazine doing what they envisioned *Ms.* could do, so they started one.

Departments

Departments offer consistency to readers by providing shorter articles, essays, and columns that offer updates, details, and perspectives on a wide variety of predetermined issues. These are grouped together under one common topic area so that an individual department may have a single article or as many as several dozen. These whet the reader's appetite for the longer features, and they also satisfy the need for a broad range of topics. The staff knows exactly what departments it must fill every issue, and the readers know which to expect. Well-planned and executed departments are often the easiest way for a magazine to maintain consistency.

Early American magazines had few, if any departments. *Scribner's*, *The Century*, and *McClure's* simply began each issue with one long feature and followed that with another long feature, consistent with their book-like approach. Articles then looked like chapters in a book.

Changing reader habits as well as the move toward specialized titles and more service journalism led to the growth of department articles beginning in the 1960s. Partially to compete with television, magazines began offering shorter articles. At the same time, specialized titles began finding that the short pieces brought readers quickly into the book and allowed the staff to add late-breaking information. Service-related departments—quick recipes, hobby tips, shopping guides—earned high reader appeal. Departments are now a staple in most magazines.

The first question to ask when planning the editorial formula is: Do departments belong in the magazine? What kinds of departments fit the magazine's editorial philosophy and fill the needs of its audience? Not all have to appear in every issue, but a consistent group of departments should regularly appear. News magazines, for example, are highly departmentalized around broad topics such as "Politics," "The Arts," and "Business." One issue may have no articles on business, while another issue may have three. Throughout the span of a year, however, the business department appears in a majority of the issues.

The second question is: What kinds of content will these short articles regularly cover? Some departments are built entirely of service articles, others of essays, and still others have a mix of article types. Department titles should give an immediate indication of what's included in that section. Cute, evasive titles such as "Dimensions" and "Frames" are an indication of an ill-conceived department. What is a *dimension* and what will the audience gain from reading about one? To-the-point names, such as *People*'s "Picks and Pans," are meaningful and, therefore, successful. There's no confusion in the reader's mind about what to expect on those pages: a series of reviews on current music, movies, books, and television shows. Department names should be the same from issue to issue and the length of department pieces should be consistent.

The third question is: What will be the length of department articles? They can be snippets of fewer than 50 words, or longer pieces that take up a whole page. Typically, department articles are shorter than 500 words. Often, one department includes a range of lengths: perhaps two pieces under 50 words, three at between 150 and 200 words, and one at 500 to 600 words. This range, however, should be consistent.

"Picks and Pans" pieces are consistently between 150 and 200 words each, with five to eight items, plus illustrations, taking up a page. *Men's Health*'s "Malegrams" department, by contrast, contains a lively mix of articles from under 100 words to more than 1,000, with some pages consisting of only one article, others being composed of eight to ten articles.

Features

Features are the bread and butter of a magazine, the content readers take time to sink their teeth into. The features in any given issue connect logically as well as aesthetically and emotionally. Over time, those features create the backbone of the magazine.

Planning for features often begins one to two years before publication. Editors look for topical issues but offer the writers enough time for planning, research, and development.

Features provide spark to a magazine by the diversity of their content and length. Some magazines plan, for example, for one major service article, one profile, and two general features. Others go for one long feature—3,000 to 5,000 words—surrounded by smaller features at 1,000 to 1,200 words.

Features have shrunk in word length throughout the past century and now average fewer than 2,000 words. They range, however from 1,000 to more than 10,000 words. The longest magazine features are typically 5,000 to 8,000 words, but a few magazines—*Rolling Stone, The New Yorker, Esquire,* and *Sports Illustrated*—have features that may exceed 10,000 words.

Some other examples:

Broadcast Technology: Under 1,500
Beer Across America: Under 2,000
Cosmopolitan: Under 3,500
Modern Drummer: 5,000 to 8,000
Nurseweek: Under 2,500
Sports Afield: Under 2,500

Children's magazines, not surprisingly, have short features:

Jack and Jill: 300 to 500
Highlights for Children: Maximum 900
Ranger Rick: Maximum 900
Sports Illustrated for Kids: Maximum 1,000

For a start-up, the essential questions are: What kinds of feature articles will be included? What kind of content will full-length articles cover? How does the magazine define a full-length article? The formula for features should be specific enough to offer the reader—and the staff—some direction but broad enough to give everybody some room to move around.

Placement of Content

There's no one "right" way to organize all this material as long as it follows a plan. Some magazines are entirely departmentalized, some have a mix of departments and features, and some combine department articles and features on similar topics into regular sections.

Think of the magazine structure as a house. The cover is the front door, the departments are the hallways, and the features are the bigger rooms. You want that front door to look inviting enough for the reader to walk in. Once in, you want her to be delighted and intrigued by what is elsewhere in the house. Then you want her to roam from room to room easily, following her own pace, being satisfied by what she finds, and curious about what is ahead. Perhaps she will go through one room twice, to study it better, because she finds it especially appealing.

Just as the interior design of a house makes it comfortable and reflective of the owner's

HARPER'S FORMULA: A TOOL OF SUCCESS

A significant part of the successful repositioning of *Harper's* is a direct result of retooling the magazine's formula. Regular departments of the magazine include "Index," "Readings," "Annotation," "Forum," and "Story." Each of these elements has a clearly articulated goal and consistent design and placement:

- The "Index" is a list of current statistics, juxtaposed against other statistics to give a quick glimpse of contemporary culture:[1]

  Number of products O. J. Simpson plans to market under his six trademarks: 463

  Number of films to be released by the end of the year in which Larry King plays himself: 8

  Ratio of The Lost World to Jurassic Park *in the amount of screen time devoted to dinosaurs eating people: 7:11*

  Lapham calls this a "plumb line" built on "our American faith in numerical measurement."[2] The "Index" is one full page in each issue, and its design is identical from issue to issue: One full page, type only, copy centered on the page, topped with an all-caps, no-nonsense headline: "*Harper's* Index."

- "Readings" are miscellaneous gleanings from such diverse sources as the Target Corporation's training manual, Dan Quayle's Christmas cards when he was vice president, transcripts from discussions in Bill Clinton's White House, Web sites, personal letters, and, of course, books and other magazines. "Readings" take up 16 to 18 pages per issue. They run in a continuous two-column flow, with an italicized introduction and with identical type treatment for headlines of each separate article. Interspersed through the department are quirky art photos and illustrations, which stand on their own as content, unrelated to the articles.
- "Forum" is a feature-length conversation the magazine tapes between people on various sides of a

personality, so too should the design of the magazine make the reader's stroll through its pages easy and pleasurable. You want a visitor to your house to sit down every now and then and just look around, perhaps at the paintings you've hung, the color of the walls, the heights of your ceilings, the shapes of your windows, and the view outside. You want her to know, just by looking around, whose house she is visiting. You want her to be comfortable, and you want her to know she's welcome.

A good magazine host plans for a smooth and comfortable pacing from article to article. A short article after a longer article gently encourages the reader to keep reading. A design with consistent signposts tells her when one department ends and another begins and helps the reader follow the articles from page to page. Editorial jumps—in which an article continues from the middle of the magazine to the end—are like serving a guest coffee in the kitchen and telling her to go through the bathroom, down the basement stairs, through the laundry room, and out the back door if she wants cream and sugar. That cream and sugar better be mighty good for her to make that trek.

Departments are usually placed either in the front of the book (FOB) or the back of the book (BOB). Advertising is often sold for placement in specific departments. In other cases, it is sold to be placed anywhere in the front or back, with ad contracts, then, requesting FOB or BOB placement. Those few advertisers with no preference simply ask for a run-of-the-book (ROB) placement.

Many departments have both advertising and editorial material on a single page. These pages, called "A and E" for advertising and editorial, may change from day to day during the final stages of a magazine's production, as editorial pages are dropped to make room for advertising or added to replace ads that don't materialize.

Features are usually structured according to **wells,** or blocks of editorial material unbroken by advertising. A **monowell** structure means that all feature material is placed together, usually in the center of the magazine, and all ads are either in the front or back of the book. American magazines used this structure when advertising first began appearing after the Civil War, keeping an obvious separation between advertising and contemporary issue. In the December 1997 issue, the topic was women in business; the eight participants included two businesswomen, a feminist theorist, a political essayist, a sociologist, and a *Harper's* editor. According to participants, women in business are winning, losing, controlling, being controlled, being marginalized, and calling the shots. Which perspective is closest to reality? You figure it out, say the editors. Intended to give enough time and space for the topic to be discussed thoroughly, "Forum" is usually eight to ten pages long. Although it is a regular feature, it does not appear in every issue.

- "Annotation" is a double-page spread with photos and annotated text putting the illustrated material into contemporary context. In December 1995, the magazine ran "Out of the Closet, And Into Never-Never Land" about gay magazines that, the writers maintained, trivialized the politics they were purporting to cover in colorful and glossy publications that serve more as marketing vehicles than as serious perspectives on issues. The spread featured the cover of *Out* magazine connected with arrows to editorial comments on the magazine's sanitized version of gay life and emphasis on celebrities. The "Annotation," while regular, is not offered in every issue. The photo of the subject to be discussed takes up the majority of the spread, with paragraphs of commentary placed around the edges of the illustration. It looks a bit like the illustrations in your car's owner's manual that point to individual parts of your dashboard and tell you which switch does what.
- "Story" covers the short fiction for which the magazine has historically been known. Stories range from 10 to 15 pages in length.
- Other regular elements include "Letters" (two to four pages), "Notebook" (Lapham's essay, two to five pages), "Acrostic" (a full page), and "Puzzle" (a full page).
- Advertising. Each magazine ranges from 88 to 100 pages, including the covers. The inside front cover, inside back cover, and back cover—called by advertisers the second, third and fourth covers—have full-color ads. Average advertising-to-editorial ratio in 1997 was 35:65.

[1] "*Harper's* Index," *Harper's* (August 1997): 13.

[2] Ibid., 8.

editorial material. *National Geographic* has a monowell structure.

More common is a **multi-well** structure, in which editorial material remains unbroken in smaller wells throughout the magazine. Advertising appears between wells. This maintains the integrity of the editorial material while allowing advertising to be placed in the middle of the publication. *Saveur, Harper's,* and *The Atlantic Monthly* use a multiwell structure. Some magazines, such as *Cosmopolitan,* modify the multiwell approach by adding jumps to longer pieces.

AUDIENCE

Before a magazine is published, the editors have to define the way in which the magazine's content is geared to the needs, interests, and motivations of its audience.

Although advertising is sold based on a clear delineation of reader demographics and psychographics, much editorial material is created based on the editors' inherent understanding of their audience. This understanding goes far deeper than the numbers created by the research department; it derives from a savvy editor's gut feeling.

In many cases, the editor *is* the reader, and the magazine is aimed at the editor's tastes, which often mesh nicely with the tastes of the larger audience. "I am the reader," *Men's Health* Lafavore says. He's a maturing baby boomer, and, like others in his generation, is "inner-directed and interested in self-improvement."

The Russian version of *Men's Health* takes a different approach from its American counterpart because its audience lives in a significantly different culture. Russian editor Ilya Bezugly says the magazine deals with topics unique to the Russian audience, such as that country's problems with alcoholism and drug abuse. "*Men's Health* in the United States seldom covers these subjects. The editors there figure that if a man is buying their magazine, he cares enough about his health not to be an alcoholic or drug addict," Bezugly says. "But we know we have big problems in this area, and we will try to be a positive influence on young men."[19]

As new audiences develop, astute magazines find ways to speak to those audiences. The alternative politics of the late 1960s and early

CATCH THEM ON THE FLY

Editor Jim Butler tries to be polite when readers mock the title of his magazine: *Fly Rod & Reel.* Naysayers note with glee that this title demonstrates the narrowness of topics in current magazines. Yuk, yuk, there's even a magazine for fly-fishing, they chuckle. Go ahead and joke, Butler says, but our readers are dedicated to their sport and to the magazine. The magazine is a hit with readers and with advertisers, so Butler can take the teasing. He's doing what successful editors are doing throughout the country: serving his audience. His 54,000 readers boast an average household income of $106,000, and advertisers of fly fishing products take the magazine very seriously.

The magazine's editorial philosophy:

Fly Rod & Reel offers readers a fresh, unique look at fly-fishing, capturing the essence of the sport through the finest writing, photography and design in the field. It looks at exciting fishing destinations near and far, the fine tackle anglers love to own and use, the latest, most effective fly-fishing techniques and the health of the environment on which the sport depends, giving readers a view of the sport provided by no other magazine.

Fly Rod & Reel covers the how of the sport, but the emphasis is on the why; it examines everything that's appealing about casting flies for whatever fish will take them.

Butler is an active part of his audience. When he applied for his first position on the magazine, he had to take a test: He had to prove to the publisher that he could cast a fly.

JANUARY/FEBRUARY 1999: *Fly Rod & Reel* covers the how and the why of the sport of fly-fishing.

1970s brought magazines for those movements: *Mother Earth News, Rolling Stone,* and *Ms.* The growth of magazines for "Generation X" readers in the 1990s has been a response to the same type of audience growth. *Details, Bikini, Wired, Vibe,* and a host of national, regional, and local magazines began to hit the newsstands in the early 1990s, aimed at Americans born from 1961 to 1981. In 1994, James Truman, *Details* editor-in-chief, said his readers, like him, were "tremendously cynical because they know the media is most often talking to them to sell them something."[20] In 1993, *Advertising Age* named *Details* "Magazine of the Year," saying it had "established itself as the leading vehicle to reach Generation X."[21]

The survival of Generation X magazines is dependent on the vitality of the audience, which could mature and buy houses in the suburbs at any time. This happened to the audiences of several noteworthy 1960s and 1970s starts, including *Rolling Stone* and *Mother Earth News.*

Better Homes and Gardens looks little like the original *Fruit Garden and Home* of 1922, just as today's high-tech refrigerators have little resemblance to the "ice making refrigerators" introduced in the magazine in July 1925. (See the "Magazine Voices" piece by Jean LemMon at the back of the book for more on the changes in *Better Homes and Gardens* in its first 75 years.) Its longevity is a result of the magazine's ability to change with the times. In April 1997, editor Jean LemMon introduced readers to Myrtle Surendonk, who had subscribed to the magazine without interruption since April 1926, four years into the fledgling publication. LemMon visited Surendonk and wrote of the meeting:

> *I could tell by the look in Myrtle's eyes that, in the brief moment before she answered my questions, her memory flitted back over all the years in her home, the raising of her family, the good times and the bad. And I was enormously proud to be there as a new friend and as the editor of the magazine that's been her old friend for 71 years.*

AUGUST 1950: *Flair* magazine pulled out all the production stops available during its brief life; these horizontal half pages allow the reader to match different skirts and tops.

ANATOMY OF A FAILURE

Flair magazine is one of the most popular failures in American history and provides an excellent case history of the importance of editorial philosophy, formula, and audience. *Flair* lasted only 12 issues, from February 1950 to January 1951. Nearly 50 years later, in 1997, *Flair*'s editor Fleur Cowles published a collection of the magazine's most popular features in a $250 book titled *The Best of* Flair. The book sold out and went to a second printing. Fleur, *Flair,* and the book were the topic of articles in 1997 in *Print, Vanity Fair, Mirabella,* and newspapers throughout the country.

Flair was a design innovator, boasting production tricks that would make today's publishers quiver: vertical and horizontal half-pages, a variety of paper stocks, die-cut covers, accordion inserts, and fold-outs. Publisher Gardner (Mike) Cowles—who was married to Fleur at the time—also published the then-successful mass circulation *Look.* Mike said he suspended publication of *Flair* because of high production costs. Fleur Cowles blamed the death additionally on poor marketing techniques.[22]

Flair took a bewildering planning route, with regular changes in concept. In September 1948, Mike Cowles spoke of creating a "new man's magazine" that would combine various elements of *Esquire, Field & Stream, Outdoor Life,* and *Holiday.* He offered Arnold Gingrich, founding editor of *Esquire,* the opportunity to work with Cowles Publishing to start such a magazine. However, Gingrich said Mike Cowles lured him to work on a "left-wing Republican magazine" and that Fleur "flanked us by turning it into what was commonly regarded as a pansy's home journal."[23]

In the early stages, content included cuisine, which was later dropped and replaced with literature. Humor was included at one point, and theater drifted in and out as a content category. Consistent throughout was an emphasis on the arts, fashion, and "decoration." [24]

Planning for design was more clearly articulated than planning for editorial content. A memo dated April 1, 1949, called the magazine a "large and luxurious publication of distinctive format." Moreover, it added, because the magazine "is itself a thing of beauty, it furnishes in its each appearance its own excuse for being."

The first issue of *Flair* was published in February 1950. In it, Fleur Cowles used a handwritten note to explain the magazine to readers. Her plan emphasized variety and graphic experimentation rather than editorial information:

> *There have been great adventures in paper and in printing and in the presentation of the graphic arts in the last decade . . . unhappily, few of them for the public at large. I have longed to introduce a magazine daring enough to utilize the best of these adventures. A magazine which combines, for the first time under one set of covers, the best in the arts: literature, fashion, humor, decoration, travel and entertainment.*
>
> *This copy of* Flair *shows that it can be done; it is proof that a magazine need no longer be stolidly frozen to the familiar format.* Flair *can, and will, vary from issue to issue, from year to year, assuring you that most delicious of all rewards—a sense of surprise, a joy of discovery. For the young in heart, men and women, I believe our efforts will help give a vital contemporary direction and fullness to American life.* [25]

When *Flair* folded, *Time* magazine noted that "journalists (no doubt including Mike Cowles) knew the real trouble: In striving valiantly for the unusual, *Flair* had too little old-fashioned journalistic flair itself." [26] *Newsweek* said the magazine was "perhaps more famous for the hole in its cover than its contents."[27]

Geared to a sophisticated audience interested in the arts, fashion, and travel, *Flair* was positioned against 10 magazines aiming at the same audience: *House and Garden, House Beautiful, Vogue, Harper's Bazaar, Holiday, The New Yorker, The Atlantic Monthly, Harper's, Saturday Review of Literature,* and *Town & Country*. An April 1, 1949, planning paper discussed the hazards of too close a resemblance to these magazines and suggested humor as a point of difference. Humor, the paper noted, was "completely lacking in all magazines in this field"—an odd comment that ignored the highly developed humor for which *The New Yorker* was justifiably famous.

The Cowles projected a circulation of 200,000, but the debut issue had only 31,000 subscribers.[28] By the end of the year, this had grown to only 90,000.[29] The magazine sold 245,000 copies at its peak.[30] By the end of 1950, according to Mike Cowles, losses before taxes were roughly $2,485,000, a loss of nearly 75 cents per copy sold.[31]

Flair contained advertising for upscale products such as diamonds, minks, and designer clothing, but the magazine did not see eye-to-eye with advertisers. Fleur Cowles requested custom-designed ads "in keeping with *Flair*'s content," but ad agencies saw too little profit in creating ads for only one magazine. Agencies avoided the magazine, she said, because it was "too new in format to be judged by any but the trail-blazers."[32]

The Cowles's plan was to market the magazine using direct mail to "carefully selected lists," which would include book club subscribers, club women, career women, professionals, and college graduates. The results of tests to such readers were successful, especially from purchasers of "quality," or high-priced, items.

Fleur suggested a cover price of 60 cents, setting the magazine apart from the competitors, which were still selling for 50 cents. She said the magazine needed a select direct-mail readership and a higher selling price. Ultimately, though, the magazine was primarily marketed through the same mass market newsstands used by its sister publication, *Look*, and was sold for the standard 50 cents.

Not only was it unclear what *Flair* was to be, it was unclear why it was to be. The two major managers, Fleur and Mike Cowles, presented both conflicting and inconsistent messages about the magazine they were planning and producing. The third manager, Arnold Gingrich, seems to have been shut out of the editorial process despite his success as a founding editor of *Esquire*.

The success of *Flair* depended on Mike Cowles's understanding of magazine publishing and Fleur Cowles's understanding of the luxury market. Mike Cowles's only regret seemed to be in starting the magazine in the first place. He said he doubted he would have done so if Fleur "hadn't been such a persuasive saleswoman." He said he was reluctant to publish the magazine because neither he nor Fleur had experience in producing a luxury magazine. His final assessment: "I'm sure I should never have started publishing *Flair*."[33]

In her memoirs, Fleur Cowles reflected on the failure of the magazine: "The money *Flair* lost will probably never again be available on the same basis. It was put into my hands by Mike Cowles to prove that artistic effort can be commercial—which for good or bad reasons it wasn't and may never be." She contended that the magazine was marketed poorly: "No magazine was ever sold by such mistaken methods." *Flair*, she said, was "born to the right parents but reared by the wrong nannies."[34]

LAUNCHES AND LIFE CYCLES

Magazine analysts say that a magazine has a chance of long-term success if it can last at least three years. The figures on how many magazines last that long are a bit blurred, because magazines are launched with great fanfare but often die quiet deaths. The field is so risky that the Small Business Administration bylaws prohibit loans for publishing.

Magazines are generally launched in three ways: on the newsstand, by subscription, or a combination of the two.

Newsstand launches can be an easy tool for large publishers. *People* was launched by Time Inc. on the newsstand and remains a strong newsstand title. When a publication does well in newsstand sales, as was the case with Meredith Publishing's *Country Home* and *Traditional Home*, it also may be launched as a subscription title. Large publishers have the distribution system already in place and have previously developed relationships with wholesalers and retailers, allowing their titles to get placement on the newsstand. Smaller or new publishers, however, have no such benefit and are well advised not to depend only on newsstand distribution.

When he was National Geographic Society president and editor, Alexander Graham Bell hoped to increase newsstand sales of *National Geographic* in 1898, 10 years after its launch. He had no luck. The magazine's legendary success came when Bell hired Gilbert Hovey Grosvenor, who revamped the magazine, added photographs, and made it an appealing perk of membership in the society.

Subscription launches offer some interesting benefits available only to magazines. Publishers can ask for payment before a reader even sees the publication, giving the publisher upfront funds for expenses. The costs of subscription launches can be daunting, however, because they often include buying a mailing list and producing and mailing an expensive brochure. Again, large publishers have the advantage because they have the operating capital.

But even the giants were once small and had to start somewhere. Innovation, in fact, is often the entrepreneur's advantage. When John Shuttleworth started *The Mother Earth News* in 1970, he knew where his readers might be—at anti-Vietnam War rallies. He headed to the rallies himself and gave away free magazines with subscription cards included. Sure enough, he ended up adding to his readership. Not satisfied with that, he wrote to other magazines offering a free ad in his magazine in exchange for a free ad in theirs. This was at a time when he had fewer than 1,000 readers. Jann Wenner of *Rolling Stone* took Shuttleworth up on the offer, ran a free ad for *The Mother Earth News* in *Rolling Stone*, and gave the magazine a needed boost in subscriptions.

Stephen Osborne and Mike Bradley left full-time jobs in advertising sales at Cahners Publishing, put their life savings on the line, and took on second mortgages to launch *Pharmaceutical & Medical Packaging News* through controlled circulation. Approaching the market with the entrepreneur's unique vision, they saw that most medical and pharmaceutical titles were highly vertical—either narrowly dealing with medical

OCTOBER 1998: *Pharmaceutical & Medical Packaging News*, a controlled circulation trade magazine, was launched in 1993 to cover medical as well as pharmaceutical issues.

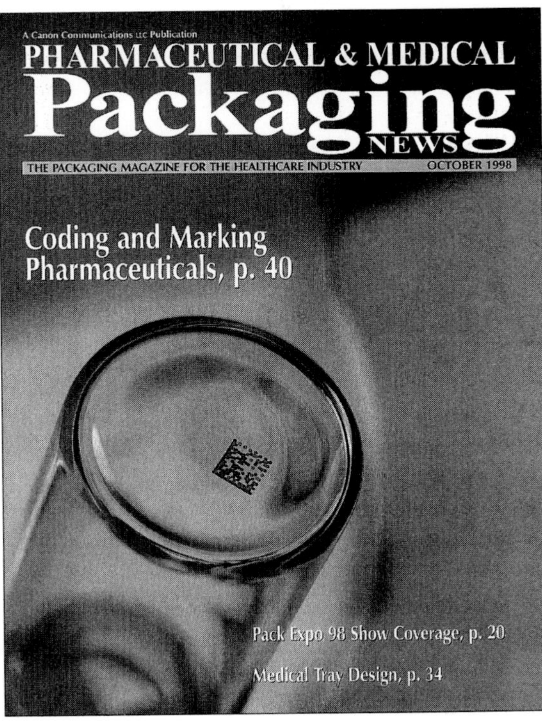

issues or narrowly dealing with pharmaceutical issues. The men decided to go "diagonal" and combine the two fields. Launched in 1993, the publication was in the black within two years, with 1995 ad revenue exceeding $1 million.[35]

The launch is just the first step; if a magazine is to keep walking, it needs to keep putting one foot in front of the other with a targeted publishing strategy. The life cycle of a magazine depends on editors who keep aware of readers' needs and social trends and who can fine-tune the magazine to deal with the vagaries of markets and social momentum.

The conditions that precede and follow a magazine's start-up—that is, the social context in which magazines operate—are important determinants of a magazine's success. Likewise, as the audience changes, the magazine must respond to that change.

How does a magazine respond to changes in society? How do such changes affect the nature of the magazine's audience as well as the nature of the magazine's content? And how do publishing realities—the necessity of making money—affect the magazine and its relationship with its audience?

A magazine and its audience develop through the same social history. Magazines have life cycles that are cyclical and unique to the magazines' relationships with their audiences. Not all magazines go through all steps of the life cycle. Some die early; some defy the odds and live on and on; some die and are restarted.

Nevertheless, looking at the patterns of a magazine's life as cyclical helps us make some sense of how a magazine and its audience change over time. The steps of this life cycle are:

- Emergence of the audience;
- Creation of the magazine;
- Growth and change;
- Refocus or death.

The Mother Earth News has gone through an entire life cycle, from birth to death; after death, it started a new cycle.

JANUARY 1970 (PREMIERE ISSUE): *The Mother Earth News* advocated a back-to-the-land philosophy in the early 1970s with practical articles for those who wanted a simple, rural life.

Emergence of the Audience

Before a magazine is started, the audience already exists. The founders of the magazine are usually members of this audience. John and Jane Shuttleworth, founding editors of *The Mother Earth News*, were self-sufficient Ohio farmers.

America was born as an agrarian nation, so in many ways *Mother*'s audience was as old as the country. *The Mother Earth News* emerged as the voice of the back-to-the-land movement of the 1970s. Other magazines were already serving small pockets of this audience by providing articles on living simple and self-sufficient lives on the land and showing respect for the environment: *Farm Journal, Vocations for Social Change, Popular Mechanics,* and *Motorhome Life.* Audience members profiled in the first issues of *The Mother Earth News* had left urban jobs for rural areas in the 1940s and 1950s—20 to 30 years before the magazine was born.

Creation of the Magazine

The creation of a magazine pulls these individuals together. The editor is closely connected with the magazine and with the audience.

The first issue of *The Mother Earth News* was published in January 1970. John Shuttleworth said he and his wife started the magazine armed

with several filing cabinets full of material "on people who have successfully walked away from the system and started living life on their own terms." The first issue was printed on newsprint and was type-heavy, with some black and white line drawings and photos. It sported a black and yellow cover with a drawing of a sun and the cover line, "a new beginning." The table of contents page introduced the magazine's tag line: "*The Mother Earth News* . . . it tells you how" and the magazine was promoted as showing readers "how to do more with less." The language throughout the magazine is representative of the 1970s counterculture, with words like "pad" and "groovy" used regularly. The magazine was referred to as "Mother," almost as though it were a person rather than a publication.

John Shuttleworth wrote to readers in a friendly-neighbor voice full of 1970s counterculture rhetoric. In May 1970 he penned a "Statement of Policy" to readers:

> *There are many paths to the Clear Light and we are all pilgrims. MOTHER exists only to present the HOW of alternate life styles not normally considered in our modern society. That's "lifestyles" not "style." Each individual must choose the way that is proper for him. We can only help to make a meaningful selection possible. Peace.*[36]

Readers began their connections with one another in the letters section of the second issue. Letters were answered in the magazine by "Mother" and readers were referred to as "Mother's children." One reader, writing in the third issue, May 1970, suggested a readers' convention. Several others asked for information on communes.

The magazine became so popular that Shuttleworth had to rein in readers who had begun to make pests of themselves. By the ninth issue, a year and a half after the magazine was started, Shuttleworth made a plea to readers indicating the popularity of the movement as well as his exhaustion and frustration with his role as the "Mother" of the movement:

> *Please! Folks, we love you . . . but please, please don't "just drop by"* Mother's *offices this summer expecting to find "a place on the floor" on which to spread your bedroll. We ain't got such a place.*

The magazine had not only solidified the audience, it had helped it become a family: connected, supportive and, occasionally, bickering. In December 1973, after one especially emotional debate about a letter defending "law-abiding hunters," *Mother* wrote in a parental voice: "For one final, last time . . . I think both sides are right and both sides are wrong on this argument and this is the last time—for now—that I want to see name-calling and finger-pointing."

Growth and Change

To grow, a magazine strives to reach a broader audience. As part of the process, the magazine may look more to advertising to help generate revenue. If not done with care, this makes the magazine less of a voice of the community it helped solidify because it may become more attuned to the needs of advertisers than to readers. At the same time, the success of the magazine leads to the development of other magazines with similar content to serve the audience. The founding editor or editors may leave the magazine, perhaps selling it.

By the sixth issue, November 1970, *The Mother Earth News* had grown to 124 pages; a year later it was regularly 132 pages. The masthead, which originally listed only the Shuttleworths and a few friends, expanded and listed the contributors alphabetically, so the Shuttleworths' names came at the end of the list. In 1975, the magazine's motto was changed to "More than a magazine—a way of life."

Early advertising in the magazine was black and white, consisting of homesteading books and organic products, often offered by people who were profiled in articles. At the beginning, Shuttleworth said he was trying to restrict advertising to 15 percent or less of every issue. Color ads started appearing in the magazine in 1975. Advertising increased gradually through the years, but editorial seriously outdistanced advertising. Ads were for home-based businesses, log cabins, seeds and gardening materials, and, occasionally, even Jack Daniel's whiskey.

The Mother Earth News agenda had seeped into the American consciousness by the late 1970s: *Better Homes and Gardens* ran articles on wood stoves and dome houses, and architects were designing high-cost, high-quality underground and solar homes. In 1978, Congress authorized a solar tax credit to encourage the

RESEARCH IN BRIEF

Teens Got *Sassy*, Advertisers Got Nervous

Sassy's concept was simple when it entered the teen magazine market in March of 1988: It would use more contemporary language and be more direct in issues such as sex than were the three dominant magazines in the market, *Seventeen, YM,* and *'Teen.* As Jane Pratt, the founding editor of *Sassy,* explained, "We'll talk to readers as peers rather than as some authority figure. . . . Teenagers will be told the truth, without euphemisms or apologies."[1]

Within six months of the magazine's start-up, circulation jumped from 250,000 to 400,000 paid subscribers. By October 1994, *Sassy's* circulation was more than 800,000. While a student at Trinity University in San Antonio, Texas, Debra Ceffalio studied *Sassy* from 1988 through 1996 to determine its impact on the teen magazine market.[2] Ceffalio points out the magazine quickly became a sensation because of its sexual frankness, breezy language, and unique relationship with its readers. Although *Time* magazine dismissed *Sassy's* editorial voice as "pajama-party journalism," teen readers appreciated the first-name relationship with writers Jane, Catherine, Karen, and Christina. Said editor Pratt (who, at 25, was only a few years older than her readers): "Other magazines have, like, a stereotypical or idealized vision of teenagers. Maybe what parents or teachers would like. Not really what teenagers are about, you know."[3]

Ceffalio's study of *Sassy* reveals an editorial staff closely in touch with its readers. For example, in September 1990, a reader wrote in wondering how a magazine that advised girls to "lighten up" about their body image could run an ad aimed at women who wanted sexier bodies. Pratt wrote that the editors really had no control over the advertising but that the ad also had made her stomach lurch. Ceffalio notes that an editorial response openly criticizing a published ad would not have been found in any of the more traditional teen magazines.

Sassy challenged the status quo that most teen magazines supported by running stories about "When We Were Depressed," "Nine Things about America That Make Us Want to Scream and Throw Stuff," and "And They're Gay," a sympathetic, accepting profile of two young lesbian couples. *Sassy* also dedicated 43 percent of its editorial content to lifestyle and general interest issues, such as an article on the Gulf War titled "The Iraq Thing," which ran in the February 1991 issue. With the subtitles "What Sadam is irked about" and "Why some Americans feel dissed enough to go to war," this article explained an important world event in the readers' own iconoclastic language.

The magazine's frank sex information set *Sassy* apart from its competitors, who, writes Ceffalio, tended to couch coverage of sexual issues in judgmental terms, if they wrote about sex at all. *Sassy* ran articles about the pros and cons of virginity, getting turned on and how to handle it, and "The Truth about Boys' Bodies." These topics got rave reactions from readers, but advertisers eventually weighed in with a thumbs down following a massive letter-writing campaign launched by two mothers from Wabash, Indiana, who were dismayed by the sexually candid articles. The campaign threatened to boycott the products of companies who continued to advertise in *Sassy.* By late 1988, at least nine major accounts, led by Levi's, Maybelline, and Cover Girl cosmetics, had pulled their ads from the magazine. To save itself, *Sassy* was forced to tone down its articles.

Ceffalio believes this marked the beginning of the end for *Sassy,* although the magazine kept its strong editorial position among teens as long as Jane Pratt remained at the helm. *Seventeen, YM,* and *'Teen* began copying ideas first seen in *Sassy*—using slang, including the personalities of the staff in editorial comments, having a less preachy approach to topics, and providing a clean look through design makeovers. But they did not emulate the emphasis on sex.

Pratt left *Sassy* in late 1994 after the magazine was sold to Petersen Publishing, owner of competitor *'Teen.* Trying to revive *Sassy,* which had experienced economic difficulties ever since the advertising boycott, Petersen hired a new staff to revamp the magazine in a more traditional fashion. This "new" *Sassy,* which debuted in August 1995, lacked the irreverent edge of its predecessor. Stated new editorial director Catherine Ettlinger, "We have underage girls reading this magazine. We are responsible. We are mainstream. We are not out to shock. We'll never be sassy gratuitously."[4]

Readers of the original *Sassy* quickly noticed the editorial difference, says

Ceffalio. In the January 1996 issue, *Sassy* published a page of letters from disgruntled readers pining for the "old" *Sassy.* "Without Jane Pratt and Co. this magazine is boring, repetitive and just like any other one on the shelf," one reader complained. Many readers expressed a feeling of abandonment: "You have sucked every ounce of what the 'old' *Sassy* stood for out of the magazine. This magazine contains nothing but superficial garbage that needs to be thrown away forever. How could you do this to us? We depended on *Sassy* month to month for advice, security and most of all, a good friend." Readers began canceling their subscriptions. In response to the barrage of negative letters, the new *Sassy* staff told readers, "Get over it! Get a clue! Get a life!" because "Jane's gone."

In a few months, even *Sassy* was gone. In December 1996, Petersen Publishing folded *Sassy* into *'Teen.* All that was left of the original *Sassy* was a 10-page section titled "*Sassy* Slant," offering the latest "hot bits on style, stars, gossip, bands and guys." Although the layout for this section was reminiscent of the original *Sassy,* the mixture of cheekiness, bravado, and vulnerability that resulted in the *Sassy* personality was missing. Then, in August 1997, a totally redesigned *Teen* (sans the apostrophe) hit the newsstands—with no evidence of *Sassy* to be found anywhere in its editorial pages.

Ceffalio's study highlights the fact that all teen magazines speak to an audience that is vulnerable. Teenage girls often are obsessed with beautiful bodies and boys and are plagued by stress, self-esteem problems, and eating disorders. *Sassy* proved that because teenagers look to magazines for support and friendship, establishing a bond of trust between the staff and readers can be a key to success. *Sassy* also demonstrated that young girls want to be treated as intelligent young women who are interested in a wider variety of topics than previously had been covered by teen magazines.

By becoming a friend to teenage girls, *Sassy* found a niche in what previously was considered a saturated market. Now that *Sassy* is dead, Ceffalio says *Seventeen, YM,* and *Teen* seem content to focus on celebrities, boys, beauty, and fashion rather than hard-edged issues such as suicide or sexual abuse. *Sassy*'s frank style of writing no longer is embraced by the three teen magazine leaders.

At least one recent teen magazine start-up, however, has aimed for *Sassy*'s editorial tone. *Jump,* in its September 1997 debut issue, emulated *Sassy*'s editorial page with a photo of and comments from its "all-girl staff of nine" who "moan about guys, groan about our bodies and whine about our bad hair and face days. I mean, girls will be girls. But when we get past all of the superficial stuff, what we really agonize over is staying true to ourselves." With a cover tag stating "for girls who dare to be real," *Jump* appears to be heir to *Sassy*'s mantle—at least for now.

As for Jane Pratt, she has her own magazine, *Jane,* which premiered in September 1997 to compete against *Cosmopolitan, Mademoiselle,* and *Glamour.* Now in her thirties, Pratt wants to do the same thing for women 18 to 34 that she did with *Sassy:* talk to them in an irreverent, edgy tone and make them feel good after reading the magazine.

[1] Geraldine Fabrikant, "Magazine to Pursue Teenagers," *The New York Times* (May 3, 1988): 4:26.

[2] Debra Ceffalio and Sammye Johnson, "Teenagers Get *Sassy* 1988–1993: A Case Study of the Teen Magazine Market," *Southwestern Mass Communication Journal* 13:2 (1998): 1–11.

[3] Suzanne Daley, "*Sassy,* Like, You Know, for Kids," *The New York Times* (April 11, 1988): 4:8.

[4] Mark Adams, "The Mainstreaming of *Sassy,*" *Mediaweek* (July 10, 1995): 18.

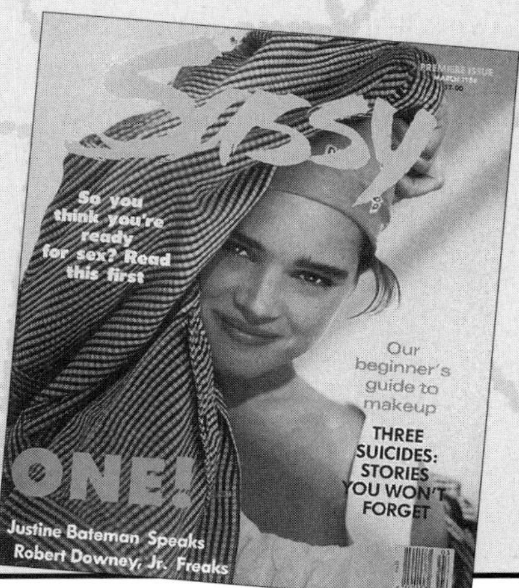

MARCH 1988 (PREMIERE ISSUE): *Sassy* blazed trails and, eventually, blazed out by talking to its teen readers as peers and by shunning euphemisms and apologies.

The Unidentified Flying Objects "field" is covered by at least five magazines, including *International UFO Reporter, UFO Files, UFO Magazine, UFO Universe Conspiracies and Cover-Ups,* and *Would You Believe.*

building of new solar homes—long a staple of the magazine's content—and the integration of solar technology into existing homes.

The mythical "Mother" continued answering letters although, as the magazine aged, fewer letters rated an answer than in early years. Content changed dramatically in the late 1970s, with emphasis on energy conservation, home building, remodeling, and organic gardening. Letters about communes disappeared, but readers were still willing to share what they had, although they were often looking for a profit. One letter offered readers the chance to buy moccasins at 20 percent to 40 percent off wholesale prices. Others offered supplementary information on previously published articles and gave suggestions for environmentally sound lifestyles.

Increasing stress colored Shuttleworth's columns, however, as he regularly talked about working 14-hour days and never having a vacation. Finally, in October 1978, he gave up the editorship of the magazine and, in 1980, he sold it to staff members.

The energy crisis of the 1970s fueled interest in the magazine's self-sufficient focus.[37] In 1980, the magazine ran roughly one page of advertising to every five pages of editorial, a formula that continued until 1985, when ad pages for the year totaled 300. Circulation grew from 490,000 in 1977 to 939,000 in 1979, going slightly over a million in 1980, 1981, and 1982. By 1983, however, energy conservation was no longer as great an issue with the American public, and *The Mother Earth News*'s circulation moved downward again, to 911,000. It inched down farther, to 893,000 by 1985.[38]

In 1985, the magazine was purchased by Owen Lipstein, founder of *American Health,* who was optimistic about increasing ad revenues because *The Mother Earth News* had "never been sold to Madison Avenue." It was, he said, like "a new launch." The motto was changed again, this time to "the original country magazine." [39] In the September/October 1985 issue, one reader was so comfortable with the magazine he referred to it as "Mom."

Refocus or Death

As social and economic realities change over time, a magazine's relationship with the audience may reach a critical point. Some readers may accuse the magazine of failing its original audience, and others accuse it of not changing enough to suit changing times. This forces either a change in the magazine or in its target audience. Failure to successfully refocus leads to the death of the magazine. No matter what the fate of the magazine, however, the audience remains, although it has changed as society has changed. This audience may be served by some form of the original magazine, or readers may have moved to other magazines more suited to their changed needs.

The 1980s were possibly the antithesis of the era in which *The Mother Earth News* was born. The ideal of living on less was replaced by the goal of accumulating more. The concept of country became associated with decorating, collecting, and living *on* the land, but not *off* it. Wall Street was king, and the term "yuppie" came to characterize many of the baby boomers who no longer were interested in activism but, rather, aspired to high-paying jobs and expensive houses and cars. Condos had replaced communes.

By the mid-1980s, as the magazine came under Lipstein's control, much of the country was comfortably entrenched in a consumerism mentality. Many of the changes in the magazine after 1985, then, reflected not only a changing culture but also changing ownership and a changing perception of readers. Lipstein succeeded in promoting the magazine to advertisers. *Advertising Age* named *The Mother Earth News* one of the 10 top magazines of 1988.

That same year, *Adweek* named *The Mother Earth News* one of the 10 hottest small magazines. According to *Adweek,* the magazine saw a 33.5 percent increase in ad pages in 1988 and a 38.7 percent increase in ad revenue. The magazine Lipstein was promoting, however, was different from the one the Shuttleworths had started. *Advertising Age* defined the magazine's focus in explaining its strength: "The continued strong interest in home and property will bode well for *The Mother Earth News,* the once back-to-the-land hippie journal that has been redesigned for yuppies." Lipstein was obviously so comfortable with this characterization he used it in promotional material for the magazine.[40]

The back-to-the land movement was partially subsumed by the environmental movement of the late 1980s, and *The Mother Earth News* became one of many voices of that movement. However, as one of many environmental magazines, the magazine competed with old standards such as *Audubon* as well as new starts like *E.* As a country magazine, *The Mother Earth News* also competed with the growing number of country magazines—*Country Living, Country Home, Country,* and *Country Journal.*

A successful new start of the late 1980s, *Utne Reader,* may have brought the alternative magazine concept full circle. Promoting itself as "the best of the alternative press," *Utne Reader,* like the early *The Mother Earth News,* was a storehouse of alternative information from other publications.

In a column in the magazine's January/February 1990 issue, editor Bruce Woods acknowledged that *The Mother Earth News* lost readers in the mid-1980s, but said these were people who were concerned only with the energy crisis and who disappeared when the crisis faded. The solid core of readers, he said, were different; they didn't change their "ideals with the seasons" but maintained their interest in the environmental movement and in *The Mother Earth News* as a "how-to" publication of that movement. He made no reference to the back-to-the-land movement. Woods presented the magazine as a practical guide for the ecologically concerned.

Letter writers, however, disagreed, saying the magazine looked like it was "aimed at 'eco-yuppies'" and had become a "bordello for lawnmower ads." In 1990, the motto was changed simply to "The original," dropping all reference to country. "The original," however, had become just one magazine among many doing the same thing. It had lost its special focus, its appeal to the frontier spirit, to individual initiative, and to the ideals of a simpler life. Articles appearing in *The Mother Earth News* could have appeared in many other country, environmental, or women's magazines.

The Mother Earth News celebrated the 20th anniversary of the magazine and of Earth Day with the March/April 1990 issue. The logo was changed to a lighter, airier typeface. The tone of the articles was professional but removed from the audience. Articles concerned the environment, but how-to tips were usually limited to the letters column. First person was occasionally

SEPTEMBER/OCTOBER 1990: After 20 years, *Mother Earth News* had lost sight of its original philosophy, as this ethereal cover demonstrates; one reader dismissed it as a "bordello for lawn mower ads."

used but in a clean, professional—certainly not chatty—tone. Covers became more dramatic and less homey. For example, the May/June 1990 issue featured a "radical fisherman" in a bright yellow slicker silhouetted against an ominously dark sky and blue-black water. Most cover models were still unknowns, although Willie Nelson popped up in May/June 1987 in an article on Farm Aid.

After Issue 125, September/ October 1990, the magazine ceased publication for a year. That issue featured a moody cover with a young couple—mother holding the baby, father drawing water from the well, with sunbeams drenching the whole family. The magazine looked like a poetic version of *Audubon.* Lisa Quinn, public relations representative for *The Mother Earth News,* said readers "freaked out" over the new issue, saying it was too urban and too slick, and canceled their subscriptions.

As with many magazines, the death of *The Mother Earth News* was gradual and was based on business decisions. But at the heart of the magazine business is the audience. Without an audience connection, a magazine has no reason to exist. When *The Mother Earth News* lost its audience, the rest was inevitable.

Reports of the magazine's death, however, were premature. In August/September 1991, the magazine was reintroduced with its former motto, "The Original Country Magazine." The "News From Mother" column speaks of audience reaction to the magazine's 1989-to-1990 changes and eventual death:

> *You rightly told us that the last three or four issues didn't deliver useful tips and practical information on how to live wisely and responsibly in the country. One subscriber compared her disillusionment with the new MOTHER to the way she felt when John Lennon was murdered. You knew it and we knew it: MOTHER no longer was MOTHER.*

Although the back-to-the-land movement had faded as an artifact of the 1970s, the interest in back-to-the-land issues remained. Americans still see nature and the country as a refuge from urban problems and as a means of reconnecting with traditional roots. Essentially, then, the magazine came full circle, returning to its roots while changing its approach to match changes in its audience and society as a whole. That audience has retained its back-to-the-land ideals but has modified them with some 1990s realism. The "new" *Mother Earth News*—the magazine had dropped "the" from its title—is geared to a new audience, one that existed before its restart. The difference in this incarnation of the cycle is that the magazine itself had a hand in creating that audience. In addition, *Mother Earth News*'s redevelopment exists in an environment full of other magazine voices competing for that audience.

Now owned by Sussex Publishers and published six times a year, *Mother Earth News* has a circulation of more than 400,000.

Readers of *Robb Report* earn an average of $755,000 a year.

LIVING TO A RIPE OLD AGE

Harper's is now in its second century and *Mother Earth News* is in its third decade. *Harper's* bears little resemblance to the book-like publication launched in 1850. It has, however, kept its emphasis on fiction alive, one of only a handful of magazines doing so, and it has outlasted many American magazines. *Mother Earth News* is far more glossy and colorful than Shuttleworth's original creation, but it still tells readers how to compost and live responsibly with and off the land.

Meanwhile, *Flair* exists only as a remarkable historical artifact. The innovations *Flair* introduced still fascinate American audiences, even those born long after the magazine died. The magazine, though, is as timely as the Edsel.

Just as cars and clothing change over time, so must magazines. *Harper's* was introduced at a time when women wore bustles. *Flair* came along in an era in which wearing mink was chic rather than dangerous. *Mother Earth News* took full advantage of its hip-hugging trendiness. Those original magazines would fit in today's society, perhaps, if women still wore basket-like contraptions on the backs of their skirts, tiny mink heads around their shoulders, and chartreuse beaded pants hanging beneath their navels.

Harper's and *Mother Earth News* stayed alive by responding to change. Magazines, Lewis Lapham said in 1992, need to move with the same speed as other forms of communication:

> *The ubiquity and accelerating speeds of the mass media had accustomed a generation of readers to the techniques of film, to shorter texts, to the abrupt juxtaposition of images as distant from one another as Madonna and Barbara Bush. Any publication that hoped to reflect the spirit of the age was obliged to align itself with a sensibility formed as much by the watching of MTV as by the reading of Marcel Proust.*[41]

FOR ADDITIONAL READING

Abramson, Howard S. *National Geographic: Behind America's Lens on the World.* New York: Crown Publishers, 1987.

Black, David. *The Plague Years : A Chronicle of AIDS, the Epidemic of Our Times.* New York: Simon and Schuster, 1986.

Burlingame, Roger. *Endless Frontiers, The Story of McGraw-Hill.* New York: McGraw-Hill Book Company, 1959.

Byron, Christopher. The *Fanciest Dive.* New York: W.W. Norton, 1986.

Cowles, Fleur., ed. *The Best of Flair.* New York: HarperCollins, 1996.

Cowles, Fleur Fenton. *Friends and Memories* . New York: Reynal, in association with William Morrow, 1978.

Cowles, Fleur. *She Made Friends and Kept Them.* New York: HarperCollins, 1996.

Cowles, Gardner. *Mike Looks Back.* New York: Gardner Cowles, 1985.

Gingrich, Arnold. *Nothing But People. The Early Days at* Esquire. New York: Crown, 1971.

The Handbook of Magazine Publishing. Stamford, CT: Cowles Business Media, 1996.

Mayes, Herbert Raymond. *The Magazine Maze.* Garden City, NY: Doubleday, 1980.

ENDNOTES

[1] William J. Garry, "The Winners. . . and the Losers," *Free Enterprise* (August 1978): 40.

[2] Ibid., 41.

[3] Ibid.

[4] James Kobak, "The Life Cycle of a Magazine," *Magazine Publishing Management* (New Canaan, CT: Folio Magazine Publishing Corporation, 1976): 35.

[5] James Kobak, "How to Destroy a Magazine: Let Me Count the Ways," *Magazine Publishing Management* (New Canaan, CT: Folio Magazine Publishing Corporation, 1976): 43.

[6] Theodore Peterson, *Magazines in the Twentieth Century* (Urbana: University of Illinois Press, 1964): 43.

[7] Milton Hollstein, *Magazines in Search of an Audience* (Magazine Publishers Association, Undated): 25.

[8] Christopher Byron, *The Fanciest Dive* (New York: W.W. Norton, 1986): 272.

[9] Lewis Lapham, "Notebook," *Harper's* (October 1992): 7.

[10] Dorothy Kalins, "Positioning: The Mission of Your Magazine," Stanford Professional Publishing Course, Palo Alto, CA (July 21, 1997).

[11] Anne Graham, "Mission Statements Light the Way," *Folio*: (March 15, 1995): 47.

[12] Kalins.

[13] Mike Lafavore, "The Art and Craft of Service Journalism." Stanford Professional Publishing Course, Palo Alto, CA (July 22, 1997).

[14] Anne Graham, "Peace Overtakes the Ad/Edit Conflict," *Folio:* (July 1998): 88.

[15] Ellen Levine, "The Editor's Business," Stanford Professional Publishing Course, Palo Alto, CA (July 24, 1997).

[16] Fred Kaplan, "Stopping the Presses," *The Boston Globe* (July 16, 1997): E2.

[17] Ibid.

[18] Condé Nast, "Class Publications," *History: The Condé Nast Publications*, (New York: Condé Nast Publications, Undated):12.

[19] Carol J. Williams, "Magazine Concept Loses Something in Translation," *Los Angeles Times*, reprinted in *Des Moines Sunday Register* (January 4, 1998): 2AA.

[20] Laura Zinn, "Move Over Boomers," *Business Week* (December 14, 1992): 79.

[21] Keith White, "How *Details* Magazine Turned Me into a Rebel Consumer," *Washington Monthly* (April 1994): 18.

[22] All references to correspondence and prepublication material on *Flair* comes from The Cowles Collection, Cowles Library, Drake University, Des Moines, Iowa. Much of this material is undated. Dates, when available, are cited.

[23] Arnold Gingrich, *Nothing But People. The Early Days at* Esquire (New York: Crown Publishers, 1971): 180.

[24] Patricia Prijatel and Marcia Prior-Miller, "An Analysis of the Failure of *Flair* Magazine" (paper presented at the annual convention of the Association for Education in Journalism and Mass Communication, Boston, MA, August 1991).

[25] Fleur Cowles, Untitled, *Flair* (February 1950): 23.

[26] "No *Flair*," *Time* (December 11, 1950): 67.

[27] "*Flair*'s Finish," *Newsweek* (December 11, 1950): 57.

[28] "Sugar and Spice," *Newsweek* (January 30, 1950): 46–47.

[29] "No *Flair*," 67.

[30] Herbert Raymond Mayes, *The Magazine Maze* (Garden City, NY: Doubleday, 1980): 199.

[31] Gardner Cowles, *Mike Looks Back* (New York: Gardner Cowles, 1985): 115.

[32] Fleur Fenton Cowles, *Friends and Memories* (New York: Reynal, in association with William Morrow, 1978): 53.

[33] Gardner Cowles, 115.

[34] Fleur Fenton Cowles, 55.

[35] Lorraine Calvacca, "No Guts, No Glory," *Folio:* (February 1, 1996): 48.

[36] "A Statement of Policy, " *The Mother Earth News* (May 1970): 9.

[37] "The Story of *Mother Earth News*," *The Mother Earth News*, (March/April 1990): 98.

[38] *The World Almanac and Book of Facts* (New York: The Newspaper Enterprise Association, 1977). Also, almanacs for 1979, 1980, 1981, 1982, 1983, and 1985.

[39] "American Health Repositions *The Mother Earth News*," *Folio:* (February 1986): 59.

[40] Promotional flyer from *The Mother Earth News*, undated.

[41] Lapham, 6.

CHAPTER 6

Magazine Business Plans

Determining the Bottom Line

"I used to use words like *lead* and *grammar*," *Good Housekeeping* editor-in-chief Ellen Levine told a group of magazine professionals in 1997. "Now I use words like *margins* and *revenue*." Levine is typical of today's editor who goes on advertising sales calls, carefully studies the magazine's profit and loss statement, and has a voice in circulation price hikes. Magazines that last in today's marketplace are managed by individuals—on both the editorial and business sides—who have a day-to-day understanding of the intricacies of their publication's budget. 📖 This is even more true of new magazines. Keith Clinkscales, president and CEO of *Vibe* magazine, is a Harvard MBA who started his career as a credit analyst. He has been with *Vibe* since its 1993 launch and saw the magazine grow from an initial circulation of 100,000 to its current 450,000. He also oversaw the creation of a one-hour late-night talk show, "Vibe," the development of an industry trade show, "Vibe Music Seminars," and the publication of books related to the magazine's focus on urban music and its multi-cultural proponents and trendsetters. Before joining *Vibe* he was a founder of *Urban Profile*, a magazine that targets 18- to 34-year-old black males. His success at that magazine, in fact, was what caught Time Warner's eye and caused them to lure him to their publishing house as the force behind the launch of *Vibe*. One of Clinkscales's many talents is the development of business plans that work.

In the summer of 1997, Clinkscales helped a group of magazine editors, writers, designers, publishers, and ad salespeople create a business plan for a hypothetical magazine. The group was part of the Stanford Professional Publishing Course, and participants who might have once considered themselves strictly word or picture people were using their calculators, computers, and heads to build an economic structure. Many, in fact, had come to the course primarily to learn about the business side of magazines.

The group's goal was to launch a magazine with a $300,000 investment. Clinkscales guided the professionals through revenues and expenses, adjusting one to make the other work. He chided an editor from *National Geographic* who had budgeted herself a $100,000 salary for the new magazine and told her to scale it down to $60,000.

"We're not launching *Worth* here," he joked. "We don't have $25 million," a reference to the budget publisher Randy Jones had for his 1991 launch of the personal business magazine *Worth*.

Clinkscales reminded the group that, even though the start-up was modest, they were not likely to get a loan for it. The money, he said, would have to come from mortgaging their houses, maxing their credit cards, and borrowing from friends. When he launched *Urban Profile*, Clinkscales asked a group of his friends for $300 each, and he threw a party for 3,000 people at $15 a head.

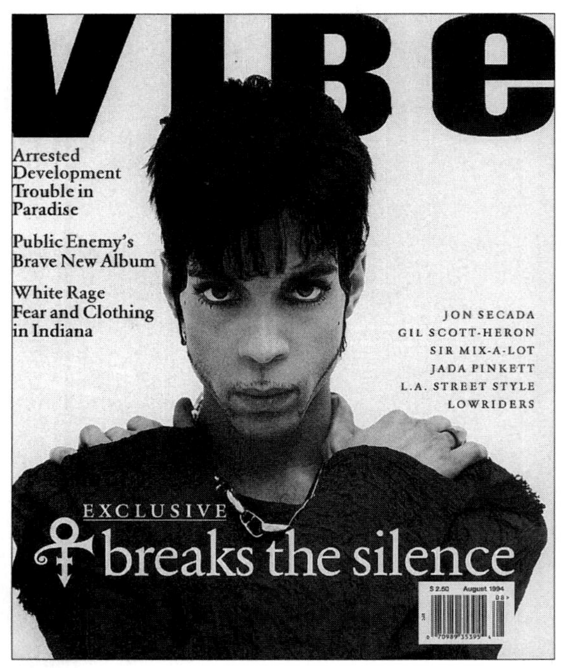

AUGUST 1994: *Vibe,* launched in 1993, built financial success by growing its circulation as well as by the creation of a one-hour late-night talk show, the development of an industry trade show, and the publication of related books.

The Stanford group eventually came up with a 20,000-circulation bimonthly magazine that would sell on the newsstand for $5.95, have a full-color ad rate of $8,000 a page, would be produced for 75 cents an issue, and be headed by an editor whose salary was more modest than she had planned.

How did they do it? They did it by following standard magazine economics.

The key to a magazine's economic foundation is the **business plan,** which outlines the publication's strategy and tactics and helps lure investors to a new magazine. It is built on a financial structure that is common to all magazines and follows budget procedures that have been well tested in the industry. To understand how to create a business plan, it is important to first understand the basic components of a magazine's budget.

THE MAGAZINE BUDGET

A magazine must eventually earn more than it spends. That is the simple part. More complex are the revenue streams on which magazines depend and the costs associated with those revenues. Table 6.1 is an overview of the areas of income and expenses in a typical magazine, illustrated with figures representing the budgets of 127 national consumer, trade, and association magazines. These figures were then used to derive a budget for an "average" magazine, plus average percentages of costs and revenues.

We will use Table 6.1 as our base in the following discussion of magazine budgets. That is, when we refer to the "average" magazine, we are referring to the averages of these 127 consumer, trade, and association magazines. Likewise, when we refer to percentages, we mean the percentages derived from these 127 magazines. The data in Table 6.1 give us a way of imagining magazine economics. Recognize, of course, that actual amounts can vary significantly from one magazine to another and from year to year on the same magazine.

Revenue

The magazines in Table 6.1 derived 45 percent of their revenue from advertising, 54 percent from circulation, and 1 percent from list rentals. Circulation income includes subscriptions—accounting for 39 percent of revenues—and single copy, or newsstand, sales—accounting for 15 percent. The average magazine earned $20.3 million a year from advertising and $24 million from circulation—$17.5 million of that from subscriptions and $6.5 million from single copy sales. It sold its lists of subscribers to other magazines, organizations, and marketing firms for $388,000.

Circulation revenue is counted according to gross receipts, that is, revenues before costs are deducted. In the case of advertising, however, net revenue—revenue after commissions for salespeople and discounts for advertisers have been deducted—is counted. All circulation expenses and some additional advertising-related costs are listed as expenses.

Table 6.1 is based on the assumption that magazines will have advertising income. Because ad-free magazines have no ad-related income, they build their overall income on circulation revenues and list rentals.

Expenses

To earn money, magazines have to spend money. In the process, they become huge employers and users of goods and services, thus pumping billions of dollars back into the economy.

The direct costs associated with earning advertising and subscription income for the magazines in Table 6.1 added up to nearly half of the magazines' expenses: advertising 9 percent, subscriptions 25 percent, and single copy sales 8 percent, for a total of 42 percent. Other costs included editorial at 10 percent, production at 21 percent, distribution at 8 percent, and administrative and operating costs at 9 percent.

ADVERTISING. The average magazine in Table 6.1 spent $4.1 million to earn its $20.3 million advertising income. That is, for every advertising dollar earned, the magazine spent 20 cents for selling, research, and promotion. Expenses included advertising salaries, development and production of media kits, and research and creation of audience demographic and psychographic profiles. Ad-free magazines, of course, have none of these expenses.

SUBSCRIPTIONS. The average magazine in Table 6.1 spent $11 million to earn its $17.5 million in subscriptions. That is, for every subscription dollar earned, it spent 63 cents on subscription costs. Expenses included postage,

TABLE 6.1

Magazine Revenues and Expenses

Responses from 127 national consumer, trade, and association magazines prepared for the Magazine Publishers of America.

	TOTAL AMOUNTS (000)	AVERAGE (000)	PERCENTAGE OF TOTAL REVENUE
REVENUE			
Net advertising revenues	$2,576,534	$20,287	45 Percent
Circulation: Gross subscription revenues	$2,220,365	$17,483	39 Percent
Circulation: Gross single copy revenues	$829,949	$6,535	15 Percent
List rental revenues	$49,284	$388	1 Percent
Total Revenues	**$5,676,132**	**$44,693**	**100 Percent**
EXPENSES			
Advertising	$526,518	$4,146	9 Percent
Subscription	$1,399,996	$11,024	25 Percent
Single Copy	$456,884	$3,598	8 Percent
Editorial	$560,479	$4,413	10 Percent
Production	$1,192,828	$9,392	21 Percent
Distribution	$468,769	$3,691	8 Percent
Administration/Operating Costs	$506,791	$3,990	9 Percent
Total Magazine Costs	**$5,112,265**	**$40,254**	**90 Percent**
Operating Profit	**$563,867**	**$4,439**	**10 Percent**

Columns 1 and 2 are reduced by thousands, or by three digits, so that the total revenue of all magazines, listed as $2,576,534, should be multiplied by a thousand, for the final figure of $2.57 billion.

Column 1 shows actual income and expenditure amounts of all 127 magazines combined.

Column 2 is an average of the 127 magazines and thus provides figures for one "average" magazine.

Column 3 demonstrates percentages that have been rounded. For example, the average magazine earns a total revenue of $45 million a year, $20 million of that from advertising. Advertising then accounts for 45 percent of that revenue. Expenses are shown as a percentage of total revenue. Total revenues add up to 100 percent, and total costs add up to 90 percent of that, leaving a 10 percent total operating profit.

creation and development of promotional materials such as direct mail flyers to potential subscribers, reminder mailings to current subscribers, and commissions to outside agencies, or fulfillment houses, that manage subscriber accounts.

SINGLE COPIES. The average magazine in Table 6.1 spent $3.6 million to earn $6.5 million in single-copy revenue. That is, for every dollar earned on the newsstand, the magazine spent 55 cents on single-copy costs. Expenses included commissions to wholesalers who provide the magazines to the newsstand, commissions to newsstand sellers, and special promotions for individual issues.

EDITORIAL. In the economic world, editors make up less than 10 percent of the budget. The average magazine in Table 6.1 spent $4.4 million on editorial expenses. Costs included salaries for editorial staff members and for freelance writers, designers, editors, photographers, and artists.

PRODUCTION. The manufacturing of the product itself takes up 21 percent of the expenses of the magazines in Table 6.1. The average magazine spent $9.4 million on production. Costs included production salaries, printing the magazine, paper, and prepress such as color separations, desktop printing, and press proofs.

DISTRIBUTION. Getting the magazine to the readers made up 8 percent of the budget for the magazines in Table 6.1. The average magazine spent $3.7 million on distribution. Costs included in-house distribution salaries, commissions given to wholesalers (outlets that sell to retailers) and retailers (outlets that sell directly to consumers), plus postage to subscribers.

ADMINISTRATION/OPERATING COSTS. This catch-all category covers everything from heating bills to computer systems to executive and administrative salaries. The average magazine in Table 6.1 spent $3.9 million on administration. Costs included offices, the requisite office equipment, the people to run the offices, and the people to run the publishing house. As technology increasingly moves into all aspects of business, more and more overhead costs include computer hardware and software, training in their use, and regular upgrading.

OPERATING PROFIT. The amount left over after expenses have been deducted from income is the **operating profit,** which rests at roughly 10 percent. For the average magazine in Table 6.1, that meant:

Total Revenues:	$44,693,000
Total Costs:	$40,254,000
Total Profit:	$4,439,000

Profit, of course, varies from magazine to magazine, and within individual titles from year to year. New magazines may operate at a loss for as long as five years. Established magazines may have a banner year at 12 percent profit, followed by a leaner one at 8 percent profit.

EDITORIAL COSTS PER PAGE

One way to determine magazine expenses is by computing the average editorial cost per page. This is the cost of all editorial matter, divided by the number of pages. Editorial costs per page are usually determined by using all nonadvertising costs: staff and freelance expense for editors, writers, designers, and photographers, as well as for production and distribution. "Editorial," in this case, means anything that is not advertising. This is a much broader definition than is standard in the field when not discussing economics.

An existing magazine can determine this figure easily, and most editors have it memorized. Craig Reiss, executive vice president and editor-in-chief of *Adweek,* says his magazine has a cost per editorial page of between $500 and $800. Peter Mitchel, finance director of *Restaurant Business,* gives a cost per page for that publication of between $300 and $400. August Home publications *Cuisine* and *Woodsmith,* with high cover rates, no discounted subscriptions, and no advertising, have costs per page as high as $3,000, according to *Cuisine* editor John Meyer.

THE BUSINESS PLAN

A business plan offers a clear statement of the magazine's strategies and tactics. It demonstrates the interconnectedness of the product and its economics. A business plan typically defines the product through the editorial philosophy, formula, and audience, as well as an outline of staff structure. The marketing plan and the summary of profitability are the primary economic planning sections of the plan.

A typical business plan would follow this type of outline:

Title (Use Chapter 5, "Magazine Concepts" as a guide.)

Magazine Type (Consumer, trade, association, public relations, custom. Use the definitions in Chapter 1, "The Magazine as a Storehouse.")

Editorial Philosophy (Purpose, type of content, and voice. Use the definitions in Chapter 5, "Magazine Concepts.")

Audience (Demographics and psychographics. Use Chapter 2, "The Magazine as a Marketplace," as a guide.)

Identity/Comparisons with Competitors' Formulas (Three to five tables of contents to show the editorial breakdown and the types of departments and features to be included in each issue. Use the guidelines in Chapter 5, "Magazine Concepts.")

Organizational Plan (Staff size, organization chart, job duties, place of magazine within the organization, if applicable. Use Chapter 7, "Magazine Structures," as a guide.)

Marketing Plan and Executive Summary of Profitability (Decisions on promotion, frequency, circulation, distribution, and budget.)

THE MARKETING PLAN

A marketing plan is the strategy, or specific plan of action, for breaking into the market. It explains how the magazine will be promoted to readers and to advertisers and how it will stand out among the other magazines competing for attention and income. It also includes decisions on frequency; costs of subscriptions, single copies, and advertising; and distribution.

Advertising Promotion

The primary advertising sales tool is the **media kit,** a direct promotion of the magazine to advertisers, who use it to compare a magazine against other magazines and other media. The media kit must reflect the magazine's identity. It is part of the magazine's promotion plan, and it sells the magazine as a brand. *Gourmet*'s 1998 media kit is an elegant burgundy book with a sleek black binding, full of luscious photos and glowing prose selling the magazine's message: "A compelling balance of life's pleasures—travel, food, culture, and entertaining—creates the focus of *Gourmet*, the Magazine of Good Living." The media kit matches the sophisticated taste of affluent readers who can afford to cook the best food and eat at the best restaurants throughout the world. *Poz*, by comparison, has a simple see-through plastic envelope in which a recent issue of the magazine is showcased. The magazine provides service and motivation to readers who have been diagnosed HIV-positive. It requires a clear, clean, and direct promotional message.

***Keyboard*'s 1999 media kit sells the magazine's audience to potential advertisers and positions the publication as "The world's leading music technology magazine."**

RESEARCH IN BRIEF

Mad Economics

Magazines without advertising "constitute an affront to conventional wisdom," wrote Vincent Norris, then an associate professor in the School of Journalism at Pennsylvania State University, in 1982. Norris studied the ad-free magazine in perhaps its most iconoclastic form: *Mad* magazine. *Mad* publisher William Gaines not only ran no advertising in his magazine, he also refused to advertise his magazine in other media, thus, notes Norris, "defying another myth—that a product must be advertised if it is to succeed."[1]

Norris studied the magazine's economics and arrived at what he describes as simple arithmetic: In 1981, the magazine, part of Warner Communications, Inc., sold an average of 1 million copies per issue, nearly two-thirds of those on the newsstand. Nearly twice as many copies were printed—1.9 million—as were sold, to allow newsstand merchants enough average copies. The cover price of each issue was 90 cents. After paying the wholesaler, distributor and retailer, *Mad* recouped 52.55 cents per copy, for a total of $525,500 for the million copies sold. The total cost of producing the 1.9 million copies was $437,000, leaving the magazine $88,500 before taxes. Multiply that by eight issues a year and it leaves a $708,000 pretax profit.[2] Add to this the income from 80,000 subscribers who paid nearly full cover price per issue, for a total of $71,600 per issue and $572,800 a year, and the magazine's total income for 1981 topped $1.2 million.

Then, add income from four "Super Specials" issued that year, at a cover price of $1.75 and average sales of 750,000 each, and nine *Mad* paperbacks issued that year, bringing the total number of paperbacks at that time to 125, with sales of roughly 60 million. Plus, there were the 12 international editions and the *Mad* board games.

No wonder Alfred E. Neuman isn't worried.

[1] Vincent P. Norris, "*Mad* Economics: An Analysis of an Adless Magazine," *Journal of Communication* 84:1 (Winter, 1984): 45.

[2] Ibid.,53.

The most common form of media kit is a folder with multiple pockets for brochures, back issues and other printed sales tools. The media kit from *Keyboard* demonstrates many standard elements:

- At least one recent issue of the magazine.
- An advertising rate card, with costs for all possible configurations of ads, specific ad sizes available, total circulation, number of subscribers, average newsstand sales, regional editions available, and regional sales rates.
- Demographic and psychographic details on the magazine's audience, including readership rates and pass-along readership data.
- An editorial calendar showing what types of articles will be covered in future issues.
- An information sheet from BPA International verifying the magazine's circulation. This could also be from the Audit Bureau of Circulation (ABC).

A media kit may also include a letter from the editor or publisher and articles about the magazine that have appeared in other publications.

Circulation Promotion

A magazine must also be promoted to readers. Because this builds circulation, it is referred to as **circulation promotion.** A successful circulation strategy is to build in efficiency. Large circulations are not automatically a sign of success, nor are small circulations necessarily a sign of failure. Well-targeted magazines are aimed at readers who make the difference to the bottom line, whether the readership is 20,000 or 2 million.

New readers can come from a variety of sources. Magazines depend for new business on direct marketing, which includes direct mail, advertising in other media, the Internet, and insert cards. Circulation consultant Stuart Jordan says 75 percent of all publishers use some form of incentives. These may include free magazines, test issues, sweepstakes, and "value-added" offers. Publishers hope to maintain existing readers through renewals.

Direct marketing is a type of advertising that includes a mechanism for reader response—a card

Nealy 55 percent of the material reproduced for college coursepacks comes from magazines, journals, and newspapers. Permission fees added $3.5 million to American magazine budgets.

DIRECT MAIL COSTS

The elements of a typical magazine direct mail piece and their average cost per mailing are:

Envelope	$.032
Order Device	$.012
Letter	$.018
Brochure	$.017
Lift Note	$.005
Response Envelope	$.009
Postage (3rd class bulk)	$.18
Label Printing/Affixing	$.04
List Processing	$.015
List	$.08
Total	$.408

Figures are based on costs-per-thousand data provided by Stuart Jordan of Circulation Specialists, Westport, Connecticut.

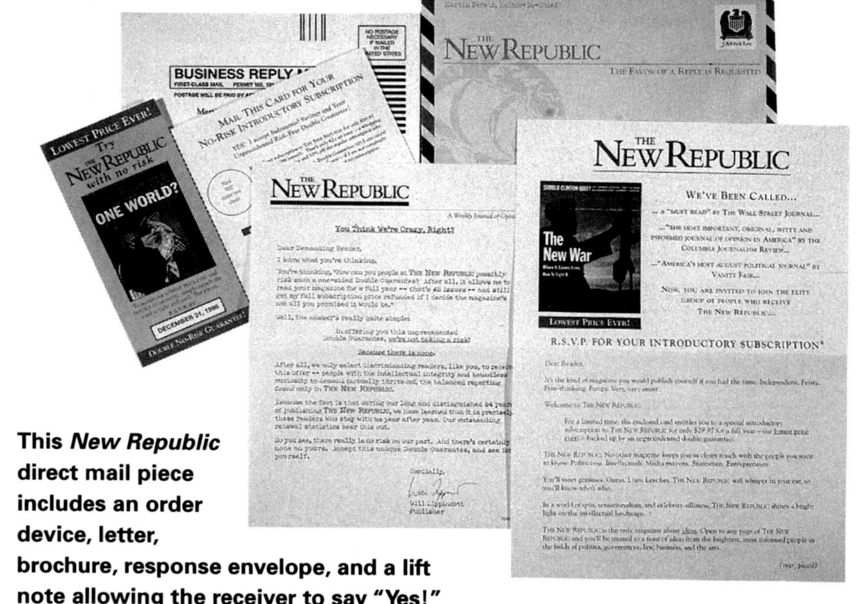

This *New Republic* direct mail piece includes an order device, letter, brochure, response envelope, and a lift note allowing the receiver to say "Yes!"

to fill out, a number to call to subscribe, a coupon to send in. Direct marketing can use all media. Direct mail is a type of direct marketing that uses the mail as its medium. The Internet has now become an additional arm of direct marketing.

DIRECT MAIL. Direct mail can be the most efficient way of matching a magazine with its audience. Because subscriptions usually get to the reader through the mail, direct mail is a logical, and the most common, approach to selling subscriptions. Magazines, catalogs, public television stations, associations, even grocery stores sell mailing lists of specific demographic groups. List houses, which advertise in the back of most industry publications, serve as brokers for a variety of different lists. Many publishing houses have **list kits:** these look like media kits but they sell lists of readers of their publications.

The successful direct mail piece has a clear and consistent message and format that sells the magazine as a benefit to the reader. Stuart Jordan of Circulation Specialists in Westport, Connecticut, says a typical direct mail package includes an envelope, a lift device ("Yes, I would like to subscribe to *Your Magazine*"), a brochure, a letter, and a response envelope. The package costs $400 to $500 per thousand mailed, or 40 cents to 50 cents each.[1]

A less expensive method is the double postcard. One part of the card includes the sales message; the other is a response card. Postage is prepaid, and the card is pre-addressed, so the subscriber simply has to mark a box and drop it in the mail. While less expensive, these usually work well only with established titles that do not need the explanatory material usually included in the more expanded direct mail package.

A typical consumer magazine direct mail response rate is 6 percent to 10 percent, with niche titles being slightly higher. Controlled circulation titles can expect an 8 percent to 14 percent response.

OTHER MEDIA. Magazines can also reach their audiences using other media. Network television may be too broad a medium for a specialized magazine, but some cable TV shows can be good buys. Radio and newspapers may be too local for a national promotion, but it is possible to buy ads in groups of stations or newspapers. The magazine can also be pitched in other magazines, especially magazines of organizations to which large numbers of the audience might belong. It may also be possible to swap ads with other magazines—that is, offer one or more ads in the new magazine in response for an ad in an existing magazine.

THE INTERNET. Guy Kawasaki, computer guru and holder of a fellowship from Apple Computer, Inc., says one of the best uses of the Internet for magazines may be to sell subscriptions.[2] The costs can be minimal for any magazine that already has a Web site.

The Internet works best, of course, for magazines whose editorial product is Internet-related. *Yahoo! Internet Life* increased circulation by 300 percent from 1995 to 1997, largely by using on-line promotion.[3]

The level and quality of responses for most magazines, however, can vary widely, because the process is still in its infancy. Until it is possible to verify the quality of a potential subscriber from the Internet—that is, the likelihood that the subscriber will actually buy the magazine—it may be safest to ask for payment upfront, with a credit card.

INSERT CARDS. Those annoying little cards that clutter your favorite magazines and fall all over the floor are there for a reason: They work. They are used by readers who have already selected the magazine on their own, so they go directly to a qualified and interested audience. Typically, an issue with high newsstand sales will yield high rates of insert card returns because it has higher initial readership and a higher pass-along readership.

Insert cards may be bound in (attached to the binding) or blown in (unattached to the binding) the issue. They work equally well for consumer, trade, and association magazines and are sometimes the choice for magazines with limited promotion budgets. They are the best source of new subscribers for *The Sciences*, a 60,000 circulation association magazine that can't afford direct mail.[4]

FREE MAGAZINES. Publishers often offer free subscriptions in the hopes that once the magazine gets into the subscriber's home, the reader will be hooked and will want to keep the publication coming. Roy Reiman, whose titles include *Country, Country Woman,* and *Reminisce*, has built a $100 million business by sending premiere issues with a letter.

Stuart Jordan cautions, however, that free offers may not always be the best business proposition. Cutting down on free responses will reduce the response rate, but it can also make the rate of payment increase. This approach can cut publishing costs significantly, because the publisher can produce fewer magazines, yet sell more. It is hard not to see that as good business. Jordan acknowledges that we live in a credit society, however, and recommends "bill me later" options. Jordan offers these examples of a free, or "soft," offer and a "hard" offer, and their response rates:

> ***Soft Offer:*** *Yes, please send me a free issue of XYZ magazine at no risk or obligation to subscribe. If I like it, I'll pay $12 for 12 issues (including my free issue). If I don't, I'll write* cancel *on the bill you'll send, return it, and owe nothing. The free issue is mine to keep with your compliments.*

This has a typical response rate of 5 percent, which is considered successful in the industry. Of those who respond, 40 percent pay, for a net response rate of 2 percent. If this mailing went to 100,000 potential subscribers, 5,000 would respond. Of those, 2,000 would pay, for a net response of 2,000. The magazine would earn $24,000 from that mailing.

> ***Hard Offer:*** *Yes! Please enter my subscription to XYZ magazine and bill me for a year (12 issues at $12).*

This has a typical response rate of 2 percent. Of those who respond, 65 percent pay, for a net response rate of 1.3 percent. If this mailing went to 100,000 potential subscribers, 2,000 would respond. Of those, 1,300 would pay, for a net response of 1,300. The magazine would earn $15,600 from that mailing.

Keith Clinkscales learned a lesson about audience appeal while promoting *Vibe*. The magazine, partially funded by well-known music producer Quincy Jones, sent a mailing

People showed a profit in 18 months. *Sports Illustrated* took nine years to show a profit, at a loss of $20 million. Both were started by Time-Life and are still published by Time Inc., which is now Time Warner.

out to potential subscribers that included a letter from Jones. Readers looked at the letter, Clinkscales said, and asked, "Why does Quincy Jones need money from *me*?"

TEST ISSUES. Publishers often create one or two test issues—actual printed magazines, with advertising content—to get an idea of subscription sales possibilities and newsstand draw. They analyze the sales results and reader reactions to determine whether the magazine should be launched as is, modified, or scrapped. As with the 1997 test of *WomanSports*, potential readers get an actual magazine to study.

In other cases, publishers will dry test, that is, send only a direct mail package announcing the magazine before the creation of an actual publication. *Latina* did a prepublication test mailing to 70,000 names, then refunded the money sent in by potential subscribers. They didn't have an actual magazine to send them yet. In the process, they found enough interest to warrant the 1996 launch of the magazine.[5]

To sell advertisers and other investors on dry-tested magazines, publishers create prototype issues, or professional-quality mock magazines. These may or may not include actual articles, but they do include representative cover lines, titles, and pull-quotes. Photos are usually picked up from another publication—easy to do for companies that produce multiple titles. Advertising may come from ad agencies at no cost or may also be picked up from other titles. The goal of a prototype is to show advertisers and other investors how the proposed title will look.

Successful magazine launches include budgets for an advertising staff that will take a prototype of the proposed magazine to potential advertisers and get commitments for future advertising. When *Wood* was still in the planning stages, editor Larry Clayton took a prototype to woodworking conventions and sold potential advertisers on the new magazine.

Michele Givens, consumer marketing director of *Outside* and *Outside Kids*, cautions that dry tests often provide the best response the magazine is ever likely to see, so new publishers might be disappointed with sales when the magazine is permanently launched. The actual launch, she says, will typically yield a response 20 percent lower than the dry test.[6]

Americans keep subscribing. A 1998 survey by *Folio:* magazine of 640 consumers found that 52 percent had begun subscriptions within the past year to magazines to which they had not previously subscribed.

SWEEPSTAKES. Publishers may sell their magazines using an organization such as Publishers' Clearinghouse as an intermediary. The sweepstakes organization gets a percentage of the sale of each magazine as an incentive. Sometimes called "dirty subscriptions," sweepstakes can yield high response rates but lower payment rates than nonsweepstake subscriptions. While sweepstakes may provide the magazine with loyal readers, more often they're the source of one-time trials from consumers who are looking for a bargain and hoping to see the Prize Patrol after the Super Bowl. Interestingly, sweepstakes offers don't have to be significantly lower than the normal subscription price to work.

VALUE ADDED. Publishers often send extra goodies as incentives to buying their magazine: *Sports Illustrated* has videotapes, *Alaska* has a full-color calendar, and *Playboy* has picture books such as *Locker Room Fantasies* and *Playmates Exposed.* Craig Reiss, editor of *Adweek*, avoids such gimmicks, however, saying they lower the intrinsic value of the magazine.

RENEWALS. The source of the original subscription affects the renewal rate. Renewals from direct mail range from 35 to 50 percent. That is, 35 to 50 percent of those who subscribed to the magazine through a direct mailing will renew once their subscriptions expire. Insert cards bring 50 to 60 percent renewals.

To cut costs and improve efficiency, publishers promote multiple-year subscriptions for renewals. Much of publishing is built on renewal rates. In general, renewals cost less than building new business. It costs about 40 cents to send an average renewal bill for a magazine—the average cost of a direct mailing. That bill sent to an existing subscriber, however, could be your only cost, while the direct mailing often has to be followed up with a bill.

PUBLIC RELATIONS TECHNIQUES: INNOVATION SELLS

Public relations experts find ways to make the magazine newsworthy so that it is covered as a news event in the media. These experts send out publicity releases to the other media and plan special events and promotions to emphasize, or even create, newsworthy issues related to the magazine. The limits of magazine public relations extend to the limits of the staff's creativity.

PUBLICITY RELEASES

A newsworthy magazine might merit a mention in the other media, especially in the many "What's New" or "People in the News" departments in newspapers, magazines, and on television. Newsworthiness might be found in content, staff, the magazine's history, its offices, in how it matches contemporary social norms, or in how it marches to a different drummer.

TALK SHOW APPEARANCES

Never underestimate the power of Oprah. What unique, lively, quirky, heartwarming, or otherwise newsworthy stories does the new magazine offer that might appeal to a local, regional, or national talk show audience?

SPECIAL EVENTS

Magazines may sponsor a cooking contest with the proceeds going to the homeless. Or organize a concert of bands on the rise. Or plan an expedition to the Grand Canyon designed specifically for urbanites. An essential element of these events is that they are newsworthy. Wouldn't "60 Minutes" love to watch a group of well-dressed New Yorkers skid down the rim of America's largest canyon?

SPECIAL PROMOTIONS

A magazine might create a board game based on the magazine's philosophy, offer design worksheets for fledgling designers based on the magazine's grid, or give schools a special discount for using the magazine in discussion groups. All have the basic goal of getting the magazine into as many readers' hands as possible.

Frequency

To be economically viable, magazines should be published at least four times a year. Magazines published less frequently have trouble building an advertising or subscription base and getting newsstand placement. Common publication schedules are weekly, biweekly, monthly, bimonthly, and 10 times a year.

Time, *Newsweek*, and *Business Week* choose the weekly frequency because they provide a great deal of timely material and compete more directly with other media produced daily, such as newspapers, radio, and television. Other titles such as *Sports Illustrated*, *The Nation*, and *The New Yorker* publish weekly to provide interpretation and analysis on breaking news and issues. *Life* changed from weekly to monthly when it was revived in 1978; the monthly schedule reduced staff and production stresses and expenses and helped keep the magazine's bottom line in the black.

Fortune is biweekly—published every two weeks. John Huey, managing editor of *Fortune*, says the biweekly schedule gives the magazine the impact of a weekly, but with the luxury of having twice the time for production.

Monthly titles, including *National Fisherman*, *Glamour*, and *The Atlantic Monthly*, offer readers and advertisers regular coverage, but at a slower pace. This allows them to reduce staff and production costs and gives them more lead time for story development.

Health, *WorkBoat*, and *Seafood Business* are bimonthly—published every two months. Some magazines customize their frequencies: *Men's Health* is published 10 times a year; *Garden Design* and *Saveur* each began as bimonthlies and now are published 8 times a year.

Karla Jeffries, assistant controller (a finance manager) of Meredith Publishing's Magazine Group, said the decision to increase frequency from six to ten times a year is primarily ad driven. Usually, the company cannot increase the subscription cost enough to justify the added production costs. Subscription buyers, Jeffries said, simply do not see enough value in added frequency to pay for it. That is, if they get a magazine six times a year for $12, they are paying $2 per issue. At that rate, they would have to pay $20 a year for 10 issues. Their magazine, then, would have gone from costing $12 to costing $20 a year;

DATABASE MARKETING

Consumer product companies are starting custom magazines for readers who have already shown an interest in a product or service and whose names appear in a database of purchases. These databases provide an intense look at demographic and psychographic characteristics of these buyers. The company then tailors the magazines to these existing interests and sends it to the existing list.

Dewar's Magazine was the brainchild of brand managers of Dewar's Scotch Whisky, who understand that drinkers develop loyalty to their brand sometime between college and the age of 30. Launched in March 1995, the 24-page twice-annual lifestyle magazine features celebrity profiles and service pieces for young professionals newly on their own. It includes eight pages of ads, plus coupons and rebates for Dewar's, and an 800-number for more information. It is mailed to 175,000 young people who attended events such as concerts and plays.[1]

Database marketing cuts both ways. Existing titles sell their lists to companies that market similar products.

Endless Vacations, started in 1975, has developed a database of 1,300,000 names of hard-core travelers. Readers get the magazine as part of their membership in Resort Condominiums International (RCI). RCI does surveys and cross-analyses of readers, and they compare income, age, and interests with travel plans. This not only helps serve members better, it also helps the company appeal to new members and to lure new advertisers into the magazine. Plus, those highly prized names can be sold to marketers of other travel-related goods or services.

[1] Lambeth Hochwald, "Have Database Will Publish" *Folio:* (November 15, 1995): 69.

the shock of the increased cost is not offset by the benefit of the four extra issues.

The 10-times-a-year frequency is often a substitute for a monthly schedule. January and July are slow advertising sales months for some magazines, so they print combined January/February and July/August issues.

Advertising Rates

Ad income is projected by determining ad rates, advertising-to-editorial ratio, costs per thousand (CPMs), and discounts.

FULL-COLOR AD RATE. New publishers may look wistfully at the ad rates for major magazines—$146,000 for a full-color page for *Sports Illustrated,* $120,000 for *People,* and $90,000 for *Cosmopolitan.* The important considerations are how much the competition charges and how closely a new launch can approximate the value given by that competitor. Like newsstand and subscription rates, these can be tested, but the tests are not scientific. Generally, they depend on committed ad salespeople getting the magazine's message to advertising agencies and product managers.

A new magazine might start with a low advertising rate or increase discounts for new advertisers, to get the magazine rolling. Occasionally publishers offer virtually cost-free advertising for the first few issues, with the promise that the advertiser will buy space in future issues. This is especially true in test issues. Some advertisers jump at this; others avoid it. No advertiser wants to be in a dead magazine—or caught in the casket with the corpse, as advertising people poetically call it.

ADVERTISING PAGES PER ISSUE. This is part of the magazine's formula. A magazine with an advertising-to-editorial ratio of 40:60 would have 40 pages of advertising and 60 of editorial for every 100 pages.

COSTS PER THOUSAND. Costs per thousand, or CPMs, is the cost for an advertiser to reach one thousand readers. (The "M" stands for the Roman numeral for thousand.) CPMs help advertisers determine the relative value of a magazine ad. CPM is the circulation divided by the ad rate. Rates are based on a full-color, full-page ad running in the magazine only once. If an ad costs $10,000 a page for a magazine with 100,000 circulation, the CPM is $10. An ad that costs $100,000 a page in a magazine with 1 million circulation also has a CPM of $10. *Outside* has a circulation of 481,000 and an ad rate of $36,990. To figure the CPM, divide 481,000 by 36,990, and you will get a CPM of $73.

Publishers want the highest CPM they can manage, and ad buyers want the lowest. Advertisers will pay a premium, however, for a premium audience. *Vibe* has a CPM of $66, *Rolling Stone,* $52, and *Details,* $75. All are dwarfed, however, by some controlled circulation titles. *WorkBoat,* for example, has 17,000 circulation and a $3,000 ad page rate, for an enviable CPM of $176. *Environmental Management,* which goes to a small but elite audience of 1,175 environmental scientists, attorneys, and engineers, sells a full-color ad for $720 a page, for a whopping CPM of $613.

Some ad agencies, such as DDB Needham, now rate magazines by **costs per point,** or CPP—the cost of a page for a specific market. Markets are rated and evaluated according to points, and the magazine reaching the target audience for the lowest cost-per-point is the best buy. It is an easy way to find the most efficient magazine for specific demographics. Rates are based on costs for full-page, full-color, and a one-time placement.

Don Peschke started *Woodsmith* when he was unemployed in 1979. In the first two years, he paid himself no salary. In the third year, he rewarded himself with $6,000. In 1985 and 1986, the company made *Inc.* magazine's list of fastest-growing privately held companies. His company, August Home Publishing, now employs more than 95 people.

For example, *Harper's Bazaar* is a great buy to reach women and a lousy choice to reach men. Looking at it based on CPPs helps enumerate what a good deal it is for the right audience:

Page rate: $51,020
Circulation: 711,000
CPM: $72
CPP: Adults 25–54: $34,242
Women 25–54: $19,037
Men 24–54: $188,963

Compare this with *Elle*:
Page rate: $52,895
Circulation: 886,000
CPM: $60
CPP: Adults 25–54: $25,553
Women 25–54: $15,790
Men 24–54: $68,695

Elle has a higher page rate but a lower CPM and a lower CPP for the target audience of women between 25 and 54.[7] So even though it might look more expensive, it could be the better buy for products aimed at that audience. DDB Needham, however, would break the decision down according to more specific demographic and psychographic details.

RATE BASE. Advertisers buy readership, so ad costs are based to a great degree on the number of readers. A magazine with 100,000 verified readers has a rate base of 100,000. Because a magazine must publish for a year before it is audited by the Audit Bureau of Circulation, the rate base for the first issue is a projection. It must be an honest projection, however, or the magazine will lose whatever advertisers it has attracted if those advertisers find that the 100,000 rate base they were promised is actually 50,000. Had the ad buyers planned for 50,000 to begin with, many of them would be satisfied.

AVERAGE DISCOUNT. Advertisers seldom pay full rate for an ad. How much is discounted per ad should be determined when the magazine is still in its planning stages. Advertising discounts are usually determined by frequency of ad placement. An advertiser who advertises in six issues pays less per ad than the advertiser who takes out an ad for only one issue. All magazines offer some sort of frequency discount.

Rolling Stone's 1998 full-color full-page rate for one-time placement was $84,445. For placement seven times, this was reduced to $81,915. For placement 100 times, it dropped to $64,180.[8]

Discounts may also be given based on the advertiser's or magazine's special circumstances. These are determined by what the market will bear and are not listed in the rate card. If you are the first magazine in your class and advertisers see that they can get to readers who are simply not accessible elsewhere, they may pay a premium. Conversely, if you are in a crowded field, you may have to offer discounts to lure some advertisers; that is, your salespeople may "sell off the card," or sell the ads for less than they are listed on the rate card.

Occasionally, a magazine faces the challenge of "selling the category," or convincing advertisers that a need—and readership—exists for such a magazine. When it was launched, *Ms.* had to sell advertisers on a whole new audience of women consumers who were looking for products advertisers hadn't yet considered targeting at women—cars, computers, and investments.

AVERAGE ADVERTISING REVENUE PER PAGE. This is the ad rate per page minus the discount. An ad that sells for $3,500 per full-color page with a 40 percent discount brings in $2,100 per page.

Circulation Rates

American newsstands sell some $4 billion in magazines annually and subscribers pay more than $5 billion a year for their magazines.[9] Publishers are increasingly asking readers to pay more of the cost of magazines, relying less on advertising income. In 1980, the average consumer magazine depended more on advertising than on circulation income. Today the opposite is true.

How does a magazine determine its cost to readers? This is a complicated formula based on reader income, the state of the economy, discounts, the advertising-to-editorial ratio, supply and demand, circulation costs, and distribution costs.

READER INCOME. In 1932, *Esquire* was founded to appeal to the man of the "new leisure class," a fellow who clearly had money in addition to time. The magazine sold for a princely 50 cents, compared with the popular *Saturday Evening Post*'s cover price of 5 cents.[10] *Esquire*'s first issue sold out.

Ida Tarbell's history of the Standard Oil Company cost *McClure's* magazine around $4,000 per article and Lincoln Steffens's stories on American cities cost $2,000 each. Both were published in *McClure's* January 1903 issue.

The cost of a magazine is directly related to the audience's ability to pay. *Architectural Digest* can ask $5 per issue because its readers are in America's top income tiers. *Field & Stream*, by contrast, sells to a middle-class audience for a middle-of-the-road $1.95 an issue. Magazines for Generation X buyers recognize that this young audience has a good deal of purchasing power, with *Wired* selling for $4.95.

STATE OF THE ECONOMY. As the economy changes and other products increase in price, so do magazines. In 1970, when one of the authors bought her first *Ms.* for $1, she also bought a brand-new avocado-green Chevy Nova for $3,000. Interestingly, the magazine is still intact, settled comfortably in a file drawer, while the Nova has long since rusted away. The 1994 hunter-green Honda Civic EX in her garage sported a sticker price of $17,000, while the *Ms.* she bought the same year cost $5.95.

Average single-copy prices have increased 83 percent since 1990, and subscription prices have increased 84 percent. This closely parallels the costs of other consumer goods, as measured by the Consumer Price Index (CPI), which rose 85 percent during the same period.[11]

Smart magazine entrepreneurs match their magazine launches with the economy. In a "down market," when other consumer goods are selling poorly, chances are a magazine won't sell well, either. The growth in magazines for personal investing, for example, was a logical development in the 1990s when personal income was up.

There is always an exception, however. *Esquire* was started in 1933 at the deepest depths of the Great Depression. Its founders expected to sell it through men's clothing stores—using the magazine almost as a catalog—with only a handful going to newsstands. The demand was so great on the newsstand that the magazine's staff took the copies out of the stores and sold them on the newsstand.

Fortune, one of America's premier business magazines, likewise saw its start in 1930, only months after the stock market crashed. Readers who were losing their fortunes needed help and perspective. For a financial magazine, the timing was excellent.

SUBSCRIPTION DISCOUNTS. Subscription prices are often discounted so that subscribers pay only 50 to 60 percent of what they would pay if they bought the magazine on the newsstand. Increasingly, though, editors are asking that subscription discounts be lowered or eliminated because they believe the discounts cheapen the value of their magazine. Many magazines succeed with no subscription discounts at all.

Men's Health sells for $21.97 year for 10 issues. The magazine offers few reduced subscriptions,

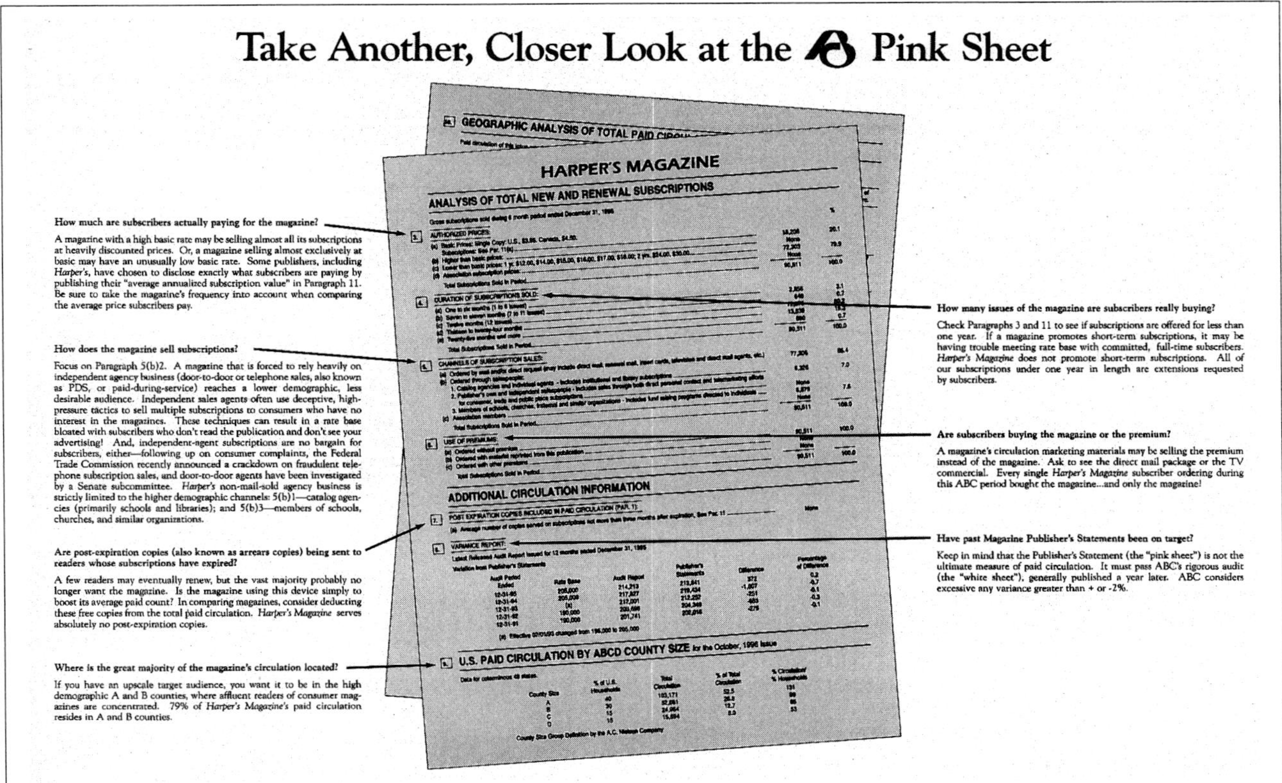

Take Another, Closer Look at the ABC Pink Sheet
HARPER'S MAGAZINE
ANALYSIS OF TOTAL NEW AND RENEWAL SUBSCRIPTIONS
ADDITIONAL CIRCULATION INFORMATION
U.S. PAID CIRCULATION BY ABCD COUNTY SIZE
How much are subscribers actually paying for the magazine?
A magazine with a high basic rate may be selling almost all its subscriptions at heavily discounted prices. Or, a magazine selling almost exclusively at basic may have an unusually low basic rate. Some publishers, including Harper's, have chosen to disclose exactly what subscribers are paying by publishing their "average annualized subscription value" in Paragraph 11. Be sure to take the magazine's frequency into account when comparing the average price subscribers pay.
How does the magazine sell subscriptions?
Focus on Paragraph 5(b)2. A magazine that is forced to rely heavily on independent agency business (door-to-door or telephone sales, also known as PDS, or paid-during-service) reaches a lower demographic, less desirable audience. Independent sales agents often use deceptive, high-pressure tactics to sell multiple subscriptions to consumers who have no interest in the magazines. These techniques can result in a rate base bloated with subscribers who don't read the publication and don't see your advertising! And, independent-agent subscriptions are no bargain for subscribers, either—following up on consumer complaints, the Federal Trade Commission recently announced a crackdown on fraudulent telephone subscription sales, and door-to-door agents have been investigated by a Senate subcommittee. Harper's non-mail-sold agency business is strictly limited to the higher demographic channels: 5(b)1—catalog agencies (primarily schools and libraries); and 5(b)3—members of schools, churches, and similar organizations.
Are post-expiration copies (also known as arrears copies) being sent to readers whose subscriptions have expired?
A few readers may eventually renew, but the vast majority probably no longer want the magazine. Is the magazine using this device simply to boost its average paid count? In comparing magazines, consider deducting these free copies from the total paid circulation. Harper's Magazine serves absolutely no post-expiration copies.
Where is the great majority of the magazine's circulation located?
If you have an upscale target audience, you want it to be in the high demographic A and B counties, where affluent readers of consumer magazines are concentrated. 79% of Harper's Magazine's paid circulation resides in A and B counties.
How many issues of the magazine are subscribers really buying?
Check Paragraphs 3 and 11 to see if subscriptions are offered for less than one year. If a magazine promotes short-term subscriptions, it may be having trouble meeting rate base with committed, full-time subscribers. Harper's Magazine does not promote short-term subscriptions. All of our subscriptions under one year in length are extensions requested by subscribers.
Are subscribers buying the magazine or the premium?
A magazine's circulation marketing materials may be selling the premium instead of the magazine. Ask to see the direct mail package or the TV commercial. Every single Harper's Magazine subscriber ordering during this ABC period bought the magazine...and only the magazine!
Have past Magazine Publisher's Statements been on target?
Keep in mind that the Publisher's Statement (the "pink sheet") is not the ultimate measure of paid circulation. It must pass ABC's rigorous audit (the "white sheet"), generally published a year later. ABC considers excessive any variance greater than + or -2%.

Magazine publishers use "pink sheets" to provide circulation and advertising information based on data from the Audit Bureau of Circulation. *Harper's* magazine offers advertisers extra help with this guide that follows the magazine's standard "Annotation" department format.

and those sell for $19.97—a mere 9 percent reduction. Editor Mike Lafavore says he wants the magazine "to have full value—to be paid for" by readers.

ADVERTISING-TO-EDITORIAL RATIO. Magazines determine upfront how much advertising will subsidize the magazine. While it might seem logical that magazines with a low number of ad pages would have higher cover prices than magazines with a high number, such is not always the case, as anybody who reads *Cosmopolitan, Harper's Bazaar,* or *Elle* knows. It all depends on what the market will bear.

SUPPLY AND DEMAND. Readers can influence the cost of a magazine through their interest in a particular title. In 1970, *Ms.* was founded with an economic philosophy that maintained that readers, not advertisers, should pay the bulk of the magazine's costs, so the editors slapped on a cover price of $1. This compared with *Woman's Day* at 39 cents an issue. *Ms.* was the first magazine of its kind, and readers signed up because it offered information and perspective not available elsewhere at the time. That first issue of *Ms.* sold out.

Magazine prices change with the times, as do prices of all consumer goods. Some magazines, though, like *Esquire* and *Ms.*, start out by pushing the envelope with a high price on an initial issue. Readers follow, and so do other magazines. Competitors sniffed when *Ms.* expected readers to spend $1 an issue. When readers anted up, these competitors turned around and raised their own prices.

At least one media critic pointed out in retrospect that Watergate encouraged *Time* and *Newsweek* to raise their cover prices. After all, the news magazines were selling the latest Watergate revelation week after week during an inflationary period when prices of everything—bread, candy bars, cigarettes—were rising. So why not the cost of news? Wrote media critic Edwin Diamond: "In April 1973, when Nixon fired John Dean, the price of a trial subscription to either [*Time* or

FINDING FULFILLMENT

Several companies nationwide are in the business of serving subscribers of magazines throughout the country. Called circulation fulfillment houses, they process all subscription-related paperwork: billings and renewals, memberships, label preparation, postal presorting, and subscription file updating. They offer customer service to subscribers and create circulation projections for publishers. In many cases, when you contact your favorite magazine about a subscription, you're dealing with a company that has no connection with producing that magazine.

Some large companies do their own fulfillment, but, increasingly, it is cheaper to have the work done by an outside company. One of the largest fulfillment houses, Communications Data Service, or CDS, grew out of the fulfillment department of *Look* magazine in Des Moines, Iowa. When the magazine folded, the fulfillment staff continued its service to outside clients. CDS now serves more than 360 magazines and 93 million subscribers.

Other large houses include Neodata in Boulder, Colorado, which serves 400 magazines and more than 100 subscribers; and JCI Data Processing, of Cinnaminson, New Jersey, which serves more than 450 consumer and trade publications with circulations from 10,000 to 400,000.

Newsweek] was pegged at 16 cents. By the fall, when the Senate Watergate hearings in the summer of 1973 had run their course, the *Newsweek* and *Time* trial-subscription price had reached 20 cents. A year later, when the House Judiciary Committee began debating articles of impeachment, the trial-subscription price hit 30 cents and the newsstand price 60 cents."[12]

According to *Newsweek* circulation director Robert Riordan, "It was a seller's market for us. We decided to seize the day."[13] By the end of 1974, *Newsweek* had reached a pricing structure of 37 1/2 cents per copy to subscribers and 75 cents on the newsstands; *Time* was close at 35 cents for subscribers and 75 cents on the newsstand. The coverage of Watergate resulted in a circulation profit center for both magazines.

Subscriptions and Memberships

Americans buy most of their magazines through subscriptions. Only 18 percent of consumer and trade magazines are sold on the newsstand, and 82 percent are sold through subscriptions.[14] Increases in postal rates have deeply affected magazine distribution. A Magazine Publishers of America Postal Committee has worked with Congress to privatize postal delivery and to make postal price setting more flexible and less time-consuming.

Most trade and organization titles are subscription-only, with the exception of some mass interest titles such as *Adweek, MacWorld,* or *Smithsonian.* Many trade publications are built primarily on controlled circulation. Association magazines depend on memberships. Both trade and association publications may have paid subscribers as well.

CONTROLLED CIRCULATION. Subscribers of *WorkBoat* magazine pay nothing for the magazine because they are highly appealing buyers of products advertised within the magazine. The magazine earns 98 percent of its income from advertising because manufacturers of commercial boats and related equipment know the magazine provides them with a select audience of readers who are buyers—commercial fishermen. Subscribers must sign a form validating the fact that they are in the fishing business.

Some trade magazines, such as *Mediaweek,* have partial paid circulation, partial controlled. Readers with high-level media positions can get the publication free; others have to pay.

Trade publications spend a great deal of time qualifying readers. It pays off for them, though, because they know exactly the size of their audience when they are producing the magazine and have to print only the magazines they will actually need.

MEMBERSHIPS. While association magazines are supported by readers in the form of memberships, some associations go beyond membership and make their publications available to nonmember subscribers. According to the

FAMILY MONEY GETS A LIFE

When Meredith Corporation staffers first began planning *Family Money,* they envisioned it as a sponsored publication produced in cooperation with Metropolitan Life Insurance Company. The outlook was so good for the new publication, however, that Meredith launched it in 1997 as a consumer magazine instead. Their relationship with MetLife evolved into an innovative marketing partnership.

The premiere issue featured an eight-page advertorial from MetLife, titled "Life Advice: Helping You Make Sense of It All." The section included short articles on budgeting for vacations, giving allowances to children, and hunting for a job in cyberspace, generously peppered with the MetLife 800-number for more advice.

Family Money editor Charley Blaine says MetLife buys the magazines in return for ad space and gives a free one-year subscription to each MetLife insurance agent. When the agent's subscription expires, Meredith sends a renewal notice and hopes to gain that agent as a regular subscriber.

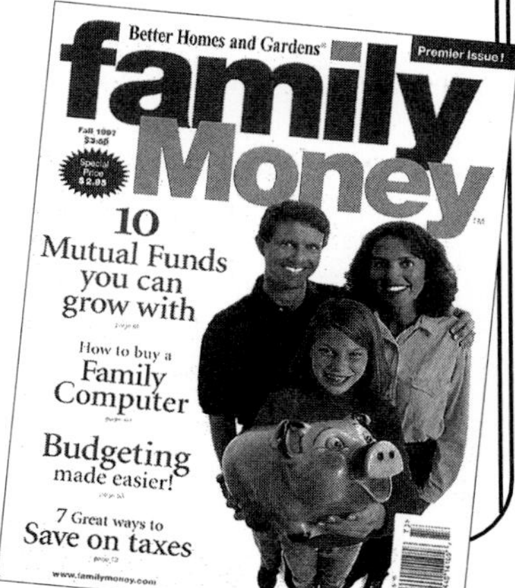

FALL 1997 (PREMIERE ISSUE): *Family Money* succeeded by giving America's families financial information in a service format.

American Society of Association Executives, nonmember subscriptions account for about 20 percent of association magazine income.[15]

The numbers may be small, as is the case with *AAUW Outlook*, the magazine of the American Association of University Women. *AAUW Outlook* goes to 150,000 members and to 300 nonmember subscribers, most of which are libraries. *The Sciences*, published by the New York Academy of Sciences, has a broader nonmember reach. The group sees part of its mission to make scientific information more accessible and understandable; the group has 12,000 nonmember subscribers, roughly 12,000 in newsstand sales, and 36,000 member subscribers.[16] *Communication World*, published by the International Association of Business Communicators, uses nonmember marketing as a means of increasing membership. They offer a one-year subscription for $39.95. This increases to $95 for a nonmember renewal. Or, the subscriber can join the IABC. Thomas Gradie, the association's director of advertising and sales promotion, says, "From a financial standpoint, we've looked at the costs associated with promotion and believe that offering nonmember subscriptions is just about a break-even prospect for us. Our primary motivation is membership enhancement."[17]

Distribution

The greatest product in the world has little value if it can't get to the consumer. Getting magazines to their readers has been a struggle for magazine publishers, with distribution costs increasing decade after decade.

SINGLE COPY. Forty percent of single-copy sales are made in supermarkets, where magazines are one of the most profitable product categories. National chain stores such as Kmart and Wal-Mart, however, are rapidly becoming the dominant retailers of magazines.[18]

Magazine distribution was restructured significantly in 1996, when the number of wholesalers who delivered magazines to the newsstands was drastically reduced. Retailers are getting increasingly picky about the titles they will sell and the wholesalers they will use to get those titles to the racks. Wal-Mart, which had been using 154 wholesalers, cut down to three in 1997.

The implications of this change is that magazine quality is more and more important, as is cover price. Smaller publishers are finding it more difficult to get on the newsstand. Retailers are also receiving more of the cover price. At the beginning of the 1990s, retailers received 20 percent of the cover price; by the end of the decade it was at 30 percent or more.

Another single-copy option is direct distribution, or selling the magazine through specialty stores either instead of or in addition to selling it through newsstands. *Cigar Aficionado* is sold through cigar stores, *Print* at art stores, and *The Source* at record stores. All are also sold on the newsstand.

Publishers offering controlled circulations are required by the United States Postal Service to show proof that more than 50 percent of all mailed magazines go to qualified subscribers.

SELL-THROUGH RATES. Newsstand marketing is an inexact science. One newsstand may sell only half its copies of an individual title, while another may not have enough to fill demand. The number of copies given to the newsstand divided by the number of copies sold is the sell-through rate. A magazine that gives 10,000 copies to the newsstand and sells 5,000 has a sell-through rate of 50 percent.

Vibe prints 845,000 copies, but has an advertising rate base of 400,000 because it can guarantee sales of only 47 percent of the number of copies printed. *Vibe,* then, has a sell-through rate of 47 percent. The premiere issue of *Latina* sold 200,000 copies on the newsstand, which was a 40 percent sell-through.

Controlled circulation magazines have no sell-through problem because their readership numbers are predetermined.

EXECUTIVE SUMMARY OF PROFITABILITY

The section of the business plan that offers an overview of finances is called the executive summary of profitability. It builds directly on the marketing plan and it typically spans five years. Keith Clinkscales recommends using modeling software to create this executive summary. Plug in the numbers you know and the programs can help determine related costs and income. Modeling software can project direct mail or insert card response rates, the relationships between ad and circulation revenue, and costs associated with each.

The magazine profiled in the business plan executive summary of profitability in Table 6.2 is a new launch that loses money the first four years and shows a profit the fifth year. This plan is based on the belief that it costs money to make money and that a series of planned losses can be the basis for substantial profit. The magazine loses money while it establishes itself.

For the first two years, the magazine will be bimonthly, which gives it a regular presence on the newsstand and in reader mailboxes while at the same time eliminating the costs associated with more regular production; as reader and advertising loyalty grow, the magazine's potential for profit grows, and its frequency is expanded to 10 times a year.

The magazine starts with a circulation of 100,000, based on comparisons of competing magazines. It grows steadily to a goal of 275,000 in the fifth year, again based on the track records of similar magazines. Throughout the five years, subscriptions outnumber newsstand sales. In the first year, the difference is negligible—55,000 subscriptions sold versus 45,000 newsstand sales. By the fifth year, however, the magazine sells almost twice as many copies through subscriptions as by the newsstand—180,000 subscription versus 95,000 newsstand sales. The logic of this approach is that new buyers will find the magazine initially on the newsstand, develop product loyalty, and become subscribers.

Income

The subscription price begins at $12 a year for six issues and grows to $24 when the magazine expands to 10 issues a year. Initially, then, the subscriber pays $2 an issue. This grows to $2.40 an issue as the magazine grows in size and popularity. The cover price increases slightly from a rather low $2.50 to an equally reasonable $2.95. The staff's philosophy is that subscribers and newsstand buyers should pay similar prices for the magazine. If this noble philosophy doesn't pan out, the subscription price can be reduced and the newsstand price increased.

Subscription income was determined by multiplying the subscription rate by the number of subscribers. In the first year, this

AAA Going Places, the magazine of the AAA Auto Club South, is linked to 68 travel agencies across the country. Readers can walk into one of the agencies and order any of the trips appearing either on the magazine's editorial or advertising pages.

TABLE 6.2

Business Plan Executive Summary of Profitability

	YEAR ONE	YEAR TWO	YEAR THREE	YEAR FOUR	YEAR FIVE
Number of Issues per Year	6	6	10	10	10
Total Circulation/000	100	150	200	250	275
Number of Subscribers/000	55	91	132	170	180
Number of Newsstand Sales/000	45	59	68	80	95
Subscription Price	$12	$12	$24	$24	$24
Cover Price	$2.50	$2.50	$2.95	$2.95	$2.95
Ad:Edit Ratio	40:60	40:60	50:50	50:50	50:50
Advertising Pages per Issue	40	48	60	70	70
Editorial Pages per Issue	60	72	60	70	70
Total Pages	100	120	120	140	140
CPM	$55	$55	$55	$55	$55
Ratebase/000	100	150	200	250	275
Full-Color Ad Rate	$5,500	$8,250	$11,000	$13,750	$15,125
Average Discount	40%	36%	36%	36%	34%
Average Revenue per Page	$3,300	$5,936	$8,256	$8,800	$11,550
Revenues					
Subscriptions/000	$660	$1,092	$3,168	$4,080	$4,320
Single-Copy Sales/000	$337.5	$442	$1,003	$1,180	$1,401
Advertising/000	$792	$1,521	$4,224	$5,280	$6,988
Total Revenues/000	**$1,789.5**	**$3,055**	**$8,395**	**$10,540**	**$12,709**
Expenses					
Advertising/000	$268	$428	$1,091	$1,370	$1,271
Subscriptions/000	$537	$886	$2,351	$2,846	$3,431
Single-Copy Sales/000	$251	$367	$923	$1,107	$1,144
Editorial/000	$179	$305	$798	$1,001	$1,207
Production/000	$376	$642	$1,763	$2,213	$2,669
Distribution/000	$197	$305	$840	$1,054	$1,207
Administrative Costs/000	$161	$275	$797	$949	$1,144
Total Expenses/000	$1,968	$3,208	$8,563	$10,540	$2,073.5
Net Income (loss)/000	**($179)**	**($153)**	**($168)**	**0**	**$635**

was $12 55,000, for a yearly subscription income of $660,000. Single-copy income is a little trickier because of retailer and wholesaler discounts. In Table 6.2, single-copy income was determined by multiplying the cover price by the frequency by the number of single-copy sales. For the first year, this is $2.50 6 45,000, for a gross single-copy income of $675,000. Magazines don't see this gross income, however; they see the net income, or income after the discounts are paid to the retailers and wholesalers. In Table 6.2, the total discount was computed at 50 percent, so the single-copy income of $675,000 was reduced by half, for a net income of $337,500.

The magazine begins with an advertising-editorial ratio of 40:60, which balances out to 50:50 by the fifth year. The magazine grows slightly in pages throughout the five years, from a

MAGAZINE SALARIES: A GLIMPSE AT THE FIELD

Today's magazine salaries reflect a field that includes both paupers and princes. Many lucrative jobs exist in New York City, which has one of the highest costs of living in the country; magazine professionals there need significantly higher incomes to be able to live at the same level as their counterparts in the heart of the country.

Folio: magazine annually surveys editors, art directors, circulation directors and managers, production directors and managers, and ad sales directors throughout the country. It then uses that data to report on average trade and consumer magazine salaries, ranked according to variables such as job title, magazine size, the editors' years of experience, and region of the country.

The amounts can be confusing because of significant differences between salaries and income. An ad salesperson may make a salary of only $5,000, the amount guaranteed by the publishing company, but earn a six-figure income from commissions.

Some highlights from the 1998 *Folio:* survey:[1]

Highest Individual Salary
- Editor-in-chief: $180,000
- Production director: $175,000
- Circulation director: $180,000
- Ad sales director: $150,000

Lowest Individual Salary
- Editor-in-chief: $12,500
- Production director: $28,000
- Circulation director: $21,000
- Ad sales director: $25,000

Average Salary for Those over 50 Years Old
- Editors-in-chief: $83,339
- Production directors: $75,417
- Circulation directors: $54,932
- Ad sales directors: $86,857

Average Salary for Those Aged 30 to 39
- Editors-in-chief $71,113
- Production directors: $59,485
- Circulation directors: $61,117
- Ad sales directors: $132,117

Area with Highest Average Salaries
- Editors-in-chief: New York City, at $88,878
- Production directors: New York City, at $85,168
- Circulation directors: New York City, at $71,023
- Ad sales directors: New York City, at $164,694

Area with Lowest Average Salaries
- Editors-in-chief: North Central, at $66,711

total of 100 to a total of 140. The second and third years have the same total pages—120—but a different ad:edit ratio, so the second year has 48 ad pages, and the third year has 60. The magazine staff feels it is important to start with a magazine that is close to the size of the final, established magazine. The product, after all, must be substantial if it is to appeal to a growing base of readers.

The CPM remains standard at $55, which is the CPM of other magazines reaching the same audience. The ad rate increases as circulation increases. In the first year, the rate base is 100—based on 100,000 projected circulation (55,000 subscription and 45,000 newsstand)—and, therefore, the ad rate is $5,500 ($55 CPM 100 rate base). As the rate base grows, so does the ad rate, to a final $15,125 in the fifth year ($55 CPM 275 rate base). The magazine projects an initial advertising discount of 40 percent, which drops in five years to 34 percent. Initially, the discount provides advertisers with an incentive for multiple ad placements. The incentive becomes less sizable as the magazine's reputation and reader loyalty grow. The ad income per page is the actual ad rate minus the discount. In the first year, the $5,500 per page rate is reduced by 40 percent, or $2,200, to yield final ad income per page of $3,300.

Expenses

Projections of magazine expenses require an ability to look into the economic future while understanding and remembering the past. Magazine staffers study past performance, analyze future trends, and use this information to build an economic plan that guides the creation of a financially feasible magazine.

Expenses are based on revenue. If you want to spend $1 million printing a magazine, you had better have a lot more than that million in revenue—usually $5 million to $7 million. New magazines must spend proportionally more

Production directors: South, at $54,625
Circulation directors: North Central, at $52,238
Ad sales directors: South, at $85,625

Age makes a difference: The only editorial job title with significant representation from those under 30 in the *Folio:* survey was managing editor, where individuals 29 and under made an average of $32,928. Those 30 to 39 made almost 34 percent more: an average of $44,077.

In recent years, editors have begun receiving bonuses from their magazines' profits. The 1998 average bonus reported was $13,252 for both trade and consumer editorial directors or editors-in-chief. Consumer magazine editorial directors received an average bonus of $15,076; trade magazine editorial directors earned an average of $11,407.

Production directors and managers also make bonuses. The average bonus for a production director at both consumer and trade magazines in 1998 was $11,286, with consumer magazine production directors making $13,176 and trade magazine production directors making $9,262.

The 1998 average bonus for a circulation director for both trade and consumer magazines was $6,065; consumer magazine circulation directors made the higher bonuses, at $6,345 average, while trade magazine circulation directors trailed at $5,824.

The individuals who sell ads often earn higher salaries than editorial staffers. Much of the salary, however, comes in the form of commissions, and the job is filled with a great deal of uncertainty. A great year of sales means a new boat. A bad year means a job search. Bonuses and commissions have long been a part of the income for the advertising staff. The 1998 average bonus for ad sales directors at trade and consumer magazines was $31,437. Trade magazine ad sales directors earned the largest bonuses, with a $32,754 average; consumer magazine ad sales directors earned $30,474.

GUILD FIGURES

The Newspaper Guild has salary guidelines for member publications. The Guild is a union that represents publishing professionals; staff members on specific magazines vote on whether or not employees at that publication join the Guild. The Guild gives the following salaries for specific magazines:[2]

Consumer Reports senior editor, $65,364
Scientific American editor, $61,568
Newsweek general editor, $54,808
The Nation associate editor, $47,788
Scholastic editor, $46,280
Time Warner, writer-editor, staff correspondent, $42,536

[1] Rolf Maurer, "Production Salary Survey," 179–83; "Ad Sales Salary Survey," 212–17; "Editorial Salary Survey," 226–31 *Folio: Special Sourcebook Issue for 1999* and Rolf Maurer, "Circulation Salary Survey," *Folio:* (December 1998) 49–54.

[2] *The Newspaper Guild-CWA Collective Bargaining Manual 1* (April 1, 1998). The Guild lists weekly salaries; these have been changed into annual salaries.

on advertising, subscription, single copy, and distribution than established magazines because they are paying to sell themselves to new readers, advertisers, wholesalers, and retailers. Editorial costs are usually proportionally the same for a new start as for an established magazine, although some new magazines may offer staff members a percentage of the profits in exchange for lower initial salaries. Some administrative costs can be reduced by renting low-cost offices and putting off major equipment buys.

Production costs are probably the least stable expenses and therefore, the hardest to project. Magazine budgets have been decimated when paper prices have risen or when production technology has changed, requiring new equipment. One tenet should serve as a guide when determining expense projections: A magazine will always cost more than you think.

In creating expense projections, staff members have to determine how much they can reasonably limit expenses in one area to support costs in another and how much loss they can sustain for how long. Magazines with major investors also have to present a plan that shows a significant enough profit in time to encourage investors to take a risk. Clinkscales said the business plan "answers the most important question of the investor, namely: How much and when are you going to pay me back?"

Table 6.2 demonstrates expense projections for a new magazine, plus an explanation of how those projections were determined. All expenses are based on total projected revenue. The staff determines how much income the magazine can make and bases expenses on that income. Projected expenses in Table 6.2 are modeled on industry standards, based on the percentages given in Table 6.1. For example, the magazines in Figure 6-1 spent an average of 9 percent of total revenues on advertising. The magazine in Table 6.2 spends 15 percent on advertising in its first

TABLE 6.3

Expense Percentages in a Magazine's First Year

Advertising	15 percent (.15 $1,789,500 total revenue = $268,425)
Subscriptions	30 percent (.30 $1,789,500 = $536,850)
Single Copy	14 percent (.14 $1,789,500 = $250,530)
Editorial	10 percent (.10 $1,789,500 = $178,950)
Production	21 percent (.21 $1,789,500 = $375,795)
Distribution	11 percent (.11 $1,789,500 = $196,845)
Administration	9 percent (.09 $1,789,500 = $161,055)
Total Costs	110 percent (1.10 $1,789,500 = $1,968,450)
Operating Loss	10 percent (.10 $1,789,500 = $178,950)

TABLE 6.4

Expense Percentages in a Magazine's Fifth Year

Advertising	10 percent (.10 $12,709,000 total revenue = $1,270,900)
Subscriptions	27 percent (.27 $12,709,000 = $3,431,430)
Single Copy	9 percent (.09 $12,709,000 = $1,143,810)
Editorial	9.5 percent (.095 $12,709,000 = $1,207,355)
Production	21 percent (.21 $12,709,000 = $2,668,890)
Distribution	9.5 percent (.095 $12,709,000 = $1,207,355)
Administration	9 percent (.09 $12,709,000 = $ 1,143,810)
Total Costs	95 percent (.95 $12,709,000 = $12,073,550)
Operating Profit	5 percent (.05 $12,709,000 = $635,450)

year, when it is trying to develop a presence, and ends up spending 10 percent on advertising in its fifth year, when it is more established. By the fifth year, then, it is close to the industry standard.

The percentages used in Table 6.2 are projections, or hypothetical figures based on the best assumptions available at the time and interpreted as wisely as possible. Because business plans are readings of the future, they have to be as close to reality as honestly possible. That reality can change, however, as the economy bumps up or down.

The magazine loses money for the first three years, spending more than it can make. It breaks even the fourth year and shows a profit the fifth year. It spends proportionally more (a higher percentages than the industry standard) on advertising, subscription, and single copy costs in the first few years to build its audience base. Costs for editorial, production, distribution, and administration remain proportionally the same through the five years.

The percentages of revenue projected as expenses in the first year are shown in Table 6.3. Operating loss can also, of course, be determined by subtracting expenses from income:

$1,789,500	projected income
– $1,968,450	projected expenses
($178,950	operating loss)

By the fifth year, expense percentages have changed to the data shown in Table 6.4. Operating profit can also, of course, be determined by subtracting expenses from income:

$12,709,000	projected income
– $12,073,550	projected expenses
$635,450	operating profit

For the first year, the magazine loses 10 percent. Losses are reduced until the magazine earns a small profit in the fifth year. The magazine loses 5 percent in the second year, 2 percent in the third year, and 1 percent in the fourth year. It earns a 2 percent profit in the fifth year. By the sixth and seventh years, the magazine should aim for at least a 9 to 10 percent profit.

The business plan, Clinkscales said, is a process, not a destination, and it will change several times before a new magazine is actually launched. A good plan must be flexible.

Most important, he said, is that the plan should be built on a quality product. A well-conceived and articulated editorial philosophy and formula are the heart of the business plan. "Without the product, you have nothing," Clinkscales said. "It is virtually impossible for good business to save a bad product."[19]

FOR ADDITIONAL READING

Compaine, Benjamin M. *The Business of Consumer Magazines.* White Plains, NY: Knowledge Industry Publications, Inc., 1982.

Greco, Albert. *Advertising Management and the Business Publishing Industry.* New York: New York University Press, 1991.

Marino, Sal. *Business Magazine Publishing. Creative Ideas on Management, Editorial, Selling Space, Promotion . . . and Boosting Profits.* Lincolnwood, IL: NTC Publishing, 1993.

Folio: Special Sourcebook Issue 1998. Stamford, CT: Cowles Business Media, 1998.

ENDNOTES

1 Stuart R. Jordan, "Building the Winning Package," Stanford Professional Publishing Course, Palo Alto, CA (July 7, 1997).

2 Guy Kawaski, speech at Meredith Corporation, Des Moines, Iowa, November 1997.

3 Joanna Lowenstein, "Direct Mail: More Expensive Less Effective," *Folio:* (December 1, 1997): 27.

4 Anne Graham, "Nonmember Subs—Or Not," *Folio:* (June 1, 1995): 47.

5 Lambath Hochwald, "Circulation Secrets," *Folio:* (February 1, 1996): 57.

6 Ibid.

7 *By The Numbers*, DDB Needham. Based on MRI Fall 1995 and SRDS January 1996 data.

8 *Rolling Stone* (Media kit, 1998).

9 *Veronis, Suhler and Associates Communications Industry Forecast* (New York: Veronis, Suhler and Associates, 1997): 274

10 Phillip Moffitt, "*Esquire* from the Beginning," *Esquire* (June 1983): 13.

11 *Veronis, Suhler and Associates Communications Industry Forecast* (New York: Veronis, Suhler and Associates, 1998): 304.

12 Edwin Diamond, "The Mid-Life Crisis of the Newsweeklies," *New York* (June 7, 1976): 56.

13 Ibid.

14 *The 1996/97 Magazine Handbook: A Comprehensive Guide for Advertisers, Ad Agencies and Magazine Marketers*, 68 (New York: Magazine Publishers of America, 1996): 16.

15 *Policies and Procedures in Association Management* (Washington, DC: American Society of Association Executives, 1996): 91.

16 Graham, 48.

17 Ibid.

18 "Magazine Wholesaler Restructuring," *MPA Consumer Marketing Newsletter* (Spring 1996): 1.

19 Keith Clinkscales, "The Economics of Magazine Publishing," Stanford Professional Publishing Course, Palo Alto, CA (July 28, 1997).

CHAPTER 7

Magazine Structures

Staff Organization

Country Home has an innovative trio of editors who were hired as a group in 1997 to replace the outgoing editor-in-chief. The magazine and its ancillary products had grown to such a degree that three people were needed to do a job that had been previously done by a single individual. By meshing three job descriptions, a unified whole was created with three talented individuals divvying up the work: The editor-in-chief has final say over the whole magazine, the creative editor oversees both the editorial and design portions of the magazines, and the executive editor is in charge of special products and projects. 📖 *The magazine workplace has changed significantly since the days of Benjamin Franklin, when the editor was also the printer, the publisher, and the proprietor. And it continues to change. While magazines historically have functioned as vehicles for information, interpretation, entertainment, advocacy, and service, their creation is usually a business decision. Their day-to-day success depends not only on editorial quality, but also on business acumen. The professionals who run today's magazines are managing complex businesses; their decisions must go beyond creation of the physical product.*

WHO'S RUNNING THE SHOW?

All magazine staffs have to complete the same basic tasks—planning, writing and editing articles, designing pages, overseeing the manufacture of the finished product, promoting the magazine to advertisers as well as to readers, managing audience needs, and making sure the bills are paid.

Look at magazine mastheads: On one magazine, a single individual may do it all, with help from outside agencies and freelancers. Another magazine may need hundreds of staffers. Some important staffers, without whom the magazine would be doomed, are never named on the publication's pages. What's more, there is little consistency in magazine job titles and the duties associated with them. A senior editor at one magazine may have the responsibilities of an associate editor at another magazine. An advertising manager at one company may be the marketing director at another.

It is a constantly changing mix, as well. The job of editor has shifted dramatically in recent years and, with it, the roles of the rest of the staff. Nevertheless, the editor's role remains pivotal. "A successful magazine is characterized by a strong editor who supplies its central thrust. There is no room for weakness or uncertainty in defining what the editor does. To some extent, then, everyone else's job description follows," says editorial consultant John Fry.[1]

The size, frequency, and content of a magazine, as well as its place within a corporate structure, determine the size and structure of its staff. A weekly magazine needs a large staff and is more likely to have staff writers and photographers than magazines published less frequently. A quarterly, by comparison, may rely on a regular pool of freelancers and purchase its illustrative material from a photo house. A highly departmentalized magazine might need several section editors, while a magazine with mostly feature material may have none.

The division of labor at a magazine traditionally falls into four areas: editorial, advertising sales, circulation, and production. Editorial involves the magazine's content—its features, departments, and illustrations from the cover to the last page. Advertising sales has the responsibility of selling ad space in the magazine and for marketing and promoting the title. Circulation is concerned with getting and keeping readers, whether they are newsstand buyers or regular subscribers. Production covers the printing and technological concerns of equipment, paper, color, binding, and delivering the magazine to the newsstand or the home. However, this traditional approach doesn't allow for the evolving roles of magazine staffers and the need for fluidity in the workplace. It assumes that every magazine has four departments, when there are many small magazines that may not even have four full-time employees because many functions are outsourced to freelancers or special service companies.

Consequently, it makes more sense to divide magazine staffs into two major groups: the

Meredith Publishing Group Organization Chart

Meredith Corporation of Des Moines, Iowa, publishes consumer and custom magazines. The company's publishing group flow chart, below, illustrates the complexity of a multiple-title publishing house. Because Meredith is a multimedia company, the magazine group is just one section of a more complex system headed by Chairman and CEO William T. Kerr, not shown on this chart.

Heading the magazine group is President Christopher Little. Reporting to Little are a series of group publishers who oversee the magazines and vice presidents who oversee strategic marketing, development, operations, finance, and administration. In addition to consumer titles such as *Better Homes and Gardens, Ladies' Home Journal, Country Home*, and *Successful Farming*, the Meredith Integrated Marketing group publishes custom magazine marketing programs, such as Sears's *Mature Outlook*, Lutheran Brotherhood's *Bond*, and four Iams Company publications, including *Your Cat* and *You and Your Dog*.

Not shown on the chart: the corporate public relations offices, through which the corporate communications magazine *Meredith Insider* is published.

Meredith Publishing Group Organization Chart

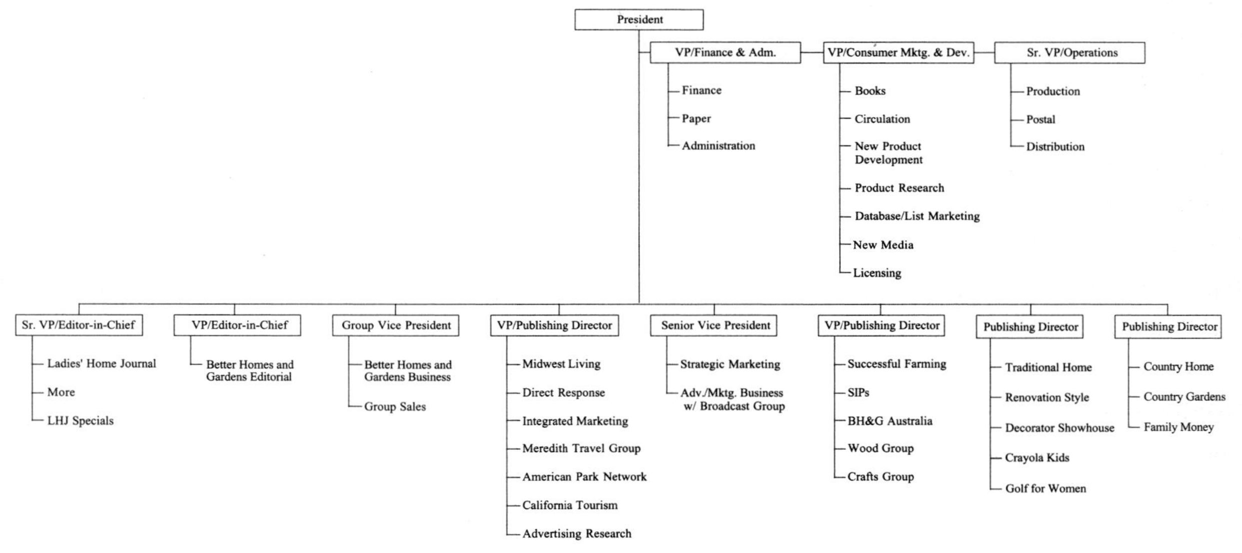

creative side and the business side. The creative side provides the magazine's content—articles, artwork, photos, and design. The business side consists of advertising, marketing, circulation, distribution, and production. Both sides report to the publisher. In large publishing houses with more than one magazine, there may be a president or chief executive officer who is the ultimate decision maker. At a small magazine, decisions may be shared by both the editor and the publisher. Regardless of set-up, a magazine's creative side and business side work together for a common goal.

The job titles and descriptions that follow are those typically found at a large or mid-sized consumer or trade magazine. Smaller consumer, trade, and organization magazines are less likely to have the entire hierarchy of titles and may

BETTER HOMES AND GARDENS FLOW CHART

The *Better Homes and Gardens* flow chart, right, breaks out the positions needed to produce America's fifth largest circulation magazine. The magazine has a new media department as well as a test kitchen, in addition to standard magazine job positions.

Because of space limitations, the managing editor tier was placed at the bottom of this page. The managing editor works closest with the editor-in-chief and is a notch higher on the organization chart than the art director and the executive editors. The executive editors are slightly higher than the manager of reader shopping and the creative director of new media/TV.

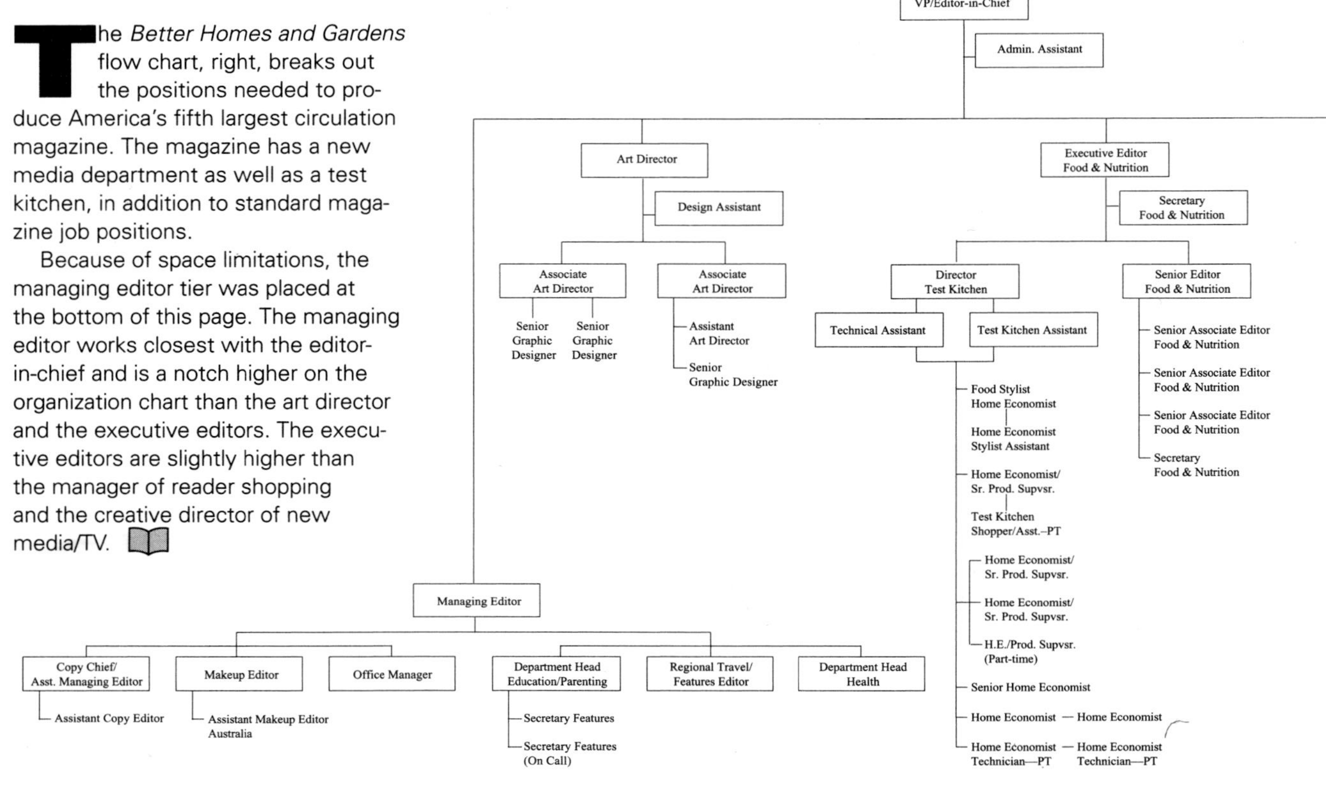

have collapsed several job responsibilities into a few positions.

President and CEO

A chief executive officer is the top title in America's corporate structure. It is a corporate title, not a traditional magazine one, so only magazines that are part of a larger company have these positions on their mastheads. The title of president is also a corporate designation and implies leadership over a major section of the organization. Sometimes the president is also the CEO; at other times the president reports to the CEO.

For example, David J. Pecker is president and chief executive officer of Hachette Filipacchi Magazines and has been credited by some in the industry with turning a struggling publishing house into a major media player. He wheels and deals in the business and advertising arena, but he has a hands-off approach when it comes to editorial content. There he fosters an entrepreneurial atmosphere.

At *Archaeology,* on the other hand, the publisher reports not only to a 40-member board of trustees, but also to a paid executive director and a volunteer president of the Archaeological Institute of America.

Publisher

This is typically the top business job on a magazine. The publisher has final responsibility for the magazine's profitability. Budgeting, strategic planning, and advertising development are the publisher's responsibilities. Traditionally, publishers

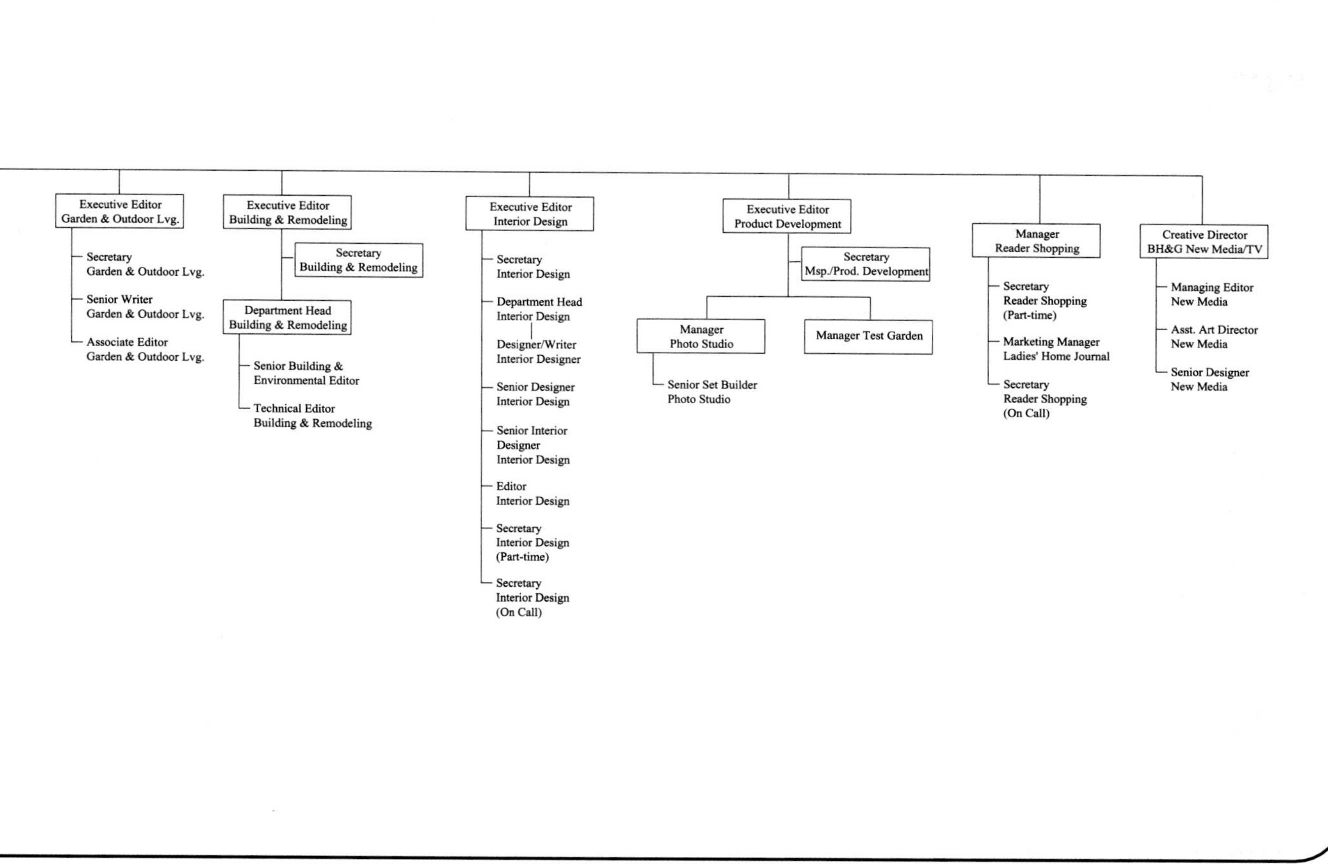

have moved up the ranks from advertising sales, where they learned how magazines build a profit base through circulation and advertising.

Jim Fishman, vice president and publisher of *Audubon,* the magazine of the National Audubon Society, says, "Ad sales people are better prepared than most, by experience and inclination, for advancement to senior management positions because the analytical, negotiating, and motivating skills they use in sales calls are critical for a president or publisher, particularly when it becomes necessary to structure and implement an unpopular plan." Fishman argues that the title of publisher has a thousand meanings, "but generally, he or she has a broad business background, and as such, determines how to boost business for the title."[2]

Increasingly, however, publishers are moving up from editorial positions. Jim Roberts, group publisher at Miller Freeman Inc., started as a freelance writer at *Guitar Player* and moved to editor of *Bass Player* when it was launched in 1989. In 1994, he was named associate publisher in addition to his job as editor of *Bass Player* and "had to learn a whole new set of ropes about the business side." Today, he is publisher of the music group at Miller Freeman, which includes *Bass Player, Guitar Player,* and *Keyboard.* "I've seen magazine journalism from just about every perspective except ad sales, although I've been involved with that on the publisher level. I'm not sure if that's the best way to train, but it worked for me," Roberts says.

Typical Magazine Job Titles

Business Positions	Creative Positions
President/CEO	Editor-in-chief/Editor
Publisher	Managing Editor
Circulation Director	Executive Editor
Marketing Director	Creative Director
Public Relations Director/ Promotion Director	Art Director
Production Director*	Senior Editor/ Section Editor
Advertising Sales Director	Associate Editor/ Assistant Editor
Assistant Publisher/ Business Manager	Copy Editor
Research Director*	On-line Editor
Advertising Sales Representative	Staff Writer
	Photographer
	Contributing Editor
	Editorial Assistant/ Fact Checker
	Freelancer

* Depending on the magazine, may be considered a business position or a creative position.

Group Publisher

Multiple magazine publishing houses such as Miller Freeman may have a group publisher like Roberts who is responsible for several magazines. Bob Brink, executive vice president and group publisher at Hearst Magazines, says his job is one of overall coordination: "I have 12 or 13 publishers reporting to me, and my responsibilities are to make sure all the titles they manage are in place for budgeting, positioning, personnel, and sales. Most important, though, is to show how a magazine fits together with sister titles in the same area."[3]

John Miller, vice president and group publisher of Hachette Filipacchi Home Group, is involved with ad sales, promotion, circulation, manufacturing costs, and the overall bottom line for the magazines in his group. "The big distinction between a group publisher and a regular publisher, though, is that you present powerful marketing opportunities and better service for advertisers via a collection of similarly themed magazines," he says.[4]

Editor-in-Chief/Editor

This is the top creative job on a magazine. At some magazines, the top title may be editor-in-chief, while at others it may be editor, or even editorial director. Whatever the title, this key person is the creative force behind the magazine.

Today's editor-in-chief or editor (the titles are interchangeable and it's a moot question why one may be chosen over the other as the name for the top title) is expected to be more than a creative and visionary editorial architect. The editor works with the publisher in planning a budget, works with advertising salespeople and the public relations manager to provide the information they need to sell the magazine, and works with the managing editor in making assignments. Not surprisingly, the editor-in-chief must be a successful manager of both staffers and freelancers. Increasingly, the position also has marketing implications, including building relationships with advertisers and creating brand extensions. As the top editorial player, the editor-in-chief reports only to the publisher.

VISIONARY. The editor-in-chief is responsible for shaping the magazine's content to suit its editorial philosophy and audience and for determining the magazine's formula. She does this by maintaining continuity with the past, while also adding an element of surprise and excitement. The final decision on what articles and artwork to assign and to accept, and what graphic approach best suits the magazine, rests with the editor-in-chief.

The best magazine editors infuse their magazines with their own personalities. They look ahead for what the audience might need in one or two years and plan an exciting and involving way to provide it. Good editors read their competition, and lots of it, and spend their lives with their ears open to the delights, vagaries, oddities, and thrills of the world around them.

Jim Roberts of Miller Freeman offers his "two cents" on the role of the chief editor: "I've always said the job consists primarily of connecting the people who read the magazine to the people who create the magazine. When that connection is broken or compromised, the magazine is in trouble."

JUGGLING ACTS

On March 12, 1998, Mike Mettler, editor-in-chief of *Car Stereo Review,* worked on four different issues of his monthly magazine. In many ways, Mettler is like a juggler in a three-ring circus, trying to provide continuity from issue to issue, while also making sure there is an element of anticipation and excitement. On this particular day, Mettler:

- Saw film for the April issue;
- Did second and third edits of articles for the May issue;
- Changed the topic for an article in the June issue and modified the deadline to accommodate the change;
- Slated and modified assignments for the July issue;
- Watched the sunset reflect off the Statue of Liberty and saw the marquees light up on Broadway, 44 floors below;
- Went home very late.

After 10 years of juggling multiple issues every day as editor of *Utne Reader,* Jay Walljasper was ready to trade in his editor role for that of writer. He wanted to remain at the magazine, but with different responsibilities. Walljasper negotiated with the magazine's founder, Eric Utne, to work three days a week, or 60 percent of the week, for 60 percent of his salary. The remaining two days of the week, Walljasper writes for other magazines such as *The Nation.*

His new title at *Utne Reader,* editor-at-large, means he writes many of the cover articles, conceives ideas, and does some editing. "Management and administration are not much a part of my life now," Walljasper says. "This is my reward for helping build up the magazine."

MANAGER. The editor-in-chief is the primary magazine "boss," managing the creative staff as well as the magazine itself. At a big circulation magazine, a good manager provides direction for his large staff and then gets out of the way by delegating as much work as possible. At a smaller magazine with a two- or three-person editorial staff, the editor is more likely to be a hands-on manager who works with the staff individually and as a group to control the direction of the magazine. Whatever the magazine's size, the editor-in-chief is responsible for staff relations and communication, editorial supervision, planning, and public relations.

Good editors nurture talent and find the right people to be both editors and writers. The editor-in-chief strives to create an environment in which they can all do their best work together. Two magazine editorial heavyweights, Tina Brown and Anna Wintour, discussed the editor's role on PBS's "The Charlie Rose Show" in 1998.[5]

Brown, who left her job as editor of *The New Yorker* in July 1998 to start her own magazine in affiliation with Miramax Films, said she believed a good editor fosters teamwork over a period of several years: "I think it takes, really, that long for an editor to grapple with all the forces at play, learn what her team is best at, form that team, forge that team, create an identity, and then have you all dancing on the same team."

Wintour, editor-in-chief of *Vogue,* emphasized that an editor is responsible for hiring and encouraging quality staff members: "I'm always looking to the people that I work with for a sense of news and for a sense of journalism because I don't feel that a magazine can be a coffee table book. It has to have a sense of urgency to make people want to pick it up every month. So, you need very competitive, newsy, journalistic people working for you that are inspiring to you and to everyone who works with you. One's always looking for young people who want to push the envelope a bit and tell you that you're an old fuddy-duddy and that we have to move on. I think it's really being open to other voices and listening to what they have to say."

MARKETER. Because today's magazines are viewed as brands that can be extended and franchised, the editor-in-chief is expected to think beyond the magazine into new products and publishing opportunities. Cathleen Black, president of Hearst Magazines Division, instructs her editors to think as marketers do by growing, leveraging, and expanding their titles, which she sees as "incredible franchises."[6] Conferences, books, and one-shot issues are just a few possibilities. "Being a magazine editor is more than just literally producing a magazine," she says.[7]

LONG LIVE *THE NEW YORKER*: AN EDITORIAL GENEALOGY

Since its founding in 1925, *The New Yorker* has had just five editorial monarchs reigning over the content of a magazine that many historians believe is one of the finest of the twentieth century. Emperor Harold Ross (1925–1951), King William Shawn (1952–1987), Prince Robert Gottlieb (1987–1992), Queen Tina Brown (1992–1998), and Prince David Remnick (1998 to present) are the royal players in *The New Yorker*'s editorial genealogy.

The wordy and cerebral magazine was founded by 33-year-old Harold Ross, a "tramp journalist" who hopped freight trains from town to town and worked on dozens of newspapers before achieving success as editor of the Army's *Stars and Stripes* newspaper during World War I. Identified as an abrasive, boorish hick from the West by *New Yorker* contributor Brendan Gill, Ross nevertheless had the acumen to create a magazine for the most exciting city in America. *The New Yorker*'s rise to prominence as a national publication for a metropolitan audience was due to Ross's ability to surround himself with the best and the brightest of the famous Algonquin Round Table: Robert Benchley as drama critic; Dorothy Parker as book reviewer; Katharine Angell White as fiction editor; and E. B. White and James Thurber as general editors and writers.

Ross himself was quirky, awkward, and unsophisticated, but his editorial style was eloquent, precise, and grammatically exact. From the start, Ross gave *The New Yorker* an urbane and urban tone, which readers and writers loved. And Ross loved his writers as long as they avoided language that was intellectually stuffy, self-consciously literary, or sexually connotative. Editorial content could be detached, whimsical, or even humorous—Ross liked cartoons—but the magazine had to be taken seriously. That Ross took it seriously was evident by the amount of money he budgeted for editorial, about $400,000 a year during the Depression.

As an editor, Ross demanded accuracy, and he was known for his long, detailed comments on manuscripts. The fact-checking department he created still has the reputation for being the best in the magazine industry.

Ross hand-picked his editorial successor, William Shawn, who joined the staff in 1933 as a "Talk of the Town" reporter when he was 26 years old. By 1939, Shawn was managing editor and he became editor after Ross's death in December 1951. Quiet and unassuming outside the office, Shawn was a powerful editor for more than 30 years; he molded *The New Yorker* into a magazine that combined the best of journalism and literature. According to *The New York Times* book critic John Leonard, "Shawn changed *The New Yorker* from a smarty-pants parish tip sheet into a journal that altered our experience instead of just posturing in front of it."[1] In the April 22, 1985, "Notes and Comment" section, Shawn laid out the editorial philosophy he had been following for years: "Amid a chaos of images, we value coherence. We believe in the printed word. And we believe in clarity. And in immaculate syntax. And in the beauty of the English language."

Shawn's editorial style was simple: He read every word published in *The New Yorker*, from original typescript to page proofs. Unlike Ross, who sent detailed memos to his staff, Shawn dealt directly with the two dozen full-time editors and about 140 fiction and nonfiction writers who worked on contract. He personally edited Rachel Carson's "Silent Spring" and Truman Capote's "In Cold Blood."

Writers said Shawn was patient and supportive, allowing them to work at their own pace while providing an atmosphere that encouraged creativity. As Shawn explained: "No writer or artist is ever given an order. When a journalistic writer undertakes a new project, it is always done in full agreement with the editor; the two have to bring to it the same enthusiasm. And no editing is ever imposed on a writer; every editorial suggestion is presented in the form of a question, and is settled by agreement between writer and editor."[2]

When the Fleischmann family, who had funded *The New Yorker* from the start, sold the magazine to Advance Publications (owners of *Vogue, Mademoiselle, Glamour, Vanity Fair,* and *GQ,* among others) in 1985, insiders suspected Shawn's days as editor were numbered. They were right. In 1987, the 80-year-old Shawn was forced to retire and an outsider, 55-year-old Robert Gottlieb, was named editor.

Gottlieb, who had been president of Alfred A. Knopf and was a respected book editor, did not make as many changes in *The New Yorker* as magazine watchers anticipated. He added color to the editorial pages in the 64th anniversary issue in February 1989—for the first time since 1926 when a two-page color cartoon ran. He tried to appeal to a younger audience through trendy book excerpts, more foreign coverage, new sections, and listings such as "Edge of Night Life" about late-night clubs. However, Gottlieb was not interested in revolutionizing *The New Yorker,* and he turned out to be a conservator who refused even to lunch with major advertisers or talk to them about his vision of the magazine.

That was a problem, for *The New Yorker* was in trouble, selling an average of 20,000 copies per week at the newsstand, versus its 1950s heyday of 100,000 newsstand copies a week. Not only was circulation down, but so was advertising. The solution was to bring in a new editor to sit on the throne.

Tina Brown earned her tiara at *Vanity Fair* by reviving a literary icon into what some critics described as a celebrity-driven, upscale *People.* Brown has long been a master of generating media buzz: She put a naked and pregnant Demi Moore on *Vanity Fair*'s cover. Brown wasn't afraid to throw tradition out the window at *The New Yorker* when she took over in 1992. The table of contents was expanded, bylines went to the front of stories, pieces on movie stars were carried, articles were shortened, a letters to the editor department was initiated, and controversial illustrations appeared on the covers while large photos ran on the editorial pages. Brown's goal was to add more variety to the editorial mix, make the magazine more timely and topical, and include an offbeat and irreverent tone to shorter, peppier pieces. Said Brown, "It's part of a pattern of reimagining and recreating *The New Yorker* while keeping the most important things intact."[3]

Brown's detractors said she took *The New Yorker* down-market, making it a vulgar celebrity magazine for insiders. They said the magazine was no longer elegant and that it had lost its quality of timelessness. Supporters, however, said the magazine was livelier, trendier, and more interesting. Brown dismissed most of the criticism, saying, "Anyone who talks about the lack of timelessness isn't reading the magazine. If they were reading it, they would see that the pieces I'm publishing are exactly those kinds of pieces that were previously published, but are now being mixed up with other kinds of pieces."[4] And despite all the talk about short articles, there were still long, 25,000-word pieces.

Certainly *The New Yorker* looked different under Brown, and that may be what critics responded to, rather than content. The 1993 Valentine's Day cover of a Hasidic man kissing a black woman, which shocked and offended many readers, has turned out to be a top-selling one so far. Circulation went up under Brown, yet the magazine still lost millions of dollars each year.

Reinforcing her reputation as the celebrity queen of buzz, Brown left *The New Yorker* in July 1998 to head her own multimedia venture in affiliation with Miramax Films. David Remnick, author of more than 100 articles for the magazine over a period of six years, was named editor. Remnick, who received a Pulitzer Prize in 1994 for his book, *Lenin's Tomb,* isn't likely to imitate Brown's celebrity approach. Although Remnick will miss being a writer, he says, "An editor needs to be in the chair, editing and reading, or out and about meeting with writers, and that's where you'll find me from now on."[5]

As for his plans for the magazine, Remnick says, "In the next several years *The New Yorker* will have a fuller engagement with the world. We're in a crazy Gilded Age of money, money, money, and we want to get much more of that story. And though we want to cover the unique aspects of our city, we also want to have a global reach." He intends to stress high-quality, brilliantly written pieces, pointing out, "There's no reason why the level of writing can't be extraordinarily high in every arena. Ostensibly glitzy subjects such as fashion can be written with the same intensity and skill as coverage of Bosnia or Rudolph Giuliani."

But along with expanded reporting and deeper literary writing, Remnick doesn't intend to forget the cartoon tradition. "Cartoons are our signature," he says, "probably the first thing people read, and we want to treat them well." He already is featuring more cartoons in larger spaces, covering a half page and even a full page.

Says Remnick, "Americans are surrounded by a blizzard of information. If you were inclined to lose your mind you could stay on the Internet all day. In the middle of this blizzard *The New Yorker* should stand as a place of clarity, coverage, intelligence, reliability—and hilarity. We don't want to forget hilarity."

[1] Eric Pace, "William Shawn, 85, Is Dead; *New Yorker*'s Gentle Despot," *The New York Times* (December 9, 1992): 1A.
[2] William Shawn, "Notes and Comments," *The New Yorker* (April 22, 1985): 35–36.
[3] Robert D. McFadden, "Eustace Tilley's on Vacation, And, My What a Stand-in," *The New York Times* (February 15, 1994): B3.
[4] Deirdre Carmody, "Tina Brown's Progress at the New *New Yorker,*" *The New York Times* (April 12, 1993): C2.
[5] Stefan Kanter, "David Remnick: 'We Don't Want to Forget the Hilarity,'" *Columbia Journalism Review* (September/October 1998): 43.

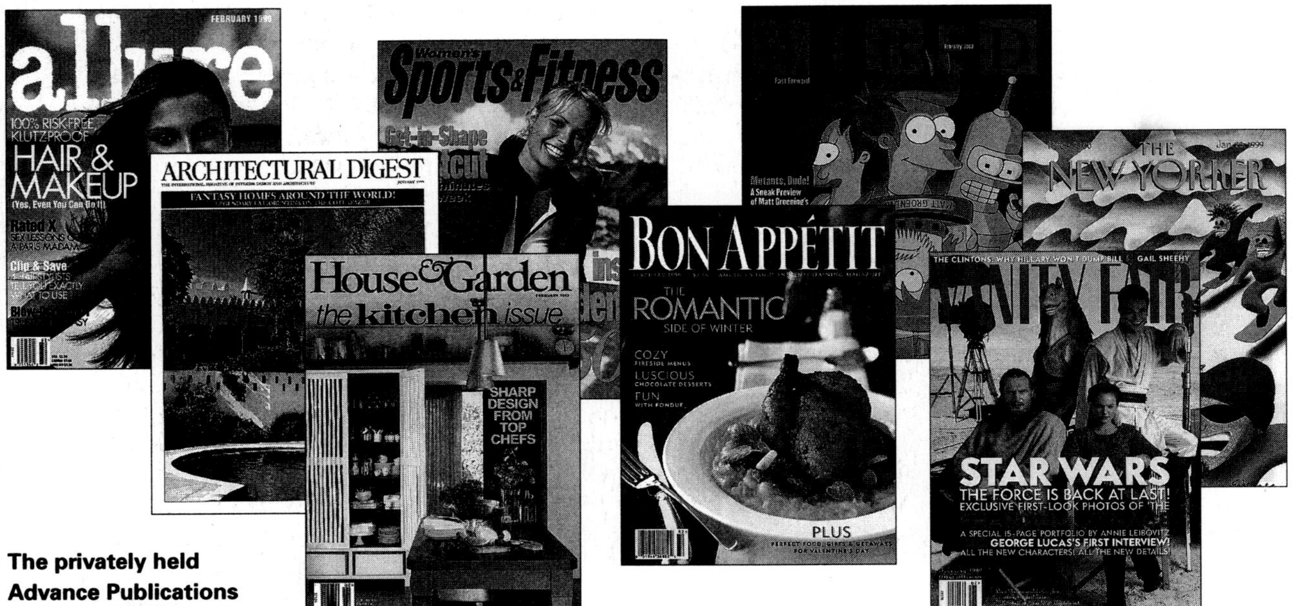

The privately held Advance Publications is the owner of the Condé Nast group of magazines, which includes *Allure, Architectural Digest, Bon Appétit, House & Garden, The New Yorker, Vanity Fair, Wired,* and *Women's Sports & Fitness.*

Today's editors are expected to be entrepreneurial market authorities who know what their readers want. This leads to credibility both inside the company and within the magazine industry. *Mademoiselle* editor-in-chief Elizabeth Crow says, "Basically, the editor is the authority on the reader; a good editor knows what her readers want to read. Presumably, she knows more about what they want to read on certain subjects than anyone else on earth." Consequently, "the lunching, the giving talks everywhere—from Harvard Divinity School to MBA conferences—is increasingly important," adds Crow.[8]

The editor-in-chief as market authority has led to editors going on advertising calls with the salespeople. Their function there, however, is to educate the advertiser on the magazine; the sales staff handles closing the sale.

John F. Kennedy Jr., editor of *George,* often goes on sales calls for his magazine. "I enjoy it," he says. *Good Housekeeping* editor-in-chief Ellen Levine also likes to call on advertisers, because, she says, she believes in the "care and feeding of major advertisers." She'd rather meet with the product manager than with an advertising agency representative, however, because the product manager has a clearer idea of his product and how it might mesh with *Good Housekeeping* content.

Editor-in-chief Dorothy Kalins of *Garden Design* and *Saveur* says she prefers to go on sales calls because she can explain the magazine's content to advertisers more thoroughly than anybody else on staff. Craig Reiss, editor-in-chief of *Adweek,* disagrees. He will not go on ad sales calls because he knows his advertisers as sources. Advertising is, after all, the subject matter of his magazine.

Managing Editor

Often called a magazine's "sergeant," the managing editor may have the toughest job on staff, spending half his time on managerial duties, half on editorial. Enforcing deadlines, hiring and firing staff and freelancers, and keeping the magazine generally on track and on schedule are all the responsibility of the managing editor, who reports directly to the editor-in-chief. In some cases, a managing editor may write articles, edit, and generally jump in to fill whatever needs exist.

It is the managing editor's responsibility to see that all work progresses efficiently and gets done by deadline. The managing editor must be aware of all problems and use discretion in either dealing with them immediately or consulting the editor-in-chief. The editor must be made aware of all problems eventually, however.

TRACKING THE STORY

The tracking chart at right shows how a managing editor keeps track of articles, photos, and designs. The assignments are grouped in tiers. This particular magazine was produced in three tiers, so that tier one had one deadline, tier two another, and tier three still another. This keeps the editors from deadline overload.

The various steps in an article's development are indicated at the top of the chart: initial draft, photo shoot, initial layout, and so on. Along the side are the positions in the magazine, starting with the editor-in-chief and moving through creative director all the way to production director.

The blocks indicate the dates when each individual must deal with each stage of the article. The shaded areas indicate "time out" for that person—stages at which they have no responsibility for the article.

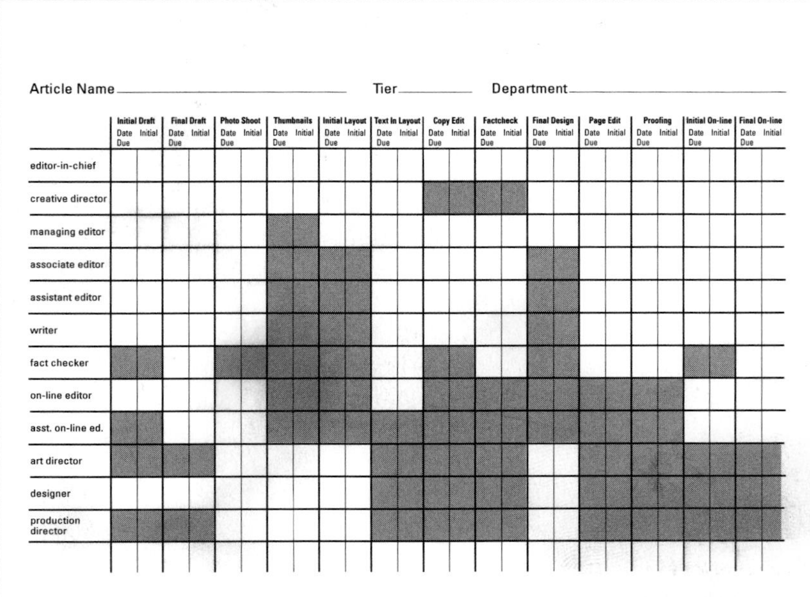

The managing editor works with the senior, associate, or departmental editors to assign and track all articles and keeps in contact with these editors from start to finish. He works with the art director in ensuring that all design and photography is well executed, on time, consistent, and appropriate for the magazine. He works with the production director to develop production deadlines and to make sure these deadlines are met.

Collette Connor, managing editor of *Videography,* says, "The managing editor is all details. You're the last person to see the magazine before it goes to print. Your proofreading must be exquisite because if anything is spelled wrong, people will come to you."[9]

The managing editor is both a buffer and a conduit between the staff and the editor-in-chief. "My job is to keep them all productive and happy—and to make sure we're out on time," Bill Marks, managing editor of *Mini-Storage Messenger,* says.[10]

Interestingly, at Time Inc. magazines, the managing editor actually functions as the editor-in-chief. This is a legacy from the days of Henry Luce when there was only one top editor in the company: Mr. Luce. Now, Norman Pearlstine is editor-in-chief of Time Inc., which puts him at the top of every masthead, from *Time* to *Fortune* to *Sports Illustrated for Kids.* The person who really runs the individual magazine is the managing editor, in this case, Walter Isaacson at *Time,* John Huey at *Fortune,* and Neil Cohen at *Sports Illustrated for Kids.*

Executive Editor

Some magazines have an executive editor in place of a managing editor. More complex magazine staffs, such as *Country Home*'s, introduced at the beginning of this chapter, have both positions.

The executive editor, who reports to the editor-in-chief, often balances the work of the editor; the

Who Has the Final Decision on the Cover?

Editors, art directors, publishers, and circulation directors spend hours trying to select the perfect cover for each issue: one that sells out at newsstands while also offering continuity and change for the subscriber. John Peter, a New York magazine consultant, says, "The most dominant [cover] factor is the image. Most people remember the image and who was on the cover last time."[1]

Who controls the cover? While choosing the topic, art, design, and cover lines may be a cooperative effort, the person with responsibility for the final decision on the cover should be the magazine's editor-in-chief. A survey of 75 editors asking who makes the final decision on cover subject, design, art, and text backs up this position. According to John Mack Carter, president of Hearst Magazines Enterprises, the majority of editors surveyed agreed that the editor has to have the final say—after input from key people such as the art director and the publisher.[2]

Greg Paul, partner of the magazine consulting firm of Brady and Paul Associates, agrees that the final decision has to be the editor's. "To make a good decision about what goes on the cover and how it is laid out, you need a creative team comprising an editor and art director who share a mutual respect. Opinions on the cover should

role of the executive editor is, therefore, often defined by the qualities of the editor. "If the editor is an authority and writer, but has a distaste for administration, for example, clearly the next person in the chain of command should be strong in areas of budgeting, scheduling, and sensing how to carry out assignments coming from the editor. For this reason, we see on more and more mastheads today the title of 'executive editor,'" says consultant John Fry.[11]

Creative Director

Not all magazines have a creative director; in fact, it's safe to say that most don't. The creative director is the liaison between the editorial and design staffs and between design and production. The creative director, who reports to the editor-in-chief, assures that all editorial and design content is in the proper tone and style. Next to the editor-in-chief, this person is the keeper of the magazine's personality.

Art Director

The art director oversees the look of the magazine, assuring that design is consistent with editorial philosophy, is logical and readable, and will appeal to the audience. The art director manages all design and photography assignments and makes sure the resultant material is well executed, on time, consistent, and appropriate for the magazine. On *Car Stereo Review,* art director Laura Sutcliffe is responsible for designing covers and features pages and for overseeing cover shoots. She has a deputy art director, an associate art director, and an assistant art director on her staff. At a small magazine, however, the art director might be the only full-time design employee; he might use freelance designers to help provide layout variety.

The art director, who reports to the editor-in-chief, works with the production director to determine production deadlines and to make sure these deadlines are met. The art director, top staff editors, and production director work together on the break-of-the-book, planning a budget, submitting requests for quotes, and selecting a printer. When the inevitable differences arise between editors and the art director, they must work together to reach a compromise, basing decisions on editorial philosophy and audience. Should they reach an impasse, the editor-in-chief has the final say at most magazines.

Senior Editor/Section Editor

This position has a variety of functions on American magazines. It also may have a variety of names, including feature editor, department editor, beauty editor, fashion editor, and so on. In general, the senior editor helps assign all articles, making sure the writer understands the topic, angle, length, tone, and other specifics.

be considered by a 'presidential cabinet' made up of the publisher and the heads of circulation, ad sales, and other pertinent departments. But the buck usually stops with the editor. It should not be a committee process, or you run the risk of producing something so watered down that nobody dislikes it—or loves it, either," says Paul.[3]

However, the editor-in-chief isn't the final arbiter at all magazines. The publisher may be the last one to sign off. At *Appliance Manufacturer,* editor Joe Jancsurak says covers are developed through consensus involving him, the art director, and technical editors before showing the final concept to the publisher. At that point, the publisher may suggest changes in placement, color, or even type size and style. Jeff Morey, president and publisher of *Nursery Retailer,* says his final input includes doing the cover design himself.

Carter reinforces the importance of the publisher's input with a true story he likes to tell: A publisher goes into the editor's office with the picture he wants to be run as the June cover. The editor says, "Now just a minute. I've been picking the covers for this magazine for 10 years and I intend to go right on making that decision, including next June, as long as I'm the editor."

The publisher agrees, adding that he just wanted the editor to know how he felt about this particular cover for that issue. Relates Carter, "Later, the editor turned the picture down—proving he had the authority. But he's no longer editor—proving something else."

[1] Mary W. Quigley. "What Sells, What Bombs: Magazine Cover Roulette," *Washington Journalism Review* (July/August 1988): 19.

[2] John Mack Carter, "Who Controls the Cover?" *Folio:* (July 1983): 99.

[3] "Cover to Cover," *Folio:* (February 1, 1998): 94.

The senior editor works with the top editors in determining what articles to assign and how to approach them and works with writers to make sure the end product suits the magazine's needs. However, the final decision on what articles to use rests with the editor-in-chief; the senior editor seldom assigns an article without first consulting the editor. The senior editor also often writes articles, usually major feature pieces. The senior editor may report to either the editor-in-chief or to the managing editor.

Associate Editor/ Assistant Editor

These two positions, while separate on the masthead, often have similar duties, which include writing, editing or assigning material for front-of-the-book or back-of-the-book departments, and writing titles and subtitles. The major distinction between the two is that, often, assistant editors have more administrative duties.

At *Family Life,* the associate editor writes the table of contents, writes and edits the "parenting" department, and writes the "contributors' page." On *Country Living Gardener,* the associate editor writes and edits columns on beauty, health, and the magazine's dream home. Associate and assistant editors typically report to the senior editor.

Copy Editor

The copy editor reads every article, cutline, title, subtitle, and pull-quote in the magazine, correcting all errors in grammar, usage, punctuation, and style. The copy editor follows the magazine's style, which may be customized, or may follow University of Chicago or Associated Press (AP) style. The copy editor, who is in charge of creating style guidelines when special problems arise, reports to the managing editor.

The copy editor also looks for problems with clarity and organization and corrects these if possible. When problems seem too massive, the article is returned to the writer, through the senior or associate editor. The copy editor helps the senior or associate editor critique articles in terms of tone, content, and development of the assigned topic. Problems in these areas are dealt with by the managing editor or senior editor, with input from the copy editor.

On-Line Editor

This position is one of the newest to surface in the magazine hierarchy over the last decade. A similar title would be Web site editor. The on-line editor typically creates and maintains the magazine's Web site, serves as the liaison between the print magazine staff and the on-line staff, and assigns or creates on-line content. The on-line editor, who reports to the editor-in-chief or to the

RESEARCH IN BRIEF

Magazine Careers 1850–1926: Inhospitable Climate for Women

What was it like to be a woman magazine writer or editor between 1850 and 1926? How did popular magazines of the period portray journalism as a career for women? To find the answer to these questions, Professor Agnes Hooper Gottlieb of Seton Hall University analyzed dozens of articles written by women journalists about their experiences, as well as features discussing the field in general. She looked at such popular consumer magazines as *Collier's, Harper's Weekly, Harper's Bazaar, The Arena,* and *The Atlantic Monthly,* as well as the journalism trade journal *The Journalist.*[1]

Although women had worked as editors, writers, and even publishers of magazines since the eighteenth century, Gottlieb points out that it wasn't until 1870 that the U.S. Census established a category for women who made their living as journalists. That year, there were just 35 women in this new category, or less than 0.6 percent of all working journalists. By 1900, 2,193 women defined themselves as journalists. Between 1920 and 1930, the number of women reporters and editors had reached 14,786. What kind of welcome did these women receive at magazines?

Some women were lured to magazine journalism, notes Gottlieb, because they wanted to defy societal conventions. Others thought it was a good place to meet a man. And some "women also thought, mistakenly as we all know, that journalism was easy," Gottlieb says.

Despite a few tales of romance and adventure, Gottlieb found that magazines of the day painted an inhospitable picture of the climate for women reporters:

> *Women journalists recounted stories of editors who paid them less than men who did similar jobs, who tried to take sexual advantage of them, who printed articles but then refused to pay for them, and who treated them pejoratively and as interlopers in their newsrooms. The women told of the drudgery they were assigned to because of their sex and about how journalism spoiled their rosy attitudes and made cynics out of the best of them.*

It definitely was not easy being a magazine editor or writer during the 75-year period from before the Civil War until after World War I. Ironically, even male editors of magazines devoted to women, and which included articles written by women, made discouraging comments about women as journalists. In a 1901 article in *Ladies' Home Journal,* editor Edward Bok discouraged women from journalistic careers, saying the field "tends to make a woman too independent, too free, too broad. It establishes her on a footing with men that is not wise; it gives her opportunities that are not uplifting."

Other male editors argued that it was "unseemly" for a woman to be out at all hours, in all kinds of weather, and in the company of men without a chaperone. Many male writers tended to feel uncomfortable competing against women for stories, plus they resented the "glory" some women received for some articles. Yet as early as 1889, *The Journalist* dedicated a 24-page issue to women journalists to signal the acceptance of women within the ranks. The trade magazine's editor, Allan Forman,

managing editor, may have an assistant who edits on-line material and creates on-line content.

Staff Writers

Fewer and fewer magazines today have staff writers. Those few individuals lucky enough to spend their lives as staff writers are talented professionals who have experience with the magazine and are entrusted with the more difficult, comprehensive articles. Staff writers consult with the managing editor or senior editor, to whom they report, in determining appropriate articles for the magazine. They also help write the titles, pull-quotes, and cutlines.

Photographers

Only a handful of magazines, such as *National Geographic, Newsweek,* and *Life,* have staff photographers. Most photographers are freelancers. Both staff and freelance photographers work under the direction of the art director, who makes photography assignments based on consultation with staff editors and writers. Photographers are responsible for all aspects of an assignment they are given. This includes scheduling; finding models, equipment and props as needed; getting photo releases; processing black-and-white photos and getting color prints processed; and doing urged women to drop the use of pen names and to build solid reputations as professional reporters.

Gottlieb reports that women writers were honest about the traits needed to succeed in the field of journalism. An article by Cynthia May Westover Alden in *Frank Leslie's Popular Monthly* described the following attributes needed by a woman reporter in 1898: "Conscientiousness, fidelity to truth, absence of hypersensitiveness, common sense in dress, self-confidence, and exemption from the hypochondriacal tendency to which so many women are prone." Eleanor Hoyt, who wrote regularly for *Collier's,* noted in an article in *Current Literature* in 1903 that women needed "good health, more than average intelligence, dogged persistence, and indomitable pluck."

Women who succeeded as magazine journalists were driven by a passion to write, an ability to write well, and a need to earn money. Gottlieb says that "uniformly among women journalists of the nineteenth century can be found an absence of family money and a real need for the woman to support herself, her parents and/or her children. This group of scribblers who turned to journalism often had never married or, if married, often divorced."

In 1901, *Ladies' Home Journal* asked 42 female working journalists whether they would approve of their daughter working in the same field. Thirty-nine said they would not approve. By the 1920s, attitudes had changed. When *Collier's* asked a woman journalist hypothetically if she'd let a younger sister be a reporter in 1922, the enthusiastic response from the journalist was, "I have one and she is." Foreign correspondent Dorothy Thompson, asked to write about women journalists overseas for *The Nation* in 1926, stated there was "nothing extraordinary" about a woman in the job. She said she was surprised this would be cause for comment, adding, "The see-what-the-little-darling-has-done-now attitude ought to be outlawed."

Genevieve Jackson Boughner, author of the 1926 book *Women in Journalism: A Guide to the Opportunities and a Manual of the Technique of Women's Work for Newspapers and Magazines,* listed dozens of possibilities for women, including society editor, home-making writer, fashion reporter, columnist, and magazine editor. Women were no longer a rarity on magazine editorial staffs.

According to Gottlieb, magazines were an appropriate forum for the debate about careers for women in journalism. Although many articles highlighted negative aspects—discrimination, low pay, and harassment—they nonetheless pointed out that some women succeeded as journalists, which popularized and glamorized the field. Additionally, Gottlieb notes, these magazine articles are invaluable primary sources from and about women journalists who left no other record of their work experiences.

[1] Agnes Hooper Gottlieb, "Grit Your Teeth, Then Learn to Swear: Women in Journalistic Careers, 1850–1926" (paper presented at the annual meeting of the American Journalism History Association, Louisville, KY, October 1998).

reshoots as necessary. Photo-heavy magazines may also have a photo editor, who is the liaison between the photographer and the art director.

Contributing Editors

Contributing editors are freelancers rather than staff members. Despite their title, contributing editors tend to be writers who are experts in the field the magazine covers. Regular freelance writers with whom the magazine wants to maintain a relationship may be given this title. They report to either the managing editor or senior editor.

Editorial Assistant/Fact Checker

This is a common entry-level position, especially for New York-based magazines. The editorial assistant does some administrative work such as research, making copies, even filing for other staffers. Some magazines have one editorial assistant for every two to three editors. These staffers open and answer the mail, so they're often the most knowledgeable about magazine gossip. Some editorial assistants write short back-of-the-book or front-of-the-book articles and may do an occasional sidebar or two. Most people stay in these positions for one or two years, pay their dues, then move up.

Wendy Naugle, senior editor at *Family Life*, says newcomers shouldn't scoff at the importance of this position in proving their talent. "If the boss doesn't think you can copy well, he won't think you can do other things well," she points out. She should know, since the editorial assistant typically reports to the senior editor or to the associate editor.

Fact Checker

Often, the editorial assistant is also the fact checker, who makes sure all information presented in articles is correct. The fact checker starts with the assumption that all writers are liars, and asks for verification for everything that is not common knowledge. This includes the spelling of names, the wording of quotes if the quote doesn't ring true to the fact checker, and all other information presented as fact. It is the fact checker's responsibility to contact sources for verification when the writer's notes do not contain adequate information. The fact checker rewrites portions of articles when it is possible to correct errors with a minimum of rewriting. When major changes are needed, the fact checker consults with the managing editor, senior editor, or associate editor, who are responsible for getting the rewrite done.

Freelance Writers/Designers

With budget cutbacks and the trend toward outsourcing, more magazines are using freelance writers and designers than ever before. Some say the same number of jobs are there, but with a shift in who does the work.

"Where we used to have five editors or writers on a magazine, you now would see three or four, with the rest of the work outsourced to freelancers or part-time employees," says Dianne Hennessy, vice president of human resources at Cowles Business Media.[12]

Freelancers usually work for a variety of magazines, striving for financial security through consistent assignments from the same titles or publishing houses. Most successful freelancers already have been staff members on a magazine, where they learned the ropes, fine-tuned their talents, built their reputations, and established contacts. Depending on the magazine's structure, freelance writers may report to the managing editor or senior editor, and occasionally to the associate editor. Freelance designers report to the art director.

Circulation Director

Circulation directors are the key to the financial success of a magazine because they connect the

***Esquire, Motor Boating & Sailing, Popular Mechanics, Redbooks, Smart Money,* and *Victoria* are published by the Hearst Corporation, a privately held company started by William Randolph Hearst and still owned by the Hearst family.**

magazine to readers. It is the job of a circulation director not only to take care of existing readers, but also to find new ones. In a nutshell, the circulation director manages all paid circulation and is responsible for expanding readership through creative use of databases, analyzing single copy and subscription programs, defining and exploring new areas of potential readership, and maintaining a high renewal rate. The circulation director reports to the publisher. Increasingly, circulation directors are moving into top management.

It is a job that can make or break a magazine. David Lee, corporate circulation director of F&W Publications, is credited with keeping the well-respected fiction journal *Story* alive. *Story*, the first to publish such American legends as J. D. Salinger and Truman Capote, ceased publication in 1967 at a time when fiction was disappearing from American magazines. F&W restarted the magazine in 1989, and Lee forged a partnership with the Quality Paperback Book Club, which advertised subscriptions to the magazine, ran a short fiction contest for members, promoted the magazine in its newsletter, and sold the magazine's yearbook as a bonus to club members. Lee also connected the magazine with Writer's Digest Book Club and Writer's Digest School. Lee's inventiveness increased readership and put the magazine in the black.[13]

Larger publishing houses may have a circulation manager as well as assistants to support the circulation director. However, some magazines hire outside fulfillment agencies to take care of circulation, finding it cheaper and more efficient to hire a group of experts than to train their own staffs. Stuart Jordan, executive vice president of one such agency, Circulation Specialists Inc., says, "We encourage the publishers to think of us as staff. For the bulk of the magazines we work with, we *are* the circulation department."[14] The circulation director is the liaison between the magazine and the fulfillment house.

Marketing Director

The marketing director is primarily responsible for publicity and promotion for the magazine, with the goal of selling the magazine to readers and advertisers. This includes promotional programs to generate ad sales and increase circulation. At some magazines, the marketing director is responsible for all budgeting and analyses of circulation programs, list rentals, and rate-base planning and maintenance. The marketing director reports to the publisher.

Public Relations Director/Promotion Director

This person is responsible for creating media kits and other special promotional efforts that create and maintain the identity of the magazine in the eyes of readers and advertisers. At a small magazine without a public relations or promotion director, the media kit would be the responsibility of the marketing director. The PR or promotion director reports to either the publisher or to the marketing director.

Advertising Sales Director

This individual manages a staff of ad sales representatives and is ultimately responsible for generating advertising in the magazine. His job includes researching and analyzing data on existing and potential audiences, creating ad sales support material, developing ad rates, overseeing ad sales contacts, finalizing contracts with advertisers, and scheduling ad placement. In a large publishing house, he may supervise advertising branch managers located throughout the United States. The ad sales director may report either to the publisher or to the marketing director.

Ad Sales Representatives

Sales reps make the actual calls on advertisers, connecting the magazine with the needs and interests of the advertiser. They service and maintain their current accounts and are responsible for finding new business. Ad sales representatives report to the advertising director.

Production Director

The production director is the magazine's technical director and manages the break-of-the-book. He is responsible for maintaining production

Martha Stewart may have the most job titles of any magazine editor. Stewart is editor-in-chief of *Martha Stewart Living,* author of a dozen books, syndicated columnist in more than 100 newspapers, television personality, radio show tipster, marketer of her own line of bed and bath linens and paints through Kmart, producer of goods and services in her Martha By Mail catalogue, and star of television commercials for the American Express card. Not surprisingly, Stewart also holds the title of CEO of Martha Stewart Living Omnimedia, which oversees all her identities.

MAGAZINE MERGER MANIA

During the strong economy of the late 1990s, a great deal of investment capital was available for buying magazines. Corporations were generating high levels of profit and were under shareholder pressure to keep earnings high. That set the scene for a round of mergers and acquisitions. The mania for merger has led to the single consumer or trade magazine title publisher being an endangered species. Magazine publishing companies that offered growth potential became investment opportunities and targets for takeovers.

"The problem is that you can't stand still in this environment," said Robert A. Amato, chairman of Jobson Publishing, which publishes pharmaceutical and eyewear magazines such as *U.S. Pharmacist* and *Optometry Today.* "Any publisher who stands still either sells out or gets knocked off."[1]

Amato's family-owned company, with 50 magazine titles, wanted to grow, but he didn't want to sell out. "We've been fortunate," he said. "We've been able to fund our growth out of cash flow. But at a certain point, you have to look to outside sources." The Amato family ended up selling a minority stake in Jobson Publishing to Boston Ventures, an investment firm with a reputation for hands-off involvement.

Miller Publishing Group purchased *Spin* for more than $40 million in 1997 from Bob Guccione Jr., who turned around and used some of his profits to launch *Gear* in September 1998. Miller also bought six titles, including *Snow Country* and *Tennis,* for $35 million from The New York Times Company.

Even magazines that were losing money attracted interest. *New Woman* posted a loss of $3 million in 1997, yet it was sold to Rodale Press for $18 million. *Wired* also had losses when it was purchased for $76 million in May 1998 by Condé Nast.

The selling frenzy extended to entire publishing houses. Reed Elsevier purchased the Chilton Business Group's 39 trade titles from Walt Disney Company for $447 million in 1997. Along with its 130 Cahners Publishing Company titles, this deal made Reed Elsevier one of the major trade magazine owners in the world. Cygnus Publishing purchased PTN Publishing, which had almost 60 trade titles, for $97 million in 1997. That one business deal put newcomer Cygnus into a different league.

By the time this book is published, who knows who will own whom. The only constant in the magazine industry is change.

[1] Mike Hayes, "A Seller's Market," *Folio:* (July 15, 1998): 28.

efficiency, helping staff members format material on the computer as needed, and assuring that all pages are completed and technically accurate. The production director makes sure as much work as possible is done before the final deadline, preparing pages on the computer as articles and photographs are completed. The production director gets all advertising and editorial material to the printer on time and in proper form and oversees the magazine's press run. Occasionally, he also is in charge of distribution, getting the magazine to subscribers and newsstands from the printer.

The production director generally reports directly to the publisher, although at some magazines, he reports to the editor-in-chief or to the art director. Some large magazines have a production manager who reports to the production director. In this case, job duties are shared by the two individuals.

Assistant Publisher/ Business Manager

In conjunction with the publisher, to whom she reports, this individual is primarily responsible for the magazine's budget, which entails cost control, financial planning and analysis, and profit and loss reviews. The assistant publisher formulates general business policy, makes salary and wage proposals, and sees that the magazine's bills are paid and its debts collected. She supervises internal office management as well as operations of ad sales, circulation fulfillment, and editorial and advertising promotion. On small magazines, this individual also may be the circulation director or public relations director, or both.

Research Director

Only large publishing houses have research directors. In smaller operations, research is done

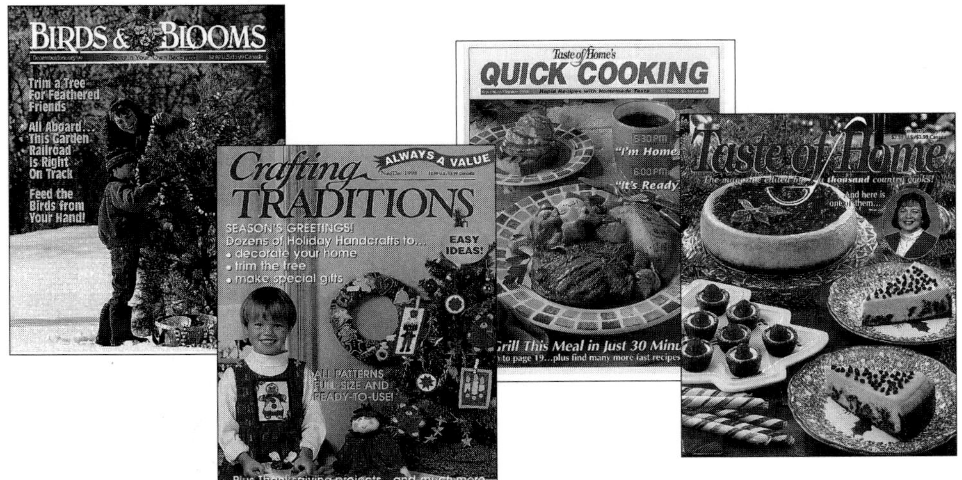

Reiman Publications, which is privately owned, publishes *Birds & Blooms, Crafting Traditions, Quick Cooking,* and *Taste of Home.*

by the editor or marketing director or by an outside agency. Typically, a research director researches the nature of the magazine's audience, which includes analyses of audience behaviors; plans and manages focus groups; presents focus group results to the staff; and makes recommendations for the magazine's response to audience attitudes. The research director either reports to the publisher or to the editor-in-chief.

A study by the American Business Press found that few magazines today have a single individual serving as research director: only five among 965 audited trade publications had a research director.[15] It wasn't that the research function was missing but that it had become the responsibility of someone in advertising sales or marketing as a result of organizational downsizing.

MAGAZINE OWNERSHIP

Magazines are published by some of the largest businesses in America. Many make profits for thousands of investors, while others must only make enough to keep one owner happy. Some magazines are nonprofit, while others see profit as part of the larger corporate picture. Increasingly, the single consumer or trade magazine, published by a single publisher, is disappearing, while conglomerates and group publishers are growing. Successful titles are sold almost weekly, and huge corporations sell entire groups of magazines, then buy others. Some of the largest publishing houses are privately owned; others are public properties with responsibility to stockholders. Ownership varies depending on the type of magazine, with different business structures possible for consumer, trade, and organization magazines.

Consumer and Trade Magazine Ownership

Many consumer and trade magazines are largely a product of a single individual's vision, even though the financing may come from other sources. In 1923, Henry Luce and Briton Hadden offered stock in their fledgling *Time* magazine to supplement their own investment. Their magazine is now part of the giant Time Warner media conglomerate and remains a public offering sold on the New York Stock Exchange.

In 1925, Harold Ross's *The New Yorker* was bankrolled by Raoul Fleischmann, who was the sole owner. Today, *The New Yorker* is still privately owned—by S. I. (Si) Newhouse Jr. and his brother Donald as part of their Advance Publications media empire.

A magazine's ownership defines the way decisions are made. Consumer and trade magazines may be publicly owned or privately owned.

PUBLICLY OWNED. Publicly owned magazines are traded on a stock exchange and must be responsive to their stockholders, who are looking for as large a return on their investment as possible. This adds an extra level of financial accountability to the magazine staff. Those investors may or may not care about editorial quality, but they are seriously interested in profit.

Some Top Magazine Publishing Houses

Below are some privately owned and publicly owned publishing houses, along with a representative sampling of some of their magazine titles.

PRIVATELY OWNED

Advance Publications/ Condé Nast
Architectural Digest
Allure
Vogue
Glamour
Self
Mademoiselle
GQ
Vanity Fair
The New Yorker
Details

Hearst Corporation
Cosmopolitan
Redbook
Good Housekeeping
Esquire
Country Living
Country Living Gardener
Harper's Bazaar
Sports Afield
Marie Claire
Town & Country

Reiman Publications
Country
Country Woman
Reminisce
Birds & Blooms
Crafting Traditions
Farm & Ranch Living
Quick Cooking
Taste of Home

Wenner Media
Rolling Stone
Men's Journal
US

Strang Communications
Charisma & Christian Life
Ministries Today
New Man
Christian Retailing
Vida Cristiana

PUBLICLY OWNED

McGraw-Hill Companies
Business Week
Hospital Practice
Modern Plastics
Electrical World
Chemical Engineering
Aviation Week & Space Technology
Byte
Power
Architectural Record
The Physician and Sportsmedicine

Meredith Corporation
Better Homes and Gardens
Ladies' Home Journal
Midwest Living
Country Home
Traditional Home
Golf for Women
Wood
Successful Farming
Family Money
More

Reed Elsevier
Building Design & Construction
Contractor
Professional Builder
Home Accents Today
Packaging Digest
Library Journal
Publishers Weekly
Variety
Broadcasting & Cable
Restaurants & Institutions

Time Warner
Time
Fortune
Life
Sports Illustrated
Money
People
Teen People
Entertainment Weekly
In Style
Sports Illustrated for Kids
People en Español

Publicly held magazines must publish their earnings in annual reports, and their editors have to report to corporate officers as well as a board of directors. Wall Street is leading the dance, and the magazines have to follow.

Some publicly owned magazines grow to become part of a conglomerate, dealing with a variety of media—and then some. Time Inc., which includes such consumer magazines as *Time, Sports Illustrated,* and *People,* is now part of Time Warner, which also owns HBO, CNN, Warner Brothers, theaters, theme parks, and music production houses. Meredith Corporation owns consumer magazines such as *Better Homes and Gardens, Ladies' Home Journal,* and *Successful Farming,* as well as broadcasting stations, custom publications, and special ancillary products. McGraw-Hill Companies owns such trade magazines as *Aviation Week & Space Technology, Chemical Engineering,* and *Electrical World,* as well as *Business Week,* Standard and Poor's business ratings services, textbook publishers, television stations, and the National Software Testing Laboratories. Reed Elsevier is a subsidiary of Elsevier Wolters Kluwer, a British-Dutch company that owns trade magazines and the LEXIS/NEXIS news and legal on-line database and is a worldwide book publisher and distributor. Reed Elsevier's publications include more than 175 business and trade print and electronic titles in aviation, manufacturing, entertainment, construction, electronics, and food service, as well as more than 1,200 scientific journals published in the United States, the United Kingdom, Australia, and Asia.

PRIVATELY OWNED. Privately owned companies do not have to publicize earnings. A single individual, a family, or a group of private investors may choose to keep the company off the stock exchange for a variety of reasons. They may enjoy the autonomy and secrecy of private ownership, they may not trust corporate buyers, or they simply may not have enough cash flow potential to go public.

Advance Publications owns not only *The New Yorker* but also the Condé Nast group of magazines, including *Glamour, GQ, Vanity Fair, Vogue,* and *Mademoiselle.* Other large privately held magazine publishers are the Hearst Corporation, Reiman Publications, and Wenner Media. Hearst, started by William Randolph Hearst and

***American Patchwork & Quilting, Better Homes and Gardens, Country Gardens, Midwest Living, Renovation Style, Successful Farming,* and *Wood* are some of the magazines published by the publicly owned Meredith Corporation.**

still owned by the Hearst family, publishes such titles as *Cosmopolitan, Good Housekeeping, Redbook,* and *Esquire.* Reiman, owned by founder Roy Reiman, publishes *Country, Country Woman,* and *Reminisce,* among others. Wenner Media, owned by founder Jann Wenner, publishes *Rolling Stone, US,* and *Men's Journal.*

Many small, niche magazines are privately owned. Strang Communications Company publishes five evangelical Christian magazines—*Charisma & Christian Life, Ministries Today, New Man, Christian Retailing,* and *Vida Cristiana* (in Spanish), as well as religious books and educational materials. Founded by Stephen Strang in 1981, the Orlando, Florida-based publishing company also produces a twice-weekly magazine-format program called "Charisma Now" on the Trinity Broadcasting Network.

Some industry insiders say that privately held magazines can take financial risks other publishers would shudder at. The buzz in publishing circles was that Si Newhouse bought *The New Yorker*—for $168 million in 1985—for the prestige of the title, and allowed it to lose tens of millions of dollars a year. Because Si Newhouse is not accountable financially to any outsiders, he can spend as much money as he wishes. It is, after all, his money.

At one point in the late 1990s, Condé Nast was known for its top editorial perks, including condos, limousines, and clothing allowances for editors. No publicly held publisher could justify that to a stockholder.

Magazine insiders say that *Glamour* has traditionally been Condé Nast's healthiest title and that Hearst's *Esquire* has lost money for years. Because private companies can keep successes and failures a secret, these comments cannot be validated. The success of both Condé Nast and Hearst titles can be measured by audited circulation or by the number of ad pages. Certainly, their titles are successful on the newsstands, but because of discounts given to advertisers, it is difficult to determine total profits and losses.

Organization Magazine Ownership

Association magazines usually are published by nonprofit entities; often, however, the magazine operates as a profit center. Public relations magazines have corporate parents, which may be publicly or privately owned. Custom magazines are marketing tools and may be outsourced; they are often produced by publishers of other consumer or trade titles.

ASSOCIATION MAGAZINES. Association members are like stockholders; they essentially own the organization and are concerned about its success. Consequently, members have a stake in the way in which their association's publication is run. They differ from stockholders significantly, however, in that they typically are more interested in the content of the magazine and the way it serves the organization than in profit. The money the magazine makes is plowed back into membership benefits and into the work of the association.

Many association publications make a substantial amount of money. "They are cash-flow centers," says Ian MacKenzie, editor of *Life Association News,* the magazine for the National Association of Life Underwriters. "They are not viewed as profit centers because they are usually run by nonprofit organizations and they cannot report profits. But these publications have to contribute to the bottom line." MacKenzie, a board member of the Society of National Association Publications, points out that many association titles have strong advertising bases in addition to substantial subscription income.[16]

Bill Otto, editor of *Arthritis Today,* says, "We are extremely profitable." Circulation and advertising revenues—millions of dollars are generated—go back to the Arthritis Foundation to fund research for a cure.[17]

Archaeology is published by the Archaeological Institute of America (AIA), which was founded in 1879 and chartered by an Act of Congress in 1906. It has been published by the nonprofit AIA since 1948. The magazine now operates as a profit center within the Institute, but it took years to develop. "The magazine is run as a separate entity. We can pull out our own records and see how we're doing financially," says publisher Phyllis Pollak Katz, who has been with the magazine since 1969. She reports to a board of trustees made up of academics and interested amateur archeologists. The central office for the AIA is in Boston; Katz operates out of New York City.

Archaeology's publisher and editor meet regularly with the AIA board. "For the most part, it's hand off. They understand the concept of editorial freedom. They tell us if there's a problem—after the fact. But they make it clear. We listen to them and we listen to our readers," Katz says.

Time Inc., a division of media conglomerate Time Warner, which is traded on the New York Stock Exchange, publishes *Asia Week, Coastal Living, Cooking Light, In Style, Progressive Farmer,* and *Sports Illustrated for Kids.*

PUBLIC RELATIONS MAGAZINES. Public relations magazines are one arm of a corporation and are generally published out of public relations, corporate communications, or human resources departments. They take their identity from the corporation and exist at the will of the corporation's management. Generally, content decisions in these magazines are made in conjunction with managers or boards of directors, not by the editors alone. When upper managers understand the goals and intricacies of the magazine, the editor's job can be smooth sailing. Often, however, management has no idea of what a magazine is, how it operates, or how it can contribute to the organization's goals. It is often the job of the editor to educate upper management on these issues.

Although the editor must make decisions based on what's good for the organization, this does not mean avoiding controversy. It may mean taking a proactive stance and being frank about problems and concerns. As with all magazines, decisions should be based on the needs of the audience. The management and the editor must make sure they agree on what those needs are.

Chronicle, the magazine of the University of Osteopathic Medicine and Health Sciences, has to be responsive to two groups: the university administration, which provides the budget, and the students and alumni, who are readers and who ultimately provide many of the university's funds through tuition and gifts. Editor David Krause gets approval of the magazine's content from university administrators, who have the final say. If Krause disagrees with administrators' decisions, the best he can do is argue that the magazine fills the needs of two of the university's major constituencies. For example, when the university came under local media scrutiny because of financial improprieties of one president and the short tenure of a replacement, Krause ran both an article and an editorial about dealing with change.

When Liz Muhler, managing editor of Walgreen's internal magazine *Walgreen World,* decided to redesign the publication, her first step was to look at the corporate mission statement and interview corporate officers. She asked them such questions as: What is the main purpose of the magazine: employee recognition? company news? feature articles? Do you think the magazine currently is fulfilling that purpose? What do you like about the magazine? What would you change?

Next, Muhler studied management's responses along with responses from a questionnaire randomly sent to employees. "What these two pieces of information showed," she says, "was that people needed company information about business goals and expansion, but they also wanted employee recognition. So, as a compromise, we are developing a quarterly newsletter geared solely towards employee recognition and trying to use the magazine for business stories." Of course, the proposed editorial plan and budget had to be presented to Muhler's department head for approval and then circulated among upper management levels for their approval.

In order to gain additional capital, the Reader's Digest Association sold 33 Impressionist and modern artworks by Monet, Van Gogh, Cezanne, Modigliani, and Giacometti for more than $86 million at a Sotheby's auction in November 1998. The paintings and sculpture were part of a collection the magazine's founders, DeWitt Wallace and Lila Acheson Wallace, had been gathering since the 1940s.

CUSTOM MAGAZINES. Custom magazines are external marketing tools designed to reach an existing database of consumers of a specific product or service. A custom magazine is usually an outsourced operation, which means it is created by an agency outside of the sponsoring organization.

The advertising implications of a custom magazine are significant. While the publication looks and feels like a consumer magazine, implicit in its publication is a marketing pitch. The creation of custom publications often resembles the creation of an advertising campaign in which the agency offers concepts and content, but the client has the final say.

Custom magazines are created by contractual agreements, which may last several years. The magazine is owned by the organization, not by the custom publisher. At the end of the contract, the client may choose to take the magazine to another publishing house. Like advertising agencies, custom publishing houses can win or lose clients in a heartbeat.

Doug Holthaus, editor of Northwest Airlines's *World Traveler,* says his job differs significantly from the jobs of consumer magazine editors. In the case of *World Traveler*, Northwest Airlines's management has the final say on all

Founder Jann Wenner's privately held Wenner Media publishes three magazines: ***Men's Journal, Rolling Stone,*** **and *US*.**

aspects, including the cover. Holthaus and his staff are often finalizing cover art only a few weeks before the magazine is printed. At most consumer magazines, this decision is made months in advance.

HOW THE WORK ENVIRONMENT HAS CHANGED

Over the last decade, the magazine landscape has changed significantly. Downsizing, outsourcing, and restructuring have eliminated many middle-management jobs. Job titles have changed, as have the responsibilities inherent in both creative and business positions. The days where an individual could specialize in a narrow topic—as a writer, an editor, or even an accountant—are gone. Today's staffs have to have broad skills and adaptable constitutions that allow them to work in a constantly changing environment. Certainly, at small magazines, editors must be generalists who can do a variety of things with little support staff.

Changes in ownership as a result of more financial players becoming involved in publicly owned publishing houses have led to increasing financial pressures on publishers. Editors are being told their magazines must be both editorially creative and financially solvent. Editorial formulas must also take into account cash-flow needs and growth. Brand extensions, or ancillary activities, sometimes produce more revenue than the magazine itself.

Marketers are not the only ones who are responsible for finding opportunities for magazines to grow through new products. "Every single person at Meredith is responsible for coming up with new products," says Chris Little, president of the Meredith Corporation Publishing Group. "We have a new product development team to find ways to encourage everyone to respond."[18]

Douglas Shore, chairman and co-CEO of Shore-Varrone, Inc., agrees with Little. Says Shore, "We have to think of ourselves as more than publishers, editors as more than editors, and salespeople as more than people selling ad space. We all have to think of how we relate to our different markets and what kind of marketing vehicles we need to create to serve those markets."[19]

Technology also has affected both the creative and the business sides of magazines. Magazine staffs may no longer be located in the same state, much less on the same floor, as a result of modems, FAX machines, and other high-tech telecommunications equipment. Anyone with a computer can be plugged into every aspect of a magazine's business environment with the touch of a key. Telecommuting has become as commonplace as the subway as a way to get to the office.

Elizabeth Crow, editor-in-chief of *Mademoiselle,* says the computer has not reduced the editorial or business workload: "The efficiencies you realize in terms of time and control increase the amount of work you end up doing. You do more research, more writing and more rewriting, and you do it longer. You do more things more efficiently."[20]

FOR ADDITIONAL READING

Gill, Brendan. *Here at* The New Yorker. New York: Random House, 1975.

Hoover's Guide to Media Companies. Austin, TX: Hoover's Business Press, 1996.

Kunkel, Thomas. *Genius in Disguise: Harold Ross of* The New Yorker. New York: Random House, 1997.

MagazineWeek 1988 Profit Profiles. Farmingham, MA: Lighthouse Communications, 1988.

MagazineWeek 1989 Profit Profiles. Farmingham, MA: Lighthouse Communications, 1989.

MagazineWeek 1990 Profit Profiles. Farmingham, MA: Lighthouse Communications, 1990.

MagazineWeek 1991 Profit Profiles. Farmingham, MA: Lighthouse Communications, 1991.

Mehta, Ved. *Remembering Mr. Shawn's* New Yorker: *The Invisible Art of Editing.* Woodstock, NY: Overlook Press, 1998.

Policies and Procedures in Association Management 1996. Washington, DC: American Society of Association Executives, 1996.

Ross, Lillian. *Here But Not Here.* New York: Random House, 1998.

Shuping, Frances, ed. *A Guide to Periodicals Publishing for Associations.* Washington, DC: American Society of Association Executives, 1995.

The Veronis, Suhler & Associates Communications Industry Forecast. New York: Veronis, Suhler & Associates, 1997.

ENDNOTES

[1] John Fry, "Supereditor: Making the Myth Work," *Folio:* (January 1987): 156.

[2] "Does Sales Produce the Best Execs?" *Folio:* (September 1, 1998): 84.

[3] "What Does a Group Publisher Do?" *Folio:* (October 1, 1996): 44.

[4] Ibid., 44.

[5] "The Charlie Rose Show," PBS (August 25, 1998), Show #2233.

[6] "40 for the Future," *Folio:* (April 1, 1996): 35.

[7] Constance L. Hayes, "Magazine Chief Shakes Things Up at Hearst," *The New York Times* (June 2, 1997): 1B.

[8] "*Folio:* Roundtable—The Editor as Market Authority," January 1, 1998, (http://www.mediacentral.com/Magazines/folio98/199801 roundtable.htm).

[9] Eric Freedman, "Manager, Editor, Candlestick Maker," *Folio:* (March 15, 1998): 44.

[10] Ibid., 45.

[11] Fry, 157.

[12] Barbara Love, "How Our Jobs Have Changed," *Folio:* (April 1, 1998): 52–53.

[13] Lambath Hochwald, "Cloudy with Bursts of Creativity," *Folio:* (March 1, 1996): 36.

[14] Jeff Garigliano, "Reach Out and Hire Someone," *Folio:* (July 1, 1997): 45.

[15] Love, 52.

[16] Lorraine Calvacca, "Five Myths of Association Publishing," *The Handbook of Magazine Publishing,* 4th ed. (Stamford, CT: Cowles Business Media, 1996): 152.

[17] Ibid., 153.

[18] Love, 50.

[19] Ibid., 50.

[20] Ibid., 47.

PART THREE

The Magazine's Content

CHAPTER 8

Magazine Editorial

Molding the Words

hen Newsweek *began in 1933, it had a hyphen between the two syllables of its name and seven photographs on the cover to depict an important event for each day of the week.* Newsweek *was started as a news magazine alternative to* Time. Newsweek *has dropped the hyphen and the seven photos as part of its news digest approach. Other cosmetic changes have occurred over the years, but* Newsweek*'s underlying character remains the same: editorially, it's not* Time. Newsweek*'s character is reflected in how editorial content—the departments and features—is molded in terms of topic, angle, style, and approach, as well as the amount of research and authority that goes into each piece. Readers are drawn to a magazine's editorial package, to the vibrant and engaging article mix that distinguishes one publication from another. While some readers may occasionally pick up a magazine because of a single department, a successful publication needs a core readership that transcends any particular article. This reader loyalty starts with a single issue and builds up over time. Readers eventually look for certain types of articles in every issue and gravitate toward magazines that provide a particular approach or way of covering topics.* *Norman Cousins, who was editor of* Saturday Review *for more than 30 years from 1940 to 1971, believed that "reader loyalty is based on the continuing maintenance of certain standards, not just on past performance." A magazine's readership, Cousins said, "rests on the quality of the relationship between editors and readers. Readers must feel respected and valued; they must feel that they are not just keys on a cash register but partners in an ongoing venture."*[1]

ARTICLE TYPES

A magazine's editorial content provides that ongoing venture from issue to issue. Specific article types occur in both the feature and department sections of magazines: service, profile, investigative reporting, essay, and fiction. The length and depth of coverage, as well as the editor-in-chief's inclinations toward a particular approach, generally determine whether the article becomes a department or a feature. Some features aren't obviously a particular type or may be a blending of types; these are referred to as "general features" by magazine editors.

Service, profile, and investigative articles typically are grounded in objective, balanced reporting that includes a context for verifiable, in-depth facts and quotes gathered from myriad sources. While some essays follow an objective path, most are intensely personal and interpretive. Fiction—short stories and novels—is the least frequent type of article found in today's magazines. Yet many of the most engaging nonfiction articles use the tools of fiction, including narration, dialogue, description, point of view, characterization, and personification.

Service

Early in the history of *Better Homes and Gardens,* founder Edwin T. Meredith coined a phrase that melodiously summed up his vision of what service was in a magazine: "No fiction, no fashion, no piffle, no passion." "Piffle" was the buzzword in the 1920s for trivial nonsense that was of little worth; "no passion" referred to a lack of sentimental short stories. The definition of service journalism was updated in 1987 by Byron T. Scott, then the Meredith Chair of Service Journalism at the University of Missouri in Columbia: "Service journalism is needed information delivered in the right medium at the right time in an understandable form, and intended for immediate use by the audience."[2] James Autry, editor of *Better Homes and Gardens* from 1970 to 1981, preferred to identify service journalism as "action journalism" because "it is journalism that goes beyond the delivery of pure information, to include the expectation that the reader will *do* something as a result of the reading."[3]

With that definition in mind, today's service pieces include expert yet practical advice, how-to information, and news and trends that empower readers and their families. While the content of

MARRIAGES STILL BEING SAVED BY *LADIES' HOME JOURNAL*

Ladies' Home Journal touts its "Can This Marriage Be Saved?" department as "the most popular, most enduring women's magazine feature in the world." The long-running column, which peeks into the problems of a different married couple each month, first appeared in January 1953.

For 30 years, "Can This Marriage Be Saved?" was written by Dorothy Cameron Disney, a pioneer marriage advice counselor and columnist. Her technique was to take the troubled couple out to dinner to learn about their marital woes, then interview each separately. No identifying names or details were ever used, and Disney contacted counseling agencies and therapists throughout the United States for source material.

What distinguished Disney's advice column was her use of intimate "he said/she said" dialogue about money problems, jealousy, infidelity, and sex, followed by her down-to-earth advice. Because of its candid language, "Can This Marriage Be Saved?" was said to be how many girls of the 1950s learned about sex.

In the 100th anniversary issue of *Ladies' Home Journal* in January 1984, Disney wrote, "The columns seem to represent a chronicle of the many changes in the institution of marriage—and the fascination it holds." She concluded that of all the marital problems she came across, "the single greatest pitfall of all times is the inability of husband and wife to communicate. 'He (or she) never listens' is universal."

Still timely today, "Can This Marriage Be Saved?" is even a registered trademark. Written primarily by Margery D. Rosen since 1984, the inspiring case studies of couples overcoming obstacles to build successful marriages were collected into a book in 1994.

service pieces may seem more micro and local than macro and global, "they can have a tremendous impact: They can change the way readers think or act, alter the way they spend time or money, influence style, eating habits and travel plans, improve relationships, diminish biases," argues Pamela Fiori, editor-in-chief of *Town & Country*. She continues, "Service magazines help the reader cope—with aging parents or one's aging self, an alcoholic co-worker, a serious illness, unemployment, change of address or change of life. They might even inspire the reader to contribute to society—by volunteering his or her services, by writing to Congress, by joining a local environmental group. Or closer to home, by spending more time with the kids."[4]

Though once narrowly associated with women's concerns and issues, service articles now can be found in most consumer, trade, and organization magazines, as ongoing departments and stand-alone features. Service articles demand accuracy and credibility in the depiction of material that is easy to read and understand. Graphic devices are important tools in service formats: lists, boxes, bullets, charts, maps, graphs, calendars, and diagrams abound in order to highlight information for the reader.

EXPERT ADVICE. The service article dates back to the advice-giving departments established in December 1883 by Louisa Knapp Curtis, the first editor of *Ladies' Home Journal*. She followed the long-established editorial formula found in successful women's magazines of the mid-nineteenth century, such as *Godey's Lady's Book* and *Peterson's Magazine*, and featured serialized novels and short stories for entertainment along with articles on motherhood, housekeeping, and fashion for women. However, the backbone of *Ladies' Home Journal* was in the household hints departments and special homemaker features written by women for women.

The women writers who suggested better ways of cleaning, cooking, needleworking, and interior decorating were considered experts in their fields. They all had many years of experience in successfully managing a home; some, like *Ladies' Home Journal* contributing household editor Christine Frederick, took a scientific approach to housekeeping, based on business and engineering principles being adopted in factories. Frederick believed women's work would be more efficient if counters and sinks were the right height, if kitchens had good light and ventilation, and if tasks were systematically organized. In almost

RESEARCH IN BRIEF

Still Cooking after All These Years

An analysis of *Better Homes and Gardens, Good Housekeeping,* and *Ladies' Home Journal* from 1905 through 1985 shows just how consistent the editorial content in women's magazines can be. Researchers Roger C. Saathoff and Julie Ann Moellering of the School of Mass Communications at Texas Tech University studied 1,420 articles from the three magazines to see what topics appeared most frequently.[1] The chart below shows the three leading topics for *Better Homes and Gardens, Good Housekeeping,* and *Ladies' Home Journal* during three different time periods.

For *Better Homes and Gardens,* cooking remained a core topic throughout the entire period. At *Good Housekeeping,* homecare/housekeeping topics continued to be important, supporting the magazine's name with panache. The most changes in topics occurred in *Ladies' Home Journal,* as shown by the four-way tie for second place during 1935 through 1955. Nevertheless, cooking remained a popular *Ladies' Home Journal* editorial subject for 50 years.

Certainly, these shifts in editorial content reflected societal changes. From 1905 through 1925, women, in general, were housewives who cooked, sewed, and took care of children. Between 1935 and 1955, editorial topics shifted, perhaps a reflection of economic change due to the Depression, World War II, and the return to prosperity. After 1965, there appears to be more emphasis on personal looks—beauty/health/diet—perhaps because more women were entering the work force. "This study gives us an idea as to where these three magazines, *Better Homes and Gardens, Good Housekeeping,* and *Ladies' Home Journal,* have been, where they are now, and in some cases, where they may be going," say Saathoff and Moellering.

These three magazines have shifted their editorial content, but in a predictable way. The choice of article topics consistently reflected their editorial identities as women's service magazines focusing on the domestic concerns of the homemaker.

[1] Roger C. Saathoff and Julie Ann Moellering, "Down the Path of Domesticity: A Content Analysis of Three Women's Service Magazines: 1905–1985" (paper presented at the annual meeting of the Association for Education in Journalism and Mass Communication, Boston, MA, August 1991).

Leading Topics in Three Magazines from 1905 through 1985

	1905–1925	1935–1955	1965–1985
Better Homes and Gardens	Homecare/housekeeping	Homecare/housekeeping	Cooking
	Garden/flowers	Garden/flowers	Interior decorating/home building
	Cooking	Cooking	Sewing/crafts
Good Housekeeping	Homecare/housekeeping	Cooking	Beauty/health/diet
	Children and their care	Homecare/housekeeping	Cooking
	Engagement/marriage	Beauty/health/diet	Homecare/housekeeping
Ladies' Home Journal	Sewing/crafts	Engagement/marriage	Beauty/health/diet
	Children and their care	(four-way tie)	Cooking
	Dress and fashion	Cooking	Public figure/movie star
		Children and their care	
		Dating/relationship	
		Homecare/housekeeping	

every issue, Frederick wrote about "the new housekeeping," which saved steps in the kitchen, whether it was washing dishes, canning fruit, or preparing dinner for eight couples. Clearly, the content of *Ladies' Home Journal* revolved around expert domestic advice as indicated in the "Practical Homekeeper" subtitle to the title. At *Ladies' Home Journal,* the practical homemaker was urged to be efficient and professional—and to take advantage of the many new appliances and products being specifically developed for the home.

When Edward Bok became editor in January 1890, the service function of *Ladies' Home Journal* was already well established. A sharp businessman and brilliant editor, Bok expanded the service departments and made the magazine an exciting blend of commerce and education. During his 39 years as editor, Bok constantly consulted his readers through informal surveys, encouraged them to write letters to the editor, and consistently responded to their wants and desires. In his third-person autobiography, Bok described his concept of service and its development: "Step by step, the editor built up this service behind the magazine until he had a staff of thirty-five editors on the monthly payroll; in each issue he proclaimed the willingness of these editors to answer immediately any questions by mail; he encouraged and cajoled his readers to form the habit of looking upon his magazine as a great clearing-house of information."[5]

It was an editor's worst nightmare come true, said *Ms.* editor-in-chief Marcia Ann Gillespie when the May/June 1996 issue of *Ms.* hit the newsstands. The problem: *feminism*—a word frequently used in the magazine known for its long involvement in the women's movement—was misspelled on the cover. The 48-point-high headline, for the 19-page lead feature, proclaimed "Mothers and Daughters: Honest Talk about Feminisim & Real Life."

For example, in the March 1914 issue readers could find advice on dealing with warts and moles, preparing ham 38 different ways, repairing fences, dressing a baby in winter, and furnishing a five-room apartment for $500. Queries about proper dating etiquette with men as well as questions about sticky social situations and cultural conundrums were answered in the regular "Girls' Affairs" column. In the ongoing department "What Other Women Have Found Out About Economy in the Kitchen," 24 readers shared their tips: Use bread crusts to grease pans, dip the knife in boiling water before cutting a slice of butter, and jot down the costs of each item on the recipe card.

The success of the service approach quickly became evident. Bok pointed out that when the practice of personally responding to every reader by return mail "was finally stopped by the Great War of 1917–1918, the yearly correspondence totalled nearly a million letters."

To the service format, then, Bok brought reader participation and trust in the editorial message, creating a magazine that became "a vital need in the personal lives of its readers" because it was grounded in information. In today's parlance, it was "news you can use." The women's service approach pioneered by *Ladies' Home Journal* was followed by other popular women's magazines. The largest in circulation and most successful practitioners in the category became known as the Seven Sisters magazines: *Better Homes and Gardens, Family Circle, Good Housekeeping, McCall's, Redbook, Woman's Day,* and of course, *Ladies' Home Journal.*

The service article is no longer exclusive to women's magazines. Other publications have adopted the service approach and made it their own. *Sunset,* the regional magazine focusing on the West, offers a mix of food, travel, home improvement, and gardening advice, termed "the four cornerstones of the magazine" by Stephen Seabolt, president and chief executive of the Sunset Publishing Corporation. Editor-in-chief Rosalie Muller Wright says *Sunset*'s strength is service to readers, pointing out that the magazine has three people who spend each day fielding phone calls from readers. Says Wright, "Far and away the largest number of them are from people who recently bought their first home. They've got a scrubby little garden; they want to do something with it, what can they do? Well, that's what we're here for. Service, service, service."[6]

WordPerfect Magazine expanded the concept of service by offering readers their own computer consultant for a day. In a "Win an Editor for a Day" contest, *WordPerfect Magazine* asked readers to send in their business cards for a drawing held each month. The winner received a visit from a *WordPerfect Magazine* editor for eight hours of computer advice, along with a one-year subscription to the magazine, ancillary products, and lunch. Editor-in-chief Lisa Bearnson said the contest fit the magazine's "how-to mission."[7]

Jeff Hadfield, editorial director of IVY International Communications, which publishes *WordPerfect Magazine,* points out that this concept is not limited to computer software magazines: "For any kind of service journalism, the editor would have some expertise that the reader doesn't, and could provide some solutions to problems. That's what service journalism is."

Glamour's 1997 National Magazine Award-winning two-part series about health management organizations is an example of the content and approach found in a service article. "Is Managed Care Good for Women's Health?" by Leslie Laurence and "Making Managed Care Work for You" by Tessa DeCarlo, which ran in the August and September 1996 issues, respectively, provided a clear and compelling examination of HMOs and their effects on consumers. The articles were designed to inspire action and to provide the information needed to act.

HOW-TO INFORMATION. It's not enough to simply advise in service journalism; explanation, interpretation, and suggestions for future action must be included through the inclusion of how-to information. Along with who, when, and where, the what, why, and how are thoroughly documented, as problems are solved or possibilities discussed.

What a reader finds applicable and of value in a service-oriented magazine like *Wood* are articles on how to use tools safely. An example is "Spotlight on Tablesaw Safety," which began: "In 1975, more than 5,000 woodworkers lost fingers in tablesaw accidents." Features editor Peter J. Stephano says that despite the narrow niche that *Wood* serves—the beginning and intermediate hobbyist woodworker—there are many subject areas to cover in the how-to approach. *Sunset* often takes the how-to approach when it goes beyond the backyard relationship with its readers

JUNE 1996: *Sunset*'s "How to Save Our National Parks: A 10-Step Guide to the Future" is an example of applying the how-to service approach to a national topic.

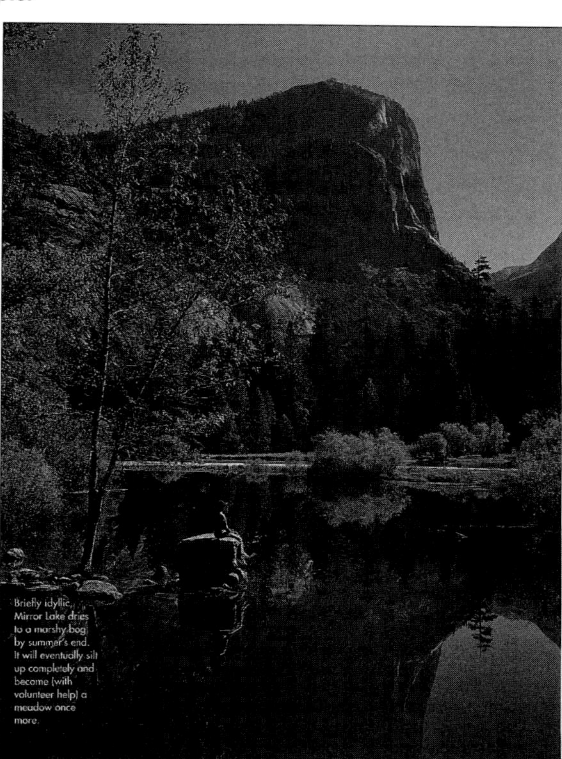

Briefly idyllic, Mirror Lake dries to a marshy bog by summer's end. It will eventually silt up completely and become (with volunteer help) a meadow once more.

Restoring Yosemite

Volunteers try to compensate for the park system's shortcomings—but for all their dedication, there's only so much they can accomplish

BY LORA J. FINNEGAN

IT'S THE JEWEL OF THE SIERRA NEVADA, AND THE PLACE WHERE OUR national conservation ethic took root. But though the granite walls of Yosemite National Park may stand for eternity, its fragile ecosystem suffers from the ailments plaguing the entire park system.

In a kind of fatal attraction, Yosemite's wonders draw 4 million visitors annually, resulting in traffic jams, pollution, and degradation of plant and animal life. Administrators can barely budget for basic needs, so the park's own support and fund-raising group, The Yosemite Fund, has stepped in to help. Its most pressing job: helping to restore damaged ecosystems and maintain species diversity.

The group's successes are evident today, deep in Yosemite Valley, as a breeze wafts across a meadow where 3-foot-tall swaths of native blue ryegrass wave gently. Patches of milkweed dot the meadow, and eye-high bushes of Western azalea edge its boundary. As executive director of The Yosemite Fund, Bob Hansen takes well-earned pleasure in a walk through this vibrant meadow, one his group helped bring back from the dead.

The fund, created in 1988, focuses on urgent resource issues unfunded by tight federal budgets: wilderness preservation and restoration, trail repair, wildlife studies. Under the supervision of park superintendent B. J. Griffin, Hansen works with the staff of the 747,956-acre park to identify projects that, when completed, will add "immeasurably to the preservation of Yosemite's natural and cultural resources" (in the words of the fund's own statement of goals). The fund has granted $7 million to park projects to date, underwriting 38 projects in 1995 alone. Though money is raised from individual donors and the sale of California's Yosemite license plate, the efforts of volunteer workers generate the most palpable bang for the fund's bucks.

Helping hands for oaks

On a sunny spring day, Hansen stands in the shade of a massive black oak, one of the few still surviving in Yosemite Valley. "Oak saplings were being trampled by visitors and browsed by deer," he explains. "And because wildfires were suppressed for many years, oaks couldn't regenerate naturally." Before The Yosemite Fund's oak-restoration project began in 1990, half of the valley's oak woodland had been lost.

Acorns supply 50 percent of the diet for a quarter of the animal species here, including black bear, black-tailed deer, and acorn woodpecker. "The oak understory also creates an environment that provides shelter and food for other animals," Hansen says. "When oaks are gone, they're replaced by conifers, and a whole component of the forest matrix disappears."

When the fund put out a call for volunteers, Chevron responded. Under ranger supervision, a total of 800 employee volunteers pitched in. First task: collecting acorns to be planted in a nursery. Next they prepared the soil in areas park resource staff had chosen for oak reintroduction—at one point uncovering an old parking lot and digging out several tons of asphalt by hand. For four weekends a year over the course of the three-year project, corporate teams returned for follow-up work: eradicating weeds and small pines, tilling soil, and planting, watering, and protecting those seedlings.

Restoration is now complete, and the volunteers can celebrate the visible results: refurbished trails through the forest, and thousands of new black oaks in Yosemite Valley.

To see the oaks, walk the paved Schoolhouse Trail between Yosemite Village and Yosemite Falls (look for signs marked with an oak leaf). A free self-guided trail brochure is available at the visitor center.

A tale of two riverbanks

Leaning over the edge of an old stone bridge behind The Ahwahnee hotel, Hansen looks down into a spring-raging Merced River, full and high on its banks. As the Merced races through this portion of the valley, it tears out small chunks of earth from the river's bare banks.

"The state's fish and game department declared this portion of the river ecologically dead," Hansen says. "The denuded stream banks leave no cover or food for fish. Plus, they're ugly." He points out rock riprap on one side of the river, remnants of a failed effort to stabilize the bank. On the other side is a campsite too close to the water's edge, helping to break down the bank.

Just downstream is Stoneman Bridge.

Stakes and plastic sleeves protect young oak seedlings grown and nurtured by volunteers in Yosemite Valley.

JUNE 1996 83

to cover national environmental concerns, as in its June 1996 article on "How to Save Our National Parks: A 10-Step Guide to the Future."

Travel magazines are built almost entirely around the how-to service approach. With almost unlimited where-to-go and when-to-go globetrotting possibilities, destination pieces can be developed that attract armchair travelers and adventurous vacationers. Both groups of readers want consumer information, entertaining copy, and lush descriptions of the settings. They also want accuracy. Recognizing this, *Condé Nast Traveler*'s "truth in travel" stance has led the way toward a more critical viewpoint and voice in travel pieces. Readers now can learn which beaches are dirty and which cities are safe from terrorist acts.

Historically, travel pieces have been a magazine staple since the eighteenth century. As early as 1784, a travel article about the South Seas was serialized for three issues in *The Gentleman and Lady's Town and Country Magazine.* The first issue of *Port Folio* featured John Quincy Adams's "Journal of a Tour through Silesia" in January 1801; the journal ran during most of the year. Later travel articles by Mark Twain in *The Century* and *The Atlantic* and by Ernest Hemingway in *Life* and *Esquire* took a subjective and anecdotal tone. However, they still performed a service for readers in terms of where to go in order to escape from the mundane and ordinary and featured informative you-are-there descriptions of places and people.

Some magazine scholars argue that travel articles, because of their descriptive nature, are closer to profiles, especially when geographic, social, political, and economic data are included. *National Geographic*'s pieces are often so exhaustively in-depth that "service," with its implication of quick accessibility and utility, seems a misnomer. Additionally, there's a strong literary tradition to be found in travel articles by Jan Morris and Paul Theroux, who both write in an impressionistic, yet highly detailed, tone about exotic locales. Their work could be described as safari-style new journalism.

David Breul, editor of *Getaways,* says travel articles shouldn't be too esoteric. Instead, he says, a successful travel magazine should be "half fantasy and half service, and that's exactly what we have. We tickle the reader in his armchair travel, and are useful in his actual travel."[8]

How to Improve Editorial Content

More than a decade ago, when she was vice president and editor-in-chief of *Woman's Day,* Ellen Levine offered 10 tips for improving magazine editorial content.[1] The tips still hold true today—and you can bet that Levine continues to follow them as editor-in-chief at *Good Housekeeping.* Levine said:

1. Cut story lengths; readers are impatient.
2. When you can't find news, try to create it by conducting surveys.
3. Sex still sells.
4. Give readers information unavailable elsewhere.
5. Strive for exclusive stories.
6. Don't focus on winning awards.
7. Lists of information are popular.
8. Don't rely on "proven" formulas for editing magazines.
9. Always be nice to advertisers.
10. Remember your magazine can make readers' lives better or worse with what it publishes. 

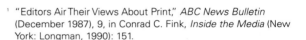

[1] "Editors Air Their Views About Print," *ABC News Bulletin* (December 1987), 9, in Conrad C. Fink, *Inside the Media* (New York: Longman, 1990): 151.

Getaways focuses on short three-to-seven-day vacations no more than 400 miles away from the reader's home. This is a different approach from *Travel & Leisure*'s expensive two-week-long jaunts to distant and foreign destinations. Even more affordable are the travel tips found in *Arthur Frommer's Budget Travel: Vacations for Real People* magazine, launched in 1998. Publisher Jacob Hill says *Frommer's Budget Travel*'s practical, bargain-orientation lacks direct competition from the "aspirational," luxury travel magazines that dominate the travel market. Edited by travel advice guru Arthur Frommer, the magazine focuses on service to readers who spend an average of $1,000 to $2,000 on trips, as opposed to $10,000.[9]

NEWS AND TRENDS. Trade and association magazines are particularly dedicated to the

Awards: An Accurate Measure of Quality?

Peer approval can be measured by awards from groups such as the American Society of Magazine Editors, which annually presents the National Magazine Awards, and the American Business Press, which hands out the Neal Awards. Both competitions are considered among the most prestigious in the magazine industry.

The National Magazine Awards are given to any magazine edited, published, and sold in the United States; these awards cover 12 categories, including general excellence, reporting, personal service, feature writing, fiction, design, photography, single topic issues, and essays and criticism. National Magazine Awards, in the form of a copper elephant (a reproduction of an Alexander Calder stabile called *Ellie*), are highly coveted and often are called the Pulitzers of the magazine world. The Jesse H. Neal Awards competition is open only to audited trade and specialized business publications published by companies belonging to the American Business Press. Neal Awards are ribboned medallions reminiscent of Olympic gold medals.

Alfred Rosenblatt, managing editor of *IEEE Spectrum,* which took the 1993 National Magazine Award in reporting for the April 1992 two-part special report, "Seeking Nuclear Safeguards," talks about the effects of the honor: "It shows we are well regarded by our peers. It is more than symbolic. It's motivation. It is something our editors can aspire to. It's like an Oscar for writers."[1] *IEEE Spectrum,* edited for the engineering and scientific professional in business, government and education, is published by the Institute of Electrical and Electronics Engineers, Inc.

Lingua Franca received the Ellie for general excellence in 1993, just three years after its 1990 debut. Says founder and editor-in-chief Jeffrey Kittay, "The immediate effect has been to give us a cachet with writers. In the long run, it operates as an effective shorthand with subscribers and particularly with advertisers to show that you are a legitimate editorial product."[2]

Bruce Rayner, editor-in-chief of *Electronic Business,* is a firm believer in the value of awards. "In trade publishing, people are always looking for a trusted source of information to get their jobs done, and awards quickly demonstrate that for those new to your title. Awards are also a measure of assurance for those already supporting the magazine," Rayner says.[3]

While adding prestige to the magazine, though, awards are not a clear indication of the magazine's economic health. Ellen Levine, editor-in-chief of

news and trends aspect of service. Dennis W. Jeffers, a journalism professor at Central Michigan University who has studied service journalism in these two magazine types, says, "Technical and educational information relating to specific practices of members is featured in these magazines in the hope that members will read it and then take specific action to adopt 'new and improved' methods or techniques."[10] According to Jeffers, readers of association magazines like *Angus Journal,* a publication of the American Angus Association, "clearly indicate that 'service' content in the form of management information has the highest priority." He says that feature stories and personality profiles are not what the majority of readers want, although editors include such material to provide variety. Above all, association readers want content that is useful.

Useful service content for trade and organization magazine readers is news—news about government regulation and legislation, market trends, technological and research innovations, and new products that might be helpful to one's business or profession. Most specialized business press service pieces focus on solving practical problems, according to Patrick Clinton who has studied this field extensively. For example, Clinton explains, when squeezable bottles became available for condiments several years ago, the mainstream press took the consumer point of view, but the trade press wrote about processes and techniques: "*Processed Foods* discussed comparative costs, how to choose the right sort of bottle for a particular product, what size opening was appropriate, what sort of glue was required to attach labels, and the problems of converting a filling machine from glass containers to the lightweight, easy-to-tip plastic."[11]

Profile

Articles concentrating on the lives and achievements of famous, infamous, and ordinary individuals have been published since American

Good Housekeeping, says awards are a "wonderful thing for editors and ad salespeople to talk about. But I've seen editors accept awards and then get fired the next month. And I have yet to meet an advertiser who buys a page because you won an award."[4]

Advertisers are wary of awards. "We have to remember it's the magazine community, not the readers, who are voting," says Ellen Oppenheim, vice president and media director at Foote, Cone and Belding advertising agency. "As much as we might want to believe there's a carryover effect with the reader, we have to marry the winning of the award with other indicators of reader appreciation."[5]

However, Valerie Bogle, manager of print buying for Western International Media, notes, "Anything that can cut through distractions and play up magazines' effectiveness would be a bonus, particularly editorial awards. Our clients pay close attention to a magazine's editorial environment to see if it serves the audience they want to reach. As a buyer, I wouldn't pass over a title that had not won awards, although it might be a deciding factor if I had several candidates."[6]

1 "Winning Responses," *Folio:* (April 15, 1994): 28.
2 Ibid., 28.
3 "What Are the Tangible Benefits of Awards?" *Folio:* (December 1998): 84.
4 Constance L. Hays, "Award Puffs Magazines' Egos but Fails to Bolster Ad Sales," *The New York Times* (April 28, 1997): C7.
5 Ibid., C7.
6 "What Are the Tangible Benefits of Awards?" 84.

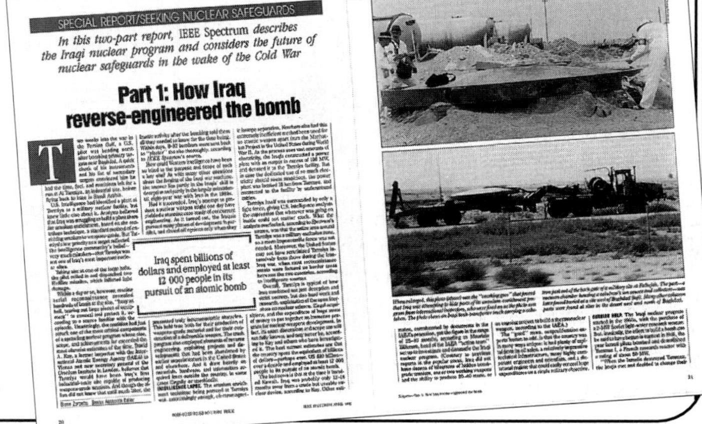

SPECIAL REPORT/SEEKING NUCLEAR SAFEGUARDS

In this two-part report, IEEE Spectrum describes the Iraqi nuclear program and considers the future of nuclear safeguards in the wake of the Cold War

Part 1: How Iraq reverse-engineered the bomb

Iraq spent billions of dollars and employed at least 12 000 people in its pursuit of an atomic bomb

APRIL 1992: *IEEE Spectrum*'s two-part article, "Special Report: Seeking Nuclear Safeguards," won the 1993 National Magazine Award in the reporting category.

magazines were established in 1741. The word *Profile* was coined by *The New Yorker* during the 1920s and even registered. But the magazine wasn't rigorous in maintaining its rights and the word passed into everyday use as an article detailing an individual's life and showing who that person is. The profile article type has a variety of approaches: biography, *New Yorker* profile, personality sketch, Q & A, no interviewer, and institutional.

BIOGRAPHY. During the eighteenth and nineteenth centuries, biographies of famous statesmen—and a few women—took a linear approach from birth to death. Alexander the Great, Napoleon Bonaparte, George Washington, and Abraham Lincoln were some of the historical figures whose lives appeared in magazines. "The last half of the present century has developed an extraordinary mania for heroes and hero worship," wrote adventurer C. Chaillé-Long in the *North American Review* in May 1887, when discussing the number of biographies found in magazines then.[12] Successful businessmen and financiers such as John Jacob Astor and John D. Rockefeller, as well as sports figures such as Babe Ruth, were predominant biographical subjects after the turn of the twentieth century. While these biographical articles were long, detailed, and often comprehensive, they lacked honesty and candor.

NEW YORKER PROFILE. Harold Ross, founder of *The New Yorker*, wanted to run a shorter, more focused form of the biography in his new magazine. Critic Wolcott Gibbs, writing in 1943, observed that *The New Yorker*'s profile gradually developed "from its very feeble beginnings [in the 1925 first issue] to its present remarkably thorough form" because of Harold Ross's "ferocious curiosity about people."[13]

Under Ross, the profile became a probing biographical study, or as critic Clifton Fadiman wrote, "a form of composition no less specific

One writer sold the same story to four different magazines. Author Ted Schwarz wrote four different versions of Kathy Miller's tragic story of being struck by a car while crossing a street. The teenager literally was knocked out of her shoes and socks; doctors gave her little chance of regaining consciousness, much less ever walking because muscles were torn from her legs. Months later, Miller had relearned to talk and walk, and eventually became a competitive long distance runner. Schwarz told the compelling story from four different perspectives, with publication in *Family Circle, Seventeen, Success,* and *Today's Christian Woman.*

than the familiar essay, the sonnet, or the one-act play."[14] Ross didn't want an impression of an individual, such as would be found in a short personality sketch. He wanted "a family history, bank reference, social security number, urinalysis, catalogue of household possessions, names of all living relatives, business connections, political affiliations, as well as a profile."[15] Writers were expected to interview not just the individual, but his or her family, friends, enemies, professional colleagues, and even servants. The profiles were so long they sometimes appeared in four to six installments. The result often was provocative and profound. To be profiled in *The New Yorker,* said Fadiman, individuals merely had to have "made a success, not of their bank-balances, but of their personalities."

That's not to say that *The New Yorker* didn't profile the famous and infamous at times. Some scholars consider Lillian Ross's May 13, 1950, *New Yorker* profile of Ernest Hemingway to be one of the most controversial magazine articles ever published. Taking the "I am a camera" approach, Ross provided a detailed account of what it was like to spend two days with the famous novelist: "I tried to describe as precisely as possible how Hemingway, who had the nerve to be like nobody else on earth, looked and sounded when he was in action, talking, between work periods—to give a picture of the man as he was, in his uniqueness and with his vitality and his enormous spirit of fun intact."[16] Hemingway fans hated the piece. Wrote one critic, "It was widely thought to be a 'devastating' portrait of the writer as an over-the-hill borderline alcoholic, whose mock-Indian lingo and constant baseball and boxing references were sad affectations."[17]

Ross, who later republished the Hemingway profile in two of her books, *Portrait of Hemingway* and *Reporting,* defended her work: "When I wrote the Profile, I attempted to set down only what I had seen and heard, and not to comment on the facts or express any opinions or pass any judgments. However, I believe that today—with the advantage gained by distance—almost any reader would see that although I did not reveal my viewpoint directly, implicit in my choice and arrangement of detail, and in the total atmosphere created, was my feeling of affection and admiration." She pointed out that Hemingway himself liked the piece and wrote to reassure her that "some people couldn't understand his enjoying himself and his not being really spooky; they couldn't understand his being a serious writer without being pompous."

Only a handful of magazines today—including *Vanity Fair, Esquire,* and *Sports Illustrated*—have the space and stamina to follow the demanding *New Yorker* profile form. Again, most editors use the word *profile* to indicate an article that is less comprehensive than a biography, more in-depth than a sketch, but not as exhaustive as a *New Yorker* piece.

PERSONALITY SKETCH. Although it is an axiom that people like to read about people, the long profile form is not as prevalent as it once was. The trend now is toward the short personality sketch (one to five pages), which was honed by *People* magazine, established in 1974. *People*'s personality sketches are a page or two in length and tightly focused. Many of *People*'s thumbnail profiles revolve around "hot" entertainment celebrities, although there are always stories about ordinary people whose lives provide an emotional impact or who have been thrust into the news for one heroic reason or another.

Wood's "Craftsman Closeup" takes about five pages to introduce woodworkers and what they do. Explains features editor Peter Stephano, "I select these people based on their originality and level of craftsmanship more than their national reputation. To me (and hopefully, our readers), a woodworker in Oregon who makes English longbows to supply to Britain's Royal Company of Archers is more interesting, entertaining, and educational than the guy in New York City who turns out one cabinet after another for Helmsley Hotels. These are meant to be inspirational (Hey, I could do that!) and to give an indication of how really enormous the woodworking field happens to be." Even wood species are profiled in *Wood:* "Wood Profile" is a two-page historical, identification, and application article about a wood used in woodworking.

Q & A. Some magazines prefer the question and answer, or Q & A, approach to profiles. *Saturday Evening Post* took a tightly focused, short Q & A angle during the late 1950s and most of the 1960s for a series titled "I Call On . . ." by Pete Martin. Martin "called on" movie stars ranging from Bing Crosby and Zsa Zsa Gabor to Jack Lemmon and Shirley MacLaine. Most of the low-key interviews took place in the stars' homes, where respondents felt comfortable being intelligent and amusing.

Playboy offers another variation on the Q & A, with its monthly question and answer format involving many hours of taped interviews with an individual. *Playboy* likes to talk to powerhouse celebrities from the political, entertainment, and literary arenas. Interviews have ranged from Tom Clancy to Tom Cruise and from Betty Friedan to Joyce Carol Oates. *Playboy*'s first interview, in September 1962, was with jazzman Miles Davis; it was conducted by a young writer named Alex Haley. Haley, who did 10 interviews for *Playboy*, including the Reverend Martin Luther King Jr., Cassius Clay (boxer Mohammed Ali), and Quincy Jones, had the tables turned when he was interviewed in January 1977 shortly after completing *Roots*.

Individuals who commit to a *Playboy* "interview of record," as the editors call it, must agree to an extended session that can range from six to 40 hours over a period as long as six months. Writer Larry DuBois spent two years interviewing actor Robert Redford—an hour here, an hour there—before the piece appeared in the December 1974 issue. Each Q & A is prefaced by a comprehensive introduction that tells where and when the interview took place, sets the tone of the profile, and establishes the perimeters of the dialogue. The published Q & A is not a simple linear transcript of the conversation; it is a judiciously edited piece that gets at the heart and soul of the subject. The journalist-interviewer—who have included such notables as Alvin Toffler, Kenneth Tynan, and Mike Wallace—serves as the magazine's voice: probing, yet neutral.

In a 1998 Internet chat, founder Hugh Hefner identified the *Playboy* interview as his favorite recurring feature (after the centerfold, of course). Said Hefner, "The one that stands out first is the interview with Jimmy Carter in the '70s [November 1976] because it became the major source of controversy before the election and he got elected." Hefner also lists the Martin Luther King Jr., Fidel Castro, and Malcolm X interviews as memorable, adding, "There have been so many over the years. They are a source of great journalistic pride for me."[18]

PLAYBOY INTERVIEW: **MILES DAVIS**

a candid conversation with the jazz world's premier iconoclast

The technical and emotional brilliance of the trumpet played by Miles Davis has made him one of the most provocative influences in modern jazz. We spent two days with Miles not long ago in his rather unusual five-story home, a converted Russian Orthodox Church on West 77th Street near the Hudson River in New York City. Miles was between gigs at the time and we accompanied him on his restless daily home routine, asking questions at propitious moments while he worked out in his basement gymnasium, made veal chops Italian style for his family, took telephone calls from fellow musicians, his lawyer and stockbroker, gave boxing lessons to his three sons, watched TV, plucked out beginner's chords on a guitar and, of course, blew one of his two Martin trumpets, running up and down the chromatic scale with searing speed. Spending time with Miles in the refuge of his own home, and seeing him surrounded by the activities and people he loves, it was hard to reconcile this reality with his sometimes flinty and truculent public posture. It was on this facet of his personality that we first queried him.

PLAYBOY: Linked with your musical renown is your reputation for bad temper and rudeness to your audiences. Would you comment?

DAVIS: Why is it that people just have to have so much to say about me? It bugs me because I'm not that important. Some critic that didn't have nothing else to do started this crap about I don't announce numbers, I don't look at the audience, I don't bow or talk to people, I walk off the stage, and all that.

Look, man, all I am is a trumpet player. I only can do one thing – play my horn – and that's what's at the bottom of the whole mess. I ain't no entertainer, and ain't trying to be one. I am one thing, a musician. Most of what's said about me is lies in the first place. Everything I do, I got a reason.

The reason I don't announce numbers is because it's not until the last instant I decide what's maybe the best thing to play next. Besides, if people don't recognize a number when we play it, what difference does it make?

Why I sometimes walk off the stand is because when it's somebody else's turn to solo, I ain't going to just stand up there and be detracting from him. What am I going to stand up there *for*? I ain't no model, and I don't sing or dance, and I damn sure ain't no Uncle Tom just to be up there grinning. Sometimes I go over by the piano or the drums and listen to what they're doing. But if I don't want to do that, I go in the wings and listen to the whole band until it's the next turn for my horn.

Then they claim I ignore the audience while I'm playing. Man, when I'm working, I know the people are out there. But when I'm playing, I'm worrying about making my horn sound right.

And they bitch that I won't talk to people when we go off after a set. That's a damn lie. I talk plenty of times if everything's going like it ought to and I feel right. But if I got my mind on something about my band or something else, well, hell, no, I don't want to talk. When I'm working I'm concentrating. I bet you if I was a doctor sewing on some son of a bitch's heart, they wouldn't want me to talk.

Anybody wants to believe all this crap they hear about me, it's their problem, not mine. Because, look, man, I like people. I *love* people! I'm not going around telling everybody that. I try to say that my way – with my horn. Look, when I was a boy, 10 years old, I got a paper route and it got bigger than I could handle because my customers liked me so much. I just delivered papers the best I could and minded my business, the same way I play my horn now. But a lot of the people I meet now make me sick.

PLAYBOY: What types of people do you find especially irritating?

DAVIS: Well, these people that's always coming up bugging me until they get me to act like this crap they heard. They ask you things, you say what you think, and if it ain't what they want to hear, then something's wrong with you and they go away mad and think you don't like them. I bet I have had that happen 500 times. In this last club I played, this newspaper reporter kept after me when I told him I didn't have

"I don't pay no attention to what critics say about me, the good or the bad. The toughest critic I got is myself ... and I'm too vain to play anything I think is bad."

"In high school I was best in music class on the trumpet, but the prizes went to the boys with blue eyes. I made up my mind to outdo anybody white on my horn."

"I don't dig people in clubs who don't pay the musicians respect. You ever see anybody bugging the classical musicians when they are on the job and trying to work?"

37

SEPTEMBER 1962: *Playboy's* first profile, with jazz musician Miles Davis, was conducted by writer Alex Haley.

NO INTERVIEWER. One of the most interesting recent wrinkles in the face of the profile has been to eliminate the interviewer altogether. *Vanity Fair*, *Vogue*, and *Premiere* ran "dear diary" jottings by, respectively, singer Madonna (while filming *Evita* in Argentina), novelist Tama Janowitz (while adopting a Chinese baby), and actress Glenn Close (while filming *101 Dalmatians*). Other magazines are letting celebrities interview themselves, such as "Nobody Does It Better: Sharon Stone on Herself" in *Harper's Bazaar* and "The Unbelievable Truth About Mel Gibson by Mel Gibson" in *US*.

INSTITUTIONAL. At the other end of the profile spectrum are the institutional profiles of small and large businesses that are the staples of trade and organization magazines. Here the focus is on the company, as an institutional

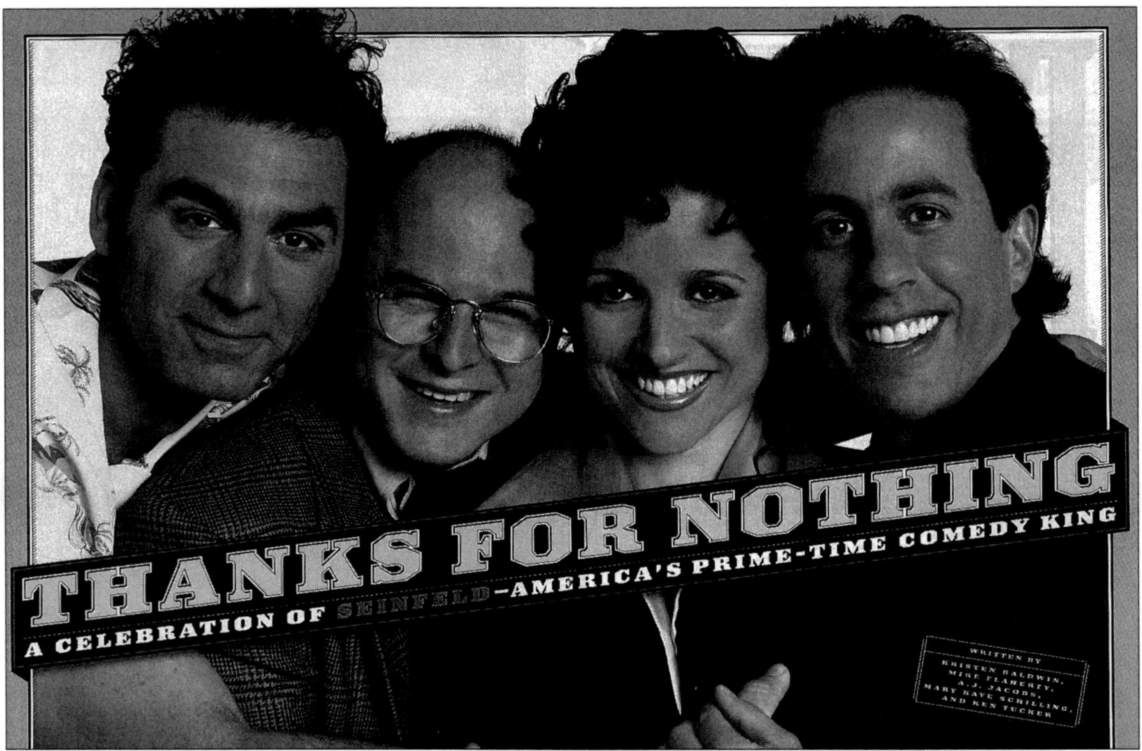

THANKS FOR NOTHING
A CELEBRATION OF SEINFELD—AMERICA'S PRIME-TIME COMEDY KING
WRITTEN BY
KRISTEN BALDWIN,
MIKE FLAHERTY,
A.J. JACOBS,
MARY KAYE SCHILLING,
AND KEN TUCKER

MAY 30, 1997: *Entertainment Weekly*'s institutional profile approach—an obsessive-compulsive report of what went on behind the scenes of 148 episodes of "Seinfeld"—won the 1998 National Magazine Award in the category of special interest.

personality, rather than the people who run it. According to Patrick Clinton, case studies and site visits are profile forms found in the trade press that increase readers' understanding of an industry. Consequently, profiles of new buildings are highlighted in *Building Design & Construction,* quarries are visited in *Rock Products,* and bakery solutions are illustrated in *Baking & Snack.*

Consumer magazines also publish institutional profiles, such as *Entertainment Weekly*'s 1998 National Magazine Award-winning "The Seinfeld Chronicles," which dominated the May 30, 1997, issue. The cover story and more than a dozen accompanying articles examined the popular television show, "Seinfeld," rather than honing in on the individual actors. Of particular interest was the "Obsessive-Compulsive Viewer's Guide to All 148 Episodes," from season one through eight, with a plot synopsis, analysis of key scenes, historic moments, critique, and "final grade." The institutional approach provided readers with more than they would ever want to know about a single television sitcom.

Investigative Reporting

Dating back to the muckraking period, today's investigative articles continue to be imaginative and enterprising pieces that tackle major social and political concerns through intensive interviews and insightful interpretations. Many investigative articles tackle topics of significant public interest in an attempt to make a difference. In 1991, *Family Circle,* a quintessential women's service magazine, won a National Magazine Award for its investigation of environmental health hazards in Jacksonville, Arkansas. Titled "Toxic Nightmare on Main Street," the August 14, 1990, *Family Circle* article by Stephanie Arbarbanel was a direct descendant of muckraking era articles in women's magazines that exposed the health dangers of patent medicines.

"The True Story of John/Joan," a 19,000-word article by John Colapinto that appeared in the December 11, 1997, issue of *Rolling Stone,* exposed a different kind of health danger. Colapinto traveled more than 20,000 miles over a period of eight months for interviews with more than 40 people for his behind-the-scenes investigation into the question of nature versus nurture in determining gender identity. The resulting report about sex-reassignment surgery on infants whose genitals either formed irregularly or were damaged by accidents won the 1998 National Magazine Award for reporting.

Most investigative articles perform a watchdog function: this particularly suits business and trade magazines. For example, the July 1995 issue of *Sales & Marketing Management* reported on the practice of salespeople taking customers to topless bars and how this wasn't fair to women in the sales business. The article, titled "Sex, Sales & Stereotypes," won a 1996 Neal Award for best investigative piece. Sal Marino, chairman and CEO of Penton Publishing, sees this watchdog function as being increasingly important for the trade magazine field:

> *The business publication, at its best, is often a crusading organ, and sometimes the conscience of the very people it serves. It was an editor in the vending industry, for example, who exposed industry-wide skimming and theft. It was a business paper editor who led a campaign against high-voltage swimming pool fixtures which were electrocuting swimmers at the rate of one a month. Our business publications conducted original research to trace hospital-acquired infections to mops and buckets and then developed tests which would help hospitals to evaluate disinfectants and set labeling standards. It was a business publication which fathered the Better Business Bureau, a business magazine which trained 40,000 mechanics in the interest of road safety through correspondence. It was a publication serving the toy industry which led the campaign to ban toy guns after the Robert Kennedy shooting.*[19]

Detailed investigative articles tend to exceed 5,000 words and sometimes are serialized over several issues. They frequently are touted on magazine covers as major features. Two currents flow in the river of investigative reporting: literary journalism and new journalism.

JULY 1995: "Sex, Sales & Stereotypes," about the practice of salesmen taking customers to topless bars and how this wasn't fair to women sales staff, won the 1996 Neal Award for best investigative article for *Sales & Marketing Management*.

CoverStory
sex, sales & stereotypes
It's often been said that sex sells—and spending a night at a topless bar provides plenty of proof. But what's the price salespeople and their companies pay when they use strip clubs to build relationships and seal deals with customers?
By Rob Zeiger
Photography by Chris Sanders
46
47

Longevity, Celebrity, and Topicality in Special Issues

Magazine anniversaries and deaths of celebrities lend themselves to special magazine issues, although an entire issue can be devoted to just about any topic. Advertisers like special issues because they have longer shelf lives on the newsstands than the regular weekly or monthly magazine. Another plus is that readers save special issues and refer to them time and again, weeks, months, and even years after their purchase.

Following the death of Diana, Princess of Wales, in August 1997, magazines as varied as *TV Guide, Entertainment Weekly, Harper's Bazaar, People, Life, Newsweek,* and *Time* all devoted special issues to a tribute. Some magazines have special issues already planned for speedy publication upon the death of a celebrity. Far from being exploitative, tribute issues generally accentuate the positive and play down the negative in individuals' lives. Readers of all ages see tribute issues as prized keepsakes.

Magazine anniversary issues also are popular collectibles. *Playboy*'s twenty-fifth anniversary issue in 1979 was a hefty 414 pages, while *Cosmopolitan*'s twentieth in 1985 (starting the count in 1965 when the "*Cosmopolitan* girl" was articulated by Helen Gurley Brown) was a whopping 484 pages. The cover of a magazine anniversary issue often shows miniatures of previous covers: *Time* followed this approach for both the sixtieth (1983) and seventy-fifth (1998) anniversary issues, as did *Sports Illustrated* for its thirty-fifth (1990), *People* for its twentieth (1994), *Vassar Quarterly* for its seventieth (1986), *Massage* for its tenth (1995), *Ebony* for both its fortieth (1985) and forty-fifth (1990), and *Town & Country* for its one hundred-fiftieth (1996).

However, the sixtieth anniversary issue of *Life* in October 1996 literally covered the most visual territory through its dramatic use of Rob Silvers's trademarked Photomosaic

LITERARY JOURNALISM. American literary journalism includes the work of Stephen Crane, Jacob A. Riis, Theodore Dreiser, Mark Twain, Lincoln Steffens, Richard Harding Davis, and John Reed. They started out as newspaper reporters whose work evolved into longer, more interpretive forms that were published in such top magazines of the day as *Saturday Evening Post, McClure's, Scribner's,* and *The Atlantic.*

The American literary journalism approach stressed the use of novelistic detail that was realistic rather than fanciful. Yet it also had an immediacy in its use of the standard news-gathering techniques of interviews, documentation, and observation. Literary journalism has been defined as "nonfiction printed prose whose verifiable content is shaped and transformed into a story or sketch by use of narrative or rhetorical techniques generally associated with fiction."[20] In a literary journalism piece, style is a critical component to the structure and organization of language. Although this approach flourished from the late nineteenth century into the 1920s, the genre dwindled with the Depression. Magazine editors wanted straight investigative news reporting—just the facts, ma'am—to match the no-frills American mood.

NEW JOURNALISM. It wasn't until the mid-1960s that some writers chose to shift from the mainstream, traditional investigative style that dominated most magazine reporting. A looser, more personal structure called new journalism was developed by such varied writers as Gay Talese, Gloria Steinem, Tom Wolfe, Joan Didion, Norman Mailer, Hunter S. Thompson, Truman Capote, and Jimmy Breslin. According to Tom Wolfe, new journalism resulted in greater flexibility and required "saturation reporting" because of the writer's willingness to immerse himself or herself in the story being told and to become part of it with first person commentary. Wolfe identified four central devices that characterized new journalism: constructing events by moving from scene to scene rather than from fact to fact; recording dialogue in its entirety; presenting events through the thoughts and emotions of the subject at the time of the happening; and recording the everyday habits, manners, gestures, and clothing that reveal an individual's status in life. The two most controversial aspects of new journalism were the presentation of the subject's interior monologue, revealing a person's inner thoughts at a certain time, and the very personal intrusion of the image which revealed Marilyn Monroe's face in relief via his arrangement of old *Life* covers. Using a special computer program at the MIT Media Laboratory, Silvers considered hundreds of aspects (color, shape, texture, contrast) of *Life*'s 2,128 covers to create the larger image of Marilyn Monroe within. You have to be just a few feet away from the cover to see Monroe's face "pop out" in a striking resemblance to the famous 1953 Alfred Eisenstaedt portrait of the blonde bombshell.

The entire August 31, 1946, issue of *The New Yorker* was devoted to "Hiroshima" by John Hersey. The 31,000-word piece, about the city's destruction by the atomic bomb as seen through six characters, was a first for *The New Yorker,* and it led the way for magazines to focus on a single topic or story in one issue. In March 1971, virtually the entire *Harper's* issue was devoted to "The Prisoner of Sex," Norman Mailer's macho musings on the Women's Liberation Movement. *Newsweek, Time,* and *U.S. News & World Report* regularly put out special issues devoted to such topics as medicine, retirement, or education that aren't part of their weekly cycle; these special issues are received by regular subscribers. *The New Yorker* has run entire issues—cover, contents, and cartoons—devoted to fiction, film, fashion, and women as part of the regular year's subscription. Annual special editions, such as *Sports Illustrated*'s swimsuit issue and *Seventeen*'s back-to-school issue primarily attract single-issue buyers, some of whom go on to become regular readers.

Trade magazines are big producers of special issues because they count on the extra revenue from both regular and new advertisers. Additionally, publishers like the extra money that comes in from reader orders for back issues and reprints following special issues. New product guides, trade show and convention exhibitions, and buyers' directories are frequent special reports developed by trade magazines. *Advertising Age* publishes well-received special reports on magazines several times a year, while *Adweek*'s hottest magazines and editor of the year issue is eagerly awaited every March. The annual sourcebook from *Folio:* is a prized reference among magazine professionals. *I.D. (International Design Magazine)* prices its annual design review issue at a princely $25; it goes on newsstands in July with a "display until November" tag on the cover.

author into the story. Many new journalism pieces revolved around the famous or near-famous as writers attempted to reveal the private side to the public persona. Or as Wolfe put it:

> *The result is a form that is not merely* like a novel. *It consumes devices that happen to have originated with the novel and mixes them with every other device known to prose. And all the while, quite beyond matters of technique, it enjoys an advantage so obvious, so built-in, one almost forgets what a power it has: The simple fact that the reader knows* all this actually happened.[21]

David Sumner, a journalism professor at Ball State University, explains how the new journalism originated in such magazines as *Rolling Stone, Esquire, Harper's,* and *New York.* The genre that emerged between 1965 and 1975 was a departure from traditional investigative articles that stressed objectivity above all else. The use of "I" by the authors matched the mood of a society experiencing upheaval ranging from civil rights marches and anti-war draft card burnings to the effects of the women's movement and the hippie counterculture. However, Sumner also argues that the inroads of television in the 1960s encouraged a group of innovative editors to take experimental risks with their magazines. Sumner writes, "High-circulation, general interest magazines such as *Saturday Evening Post* and *Collier's* had already closed, while *Life* and *Look* faced declining circulations and revenues. For many magazines, especially *Esquire* and the fledgling *New York* and *Rolling Stone,* experimentation held the key to survival."[22]

Sumner quotes *New York* founding editor Clay Felker as stating in a 1996 telephone interview that television played a role in editors deciding to try out the new writing approach:

> *What New Journalism did was to recognize that there was new competition for print. That competition was television. That brought the news to people quicker than a daily newspaper or a national newsmagazine. And so what you had to do was give another interpretation. You had to present the news in a more emotional, interpretive conceptual*

More than 15,000 short stories a year are submitted to *The New Yorker,* and about 13,000 each to *The Atlantic* and *Mademoiselle.*

RESEARCH IN BRIEF

Hidden Biases and Shattered Myths

More than half of all magazine research published in academic journals centers around editorial content analyses. Magazine researchers have studied the coverage of AIDS in men's magazines, analyzed presidential campaign accounts in news magazines, documented the progress of feminism during the 1920s, deconstructed the work experiences of short story heroines in the 1940s, and investigated racial attitudes in civil rights articles of the 1960s.

The analysis of the editorial content of magazines is extremely accessible—at its most basic level, a researcher needs only a topic, a consistent way of coding or counting what is being studied, and the magazines themselves. However, at its most sophisticated level—as the following three studies show—a researcher may reveal hidden biases and shatter myths about editorial content.

Joseph P. Bernt, a professor at Ohio University's E. W. Scripps School of Journalism, was curious whether trade magazines were doing a better job than other media in balancing race and gender in their editorial and advertising pages. Pointing out that trade magazines play an important role in America's economic and business life, Bernt also wondered if the business magazines' percentages matched race and gender numbers found in the overall labor force. So, he studied editorial and advertising photographs, mastheads, and bylines in 164 trade magazines to see how many Asians, blacks, whites, men, and women appeared.[1] His analysis of race and gender diversity in trade magazines revealed that editors under-represent blacks and women.

Bernt found that whites were over-represented in trade magazine editorial, cover, and advertising photography and that men were dominant as both staff members and writers. Whites made up about 86 percent of the labor force, yet they were found in 95 percent of the photos. Men represented 55 percent of the 1990 U.S. labor force, but they were dominant in 75 percent of the photos. Clearly, people of color and women were not being represented in the numbers expected if diversity and balanced representation were important factors.

Bernt says his research has practical implications for trade magazines interested in global expansion. Calling attention to studies that predict jobs will be increasingly filled by people of color and women, Bernt argues, "To retain the attention and respect of tomorrow's work force—to continue to inform and train that work force—trade periodicals must allow their readers to find themselves and their colleagues in their pages."

Barbara Straus Reed, a professor in the Department of Journalism and Mass Media at Rutgers University, has done numerous studies on how magazines have presented health issues, such as breast cancer and eating disorders. In 1995, Reed and coauthor Christine Morrongiello evaluated just how accurately consumer magazines interpreted scientific and technical information about breast cancer and how they presented it to readers.[2] They studied 232 articles in five consumer magazine areas: science, women's, news weekly, health/sports/fitness, and alternative/journals of opinion and compared their content with original research reports about breast cancer. Among the magazines studied were *Ladies' Home Journal, McCall's, Redbook, Vogue, The Nation, The New Republic, Prevention, Health,* and *Science News.*

---

context. And also it had to be more dramatic and emotional so that the reader not only got the intellectual argument behind it, but the reader was connected emotionally to the story.

Sumner points out that a few key magazines made a difference in journalism history by experimenting with new forms and publishing such controversial nonfiction as Hunter S. Thompson's "Fear and Loathing" series during the 1972 presidential campaign in *Rolling Stone,* Tom Wolfe's "Kandy-Colored Tangerine-Flake Streamlined Baby" in *Esquire,* and Norman Mailer's "The Steps of the Pentagon" in *Harper's.*

Essay

Essays are the oldest of magazine article types, dating back to the English periodicals of the eighteenth century. Essays have always been slippery beasts, being commentary on manners, morals, modes, and matters of everything from architecture to zoology—in voices ranging from serious to slapstick. All magazines of the eighteenth and nineteenth century printed essays that essentially were the opinions of the educated and the elite. Early essays had little research or documentation to back up the author's personal experiences and thoughts. For example, in an October 1784 essay in *The Gentleman and Lady's Town and Country Magazine,* Judith Sargent

Reed and Morrongiello found that breast cancer articles in consumer science magazines contained the lowest number of errors compared to the other magazines studied. They also found that errors of omission (incomplete information about results or methodology, lack of full identification of a source or research team members, or lack of attribution of fact to a source) were more likely than errors of commission (misstatement or misquoting of fact or report, misleading headline, or speculation treated as fact). Omission of sources and omission of relevant information about results were the most common errors, particularly in women's and alternative magazines. The bottom line was that consumer science magazines may be the best source for information about health research and medical news.

Reed also wanted to know how service information on eating disorders was being presented in women's magazines.[3] She asked whether the emphasis was on simple presentation of data and biographical accounts of women who suffered anorexia nervosa and bulimia or on presenting information that might motivate or mobilize sufferers to do something about their problem.

Reed examined 51 articles about eating disorders in 14 popular women's magazines during the 1980s; 12 of the articles were in young women's magazines, such as *'Teen* and *Seventeen,* and 39 in magazines with an older target audience, such as *Harper's Bazaar, Glamour, Ms., McCall's,* and *New Woman.* She found that fewer than half the articles, 47 percent, included specific mobilizing information, although 88 percent of them stated that eating disorders were detrimental to both physical and mental health. Where there was mobilizing information—names, addresses, phone numbers, specific health tips—it took the form of boxed, highlighted information at the end of the piece, a design approach found in many service articles.

What surprised Reed was the sparsity of articles about eating disorders during the decade of the 1980s. "Women's popular consumer magazines appear to be presenting informational/educational material, but 51 articles over a 10-year period does not seem sufficient, given the enormity of the problem," Reed said. She pointed out that editors have said they don't want to publish material that makes readers feel guilty or depressed, adding that articles about eating disorders clash with upbeat editorial content and tamper with the success of popular articles about diets by presenting the extremes to which some women go in terms of dieting.

1 Joseph P. Bernt, "Race and Gender Diversity in Trade and Business Periodicals as Reflected in Editorial and Advertising Images, Mastheads, and Bylines" (paper presented at the annual meeting of the Association for Education in Journalism and Mass Communication, Washington, DC, August 1995).

2 Christine Morrongiello and Barbara Straus Reed, "The Accuracy of Breast Cancer Reports in Consumer Magazines" (paper presented at the annual meeting of the Association for Education in Journalism and Mass Communication, Washington, DC, August 1995).

3 Barbara Straus Reed, "The Link Between Mobilizing Information and Service Journalism as Applied to Women's Magazine Coverage of Eating Disorders" (paper presented at the annual meeting of the Association for Education in Journalism and Mass Communication, Minneapolis, MN, August 1990).

Murray, writing under the pen name of Constantia, described her plan for the education of young women in "Desultory Thoughts Upon the Utility of Encouraging a Degree of Self-Complacency, Especially in Female Bosoms." In women's magazines of the early to mid-nineteenth century, most essays explored sentimental concerns of women: a lady's character, a wife's sacrifice, a mother's love. Magazines with a predominantly male audience at this time published essays about meditation and repose, city versus country life, and dialectical encounters with people of different classes and ethnicity.

The modern essay found in twentieth-century magazines, however, is a more challenging approach to topics that affect readers' public and private lives. Editors expect essayists to provide wit and imagination as well as examination, dissection, and contemplation of events and ideas grounded in a believable authority. Pulitzer Prize-winner Annie Dillard, a contributing editor to *Harper's* who has also written for magazines as varied as *Cosmopolitan, Sports Illustrated, The American Scholar, Travel & Leisure,* and *The Atlantic,* describes the essay's function: "The essayist does what we do with our lives; the essayist thinks about actual things. He can make sense of them analytically or artistically. In either case he renders the real world coherent and meaningful, even if only bits of it,

MAGAZINES WITH THE MOST AWARDS

From 1966 through 1998, 55 magazines have won more than one National Magazine Award (Ellie) each. These 55 magazines racked up 235 awards out of a total of 320 Ellie awards given by the American Society of Magazine Editors. The top 13 multiple winners are shown at right.

From 1954 through 1997, 28 magazines have won more than one Jesse H. Neal Award (Medallions) each from the American Business Press. Here are the top 13 multiple winners.

The Most Ellies	
The New Yorker	23
The Atlantic Monthly	12
Harper's	10
Esquire	9
Life	8
National Geographic	8
Rolling Stone	8
Texas Monthly	8
Business Week	7
Newsweek	7
Outside	7
Philadelphia	6
The Sciences	6

The Most Medallions	
RN	26
Jewelers' Keystone-Circular	16
Modern Jeweler	12
Medical Economics	11
Heavy Duty Trucking	10
Progressive Architecture	9
Pork	9
Patient Care	8
Commercial Carrier Journal	8
Machine Design	8
Restaurants & Institutions	8
PC World	8
Book Production Industry	8

and even if that coherence and meaning reside only inside small texts."[23]

Today's essays fall into two broad types, critical and personal. A magazine's content may lean more toward one type than the other, but the approach is popular in both departments (short form of 1,000 words or less) and features (long form of more than 2,500 words). Editorial and opinion columns may follow either the critical or the personal essay form.

CRITICAL. Critical essays tend to discuss literature, plays, and the arts in general. Unlike the thumbs-up, thumbs-down scorecard reviews found in a *Premiere* or *Entertainment Weekly*, critical essays of books and movies in *The New Yorker* or *Civilization* generally are built around a theme. For example, film critic Pauline Kael's frank, wickedly witty, and passionate discussions of just-released movies transcended the term "review" because of the thematic approach she took. For example, she once linked "On the Waterfront," "East of Eden," and "Blackboard Jungle" under the title "The Glamour of Delinquency" to show how the literary theme of alienation had invaded the mass culture medium of film. For many years, her work appeared in *Life, Vogue, The Atlantic, Film Quarterly, McCall's, Mademoiselle,* and *The New Yorker.*

The thematic approach frequently is taken in *Civilization*'s ongoing book reviews. In the February/March 1998 issue, Richard Todd used Henry David Thoreau and his writings as the contextual framework for a discussion of three just-published books about contemporary nature. Obviously, Todd had to be familiar with Thoreau's works, as well as the background of classic American nature writing in general. The result was a very satisfying essay because the reader learns about comparative writing style and depth of content for each book while also having the great outdoors placed into context.

PERSONAL. Personal essays are just that: individualistic, often one-of-a kind exercises in tone, topic, and territory. Personal essays, unlike critical ones, tend not to have an obvious thematic center, but they do have a point. They often ramble, metaphorically growing from small to large and back again in connections that are charming in the hands of a cosmic writer. A popular topic in the personal essay genre is outdoor life and all of its ramifications: natural history, the environment, the wilderness, ranching, farming, and camping. Annie Dillard has distinguished herself in this area, as have John McPhee, Edward Abbey, and Gretel Ehrlich. Their works have appeared in *Time, The Atlantic,*

Harper's, New Age Journal, Antaeus, and *The New Yorker,* to name a few.

Anne Fadiman's "The Common Reader" column in *Civilization* was an example of an uncommon personal approach to books and writing that delighted readers for four years; she left the magazine in April 1998 to become editor of *The American Scholar,* published by the Phi Beta Kappa Society. However, aficionados can read the collection of her *Civilization* columns in *Ex Libris: Confessions of a Common Reader.* Bruce Vilanch's "Notes from a Blond" column in *The Advocate* takes the essay approach to gay and lesbian topics with more than an occasional tongue in cheek because of his background as a comic writer for Bette Midler, Billy Crystal, Andy Williams, and the televised Oscar awards presentations.

Truman Capote spent six years interviewing people in Holcomb, Kansas, including the two killers of the Clutter family, for "Annals of Crime: In Cold Blood," which ran as a four-part series in the September 25, October 2, October 9, and October 16, 1965, issues of *The New Yorker.* Published as a book later that year, *In Cold Blood* has been called "the first successful nonfiction novel" because of its use of literary devices.

EDITORIALS. Editorials and opinion columns generally fall under the essay rubric, where they offer a splendid way to strengthen ties with readers. For trade and business magazines, opinion columns and editorials are where professional issues, ethics, and standards are debated and put before the readers. Former *Internal Auditor* executive editor Anne Graham urges association magazine editors to avoid writing editorials that rehash the material found inside each issue: "Editorials can be powerful agents for persuading, inspiring, illuminating, informing and connecting with readers." She says the best editorials are "highly personalized—the more personal, the better."[24]

Fiction

Serialized novels, short stories, and poems were a dominant part of magazines for many years, occupying a significant amount of space as early as 1741. Fiction could be found in just about every magazine published during the eighteenth and nineteenth centuries.

The role of magazines in supporting book publishing was recognized as early as 1885 when a leading book publisher testified before a Senate committee: "It is impossible to make books of most American authors pay unless they are first published and acquire recognition through the columns of the magazines. Were it not for that one saving opportunity of the great American magazines . . . American authorship would be at a still lower ebb than at present."[25] Magazine editors also praised magazines' role in promoting and popularizing fine literature. In 1908, *Harper's* editor Henry Mills Alden proclaimed: "With scarcely an exception, every distinguished writer of books during this period has been also a contributor to magazines. Periodical literature has done more for the American people than any other."[26]

SERIALIZED NOVELS. Serialized novels became especially popular following the Civil War. Magazines published the serialized works of England's greatest writers, Charles Dickens, William Thackeray, and Wilkie Collins, as well as popular American novels by Henry James, William Dean Howells, Edward Everett Hale, and Bret Harte. By the 1870s, it was not unusual to find as many as three different serial installments running in *The Atlantic.* Other general magazines of the period, as well as all women's magazines, carried at least one chapter of a serialized novel per issue. Some magazines, such as *The Galaxy,* regularly carried fiction in more than one-third of their editorial content.

SHORT STORY. By the twentieth century, the short story, with its tighter framework and compact narrative form, had become the primary type of magazine fiction. In 1919, the weekly *Saturday Evening Post* published 308 short stories, while the monthly *Harper's* ran 60. Consequently, some magazine historians credit *Saturday Evening Post* with making the short story a medium of mass culture by publishing hundreds of mysteries, westerns, romances, and even science fiction every year. Yet the *Post* also ran serious works, publishing more than 60 short stories by F. Scott Fitzgerald, and took a chance on William Faulkner long before other magazines did.

After World War II, fewer and fewer editors published novels in the face of the short story's popularity. *Town & Country* serialized Evelyn

FISHING FOR FICTION

Fly Rod & Reel is something of a maverick among fly-fishing magazines due to its publication of a fiction issue every year. Pointing to a long American tradition of fine sporting fiction—by Ernest Hemingway, Norman Maclean, Robert Traver, and Tom McGuane—editor Jim Butler admits that "most outdoor magazines have gotten away from that sort of thing. They're generally service magazines now."

However, since 1988, *Fly Rod & Reel* has devoted its September/October issue to five short stories. "Over the past two years, we've waded through more than 200 manuscripts each year for five pieces," Butler says. "Getting enough material is generally not a problem."

Butler says he writes to most of the good sporting fiction writers he knows of in advance, reminding them of the submission deadline. Plus an announcement is put in the magazine every year calling for submissions: "Every once in a while a complete unknown writes a real gem . . . really," says Butler.

As for reader response, "naturally, we hear from the how-to zealots who want to know what this god-damn fiction is doing in a fishin' magazine," Butler admits. "But I don't think *Fly Rod & Reel* has too many of those kinds of readers."

Butler points out that they hear from plenty of people who just love the fiction issue, so he has no plans to discontinue it. In fact, he sees the fiction issue as a way of resisting a disturbing trend among magazines today.

"There is the unfortunate phenomenon of the *USA Today* mentality toward all journalism: everything short, nothing in-depth, no room for great writing, never let accuracy get in the way of being brief. But we're resisting it," says Butler. "The editorial directions of the other fly-fishing magazines allow us to have our editorial direction, which I think is distinctly different."

Waugh's *Brideshead Revisited* in 1945 and *Life* published Ernest Hemingway's *The Old Man and the Sea* novella in a single issue in 1952. *Rolling Stone*'s publication of all 31 chapters of Tom Wolfe's *The Bonfire of the Vanities,* from July 19/August 2, 1984, through August 29, 1985, harked back to the Dickensian tradition of a lengthy serial.

EXCERPTS. Today's magazines are more likely to run excerpts of nonfiction books, such as Gail Sheehy's *Understanding Men's Passages* in *Men's Health* and Bob Woodward's *The Choice* in *Newsweek. The New Yorker,* on the other hand, often prints an adaptation of a piece of fiction rather than an excerpt. This process involves taking sections of the book and creating a similar, but shorter, whole.

The decline in consumer magazine fiction occurred with the decline in mass-market magazines during the 1950s and 1960s. Consequently, according to magazine critic Deirdre Carmody, only a handful of magazines now publish serious short stories on a regular basis: *The New Yorker, The Atlantic, Harper's, Playboy, Esquire, GQ, Seventeen, Mademoiselle,* and a few others. "Fiction is perceived to be costly because, unlike service features, it does not directly attract advertisers," says Carmody.[27]

Publishing serious fiction requires a major commitment on the part of a consumer magazine; trade and organization magazines rarely run fiction. Some women's magazines, such as *Good Housekeeping, Ladies' Home Journal,* and *Redbook,* continue to publish an occasional short story, but their material has been criticized as being too formulaic—romantic and upbeat—to be taken seriously. Of course, that's what those editors believe their readers want. *Seventeen* and *Mademoiselle,* which have published stories by Katherine Anne Porter, Margaret Atwood, and Joyce Carol Oates, are said to be exceptions to the women's sentimental fiction rule.

"There are very few magazines that pop up and start publishing good fiction," says *Texas Monthly* editor Gregory Curtis, who has been a judge in the National Magazine Award fiction category. "Those magazines that value fiction as an integral part of the magazine have always assumed that their readers are buying the magazine for the totality of the magazine and that totality includes fiction. Magazines that publish good fiction must have the confidence of the main editor."[28]

Literary journals and quarterly reviews, or "little magazines" such as *Sewanee Review,* are the primary outlet for writers of fiction. Approximately 500 of these journals exist, and few have circulations over 12,000. These publications tend to pay their writers poorly, if at all; sometimes payment is in copies. *Story,* with a circulation of 37,000, is currently the most successful magazine publishing only mainstream short fiction. Founded originally in 1931, this literary magazine is credited with helping discover J. D. Salinger, Carson McCullers, and William Saroyan. *Story* died in 1971, but was revived in 1989.

THE EDITOR AND THE READER

Norman Cousins argued that there were two general theories about editors and the way they edit for their readers: "One is that an editor should engage market research to find out what readers want to read. The other is that an editor must edit to please himself or herself. If there are enough people who share his or her tastes, the latter method is apt to be more successful. If there are not enough people to share those tastes, the editor should get out of the way and make room for someone else."[29] In his final comments as editor of *Saturday Review* in 1971, Cousins wrote, "The one thing I learned about editing over the years is that you have to edit and publish out of your own tastes, enthusiasms and concerns, and not out of notions or guesswork about what other people might like to read."[30]

The role of the editor as a middle person between the article and the reader is an important one. In a 1994 speech, Reginald K. Brack Jr., then chairman of Time Inc., observed: "Editors—those gifted middle-men and women—are the difference between the stock tables and *Fortune* magazine. The difference between the box scores and *Sports Illustrated.* The difference between the Wednesday food coupons in the newspaper and *Martha Stewart Living.* The difference between an on-line bulletin board and *Wired* magazine."[31]

Former *Time* editorial director Ray Cave says editors should give readers what they ought to read as well as what they want to read. "As editor, I make the choice of subject matter in a magazine, but I still must make the reader want to read it," Cave says. "In this respect the editor is a packager, a con man, a huckster and a whole lot of other things that journalists don't want to think they are."[32]

Because editors are expected to understand and fulfill the expectations of their readers, some editors want to hedge their bets through extensive market research about reader thoughts, attitudes, and habits. Yet editors also are concerned that research can lead to focusing on the lowest common denominator, much as network

NATIONAL GEOGRAPHIC'S EDITORIAL STANDARDS

In the March 1915 issue of *National Geographic,* editor Gilbert H. Grosvenor published a list of standards, or seven guiding principles, to give readers a sense of the editorial path he followed:

1. The first principle is absolute accuracy. Nothing must be printed that is not strictly according to fact.
2. Abundance of beautiful, instructive, and artistic illustrations.
3. Everything printed in the Magazine must have permanent value, and be so planned that each magazine will be as valuable and pertinent one year or five years after publication as it is on the day of publication.
4. All personalities and notes of a trivial character are avoided.
5. Nothing of a partisan or controversial character is printed.
6. Only what is of a kindly nature is printed about any country or people, everything unpleasant or unduly critical being avoided.
7. The contents of each number is planned with a view of being timely. Whenever any part of the world becomes prominent in public interest, by reason of war, earthquake, volcanic eruption, etc., the members of the National Geographic Society have come to know that in the next issue of their Magazine they will obtain the latest geographic, historical, and economic information about that region, presented in an interesting and absolutely non-partisan manner, and accompanied by photographs which in number and excellence can be equaled by no other publication.

THE ENVELOPE PLEASE: MAGAZINE AWARDS EDITORS LIKE TO WIN

There are myriad magazine awards presented each year. In addition to awards from the American Society of Magazine Editors and the American Business Press, awards are given by editorial associations within a narrow field, such as the American Horse Publications, Livestock Editorial Council, Parenting Publications of America, National Panhellenic Editors Association, American Jewish Press Association, Catholic Press Association, and Evangelical Press Association, to name just a few. There also are awards given by hundreds of nonprofit and advocacy groups for recognizing specific topics; these competitions usually include all media coverage of the topic, with categories for television, radio, newspapers, and photojournalism, as well as magazines.

Here is a selection of major magazine awards editors like to win:

ACRES OF DIAMONDS AWARD FOR MAGAZINE DEVELOPMENT

Sponsored by Temple University School of Communications and Theatre. Recognizes the best new consumer magazine launched in the previous five years, based on creativity, innovation, contribution, and business success. *Sports Illustrated for Kids* received the first award in 1992. Other winners include *SmartMoney, Family Fun, Martha Stewart Living, Cigar Aficionado,* and *In Style.*

ALTERNATIVE PRESS AWARDS

Sponsored by *Utne Reader.* Open to alternative press publications with awards in such categories as general excellence, reporting, writing, design, and coverage of lifestyle, cultural, scientific and environmental, political and social, international and spiritual issues. Winners include *Lingua Franca, DoubleTake, Adbusters, Hope, Blind Spot, Bust,* and *Hip Mama.*

AMY WRITING AWARDS

Sponsored by Amy Foundation, established in 1976 by W. James Russell and his wife Phyllis and named after their daughter. Recognizes writing that presents in a sensitive, thought-provoking manner the biblical position on issues affecting the world today. Articles must be published in a secular, nonreligious publication. Winning articles have been published in *Reader's Digest* and *Time.*

ANNUAL BUSINESS PRESS COMPETITION

Sponsored by American Society of Business Press Editors (ASBPE) for more than 20 years. Encourages excellence in writing, reporting, and layout and design among trade and professional publications. Winners include *CFO, Computerworld, Restaurant Business, Meat & Poultry, Game Developer, Successful Meetings, Federal Computer Week, Golf Shop Operations, California Lawyer, CIO,* and *Restaurants & Institutions.*

ASJA AWARDS

Sponsored by American Society of Journalists and Authors (ASJA). Awards are given to authors of outstanding service, profile, and essay articles. Winning articles have been published in *New Republic, Redbook, Penthouse, Consumers Digest, National Geographic Traveler, Psychology Today,* and *New Choices.* The Editor of the Year Award honors the "sensitive, intelligent magazine editor whose dedication is so important to the professional writer, and whose good work too often goes unrecognized and unrewarded." Past winners include Maureen McFadden (*Woman's Day*), David Sendler (*New Choices*), and Stephanie von Hirschberg (*New Woman*).

CITY AND REGIONAL MAGAZINE ASSOCIATION AWARDS

Sponsored by City and Regional Magazine Association (CRMA) and administered by the University of Missouri School of Journalism. All city and regional magazines that are members of CRMA or that qualify for membership are eligible. Eighteen awards cover editorial content and design with

television does. "Computer-printouts-as-gospel make no sense in an industry built on gut feelings," says George J. Green, president of Hearst Magazines International and the man responsible for the overseas editions of *Cosmopolitan, Esquire,* and *Marie Claire.* "Too many people complicate this business with too many meetings and endless debate where common sense and pragmatic thinking are what is needed," Green says.[33]

Helen Gurley Brown, who edited *Cosmopolitan* for 32 years until 1997 and now is editor-in-chief of international editions, agrees that too many editors try to edit by feeling the pulse of their readers.

general excellence entries grouped by circulation. Winners include *Yankee, Milwaukee Magazine, San Francisco, Boston Magazine, Indianapolis Monthly,* and *Pittsburgh Magazine.*

CLARION AWARDS

Sponsored by Association for Women in Communications (AWC). Fourteen magazine awards for outstanding editorial achievement in external, internal, corporate/for-profit, and nonprofit categories. External winners include *Discover, Newsweek, Business Week, Cooking Light,* and *Glamour,* while internal winners include Sigma Theta Tau International's *Reflections Magazine,* Pacific Telesis Group's *Business Digest,* and Michigan Consolidated Gas's *Beneficial Magazine.*

CRAIN AWARD

Sponsored by American Business Press since 1969. Given to an individual who has made outstanding contributions to the development of editorial excellence in the business press. Those honored include Bob Haavind (*Computer Design*), Marianne Dekker Mattera (*RN Magazine*), David C. Smith (*Ward's Auto World*), Robert J. Dowling (*The Hollywood Reporter*), and Ronald Khol (*Machine Design* and *American Machinist*).

EDITORIAL EXCELLENCE AWARDS

Sponsored by *Folio:*. Open to consumer and trade publications in 50 categories. Magazines are judged against standards that they define for themselves, rather than against one another. Judges rate how clearly entrants' mission statements are defined, then look at how well and how creatively each magazine's editorial content fulfilled its mission statement. In the trade area, winners include *Incentive, ABA Journal, Real Estate Today, Architecture, Prairie Farmer, Remodeling, Instructor, Plant Engineering, Strategy & Business, Skiing Trade News,* and *Restaurant Hospitality,* while consumer magazine winners include *Art & Antiques, Out, Health, Birder's World, Wired, Essence, Prevention, Sky & Telescope, The Advocate, National Geographic Traveler, Atlanta, DoubleTake, Scientific American,* and *Backpacker.*

GERALD LOEB AWARDS

Sponsored by G. and R. Loeb Foundation, administered by the John E. Anderson Graduate School of Management at UCLA. Six categories cover business, economics, and financial journalism, but are not limited to business publications. Winners include *Fortune, Business Week,* and *Florida Trend.*

GOLD QUILL AWARDS

Sponsored by International Association of Business Communicators. Categories include internal, external, for-profit, and nonprofit corporate and public relations magazines. Magazines published by Hewlett-Packard, Allstate Insurance, Raytheon, Exxon, Pacific Gas and Electric, and Mount Carmel Health have won.

HALL OF FAME

Sponsored by American Society of Magazine Editors. Inaugurated in 1996 to celebrate the career-long accomplishments of extraordinary magazine editors who have played leading roles in shaping and defining the magazine industry. The first inductees were Helen Gurley Brown (*Cosmopolitan*), Osborn Elliott (*Newsweek*), Clay Felker (*New York*), Richard Stolley (*People*), and Ruth Whitney (*Glamour*). More recent additions are Sey Chassler (*Redbook*), Jann Wenner (*Rolling Stone*), Henry A. Grunwald (*Time*), Hugh Hefner (*Playboy*), Gloria Steinem (*Ms.*), and Byron Dobell (*American Heritage*).

HENRY JOHNSON FISHER AWARD

Established by Popular Science Publishing Company in 1964 and administered by the Magazine Publishers of America. Named after the founder of *Popular Science,* the award honors a magazine leader who has made significant and long-standing contributions to the magazine publishing business. Winners include Malcolm Forbes (Forbes Inc.), S. I. Newhouse Jr. (Advance Publications), William B. Ziff Jr. (Ziff Communications Company), Robert D. Rodale (Rodale Press, Inc.), Gertrude R. Crain (Crain Communications, Inc.), Alexander Liberman (Condé Nast Publications), Robert E. Petersen (Petersen Publishing Company), and George J. Green (Hearst Magazines International).

INTERNATIONAL JOURNALISM AWARDS

Sponsored by Overseas Press Club of America. Recognizes outstanding coverage of foreign affairs and events

"Everybody is researching himself to pieces to find out what to do in life, and depending on others to give the answers for what the editor-in-chief should be finding out for herself/himself. You can't edit a magazine by committee. It's not a democracy," Brown explains. She says surveys can tell you where you went the most wrong or the most right with an issue, and that information can be helpful. But, she adds, in the final analysis it all boils down to basic gut instinct and intuition.[34]

But do intuitive editors also have to have a close, personal connection with the magazine's subject matter? Bob Mackowiak, editor and publisher of *P.I.*, points out that he's not a private investigator, from abroad. Winners include *Time, Newsweek, Fortune,* and *National Geographic.*

INVESTIGATIVE REPORTERS AND EDITORS AWARDS

Sponsored by Investigative Reporters and Editors, Inc., at the University of Missouri School of Journalism. Magazine category focuses on investigative articles that show initiative, originality, persistence, and importance of topic. Winners include *Money* and *Vibe.*

JESSE H. NEAL EDITORIAL ACHIEVEMENT AWARDS

Sponsored by American Business Press since 1954. Rewards editorial excellence in audited specialized business publications published by companies belonging to the American Business Press. Seven award categories focus on editorial content in three classes of advertising/circulation revenue. Winners include *Ophthalmology Times, PC World, Industry Week, Restaurant Hospitality, RN Magazine, Professional Remodeler, HomeCare, Architectural Record, Restaurants & Institutions,* and *Fire Engineering.*

JOHN BARTLOW MARTIN AWARD FOR PUBLIC SERVICE MAGAZINE JOURNALISM

Sponsored by Northwestern University's Medill School of Journalism. Established in 1988 to honor the writer(s) of stories that explore causes, consequences, or solutions to a problem in American society. Winning articles have been published in *Technology Review, Time, Life, Esquire, Newsweek,* and *The New Yorker.*

MAGGIE AWARDS

Sponsored by Western Publications Association. Must be published or distributed only in states west of the Mississippi River (Alaska, Arkansas, Arizona, California, Colorado, Hawaii, Idaho, Iowa, Kansas, Louisiana, Minnesota, Missouri, Montana, Nebraska, Nevada, New Mexico, North Dakota, Oklahoma, Oregon, South Dakota, Texas, Utah, Washington, and Wyoming). Consumer and trade publications and their promotional materials are judged in a variety of editorial and design categories. Winners include *Buzz, California Lawyer, Southwest Airlines Spirit, Sunset, HomeCare, Arizona Highways, InfoWorld, Islands,* and *Publish.*

NATIONAL HEADLINER AWARDS

Sponsored by Press Club of Atlantic City, New Jersey. Magazine categories focus on reporting, feature writing, graphics, and photography. Only paid circulation publications are eligible. Winners include *Philadelphia, Fortune, Newsweek, Time,* and *Baltimore.*

NATIONAL MAGAZINE AWARDS

Sponsored by American Society of Magazine Editors since 1966 and administered by the Graduate School of Journalism of Columbia University. Magazine must be issued at regular intervals at least four times a year. Newspaper supplements, in-house company publications, newsletters, and foreign language publications are not eligible. Fifteen awards in 12 categories recognize the variety in magazines' editorial content, visual presentation, and the move into electronic publishing. The "General Excellence" award is given in four circulation groups: under 100,000 (winners include *DoubleTake, The Sciences, I.D. Magazine, Print, Lingua Franca,* and *New Republic*); 100,000 to 400,000 (winners include *Prevention, Wired, Civilization, Men's Journal, American Photo,* and *Texas Monthly*); 400,000 to 1,000,000 (winners include *Outside, Condé Nast Traveler, The New Yorker, Health,* and *The Atlantic Monthly*); and over 1,000,000 (winners include *Rolling Stone, Vanity Fair, Business Week, Entertainment Weekly, Newsweek,* and *National Geographic*). A "General Excellence in New Media" category was added in 1997, with the first award going to *Money.*

SIGMA DELTA CHI AWARDS

Sponsored by Society of Professional Journalists. Two categories cover magazine public service and reporting. Winners include *U.S. News & World Report* and *Time.*

but he does have a strong appreciation of the field and the needs of his readers. "Eighty percent of *P.I.* is written by top professionals in the detection business. Although I don't presume to comment on the technical side of things, I know qualified people in the business who can, and I'm able to smooth out rough spots in their submissions. It's all a matter of knowing what questions to ask of whom, and applying another layer of skill to the information, through its editing and ultimate dissemination," Mackowiak says.[35]

Tim Schreiner, editor of *Fine Woodworking,* agrees. "Some past editors of *Fine Woodworking* have been professional craftsmen, while I am a hobbyist and am lucky to have experience in both journalism and woodworking. But it's my reliance on a newspaper background that is just as important, if not more so, as any woodshop experience in creating a magazine that's profitable and on the cutting edge."[36]

Both Schreiner and Mackowiak are a step removed from the days when authorities were turned into editors rather than editors into authorities. "A magazine can serve its readers well, despite having an editor with no experience pertinent to its editorial, so long as those under him do. In my case, it's my associate editor, an expert witness and a prominent name in the P.I. profession," Mackowiak says.

Or, as Cave puts it, "What matters most is not what the editor puts into a publication, but what the reader takes away."[37]

FOR ADDITIONAL READING

Applegate, Edd, ed. *Literary Journalism: A Biographical Dictionary of Writers and Editors.* Westport, CT: Greenwood Press, 1996.

Can This Marriage Be Saved? By the editors of *Ladies' Home Journal* with Margery D. Rosen. New York: Workman Publishing, 1994.

Capote, Truman. *In Cold Blood.* New York: Random House, 1965.

Clinton, Patrick. *Guide to Writing for the Business Press.* Lincolnwood, IL: NTC Business Books, 1997.

Connery, Thomas B. *A Sourcebook of American Literary Journalism: Representative Writers in an Emerging Genre.* New York: Greenwood Press, 1992.

Edgren, Gretchen. *The* Playboy *Book: Forty Years.* Los Angeles: General Publishing Group, 1998.

Fadiman, Anne. *Ex Libris: Confessions of a Common Reader.* New York: Farrar, Straus & Giroux, 1998.

Golson, G. Barry, ed. *The* Playboy *Interview.* New York: Playboy Press, 1981.

———. *The* Playboy *Interview.* Vol. 2. New York: Perigee Books, 1983.

Kael, Pauline. *I Lost It at the Movies.* Boston: Little, Brown, 1965.

Kerrane, Kevin and Ben Yagoda, eds. *The Art of Fact: A Historical Anthology of Literary Journalism.* New York: Scribner, 1997.

Mailer, Norman. *Armies of the Night.* New York: New American Library, 1968.

Marino, Sal. *Business Magazine Publishing.* Lincolnwood, IL: NTC Business Books, 1992.

Playboy *Interviews.* Selected by the Editors of *Playboy.* Chicago: Playboy Press, 1967.

Ross, Lillian. *Portrait of Hemingway.* New York: Simon and Schuster, 1961.

Thompson, Hunter S. *Fear and Loathing on the Campaign Trail '72.* San Francisco: Straight Arrow Books, 1973.

Wolfe, Tom. *The Electric Kool-Aid Acid Test.* New York: Farrar, Straus and Giroux, 1968.

———. *The Kandy-Colored, Tangerine-Flake Streamlined Baby.* New York: Farrar, Straus and Giroux, 1965.

———. *Radical Chic and Mau-Mauing the Flak Catchers.* New York: Farrar, Straus and Giroux, 1970.

Wolfe, Tom and E. W. Johnson, eds. *The New Journalism: With an Anthology.* New York: Harper and Row, 1973.

ENDNOTES

1. "How to Win and Hold Reader Loyalty," *Media Management Monograph*, no. 6 (February 1979): 7–8.
2. Byron T. Scott, "Service Journalism: Toward a Heuristic Agenda: A Speculative Paper" (paper presented at the mid-year meeting of the Association for Education in Journalism and Mass Communication, Washington and Lee University, Lexington, VA, March 1987).
3. Ibid.
4. Pamela Fiori, "Celebrating Service Magazines," *Folio:* (May 1992): 78–79.
5. Edward Bok, *The Americanization of Edward Bok* (New York: Charles Scribner's Sons, 1920): 174.
6. John Burks, "At *Sunset*, Another Day Is about to Dawn," *The New York Times* (October 7, 1996): C9.
7. "Start a 'Win an Editor' Contest," *Folio:* (July 1, 1996): 10.
8. Ellen Sturm, "*Getaways* Celebrates the Quick Trip," *Folio:* (October 15, 1996): 39.
9. Rolf Maurer, "Travel on the Cheap," *Folio:* (June 1998): 31–32.
10. Dennis W. Jeffers, "Service Journalism in the Association Magazine: A Case Study of the *Angus Journal*" (paper presented at the annual meeting of the Association for Education in Journalism and Mass Communication, Portland, OR, July 1988).
11. Patrick Clinton, *Guide to Writing for the Business Press* (Lincolnwood, IL: NTC Business Books, 1997): 13–14.
12. C. Chaillé-Long, "Heroes to Order" (*North American Review*, May 1887): 507.
13. John E. Drewry. " A Study of *New Yorker* Profiles of Famous Journalists," *Journalism Quarterly*, 23: 4 (December 1946): 372.
14. Ibid., 373.
15. Russell Maloney, "A Profile of *The New Yorker*," *Saturday Review of Literature* (August 30, 1947): 30.
16. Lillian Ross, *Portrait of Hemingway* (New York: Simon and Schuster, 1961): 14.

[17] Kevin Kerrane and Ben Yagoda, eds., *The Art of Fact: A Historical Anthology of Literary Journalism* (New York: Scribner, 1997): 129.

[18] "Chat with Hugh M. Hefner, *Playboy* founder and editor-in-chief," April 21, 1998 (http://www.playboy.com/features/hef/1998-04-21-hmh.html).

[19] Sal Marino, *Business Magazine Publishing* (Lincolnwood, IL: NTC Business Books, 1992): 12–13.

[20] Thomas B. Connery, ed. *A Sourcebook of American Literary Journalism: Representative Writers in an Emerging Genre* (New York: Greenwood Press, 1992): xiv.

[21] Tom Wolfe, and E. W. Johnson, eds. *The New Journalism: With an Anthology* (New York: Harper & Row, 1973): 34.

[22] David Sumner, "*Esquire, Harper's, New York, New Yorker,* and *Rolling Stone*: Innovators of the 'New Journalism'" (paper presented at the annual meeting of the Association for Education in Journalism and Mass Communication, Anaheim, CA, August 1996).

[23] Annie Dillard, "Introduction," *The Best American Essays 1988* (New York: Ticknor & Fields, 1988): xvii.

[24] Anne Graham, "The Power of a Good Editorial Page," *Folio:* (Special Sourcebook Issue 1998): 226–27.

[25] Frank Luther Mott, *A History of American Magazines, 1741–1850,* vol. 1 (Cambridge, MA: Harvard University Press, 1939): 3.

[26] Henry Mills Alden, *Magazine Writing and the New Literature* (1908; reprint, Freeport, NY: Books for Libraries Press, 1971): 49.

[27] Deirdre Carmody, "The Short Story: Out of the Mainstream but Flourishing," *The New York Times* (April 23, 1991): B1.

[28] Ibid., B2.

[29] "How to Win and Hold Reader Loyalty," 8.

[30] Norman Cousins, "Final Report to Readers," *Saturday Review* (November 27, 1971): 32.

[31] Reginald K. Brack Jr. "Magazines and a New Ethic of Communication," Speech given at Acres of Diamonds Award Luncheon, New York, October 31, 1994.

[32] Ray Cave, "Good Journalism vs. What Sells," *Folio:* (December 1987): 177.

[33] "MPA Draws Crowd of 800+ for Day-Night Doubleheader in NYC," *Folio:* First Day email edition, February 2, 1998 (http://www/foliofirstday@emailpub.com).

[34] "Editing a Magazine: 'It's Not a Democracy,'" *Folio:* (August 1, 1996): 9.

[35] "The Affinity Factor," *Folio:* (May 1998): 94.

[36] Ibid., 94.

[37] Cave, 177.

CHAPTER 9

Magazine Designs

Creating the Look

From 1934 until 1958, the page layouts at Harper's Bazaar *were orchestrated by art director Alexey Brodovitch to have a musical feeling and a rhythm that would carry the reader through the magazine like a series of dance steps—a tango here, a cha-cha there, a waltz or a polka for variety. Brodovitch expected magazine design to have spontaneity, vitality, and movement. Yet he also provided unity and continuity through the use of large amounts of white space and consistent typefaces and through his treatment of the open magazine as a two-page spread. Mehemed Fehmy Agha, who designed* Vogue *from 1929 through 1942, also created a distinctive look for that magazine. Agha stressed the synergy between editorial copy and design by cutting across the spine of* Vogue *to unite two single pages into one double-page spread through the use of photo bleeds across margins and gutters. 📖 Both Brodovitch and Agha instinctively understood what makes magazine design different from that in books and newspapers: a reader focuses on two pages at a time as the frame of reference. Earlier art directors used the two-page spread as a design unit, but they didn't push the horizontal envelope the way that Brodovitch and Agha did. For Brodovitch and Agha, the two-page spread naturally led to other two-page units to create a depth and continuity that transcended each two-dimensional sheet of paper.*

They also designed with a clear understanding of their magazines' editorial missions, so that each issue had a strong visual identity. During Agha's tenure, *Vogue* was dedicated to presenting fashion reporting and was a showplace of fashion photography. At Brodovitch's *Harper's Bazaar,* fashion pictures were shot on location with models in action; articles about fashion trends were tempered by the writings of Virginia Woolf, Eudora Welty, and Carson McCullers. The two magazines were, and continue to be, rivals for readers interested in women's fashion and style. More important, their visual identities still honor the legacies of Agha and Brodovitch.

A strong visual identity helps differentiate a magazine from its competitors. *Ray Gun* and *Rolling Stone* are both music culture magazines. They both have distinctive design looks and no one would confuse an issue of *Ray Gun,* with its randomly skewed images and graffitiesque layering of type, with *Rolling Stone*'s striking photography and trendy yet sophisticated design. Nor would either be confused with *Vibe,* another music culture magazine. *Vibe* stresses urban culture and has a different editorial direction, which is reflected in how the magazine saunters between alternative and mainstream design with photos that stare directly into the lens and challenge the reader to stare back.

A magazine's visual identity derives from its editorial mission; in a very real sense, form follows function here. Design is integral, not incidental, to a magazine's editorial voice. If there's a lack of clarity in the editorial content, there's also likely to be weakness in the visual element.

Magazine design has to offer both change and continuity to readers. On one hand, the magazine must look familiar from issue to issue, with thoughtful, planned content to aid in reader recognition. At the same time, the magazine can't appear boring or static. The integration of words and pictures—the use of titles, photos, cutlines, illustrations, cartoons, and infographics—has to consider readers' content expectations as well as their willingness to be challenged through the manipulation of key design principles.

Eric Utne, president and founder of *Utne Reader,* likes to recall a conversation he had with anthropologist Margaret Mead when he considers magazine design. Mead told him there was "a difference between entertaining readers, which she defined as giving them what they wanted,

YOU SAY TITLE AND I SAY HEADLINE

The terminology used to discuss design readout matter—the titles, subtitles, cutlines, subheads, and other words that draw a reader into the body copy—varies from magazine to magazine, and often depends on whether the editor-in-chief majored in journalism or English. Many magazine editors have an English or book background, although some come to the field from journalism and mass communications programs or the features departments of newspapers. Art directors often have some newspaper experience as part of their publication background.

This is not a definitive list, and there are instances where the newspaper term may dominate, particularly in the use of *caption* for the name of the text matter that accompanies illustrations. The term *cutline* dates back to the nineteenth century, when magazines used woodcuts as illustrations; the cutline was the material identifying what was in a woodcut.

MAGAZINE	NEWSPAPER	MAGAZINE DEFINITIONS
Logo	Nameplate, flag, banner	**Logo:** *the design of the magazines name.*
Cover lines	Main head	**Cover lines:** *short titles or teasers that appear on the cover of a magazine.*
Title	Headline, head, display type	**Title:** *identifying words that usually go above the start of an article or story and provide information as to the article's topic and content.*
Subtitle	Deck, drop head, subhead	**Subtitle:** *words that immediately follow the title and that are usually located just before the start of an article; subtitles provide additional clues as to the nature of the article.*
Pull-quote	Panel quote, pull-out, breakout, callout	**Pull-quote:** *words pulled from the article that are used as a design element to break up large blocks of text.*
Subhead	Slug	**Subhead:** *short phrases or words used to provide organizational information between paragraphs.*
Cutline	Caption	**Cutline:** *words underneath a photo that provide information about the image or its context.*
Dingbat	Endmark	**Dingbat:** *a small design device at the end of each article.*
Initial caps	Large initial letter, drop-in	**Initial caps:** *the first letter of a word used in a large size to make it stand out.*
Byline	Byline	**Byline:** *identification of the author of the article.*

and delighting readers, which she said was giving them what they didn't know they wanted."[1]

FORM FOLLOWS FUNCTION

The function of a magazine has little to do with art and much to do with business, which is determined by a magazine's mission or philosophy. That is why editors and art directors talk about designing a page rather than decorating it. It is also why there's a difference between magazine editorial page design and advertising design. An advertising designer has to catch the reader's attention just once, while a publication designer has to grab that reader over and over, from page to page, and from issue to issue. Design helps readers navigate their way through the pages to find the articles they want to read; it also lures them to articles they may not have intended to read. While design may be what holds a magazine together into a unified package, design alone doesn't keep readers coming back. Think of design as the means and editorial content as the important end result.

Jan V. White, who has designed the format of hundreds of magazines, says, "The purpose of editorial design is not to make a handsome piece, but a piece that *says something*. Good design should make the reason for publishing the message flare off the page at first glance. This should be the editor's primary goal."[2]

This is why the editor and the art director have to work as a team, with the editor defining and articulating each story's message to the art director, who then determines which visual tools will quickly, clearly, and effectively transmit that message to the reader. The magazine's raw material—white space, type, pictures, color—is shaped into an intellectually consistent and visually pleasing whole.

That visual whole, or the magazine's visual identity, is typically enhanced by a visual hierarchy found in every spread. This hierarchy is based on how most readers skim a story—generally the pictures first, then the title, perhaps over to the cutlines or pull-quotes, then back to the subtitle. Key hierarchical elements, such as the photo or title, generally provide instantaneous communication with the reader and are the subliminal equivalent of an article saying, "Read me."

Today's readers are visually sophisticated and they expect design to be effective, efficient, and engaging. A magazine with a strong visual identity and a clear visual hierarchy has a design that creatively juxtaposes words and images, features and departments, and articles and advertisements. The result is a sequential organization—most of the time. Magazine design is not rigid, and rules are broken every day. When discussing design principles, the phrase "everything's relative" must be recited as if it's a mantra.

Eighty-five percent of men ages 25 to 30 years old know magazines airbrush photos, according to a 1994 Stanford University survey. And 61 percent say they still want real women to look like the models they see.

On the one hand, most art directors agree that every page should have a single, important element that pops out at the reader. On the other hand, not all magazines have a visual hierarchy that quickly draws the reader into the layout and into the article. *Ray Gun* and *blue* are two magazines that have a lack of hierarchy on their pages. David Carson, former *Ray Gun* art director who is now design consultant for *blue,* challenges how people read magazines. He takes the constant visual barrage of images, messages, advertisements, and graffiti seen or heard while walking down the street or watching television and renders them on paper. His lack of a hierarchy in magazine page design is based on his belief that art directors tend to underestimate the sophistication of magazine readers and that readers are willing to view a magazine as graphic performance art.

Carson's contortionist approach is popular in trendy, iconoclastic alternative music and counterculture magazines. Magazine art director Rhonda Rubinstein points out that *Ray Gun*'s world lets readers be "hip to cool music, style and the end of print" as they "experience the raucous confrontation of type and image slamming onto the page. The consistent lack of consistency in its disturbed type, random grid, layered images and overall graphic irreverence make a direct hit on the jagged nerves of youth. Like music, where the lyrics are harder to decipher than the sound and experience, the visual experience is used to challenge the reading of *Ray Gun*."[3]

THE COMING OF AGE OF MAGAZINE DESIGN

The acceptance of an "anything goes" design approach among readers, editors, and art directors is a recent phenomenon. The evolution of magazine design cannot be separated from changing patterns of reader interest that developed following World War II—from an acceptance of broad, general editorial content to a demand for highly specific and informative niches and topics. The audience drives both editorial content and visual identity, and art directors have had to respond to the specific challenges that arose with a new generation of readers who were experiencing a fast-changing environment at home and at work.

Design Golden Age

Design historian William Owen dubs the period from 1945 to 1968 as the golden age of magazine design. He points out that magazine design matured quickly, with a short adolescence of less than 50 years from the introduction of the photograph as a regular design entity at the turn of the twentieth century.

THE INNOVATORS. The golden age of magazine design was preceded by three innovative designers: T. M. Cleland, who created *Fortune*'s modernistic and functional format; Mehemed Fehmy Agha, who gave a new graphic language to *Vogue* and *Vanity Fair;* and Alexey Brodovitch, who brought a sense of music and rhythm to the pages of *Harper's Bazaar.* These three greatly influenced the work of the golden age art directors.

Cleland laid out his design approach to *Fortune* in the February 1930 first issue:

> *The design of* Fortune *is based upon its function of presenting a clear and readable text profusely illustrated with pictures, mostly photographic, in a form ample and agreeable to the eye. It is planned upon an economic scale which permits it to go toward that end beyond the technical limitations of most periodicals. . . . The size and proportions of the magazine are designed to give scope to its illustrations and text without crowding and margins to its pages which shall be in accord with the best principles of fine bookmaking.*[4]

The 14-by-11-1/4-inch *Fortune* had a commanding physical presence: Averaging 200 pages, the magazine weighed in at three pounds due to the use of heavy, uncoated paper stock. The design stressed simplicity and consistency throughout the magazine via the use of the same typeface (Baskerville, which dates back to the eighteenth century), and the use of a thick black border around all the oversized photos. This was a departure from the myriad typefaces, decorative borders, and small photos found in many magazines of the time in their attempt to be exciting. Clearly, *Fortune*'s design matched the serious business topics being covered and the "less is more" philosophy of the time.

Agha's deliberate union of two single pages into one double-page spread by crossing the gutter was a new and dramatic way of making photos larger and bolder, as was his penchant for fanning action photos sequentially across a *Vanity Fair* or *Vogue* page to suggest movement. He eliminated column rules and decorative borders, simplified typography, and used lots of white space at the margins of pages. Agha demanded and achieved an elegant perfection in his layouts; in fact, "elegance" was the word used by peers to describe his work.

Brodovitch is considered the dean of art directors by many magazine designers. According to Owen, "Most of the techniques used in contemporary magazine design were pioneered or exploited at some time or another by Brodovitch—an undogmatic and instinctive rather than rational designer, who obsessively pursued change and modernity, and whose watchword was 'Make it new.'"[5] He used handheld cameras, over-exposed photographs, and image repetition long before Andy Warhol burst onto the art scene. Brodovitch's cover for the August 1940 *Harper's Bazaar* repeats a woman's face with blue, green, red, and yellow lips, predating Warhol's variously colored Marilyn Monroes in a far more lyrical and powerful format. Plain backgrounds with large photos and ragged type were juxtaposed with inanimate and animate forms to give depth to the pages. A sense of pacing always is felt when viewing Brodovitch's work because he viewed the page as three-dimensional rather than two-dimensional, depicting depth along with height and width.

THE HEIRS. A number of photographers and art directors were the heirs of Cleland, Agha, and Brodovitch and became key players during the golden age of magazine design. Concentrated in New York City, "designers of this period were distinguished primarily by their positive commitment to information design in the popular press, and were hidebound neither by stylistic fetish nor slavish adherence to the typographic dogma which sometimes encumbered European contemporaries," said Owen.[6] Some names to remember here are Otto Storch of *McCall's;* Bradbury Thompson of *Mademoiselle;* Henry Wolf of *Esquire, Harper's Bazaar,* and *Show;* and Alexander Liberman, who followed Agha as art director for all the Condé Nast magazines, including *Vanity Fair* and *Vogue.*

Storch, who was art director of *McCall's* from 1954 until 1967, reinforced the idea that copy, art, and typography were one unit; he was particularly adept at linking typography with photography for a unique design approach. For example, to illustrate an article titled "Why Mommy Can't Read," those words were written on the lens of a pair of eyeglasses. In "The Fortywinks Reducing Plan," a woman is shown reclining on her side on a cutaway mattress made of type, with the words of the article curving along

WINDOW TREATMENT AND THE PROPPING OF WONDERLAND

Jill Waage, editor of *Window & Wall Ideas,* at the Better Homes and Gardens Special Interest Publications, faces the same problem with each issue of her quarterly magazine: finding new ways to display curtains. For the Winter 1997 issue, Waage faced another problem: overseeing a photo shoot in New York City from her office in Des Moines, Iowa.

The firm Waage was highlighting in the feature story was Martin Albert Interiors of New York City, which creates custom draperies from designer fabrics. Waage couldn't take time off to handle the photo shoot herself, so she hired Patricia O'Shaughnessy as project coordinator.

Illustrator Geoffrey Howell painted the backdrop of windows, walls, and floor on thin, white theatrical fabric and created "furniture" from foam core. Waage hired New York photographer Jeff McNamara, who helped find studio space. Originally, Waage had planned to look for a photo space with lots of windows; she would then bring in an ottoman or ferns for simple, style-setting props. O'Shaughnessy suggested the idea of the painted set, found Howell to illustrate it, and faxed Waage ideas and sketches for approval. Waage says O'Shaughnessy was her "eyes and hands on the project."

The shoot took two months to plan and a full day to photograph. It was actually a quicker photo shoot than normal for *Window & Wall Ideas.* The backdrop arrangement simplified the process because, Waage says, the staff "didn't have to haul in flowers or rearrange the room."

That kind of propping (as it's called in the industry) of flowers and rooms often occurs in shelter magazines such as *Elle Decor, In Style, House Beautiful,* and *Martha Stewart Living.* Propping is used when the design editor or interior stylist decides that an existing interior decor is not quite a 10. So a chenille throw will be tossed over a sofa or a wicker chair placed in the corner of a sunroom, making a room look more homey or more finished.

"Editors call us all the time when they need an extra dining chair or an end table," says James Rosen, executive vice president of Pace Collection, which specializes in twentieth-century classic furnishings. "We're always happy to help them enhance a photo."[1]

Flowers are a frequent enhancement used by shelter magazines for interior room shoots. Often, hundreds of dollars worth of flowers will be purchased the day of the photo shoot, which can take as long as three days to complete.

her body from the pillow to her feet. Storch also regularly built two-page spreads around a single **bleed photo**—extending past the edge of the page—which served as both the background for the text and its illustration.

Thompson found new applications for type while at *Mademoiselle* from 1945 to 1959. He experimented with type both as an illustrative tool and as an alliterative form to create movement, volume, place, and mood. Plus, he used large horizontal and vertical grids to fashion layouts dominated by blocks of primary color, mimicking the paintings of the Dutch artist Piet Mondrian.

Wolf, who served as art director at *Esquire* (1952 to 1958), *Harper's Bazaar* (1958 to 1961), and *Show* (1961 to 1964), took a surrealistic approach to his pages. To illustrate *Esquire*'s July 1958 cover story about "The Americanization of Paris," Wolf shot a photo of a packet of "instant vin rouge" being poured into a goblet of water. Although it was meant to satirize the spread of American conveniences and customs, letters were sent to the editor asking where instant wine could be purchased. A May 1959 *Harper's Bazaar* cover touting "The Wonders of Water" found Wolf creating a refracted image of a woman's face in a large glass of water; the real face loomed behind the glass. Where the logo touched the glass, it, too, was refracted.

Liberman had the title of editorial director at *Vogue* and *Vanity Fair,* which allowed him to take a journalistic approach to design and to recognize the need to meld commercialism and circulation sales with fine art. He liked dramatic layouts that were classically bold and crudely aggressive at the same time. That was possible at fashion magazines where the photograph or

"We don't bring in just a few flowers," says Marian McEvoy, editor-in-chief of *Elle Decor.* "We bring all the colors we can find, because if you need a shot of marigold, you'd better have it."[2]

During the 1980s, flowers weren't enough. Entire rooms would be emptied of their furnishings, truck loads of museum-quality pieces substituted, and walls repainted or papered. "Those days are over," says McEvoy. "Today, people respond more to real people in real rooms with real personality. I can't fabricate that much personality."

Yet *In Style* successfully fabricated reality for a July 1996 cover story about Christie Brinkley's summer home in the Hamptons. The problem was that Brinkley hadn't moved in yet, so her home had only a few items in place. *In Style* found itself having to make an exception to its rule of capturing celebrities as they really live. An interior decorator was sent to get things in shape for the shoot by adding furniture from various antique stores in the region to Brinkley's own things. When Brinkley saw the final result, she decided to keep it just the way it had been created. She purchased all the furnishings and props, including antique English inkwells placed on her desk.

Of course, each magazine has to draw a line as to how much propping it will do. "We don't rearrange houses. We're not decorators. We're reporting on a place that already exists," says *Elle Decor*'s McEvoy.[3]

However, she admits that she does draw the line with bed sheets: "Real people's sheets are not going to make it for a shoot. They need to be pristine." And propped.

[1] Julie V. Iovine, "Making the Imperfect Picture Perfect," *The New York Times* (July 17, 1997): C9.
[2] Ibid., C9.
[3] Alex Witchel, "Having a Way With Décor, and a Way With *Elle Decor*," *The New York Times* (February 19, 1998): B9.

WINTER 1997: This fun and fake scene was created for *Window and Wall Ideas* with foam core "furniture" and a painted backdrop of windows, walls, and floor; the goal was to highlight window curtains—the only "real" element in the room.

illustration of clothing had to speak as loudly as the copy describing each garment.

Speaking in 1958, Wolf said the fashion magazine offered "the highest form for art direction: it is the art director's ideal showcase. The fantasy inherent in fashion stimulates creative designing, and furthermore, the photography and its layout are the means of 'talking' fashion. Since the picture can and must say it all, the copy in a fashion magazine plays a subordinate role. What a rare privilege for an art director! The only objective to present something visually beautiful!"[7]

But even when accentuating the visual, art directors from 1945 to 1968 wanted a gestalt, or integration of various parts into a functional unit. A gestalt occurs when editorial and design are in harmony, so that the layout's whole—the spread—is greater than the sum of its individual parts (copy, title, subtitle, photos, cutlines). With a gestalt, the design reflects or builds upon the editorial content by helping tell the story rather than just embellishing it.

The golden age of design, then, clearly linked all the elements of a page into a synergistic whole. Preliminary editorial conferences defined the feature copy and thinking that went behind each piece; design was supposed to express the concepts and ideas of each article. Next, the art director worked with photographers, illustrators, and graphic artists to plan and to visualize how the material could be presented imaginatively. Advertising tended to be clustered at the front and back of the magazines, and departments were few. There was usually a 40- to 50-page editorial well to work with and, although stories had to jump to the back of the magazine, a lavish start using four or five pages could be achieved. The assumption was that readers spent an unhurried, relaxing visit with their favorite magazines, and they would become absorbed by the visual and verbal spectacle on each page. Adding to the elegance and drama was the large size of the magazines themselves, averaging 10 1/8 inches by 13 1/8 inches. Although lavish, physically imposing, and slick, there nonetheless was always a sense of logic to the most opulent pages produced during the period from 1948 through 1967.

The choice of typeface makes a difference in how fast people read. Reading speed increases an additional seven to 10 words a minute when a serif type like Times is used rather than a sans serif type such as Helvetica.

Design Turning Point

Many designers believe the launch of *New York* in 1968 was an important turning point in magazine design. Founder Clay Felker says *New York*'s design and content were based on his belief that magazines had to compete in new ways for readers' time and attention. Certainly, there was enough going on in American society during the late 1960s to co-opt leisurely reading: the Vietnam War, civil rights sit-downs, women's liberation marches, and the increasing dominance of television to tell the stories of the day all affected the kinds of magazines being developed. Some pundits were even predicting the death of the magazine as a significant communications medium.

The time was right for highly specialized, smaller scaled, tightly formatted magazines like *New York* that took readers' needs into account. Calling the design formula simple enough to work on a weekly basis, yet sophisticated enough to compete for a busy metropolitan reader, Felker explained how it worked:

> *It was a magazine that had to give the reader a feeling of getting something out of the magazine just by paging through it—without reading anything, on the surface. And then if they decided to read something more, they would get another experience on a deeper level. It had to operate on two levels and it had to operate very quickly. We assumed that the readers we had didn't have a lot of time; we had to get our message across very quickly, to intrigue those readers enough to get them to read the magazine in the subsequent paging through. We designed the magazine with that in mind.*[8]

Founding design director Milton Glaser said he created *New York* according to an assumed attention span of seven minutes, which, he observed, "coincided exactly with the interval between television commercials during most TV programs. So we designed *New York* to be read by somebody with that temperament, for the television generation. It had constant interruptions—titles, subheads on every page, everything was designed for easy access."[9]

New York moved away from the graceful, sweeping, primarily visual approach of the golden age. Its compartmentalized pages eliminated jumping features to the back of the magazine and allowed advertising to run throughout the publication rather than just in the front and back. A lot more text, including sidebars, filled each page. Glaser's design format was very functional: readers knew precisely where to go to get information, and they could get it in short, but dense, chunks without having to jump to the back of the magazine to find it.

Wildly colorful psychedelic art was balanced by such type paraphernalia as initial caps, column rules, boxes, and a variety of decorative types for feature titles, although standing department titles tended to use traditional typefaces. Reverse type, bolded first sentences, and squared-off, boxed-in pages became the norm. There were fewer bleed photos and more illustrations, along with a willingness to break the sweeping unity of type and image used earlier.

Many city and regional magazines copied *New York* down to the last dingbat detail. Magazines as disparate as *Esquire, Playboy, Redbook,* and *Adweek* began playing around with what some critics dubbed as "fusspot" typography and flat graphic design. However, the sixties and the seventies were about letting go and experimenting, even if there was a surprisingly homogenous quality to the "revolution." So why should magazines be any different?

Computers and Design

The real revolution was still to come, and it was a technological one in 1984 that forever changed the magazine design process. In that year, the first generation Macintosh computer was introduced by Apple; type letterforms were primitive dot matrixes, and icon choices to click on were few. But it was clear that an innovative tool had arrived on the art director's desk, one that was transformed into the powerful graphic desktop by the late 1980s.

As an interactive tool, computers enable text to be simultaneously edited and designed on screen. All the components of design choice—words, photos, illustrations, typefaces, colors, textures, rules, and boxes—are integrated into a single system. This does not necessarily make magazine design easier, nor does it make the process faster. Design combinations and choices still have to be made, but now the possibilities are almost limitless.

Designer Henry Wolf calls the computer a "seductive piece of equipment that too easily facilitates excess." Referring to the golden age of design, he says, "In my world, the idea was to communicate with clarity, to dramatize your point. I think what the computer does is obfuscate the point, make it more difficult, more layered, instead of bringing out the thing that clarifies it. The computer adds. For us, it was always to subtract."[10]

"More Is Better"

Experimental design and lack of reference points to long-held design standards have resulted in a "more is better" approach in the late 1990s. Carol E. Holstead is a professor at the William Allen White School of Journalism at the University of Kansas who studies contemporary magazine design. She argues that the historical perspective of "less is more" has been sacrificed for flashy newsstand cover graphics featuring a plethora of cover lines (as many as 10) and colors (as many as six different single colors to highlight a word, sentence, or image) on top of the main cover photo in such women's magazines as *Family Circle, Woman's Day,* and *McCall's.* Inside pages aren't much better, she notes, with departments and features using four or five different colors per page, irregularly cut-out photos, decorative borders, numerous type weights and styles, and rakish title angles.[11]

Holstead says fashion magazines, too, have fallen into this "more is better" approach and abandoned their historic legacy. She cites *Allure*'s

JANUARY 1999: ***Ray Gun*'s distinctive design challenges how people read magazines.**

March 1994 "Reporter" department, with its collection of short pieces and titles printed in five different colors and five typefaces, as a design that "created communication obstacles for readers." Some contemporary magazine design critics refer to such busy, cluttered pages as the "MTV-ing of the printed page."

Interestingly, Holstead argues that some alternative music and culture magazines reflect historic influences, although it might not appear that way at first glance. Magazines such as *Ray Gun, blue, Black Book,* and *Bikini* seem to blast conventional design to smithereens with their densely imbedded layouts filled with images and colors; lack of formatting with randomly placed columns; photos that tilt or bleed off the page in mid-image; and type that changes style or size in the middle of a sentence or simply disappears into an illustration. Although the readability and harmony of the material is called into question, Holstead says the "startling confrontational design" found in *Ray Gun* in particular harks back to the Dadaists and Cubists. She sees a clear link between computer-generated type forms and the Cubist concept of letterforms as a visual experience, while the layered type pages reflect the disorder and societal disdain of Dadaists.

Relationship with the Reader

Readers know when a magazine title misrepresents or over-hypes a story, and they recognize graphics that are superficially startling. Today's readers may still read words the same way as those in 1741, but they also read images and typography—and, therefore, design. It takes discipline to maintain a visual identity that resonates with readers without boring them. Fortunately, there's plenty of room in the magazine industry for designs that are spare, simple, and classic as well as designs that are pyrotechnic, deconstructive, and confrontational—from magazines as disparate as *Martha Stewart Living, Harper's Bazaar, Civilization, Rolling Stone, Vibe,* and *Ray Gun.* After all, the reader can choose whether she wants to be soothed by uncluttered, color-coordinated pages of still life fruits, perfectly posed fashions, and historical print collections or challenged by the unconventional perspective of story-specific typography, street-smart attitudes, and unbalanced, obliterated typefaces that shatter the way she was taught to read.

David Carson says the nonformatted style of a *Ray Gun,* with its collision of images and letterforms, "humanizes the magazine because it requires interactivity, having to spend time with it, figuring it out."[12] That's a long way from the safe, comfortable embrace of a picture-perfect spread in *Martha Stewart Living.* But whether the design is that of a *Ray Gun* or a *Martha Stewart Living,* the relationship with the reader is paramount. Despite the design extremes found in magazines today, art directors and editors take into consideration how the publication is used, when and where it is read, what the reader wants, how it is held, and how quickly it is read when they design each spread in each issue.

Consequently, the best magazine design operates on a continuum, taking into account that a magazine offers a series or sequence of impressions through its content and its images. Jan White sums up the complex relationship between the reader and the magazine:

> *The best presentation is so natural and obvious that the readers are aware only of the wonders of the information they are reading. If they are tempted to notice the design, then that design has interposed itself and is therefore a failure—no matter how exciting or pretty. The medium is not the message. The message is the message.*[13]

DESIGN ELEMENTS

The impact of visual literacy, where people read images, typography, and design as much as they do a story's words, has led designers to consider one of two broad approaches: ordered versus diversified designs. Ordered designs stress unity from page to page, with relatively few frills or complications. Ordered magazines have tightly organized pages with consistent typography and page margins, but that doesn't mean they are dull or unattractive. The order results in a crisp, clean, and attractive format that appeals to many readers. Magazines using this approach include *Scientific American, The New Yorker,* and *The New Republic.*

Diversified designs still use basic design principles but with a lot more variety and liveliness. Although some diversified approaches may seem like a three-ring circus, there usually is order within the appearance of chaos. Designers taking a diversified approach use varying typefaces and are willing to change page margins to suit their needs. Examples of magazines taking a diversified approach are *Rolling Stone, Esquire,* and *Allure.*

Both approaches take into consideration such design elements as eye movement, grid, typography, color, and the basic design principles of unity, balance, proportion, sequence, and contrast. And both approaches revolve around the two-page spread, which is the primary unit of design in magazines since readers almost always view two pages at a time when reading.

Eye Movement

In general, people in the Western world read from left to right and top to bottom. Research shows that magazine readers also read from big to little, from heavy to light, and from color to black and white. Consequently, a large, colorful focal point, such as a full-color photograph or even a single color drawing, can pull a reader into a story.

Another eye path involves intentional or unintentional lines of direction, such as eyes in a photograph, raised capital letters in the middle of text, subtitles or subheads between paragraphs, or bulleted paragraphs. When a reader initially scans a page, his eyes tend to follow a "Z" formation. Because readers automatically gravitate toward the upper left quadrant of a page as a starting point, this is where many designers place an article's title.

However, designers at magazines such as *Bikini* and *Ray Gun* choose to ignore traditional eye movement as part of their lack of conformity. Articles in those magazines may start at the end and work back to the top of the left-hand page, or begin in the middle of the right-hand page. This approach makes a story harder to read, admits David Carson, who adds, "The starting point is about trying to interpret something about the article. In doing so, it may become hard to read. But our audience seems to enjoy that."[14]

The Grid

The **grid** establishes margins, number of columns per page, widths of columns, cutline and photo placement, title placement, and most important, the use and placement of white space, or air, in a layout. Essentially, a grid provides structure and discipline for each page, as well as an ongoing format to follow from issue to issue. A well-designed grid system can produce a sense of continuity and balance while still allowing for contrast, variety, flexibility, and the use of **sidebars,** or short accompanying pieces, to support main articles. However, a poorly designed grid, or one that is not used effectively, can result in monotonous, rigid, and crowded layouts.

Will Hopkins, a partner in the New York design firm of Hopkins/Baumann, explains why the majority of art directors use grids: "Think of the grid as a container into which you pour content. It's difficult to carry water without a bucket, and it's difficult to carry content without a grid. It's a structural and visual aid that should be flexible, and not a straitjacket."[15]

The editorial staff benefits from a grid because it creates a design standard, allowing everyone to speak the same language in terms of column widths, photo sizes, and space requirements. The reader benefits from pages that are logical, organized, readable, and visually appealing. There are three grid possibilities, but because most magazines customize their grids depending on their page size, determining an exact system is difficult.

TRADITIONAL. A traditional grid has standard margins and divides space into a two- or three-column format for a page size of about 8 1/2 inches wide and 11 inches deep (keep in mind that few magazines are exactly that size). There are no horizontal lines on a traditional grid, and the space inside the margins becomes the type page. In a traditional grid, margins often are progressive, with the most white space at the bottom of the page and the least in the gutter area separating the two pages. Photos fill one, two, or three columns of space; bleeds are possible but not frequent on editorial pages.

A traditional grid may designate a three-column format for departments and two columns for features, or allow for either two- or three-column features. All design elements end at the same place from page to page, which provides a strong unifying factor and creates an orderly relationship of typography, photography, and illustration. Some traditional grids resemble book designs because of the emphasis on verticality and the tendency to treat each page as a separate entity rather than as a two-page unit. The traditional grid results in formal-looking layouts.

Between 250 and 350 rolls of 36-exposure color film are shot during an average *National Geographic* assignment. A more demanding assignment can result in as many as 1,000 rolls of film, the majority of which are properly exposed, in focus, and interestingly composed. A cover feature in the magazine typically uses 30 to 40 illustrations.

NONTRADITIONAL. The nontraditional grid starts off with the traditional vertical two- or three-column format, but it also uses horizontal lines for a modular approach to design. Because there are numerous horizontal units to consider, column width can expand or contract as needed, type can be wrapped around photos or set in varying widths, photos can cut across columns, and page margins can be changed. The nontraditional grid offers more options for the use of sidebar material than the traditional grid.

Unity and continuity are still emphasized in a nontraditional grid, although there are more design possibilities. The ability to manipulate white space is the strongest aspect of the nontraditional grid. With more emphasis on the horizontal flow of the pages, a sense of sequencing or movement can be developed. The majority of magazines—consumer, trade, and organization—use a nontraditional grid.

12-PART GRID. Developed in Germany by Willy Fleckhaus and brought to the United States by Will Hopkins in 1968 when he was art director at *Look,* this grid starts with 12 equal parts per page, which allows for a great deal of flexibility

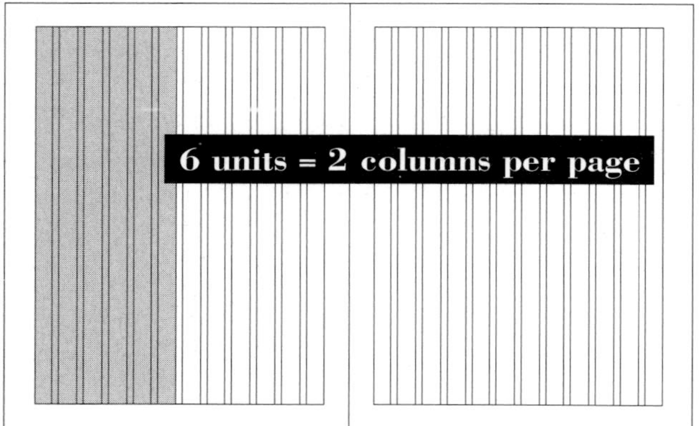

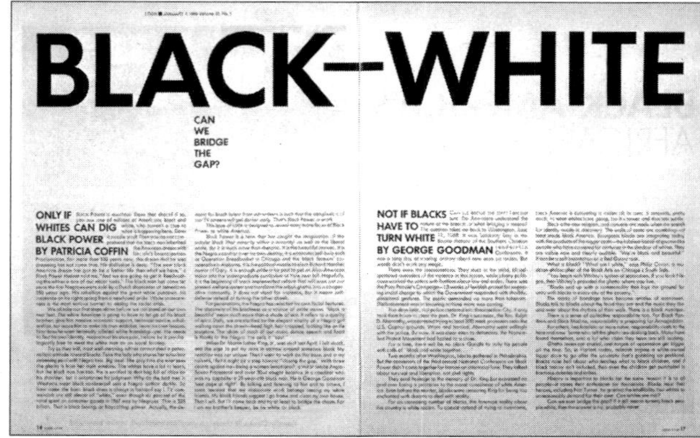
BLACK—WHITE

CAN WE BRIDGE THE GAP?

ONLY IF WHITES CAN DIG BLACK POWER BY PATRICIA COFFIN

NOT IF BLACKS HAVE TO TURN WHITE BY GEORGE GOODMAN

Will Hopkins says the 12-part-grid gives art directors both design flexibility and consistency. The "Black-White" layout (*Look*, January 7, 1969) uses six units of the grid to create a two-column format per page. The "Japan" layout (*Look*, February 7, 1967) takes just two units of the grid for a small copy block, allowing photos to take four, six, and 12 units—or one page—of the grid.

while still having precise margins and columns. The 12-part grid can operate with two, three, four, or six columns per page, and it encourages the use of sidebars, thumbnail photos, and skinny design elements as well as large-scale visuals, contrasting shapes, and dramatic bleeds. The 12-unit grid controls overcrowding of material and positions white space in powerful and surprising ways.

NO GRID. David Carson eschews grids of any form. His hyperkinetic page layouts take a lot more time to create, he says, because "it's not just this horrible grid where things are dropped in, which I think represents a certain amount of laziness. It's very work-intensive to do a magazine in which every page is completely different."[16]

Typography

Typography is the primary visual component in the communication of words on a printed page. Whether a single typeface or series of typefaces are used for body copy, titles, and cutlines, a message is conveyed to readers about a magazine's character. Some art directors think of typography as an art form that allows for the musical expression of words.

Designers can choose among thousands of typeface possibilities, each with its own tone of voice. Type can shout, whisper, stammer, bawl, growl, or converse in a gently modulated pitch. In deciding which typefaces to use, several factors must be considered: legibility, suitability, font, size, line length, and spacing of letters and lines.

The advent of computers has made it difficult to identify or classify typefaces by design attribute or even by name. More than 10,000 typefaces are available, and computers allow for the modification of existing ones as well as the creation of new ones every day. While this unprecedented variety of available typefaces has had its greatest effect on advertising and promotional material, the fact remains that all sorts of typographic idiosyncrasies can be—and are—catered to in magazine page design. David Herbick, former art director of *Civilization*, observed, "It's very easy to get carried away with special effects. Take type. You can stretch it or bend it, vary its color, give it a shadow or a color outline, make it semi-transparent—all with a few clicks of the mouse."[17]

LEGIBILITY. The ability of a typeface to jump off the page at a quick glance and into the reader's consciousness is its **legibility.** The term *legibility* describes how easily type can be read and comprehended. Yet even the most legible typefaces can become unrecognizable through the poor arrangement of typography on a page. Serif and sans serif are the two main categories of type to consider for body copy.

Serif. If there is a large amount of text to digest, the type must be easy to read, which is why most magazine feature articles are set in a serif typeface. **Serif** typefaces have delicate vertical and horizontal lines, or "feet," at the end of letter strokes. These serve as a guideline for the eye; the finishing strokes are the serifs. If you cover the bottom half of a line of serif type, you still can discern the words because of the clues

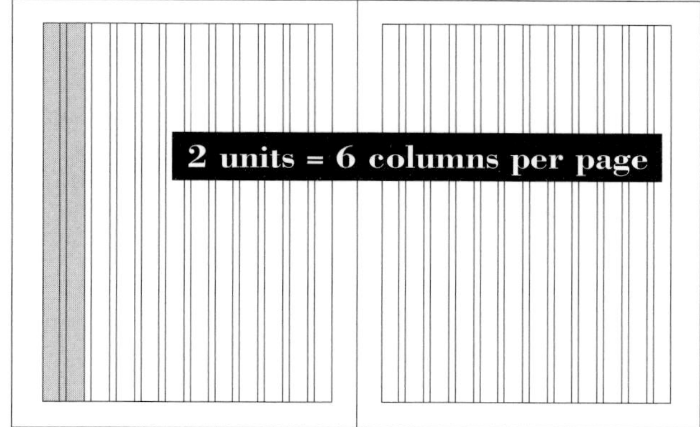

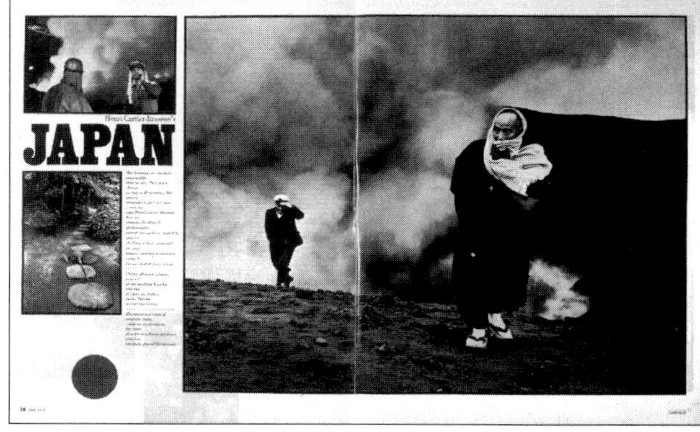

provided by the thick and thin finishing strokes. Most books, daily newspapers, and the majority of magazines use serif typefaces for their body copy. Typical serif typefaces include Times Roman, Bodoni, Baskerville, Palatino, and Century Schoolbook. Such typefaces connote stability, tradition, and formality.

Sans serif. Typefaces, such as Helvetica, Futura, and Avant Garde are **sans serif**—and geometric in appearance. As their name implies, they lack serifs. Sans serif typefaces work best when used in short copy blocks, such as sidebars, lists, photo cutlines, and titles. They suggest a modern, contemporary, and upbeat attitude.

SUITABILITY. The effectiveness of type in enhancing the message is its suitability; choice often is intuitive rather than grounded in research. Typefaces can create moods and motifs as a result of different characteristics involved in the shape and weight of the letterform. Some typefaces are said to be masculine, while others are feminine; some are powerful, while others are delicate. In reality, the psychological considerations of typefaces depend on individual interpretation by the art director—with the reader ideally in agreement. Certainly, the tone or shape of a typeface should match the mood of an article.

Cursive and script typefaces, such as Murray Hill Bold and Palace Script, look like hand lettering or ornate handwriting, while Old English seems to have come straight out of the King James Bible. Decorative or novelty typefaces, with names and shapes that reflect their attention-getting appeal—Circus, Earthquake, Paper Clip, and Jumbo—find usage as titles that reinforce an article's message. In general, cursive, script, and decorative typefaces are too difficult to read as blocks of body copy, although they can be effective when used for titles.

FONT. The name of an individual typeface is its **font. Style** refers to the various individual options within the font. A type font can have numerous style variations, such as italic, bold, extra bold, bold italic, extra bold italic condensed, extra condensed, and ultra condensed (the possibilities boggle the mind), which affect the look, shape, and the weight of the letters. However, all of the various styles in a font have the same design. One way to have a bit of variety with strong consistency is to use a font that has several style variations: Bodoni Regular for body copy, Bodoni Bold for titles, Bodoni Bold Condensed for subtitles or subheads between paragraphs, and Bodoni Italic for cutlines. Bodoni is the name of the typeface, while the various bold, condensed, and italic labels are descriptions showing weight, such as light or bold; width, such as condensed; and stance, such as italic. Since almost every typeface has several styles, it's estimated that there are upwards of 100,000 type possibilities available.

The use of computers in design has led to some changes in type terminology. At one time, *family* was the name of a particular typeface, and *font* referred to the various individual styles within the family. However, for Macintosh computer users, font has come to mean a typeface in every size and every style. Consequently, when some designers talk about changing the size or style of type, they don't think of it as changing the font; depending on the computer design software program being used, each variation may be listed as a font. For example, in some computer

Which magazine cover is the one rock groups want to be on? In 1973, rock group Dr. Hook and the Medicine Show answered the question by singing "*Rolling Stone*—Gonna see my picture on the cover. *Rolling Stone*—Gonna buy five copies for my mother. *Rolling Stone*—Gonna see my smiling face on the cover of *Rolling Stone*." After "Cover of *Rolling Stone*" hit the Top 40 charts, the magazine did indeed feature Dr. Hook on the March 19, 1973, cover. Life further imitated art when Hook bought five covers for his mother at *Rolling Stone*'s San Francisco office.

programs, Bodoni Bold is designated as a specific font and is different from the effect achieved by selecting Bodoni and bolding the words.

In general, copy that is set in uppercase and lowercase type is easier to read than all caps. Researchers say people don't like to read large blocks of italic type because it slows their reading speed. Italic tends to be used for emphasis or contrast. Bold, because it also slows readers, likewise tends to be used for emphasis, primarily to punch up titles for features and departments. The most popular weight and style choices for large masses of body text are the medium weight, regular width, and regular (or upright) version of a serif typeface, such as Times Roman, Palatino, Baskerville, or Garamond.

SIZE. Points and picas are the two units of measurement in design. The **point** is the unit of measurement for type and is used to indicate size. There are 72 points in one inch, that is, one point equals 1/72 of an inch. **Picas** are used to indicate width and depth of columns, photos, and page space. There are 12 points in one pica; 6 picas equal one inch.

1 point = 1/72 of an inch
72 points = 1 inch
12 points = 1 pica
1 pica = 1/6 of an inch
6 picas = 1 inch

Type size and point size are not interchangeable. This is because point size historically refers to the measurement of type as if it were cast in metal (although it isn't anymore). The actual height, or type size, of individual letters can vary significantly among typefaces that have the same point size. This size factor is the type's x-height, or measurement of a lowercase *x*. This affects how large the type looks on the page. For example, 12 point Times Roman is actually smaller—takes up less space on the page—than 12 point Palatino. Ten point Baskerville has a smaller x-height than 10 point Times Roman, which is smaller than the x-height of 10 point Helvetica. This has an impact on readers because type that is too large slows down readability as well as comprehension of text. Type that is too small impedes word recognition and reduces visibility.

Most art directors opt for body type that is either 9, 10, or 11 points in size, assuming an audience that is not very young or very elderly. Both of those age groups prefer larger type sizes. Display type refers to type that is larger than 14 points and used for titles and subtitles. Myriad computer adjustments in size are possible so that the best solution can be found for a magazine's readers.

LINE LENGTH. The number of letters in a line is the line measure or line length. The width of columns is a factor here, but art directors have to remember that lines that are too short are tiring to read because they create a jittery feeling. Lines that are too long also are tiring because readers' eyes may find it awkward to return to the following line. "Doubling" can occur after reading a very long line: when the eyes swing back to the left margin, they lose track of where they are and begin to read the same line again. This is not only irritating, but it also can result in a reader giving up on the entire article.

Because eyes take in several words, usually three or four at a time, a rule of thumb for line length has been identified as being about 40 characters. That would take up about 13 to 15 picas of space, depending on the size of the type (assuming 9, 10, or 11 points). This translates to a three-column format of about 15 picas each, on a page size of about 8 1/2 inches, which is used by many magazines. Magazines generally don't set large blocks of body copy more than the width of two columns, or about 30 picas wide.

Another factor in line length is whether copy is set justified, where all lines are set flush at both the left and right edges of the column (as found in books), or is set ragged right, where lines are flush on the left side, but have varied lengths on the right side. Justified type creates a formal, traditional look, while ragged right seems more casual and contemporary. However, numerous studies reveal that it really doesn't matter whether justified or unjustified lines are used. Both are equally readable, so which to use becomes an artistic decision rather than a functional one.

SPACING OF LETTERS AND LINES. The amount of space between letters affects readability, as does the amount of space between lines. Computers have made **kerning**—the reduction or enlargement of space between letters—a simple operation. **Tracking,** on the other hand, involves adjustments to the amount of space between words, making them tighter or looser overall. Excessive spacing may look decorative, but it may not be readable. Tracking or kerning that is too tight can distort letter forms; some art directors call this "traumatizing the type."

Leading (pronounced *ledding*) is the amount of space between lines of type. In the days of hot metal type, leading was done by inserting a thin strip of metal (called a lead) between lines. Today's computers automatically build in that space beneath the type lines. This is somewhat like double- or triple-spacing your copy when you type a paper or article. One rule of thumb is that there should be at least 1 point of leading between lines: Using a 10-point typeface for body copy would call for 1 point of leading, resulting in 11 points of space in each line. This creates an unconscious river of white that provides stability for the eyes. Again, computers have made a difference here, allowing for more or less leading. Too much or too little line space slows reading, and excessive line spacing results in a loss of reading function.

For former *New York* art director Robert Best, the relationship of typography to layout is critical. "Part of what we do, and what many other magazines do, with type is done to draw the reader in, to get them to read a story they might not actually have read if they hadn't been attracted by a catchy head, a catchy subhead, or some other spot," said Best. He added, "For us the type is the first and the last part of the design. It's the first part because it's the story everything is built around; but it's last because the format, the pictures, and the layout all have to be done before anything else. It's really the type and the look that pull the page together, but you don't get those things until the page is complete."[18]

Color

Black type on a white background is standard, and the use of any color other than black for type is risky. Black on white is the most legible choice for large blocks of printed information. It once was a "never" to run body type in anything but black, with a short and very occasional use of **reverse type**—white type on black background—being acceptable. But many art directors today are willing to take risks, using such combinations as maroon type on pale blue or orange type on green for shock, surprise, or just sheer serendipity.

Color provides identification, creates associations, and attracts attention. The use of color adds visual excitement to pages, and readers say they prefer a page with full color to one with just black and white.

IDENTIFICATION. The red border around *Time*'s cover and the yellow one around *National Geographic*'s are examples of how color provides editorial identification. *Time* first used a red border around the January 3, 1927, cover featuring a black-and-white head and shoulders drawing of Leopold Charles Maurice Stennett Amery, who was identified as Great Britain's secretary of state for the colonies. Yellow has belonged to *National Geographic* since February 1910, although the earliest covers had a much paler hue than today's issues, as well as a border design with acorns, oak and laurel leaves, and four globes representing the four corners of the world.

Life's name is quickly identified by all capital white letters within a bright red rectangle in the upper left-hand corner of the cover. There have only been three exceptions in *Life*'s more than 60 years: a logo-less cover photo of a leghorn rooster on April 26, 1937; a black rectangle for the November 29, 1963, issue about the assassination of President John F. Kennedy; and a green rectangle for the May 1990 Earth Day issue.

Since November 25, 1985, *Newsweek*'s name has been set in white type against a red block, with a thin red border just inside the cover's edges; a variety of different colors for the name was used during the 1960s and 1970s. *Kiplinger's Personal Finance Magazine* uses red type against a background of varying colors each month. While most magazines use color in the **logo,** or name design, that color tends to vary from issue to issue depending on the dominant colors in the cover photograph or illustration.

ASSOCIATION. Color has basic associations: red is active and hot, while blue is peaceful and cool. Researchers have found that looking at red raises breathing rate, blood pressure, and number of eye blinks, while blue lowers all three.[19] Red has the connotation of passion ("red hot mama"), vitality, anger, and love, while blue connotes serenity, loyalty ("true blue"), reserve, and gloom ("blue funk"). If you ask people to name their favorite color, most will answer blue, with red second.

Yellow is cheerful and optimistic ("sunny"), but also can mean caution and coward. Large blocks of bright yellow are hard on adult eyes, although yellow is a good color choice in children's magazines. Green has a tranquilizing and earthy effect and is often associated with spring. But green, too, has some negative associations: envy, mold, seasickness, and the skin of monsters and witches (the Wicked Witch of the West in *The Wizard of Oz*). Orange is almost always associated with Halloween and autumn, while purple belongs to royalty. Some art directors consider these associations when using colors in page layouts, although others ignore them.

ATTENTION. Color makes a page look special, and browsers often become readers after being hooked into a story through the use of color. Full-color photographs, in particular, attract attention because they suggest immediacy and drama. A single spot color can make a word in a title, a portion of line art, a chart, or a sidebar pop out at a browser and say "read me."

Remembering that the natural reading pattern is to start in the left corner, move to the right, and then down, some designers automatically place the biggest and brightest use of color slightly above and to the right of the geometric center of a spread. This creates a focal point or center of interest that eyes are drawn to when browsing. And, because the bottom right corner of a spread is seen as "the end" by readers, most designers tend to avoid placing bright color there. They don't want to take the reader away from the article before he or she even starts reading it.

Jan White says the use of color should be disciplined and meaningful, with shades and tints representing certain kinds of information to help readers interpret and grade material. "Using lots of color isn't useful," he says. "It is just gaudy. Readers don't want gaudiness; they want guidance."[20]

Design Principles

Because the magazine's mission and audience must be considered when making design decisions, some art directors can ignore basic design principles and still produce a creatively designed magazine. Most, however, follow five established design principles, to one degree or another, because they believe that creativity is a matter of discipline, of knowing the rules and knowing when to modify or break them. These principles are unity, balance, proportion, sequence, and contrast.

UNITY. Unity is uppermost in an art director's thoughts when designing a magazine. Readers come to each issue expecting similarity and continuity in the format; where they want change is in the topics and issues that are covered. Using a grid can provide unity; it also is cost and time effective because the art director is merely modifying the wheel each time, not totally reinventing it.

Consistency in typeface also provides unity: just having the same type for the body copy of both features and departments goes a long way toward providing a unified product, even when titles may have wildly varied typefaces. Certainly the most controlled use of typeface consistency involves using a single font that has a variety of style possibilities throughout the magazine. With a controlled and unified design approach, even the cover logo and department titles use the same typeface; this results in a unification of the outside and inside pages. Ornamental column lines, or rules, and borders offer both unity and variety. There are numerous options here beyond the standard line, such as Oxford rules (consisting of a thick and a thin line), Scotch rules (a thick line with a thin line on either side), and dotted rules. Equally abundant are the border possibilities, although graphic design consultant Roger Black, who has been art director at *Newsweek, Rolling Stone,* and *New York,* points out, "If you don't watch out, ornaments will make a layout look canned, like clip art."[21]

Unity is possible even when trying to provide variety through typography. One route is to have

FLIPPING THROUGH FOLIOS

The placement of folio lines (page numbers, name of magazine, and date of issue) can be a unifying characteristic as well as a creative design element. Folios don't have to fall at the bottom left- and right-hand corners, although readers tend to expect that location, and most magazines place them there. The choice of typeface for folios is a stylistic decision, as are deciding whether to include the issue date and name of the magazine, and in what order.

Time puts numbers on the outside bottom corners and centers the name and date on editorial pages. *Mode* has numbers on both outside bottom page corners, but positions the name of the magazine and date only on the left-hand page following the number. *Esquire* locates the number, magazine name and date on both pages for a mirror image look. *The New Yorker* places only numbers on the upper right- and left-hand corners of each page. *Black Book*'s folios look like they were typed on an old Smith-Corona typewriter that hasn't had its keys cleaned in a long time; a period is placed before the number, which is followed by the name, but no date. Although *blue* has folio numbers on the pages, there's no consistency in placement, size, typeface, or color of type. Don't even look for folios in *Ray Gun*.

Unfortunately, magazines in general aren't good about placing page numbers on every page. A bleed page or an page with an advertisement generally does not receive a number, leaving a reader who is hunting for a story "continued on page so-and-so" to have a difficult time finding it. Readers shouldn't have to flip back and forth trying to find a page number. After all, page numbers are supposed to help establish the proper sequence of material and should be there to let readers find and follow-up on every article.

one typeface for department titles and body copy and another typeface for all the features. A third typeface could be used for all the photo cutlines and a fourth for sidebars. There would still be consistency because the use of type would be predetermined by where the material is placed. This diversified approach to unity takes care since too many typefaces can hurt readability and cause confusion. Some art directors try to match type with the mood of the article, so that each story has a different typeface. *Rolling Stone* successfully uses different typefaces for articles and remains elegant rather than messy.

David Carson ignores all typography rules when creating layouts for magazines such as *Ray Gun* and *blue.* He says his primary concern is expressing the tone of an article. "When the tone of the type and layout match the attitude of the article, you get the most powerful form of communication," he says. "I think it's a disservice to a writer to just flow his article into three columns of type because you've found that command on QuarkXPress. A secretary can do that. If a story is not presented in a compelling way, people bypass it."[22]

Unity also comes into play when determining how much white space to use around photos, whether to frame photos with rules (using the same size and same kind each time), and whether to have justified or ragged margins throughout the magazine. A dingbat, or small design device at the end of each article, provides unification while clearly indicating the end of each piece. Other repetitive devices include starting all features with an initial cap, or large initial letter, or always making the first sentence in bold. These design devices draw the reader's eye to the start of the text. Color, also, can provide a connection, whether it's to pull together a particular spread or to make departments stand out from features.

BALANCE. The principle of balance in magazine layout has to do with whether the various elements on a page look natural and contained. Some readers notice if a page with several large photos appears top-heavy or bottom-heavy; their preference is for pleasing (if not orderly) boundaries that bring all elements together. Other readers like the juxtaposition of unequal shapes and see a dramatically exciting layout effect. Again, the use of basic design principles, successfully or not at all, is relative to the needs and demands of a magazine's audience.

Balance can be either formal or informal, with most magazines gravitating toward the asymmetrical approach of informal layouts. Formal balance requires placing elements of equal weight above and below the optical center of a layout in a mirror image effect; what's on the left page is repeated on the right-hand one. Informal balance is intuitive and involves a dynamic relationship rather than a static one. Informal balance takes the teeter-totter effect into account: a 90-pound child can achieve horizontal board balance with a 45-pound child if the heavier child sits closer to the center of the teeter-totter.

The effective use of balance is subtle. For example, using the mathematical center as a focal point makes a layout appear off-kilter since readers visually perceive the optical center as being about one-third of the way down from the top of a page. When the principle of balance is ignored—if photos or type appear to fall off the page—readers may become frustrated and stop reading. More serious, they may lose confidence in the magazine's mission.

The *Sports Illustrated* annual swimsuit issue is purchased by 19 million women—and twice as many men. Women see the issue as the most extensive catalogue of swimsuit trends being published. Men, on the other hand, see drop-dead gorgeous models showing a lot of flesh in provocative poses.

PROPORTION. Proportion has to do with the shapes of things and is derived from the golden rectangle principle dating back to early Greece. The proportion of the golden rectangle is about three to five, and historically it has been considered more interesting than the one-to-one ratio of the square.

A magazine's two-page spread starts out as a horizontal shape. Art directors generally try to maintain that shape through the use of generous white space around copy blocks, type wrapped around photos, and the way photos are grouped together or isolated. However, because the golden rectangle is a standard, some art directors gravitate toward the square to distinguish their magazines. While conventional theory states that a horizontal long shot showing a person's entire body as he strides across a room has more vitality than a square mug shot of his head and shoulders, that convention makes no sense if the mug shot is by a photographer noted for dramatic close-up face shots, such as Richard Avedon or Annie Leibovitz.

SEQUENCE. Most readers have a sequence of expectations when they read: title first, followed by a subtitle, byline, and the start of the article. That doesn't mean that layouts have to be rigidly hierarchical, but it does suggest that readers prefer a pattern that can be creatively modified. The logical arrangement of material is usually more readable than a complex one that ignores eye movement.

Departments usually are highly sequenced, with standing titles for each topic and standard formats involving similar images, shapes, or color that are repeated from issue to issue. Sequencing even involves the words of a title. There's a basic rhythm to writing titles that are on target. Words are read as groups of phrases with automatic pauses between certain words; readers expect a natural reading sequence to the material. Consequently, both readability and design considerations come into play when deciding how to divide a long title into more than one line.

CONTRAST. When contrast is used effectively, readers quickly realize what the most important elements in a story are. Contrast also helps readers remember those elements. Usually the title or the photo in an article is played "big" with an ample amount of white space. Contrast can be achieved through variations in typography, color, photograph sizes, irregularly shaped images, and the interplay of horizontal elements against vertical elements.

The editorial placement of features also offers an element of surprise through pacing and the unusual juxtaposition of content and form. Art directors see the magazine spread as a large, open canvas on which to work; that's why opening feature pages do not carry advertising. But the canvas needs some boundaries, explained David Herbick, who tried to make *Civilization* look customized and hand-crafted rather than cybernetic and computerized. "The key is restraint," he said. "I developed a standard color palette, limited the number of fonts we would use, and ruled out many of the design gimmicks made possible by the computer."[23]

INTEGRATION OF WORDS AND PICTURES

After all design decisions have been determined, the visual impact of a magazine depends on the integration of words and pictures. Decisions have to be made on the illustrative use of images—the photos, artwork, and infographics to complement the words in the articles. Readout material has to be written in order to achieve a synergistic relationship of titles to stories, subtitles and pull-quotes to body copy, and cutlines to photos. How to approach special materials such as the table of contents and the last page of editorial copy also come into play here.

While there are some readers who read every issue from cover to cover, most are selective. In today's busy world, most readers leaf through a magazine, scanning the pages before honing in on a particular article to read in its entirety. "The optimum goal of every editorial staff would be to have every reader read everything in every issue," says design consultant John Peter. "The realistic and more reasonable goal is to signal the text in such a way that every reader who would find it interesting or useful would read it. This demands sufficient information at the glance level for the readers to make their own decisions."[24]

Illustrative Images

Art directors and editors have to determine what is the best illustrative material for the words of each article: artwork, photographs, or infographic charts and diagrams. Historically, magazines offered a true rendition of what was happening at the time the illustration was drawn or the photo was shot. However, the choice of which image or angle to use has always been deliberate in order to evoke specific responses on the part of readers.

ARTWORK. Drawings dominated the magazines of the eighteenth and early nineteenth century. Illustrators added a silhouette of a famous person, a satirical cartoon, or a detailed landscape etching as the visual component to masses of gray type. From the start, few readers demanded absolute accuracy in a drawing of a place, person, or thing. Consequently, artwork tended to be interpretive and suggestive, although there was an early tradition of the illustrator as reporter, particularly in the works of Frederic Remington and Winslow Homer.

Illustrators at the turn of the twentieth century were highly paid and admired, with Charles Dana Gibson receiving $100,000 for 100 pen-and-ink illustrations drawn between 1903 and 1907. Other famous illustrators were Maxfield Parrish, J. C. Leyendecker, Sarah Stilwell-Weber, and N. C. Wyeth. These artists broke away from realistically illustrating an article to presenting images that also were appealing in their own right. They offered fantasy, drama, excitement, and warmth, making magazines more accessible and popular than books because they were more visual.

The magazine illustrator who united realism and appeal was the most beloved, and his work still resonates with middle America: Norman Rockwell. He is forever linked with the more than 300 covers he contributed to the *Saturday Evening Post,* from his first one on May 20, 1916, to his last on December 14, 1963.

Commissioned artwork still appears in today's magazines, but certainly not as frequently as it did before the camera lens came to dominate layouts. That's because working with an imaginative illustrator involves not just visual flair but editorial effectiveness. A custom-made illustration has to fit the content of the article—and if it doesn't, it's bad art even if it's graphically superb. For profiles, caricatures tend to be an accessible form of commissioned artwork. *Time*'s illustrated—as opposed to photographed—cover portraits reveal a wide range of design styles and media over the years.

A lot of art directors turn to old engravings in the public domain when they want to illustrate a historical piece or provide an interesting visual juxtaposition between the old and new. Line engravings more than 75 years old generally can be reproduced for free, and because of the techniques used (cut from wood or etched from metal), they can be reduced or enlarged without becoming muddy.

Numerous artwork possibilities can also be found in clip book services and computer software art programs that offer ready-made illustrations for just about any topic. Unfortunately, the use of clip art can be cheesy and embarrassing unless a good deal of creative change is applied to the original piece.

The New Yorker and *Playboy* are primary users of cartoons now, although cartoons were wonderfully serendipitous layout fillers during the

1930s, 1940s, and 1950s in magazines ranging from *Redbook* to *Collier's*. Today, *Reader's Digest* tends to use only a few cartoons per issue, relying more on short, anecdotal material for laughs. *Esquire*, once known for its risqué cartoons, no longer uses them.

The decline of artwork as magazines' primary illustrative option didn't occur with the development of the photograph at the turn of the twentieth century. Rather, drawings remained a visual star until after World War II, when a changing societal mood led Americans to demand realistic facts over lifelike fantasy. Only photography could offer the raw visual power desired by many readers.

PHOTOGRAPHY. Photos confer additional power to words on the page because most readers accept photographic images as an objective reflection of reality with built-in credibility and authority. In 1859, when he was 50 years old, author Oliver Wendell Holmes identified photography as "the most remarkable achievement" of his time because "it allowed human beings to separate an experience or a texture or an emotion or a likeness from a particular time and place and still remain real, visible, and permanent." It quickly became an axiom that a photo does not lie, although Holmes cannily observed that this new technology "marked the beginning of a time when the image would become more important than the object itself and would in fact make the object disposable."[25]

Yet even if the photo didn't lie, liberties in providing a true rendition occurred as early as the Civil War. When woodcuts depicting Alexander Gardner's battlefield photos were made prior to printing, bodies were added for dramatic effect. But for the most part, early photos provided a window on reality that readers appreciated in modest doses at the turn of the twentieth century. During the 1920s and 1930s, editors reserved the most layout space for fashion photography, where the alteration of reality was acceptable. The great fashion photography of the 1950s, 1960s, and 1970s, with boldly posed and arranged bodies and spaces, made the visual image the predominant message. While photography remains a prime component in women's fashion magazines, shelter magazines are the ones now pulling out all the stops in their use of both surreal and super-real images that pack a visual wallop. A perfect world is created through enhanced computer and camera technology and saturated color coding.

National Geographic's early use of photography gave the new form aesthetic dignity by linking it to the geographical and social documentation of reality. Photography in *National Geographic* was semi-scientific rather than titillating, even if there were bare-breasted native women shown working in fields as early as 1903. Certainly, *National Geographic*'s booklike size was a factor in its academic as opposed to sensational ambiance. It was up to the oversized *Life* magazine to provide interpretation and commentary to dramatic photographs by articulating a new photojournalistic way of documenting reality in its grandiose mission statement in 1936:

> *To see life; to see the world; to eyewitness great events; to watch the faces of the poor and the gestures of the proud; to see strange things—machines, armies, multitudes, shadows in the jungle and on the moon; to see man's work—his paintings, towers and discoveries; to see thousands of miles away, things hidden behind walls and within rooms, things dangerous to come to; the women that men love and many children; to see and take pleasure in seeing, to see and be amazed; to see and be instructed.*[26]

Enthusiastic magazine readers quickly realized *Life* was offering something new in the world of photography, bringing concise visual information into the home long before television. *Life* set the photojournalistic standard for many years, a standard that would be approached, but never surpassed, by news magazines during the Vietnam War.

The shift to a celebrity or personality photographic approach occurred in 1974 when *People* became the newest picture magazine on the scene. Although Richard P. Stolley, *People*'s first managing editor, was a *Life* editor for many years, he soon found himself using a different set of photo rules for his page images. Because *People* focuses on celebrities and ordinary people who have been thrust into extraordinary situations, *Life*'s documentary photojournalistic approach isn't appropriate. Instead, *People*'s photographers stage a lot of offbeat shots to get outrageous or exuberantly posed celebrity pictures

Art in American Magazines

America's magazines have long enjoyed a close relationship with contemporary artists, from Salvador Dali to Annie Leibovitz. The magazine cover itself is an art form; when that cover showcases museum-quality art, it becomes part of America's cultural heritage. This section offers a brief walk through twentieth-century American magazine covers that featured world-famous artists who created variations of their trademark images and landscapes.

SEPTEMBER 1904: Artist Maxfield Parrish offered fantasy and drama through beautifully illustrated magazine covers for *Ladies' Home Journal* at the turn of the twentieth century. This one is an example of a poster cover with no cover lines to take away from the image; also known as an art cover, the poster cover was often framed and hung on living-room walls.

APRIL

SCRIBNER'S

William de Mille on the Talkies

An African Savage's Own Story by Ibn LoBagola

How Mad was Anthony Wayne? by Thomas Boyd

Homesick Ladies by Sidney Howard

What's on Working Woman's Mind?

APRIL 1929: Like many magazines at the beginning of the twentieth century, *Scribner's* used woodcuts as art. The "cover decoration"—as it was called on the table of contents page—of this well-read and well-worn issue is by artist Rockwell Kent.

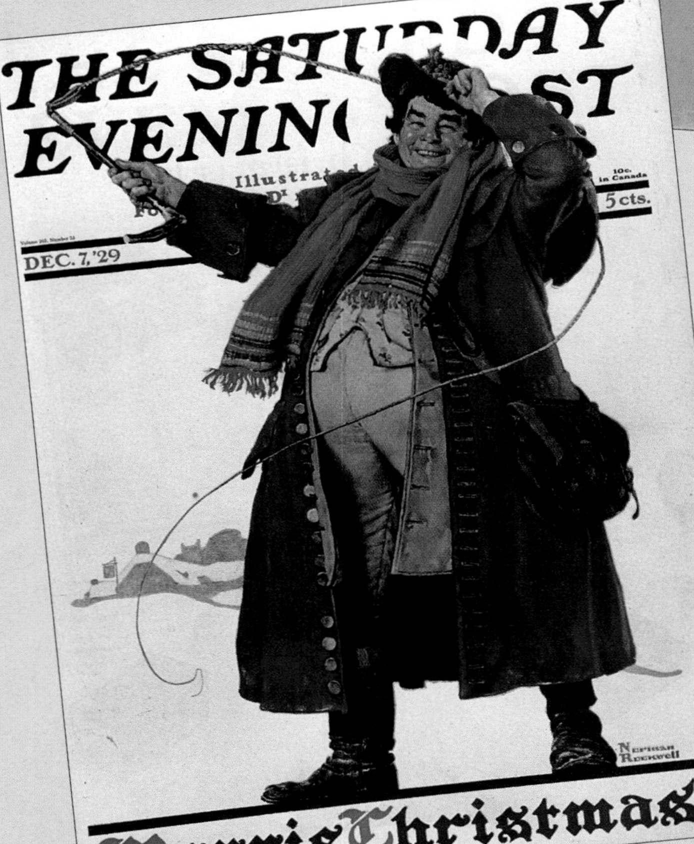

DECEMBER 7, 1929: Illustrator Norman Rockwell drew more than 300 covers for *Saturday Evening Post.* This particular issue was so ad-heavy that it weighed nearly two pounds; merchants bought extra copies to use as wrapping paper because it cost less than a roll of paper.

JUNE 1, 1939: Salvador Dali's surrealistic bridal cover for *Vogue* is eerily similar to his renowned *Persistence of Memory* painting.

AUGUST 1940: ***Harper's Bazaar*** **art director Alexey Brodovitch used color and repetition as a powerful and lyrical artistic device long before Andy Warhol's photomontages of Marilyn Monroe.**

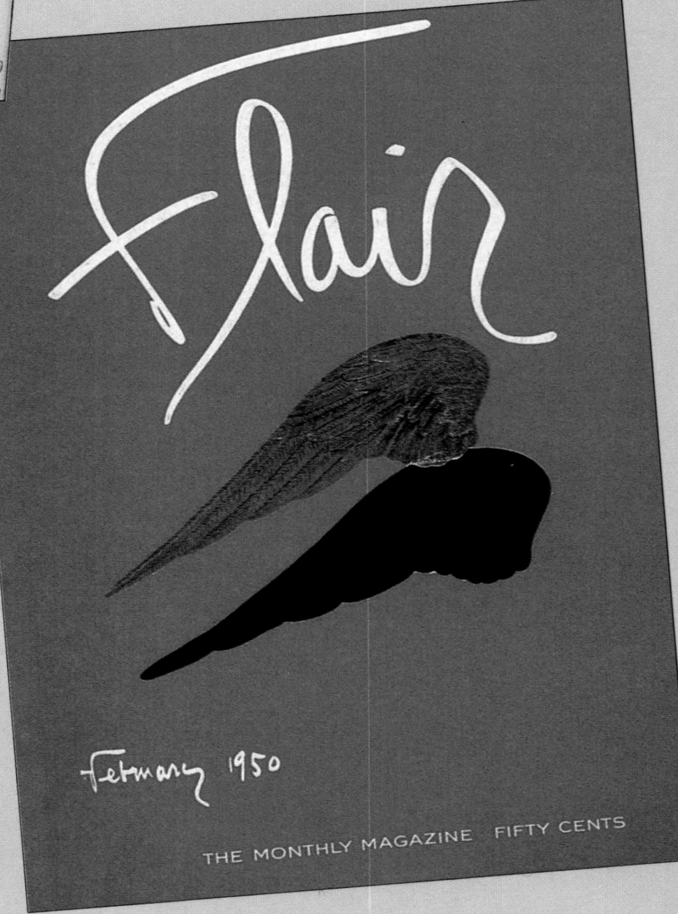

FEBRUARY 1950: The cover of the premiere issue of ***Flair*** **was—like all subsequent issues in the magazine's year-long run—embossed and die cut. The illustration forming the die cut was modeled after a favorite pin owned by editor and founder Fleur Cowles.**

(Far right) Through the hole formed by the die cut, readers could see the second part of the cover, a drawing titled ***The Spirit of Flair*****, by Rene Gruau.**

MAY 24, 1968: Pop artist Roy Lichtenstein used his colorful comic book style to illustrate *Time*'s cover story about Robert Kennedy's fast-paced presidential campaign.

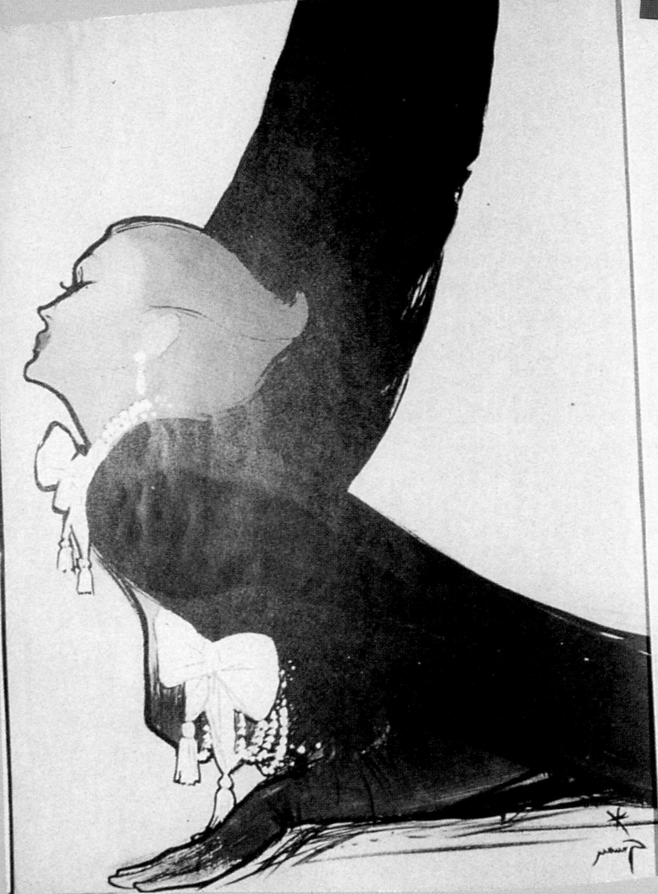

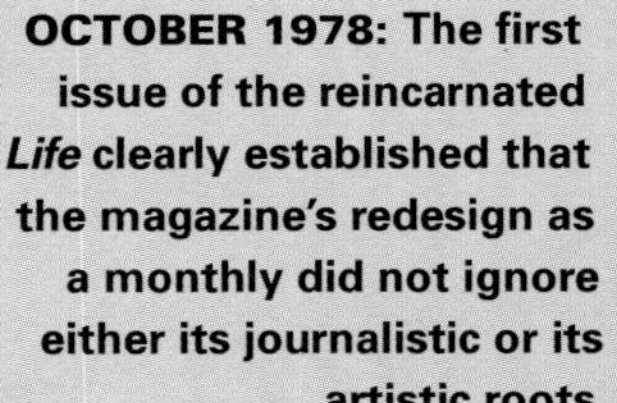

OCTOBER 1978: The first issue of the reincarnated *Life* clearly established that the magazine's redesign as a monthly did not ignore either its journalistic or its artistic roots.

LIFE
'Godfather' Puzo's New Novel
Spectacle in Rome: Pope John Paul I
'The Wiz'— Most Expensive Musical Ever
October 1978/$1.50
EI-BFA
Balloons are bustin' out all over!

JANUARY 22, 1981: John Lennon said Annie Leibovitz's portrait of himself and his wife Yoko Ono for the cover of *Rolling Stone* "captured our relationship perfectly." Lennon was killed shortly after the photo was taken.

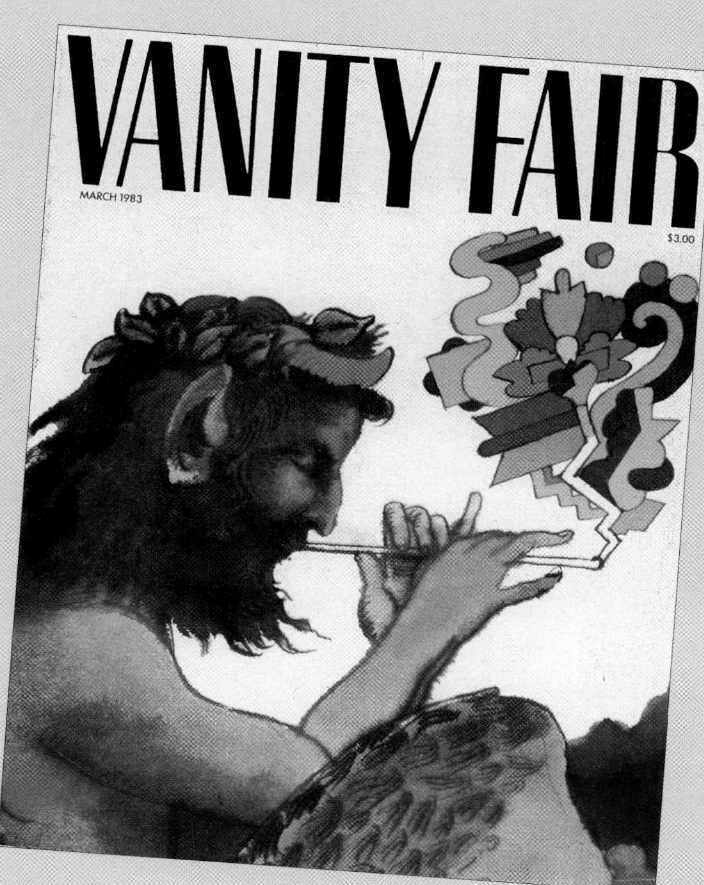

MARCH 1983: *Vanity Fair* magazine has had two lives. The first began in 1914 and ended in 1936, during which time the magazine published legends such as Edna St. Vincent Millay, Noel Coward, Carl Sandburg, T. S. Eliot, Theodore Dreiser, and Alexander Woollcott. The second life began in 1983 and included this whimsical cover illustration by designer Milton Glaser. The "new" *Vanity Fair* publishes contemporary literary and artistic greats such as—in this issue alone—Richard Avedon, Annie Leibovitz, Andy Warhol, Gore Vidal, Nora Ephron, and Gabriel García Márquez.

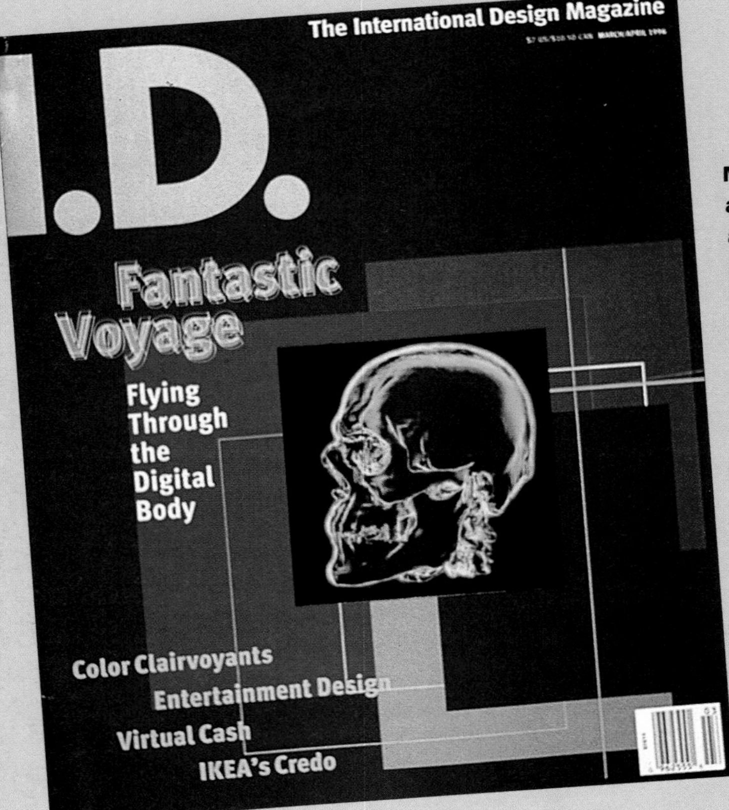

MARCH/APRIL 1996: Designer and artist Alexander Tsiaras used autostereoscopic, or three-dimensional, technology to photograph his own head as part of *I.D.*'s article on *Anatomical Travelogue,* a multimedia project Tsiaras created to provide a digital view of the human body.

RESEARCH IN BRIEF

Life's Photojournalism Essay Formula

Almost from the start, *Life* magazine offered readers something different from the traditional news photo that was a result of a photographer simply reacting to an event as it happened. Caroline Dow, a journalism professor at Flagler College in St. Augustine, Florida, says *Life* distinguished itself by providing readers with a system of visual reporting that anticipated and planned the coverage of events.[1]

Although "*Life* had been envisioned as a showpiece of previously published photographs gathered on a pick-up basis," Dow says the weekly magazine quickly used up the available stock of photos and news. So the magazine began generating its own stories and photographs. The result was the "mind-guided camera," a photo formula that grew out of *Time* magazine's use of group reporting (and its "round-up" news format) while also incorporating photographer Roy Stryker's Farm Security Administration documentary approach. Stryker believed that photographers should be provided extensive background before they went out on a shoot so they would understand the people they were recording.

Thus, several concepts drove the "mind-guided camera" approach, which was a cooperative project involving staff editors and photographers who decided on a story, did background research, and prepared a shooting script. The script was designed to help the photographer understand the types of photos needed, their purpose, and the mood of the topic. More photos would be shot to go along with the story than actually would be used since no amount of previsualization could predict what would occur on site.

No longer were photos an adjunct to print. "*Life* elevated the photograph to an equal partnership with words," says Dow.

Dow discusses the "*Life* process," pointing out that "the essence of the *Life* method was that a photographic feature had to be defined in words first. Then the idea was researched. When the idea or experience was clear to everyone, a script of possible scenes would be prepared and approved." Following approval by an editor, a photographer would be assigned and a reporter selected; they would work together as a team.

"The specific *Life* scripting formula has not been published. Perhaps it was not considered necessary to record it because it was so well understood by those who practiced it," says Dow. She studied the formula by researching how it was taught by Robert L. Drew, *Life*'s first Detroit bureau chief, in his photography workshops from 1949 to 1951. Dow took oral histories from participants in the Detroit Workshop and combined them with documentary research to discern just what *Life*'s photojournalism essay formula involved.

Dow's research reveals a list of eight types of photos that had to be part of the rolls of film shot by the photographer after the concept or story idea had been researched to see if it had news and/or social value. These eight photos of the scripting formula included the following:

1. An introductory or "overall" shot, usually a wide angle, often an aerial.
2. A middle distance or "moving in" shot, such as a sign, a street, or a building.
3. A close-up, usually hands, face, or detail.
4. A sequence or how-to shot.
5. A portrait, usually environmental.
6. An interaction shot of persons conversing or action portrayed.
7. The signature picture—the decisive moment, the one picture that conveyed the essence of the story.
8. The clincher or "good-bye" shot signifying the end of the story.

"By thinking about the picture story in these terms," Dow says, "a photographer would prepare himself to see a story." Prethinking, or previsualizing a story, encouraged a photographer to shoot different views and angles of the same scene. The event was more likely to be covered in greater depth since the photographer, having thought through the obvious pictures, was prepared to see the unusual or unique picture as well as to recognize the signature shot when it happened, even though it might not be what was planned.

This formula helped define *Life*'s design personality as well as its editorial value. The relationship of the photos to the page and to the copy resulted in a distinctive narrative design that made *Life* a success with readers and advertisers from the start.

[1] Caroline Dow, "*Life*'s Photojournalism Essay Formula" (paper presented at the annual meeting of the Association for Education in Journalism and Mass Communication, Houston, TX, August 1979).

that seldom have the candor or the conscience found in photojournalism. Likewise, *TV Guide*'s covers frequently show celebrities with their feet off the ground: "It's high energy that really captures your eye and conveys your authority," says the magazine's editor-in-chief Steven Reddicliffe. "Jumping is good."[27]

Star treatment isn't limited to *People* or *TV Guide.* More and more celebrities are demanding approval of the layout and photographs as a condition of publication. *Rolling Stone* gave Madonna photo approval and copyright to the photographs used for a thirtieth anniversary cover story about women in rock on November 13, 1997, but refused to give her layout approval. For photo shoots, publicists of the top celebrities may specify makeup, clothing, food preferences for snacks, and even the lenses used by the photographer.[28]

The trend in the use of photos is to run them big: *Life* and *Look* initially led the way here, with *Sports Illustrated* and *Rolling Stone* continuing the tradition. Of course, the corollary to larger photos is fewer ones, which means the selection and cropping processes become very crucial. Large, tightly cropped head shots can make even a mundane photo vibrant, although small, one-column mug shots (head-on, static head and shoulder photos) still get published, as do boring group shots, awkward grip and grin award photos, and the ultimate in blandness, pictures of individuals sitting at their desks (pretending to be on the phone does not negate the cliché). The best photographers, such as award-winners Richard Avedon and Annie Leibovitz, provide the large vistas of environmental portraits that combine fashion, place, and personality into one dramatic shot.

Magazines that can't afford an Avedon or Leibovitz turn to stock photo houses such as Image Bank, Black Star, or Comstock. These picture agencies offer editors photographic variety and clarity at a reasonable cost. Historical collections at the Library of Congress provide a wealth of photo possibilities, although care must be taken when using historical shots to document them and make sure that no misinterpretations occur.

The choice of which photo or photos to run is both emotional and intellectual. Potentially more problematic is when **cropping,** or the figurative cutting away of portions of a photo, is applied. Effective photographers crop in the camera viewfinder, but art directors frequently go beyond the limitations of the original photo through creative cropping to enhance or refine the message already present. Photo cropping is an important editorial tool because strong verticals or horizontals can be created, or the focus of the frame shifted to suggest a new meaning. In deciding how closely to crop a scene, it's important to know the photo's purpose: Is it a documentary shot for an investigative article or a fashion shot showing elaborate evening wear? Is the intent to show reality or fantasy?

Photo retouching is another editorial tool with a lot of power. When used to airbrush a sign behind a model's head in a fashion photo, or to remove an extraneous foot that could not be cropped out for a cover, retouching may be appropriate. Again, the content, intent, and goal of both the article and the photo must be considered before any changes are made in an image.

Unfortunately, computer digital manipulation has changed the boundaries of photo cropping and retouching and destroyed the belief that photos don't lie. Some magazine editors use the term *photo illustration* to distinguish a picture that has been staged, retouched, or manipulated in some way from the news photo resulting from photojournalism. One of the earliest instances of photo illustration via electronic retouching occurred in February 1982 when *National Geographic* moved a Great Pyramid of Giza to fit the vertical shape of its cover. Since then, digital imaging technology has been used on covers featuring O. J. Simpson (*Time*), Cher (*Ladies' Home Journal*), Bobbi McCaughey (*Newsweek*), and Princess Caroline of Monaco (*Harper's Bazaar*).

INFOGRAPHICS. Complex statistical data can be explained and compared through the use of charts, diagrams, and graphs—or **infographics.** Pie charts are the easiest explanatory visuals to use, with bar charts not far behind. Schematic diagrams can show how things work, while line graphs often reveal trends over time. Colorful maps pinpoint the location of exotic cities. Infographics can make relationships that would be boring if spelled out in words become clear and comprehensive through a few visuals.

The information value of the material must be kept uppermost when using charts and graphs in magazine layouts. For example, a chart used to illustrate a story about improved mathematical test scores should not only show this year's scores but also scores from previous years so readers can visualize the relationship of the data. Pitfalls can occur with the use of infographics. Cramming too many figures into a graph is as bad as not giving enough information. Every infographic device needs a title to tell what it is about, a scale line to tell what measurement is being used, and the source of the information.

Information graphics designer Nigel Holmes offers several rules for the successful use of infographic material in magazine layouts. First and foremost, he says, is to keep it simple. "Make it a little self-contained story," is Holmes's second rule. Third, he suggests using small images that are easy to understand and that simplify the complicated. Finally, he restricts the use of color in the infographic. The result, he argues, is visual information that is likely to be read because the reader has been provided with "little jewels that pack a punch."[29]

Readout Synergy

Titles, subtitles, subheads, pull-quotes, and cutlines are the readout materials that should convert a scanner into a reader. A test of good design is how well the editorial copy meshes with the typographic format of readout tools. Good illustrations—photographs and artwork—are not enough to turn browsers into readers. Today's magazine audiences are bombarded with images and sounds; short attention spans must be factored into page design because readers will not stay with a magazine article that consists only of 9 point body type. The use of sidebars to support main articles is one way to deal editorially with reader hyperactivity.

Readouts are the ultimate readership design devices. Time-consuming and sometimes difficult to write, readout material virtually shoves words at people to get them intrigued enough to start reading the article. The creation of exciting and precise readout matter—particularly the title and subtitle—forces editors to confront what an article is all about in concise yet interesting words.

TITLES. Editors agree that the title is the most important typographic design tool in getting a magazine subscriber or browser to read a particular article. Many good stories are never read because the titles and subtitles (the information immediately following the main title before the start of the article) fail to interest the reader. Consequently, a lot of titles and subtitles feature "sell" language, essentially advertising words—best, most, newest—that help sell the story to the reader. The title should either entice readers to read the story or provide enough information to tell them they aren't interested in the topic. Titles can be as short as a single word or as long as several complete sentences taking up to five lines at the top of the spread.

"We try to get at the essence of the story and say it in an easy to read, appealing way so that the reader will pick the story up and read it," said Cynthia Kellogg, former special projects editor at *Woman's Day*. "We try to tell her what is in it truthfully, not to mislead her in any way. I can't advertise in a title that an article says something just because it sounds very glamorous, when in actual fact it is a service piece."[30]

An editor at a monthly magazine will write between 400 to 500 titles during a year—and they will begin to sound alike. It becomes a challenge to write a title that is descriptive, inviting, and accurate. "The thing that we try to work for in titles is, first of all, distinctive words and phrases," said Don L. Berg, former executive editor of *Medical Economics*. "We may have written 17 other stories in the same particular field in the course of a year. We look for something that is evocative and distinctive in the particular story. Beyond that we look for words that are stoppers or grabbers—the ones that arrest the reader."[31]

Take a *Medical Economics* story that was given the title of "My Million Dollar Malpractice Ordeal." That was rejected, Berg said, because "we decided that anybody can have an ordeal. It's not very specific and there is nothing there evocative or grabbing that's going to get you into the story. There's no grabbing word except 'malpractice.'" So the title was changed to "My Million Dollar Malpractice Lesson: Trust Nobody." That title was not only provocative but also gave a reasonable expectation of what the article would contain.

SUBTITLES. Most titles are supported by a subtitle, which provides additional clues as to the

Ninety percent of readers between 18 and 24 insist on the use of color in magazine spreads. Only 53 percent of readers who are 65 years or older make that demand, according to research studies by *Communication Briefings*.

Cutlines Capture the Moment

A picture really isn't worth an entire 1,000 words; the accompanying cutline takes at least 20 to 30 of those words. At many magazines there's a law: Every photo needs a cutline.

Cutline styles vary from magazine to magazine, but there are at least seven used by editors today: identification, information, question, teaser, mood, redirection, and contradiction.

Identification cutlines are the workhorses, but they don't have to be nags. Magazines such as *US, People,* and *Town & Country* make an effort to stay away from the obvious when providing identification by including an interesting tidbit along with the necessary name, title, or place. But there are still numerous magazines that use label cutlines, simply providing a name or a location without any context or even a complete sentence.

The best information cutlines are found in *National Geographic.* Captions here are so complete that some readers never get around to reading the entire article. Information cutlines expand on the identification approach by offering details about a landscape, an interior, or an individual. They are frequently used in travel and shelter magazines. This cutline style, which provides context to a photo, tends to be the longest, sometimes up to 100 words.

A quotation cutline frequently is used with a head-and-shoulders photo of an individual, and it involves using a controversial or illuminating quote from the main story. Usually, the cutline begins with the quote, which makes it more of an attention-getter than starting with the name would. *Playboy's* interviews always use quote cutlines under the subject's photo; the magazine's most famous cutline ran under a photo of a pensive Jimmy Carter, who admitted in November 1976, "I'm human and I'm tempted. I've looked on a lot of women with lust. I've committed adultery in my heart many times. This is something that God recognizes I will do, and God forgives me for it."

Some teaser cutlines begin with a question, while others parody a quotation or put a spin on a cliché. But more frequently, the teaser cutline features the most intriguing detail from the story and is likely to drive the reader into the text to find the answer or get additional details.

Mood cutlines allow editors to remind readers of a story's ambiance

nature of the article—service, profile, investigative reporting—and pizzazz to intrigue the reader. The subtitle is where the modifying or qualifying information goes. For the "My Million Dollar Malpractice Lesson: Trust Nobody" title, a subtitle might have the qualification, "Perhaps you can trust your own attorney."

Subtitles either summarize the article in a straightforward way or tease readers through an intriguing phrase or play on words. The best subtitles build on the title and draw readers into the first paragraph of the article. The subtitle usually appears after the title, but not always. When a subtitle appears above the title, it is called a **kicker.** In its May 1988 issue, *Reader's Digest* placed this kicker above the title: "Banks love you for all the fees they can charge you. Here's how to cut your costs." The title, in large capital letters, was "IS YOUR BANK RIPPING YOU OFF?"

SUBHEADS. **Subheads** help break up large blocks of text by providing organizational cues between paragraphs. When written in a clever as opposed to perfunctory tone, they also attract attention. The subheads in "Is Your Bank Ripping You Off?" were intriguing: "The ATM Junkie," "The Merger Orphan," "The New Saver," "The Workaholic," and "The Cyber-Banker."

Subheads can be large or small in type size; they don't have to fall at a natural pause in the story, but they should be consistent in tone. Subheads don't even have to have their own line—they can start on the first line of the paragraph in type that's larger, bolder, in color, or all three.

PULL-QUOTES. **Pull-quotes** are another way to break up large blocks of text by taking an interesting or important sentence or two from the story and setting it off graphically within the body copy. Sometimes the pull-quote is an actual quote from an individual in the article; when that happens, quote marks are used around the words and attribution is included.

Roger Black especially likes pull-quotes, saying, "Skillfully extracted from the piece, these devices allow a reader to get an idea of what a story is about before taking the cold bath of and point of view. Some mood cutlines become mini-editorials, suggesting how a photo should be viewed or evaluated. Mood cutlines can even highlight the less obvious artistic values of a photograph. *Life* has used mood cutlines effectively for many years.

David D. Perlmutter, a professor at the Manship School of Mass Communication at Louisiana State University, says some mood cutlines go beyond the photo's image to provide intensification of the scene. He studied photos and cutlines of China in *Time* and *Newsweek* from 1949 through 1989 and discovered that intensification occurred when the information in the photo "was embellished through affective language. For example, a picture of a policeman hitting a protester was captioned, 'A policeman mercilessly beats a helpless hunger striker.'"[1]

Redirection, says Perlmutter, occurs when the photo and the cutline seem unconnected because "an action referred to was absent from the pictures." He says portrait shots often have seemingly unrelated cutlines and gives as an example a photo of Nationalist Leader Chiang Kai-Shek posing in front of his flag. The cutline: "Can he stop a Communist peace?"

A cutline that contradicts definitely goes beyond the photo frame by totally changing its visual meaning. As a contradiction example, Perlmutter refers to a photo of a smiling Chiang waving to a saluting crowd with this cutline, "Chiang's days were numbered as the Communists roll on to victory."

Perlmutter found in his study that photos created by the Communist Chinese government from 1950 to 1972 were more likely to receive a contradictory cutline when used in American magazines. The editorial view of the magazines toward Communist China came into play with the addition of the phrase "claims to show" or through citation of a "Red Chinese" source to cast doubt upon the veracity of the image. Until 1972 very few American journalists were allowed into mainland China, but pictures shot by Western photographers did not receive contradictory cutlines. "In sum," comments Perlmutter, "the enemy's pictures were propaganda; ours were photojournalism."

Perlmutter argues that the editorial slant of a magazine can strongly affect how cutlines are written and can be an important indicator of a publication's ideology, perhaps even more so than the image. "No lens is wide enough to reveal all of any reality, but the caption can enhance or distort the engagement between the photographer and subject, and between publication and public," Perlmutter says.

[1] David D. Perlmutter, "A Picture's Worth 8,500,000 People: American News Pictures as Symbols of China," *Visual Communication Quarterly* (Spring 1997): 5.

actually reading it. In a magazine you can't expect everyone to read everything, and a pull-quote will help people get something out of an article they only glance at."[32]

CUTLINES. Some people read the **cutlines,** or captions, of photos before they read anything else. Unfortunately, many editors wait until the last minute to write them, so the result can be unclear or cryptically short text. Because the photographer usually is not around to aid in identification, cutline writing can result in unintentional bloopers. In 1981, *National Review* found a hilarious cutline correction in *Community Life* and reprinted it as a filler: "Mai Thai Finn is one of the students in the program and was in the center of the photo. We incorrectly listed her as one of the items on the menu."[33]

A mislabeled photo cutline in the February 22, 1993, issue of *Time* created an international outcry. Accompanying an article by Lance Morrow titled "Unspeakable" about rape as a weapon in war was a black-and-white photo of a young girl who apparently was a victim of rape; the cutline underneath read, "Traditions of atrocity: A Jewish girl raped by Ukrainians in Lvov, Poland, 1945." Ukrainians in the United States and Canada were angered by the cutline, which they felt was a blanket indictment of Ukrainians as rapists over time due to the phrasing of the sentence. Plus, although Ukrainians were singled out in the photo, they were not mentioned in the article at all.

After receiving more than 750 letters, *Time* ran an apology in the April 19 issue in which it admitted that the photo was taken in 1941, not 1945, and that the city of Lvov was not a part of Poland at that time but was a Ukrainian city. Most damning was the admission that "despite our best efforts, we have not been able to pin down exactly what situation the photograph portrayed. But there is enough confusion about it for us to regret that our caption, in addition to misdating the picture, may well have conveyed a false impression."

A cutline should do more than describe what is obviously in a photograph. Cutlines should not

TABLE OF CONTENTS: LOCATION, LOCATION, LOCATION

There are five yardsticks—location, length, logic, linkage, and look—to use when measuring the design impact of a table of contents, or TOC. Of these, location is the most important (as in the real estate mantra of "location, location, location").

For 75 years, *Reader's Digest* used the table of contents as its bland but useful cover, with all the yardstick components in a single place. As part of a major design overhaul unveiled with the May 1998 issue, the magazine switched to a full-page photo on the cover with a few cover lines, and located its now colorful, detailed two-page table of contents inside. *Reader's Digest* editor-in-chief Christopher Willcox says, "When you have the table of contents on the cover, it limits what you can say about what's in the magazine."[1]

A right-hand side, front-of-the-magazine location is the best spot for the TOC, says design consultant John Brady. He calls it "an unfortunate marketing blunder" to put the TOC on the left, reserving all front right pages for advertisers. "A left-hand table of contents is consumer unfriendly. Subliminally, these magazines are saying to their readers: Our advertisers are more important than you," Brady says.[2]

However, international editorial and design consultant John Peter disagrees, saying, "There is no real evidence that the right-hand page is a better position for the contents page, but people think it gets more attention there. And the legend among advertisers is that the right-hand page is better."[3]

There are many successful and popular magazines with left-hand contents pages: *Premiere, The Atlantic, George, Psychology Today, Robb Report,* and *Latina.*

A TOC with a two-page spread is a "stronger trumpet blast," says Peter, if there is something dramatic and visual that follows. A two-page spread does have visual impact, agrees Brady, although he says starting with a right-hand page and jumping to a second TOC page conveys "a jam-packed, value-added feeling to the reader." *Redbook*'s right-hand to left-hand jump has just that feeling, as do the TOCs for *Esquire, Entrepreneur, New Woman, Wired,* and *Mode.* Some magazines with just a single right-hand TOC are *Ms., Country Woman, Wood,* and *Chile Pepper.*

Never use less than one full page for the TOC, say both Brady and Peter; no extraneous material such as a masthead or letter from the editor should compete for the reader's attention. During the 1920s and 1930s, *The New Yorker*'s TOC seemed to be an afterthought, a mere dollop of copy in the middle of entertainment listings, with page numbers only for such standing departments as books, cinema,

be omitted, however, because of the risk of photo misinterpretation. Cutlines can point out something that may be overlooked by readers ("standing behind so-and-so is") or supply information that is missing ("John Jones painted the oil held by"). Some editors even use the cutline as an opportunity to include information that has been omitted from the original article. More frequently, though, the cutline reinforces the tone and thrust of the article by supplying material not elaborated on in the text. This gives the cutline a vital and synergistic role in overall layout design.

WRITING THE READOUTS. Who writes the titles, subtitles, subheads, pull-quotes, and cutlines? At a very small magazine, the writer may be asked to supply that material. At many magazines, the editor who conceived, assigned, and edited the particular article is responsible for all the readout material. Sometimes, the copy editor completes this part of the editorial circle, although the final word on titles usually belongs to the editor. Readout material tends to be written and placed in the layout last so the editor can take advantage of having selected the photos and determined how much copy is going to be used.

All readouts have to match the tone of each article and reflect the magazine's editorial philosophy. Editors at *Harper's* and *The Atlantic* strive to be clever without being facetious or cute in their readout material. There's a fine line between a clever play on words and being obscure, too. When she was at *New York,* Elizabeth Crow, now editor-in-chief at *Mademoiselle,* recalls, "If you're dealing with puns, there's a difference between the sound of a pun and the way it looks. For instance, we did a head for a dog-walking school that was 'The Paws That Refreshes' which was very funny, theatre, and art. The first "real" TOC, with titles of articles and bylines, appeared in the March 22, 1969, issue. Even now, *The New Yorker*'s left-hand TOC still doesn't occupy a full page of space and shares the page with a one-third-sized advertisement.

Lack of logic in the TOC is a big turn-off for readers. TOC design nightmares have unidentified photos, no page numbers, haphazardly placed artwork, and punning titles that have no relationship to the content of the article. Brady urges art directors to organize the copy either chronologically by page number or editorially by features, departments, columns, and miscellany. More important, article titles on the TOC page should be identical to what's inside; descriptive subtitles, however, should be different. Fresh text should market each article "by emphasizing the benefits—insight, information, income—to be derived from reading on," he says.

Closely related to logic is cover linkage. Readers should be able to find all stories mentioned on the cover quickly and efficiently without having to wade through cute or remote connections.

Finally, the TOC must have a distinct look, "like a great menu in a fine restaurant," says Brady. Peter suggests color on the TOC, particularly if the magazine itself is a "colorful" one. "If the editorial content deals with subjects such as food or fashion, it certainly makes sense to publicize that with a colorful contents page. But color is less important for a magazine whose emphasis is on information—such as a business magazine," Peter says.

The TOC should reveal that the magazine's whole is greater than the sum of its parts. Some magazines that succeed in doing this are *People*, *Saveur*, *Cigar Aficionado*, *Scientific American*, and *SmartMoney*—all have very dramatic and colorful two-page spreads.

1 "*Digest* Puts Contents Table Inside," *San Antonio Express-News* (March 31, 1998): B1.

2 John Brady, "Perusing the Table of Contents," *The Handbook of Magazine Publishing*, 4th ed., compiled by the editors of *Folio:* (Stamford, CT: Cowles Business Media, 1996): 197.

3 Douglas A. Learner, "Contents Page," *Folio:* (July 1982): 38.

ISSUE NO. 111 WINTER 1998

Better Homes and Gardens

WOOD

THE WORLD'S LEADING WOODWORKING MAGAZINE

CONTENTS

WOOD MAGAZINE WINTER 1998

1

WINTER 1998: *Wood*'s table of contents packs a lot of information and photos about what's inside on a single right-hand page.

but it really didn't quite work. We used it anyway because we thought it was so funny. Occasionally, we're too clever by half and we try to slap ourselves down when we see that happening. Other times it will work out perfectly."[34]

Special Material

The table of contents and the last editorial page in the magazine require special consideration in the merging of words and pictures. Unfortunately, these pages can look haphazard and unappealing if enough attention isn't paid to their role in the magazine's editorial and design package.

TABLE OF CONTENTS. While newsstand sales success usually is judged on the basis of cover content, the table of contents may pack the real wallop. Most browsers move quickly from the cover to the table of contents, where they pause for as long as a minute before making a financial commitment to the magazine. The cover may be the door-opener, but the table of contents is the marketing page that must be well designed to motivate purchase and reading.

The structure of an editorial formula is most obvious in the table of contents, or TOC. From issue to issue, year to year, the TOC of a successful publication demonstrates its continuity. Technically, the TOC tells what's inside and where things can be found. Of all the pages inside a magazine, the TOC has a clearly defined function as well as emotional and informational value. Consequently, it requires clarity in presentation and vision in structurally highlighting special articles.

"A lot of people read the contents page at the newsstand to decide if they want to buy the magazine. If the contents page is difficult to read—if it is difficult for the reader to find specific articles—someone might be deterred from buying the magazine. We have a lot of copy on our contents page because we have a lot to say in the magazine. We want it to look packed with information," said *Car and Driver*'s former art director Linda Moser.[35]

LAST EDITORIAL PAGE. For some readers, the last editorial page, opposite the inside back cover, is their first impression of the magazine, so it, too, needs special attention. Probably the best known closing page is *Life*'s "Parting Shots," usually with one large photo and a short amount of copy ending each issue. Magazines as varied as *George, Jump, Travel Holiday,* and *Time* all use their last single editorial page effectively: as a whimsical Q&A interview, as a hodgepodge of last-minute quips, as a globetrotter's detailed index, and as a thoughtful essay.

Using the last page for a strong editorial focus gives readers who flip from the back of the magazine forward a full editorial page to start with rather than jumped articles and fractional advertising. It adds to the illusion of having a magazine filled with information, from front to back; a very high page number listed in the table of contents further reinforces the jam-packed image. Plus, those readers who start with the first page and read sequentially through the magazine are rewarded with a strong final page.

Advertisers benefit also because a strong last page tells them the editors place value on the entire magazine, not just the front half. It also indicates that the magazine is read from cover to cover, so there are no "bad" pages.

COVERS

The cover is the most important editorial and design page in a magazine. The cover, as the magazine's face, creates that all-important first impression. It also provides both continuity through format recognition and change through intriguing cover lines from issue to issue. Editors, art directors, publishers, and circulation directors spend hours trying to select the perfect cover for each issue—one that sells out at the newsstands and creates a media buzz.

"The business of editorial demands that we pay as much attention to our covers as we do to our content," says David Pecker, president and CEO of Hachette Filipacchi Magazines. "Remember the old adage, 'You can't tell a book by its cover'? Well, you can't sell a magazine anymore without a good one."[36] Pecker argues that since 80 percent of consumer magazines' newsstand sales are determined by what is shown on the cover, a cover that sells can mean the difference between a magazine's life or death.

A panel made up of design consultant John Peter, circulation consultant Ron Scott, and Hearst Magazines Enterprises President John Mack Carter, who has been editor-in-chief at both *Ladies' Home Journal* and *Good Housekeeping,* offered the following cover bromides:

- Photos sell better than artwork.
- Sex sells better than politics.
- Timeliness is a critical sales factor.
- Solutions sell better than problems.
- Subtlety and irony don't sell.
- Bylines don't sell.
- Puns don't work well in sell lines.[37]

Yet every editor can cite wildly successful cover exceptions to this conventional wisdom, or offer their own cover formula. Richard Stolley, who is now senior editorial advisor at Time Inc. Magazines, is recognized as a cover guru by his peers. He recalls that when he was at *People,* the cover mantra went: "Young is better than old. Pretty is better than ugly. Rich is better than poor. TV is better than music. Music is better than movies. Movies are better than sports. Anything is better than politics. And nothing is better than the celebrity dead."[38]

Speaking of the need for a cover with a persona who grabs the newsstand browser, Stolley says, "The face had to be recognizable to 80 percent of the American people. There had to be a reason for the person on the cover. There had to be something happening in the person's life the week it was out there. And then there was this *X* factor. There had to be something about that person that you wanted to know."

The quest for a recognizable *X*-face has led to more and more celebrities appearing on magazine covers. But not just any celebrity will do. Stolley points out that Mary Tyler Moore was never a successful cover subject, even when she was at the pinnacle of her television success.

"There was nothing left of interest about her that people did not already know," he says. "They loved her, but that wasn't enough for *People*'s cover."

Of course, there is more to designing a cover than just slapping a celebrity's face on the page, just as there are many magazines that stay away from recognizable faces. Deciding what to put on the cover, and the type of cover to use, generally are determined by the magazine's editorial mission. No matter what is on the cover, it has to be backed up by solid editorial material. Regardless of how exciting the cover is, it doesn't guarantee a return customer or a satisfied reader. Only content can do that.

Logo

The design of the magazine's logo, or name, is critical because it is the most important word on the cover. The typeface used for the logo helps set the tone and the mood of the entire magazine; the design has to visually match what the word or words of the title say. It also has to provide instant recognition of a magazine. Because the logo also appears in circulation promotion, in advertising, and on stationery, it becomes an important identification symbol of the magazine. The magazine title is like a corporate logo or trademark; it represents a product that has both recognition and value as a brand in the marketplace.

Naming a magazine with an identifying color that became part of the design was an early cover option for *The Yellow Book, The Blue Book, The Golden Book,* and *The Red Book* (which later adopted the more familiar spelling and name of *Redbook*). Many consumer magazines have a one-word title—short, catchy, and to the point: *Time, Vibe, Esquire, Playboy, Jump, Ebony, Latina, Elle,* and *Mode.* Two-word titles also abound among consumer magazines: *Rolling Stone, Ray Gun, Utne Reader, Reader's Digest.* A one- or two-word logo can take advantage of specially designed typefaces that can be set in a type size large enough to be clearly seen and recognized at a distance of eight to 10 feet away. Establishing a high contrast between the logo and the background also makes a cover pop out when it is on a rack with hundreds of other magazines, and all that might be seen is the top one-third of the cover.

A distinctive, appropriate logo is one that will hold up over time. Consequently, most logos tend to be derived, and modified, from serif or sans serif typefaces rather than decorative or novelty ones. There are good arguments to be made for never changing a logo, although periodic and gradual refinements usually make sense to keep it up to date. *Time*'s logo has been modified over the years—it has generally become heavier and bolder—but the logo's recognition value is essentially the same as it was in 1923.

Cover Types

There are five recognizable cover types: poster; one theme, one image; multi-theme, one image; multi-theme and multi-image; and all-typographic. Regardless of which cover type is used, a cover has to be uniform from issue to issue in size, paper stock, logo, and placement of date and price. These items provide consistency for the magazine, while the cover images and cover lines, provide change from issue to issue.

POSTER. A poster cover is one that has only a drawing or a photograph along with the name of the magazine, date, and possibly the price. There are no cover lines or themes announced, and the image generally is not covered by the logo. Also referred to as art covers, poster covers were dominant during much of the early part of the twentieth century as artwork. Indeed, magazine covers were treated as mini-posters to be framed from 1890 to about 1930. While poster covers for *Ladies' Home Journal, Good Housekeeping,* and *Redbook* were commercially inspired, Steven Heller and Louise Fili, writing in *Cover Story: The Art of American Magazine Covers 1900–1950,* state that many of them "transcended their ephemeral natures and became documents of their times—represented a high-level artistic endeavor."[39] These covers sold because they were aesthetically appealing.

Most poster covers between 1890 and 1940 didn't even relate to a story inside the magazine. Rather, the poster cover depicted a season or a conveyed a general mood. Poster covers are rarely used now by consumer magazines. *The New Yorker* stands alone in its use of a poster cover with no cover lines, at least in the version mailed to subscribers; a plain flap with cover lines overlays almost two-thirds of the image on newsstand copies. However, several association magazines use the poster format. *Texas Highways,* published by the Texas Department of

Transportation, almost always has a lovely landscape photograph on the cover, while *Gems and Gemology,* the journal of the Gemological Institute of America, features unusual stones.

JAMA: The Journal of the American Medical Association has used original art for its poster cover for more than 30 years. The works of fine art range from American Primitive and German Expressionist paintings to photographs of elaborately decorated porcelain eggs and ornate silver tea sets. Senior contributing editor Dr. M. Therese Southgate, who discusses the covers in each issue, says, "Contrary to what some readers may believe, most of the works of fine art that appear on the covers of *The Journal of the American Medical Association* are not intended to reflect the content of the particular issue. When one or another seems to do so it is usually because of some accident of timing or interpretation by especially astute or creative readers."[40]

Only occasionally—a mere handful out of some 1,500 works of art that have been reproduced through the years—has *JAMA* intentionally used a cover related to content, usually for an issue dedicated to a single topic. Southgate calls these "signature covers," or "covers that through repetition call attention to and identify on sight the special topic of that issue. In the past these 'dedicated' issues have concerned such perennial medical concerns as nuclear war, gun violence, tobacco, health care for the underserved." For example, Vincent Van Gogh's *Skull with Cigarette* was used for the March 28, 1966, and February 28, 1986, issues, which both were devoted to tobacco concerns.

ONE THEME, ONE IMAGE. In the one theme, one image cover approach, there's a photograph or drawing with a two- or three-word identification of the subject or a short descriptive phrase. The depicted cover image is featured in a major inside story. From 1936 through most of 1949, *Life*'s covers featured one theme and one image. A few *Life* covers during 1949 had a second story titled in the upper right-hand corner, and the practice become more prevalent during the 1950s. Once a second title is added to a single image cover, it becomes a multi-theme, one image format.

The majority of *Time*'s covers tend to be one theme, one image in format, although a slash was used sporadically in the left or right corner beginning in the 1940s. The use of an occasional flapped right corner with a small thumbnail photo to signal a story of secondary importance didn't occur until 1977. In recent years, at least half of *Time*'s covers in a given year will be one theme, one image. *Physics Today* and *Smithsonian* are two magazines that consistently use the one theme, one image cover.

MULTI-THEME, ONE IMAGE. The majority of magazines use a multi-theme, one image cover. From *The Sciences* to *Tikkun* to *Vogue,* this is the prevailing approach. Most designers believe that the image grabs the reader's attention, but the multi-theme aspect of cover lines is what clinches the sale.

How many cover lines are enough? The number of cover lines is at an all-time high these days, but six seems to be the average number. "We know from research that the reader will buy a magazine for a single cover line," says Ron Scott. "Using cover lines effectively is like being a politician. You have a certain number of constituents and you must let each one of those constituents know in each issue there's something important in the magazine for him."[41]

Designer Mary Kay Baumann of Hopkins/Baumann says where editors place cover lines ultimately depends on where the magazine is displayed most. If it's at the checkout counter, where magazines are displayed in individual racks, the entire cover space can be used for cover lines. Cover lines may be placed along the left-hand side of the cover because many newsstands shelve magazines horizontally and fan the covers so they overlap along the left edge.

"That upper left-hand corner can be a valuable piece of real estate because that's where sales start," observes Scott. He adds that at some newsstands, stacking may occur vertically, so a few editors also consider the skyline area above the logo as an important design space, and cover lines may be placed there for increased interest.

"Newsstand magazine buyers are fringe buyers, so you need to do something to catch their eye," Baumann says. "The cover must have a package concept with a strong identity formed by the logo and the cover lines. The logo and cover lines must lead to fast recognition."

Cover lines are just as important for specialized trade magazines with controlled circulations. The magazine competes with all the other mail a busy manager receives each day. Effective cover lines can mean the difference between reading an issue immediately or tossing it aside for a later read—or the recycling bin.

MULTI-THEME AND MULTI-IMAGE. The second most popular cover format is multi-theme and multi-image. Here, there is more than one photograph, or more likely, a collage of cropped photos or cut-outs, along with numerous cover lines. *People, Consumer Reports, PC Magazine, PC World, Metal Edge, Teen Beat, 16,* and *Bop* are the most frequent users of this cover approach, although other magazines use it from time to time.

ALL-TYPOGRAPHIC. The all-type cover is the exception to the rule of using a strong visual illustration. All-type means just that: not a single photo or drawing on the cover, just words. *Rolling Stone, New York,* and *Esquire* have had big sellers with all-type covers. These usually tout a special topic, such as *Rolling Stone*'s November 17, 1994, "The Future of Rock: Generation Next" and *Esquire*'s October 1993 "60 Things Every Man Should Know" sixtieth anniversary collector's edition.

Time's editors grappled with the concept of an all-type cover for a year before running its first one, on the April 8, 1966, issue, asking "Is God Dead?" It would be 17 years before *Time* would use another all-type cover. This time the editors decided to run the first paragraph of the "Death Penalty" story on the cover of the January 24, 1983, issue:

> *The chair is bolted to the floor near the back of a 12-ft. by 18-ft. room. You sit on a seat of cracked rubber secured by rows of copper tacks. Your ankles are strapped into half-moon-shaped foot cuffs lined with canvas. A 2-in.-wide greasy leather belt with 28 buckle holes and worn grooves where it has been pulled very tight many times is secured around your waist just above the hips. A cool metal cone encircles your head. You are now only moments away from death.*

A whimsical approach to an all-type cover is also possible. *Print*'s May/June 1998 cover features a 300-word essay about the various ideas the art director thought about for the cover. Starting with the words "This is my best idea yet," and sounding as if the art director is in his office thinking out loud, the reader is treated to possibilities ranging from blowing up the logo to cover the entire page, to making the cover all one color, just black on white. Each new idea is "my best idea yet." The essay, which takes up the entire cover except for the logo, is set in about 24 point Helvetica. Of course, it ends, "This is my best idea yet."

Magazines that use all-type covers all of the time tend to take a serious approach to their topics. *Commentary, Dissent,* and *Foreign Affairs* list a few articles and their authors on the covers, but they do not include page numbers. Each has a regular table of contents page inside. Most academic journals use their covers either as a table of contents or as a short listing of some of the articles inside; *New England Journal of Medicine* and *Harvard Business Review* are two examples.

According to professor Samir Husni of the University of Mississippi, new magazines tend to use the multi-theme, one image cover format about 63 percent of the time; multi-theme,

Print America's Graphic Design Magazine

"This is my best idea yet. No, wait! I've got a better one! First I'll blow up the logo huge to fit across the whole page, and put a drop shadow on it. Or get someone to redraw it. No. No. No. They'll never let me do that. At least I'll get to tweak that little spaghetti type at the top. OK, then I'll take a picture and do a Photoshop number on it. Not one of those OJ things, something hip. What a brilliant idea. This is my best idea yet. Oh man, maybe a type thing would be cooler. I need a headline that's just one short word, but they'll probably give me something that's way too long and doesn't fit. And then of course I'll get a subhead that's as long as a novel. People aren't stupid! You don't have to tell them the whole story. I should run the type vertically up the side. I know it's hard to read, but so what. No, wait! I'll make the cover all one color, just black on white. This is my best idea yet. If they weren't so cheap I could get a fifth color and use it just for the period at the end of the sentence. This is definitely an award-winner if they let me do exactly what I want. But everybody wants to be an art director. And after all this, the printer will probably mess up the separations and the registration anyway. What's pathetic is that the cover could be butt-ugly and people will still like it. What I need is a really cool illustrator who can come up with a great idea so I don't have to. This is my best idea yet."

MAY/JUNE 1998: *Print* took a whimsical approach to an all-typographic cover with a 300-word essay telling how an art director thinks through the possibilities of what to put on a cover.

DESIGN EXCELLENCE

Visual excellence in magazine design has to have a recognizable sense of self. Design consultant Jan White believes a magazine's design character "is defined by the underlying styling system, which is a subtle mix of titles, logos, slugs, display type, body copy type, spacing, columns, and color. Its success depends on disciplined self-control of the patterning, which causes the reader to say, 'Of course, it couldn't be any other way.'"[1] Photographs and illustrations also play a major role in the vivacity or subtlety of a magazine's design personality.

Several awards listed in "The Envelope Please" sidebar in Chapter 8 include design and photography honors as well as editorial kudos. Here is a listing of which ones include special awards for design excellence, as well as awards from groups that exclusively honor design and photography.

ALFRED EISENSTAEDT AWARDS FOR MAGAZINE PHOTOGRAPHY

Administered by Columbia University Graduate School of Journalism under a grant from *Life.* Established in 1998, these awards for visual excellence in American magazine photography are named after Alfred Eisenstaedt, one of the greatest photographers in magazine history. Awards are given in nine categories with some subcategories: our world (essay, nature, and science), human spirit (essay and single image), eyewitness (news essay, news single image, and sports), journalistic impact, portraiture (essay and single image), humor, style (essay, design, and single image), cutting edge (essay, single image, and photo illustration), and cover of the year. Additionally, the *Life* Legend Award is given to a photographer whose work has elevated magazine photojournalism. The first one went to Sebastiao Salgado.

Winning photographers had their work published in *DoubleTake, National Geographic, Newsweek, Time, Astronomy, Sports Illustrated, Natural History, W, The New Yorker, Life, 2wice, Vanity Fair, Detour,* and *Details.* The winner of the 1998 best cover of the year was *Rolling Stone*'s powerful January 23, 1997, photograph of outrageous rocker Marilyn Manson by Matt Mahurin.

ANNUAL BUSINESS PRESS COMPETITION

Sponsored by American Society of Business Press Editors (ASBPE). Graphic design awards are given for best cover photo and cover nonphoto, contents page, spread, publication redesign, and new publication design. Winners include *Pest Control Magazine, Beyond Computing, Distribution Channels, Electronic Engineering, Big Builder, Fresh Cup, PC World, Communicator, Restaurants & Institutions,* and *Residential Architect.*

CITY AND REGIONAL MAGAZINE ASSOCIATION AWARDS

Sponsored by City and Regional Magazine Association (CRMA) and administered by the University of Missouri School of Journalism. Design award winners include *Yankee, Los Angeles Magazine,* and *Colorado Homes & Lifestyle.*

OZZIE AWARDS

Sponsored by *Folio:*. Categories for magazine design excellence include cover, overall design, redesign, new magazine, feature design, photography, illustration, digital imagery, typography, and table of contents. *Folio:*'s awards are comprehensive, breaking out each

multi-image 29 percent; one theme, one image 7 percent; and poster 2 percent.[42] So, what makes a good cover?

Cover lines should be clever and not too long. Issues with several cover lines tend to sell better than those with just one. However, the cover shouldn't be crowded with so many cover lines that it looks cluttered or junky. Like the logo, cover lines should be easy to read from a distance and should contrast with the background color. When there is a single image on the cover, editors have found that a photograph of a woman's face tends to sell better than a man's on newsstands; whatever gender, though, the person on the cover should be making eye contact with the reader. A crisp photo with an innovative use of color generally sells better than a drawing, and a realistic drawing usually grabs more readers than does an abstract one.

Although cover design is more of an art than a science, studying previous covers and how they sold on the newsstand can provide insight. Circulation consultant Jeff Williams advises examining every copy for the last five or 10 years and writing down each issue's newsstand sell-through as a simple percentage. Then, says Williams, examine each cover: "What backgrounds have sold best? Are keywords more emotional or intellectual? Do illustrations do better than photos? The results may surprise you category into consumer, trade, and association/nonprofit magazine winners, with the consumer and trade magazines also grouped by circulation.

Consumer winners include *Icon Thoughtstyle Magazine, Shape, Hemispheres, Discover, New Jersey Monthly, Adirondack Life, Men's Health, New Mobility, Travel Holiday, Wine Enthusiast, Jazz Times,* and *World Art.* Trade magazine winners include *ProSales, Residential Architect, Communicator, Architecture, 3D Design, Eyecare Business, Software Strategies, CFO, Iridium Today, Fly Tackle Dealer, Bank Systems + Technology,* and *The Gourmet Retailer.* Association/nonprofit magazine winners include *Angels on Earth, Jewish Woman, Arthritis Today, Wildlife Conservation, Internal Auditor, California Schools, Preservation, Nature's Best, Home Healthcare Nurse, Symphony, Northeastern University Magazine,* and *Pitt Magazine.*

MAGGIE AWARDS

Sponsored by Western Publications Association. Awards are given to both consumer and trade magazines for black-and-white layout, color layout, table of contents, illustration, photograph, cover, overall design, and most improved. Winners include *HomeCare, Living Fit, PC World, Sunset, California Lawyer, Diablo, Outdoor Retailer, American Way,* and *Arizona Highways.*

NATIONAL MAGAZINE AWARDS

Sponsored by American Society of Magazine Editors. Publications are recognized "for excellent and innovative visual presentation that enhances the magazine's mission." The design category requires submission of three entire issues along with a statement explaining how design enhances the overall editorial presentation. Magazines that have won in this category, which was called visual excellence from 1970 to 1979, include: *Entertainment Weekly, I.D. Magazine, Vogue, Newsweek, Country Journal, National Lampoon, Architectural Digest, Audubon, New York, Forbes, Time, Elle, Life, Condé Nast Traveler, Vanity Fair, Harper's Bazaar, Allure, Martha Stewart Living,* and *Wired.* Some winners—*Look, Horizon, Geo, Attenzione,* and *Nautical Quarterly*—are no longer published. Only two magazines have won twice, *Esquire* (1972 and 1990) and *Rolling Stone* (1977 and 1989).

A magazine's excellent use of photography as part of its editorial mission is also recognized. Winners include *Life, Vogue, National Geographic, Rolling Stone, Texas Monthly, Harper's Bazaar, Martha Stewart Living, Saveur,* and *W.* The only five-time winner in this category is *National Geographic.*

[1] Jan White, "Self Test: Do You Design for Your Readers?" *The Handbook of Magazine Publishing*, 4th ed., compiled by the editors of *Folio:* (Stamford, CT: Cowles Business Media, 1996): 324.

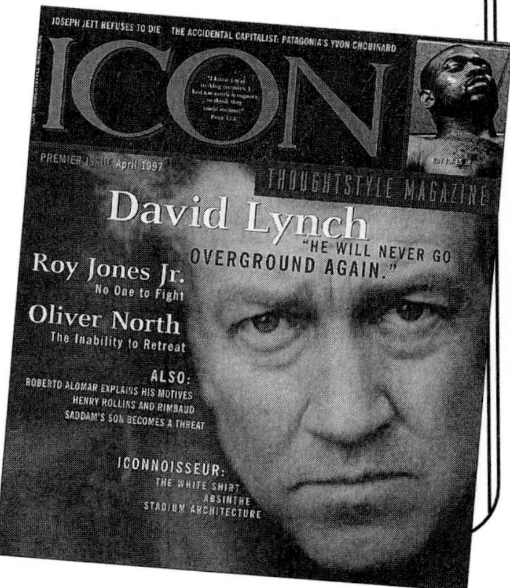

APRIL 1997 (PREMIERE ISSUE): *Icon Thoughtstyle Magazine* won the 1998 Ozzie Award for best overall consumer magazine design (over 100,000 circulation) after just a year of publication.

and will give you some critical information when trying to boost your newsstand sales."[43]

REDESIGNS

Magazine experts say that publications should be redesigned every five or six years, both as part of their evolutionary process and in order to stay current. Sometimes a full face-lift and major body overhaul occurs, but more frequently a magazine has little nips and tucks, such as updating the contents page, tweaking the logo, adding more color, or changing to a different paper stock. While a redesign tends to be aimed at attracting new readers, editors have to be careful that old, loyal readers aren't alienated. As for the advertisers, media buyers agree that publication touch-ups are really an appeal to new advertisers, who, of course, are concerned with readers' reactions.

A redesign can be introduced from one issue to the next, or it can evolve over several issues. A redesign will not help an ailing or unfocused magazine or one that's in trouble with declining subscription renewals, low newsstand sales, and evaporating advertisers. Several major changes over a few years may signal the last gasps of a magazine on the verge of folding. *Saturday Evening Post* went through two major redesigns (including a new logo) in 1961 and 1968 yet wasn't able to keep up with shifting audience needs, societal expectations, and economic downturns. The magazine folded in 1969.

Fortune has had at least 20 redesigns since 1930, the most recent one in 1996 under managing editor John Huey. *Time,* on the other hand, had minor modifications, but for all practical purposes remained the same for 69 years until a radical redesign in 1992. Yet, it is still unmistakably *Time.* Most consumer magazines do an in-house tweak of their designs every few years, a process so subtle that few readers or advertisers notice the change. It seems to make the magazines a little brighter and a little more contemporary, though.

Smithsonian, the official magazine of the Smithsonian Institution, got a face-lift in July 1997 after 27 years of publication. Designer Don Morris, who redesigned *Popular Science, PC World,* and *Golf,* was hired to put a contemporary spin on *Smithsonian*'s editorial pages, which had been designed by Bradbury Thompson in 1970. Morris, who added full photo bleeds, more color, and varied type styles for features and departments, says the magazine was projecting "an institutionalism that didn't reflect the diversity of its stories—lifestyle, history, art, science, and other areas—that made the magazine so interesting. The challenge for me was to bring out the warm editorial voice through design."[44] *Smithsonian*'s cover was slightly modified, with its traditional Baskerville logo enlarged from 4.9 picas to 7.6 picas and a gold outline placed around the name to increase legibility.

Scientific American, on the other hand, didn't touch its logo when it updated its look in 1995, choosing to add more cover lines instead. Calling it a mature magazine which had not been modified since 1948, editor-in-chief John Rennie (only the seventh editor in the magazine's history) wanted to keep *Scientific American*'s mandate as a forum for scientists and experts to write about inventions and discoveries for the general public. "Magazine publishing is not taxidermy," says Rennie in justification of the redesigned publication. "We're not sending these people some sort of embalmed thing they can put on their coffee table once a month and pretend they're intelligent. We want people to read the magazine and come away better for it."[45]

Rennie worked with art director Edward Bell, who had designed the magazine for 28 years, in adding more color. Rennie shortened the long, complex articles the magazine was famous for and introduced sidebars as well as an "In Brief" section. He also started using some articles written by journalists in conjunction with scientists; previously only scientists—more than 100 of *Scientific American*'s authors have won Nobel Prizes—wrote for the magazine.

Rob Sugar, president of AURAS Design, a full-service design studio in Washington, D. C., says there are good and bad reasons for a magazine redesign.[46] Some of the bad reasons have nothing to do with creating a better-looking magazine:

- Marking territory: A new editor, publisher, or art director may want "to alter the look to inaugurate a new administration." Sugar says this is self-serving and usually adds nothing to the magazine, particularly if the changes are cosmetic and ungrounded.
- Anniversary coming up: Some editors will use an anniversary as an impetus for a makeover. "It's never a good idea to change the look just for the sake of novelty," Sugar says.
- Not trendy enough: Someone will say the magazine doesn't seem cutting edge. Sugar points out that trendiness "is actually a copy of someone else's idiosyncratic and successful look" and may be inappropriate for any other magazine.

Editors agree that good reasons for a redesign revolve around knowing the magazine's editorial mission, audience, and advertisers. The best reasons to redesign include:

- Fine-tuning the design to reflect changing editorial content. Even if the magazine's mission remains the same, departments and features may need to be updated and made visually interesting.
- Showing prospective and current advertisers the magazine is always improving. Theme issues, new columns, or special advertising sections may demand changes in layout and design.
- Boosting readership within a certain demographic group or expanding a current base of readers. "If a magazine changes its mission to include new readers, redesign is the best outward signal that a potential audience member's opinions have been re-evaluated," Sugar says.

▶ Needing a full relaunch because shrinking newsstand sales and dwindling renewals show readers are dissatisfied. Other signs pointing to the need for a complete makeover include advertisers who say they aren't getting the response they want from the readers and competition that is outperforming the magazine.

Some magazines have a signature design style that's like the perfect outfit for an exclusive charity ball, from the diamond earrings down to the silver heels and beaded purse. Others look organized, classic and disciplined, as if they're wearing a tailored suit with necktie knotted just so and shiny wingtips. Some magazines opt for flamboyant colors and a retro appearance, mixing a trendy whizbang dress with a vintage kimono and Doc Martins boots to wear to an outdoor rock concert. And still others have a casual look that is as comfortable as wearing sweats and sneakers on a Sunday afternoon at home.

Magazine art director Rhonda Rubinstein says that design turns content into an experience. She describes the relationship that has developed between design and editorial:

> *It's a kind of temporal, emotional connection that is the essence of today's magazine. The best magazines are creating this complete experience. In these highly competitive times, seductive covers, provocative images or compelling writing alone cannot make the magazine and garner impressive doorstop-size awards. It's the total product with a consistent voice and imagery. It's all about look and feel. The cover, the page-flipping and the skim-reading all lead to a particular world with its ideals and attitude.*[47]

FOR ADDITIONAL READING

Abramson, Howard S. National Geographic: *Behind America's Lens on the World.* New York: Crown Publishers, 1987.

Bryan, C. D. B. *The National Geographic Society: 100 Years of Adventure and Discovery.* New York: Harry N. Abrams, 1987.

Carlebach, Michael L. *American Photojournalism Comes of Age.* Washington, DC: Smithsonian Institution Press, 1997.

Cohn, Jan. *Covers of the* Saturday Evening Post: *Seventy Years of Outstanding Illustration from America's Favorite Magazine.* New York: Viking Studio Books, 1995.

Davis, Laurel R. *The Swimsuit Issue and Sport: Hegemonic Masculinity in* Sports Illustrated. Ithaca, NY: State University of New York Press, 1997.

Heller, Steven and Louise Fili. *Cover Story: The Art of American Magazine Covers 1900–1950.* San Francisco: Chronicle Books, 1996.

Kessler, Judy. *Inside* People: *The Stories behind the Stories.* New York: Villard Books, 1994.

Kozol, Wendy. Life'*s America: Family and National in Postwar Journalism.* Philadelphia: Temple University Press, 1994.

Owen, William. *Modern Magazine Design.* Dubuque, IA: Wm. C. Brown, 1992.

Rolling Stone: *The Complete Covers 1967–1997.* New York: Harry N. Abrams, 1998.

White, Jan V. *Editing by Design*, 2nd ed. New York: R. R. Bowker Company, 1982.

———. *Mastering Graphics.* New York: R. R. Bowker Company, 1983.

ENDNOTES

1 Tim Bogardus, "Define Your Redesign," *The Handbook of Magazine Publishing*, 4th ed., compiled by the editors of *Folio:* (Stamford, CT: Cowles Business Media, 1996): 335.

2 Jan V. White, "Editors Don't Know Design? Nonsense!" *Folio:* (April 1983): 66.

3 Rhonda Rubinstein, "Branding in Print," *U & lc* (Fall 1997): 102.

4 "Note on *Fortune,*" *Fortune* (February 1930): 180–81.

5 William Owen, *Modern Magazine Design* (Dubuque, IA: Wm. C. Brown, 1992): 50.

6 Ibid., 56.

7 "*Harper's Bazaar* at 100," *Print* (September/October 1967): 47.

8 Jim Nelson Black, "Magazine Design: The Evolution," *Folio:* (November 1983): 80.

9 Owen, 111.

10 Carol E. Holstead, "What's Old Is New: The Need for Historical Inspiration in Contemporary Magazine Design," *American Periodicals* (Vol. 7, 1997): 74.

11 Ibid., 79-81.

12 Michael Kaplan, "Carsonogenic," *Folio:* (March 1, 1995): 51.

13 Jan White, "Self Test: Do You Design for Your Readers?" *The Handbook of Magazine Publishing*, 4th ed., compiled by the editors of *Folio:* (Stamford, CT: Cowles Business Media, 1996): 324.

14 Kaplan, 51.

[15] Will Hopkins, "Design Basics: Magazine," Stanford Professional Publishing Course, Palo Alto, CA (July 25, 1997).
[16] Kaplan, 51.
[17] Stephen G. Smith, "From the Editor: A Farewell to Hot Wax and X-Acto Knives," *Civilization* (May/June 1996): 6.
[18] Jim Nelson Black, 90.
[19] Robert Bohle, "Readers Tell Us About Color," *The Journal of the Society of Newspaper Design* (No. 21, 1985): 9.
[20] Jan V. White, "Using Color to Carry the Message," *Folio:* (April 1991): 89.
[21] Roger Black, "Pulling Out the Stops," *U & lc* (Summer 1997): 17.
[22] Kaplan, 84.
[23] Smith, 6.
[24] John Peter, "Stop! Read This Article," *Magazine Publishing Management,* compiled by the editors of *Folio:* (New Canaan, CT: Folio Magazine Publishing Corporation, 1976): 201.
[25] Elizabeth Thoman, "Rise of the Image Culture: Re-Imagining the American Dream," *Media & Values* (Winter 1992): 7.
[26] Loudon Wainwright, *The Great American Magazine: An Inside Story of* Life (New York: Alfred A. Knopf, 1986): 33.
[27] Kathryn Shattuck, "Museum as Reprieve from the Recycling Bin," *The New York Times* (July 2, 1998): B3.
[28] Robin Pogrebin, "Magazines Bowing to Demands for Star Treatment," *The New York Times* (May 18, 1998): A1.
[29] Nigel Holmes, "Visual Information," Stanford Professional Publishing Course, Palo Alto, CA (July 25, 1997).
[30] Peter, 201.
[31] Ibid., 201.
[32] Roger Black, 17.
[33] Roy Paul Nelson, "Tracing the Circuitous Route of Publication Design," *IABC Communication World* (May-June 1990): 50–51.
[34] Peter, 202.
[35] Douglas A. Learner, "Contents Pages," *Folio:* (July 1982): 38.
[36] "Pay As Much Attention to the Cover As the Contents," *Folio:* (February 1, 1998): 9.
[37] "What Makes a Cover Sell?" *Folio:* (September 1986): 51.
[38] Judy Kessler, *Inside* People: *The Stories Behind the Stories* (New York: Villard Books, 1994): 11.
[39] Steven Heller and Louise Fili. *Cover Story: The Art of American Magazine Covers 1900–1950* (San Francisco: Chronicle Books, 1996): 11.
[40] M. Therese Southgate, "The Cover," *JAMA: The Journal of the American Medical Association* (July 1, 1998): 5.
[41] Mary W. Quigley, "What Sells, What Bombs: Magazine Cover Roulette," *Washington Journalism Review* (July/August 1988): 20.
[42] Samir Husni, "The New Consumer Magazines of 1984: A Fact Sheet" (paper presented at the annual Association for Education in Journalism and Mass Communication, Memphis, TN, August 1985).
[43] Jeff Williams, "The Art and Science of Covers That Sell," *Folio:* (October 1998): 39.
[44] Rolf Maurer, "A Classic Title Gets a Little Pizzazz," *Folio:* (September 15, 1997): 27.
[45] Steve Wilson, *"Scientific American* Creates a New Chemistry," *Folio:* (September 1, 1997): 29.
[46] Rob Sugar, "Looks Can Kill," *Folio:* (November 1, 1997): 64.
[47] Rubinstein, 102.

C H A P T E R 10

Magazine Production

Manufacturing Issues

On the fourth floor of a Manhattan office building a block from Central Park, the production staff of Country Living Gardener, *part of Hearst Publishing, pores over thumbnail-size pages, puzzling about where to place an adverting insert so that it doesn't cut into the magazine's editorial content. The decision goes through the publisher, editor-in-chief, art director, advertising director, electronic production director, and production staff. The decision is a collaborative effort, but the production staff actually makes the placement. A thousand miles away, in an office building a block from Greenwood Park in Des Moines, Iowa, the staff of* Chronicle, *the magazine of the University of Osteopathic Medicine and Health Sciences, also pores over thumbnails, determining how to make the article on employee morale full-color throughout while keeping within budget. The decision is made by the editor and art director because they are the magazine's entire staff. All types and sizes of magazines must go through the same basic manufacturing stage, called the production process, for the creation of the printed and bound publication. At the same time that the editorial, design, and advertising staffs are planning the magazine's content, the production staff is planning the most efficient and precise method of making that content into a tangible product. On a small magazine, all the work is done by a handful of people, sometimes only one or two. In a large publishing house, an entire floor of the building may be reserved for the production staff. Once the magazine closes—that is, reaches its final deadline for content—the production staff kicks into high gear.*

THE PRODUCTION PROCESS

The production process includes placing all content, choosing paper and color, preparing art for reproduction, and overseeing printing and binding. It is a high-tech operation that depends on human skill as well as on an array of machines ranging in size from desktop computers to printing presses the size of a house. Many production staffers fall into their jobs accidentally and end up loving the work for its mix of creativity and scientific problem-solving.

The production of *Country Living Gardener* provides a clear overview of the process. At the planning stage, the production staff works with a computer, pencil, and paper to organize the placement of articles and advertising in the magazine. They follow the magazine's established editorial formula as well as directions from the editor and art director in determining the flow of articles; they place advertising according to the ad contract, making sure advertising and editorial mesh logically and serve the reader with a clear and consistent message. Once placement has been established, the staff takes the computer-designed pages from the art director and formats all art and type in preparation for production. They send the finished pages on disk,

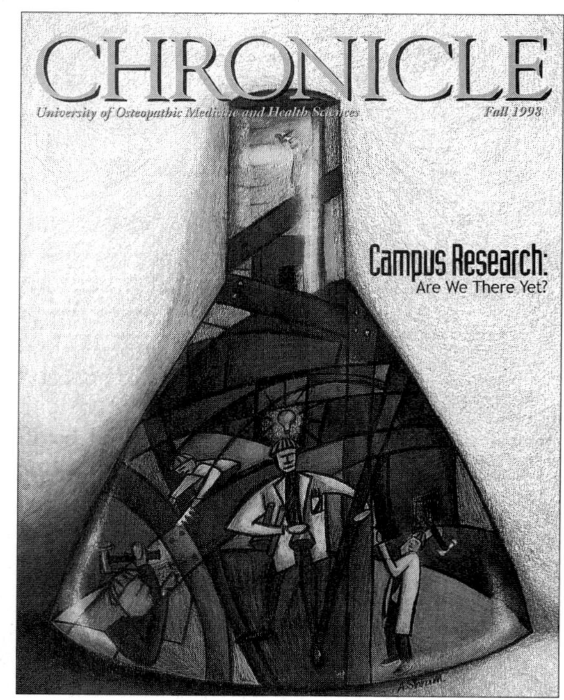

FALL 1998: On the *Chronicle,* which has a small staff, most of the production work is done by the art director.

Advertisers Know Their Place

In addition to specific ad placement requests, production staffers have to keep their eyes open for ad-related problem areas. For example:

- Most consumer magazines make sure at least six pages separate two car ads.
- Coupons must back up to editorial or to another part of the same advertiser's message. No coupons can be placed behind another ad. In that way, when a consumer cuts out a coupon, part of the magazine's editorial content is sliced out, not part of another ad.
- Magazines must "make good"—that is, run the ad for free—on ads that are placed contrary to the ad contract.
- Advertising inserts—preprinted groups of pages—should not break up an article but should come between articles or departments. Because they are preprinted, these inserts are numbered differently from the rest of the magazine.
- Regional advertising pages cannot be numbered as part of the magazine. U.S. postal regulations require that only those pages that are part of every edition of the magazine can be sequentially numbered. Pages in regional editions, then, typically bear a letter as well as a number, with the letter being the production staff's code for that particular edition. At *Good Housekeeping*, NC1 refers to the first page of the North Central edition.

plus all art, to a production company in Tennessee, which scans and places the photographs. The production company converts the pages to film and sends them to a printing plant in Kentucky, which prints, binds, addresses, and transports the magazines by truck to newsstands and subscribers. Postal workers have an office in the plant so they can determine postage and inspect the magazines to make sure they meet postal regulations.

On the *Chronicle,* the process is the same, but most of the production work falls on the art director. The editor and art director also use the magazine's established formula as their guide in placement of elements, being sure that they represent the goals and philosophy of the university. The art director designs all the pages on her computer, then sends them to the printing plant, which scans and places all photos, and prints and binds the magazine. The printer sends the finished product to a mailing house, which sends it to faculty, students, staff, and alumni of the university.

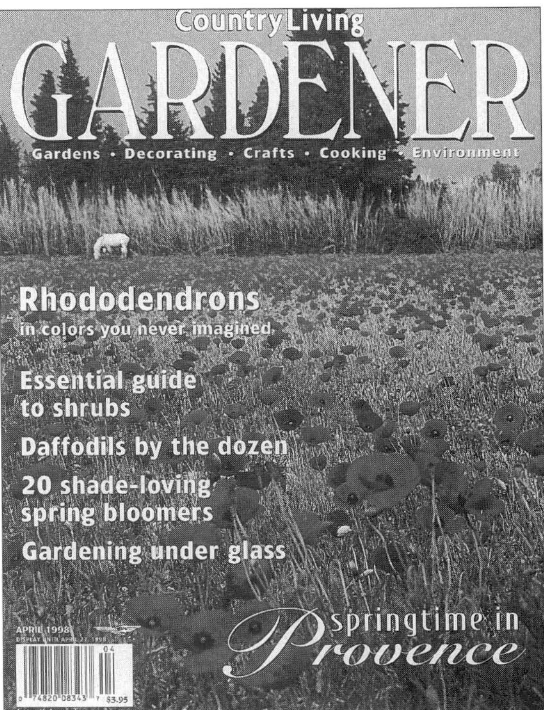

APRIL 1998: Much of the production work for *Country Living Gardener* is done by a production house in Tennessee, which receives all editorial and art finished pages on disk from the New York office.

PRODUCTION PLANNING

The production planning process for each issue requires deciding on the placement of pages in the magazine. Each issue builds on decisions about paper, color, art, special effects, printing process, and binding, which are made when the magazine is launched or redesigned. These decisions usually stay in place for years, unless budget changes require a modification of size or paper. The whole process has one goal: creating a quality product that serves the reader.

Break-of-the-Book

The determination of which article or advertisement goes on what page is called the **break-of-the-book;** it is occasionally also called the *ladder* or *map*. As explained in Chapter 5, a well-planned magazine has such a consistent formula that the placement of elements from one issue to another is a natural process. At large publishing houses, the break-of-the-book is done by a production manager, following an outline given by the editor and art director. At smaller magazines, it's done directly by the editor and art director. No matter who creates it, the editor, art director, and publisher all must approve the break-of-the-book.

At *Country Living Gardener*, one production staff member is concerned only with editorial, another with advertising. The two coordinate their work, which is overseen by the editor and art director. *Chronicle* has no advertising.

For each issue, the staff starts with a blank worksheet—usually a tiny thumbnail showing all pages of the magazine—and begins to fill it with specific content. The break-of-the-book is initially done in pencil because it changes often. An article that had been planned for four pages suddenly becomes a major story and is expanded by three pages. That means a six-page photo spread is cut to three pages. Then two pages of ads come in at the last minute, forcing the staff to postpone one entire feature until the next issue. *Country Living Gardener*'s March/April 1998 break-of-the-book is shown below. The "Xs" indicate pages that are complete. Typically, *Country Living Gardener* runs 120 pages, 90 of them editorial. Notice the "Final—Really!" note at the top. The staff uses humor to deal with the many versions of the plan they have created.

Editorial Needs

The staff plans the magazine's editorial content months, often years, in advance. Editors and art directors make assignments according to the editorial formula; magazine editors often assign more articles than needed to make sure they have a back-up in case one falls through. They also generally have a file of extra articles—an article "bank"—to use if they need to add pages in the happy event that ad sales go beyond expectations.

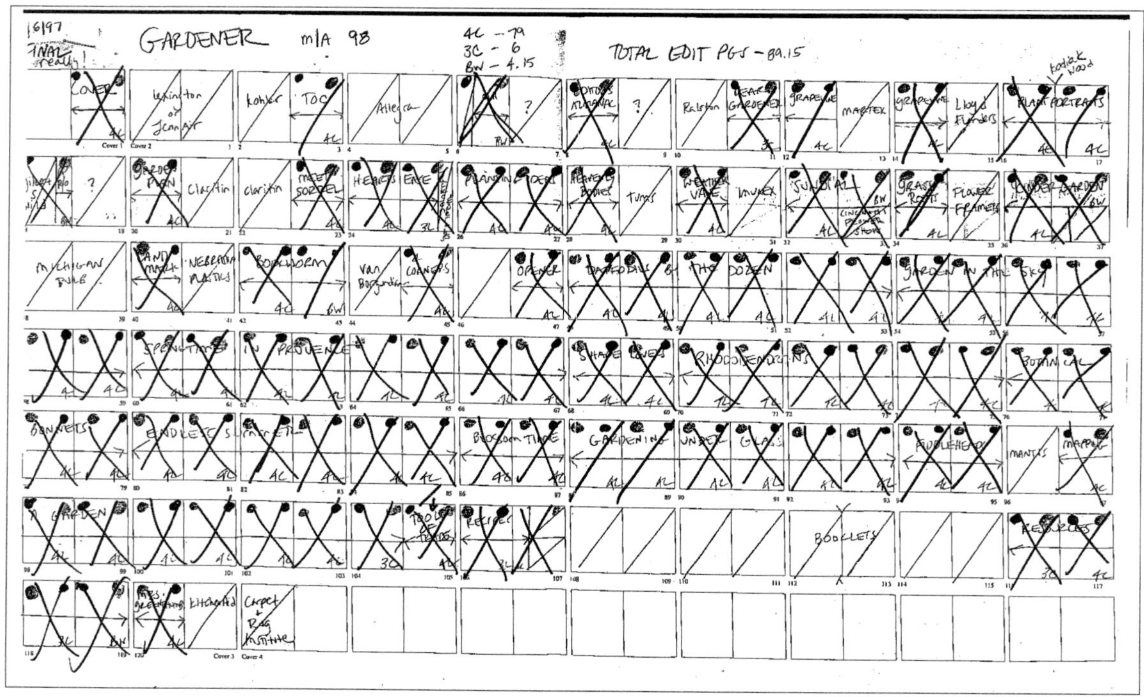

This break-of-the-book from *Country Living Gardener* shows the final page layout for an issue.

Adding Pages: How Many Before It Pays Off?

In an ideal world, ad sales would be finalized far enough in advance to give editorial, design, and production staffs the time to prepare the right amount of editorial material to keep the magazine's advertising-editorial ratio consistent. Too often, however, ads come in late and the staff is left scrambling to fill extra pages. Worse yet, ads may be pulled out late, leaving the magazine with a gap.

Magazine staffs know at what point it makes sense to add pages when extra ads come in and at what point it makes sense to simply take the ad and cut an editorial page or two. For example, a magazine with a 40:60 advertising-editorial ratio plans 60 pages of editorial for every 40 pages of advertising. If, at the last minute, two extra pages of ads come in, the magazine staff usually cuts two department pages or replaces a six-page feature with a four-page feature, if possible. The six-pager can then be placed in a subsequent issue.

Partial-page ads are less problematic because magazines traditionally plan "advertising and editorial" (A&E) pages, which have partial-page ads and short articles all on one page. An additional ad might mean simply losing one of the articles, which can then be placed in a later issue.

Six or seven pages of extra ads, however, may require a whole new signature. This will consist of the ads, plus extra editorial pages with content from the magazine's editorial *bank,* which is its store of articles of varying sizes that can be put in at any time to fill space. The magazine staff goes to this bank again when ads are lost at the last minute.

Each editorial element has a predetermined spot in the magazine, so while the editor is making sure the article reads appropriately and the art director is overseeing design, the production staff is already assigning space to that article. Departments may fall on the same page from issue to issue, or they may fall within a general range. In some magazines, a particular department is the same length in every issue; in others, the length varies according to the amount of material available, the importance the editors want to place on that department, or the design effect the art director is planning. Features are placed within the feature well, with lengths and pacing determined by the editor and art director.

Advertising Placement

Advertisers who buy specific placement in the magazine must be given that placement; they have a contract. The ad staff strives to sell specific pages—the covers, especially—and not to oversell other areas. That is, they try not to sell eight full-page ads to food advertisers who want to be in a food section that normally has only two editorial pages. Should these problems occur, the staff tries to accommodate advertisers; they may decide to reevaluate the formula and add more food pages on a regular basis, or they may encourage the ad staff to sell food advertisers on placements throughout the magazine.

Some magazines limit the number of partial-page ads. At *Classic Automobile,* the production manager places fractional ads next to the masthead or at the back of the book. Where there is a deviation from this norm, the editor makes the call.

The production manager places ads first, to assure all contracts are honored. The typical ad placement requests are:

- The second, third, or fourth covers, also known as the inside front, inside back, and back covers.
- Next to a specific department. Occasionally magazine ad sales staffs will sell ads next to features, but this can be tricky if the feature falls through; it also can look like that advertiser is getting preferential treatment.
- Front-of-the-book (FOB): before the table of contents or in the departments at the beginning of the magazine.
- Back-of-the-book (BOB): in the departments or columns at the end of the magazine.
- Run-of-the-book (ROB): anywhere in the magazine.

Some publishers will eliminate perfume strips from magazines if subscribers complain that they are sensitive to scents. These magazines are selectively bound and labeled.

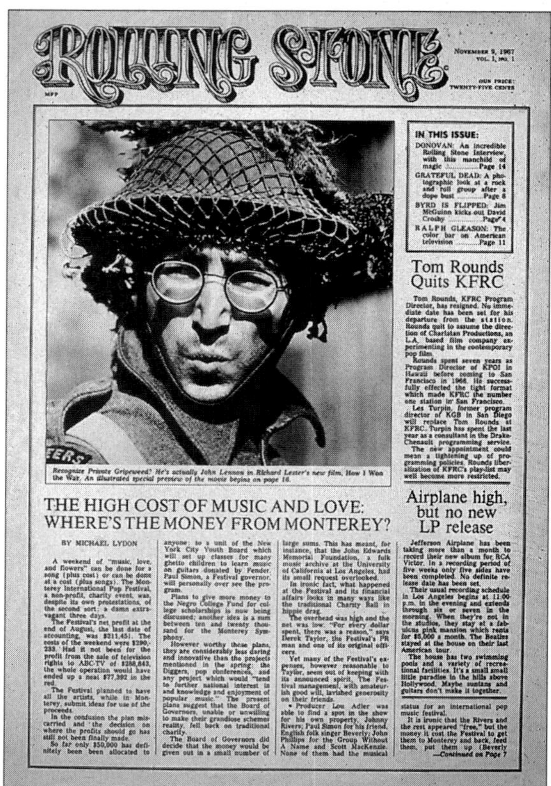

ROLLING STONE

November 9, 1967
Vol. 1, No. 1

Our Price: Twenty-Five Cents

IN THIS ISSUE:

DONOVAN: An incredible Rolling Stone interview, with this manchild of magic ......Page 14

GRATEFUL DEAD: A photographic look at a rock and roll group after a dope bust ......Page 8

BYRD IS FLIPPED: Jim McGuinn kicks out David Crosby ......Page 4

RALPH GLEASON: The color bar on American television ......Page 11

Recognize Private Gripweed? He's actually John Lennon in Richard Lester's new film, How I Won the War. An illustrated special preview of the movie begins on page 16.

THE HIGH COST OF MUSIC AND LOVE: WHERE'S THE MONEY FROM MONTEREY?

BY MICHAEL LYDON

A weekend of "music, love, and flowers" can be done for a song (plus cost) or can be done at a cost (plus songs). The Monterey International Pop Festival, a non-profit, charity event, was, despite its own protestations, of the second sort: a damn extravagant three days.

The Festival's net profit at the end of August, the last date of accounting, was $211,451. The costs of the weekend were $290,233. Had it not been for the profit from the sale of television rights to ABC-TV of $288,843, the whole operation would have ended up a neat $77,392 in the red.

The Festival planned to have all the artists, while in Monterey, submit ideas for use of the proceeds.

In the confusion the plan miscarried and the decision on where the profits should go has still not been finally made.

So far only $50,000 has definitely been been allocated to anyone: to a unit of the New York City Youth Board which will set up classes for many ghetto children to learn music on guitars donated by Fender. Paul Simon, a Festival governor, will personally over see the program.

Plans to give more money to the Negro College Fund for college scholarships is now being discussed; another idea is a sum between ten and twenty thousand for the Monterey Symphony.

However worthy these plans, they are considerably less daring and innovative than the projects mentioned in the spring: the Diggers, pop conferences, and any project which would "tend to further national interest in and knowledge and enjoyment of popular music." The present plans suggest that the Board of Governors, unable or unwilling to make their grandiose schemes reality, fell back on traditional charity.

The Board of Governors did decide that the money would be given out in a small number of large sums. This has meant, for instance, that the John Edwards Memorial Foundation, a folk music archive at the University of California at Los Angeles, had its small request overlooked.

In ironic fact, what happened at the Festival and its financial affairs looks in many ways like the traditional Charity Ball in hippie drag.

The overhead was high and the net was low. "For every dollar spent, there was a reason," says Derek Taylor, the Festival's PR man and one of its original officers.

Yet many of the Festival's expenses, however reasonable to Taylor, seem out of keeping with its announced spirit. The Festival management, with amateurish good will, lavished generosity on their friends.

• Producer Lou Adler was able to find a spot in the show for his own property, Johnny Rivers; Paul Simon for his friend, English folk singer Beverly; John Phillips for the Group Without A Name and Scott MacKenzie. None of them had the musical status for an international pop music festival.

It is ironic that the Rivers and the rest appeared "free," but the money it cost the Festival to get them to Monterey and back, feed them, put them up (Beverly

—*Continued on Page 7*

Tom Rounds Quits KFRC

Tom Rounds, KFRC Program Director, has resigned. No immediate date has been set for his departure from the station. Rounds quit to assume the direction of Charlatan Productions, an L.A. based film company experimenting in the contemporary pop film.

Rounds spent seven years as Program Director of KPOI in Hawaii before coming to San Francisco in 1966. He successfully effected the tight format which made KFRC the number one station in San Francisco.

Les Turpin, former program director of KGB in San Diego will replace Tom Rounds at KFRC. Turpin has spent the last year as a consultant in the Drake-Chenault programming service.

The new appointment could mean a tightening up of programming policies. Rounds liberalization of KFRC's play-list may well become more restricted.

Airplane high, but no new LP release

Jefferson Airplane has been taking more than a month to record their new album for RCA Victor. In a recording period of five weeks only five sides have been completed. No definite release date has been set.

Their usual recording schedule in Los Angeles begins at 11:00 p.m. in the evening and extends through six or seven in the morning. When they're not in the studios, they stay at a fabulous pink mansion which rents for $5,000 a month. The Beatles stayed at the house on their last American tour.

The house has two swimming pools and a variety of recreational facilities. It's a small small little paradise in the hills above Hollywood. Maybe suntans and guitars don't make it together.

NOVEMBER 9, 1967 (PREMIERE ISSUE):
Rolling Stone **began as a newsprint publication and gradually moved to coated paper stock to appeal to advertisers.**

Paper Stock

On a regularly published magazine, the art director or production manager may not even know exactly what type of paper is used because it has been standardized for so long. The initial decision about paper—also called **stock**—is based on precise magazine needs and budgetary restrictions.

It is an important decision. Readers often have a visceral reaction to paper. They eye it, touch it, rub it between their fingers, and hold it up to the light. Even the least sophisticated reader notices paper quality. Paper is evaluated on its finish, grade, and weight.

FINISH. Paper can be coated or uncoated, which refers to the outer layer of finish applied to one or both sides. This coating is then polished to various levels of sheen on a machine called a **calender**, which smoothes the paper by compression.

Coated paper generally tends to hold ink better than uncoated, resulting in sharper, brighter images; its surface also allows more even reflection of light. Uncoated paper, such as newsprint, generally allows both ink and light to soak in, resulting in dull final images. Some magazines use coated inks for the main editorial well and uncoated for certain departments. *Wood,* for example, is printed on a coated stock except for the project patterns, which are printed on uncoated. *Rolling Stone* started as a newsprint publication but ultimately moved to coated stock as the magazine matured and appealed to more upscale readers and advertisers; it now uses paper that has a mix of uncoated and coated qualities.

Coated stocks can have a high gloss, a dull finish, a matte finish, or they can be coated-uncoated hybrids. Coated stocks are further defined according to grades of quality.

- ***High gloss*** A high gloss paper is lustrous and shiny; this is the result of coating as well as the amount of calendering. A gloss sheet is highly reflective and is a good choice for photos because it can make printed images sparkle. It may be less appealing when reproducing type, however, because it can cause too much glare. *Classic Automobile,* which features ads and articles focusing on dream cars—Bentleys and Rolls Royces—uses high gloss paper.
- ***Dull coat*** A dull sheet is slightly less coated and less calendered. It may hold the ink well, but it is less reflective; colors are less brilliant but the sheet also has less glare. It can be a good choice for magazines with both photographic appeal and large amounts of type. The Osteopathic University's *Chronicle,* with an emphasis on educational material for an audience of health care professionals, uses dull paper.
- ***Matte coat*** A matte sheet has even less coating and polish, so it has the least gloss and the least reflectivity. It can be a good choice for magazines that want the understated effect of newsprint with the printing quality of a coated stock. Farm Bureau's *Family Ties* moved from a high gloss to a matte coated stock when readers complained about paper glare.
- ***Super calendered*** Called "super cal" sheets by printers, these papers have less coating

GREEN MAGAZINES

Magazines are huge users of natural resources—notably ink and paper. Publishers can be responsible citizens by using safer printing inks that create less air pollution, by printing on recycled paper, and by recycling both paper and ink.

Traditionally, printing ink has been made with petroleum products, which are nonrenewable and can be toxic to the environment as well as to the individuals working in the printing plant. Most contain Volatile Organic Chemicals (VOCs), which have been implicated in many types of cancer. In the past, cadmium, a heavy metal, was also used; it has virtually disappeared from the American printing scene. Soy oils are reducing some printers' reliance on petroleum products. The American Soybean Association offers a seal of approval for printing ink that uses at least 7 percent soy. Soybean oil is a renewable resource, usually produced by Midwestern farmers, and its use reduces reliance on nonrenewable resources at the same time it supports our agricultural economy. Ink developed by Quad/Graphics, a major magazine printer, uses corn, linseed, and soy oils to replace some of the petroleum-based oils.[1]

Soy-based inks may be of uneven quality, however, so the majority of ink used today is petroleum-based and includes VOCs. Quad/Graphics minimizes air pollution from this ink with emission control equipment. Both Quad/Graphics and R. R. Donnelley are reducing the amount of ink waste and are storing used inks in drums that can be disposed of more safely than in the past.

In 1993, the American Society of Magazine Editors and the Magazine Publishers of America established the Task Force on Magazines and the Environment, with an emphasis on paper production and recycling. Among other findings, the task force concluded that "minimum environmental impact is the broad goal for all phases in the life of a magazine, from forest to recycling fiber. This should be the standard by which we as an industry ultimately evaluate the processes used both by our suppliers and ourselves."[2]

Audubon magazine and Quad/Graphics have been testing recycled paper, vegetable-based inks, and cover coating since 1991, in search of environmentally safe materials that meet the magazine's high reproduction standards. The magazine switched from ultraviolet-coated covers to varnish in 1992 so the finished product would be recyclable. In 1993, *Audubon* switched to vegetable-based ink; in 1994, it moved to a recycled paper.

Printers such as R. R. Donnelley reduce paper waste by shipping all paper scraps—printed and unprinted—to recycling houses for use in cardboard, toilet paper, paper towels, and other products.

Environmentally safe printing is an ongoing process, and each success comes at something of a price. Recycled paper may cost more than other types because it has been so slow to gain favor that it is produced only in small quantities. With the law of supply and demand, short supplies mean high prices. And, some producers say, recycled paper is a mixed blessing: It has to be whitened to be usable in magazines, and the bleaching process requires chemicals.

[1] *Enviro/News* (Pewaukee, WI: Quad/Graphics, ND): 3.

[2] Magazine Publishers of America and the American Society of Magazine Editors, *The Magazine and The Environment* (New York: Magazine Publishers of America and the American Society of Magazine Editors, Boston, September 1996).

and finish than coated stocks, but more than uncoated. They are increasingly the choice of large circulation magazines such as *Rolling Stone, Family Circle,* and *McCall's.*

The move to super cal sheets has caused a bit of a controversy in the paper industry. In 1997, Champion papers ran an ad in *The New York Times* telling advertisers that publishers were cheapening the paper they were using without telling the advertisers, by moving from coated to "super calendered" sheets. The ad's message: "For years, magazines have been selling advertisers on the excellent reproduction quality of coated paper. It'll be interesting to see how they'll try and sell you off it."

Many magazines print on coated stocks because of the quality of printing they provide. Yet some uncoated stocks are of extremely high quality and appeal, with a matching high price tag. These uncoated stocks usually offer an artistic appeal that is more appropriate for advertising brochures and public relations materials than magazines, however.

If all other elements are equal, gloss coated papers are the most expensive, followed by dull, then matte, then super cal. Often, the cost of paper simply has to do with the kind the printer has in stock. When the printer can buy in huge

TABLE 10.1 Paper Weights of Magazines

MAGAZINE	TEXT WEIGHT/LBS.	COVER WEIGHT/LBS.
Car and Driver	38	60
Country Home	45	100
Family Ties (Farm Bureau)	60	60 text (self-cover)
National Geographic	55	100
Successful Farming	40	60
Traditional Home	45	130
Vibe	38	70
Rolling Stone	40	60
World Traveler (Northwest Airlines)	40	120

quantities, his costs go down, and he passes the reduction on to customers.

GRADE. Top-grade papers have high brightness, whiteness, smoothness, and opacity:

- ***Brightness*** Paper with high brightness reflects light, resulting in photos that look clean and brilliant.
- ***Whiteness*** Paper with high whiteness evenly reflects all colors in the spectrum; it does not reflect any one color more than another.
- ***Smoothness*** Smooth paper absorbs the ink evenly, which means even printing of photos as well as type.
- ***Opacity*** A highly opaque sheet lets little light shine through; it has little show-through of images from one side to the other side.

Coated paper is offered in six grades: premium, and grades number 1, 2, 3, 4, and 5. The quality of the sheet lowers as the grade number gets higher. Brightness, whiteness, smoothness, and opacity are reduced gradually from grade to grade. Even the lowest quality grade—number 5—still offers viable printing, however. Many large circulation magazines, in fact, are produced on numbers 4 and 5.

- ***Premium, Number 1, and Number 2*** These papers are generally used for annual reports; they are usually too expensive for magazines. Some corporate communications magazines, however, which are printed in small quantities, can afford a number 1 or number 2 sheet. Farm Bureau's *Family Ties* uses number 2 paper.
- ***Number 3*** This paper still has a high-end look, and is used by magazines such as *Classic Automobile* and *Vibe*. Most consumer magazines printed by R. R. Donnelley, one of the country's largest printing companies, use this sheet for covers.
- ***Numbers 4 and 5*** These grades are affordable while still offering good quality. They may leave fibers—small black spots that printers call "hickeys"—on the printed product, however. *Rolling Stone, Country Home*, and *Elle* use number 4 paper. *Car and Driver* uses number 5.

WEIGHT. Paper weight is determined by the weight in pounds of a ream—500 sheets—of paper cut to a standard size. That is, 500 sheets of a 40-pound paper weighs 40 pounds. Today's magazines are published on anything from 32-pound to 130-pound paper.

Paper is available either in cover or text weights. Cover weight papers are heavier than text papers. A 60-pound cover sheet is noticeably thicker than a 60-pound text sheet. A common choice for consumer magazines is 40-pound text stock with an 80-pound cover. Some specific examples of the paper weight of consumer, trade, and organization magazines are shown in Table 10.1.

Special Effects

Special processes that add to the impact of paper include coatings that can reduce smears and add gloss.

UV COATING. A coating is added to the printed product, which is dried using ultraviolet (UV) lights; it adds gloss to the page and is often used for magazine covers.

VARNISH. A slick coating is printed atop a finished sheet. It is used to prevent ink from running or for special effects, usually on covers. Occasionally an uncoated or matte sheet is highlighted with varnish, which acts almost like a subtle ink.

Color

Color may be process or spot color. Process color is more expensive than spot color; both can add energy and personality to a magazine.

GARBAGE IN, GARBAGE OUT

Even the best printing plant can't be expected to save a grainy photograph or a fuzzy illustration. Quality reproduction of art in magazines is largely determined by the type and condition of the original. When planning art, consider the following:

- Pencil drawings may be difficult to reproduce. Because they have gray tones, they are treated like continuous tones and therefore have to be screened. However, the original itself has a natural dot pattern from the texture of the lead. That means the drawing is essentially screened twice. The printed product may lack definition and detail.
- Slide film reproduces better than prints. Printers call slides **transparencies,** for obvious reasons. Transparencies produce clearer images because they are first-generation art, whereas prints are second-generation art, being created from negatives. First-generation images are, by nature, more precise.
- 35mm film can be used for magazine photographs, but the images it produces have to be enlarged to such a degree—sometimes up to 2000 percent—that they get grainy. Professional photographers avoid this problem by using large-scale cameras that produce transparency images up to 8 × 10 inches.
- Using already-published art is dangerous, not only because of copyright issues, but because of quality problems. A printed image has already been screened; to use it again would mean screening it once more. This double screening could create a **moiré pattern**—a wavy, shadowy pattern imprinted in the image—on the photo.

PROCESS COLOR. Full-color photographs in the printing world are referred to as four-color photos because they must be separated into the four **process colors**—magenta (red), cyan (blue), yellow, and black—for printing. This can be done in-house or by outside experts.

Color separations. Color photos that have been scanned and separated into the four process colors are called color separations. These can be costly additions to the magazine budget because each color has to have its own film and print run. A one-color photograph needs only one sheet of film and one press run. A four-color photograph, however, needs four sheets of film and four press runs.

Photographs can be scanned—or separated into process colors—by the magazine staff itself, using a digital scanner, photo manipulating software, and page film processing equipment. This can save the cost of hiring outside experts. The savings may come at the expense of quality, however, because of the limitations of the equipment and because magazine staffers may not have the time and training necessary to create high quality film.

A prepress house, also called a production house, does color separations and turns the photographs into film. While they may be more expensive than in-house scanning, prepress houses offer color correction capabilities that may provide much higher quality reproduction.

Low-resolution scans. The art used in most photo-heavy magazines takes up so much memory that production managers can't store it in their computers. The art staff, therefore, uses low-resolution (low-res) scans for placement only (FPO) when creating their pages. Low-res scans have fewer dots per inch (DPI) than high-res scans, so they take up less memory. The production staff then gives the page with low-res scans to a printer or prepress house, which replaces them with the high-resolution (high-res) scans necessary for quality printing. Automatic Picture Replacement (APR) software can instantly replace low-res scans with high-res scans, retaining the exact cropping, sizing, and placement on the page.

Photo blocks. Often, pages are sent to a printer or production house without scanned art, but with blank blocks left open for photographs and other page elements requiring special processing. These are scanned by the printer and then spliced into the rest of the page to create a final page of

Some magazines choose paper based on the "plop factor," or the sound the magazine makes when dropped. A wimpy magazine makes a tiny "plop," while a magazine with presence makes a strong, sturdy "PLOP." A magazine can improve its plop factor by increasing pages or paper weight.

THE $450,000 WORD CHOICE

In 1997, an insert placed in *Woman's Day* carried the small word *catalogue* at the front. As an insert, it would have been considered by postal authorities as part of the publication, and the magazine could then be mailed periodical class for 23 cents, based on its weight. Catalogues, however, must be mailed third class. Because the insert was called a catalogue, the entire magazine had to be mailed third class, for an additional 32 cents a copy, or a total of $450,000 extra postage.

Charlie Lake, production director at Hachette Filipacchi, which publishes *Woman's Day*, says it's critical for the production staff to see inserts before they are bound. Product samples—the CDs used in some computer magazines—may have to be mailed third class. Perfume strips, however, are not considered samples, so they can be included as regular advertising content.

film, or a **composite.** This is the process of choice for small magazines that don't create enough publications for in-house imaging to be cost-effective.

SPOT COLOR. **Spot color** is added to the page for special effect, usually for type or color blocks. Spot colors are standardized and given PMS (Pantone Matching System) numbers. PMS 122 is yellow-gold; PMS 512 is purple. Art directors select PMS colors the way interior designers choose paint—by looking at a swatch book, in this case a PMS book. PMS colors are included on most desktop computer software.

If spot color is used on a page that will be printed by the four-color process, the printer usually tries to create a match color, or match a PMS color by using a combination of process colors, in much the same way a hardware store mixes paints.

Adding spot color to a black-and-white page requires an additional press run and increases printing costs. Printing only in black is considered printing in one color. Printing in black and red is printing in two colors. When a printer gives a bid for a two-color job, that usually means black and one spot color. A three-color job usually means black and two spot colors.

Adding spot color to a full-color page should add very little, if anything, to the printing costs.

Art

Artwork can be simple line drawings or photographs and may be printed in color, black and white, or black with a second color.

LINE ART. Art created with no gray tones is line art. This includes most cartoons, maps, and pen-and-ink drawings. When placed on the page in the correct size, line art is reproduced as part of the page and requires no extra preparation. Line art can be reproduced with any color ink.

CONTINUOUS TONES. Any black-and-white art that includes gray tones is considered a continuous tone. This includes photographs, paintings, and water colors. Continuous tones must be screened for printing, which turns them into a series of dots. Screened black-and-white continuous tones are called **halftones;** they are the one-color equivalents of color separations. Printers never speak of photographs, calling them halftones instead. The screening process to create halftones adds preparation time and, therefore, adds to the cost of the printing job.

The quality of halftones is determined by the fineness of the screen that is used to create them. In most cases, the finer the screen, the better the reproduction, although occasionally a too-fine screen can cause ink smears. Screens traditionally have been measured by lines per inch, with most magazines using at least a 133-line screen. For best reproduction, photographs should be scanned at twice the final screen resolution, which means a photograph to be reproduced with a 150-line screen would be scanned at 300 dots per inch (DPI).

Occasionally, a magazine may reproduce a halftone using the four process colors to give it special definition. To create this effect, the original photograph is screened four times. The casual reader only notices a high-quality photograph. Closer inspection with a magnifying glass reveals the tiny dots of the process colors within the halftone. *Classic Automobile* has done this to add emphasis to photos of antique cars painted in deep black.

DUOTONES. Black-and-white photographs can be printed with additional spot colors to create **duotones**, or halftones that are printed twice, once usually in black, and once in a second color. Duotones retain the same level of gray tones as the original, so that if the original has large expanses of white, so does the duotone. A duotone can also be printed with two runs of black—that is, black is both the first and second color—to add punch to a black-and-white photograph.

DUOTINTS. When spot color is added as a block over the halftone, this creates a **duotint**. Duotints have an even coverage of the second color over the entire halftone. If the original has large expanses of white, the duotone will cover that white with a second color.

SCREENS. Color blocks can be added behind type, creating the same effect duotints create with photographs. When the color is applied full strength, it is called 100 percent color. If it is applied at less than full strength, it is called a screen, referring to the screen through which the printer diffuses the color. Screens are measured by percentages of full color, so that a 50 percent screen has half the coverage of 100 percent color. On a one-color page, with the color usually being black, a screen can add interest with little extra cost. On a multiple-color page, a variety of screens can add almost as much life as full-color art. Duotints can also be screened.

The wise designer plans screens carefully. A vibrant red turns into a timid pink when screened. Hunter green turns pastel lime.

THE PRINTING PROCESS

Everything comes together during the printing process, in which printing presses transfer ink onto paper, creating the final images the reader will see. In their early history, magazines were printed in-house, often by the editor using a slow hand-operated press. Almost all magazines are now printed at printing plants devoted entirely to printing, binding, and mailing the finished product. Magazines are produced either on sheets or continuous rolls of paper using either offset or rotogravure printing presses.

Sheet-Fed

Small magazines—those under 10,000 circulation—are usually produced on sheet-fed presses. These presses take one sheet of paper at a time. These are oversized sheets on which multiple pages are printed. A typical sheet of cover stock measures 20 by 26 inches and a typical sheet of text paper measures 25 by 38 inches, although individual paper producers may offer additional and varied sizes. Sheet-fed presses usually require at least a 50-pound sheet because thinner paper might get jammed in the press.

Web

Magazines above 10,000 circulation can be printed on web presses, which use a continuous roll of paper. Web presses are much faster than sheet-fed presses and can print on thin paper with accuracy. Web paper usually comes in 22.75-inch or 21.5-inch widths.

Offset

The majority of magazines today are printed on offset presses, which work well for small or large runs. The process gets its name from a rubber plate onto which the image is transferred—or offset—from the metal image plate; the paper comes into direct contact with the offset plate. Offset presses may be either sheet-fed or web. Large presses—those that run 16 pages to 32 pages at once—print both sides of the sheet at the same time. The offset process is shown below.

Rotogravure

Magazines with circulations above one million may be printed on rotogravure, or gravure, presses, which move with high speed and precision. Gravure presses use highly fluid ink, which can give better

The offset process uses the principle that ink and water do not mix to print images on paper.

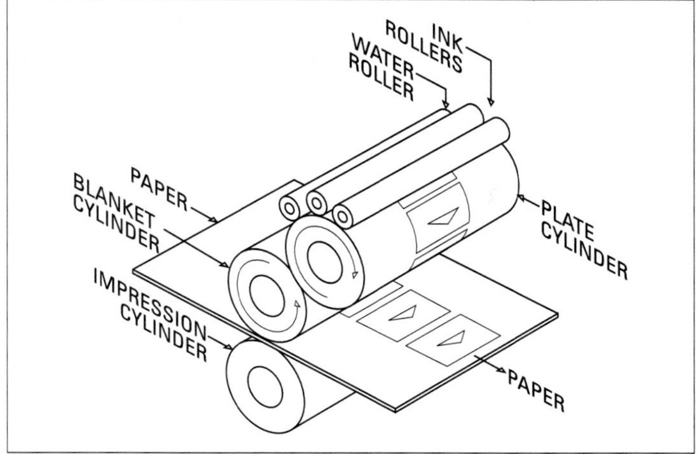

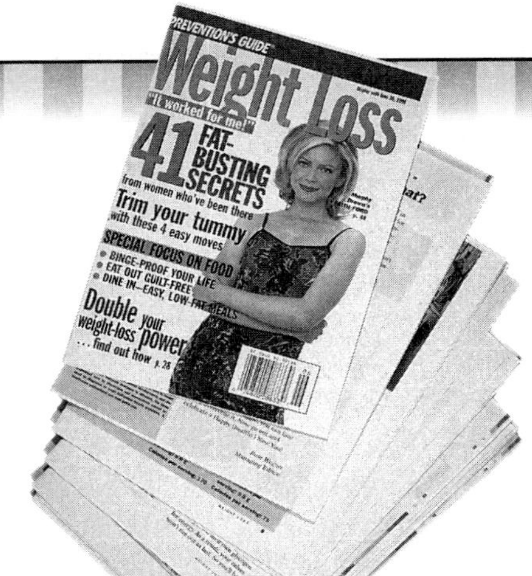

SIGNATURES AND IMPOSITION: SADDLE-STITCH

A saddle-stitched publication places one signature within another, which means that the first and the last page of the magazine are on the same signature. In this example, a 32-page saddle-stitched magazine is produced using two 16-page signatures; each signature has eight pages on one side. Signature 1 contains the outer 16 pages of the magazine, or pages 1 through 8 and 25 through 32. Signature 2 contains the inside 16 pages, or pages 9 through 24. Signature 2 fits inside signature 1. Additional signatures would be placed inside signature 2.

A saddle-stitched magazine contains only one "natural" spread, that is, a spread in which the pages are actually printed side-by-side. In this case, the natural spread falls on pages 16 and 17, at the exact middle of the magazine. *Prevention's Guide—Weight Loss* is a saddle-stitched magazine, as you can see from the way the pages fit within one another inside the magazine. A saddle-stitched magazine can have a self-cover.

5	28	25	8
4	29	32	1

Signature 1, Side A: Saddle Stitch

7	26	27	6
2	31	30	3

Signature 1, Side B: Saddle Stitch

13	20	17	16
12	21	24	9

Signature 2, Side A: Saddle Stitch

15	18	19	14
10	23	22	11

Signature 2, Side B: Saddle Stitch

printing quality than offset presses. This creates a finished product with excellent correlation to the original. Gravure also allows magazines to use less expensive paper without a loss of printing quality. A magazine that used a 40-pound sheet for offset printing can drop to a 34-pound when using gravure. Moreover, because in gravure printing the image plate is mounted on a cylinder that makes direct contact with the paper, the impression is more exact than in offset.

Historically, gravure has been an expensive choice because of high preparation costs and because the image plates must be etched, or recessed. Engraving the plates and creating the proper viscosity of ink is time-consuming because of its precision and complexity. Also, gravure presses print with great speed, so it's essential that they be perfectly aligned before printing starts because stops and starts are costly. With recent changes in technology, however, printers have been reducing preparation costs so lower circulation magazines are increasingly using gravure. Most European magazines, even those with circulations as small as 200,000, are printed on gravure.

Gravure presses are always web presses. They print only one side of a sheet at a time and generally run four-color only.

BINDING

The binding process turns a bunch of loose pages into a publication. Magazines may be stapled in

Signatures and Imposition: Perfect Bound

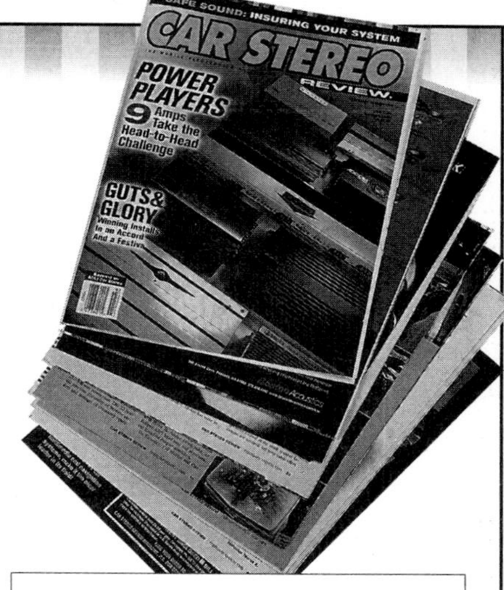

In a perfect-bound publication, signatures are placed on top of one another, which means that the first pages of a magazine are all on the same signature, and the last pages are on a different signature. In this example, a 32-page perfect-bound magazine is produced using two 16-page signatures; each signature has eight pages on one side. Signature 1 contains the first 16 pages of the magazine, or pages 1 through 16. Signature 2 contains the last 16 pages, or pages 17 through 32. Signature 2 is placed after signature 1. Additional signatures would be placed after signature 2.

Each signature of a perfect-bound magazine contains one "natural" spread, that is, a spread in which the pages are actually printed side-by-side. A perfect-bound magazine, then, has as many natural spreads as it has signatures. In this case, the natural spread in signature 1 falls on pages 8 and 9, at the middle of the signature; the natural spread in signature 2 falls on pages 24 and 25. *Car Stereo Review* is a perfect-bound magazine, as you can see from the way the signatures fit atop one another. A perfect-bound magazine also requires a separate cover.

5	12	9	8
4	13	16	1

Signature 1, Side A: Perfect Bound

7	10	11	6
2	15	14	3

Signature 1, Side B: Perfect Bound

21	28	25	24
20	29	32	17

Signature 2, Side A: Perfect Bound

23	26	27	22
18	31	30	19

Signature 2, Side B: Perfect Bound

the middle or bound like a book. The type of binding affects the way pages are organized within the magazine.

Saddle-Stitch

Magazines that are saddle-stitched are stapled in the middle. All pages are placed within one another. Saddle-stitched magazines can have self-covers, which are covers that are made from the same paper stock as the rest of the magazine. *Playboy* was saddle-stitched for years to allow the reader to easily pull out the centerfold. The magazine is now perfect-bound, with the centerfold printed as a **gatefold,** or a fold-out sheet.

Perfect

Perfect-bound magazines have a booklike binding; they require separate covers. Pages are stacked on top of one another, the edge is glued, and a cover attached. Cover lines, volume, and issue numbers are often printed on the spine. Magazines should be at least 1/8-inch thick to use perfect binding to allow enough surface area for the glue to work.

Perfect binding makes it easier to add inserts because they can simply be placed between two stacks of pages. However, perfect binding is usually more expensive than saddle-stitch, especially for small magazines.

RESEARCH IN BRIEF

When Desktop Publishing Was New

Imagine making rule lines by pressing printed tape evenly and precisely onto the page. Or creating headline type by rubbing one letter at a time onto a layout sheet. Or making type wraps by carefully measuring the number of characters to appear in each line and sending those calculations to a typesetter—a person who spent all day at a huge typesetting machine.

That was the mid-to-late 1980s. By the early 1990s, the picture had changed and graphic designers no longer had to learn drafting skills; instead, they had to learn to use the computer. The movement from hand tools to computer tools was swift and complete. Little is left of those pre-computer artifacts. What was commonplace at the beginning of the 1980s was almost obsolete a decade later. Art directors who have seen it both ways are not so sure of the benefits of computerized design.

In the midst of the change from hand to computer—1991—Patsy Guenzel Watkins of the University of Arkansas studied the impact of computers on graphic design,[1] surveying art directors at more than 100 consumer, trade, and organization magazines.[2]

The art directors said they had moved to the new technology to save money and time and to gain more control over the finished product. Interestingly, some said it was difficult to assess the amount of time saved because their jobs had changed with the new technology, and they were now responsible for other tasks. Many said a major impact of desktop publishing was an increased workload for designers.

The position of typesetter had been virtually eliminated by 1991, Watkins said. In addition, computers had blurred the distinctions between design and production jobs. It was less clear where the designer left off and the production manager took over. More and more designers were doing tasks that had been the domain of the production staff.

The art directors in the survey agreed that desktop technology had speeded up the production process and allowed them to experiment with different designs and ideas. "In fact, there is some sense that design skills are sharpened in this rapid evaluation of design alternatives," Watkins noted.

For all its heralded power, however, the computer has significant limitations, the art directors said. Losing the typesetter meant losing the expertise of an individual whose life revolved around type. Also, some designs might be easier to create by hand. Lisa Bowser, art director of *Kansas City Live,* showed Watkins one page that took nearly 10 hours of computer time to produce; it was a complex five-color design with five overlays. That page, Bowser said, could have been done much faster by hand.

[1] Patsy Guenzel Watkins, "Assessing the Impact of Microcomputers on Magazine Design" (paper presented at the Annual Meeting of the Association for Education in Journalism and Mass Communication, Boston, MA, August 1991).

[2] Watkins grouped the magazines according to circulation: Group 1: circulation of half a million or more; Group 2: 100,000 to 499,000; Group 3: 50,000 to 99,999; Group 4: 20,000 to 49,999; and Group 5: circulations below 20,000.

Because of its perfect binding, *National Geographic* stacks easily on a shelf, and specific issues are easy to spot by reading the spine. Mike Mettler, editor-in-chief of *Car Stereo Review,* began printing a message on the spine to his readers in 1997, one letter at a time: T-H-E M-O-B-I-L-E-E-L-E-C-T-R-O-N-I-C-S-A-U-T-H-O-R-I-T-Y, which is the magazine's motto. *Guitar Player* began spelling its name, also one letter at a time, on the spine in 1991. Conveniently, the name of the monthly magazine is 12 characters long.

Signatures

Magazine pages are printed in multiples of four, with as many as 128 pages printed at one time. The sheets of multiple pages are called **signatures** or forms. Sheet-fed presses typically print signatures of 4, 8, 16, or 32 pages; some new sheet-fed presses can run 48 pages. Web presses typically print signatures of 28, 56, 96, or 128 pages.

Both sides of the sheet are counted in the signature: A 16-page signature has eight pages on each side. An 8-page signature has four pages on each side.

A typical 224-page *Better Homes and Gardens* is printed at R. R. Donnelley Printing on four 56-page signatures using the gravure method. An additional gravure run would require at least 28 additional pages for efficiency. The production staff increases its options by printing part of the magazine on offset presses. That means print runs of eight pages become a possibility. In fact, the regional editions of the magazine are printed offset on a regular basis. Those editions add significantly to the magazine: The May 1998 issue had some regional editions with 282 pages

SIGNATURES AND COLOR PLACEMENT

If a 64-page magazine can afford only eight pages of color, it has several options. It can:

- Use four 16-page signatures, with one side of one signature printed in color.
- Use three 16-page and two eight-page signatures, with one entire eight-page signature in color.
- Use three 16-page and two eight-page signatures, with one side of each of the eight-page signatures in color.
- Use three 16-page signatures, one eight-page signature, and two four-page signatures, with color on both sides of the four-page signatures.

Smaller signatures allow the color to be placed throughout the magazine; however, they take more binding time, which will cost extra.

Binding affects the placement of color. Using the same example of the 64-page magazine with eight color pages:

- If the magazine is saddle-stitched, it will have half of the pages of color at the front of the book, half at the back of the book. Every color page in the front will have a corresponding color page in the back. If the color is all in the middle signature, the magazine cannot have a color table of contents.
- If the magazine is perfect-bound, the color signature or signatures can be placed anywhere in the stack. If the color is all in one signature, it will be blocked together sequentially.

and others with 372 pages.

Penthouse, another Donnelley product, also uses both gravure and offset. A typical gravure print run of the magazine is two 56-page signatures, creating a basic 112-page book. Additional ad pages are printed by offset.

Magazines that use limited color should use that color efficiently by placing it on the same signature. Most national magazines print the entire publication in full-color; smaller magazines don't have that luxury. Signatures are folded, then stacked in preparation for binding. The type of binding has significant implications for placement of color.

Imposition

The way pages are printed on the signature is called the **imposition.** Pages are not printed sequentially; pages that follow one another in the magazine may not even be on the same signature. Imposition is determined by the binding method as well as the number of pages, and it affects the placement of color. For example, a saddle-stitched magazine will have the pages from the front of the book on the same signature as the pages from the back of the book, with the first and last pages printed next to one another. Even-numbered pages are always on the left, odd-numbered on the right. Page 1, then, is a right-hand page. Look again at the illustrations on pages 260 and 261: the first demonstrates the imposition for a 32-page saddle-stitched magazine printed in two 16-page signatures. The second demonstrates the imposition for the same magazine if it is perfect bound.

IMAGE TRANSFERS

Before printing, images on the camera-ready pages are transferred to film, then to printing plates or cylinders. The production staff checks a variety of proofs for printing accuracy and color clarity.

Camera-Ready Pages

These pages, almost always created on the computer, contain all finished art and type; they look essentially like the finished product, except for some final touches such as color and, occasionally, art.

Film

Camera-ready pages are usually turned into film, or negatives, in preparation for printing. In fact, the source of the term "camera-ready" is the fact that these pages are ready to be photographed, or made into film. Four-color pages require four sheets of film, or one for each color; duotones require two sheets of film. Spot color pages require as many sheets of film as the number of

Request for Printing Estimate

Printing costs can vary significantly depending upon paper, color, binding, art, special effects, and the printing company. The form below offers a format to use when asking a printer for a cost estimate. Large publishing houses have such a form standardized; correspondence with the printer is handled by the production staff. On smaller magazines, the editor or art director deals directly with the printer. Multiple requests for bids are usually submitted, with the printer offering the best quality at the most reasonable price being the one chosen for the job. Often, placement and use of color in the magazine changes, requiring another estimate.

Company Name: ______________________

Address: ______________________

City, State, Zip: ______________________

Phone/Fax: (___) __________ (___) __________

Attn.: ______________________

Description:

Trim Size:

Quantity:

Number of Pages:

Color:

Cover:
____ pages process color
____ pages PMS
Number of PMS colors: ____
____ pages one color

Interior:
____ pages process color
____ pages PMS
Number of PMS colors: ____
____ pages one color

Number of separations:

____ (9×12); ____ (8×10); ____ (5×7); ____ (3×4); ____ (2×3)

Number of halftones:

Paper type:

Binding:
____ Perfect
____ Saddle-stitch

Proofs needed:
____ Blueline
____ Contract proof
____ Iris
____ Match print

____ **Camera-ready art provided**
____ **Disk provided**
____ **Material submitted electronically**

Deliver to:

colors used; a two-color page requires two sheets, a three-color requires three, and so on.

Plates or Cylinders

The final step before printing is the creation of printing **plates** for the offset process or **cylinders** for the gravure process. These metal plates or cylinders contain all the images to be printed. One plate or cylinder is required for every color used.

In the offset process, the metal plates have been chemically treated to repel water and accept ink. During printing, the plates are lubricated with water, then inked. All nonprinting surfaces soak up the water, and all printing surfaces accept the ink. The inked image is offset onto the rubber plate, paper is fed through the press, and the ink is then transferred to the page.

A gravure cylinder has tiny wells etched into its surface. The depth of each well determines the amount of ink to be used in a particular spot. The flow of the fluid ink is controlled by razor-thin wipers to ensure precise printing.

In most cases in the past, plates or cylinders have been processed from film. Increasingly, offset printers are using computer-to-plate (CTP) technology, which eliminates the film stage. Gravure printers have been eliminating film for several years, using software such as Donnelley's patented NKI, or New Klisch Interface. In both CTP and NKI, camera-ready pages are digitally transferred directly on the plate or cylinder. In 1993, *Family Circle* became the first magazine to create an image on a gravure cylinder without film. A year later, in 1994, *Scientific American* was the first to do so with web offset.

Richard Sasso, associate publisher and vice president of production for *Scientific American*, says CTP can improve quality and reduce costs. One hitch with the process, though, is that advertising agencies have been slow to make the transition and continue to provide advertising film rather than digital data.[1]

STANDARD DEVIATIONS

What's the typical size of an American magazine? Conventional wisdom holds that the average is 8.5 × 11 inches. As paper costs rise, however, many magazines have been reducing their page sizes, especially those printed on web presses.

A reduction in page size can be a huge budget saver. *Woman's Day* saved $500,000 a year by trimming 1/8 inch off its width. In the 1970s, the magazine measured the standard 8.5 × 11 inches. Through the years it has dwindled to 7.87 × 10.5 inches.

A sampling of page sizes of consumer, trade, and organization titles that are variations of the 8.5-×-11-inch norm:

Adobe	8.25 × 11.875 inches
@issue (Potlatch Papers)	8.50 × 12 inches
Folio:	8.50 × 10.875 inches
Hemispheres (United Airlines)	8.00 × 10.75 inches
Penthouse	8.00 × 10.875 inches
Time	8.00 × 10.5 inches
Town & Country	9.00 × 11 inches
Video	8.00 × 10.5 inches

Proofs

The production staff may ask for page proofs and color proofs, which come in a wide variety of forms:

- ***Blueline*** This shows all type and art, and is produced on light-sensitive paper in blue ink. It offers an accurate proof of the position and registration of color as well of the accuracy of binding. For magazines that use only black-and-white or spot colors, a blueline is the only proof they need. A blueline is created from the final film, which means it comes after a great many highly paid technicians have spent a great many hours on the page. Most changes at this stage are expensive.
- ***Contract proof*** This shows the accuracy of color reproduction; it gets its name from the fact that it is actually a contract between the magazine and the printer that the final printed color will match the contract proof. Magazines that are mostly in color will receive an integral or composite proof—a proof of the entire piece. Magazines with limited color will get scatter or random proofs, which show only the sections to be reproduced in color.
- ***Iris print*** This is usually used early in the proofing process, primarily for placement and design issues, not as final proof of the accuracy of color.
- ***Match print*** A true representation of color; usually given for art only, not entire pages. Match prints are usually contract prints.

THE QUALITY PRODUCT

When one of the authors of this book edited a small Catholic magazine, she avoided looking at the printed product until somebody else on staff checked it over and gave it an A-OK. She worked with a tiny staff and often served as editor, designer, and production manager. By the time the magazine was printed, she had seen it in so many forms she no longer could read it clearly. No matter how carefully she had edited the magazine, however, she was terrified she might have missed something outrageous, such as a

THE UPC BAR: CHECK IT OUT

All magazines sold through retail store checkout counters must have a Universal Product Council (UPC) bar. In 1975, *Family Circle* became the first magazine to use the UPC bar. At that time, UPC bars revealed only the title of the publication. Other information such as issue date and cost would come later. Now the UPC code is so universal that readers barely notice it when they scan a magazine's cover lines.

Production managers and art directors, however, pay close attention to this addition to the cover. For the store's register to read the bar correctly, it must be printed following rigid specifications, which include:

- ▶ Bars must always be 100 percent black, and black only.
- ▶ The maximum tint behind the bars must be:
    - Yellow alone, up to 100 percent
    - Magenta alone, up to 100 percent
    - Cyan alone up to 10 percent
    - Black alone up to 10 percent
    - Combined values of: yellow and magenta, up to 160 percent together; cyan and black, up to 10 percent together
- ▶ The preferred location is the left side of the front cover, although right is acceptable.
- ▶ Actual issue number to be on:
    - Top for vertical bars
    - Left for horizontal bars
- ▶ Adequate quiet zone around bars (specified for vertical bar position):
    - Left and right: minimum space (other than background tint) to be 5/64 inch.
- ▶ No space is necessary between top and bottom of bars and surrounding image.

Each issue of a magazine has a different code, which allows magazine staffs, as well as retail outlets, to track sales of individual issues. When magazines run split covers—one cover for a specific region, for example, and another cover for a different region—tracking gets complicated. The magazine must use the same code for both covers, which means circulation managers can only tell which cover sells best by placing specific covers in specific stores and tracking sales through those stores. When the same covers are sold in the same stores, it is difficult to precisely measure effects of different images.

headline that used "bizarre" instead of "bazaar" or "pubic" instead of "public."

She clearly remembers the newly printed magazines arriving at the office one day when an archbishop was visiting. She watched as he opened the box, pulled the magazine out, smelled it, felt the paper, looked at the cover, turned the magazine over to see the back, then opened it up and began reading, all the while leaning up against the office refrigerator. He was so engrossed he didn't even notice her watching him. She left him to his reading, satisfied that she had done her job.

The archbishop had no idea how many mistakes the editor had caught before the magazine's final printing. The delicate pencil drawing on page 14 he was admiring had to be screened four times before it reproduced well. At one point, the printer had cropped one photograph wrong, cutting out what she wanted enlarged and enlarging what she wanted highlighted. Instead of a bucolic scene of cows, farm, silo, and barn, the page had only the picture of the top of a silo and a lot of sky. She caught the mistake on the blueline.

What's more, the archbishop did not care about the editor's production problems. He wanted his magazine to be of top quality and he wanted it on time. How it got that way was the editor's problem, not his.

Production is a process built on technology. Whoever is in charge of a magazine's production must know far more about printing technology than the great majority of people who roam the earth. As technology changes, the magazine staff has to change with it. And computer-generated change happens regularly and often.

But no matter how complicated the technology becomes, the bottom line on a magazine remains the readers. Jan White, award-winning designer for national magazines such as *Time*, says the reader is oblivious to the intricacies of printing. To the reader, an iris is something that grows in the garden and a hickey has nothing to do with paper. White observes:

> ***Let's remember the fundamental truth: It is not the technology that matters, but the message. No matter how the message is produced or***

transmitted, it is its content that makes it useful and worthy. Recipients of communication couldn't care less about how or where the piece was produced. All they want is information, and they want it fast, to the point, easy to understand, easy to absorb, easy to use. To them, its technological provenance is immaterial.[2]

FOR ADDITIONAL READING

Beach, Mark, Steve Shepro, and Ken Russon. *Getting it Printed.* Portland, OR: Coast to Coast Books, 1993.

Bivens, Thomas, and William E. Ryan. *How to Produce Creative Publications: Traditional Techniques and Computer Applications.* Lincolnwood, IL: NTC Business Books, 1990.

Click, J. William and Russell N. Baird. *Magazine Editing and Production,* 6th ed. Madison, WI: Brown & Benchmark, 1994.

Georgia-Pacific Papers Stock Item Pocket Guide. Atlanta, GA: Georgia Pacific Papers, July 1998.

White, Jan V. *Graphic Design for the Electronic Age.* New York: Watson-Guptill Publications, 1988.

Words on Paper. Stamford, CT: Champion International Corporation, 1993.

ENDNOTES

[1] Richard Sasso, "Computer-to-Plate Printing," *The Art of Production* (Summer 1997): 4.

[2] Jan V. White, *Graphic Design for the Electronic Age* (New York: Watson-Guptill Publications, 1988): ix.

CHAPTER 11

Magazine Legalities

Understanding the Law

In 1948, salesman Jack Breard was arrested in Alexandria, Louisiana, for selling magazines door to door. He was later convicted under a law that prohibited all such soliciting in the town. In his defense, though, Breard asserted that the law violated his constitutional rights because as a magazine subscription salesman he was protected by the First Amendment's guarantee of a free press. The case went all the way to the United States Supreme Court, where the justices ruled against Breard's interpretation of the First Amendment. The court declared that when a general law such as this one is applied to magazines it does not violate the First Amendment because the effect of the law falls evenly on the magazine subscription seller and the vacuum cleaner seller alike. "It would be, it seems to us, a misuse of the great guarantees of free speech and free press to use those guarantees to force a community to admit solicitors of publications to the home premises of the residents," wrote the Supreme Court.[1] *The Breard case stands for a fundamental principle that shapes the legal environment in which magazines operate: The First Amendment's protections for magazines do not exempt magazines from obeying laws that are generally applicable to all citizens. The Constitution's free press guarantee will not allow magazine publishers to flout labor laws in dealing with employees, ignore contract laws in working with advertisers or printers, or skirt postal regulations in mailing their magazines to subscribers.*

By the same token, the Supreme Court ruled in 1987 that generally applicable tax law must be enforced fairly against magazines, or else the law violates the First Amendment. In that case, the monthly *Arkansas Times* challenged a law that required general interest magazines to pay a state sales tax while religious, sports, professional, and trade magazines paid no sales tax at all.

The Supreme Court sided with the magazine, ruling that the tax scheme unfairly singled out some publications while letting others off. The Court said the First Amendment did not prevent states from taxing magazines, but it did require that taxes on magazines be applied in a neutral way, without considering their editorial content. The Court said the First Amendment prohibits government from burdening one kind of editorial viewpoint or content with a tax while favoring another with a tax break.[2]

Editors don't need to be lawyers. Many of the legal issues involved in publishing a magazine can be handled adequately and safely by editors because many of the legal decisions editors make are also commonsense editorial decisions. At the same time, though, publishers and editors need to understand enough about the specifics of the law to know when they need to call in their lawyers for help. Those decisions—whether to go it alone because good editing is also good law, or to seek outside help because an editor knows she is in risky territory but unsure how risky it is or how far into it she has crept—require editors to pick up a working knowledge of the basics of the law of publishing. These basics include an understanding of laws and key decisions related to prior restraint, libel, invasions of privacy, intentional infliction of emotional distress, third-party liability, copyright, access to information, and obscenity.

PRIOR RESTRAINT

A basic principle under the First Amendment is the general ban on prior restraints. **Prior restraint** means a government official—a police chief, a judge, or any other censor—reviews stories and articles before publication and has wide discretion in deciding what should not be published. Thus the origin of the phrase: Prior restraint is a restraint prior to publication.

The injustice of such a system seems obvious to journalists, writers, and editors. Prior restraint

The H-bomb secret

To know how
is to ask why

Howard Morland

(Copyright © 1979, Howard Morland.)

What you are about to learn is a secret — a secret that the United States and four other nations, the makers of hydrogen weapons, have gone to extraordinary lengths to protect.

The secret is in the coupling mechanism that enables an ordinary fission bomb — the kind that destroyed Hiroshima — to trigger the far deadlier energy of hydrogen fusion.

The physical pressure and heat generated by x- and gamma radiation, moving outward from the trigger at the speed of light, bounces against the weapon's inner wall and is reflected with enormous force into the sides of a carrot-shaped "pencil" which contains the fusion fuel.

That, within the limits of a single sentence, is the essence of a concept that initially eluded the physicists of the United States, the Soviet Union, Britain, France, and China; that they discovered independently and kept tenaciously to themselves, and that may not yet have occurred to the weapon makers of a dozen other nations bent on building the hydrogen bomb.

I discovered it simply by reading and asking questions, without the benefit of security clearance or access to classified materials. There may be some missing pieces here and there — some parts of the puzzle that eluded my search — but the general accuracy of my descriptions and diagrams has been confirmed by people in a position to know.

Why am I telling you?

It's not because I want to help you build an H-bomb. Have no fear; that would be far beyond your capability — unless you have the resources of at least a medium-sized government.

Nor is it because I want India, or Israel, or Pakistan, or South Africa to get the H-bomb sooner than they otherwise would, even though it is conceivable that the information will be helpful to them.

It isn't so much because the details themselves are helpful to an understanding of the grave public policy questions presented by hydrogen weaponry — though they may well be essential.

'A complete one-megaton bomb ...would fit under your bed'

I am telling the secret to make a basic point as forcefully as I can: Secrecy itself, especially the power of a few designated "experts" to declare some topics off limits, contributes to a political climate in which the nuclear establishment can conduct business as usual, protecting and perpetuating the production of these horror weapons.

The pernicious effects of hydrogen bomb secrecy are well illustrated by an incident that occurred in Washington five months ago.

On October 24, 1978, Representative Ronald V. Dellums, a member of the House Armed Services Committee, sent a letter asking the Department of Energy to explain publicly why it expects a shortage of plutonium in its nuclear weapons production program.

Would the neutron bomb, which was then going into production, require more plutonium than the standard tactical nuclear weapons it is designed to replace?

Had the shortage been induced by the plutonium requirements of a new generation of multiple-warhead ballistic missiles — the Navy's Trident (successor to Poseidon), and the Air Force's M-X (successor to Minuteman III)?

What were the weapons specifications that had led the Department of Energy to contemplate a massive industrial retooling: the rebuilding of its old plutonium production plant at Hanford, Washington, and the restarting of a standby reactor at Savannah River, South Carolina?

"Each of these options will involve both financial costs and environmental costs," the letter stated. "The American people need to know the reasons for the anticipated plutonium shortage in order to have informed opinions on the cost-benefit aspects of the plutonium shortage issue."

As chairman of the Subcommittee on Fiscal and Government Affairs, and as a Congressman whose California district includes one of the nation's two nuclear weapons laboratories, Dellums had more than a casual interest in such questions.

Three weeks later he received the Energy Department's reply:

"...It is not possible to respond to most of the questions in an unclassified manner. The enclosure to your referenced letter contains 'secret/restricted data' and should be so classified." The enclosure was the list of questions. *It* is now a secret.

Had Dellums invoked the security privileges available to Representatives and Senators with a "need to know," he could readily have obtained the answers. But he did not choose to do so. The response he received demonstrates the lengths to which the keepers of the secrets are prepared to go in dealing with the public: They do not simply withhold the answers; *they can also confiscate the questions.*

Such tactics have served since the dawn of the atomic age to shield nuclear weapons policies from public scrutiny and debate, giving an advantage to those who formulate the policies and have a stake in their perpetuation. And yet the advantage is one gained mostly by default. It results as much from the self-imposed restraint of those who are not members of the classification elite as from the weapon makers' own complicated security system. The importance of looking behind "secret/restricted" curtains, the relative ease of doing so, and the value to be gained from the exercise are lessons we have still to learn.

The self-serving purposes of official secrecy — not the least of which is its paralyzing effect on the spirit of public inquiry — can best be understood by examining the most momentous official secret of them all: the mechanism of a hydrogen bomb.

Of all the world's nuclear weapons secrets, none has eluded publication more successfully than the secret of the H-bomb. In the twenty-five years since its first successful field test in the South Pacific, no description of how it works has ever been made public.

The diagrams that accompany this article are a close approximation of that process. They show the progression of events that occur during the detonation of a hydrogen weapon. The energy of an exploding fission bomb, the circular object near the top of each drawing, is transferred by means of radiation pressure to the hydrogen part of the weapon. Radiation pressure — a term never mentioned in the open literature — is

Somebody talked

"Does anyone know the secret of the H-bomb?"

Howard Morland didn't really expect an answer when he threw the question out half-seriously one night a year ago in a dormitory at the University of Alabama at Tuscaloosa.

About thirty students had gathered to see his traveling slide show on atomic power and the arms race; in the discussion that followed he was explaining that his next project would be to find out more about nuclear weapons.

"Sure, I know," said a young man in the back of the room. "The secret is in the radiation reflectors."

The student went on to explain that he knew some of the people who worked at the big Union Carbide plant in Oak Ridge, Tennessee, where most of the components for hydrogen weapons are built, and that they had told him the reflection of x- and gamma rays was the key to how the weapons work.

The explanation made little impression on Morland at the time, and he didn't even bother to get the student's name. But later on it helped him crack what the weaponmakers consider to be one of their best-kept secrets.

Such chance remarks were part of the mosaic of information from which Morland, a thirty-six-year-old peace activist, constructed the report on these pages — a report confirmed by people who are knowledgeable about the hydrogen weapon program but are not at liberty to discuss it openly. He undertook the project on assignment from *The Progressive* to demonstrate that official secrecy in this area serves no useful public purpose.

A 1965 graduate of Emory University in Atlanta, Morland has had only a smattering of science education: two courses in physics, two in chemistry, and one in quantum mechanics. As a journalist, it was only this winter that he published his first article ("Tritium: the New Genie," in the February issue of *The Progressive*). What knowledge he has of military affairs comes largely from the two years he spent piloting Air Force cargo planes between California and Vietnam.

But Morland put his training and experience to use in an intensive six-month self-education project in which he read virtually every scrap of information available on the subject, visited every production plant to which he could gain access, and interviewed scores of scientists and engineers in and out of the weapons program.

Every technical fact was double-checked; none was printed unless it could be authenticated by at least two knowledgeable sources. His diagrams and descriptions received widespread review in the scientific community prior to publication. Copies also were submitted to the Department of Energy for verification as to technical accuracy. The Department declined to do this.

Morland's research was supported by donations to *The Progressive*'s arms race investigation fund. He also received research assistance from a colleague, Louise Franklin Ramirez.

14 / NOVEMBER 1979

THE PROGRESSIVE / 15

NOVEMBER 1979: Although the federal government got a prior restraint order to stop *The Progressive* from publishing its article about the technology of hydrogen bombs, the piece eventually ran because other magazines printed similar articles about the H-bomb; the injunction against *The Progressive* became moot and the government dropped the case.

keeps an idea, a fact, or an opinion from ever getting into the hands of readers. It flies in the face of the First Amendment ideal of a public who are free to inform themselves and then to make decisions based on the information they have. Because the free flow of information was always seen as important to civic, political, and commercial life in the United States, American law has always favored punishment after publication for articles that were libelous, invasive of someone's privacy, or in some other way deserving of liability.

In 1963, the U.S. Supreme Court said a prior restraint challenged in court faces "a heavy presumption against its constitutional validity."[3] So the threat of prior restraint is rare, but it is not unheard of these days. Examples from two areas where magazine editors have run into problems in recent years—national security and the administration of justice—help illustrate the dangers of prior restraints and the general rule that gag orders against magazines are not usually upheld by appellate courts.

National Security

For national security reasons, *The Progressive,* a leftist political magazine, was ordered in 1979 not to publish an article about the technology of hydrogen bombs. Editors had titled the piece "The H-Bomb Secret: How We Got It; Why We're Telling It" and said they were publishing the article to spark a national debate about nuclear arms policy.

Before publication, though, the editors sent a copy to the federal Department of Energy for help in fact checking the technical information about atomic physics. Without returning the article, Energy Department officials contacted the Justice Department, which sought an injunction from the federal court in Madison, Wisconsin, where the magazine was published, claiming that the article contained information classified as secret under the Atomic Energy Act.

The Progressive's editors argued in court that the article was based on information taken from public records that the writer, a freelancer, had compiled after many of hours of research in libraries and at national research laboratories. But the judge, applying a test taken from a 1971

GOVERNMENT CENSORSHIP AND *THE MASSES*

The 1917 Espionage Act, which allowed the United States postmaster general to declare unmailable any publications that interfered with the war effort, led to the death of *The Masses*, a socialist magazine produced by an editorial cooperative. The Espionage Act primarily was directed at the left-wing socialist press, which tended to advocate pacifism or noninterventionalism during World War I. Administered by the Post Office Department, the act made it a crime to oppose the government and the war; any opposition to conscription or censorship could be construed as obstruction:

> *Whoever, when the United States is at war, shall willfully make or convey false reports or false statements with intent to interfere with the operation or success of the military or naval forces of the United States or to promote the success of its enemies and whoever, when the United States is at war, shall willfully cause or attempt to cause insubordination, disloyalty, mutiny, or refusal of duty, in the military or naval forces of the United States, or shall willfully obstruct recruiting or enlistment service of the United States, to the injury of the service or of the United States shall be punished by a fine of not more than $10,000 or imprisonment for not more than 20 years, or both.*[1]

The Espionage Act essentially voided the First Amendment and the right to disagree with the U.S. government.

The Masses was radical and irreverent for its time. It was critical of war, racism, sexism, and religion, and it supported free love, birth control, and divorce. Understandably, there were no advertisers. Many libraries refused to subscribe to it or even give it shelf space. Contributors to *The Masses* included John Reed, Amy Lowell,

Supreme Court case (in which the high court had denied the government's request for a prior restraint[4]) ruled that the publication must be blocked because it presented "grave, direct, immediate and irreparable harm to the United States."[5] The judge conceded that the article was not a "how-to" piece about hydrogen bombs, but he said the article's synthesis of all the available information could make it easier for a medium-sized country or a terrorist organization to develop nuclear weapons.

The case was never decided by an appellate court because in the months after the judge issued the injunction, other writers, incensed by what they considered the heavy-handedness of this prior restraint, prepared similar articles. Newspapers and magazines eager to flout the court's injunction published them. Soon the injunction against *The Progressive* was moot, and the government dropped the case. *The Progressive* ran "The H-Bomb Secret" in its November 1979 issue.

Administration of Justice

Another case in 1996 illustrates the prior restraint risk when a magazine disrupts the smooth administration of justice. Through a combination of good reporting and good luck, *Business Week* acquired documents from a high-profile civil fraud case between two large corporations in 1995. Unknown to *Business Week*, though, the documents, which were fairly standard filings in a court case, had been sealed by order of a judge to protect the interests of the two corporations. In other words, the papers were not available for public viewing at the courthouse.

After obtaining the papers, *Business Week* called each side in the lawsuit for comments, but the lawyers for the corporations promptly ran to a judge seeking a restraining order. Just three hours before *Business Week*'s weekly deadline, the district judge faxed a restraining order to the magazine's offices forbidding publication of the article. On appeal, the federal circuit court quickly struck down the prior restraint order but also took advantage of the case to lay out some important principles about prior restraints.[6]

First, the court emphasized that judges must not drag their feet when considering prior restraints. With a magazine blocked from publishing an article by court order, there is no time for a deliberate judicial process of holding hearings and gathering evidence. The court said all

Sherwood Anderson, Bertrand Russell, Max Eastman, Walter Lippmann, Carl Sandburg, Pablo Picasso, and Upton Sinclair. Although editors and writers worked without pay, contributors had full control over their work, a luxury they didn't enjoy at other magazines.

When the August 1917 issue was barred from the mails by the postmaster general, the magazine's editors found few newsstands or book stores willing to carry *The Masses.* They feared that they, too, could be shut down and found guilty of trading with the enemy.

The Masses stopped publishing in December 1917 and five editors went on trial for personally violating the Espionage Act. They were charged with conspiracy against the government and with unlawfully and willfully obstructing the recruitment and enlistment of soldiers in the armed forces. Articles in *The Masses* supporting conscientious objectors, editorials calling on President Woodrow Wilson to repeal conscription, and antiwar cartoons (one showed a skeleton measuring a military recruit) were the government's exhibits at the trial.

Fortunately, content was decided collectively at monthly meetings where editors and visitors voted on what would be in the next month's issue. This haphazard editorial approach made it difficult for the government to prove a conspiracy to disrupt the war effort existed on the part of the magazine. The trial resulted in two hung juries before the case was dropped.

Was the outcome a victory for free speech? It was a small start. Although the constitutionality of the Espionage Act was upheld in 1919, Justice Oliver Wendell Holmes did articulate the "clear and present danger" standard for determining when the government could limit free speech. That led to greater protection of civil liberties for all.

Sadly, mainstream—or capitalist—magazines failed to rally behind the challenge to *The Masses.* They simply didn't understand that First Amendment rights cannot be applied selectively; when one magazine is suppressed, all others are threatened.

[1] Kirk Heinze, "Left-wing Tragedy or Comic Opera?: A New Look at the Demise of *The Masses*" (paper presented at the annual meeting of the Association for Education in Journalism and Mass Communication, Boston, MA, August 1980).

other matters should be cleared from the docket so the prior restraint can be considered on an emergency basis.

Second, the appeals court said the judge should not have issued the restraining order without giving the magazine's lawyers a chance to argue their position. The order against *Business Week* was issued after the judge had talked only to the corporations' lawyers.

And finally, the appeals court emphasized the difference between a restraining order in a run-of-the-mill court case and one issued against a magazine forbidding publication. Ordinary restraining orders are issued by courts when there is a threat of irreparable injury that the court wants to prevent. But in the case of a prior restraint, the risk arising from the publication must be even more grave than a threat of irreparable injury. The court said: "Publication must threaten an interest more fundamental than the First Amendment itself."[7]

The *Business Week* case reiterates the "heavy presumption" courts have against prior restraints and stands for the proposition that while prior restraints issued by judges against magazines are rare, prior restraints upheld by appellate courts are rarer still. The *Business Week* example also shows the hurdles built into the law to keep prior restraints rare.

LIBEL

Without a doubt, the biggest legal problem facing magazines today is libel. Attorneys' fees can be astronomical because cases can last more than a decade, and the threat of losing a multimillion-dollar judgment creates a "chilling effect" on the way a magazine exercises its right to publish. It is so serious that some editors have decided that it is easier and cheaper not to run controversial pieces than to raise the specter of a libel suit: It's good business to avoid the risk—even though it might be bad journalism.

Libel means publishing a false statement about a person that hurts the person's reputation in the community. Of course, responsible writers and editors never intend to run a false statement in their magazines, but potential libels crop up in every issue. Every article, photo and cutline, title, and illustration that runs in a magazine should be evaluated for libel risks, no matter how routine it is.

Libel is (1) a false statement that injures the reputation (2) of a specific person (3) when it is published. All three elements of that definition must be found in an article or photo before there is libel.

Damage to Reputation

A story damages a reputation if the false statement in it exposes the person to hatred, ridicule, or shame among the members of the community. That can happen in any number of ways, such as false reports that a person was charged with a crime, carries the AIDS virus, is an alcoholic, or filed for bankruptcy. False accusations that a person is insane or mentally ill have traditionally been found by courts to be libelous. Former senator and presidential candidate Barry Goldwater sued *Fact* magazine over an article during the 1964 presidential campaign that said Goldwater was paranoid, anti-Semitic, sadistic, and uncertain about his sexuality. The jury found the statements, which Goldwater proved false, to be damaging to his reputation.[8]

Similarly, a false statement that a person is sexually promiscuous is libelous, as an action against *TV Guide* illustrates. When author and TV personality Pat Montandon agreed to appear on a talk show, the talk show's producers submitted a blurb to *TV Guide:* "From Party Girl to Call Girl? How far can the 'party-girl' go until she becomes a 'call-girl' is discussed with TV personality Pat Montandon, author, 'How to Be a Party Girl' and a masked anonymous prostitute!" *TV Guide* edited the item in its September 14, 1968, issue in such a way as to make Montandon sound like the only guest on a program about call girls: "From Party Girl to Call Girl. Scheduled guest: TV Personality Pat Montandon and author of 'How to Be a Party Girl.'" Testimony at the trial showed that average readers would conclude that Montandon had gone from being someone who liked to have fun at parties to being a prostitute. The jury awarded her more than $250,000, and an appeals court upheld the verdict.[9]

But not every statement that makes someone angry is libelous, even though the plaintiff may feel it impugns his reputation in his profession. When *Newsweek* criticized Professor Stanley Kaplan's criminal law class at Stanford Law School as "the easiest five credits" at Stanford University, the professor sued. The *Newsweek* article reported that some students listened to the lectures over the radio while sunning by the pool and that two students took the exam while wearing top hats and sipping champagne. In 1985, the Ninth U.S. Circuit Court of Appeals ruled that the statements did not damage the professor's reputation for integrity or his ability as a teacher.[10]

Send in the fact checkers. In his September/October 1998 premiere issue of *Gear*, a magazine for young men, editor and publisher Bob Guccione Jr. gushes, "The exciting thing about starting this magazine is that we have no idea where we're going." He also has no idea where "King of the Wild Frontier" Davy Crockett was born. It wasn't in Crockett, Texas, as stated in an article about Texas Governor George W. Bush and his political aspirations. Pioneer scout Crockett was "born on a mountain top in Tennessee."

Identification

Damage to reputation is a personal offense. For a statement to be libelous, it must be made about a specific individual. People are most obviously identified by their names. To avoid confusion about the identity of people, editors like to use middle initials, ages, job descriptions, titles, and other specific information in articles. Fact checking to make sure all these small facts are scrupulously correct is an important part of preventing libel by misidentifying a person.

People also can be identified by their photographs, so using a generic file photo to illustrate a story can be risky if the story contains any statement that might be construed as applying to a person who can be clearly identified in the picture. For example, using a file photo of a man under arrest to illustrate an article about the effects of plea bargaining on the courts could be libelous if the pictured man was never charged with a crime. The implication of a story about plea bargaining is that the man in the photo entered a guilty plea as part of a bargain for a reduced sentence.

As a rule, members of a large group of people, such as "all the students at the university" or "all the patients treated by Dr. Kilroy," cannot claim they were libeled unless they have been personally identified. For example, several businessmen in Butte, Montana, sued *Time* over a story in the September 22,

1975, issue that said arson was common in the city. The businessmen owned two buildings that had burned accidentally; the *Time* article said the local economy was so depressed that owners had taken to burning buildings to collect the insurance. The owners were not identified in any way in the article, and the Montana Supreme Court ruled there were too many people who owned burned buildings in Butte for the plaintiffs to assert that the article referred to them.[11] There is no hard and fast number for the group identification rule, but usually in groups of more than 25 people, individuals would have a hard time convincing a court they were identified if an article referred only to the group as a whole.

In the final analysis, whether a person is identified or not boils down to a simple proposition: Do the people who know the plaintiff understand the statement, whether a story or photo, to refer to the plaintiff?

Publication

To be libelous, a statement must be communicated to someone other than the writer and the person it is written about. That is easy to prove when the article is published in a magazine. A statement doesn't have to be published to a large audience to meet the requirement of libel law, however. A memo from a writer to an editor could be the basis of a libel suit if the memo includes defamatory statements about another person. The memo would be "published" for the purposes of the law the minute it went from the writer's hands into the editor's hands because it went to a third person.

Magazines are also responsible for libelous statements they "republish," such as libelous quotations included in an article. A magazine is responsible even if the writer is simply repeating verbatim the words of a source. If a source says, for example, that investigators are sure Jones committed fraudulent stock dealings, the source has defamed Jones. But the writer commits a new libel by including the direct quotation in an article about the investigation.

Negligence and Actual Malice

Some confusion about libel comes from a series of U.S. Supreme Court decisions in the 1960s and 1970s to make the law of libel conform with the free press guarantees of the First Amendment. In the first of those cases, *New York Times v. Sullivan* in 1964,[12] the Supreme Court introduced the principle that, in addition to showing reputational damage, identification, and publication, libel plaintiffs who are public officials must show the defamation was published with **actual malice**, that is, with the publisher knowing it was false or with a reckless disregard for the truth. The actual malice rule, the Supreme Court reasoned, would require plaintiffs to prove that the publisher's decision to print the libelous statement was so outrageous that the publisher did not deserve First Amendment protection.

Before *New York Times v. Sullivan*, a publisher could lose a libel suit just because the defamatory statement got into print, whether by an innocent mistake or malicious intent, whether the damage to the plaintiff's reputation was great or slight. In the Sullivan case, the court recognized that there will be errors that creep into print as part of robust public debate, but some of them, while serious enough to injure a potential libel plaintiff, are not so serious that the First Amendment should allow the publication to lose a libel suit.

Following Sullivan, the Court extended the actual malice rule to "public figures," those persons who by their prominence affect public debate about public issues. Then, in 1974, the Supreme Court took advantage of the case of *Gertz v. Robert Welch, Inc.*[13] to distinguish the treatment of public officials and public figures as opposed to private figures in libel law. In that case, Elmer Gertz, a prominent lawyer in Chicago, sued *American Opinion* over an article that described him as a key player in a worldwide communist conspiracy to undermine the authority of American police. After a Chicago police officer killed a young child and was convicted of murder in the case, Gertz represented the child's family in a civil lawsuit against the officer. The article in *American Opinion*, the monthly magazine of the John Birch Society, described Gertz as a communist and said he had a long criminal record. Both accusations were false, and both fell into those categories of aspersions that courts have traditionally found to be libelous. So Gertz sued.

In Gertz, the Court pointed out that the actual malice rule was originally applied to public officials because they have such influence on the outcome of public issues. Then it was extended to public figures for the same reason. In *Gertz v. Robert Welch, Inc.*, the Court said that public figure libel plaintiffs have voluntarily thrust

RESEARCH IN BRIEF

Fact Checking Is More Than a "Fetish of Facticity"

In 1891, a boy rode the New York City rails going through both Grand Central and Penn Stations, according to the short story "The Boy on the Train" by Arthur Robinson. Wrong, said a *New Yorker* fact checker. Why? Because neither station existed in 1891. Ever vigilant, the fact checker hunted down nineteenth-century railroad schedules to correct those and other details. Presented with the facts, the writer made the necessary changes to his story before it ran in the April 11, 1988, issue of *The New Yorker*.[1] Of course, fact checkers at *The New Yorker* also verify the obvious, such as the latest population figures for Sweden or the number of homeless people in Manhattan who stayed overnight in shelters during Thanksgiving.

Fact checkers are the gatekeepers of truth at magazines, with responsibility for verifying every name, number, and quote in a story before it is published. Should they fail in their job, a magazine will suffer the consequences of diminished respect from readers who expect accuracy and fairness in articles and from advertisers who want to be associated with a reputable product. Fact checkers offer some legal protection against lawsuits due to the paper trail that grows from every verified fact, but it is not an absolute one.

Editors who have dozens of fact checkers on staff—at *Time, Newsweek, The New Yorker, Reader's Digest, Rolling Stone,* and *National Geographic,* among others—believe a magazine's credibility is enhanced by the existence of such a department. There may be as many as one fact checker for every three writers or correspondents, and more than one million dollars a year may be budgeted for fact checker salaries alone at a large weekly magazine, says sociologist Susan P. Shapiro, who studied fact checking at three large weekly magazines—two general news magazines and one specialized sports publication.[2]

Magazines that can't afford to have a slew of fact checkers on board because of budgetary restraints still care about accuracy. Editors there, however, will involve the entire editorial staff in the verification process, from editor-in-chief down to editorial assistant. Small magazines tend to trust the writers to get it right. A copy editor still checks for inconsistencies and misspelled words in the article, but without the extensive double and even triple checking of material that occurs in some fact checking departments where nothing is taken for granted.

Some trade magazines use professional peer review as a fact checking mechanism, and a few even run routine accuracy checks with sources after the article has been published. Others have lawyers read each article before it goes to press. At most consumer and trade magazines, however, legal review occurs only if a fact checker or editor requests it because of concerns about libel, privacy, or potentially sensitive assertions.

Shapiro's report about the "long, tedious, ambitious, very expensive, and labor-intensive operation that saps the energy of scores of young journalists every week" reveals that fact checkers do more than verify straightforward assertions such as a person's name or title and unambiguous facts such as an individual's birthplace or the number of floors in a building. Contrary to popular thought, they are not obsessed with mindless nit-picking nor do they have a "fetish of facticity." Rather, they also "contribute valuable intelligence to questions of *subjective* fact, the kinds of questions that editors often agonize over and that can put a publication's reputation at risk." Shapiro writes:

> *They painfully struggled over more subtle questions: Is the evidence credible? Does it support the conclusions drawn? Is the datum or quotation presented in the appropriate context? Is a word being misused or does a vague turn of*

themselves into the center of a public debate with the objective of influencing its final outcome. Such people are not public figures all the time, but they can be public figures if they sue for libel over an article about their public issue. These limited-purpose public figures must also prove actual malice to sue for libel.

But Gertz himself, the Court ruled, was not a public figure for purposes of the *American Opinion* article. He had only taken on a client—an everyday activity for a lawyer. He had not inserted himself into the debate about police authority and social order that *American Opinion* had written about. So requiring him to bear the heavy burden of proving actual malice on the part of the magazine struck the Court as too harsh. Private figures like Gertz, the justices reasoned, should not have to endure harsh public criticism in order to protect the First Amendment ideal of public discussion.

phrase permit an inaccurate interpretation? Does a sequence of verified facts lead to a false conclusion? Is an assertion fair and balanced? Does the story show all sides of the controversy?

Shapiro shadowed fact checkers from morning until late at night—spending 16-hour days—as she read, observed, and listened to their formal and informal interactions with writers, editors, and the computer screen. After spending more than five weeks studying fact checkers, Shapiro argues that their "ritualistic methodological routines" make it possible for magazines "to move through an extraordinary empirical morass on deadline."

Shapiro estimates that fact checkers pause—stop and evaluate an item—three times per column inch: "Half the words ultimately printed in an average story generate a pause." She says the fact checkers she studied investigated every item for accuracy.

About 16 percent of the pauses are clearly objective matters such as names, titles, and other proper nouns and their spelling (even if the reference is to the president of the United States, it is checked); 35 percent of the pauses are over relatively objective questions such as number, place, or date, which are slightly more difficult to verify; 24 percent are for less objective questions such as descriptions of people or events that may have fewer authoritative sources for verification or are comparative statements; and finally, 25 percent of the pauses are for subjective questions, the gray area that includes statements of feelings, future predictions, loaded adjectives, analogies, and qualifications that "lack a firm evidentiary basis." Shapiro says fact checkers spend more effort evaluating those subjective concerns than they do on routine objective ones.

What is the result of all this fact checking? Shapiro reports that more than half of the pauses (56 percent) are judged accurate, proper, or acceptable. That's to be expected since so many pauses are for clearly objective or relatively objective matters. But more significant, she says, is that about one-third of the pauses (32 percent) are found to be wrong (statements for which it is generally obvious how they ought to be corrected) or improper (the choice of remedies is problematic).

Fact checkers, writers, and editors (who have the final say on disagreements between the fact checker and the writer) have four basic options when they find a problem: leave it as it is, change it, cut it, or kill the story. The last option seldom occurs, Shapiro says, and even cuts are limited. "Editorial surgeons are more apt to repair the damaged organ than to excise it," she points out. Consequently, most stories are changed by the addition of information for clarification or a modification in wording.

Shapiro concludes that "other news media could benefit from magazine-like fact checking" to decrease the number of inaccurate accounts. She says the argument that fact checking is a luxury for weekly or monthly publications doesn't hold up: she found that "most magazine stories are written, edited, and checked in the last 48 hours before publication, often requiring fact checkers to work the equivalent of a full-time job in two days' time." Finally, she adds, fact checking not only ensures accuracy, but it is an important part of the editorial process because it is clear that fact checkers see both the forest and the trees.

[1] "Check the Facts: Fact Checking at *The New Yorker*," *The New Yorker* Education Program (1988).

[2] Susan P. Shapiro, "Caution! This Paper Has Not Been Fact Checked! A Study of Fact Checking in American Magazines." (New York: Gannett Center for Media Studies, 1990).

Nevertheless, it seemed to the Supreme Court that Gertz's suit could have a chilling effect on *American Opinion*, just as Sullivan's suit had on *The New York Times* if he had to prove only defamation, identification, and publication. So it didn't seem reasonable to let Gertz go forward with his libel action without showing some level of fault on the part of the magazine. To solve the conflict, the Court struck a compromise by ruling that private figures like Gertz, those people who have not made themselves part of the public discussion about a public issue, must show only that the defamatory statement was published negligently.

IDENTIFYING PUBLIC OFFICIALS. Public officials are fairly easy to identify, for purposes of libel, thanks to the several public official libel cases American courts have heard through the years. The clearest test for defining a public official came out of the 1966 case of *Rosenblatt v. Baer*, where the U.S. Supreme Court said public officials are government employees "who have, or appear to the public to have, substantial responsibility for or control over the conduct of governmental affairs."[14] Elected officials and officials who control the use of public funds will almost always be considered public officials. But court decisions throughout the United States have applied the Supreme Court's test to find that public officials include school superintendents, county medical examiners, financial aid directors at public universities, and law-enforcement officers and agents.

IDENTIFYING PUBLIC FIGURES. Public figures can be a little more slippery to define. The Gertz case made it clear, though, that public figures come in two categories: all-purpose public figures and limited-purpose public figures.

All-purpose public figures are those whose influence over public issues is both broad and ongoing. For example, in the first case to extend the actual malice rule to public figures, the U.S. Supreme Court ruled in *Curtis Publishing Co. v. Butts* in 1967 that a high-profile football athletic director at the University of Georgia must prove actual malice on the part of the *Saturday Evening Post* to win his libel action against the magazine. Athletic Director Wally Butts, who was not paid with public funds, was sufficiently prominent to be a newsworthy figure in all regards.

All-purpose public figures are rare, though courts around the country have found that celebrities as diverse as comedian and television personality Johnny Carson, political pundit William F. Buckley, and actress Carol Burnett are all-purpose public figures. General Colin Powell and the Reverend Jesse Jackson, for example, might be safe bets to be all-purpose public figures as would others of comparable renown.

Notoriety and celebrity do not necessarily make a person a public figure however. For example, in 1976, the U.S. Supreme Court found that Mary Alice Firestone, a high-profile Palm Beach socialite, was not a public figure in her libel suit against *Time*. On December 22, 1967, *Time* ran a "Milestones" piece stating inaccurately that Mrs. Firestone's husband, Russell Firestone, heir to the Firestone tire fortune, had been granted a divorce on grounds of cruelty and adultery. In reality, the court had not given a reason for granting the divorce, even though evidence of adultery and cruelty was presented at trial. So Mrs. Firestone sued for libel.

The Supreme Court ruled that for purposes of her divorce Mrs. Firestone was not a public figure even though she was a prominent member of Palm Beach high society. Although she held news conferences during the divorce trial and subscribed to a news clipping service to keep track of her mentions in the media, the Supreme Court said she was just like all other people forced into court to dissolve her marriage. She otherwise held no position of special prominence in public affairs, the Court said.[15]

Similarly, a person's standing as a public figure can fade as his or her prominence fades. In a case against *Reader's Digest*, the Supreme Court held in 1979 that a man who received substantial news coverage in 1958 for refusing to testify before a grand jury was not a public figure for purposes of a *Reader's Digest* book published 16 years later. Ilya Wolston refused to testify during an investigation of Soviet spy activities but did not voluntarily thrust himself into the spotlight. After the controversy, he returned to his anonymous station in life until he was brought into the public eye again by *Reader's Digest* in its 1975 book, *KGB: The Secret Work of Soviet Agents.*[16]

Limited-purpose public figures, the Supreme Court explained in the Gertz case, are those people who voluntarily insert themselves into an existing public issue in hopes of influencing its outcome. They might otherwise be considered anonymous citizens, although as a practical matter many of the limited-purpose public figures identified by courts in libel cases have been well known. The key factors have been that a public controversy existed and the plaintiff had voluntarily entered the controversy in hopes of affecting its resolution.

Elmer Gertz was a good example of a person being widely known in certain circles, but for purposes of his libel action he was not a public figure. The Supreme Court acknowledged that Gertz was a prominent attorney who had represented controversial clients in Chicago. He also had served without pay on a city board, and he had published articles on local affairs. But because Gertz had not tried to influence public opinion about the police officer's murder trial that *American Opinion* wrote about, he was a private figure in his libel action, the Court ruled.

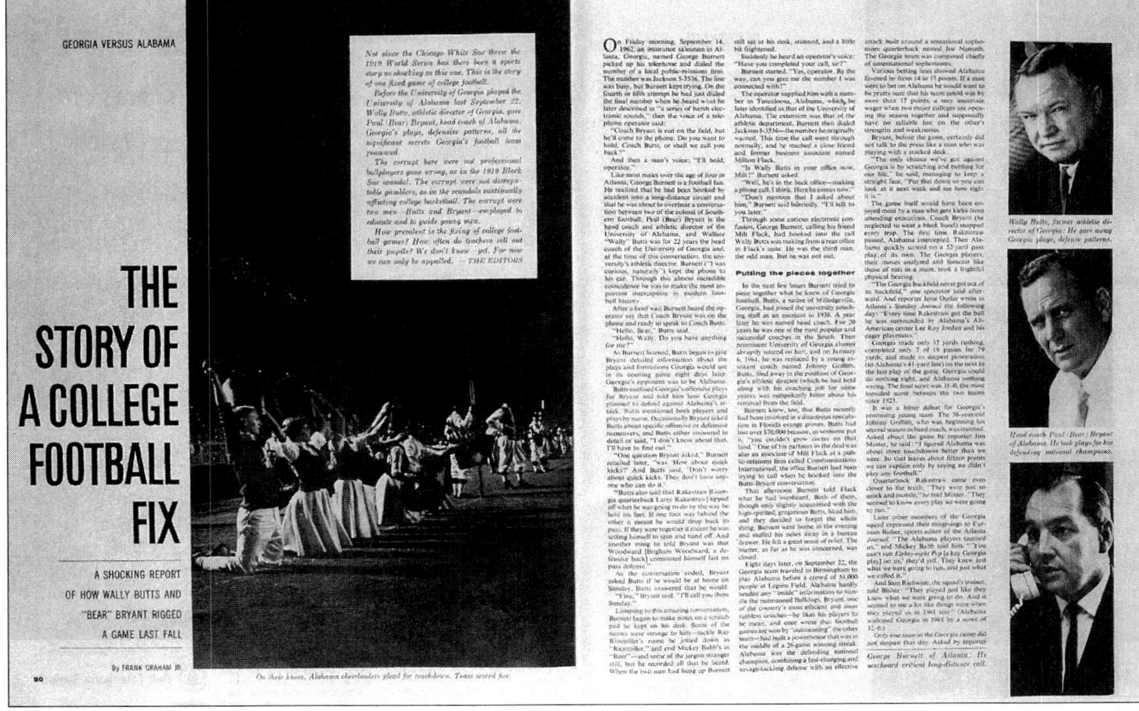

GEORGIA VERSUS ALABAMA

THE STORY OF A COLLEGE FOOTBALL FIX

A SHOCKING REPORT OF HOW WALLY BUTTS AND "BEAR" BRYANT RIGGED A GAME LAST FALL

By FRANK GRAHAM JR.

Not since the Chicago White Sox threw the 1919 World Series has there been a sports story as shocking as this one. This is the story of one fixed game of college football.

Before the University of Georgia played the University of Alabama last September 22, Wally Butts, athletic director of Georgia, gave Paul (Bear) Bryant, head coach of Alabama, Georgia's plays, defensive patterns, all the significant secrets Georgia's football team possessed.

The corrupt here were not professional ballplayers gone wrong, as in the 1919 Black Sox scandal. The corrupt were not disreputable gamblers, as in the scandals continually afflicting college basketball. The corrupt were two men—Butts and Bryant—employed to educate and to guide young men.

How prevalent is the fixing of college football games? How often do teachers sell out their pupils? We don't know—yet. For now we can only be appalled. —THE EDITORS

On their knees, Alabama cheerleaders plead for touchdown. Team scored five.

Wally Butts, former athletic director of Georgia: He gave away Georgia plays, defense patterns.

Head coach Paul (Bear) Bryant of Alabama: He took plays for his defending national champions.

George Burnett of Atlanta: He overheard critical long-distance call.

MARCH 23, 1963: The Supreme Court ruled that *Saturday Evening Post* had published a libelous statement in "The Story of a College Football Fix" when it said Athletic Director Wally Butts of the University of Georgia intentionally lost a football game against the University of Alabama in exchange for a huge payoff.

DEFINING ACTUAL MALICE. Editors publish a libelous statement with actual malice, the Supreme Court said, when they knowingly publish an out-and-out lie or when they publish an article even though they have a serious doubt about its truth or accuracy. In the Butts case, the *Saturday Evening Post* was found to have published its article, "Story of a College Football Fix" in the March 23, 1963, issue, with actual malice when it said Athletic Director Wally Butts of the University of Georgia intentionally lost a football game against the University of Alabama in exchange for a huge payoff. The Court chastised the magazine because it made no effort to verify the article, even though the freelancer said he uncovered the conspiracy only after he was inexplicably tapped into a telephone conversation between Butts and the Alabama coach. To make matters worse, the writer had a police record for fraud, yet the magazine showed no skepticism toward his work. Working with a longer deadline, the Court noted, a magazine is also in a much better position to verify facts than a wire service, which has deadlines around the clock.[17]

In Senator Goldwater's case against *Fact*,[18] a federal appeals court found the magazine had published its accusations about Goldwater with actual malice when evidence during the trial showed the publisher and managing editor agreed to attack Goldwater as mentally unstable long before they started researching the articles. Their accusations were not based on their consultations with mental health professionals, and they altered psychiatrists' answers to questionnaires to make them look more critical of Goldwater than they really were.

However, in a case important for magazine writers and editors, the Supreme Court ruled in 1991 that altering direct quotations was not evidence of actual malice. Psychoanalyst Jeffrey Masson sued *New Yorker* writer Janet Malcolm, alleging that she defamed him by changing and rearranging his own words to make them sound more damaging than they were originally in the interviews. The quotations in Malcolm's article, which ran as a two-part profile in the December 5 and December 12, 1983, issues of *The New Yorker,* had Masson calling himself an "intellectual gigolo" and "the greatest analyst who ever lived." He said she exaggerated his words in a way that made him look irresponsible, vain, unscholarly, and dishonest.

The April 11, 1938, issue of *Life* was banned in more than 50 locations, including Boston, Chicago, Brooklyn, Memphis, Savannah, New Orleans, all of Pennsylvania, and Canada. The controversy was over the publication of photos from an educational film titled *The Birth of a Baby.* All charges of obscenity and/or decency eventually were dismissed. A Gallup poll later showed that 76 percent of the American public approved of the story.

The Supreme Court did not find the alterations to be libelous, though. It said all writers alter quotations to some degree, whether it is to insert punctuation, correct grammatical mistakes, or clean up sloppy diction. Words within quotation marks are often incomplete or inexact, so only those alterations that create defamatory meaning where none existed would constitute actual malice. Malcolm maintained that the quotations were accurate.[19]

DEFINING NEGLIGENCE. The Supreme Court has said that libel plaintiffs who are ordinary citizens—not public officials or public figures—should be able to win a libel suit more easily than public officials or public figures. Because they haven't voluntarily entered public life, they can't be expected to endure the same kind of criticism public officials and public figures must endure. Private figures must show, however, that a libelous story was published with **negligence.** That means that a private figure libel plaintiff must prove that the writers and editors who published the story did not prepare the piece with the level of professional care and behavior usually used for that kind of story. One academic study of negligence in libel found three ways courts have found journalists to be negligent:

1. They fail to contact the person who is being defamed, unless there was a thorough investigation otherwise.
2. They fail to verify information through the best sources available.
3. There is an unresolved disagreement between the source and the writer over what the source told the journalist.[20]

Actual malice and negligence have been topics of debate and discussion by media professionals, attorneys, and legal scholars. But for editors worried about meeting a production deadline, they can be demystified to a simple rule: In preparing and editing all stories, insist on fairness and accuracy, without exception and without failure.

Libel Defenses

The law recognizes several defenses to a charge of libel. These defenses do not guarantee that a magazine won't be sued for libel. The mire of a libel suit can be long and dirty before it gives the defendant the chance to present defenses to judge and jury. In many cases, too, these defenses may give a magazine only partial protection from losing a libel suit by serving only to reduce the damages the magazine must pay. Nevertheless, understanding the defenses to a libel claim should help editors think through a libel problem.

TRUTH. Truth is the first defense to a libel suit. If a published statement is true, by definition it is not libelous, even though it may damage a person's reputation. For an editor to rely on the truth defense, however, it is essential that each statement be provable in court, and that is how editors should think about every statement of fact in an article: Is there solid evidence to back up what the writer is saying? At the same time, though, errors in insignificant facts, that is, facts that don't change the gist of the story if they're wrong, will not sabotage a truth defense.

FAIR COMMENT AND CRITICISM. A second defense to a libel charge is that the statement was published as a **fair comment or criticism**. The law of libel allows public expression of opinions about public events and issues because it is in society's best interest to encourage open debate and discussion on public matters. Many articles and opinion columns operate under this protection. A bill to be introduced in Congress, a recently published book, or a controversial candidate for governor all can be commented on because each in its way was presented to the public for viewing and discussion.

The key technicality for claiming that a libelous opinion is justified by the fair comment and criticism rule is that the article, column, or review must outline all pertinent facts before the opinion is stated. In other words, each article or column should contain within it the answer to the question: "How did the writer come to hold this opinion?" It's not enough for a restaurant reviewer to opine that a new restaurant serves bad food and has lousy service. The reviewer must also explain why: Was the food cold? Were the rolls stale? Were the water glasses left unfilled? Was the calamari burned? If an editor can't find the facts underlying the opinion in the review, then the column needs to be rewritten. And, of course, since libel is meant to punish false statements, it should go without saying that the factual statements underlying the opinion must be true and accurate. Simply stated, however, the key to the fair comment and criticism defense is that every reader should be able to understand why the writer reached the opinion being offered.

PRIVILEGE. The courts have recognized through the years that there are times when it is in society's best interest to excuse an admittedly libelous statement and let it go unpunished. Such libelous statements are said to be **privileged**. Privileged statements generally are those taken from a government meeting or document and reported in an accurate and balanced article. Privileged libelous statements might be found in testimony given under oath during a court proceeding in which a witness accuses another person of a crime. They might be accusations made at a legislative hearing alleging corruption in the state's low-income housing agency. To rely on the privilege defense, editors must make sure several conditions are met:

- The libelous statement must be taken from an official meeting or document. In some states, the privilege also applies to nongovernment meetings that are open to the public to discuss an issue of public concern.
- The article must be balanced. That is, people libeled in the public meeting or document must be given a chance to respond in the article, even if they were not at the meeting to offer a public rebuttal.
- The article must be a fair and accurate report of what happened at the meeting. The writer cannot sensationalize or distort the libelous comment or the role it played in the meeting as a whole.
- Some states also require that a magazine publish the statement without any malice toward the person defamed to make sure that the magazine and its editors are truly motivated by their duties to inform the public about public business rather than by a desire to get even or bring down the defamed person.

STATUTE OF LIMITATIONS. A state's deadline for filing a lawsuit, called a statute of limitations, is a sure-fire defense, because if a plaintiff lets the time lapse, a court will refuse to hear the case. In most jurisdictions, the statute of limitations is one or two years. Most states start clocking the statute of limitations on the first publication of the libelous statement, so a later publication, distribution, or display of a libelous article cannot be used to calculate the plaintiff's deadline for filing.

A libel action against *Hustler* in 1984 illustrates a quirky aspect of statutes of limitations for magazines with national distribution. Kathy Keeton, associate publisher of *Penthouse*, sued *Hustler* for a series of articles and cartoons, including a cartoon that charged that *Penthouse* publisher Bob Guccione infected her with a sexually transmitted disease. Keeton, a resident of New York, did not file her suit in time to sue *Hustler* in its home state of Ohio, so she filed in New Hampshire, which had a longer statute of limitations. On appeal, the U.S. Supreme Court permitted the case to go forward, ruling that *Hustler*'s circulation of 10,000 to 15,000 issues in New Hampshire was enough to permit the libel action to go forward in New Hampshire courts.[21]

INVASIONS OF PRIVACY

The **right to privacy** is the right of people to be left alone or to control the way they are portrayed to others. As a legal action, the right to privacy takes many forms, each of them significantly different from libel. Like libel, however, the law of privacy sets a minimum standard of acceptable behavior for magazines. And as in libel, writers and editors can prevent most legal problems by acting ethically or responsibly in gathering, writing, and packaging their articles.

The right to privacy consists of four different legal offenses:

- Offensive publication of embarrassing private facts about individuals.
- Physical intrusion or trespass into individuals' sphere of privacy, such as their homes.
- Publishing offensive information about individuals that portrays them falsely to the public or, as the law says, puts them in a false light before the public.
- Appropriating a person's name, image, or characteristic for the publisher's advantage.

One Way to Prevent Libel Suits: Be Polite

One way to prevent a libel suit is to be polite and respectful when a person calls with a complaint about a story. A study by the University of Iowa Libel Research Project found that before libel plaintiffs filed a lawsuit, all they really wanted was some satisfaction. Most of them simply wanted the publishers to admit their mistakes and apologize for the hurt they caused. When the plaintiffs didn't get that, they called their lawyers.[1] The lesson from the Iowa study is significant: When editors or writers get complaints alleging a libelous inaccuracy, they should take it seriously. The study recommends following these guidelines to keep a complaint from becoming a libel action.

- *Don't insult the caller, don't talk condescendingly, and don't hang up.* That may sound simple, but complaining phone calls have not always been warmly received by journalists.
- *Don't let writers handle complaints about their own stories, and don't let editors or designers handle complaints about their own titles or page designs.* Writers, page editors, and designers have too much invested in their work to be expected to talk dispassionately with an angry caller. Have the next editor up the chain of command—one not directly involved in the article—take the call.
- *If it is a problem that cannot be resolved in one conversation or if there is a question that should be investigated, tell callers an editor will phone them back—then make sure one does.* Don't leave an angry caller waiting more than one day.
- *If, after some investigation, supervising editors find there was an error in an article, writers and editors need to support them when they tell the caller that the magazine is sorry.* The management should get the right information—verifying it as carefully as an editor would verify a writer's story—and promptly prepare an accurate and carefully worded correction, admitting the error and taking responsibility for it. Hidden mistakes might be exposed later before an unsympathetic jury.
- *If an internal investigation proves the story was accurate, don't cram it down the complainer's throat.* Calmly explain the facts, the supporting evidence, and the reliability of the sources. Standing behind a writer's story doesn't mean adding insult to the injury the caller already feels.
- *If it's appropriate, the editor or managing editor may offer an angry caller a chance to write a brief rebuttal piece.* The editor can explain, of course, that the rebuttal will have to be edited to comply with style rules and libel laws and to fit the allowed space.
- *If a caller mentions the word "lawsuit" or "lawyer," immediately pass the call on to the top editor.* Those editors get paid to handle the really hot items.

[1] Randall P. Bezanson, Gilbert Cranberg, and John Soloski, *Libel Law and the Press: Myth and Reality* (New York: The Free Press), 1987.

Embarrassing Private Facts

An article can be a legal invasion of privacy when it contains information that would be highly offensive to a reasonable person and that is not legitimately newsworthy. Unlike libel, **private facts** are true. For example, in 1942 *Time* was found to have published private facts about Dorothy Barber when it ran an article in its March 13, 1939, issue about her strange eating disorder. *Time* also published a photo of her taken against her wishes as she lay in her hospital room.[22] Few plaintiffs win private facts cases, although those most likely to prevail, like Barber, sue over a revelation about their health or hospitalization.

An important defense in private facts cases is the simple fact that the information is "newsworthy." Courts have defined "newsworthy" broadly, often leaving it up to editors to decide whether a fact is newsworthy or not. For example, a federal court in California ruled for *Sports Illustrated* in 1976 in a private facts case filed by Michael Virgil, one of the most well-known surfers along the California coast. The *Sports Illustrated* article said Virgil ate insects, dived headfirst down stairs to impress women, and extinguished cigarettes in his mouth. It said he intentionally hurt himself to collect unemployment payments so he would have free time for surfing. The court ruled that the disclosures of Virgil's bizarre behavior were based on more than morbid fascination or voyeurism; they were a journalistic attempt to explain to readers Virgil's aggressive and daring surfing style.[23]

An old case against *The New Yorker* also illustrates that once people are newsworthy, they remain newsworthy for purposes of a private facts lawsuit. On August 14, 1937, *The New Yorker* ran a piece about William James Sidis. Twenty-seven years earlier, Sidis had been a child prodigy who lectured in the Harvard University math department when he was 11 years old. *The New Yorker* article described Sidis as being reclusive and eccentric, living in a disorderly apartment surrounded by his collection of street-car transfers. When Sidis sued, a federal appeals court ruled he was still newsworthy.[24]

Photographer Annie Leibovitz sued Paramount Pictures for copyright infringement after they used her *Vanity Fair* cover of a nude and pregnant Demi Moore in an ad for the movie *Naked Gun 33-1/3: The Final Insult.* The advertisement, which appeared in *Sports Illustrated* and other magazines in 1994, featured actor Leslie Nielsen in the same proudly pregnant pose as Leibovitz's controversial 1991 photo. The judge ruled that because the ad was a parody, it fell under fair use protection and was not copyright infringement because it was commentary and clearly a satire.

Intrusion

Invasion of privacy by **intrusion** might be compared to trespassing. The difference is that trespass is a criminal violation and intrusion is a civil cause of action, but both involve entering a place not open to the public. The classic case illustrating intrusion involved a *Life* reporter and photographer who were invited into the home of a "healer" under the pretense that they wanted medical care. As the healer examined the woman for breast cancer, the photographer used a small camera to record the session. After their article ran in the November 1, 1963, issue, "Dr." Dietemann sued for intrusion. In 1971, the federal appeals court found for Dietemann, ruling that his den, where he received his patients, was a private place in which he could determine who saw or heard him practicing his brand of medicine.[25] The court said: "The First Amendment has never been construed to accord newsmen immunity from torts or crimes committed during the course of newsgathering. The First Amendment is not a license to trespass, to steal, or to intrude by electronic means into the precincts of another's home or office."[26]

Technology is making it easier for writers and photographers to "intrude" on people by tape-recording conversations or shooting pictures from far away. As a general rule, people in public places can be photographed or tape-recorded without concern for intrusion. A person who can be seen by the public must accept the risk that actions or words may be captured in some form and passed along through publication. But photographers, some of whom are notorious for their antics to get a good photo, can cross the legal line if they hound or harass their subjects. Aggressive newsgathering and confrontational interviewing alone are not intrusion, however.

False Light

Invading privacy by placing a person in a **false light** often stems from publishing offensive statements or photos out of context. Stories that embellish the facts or leave out important facts run the risk of putting people in a false light. In one false light case, for example, *Life* published an article in February 28, 1955, about the link between an actual crime and the Broadway play, *The Desperate Hours,* it inspired. A family was held hostage in their home by escaped convicts for many hours. While the experience was difficult, the convicts actually treated the family well and released them unharmed. But *Life*'s article presented photos and a description of the play, saying the Hill family had been "besieged" in their home but that they rose to heroic heights to defend themselves. The Hills sued, saying they were not intimidated by the convicts, nor did they fight off the intruders as the *Life* piece portrayed. Lower courts supported the Hills's false light claim, but the U.S. Supreme Court reversed for other reasons in 1967. The high court did not find for *Life* because the Hills were wrong in their false light claim; rather, the Court said false light claims must be proven with the same actual malice required by *New York Times v. Sullivan.*[27]

In a false light case against *Penthouse,* a federal appeals court ruled in 1982 that a former Miss Wyoming of 1978 could not sue because of the magazine's 1979 fictional story about a Miss Wyoming who twirled batons during the talent portion of the beauty contest and who levitated

Rolling Stone's annual "hot issue" became too hot for some stores to handle in 1998. The August 20 cover featured model Laetitia Casta in the nude and kneeling on a bed of pink rose petals. Her pose, reminiscent of Marilyn Monroe in one of those old calendar pin-up shots, was photographed from the side and looked artistic rather than erotic. Nevertheless, *Rolling Stone* sent it to the newsstands draped with a red paper band that covered Casta's body from the shoulder blade down. But that wasn't good enough for Wal-Mart, Kmart, Target, and other national chains. They banned the magazine from their newsstands and check-out counters.

her coach as she performed a sexual act with him on national television. The court said the real Miss Wyoming, who had also twirled batons as her talent in the contest, was not put in a false light because readers would recognize the story as pure fantasy.[28]

Appropriation

The privacy offense of **appropriation** is usually a greater problem for advertisers than it is for magazine editors. Most commonly, it arises from the unauthorized use of a person's name, picture, or voice to endorse a commercial product or service. For magazines, courts have said they can use newsworthy photos on their covers and in their advertising for upcoming issues. For example, *New York* won an appropriation action brought by a man who participated in the city's famous St. Patrick's Day parade. A freelance photographer took a picture of the man, and *New York* ran the photo on its cover. In 1971, the New York Court of Appeals said the picture was newsworthy because the parade is of broad public interest to New Yorkers.[29]

In a well-known case involving magazine promotions, *Holiday* successfully resisted an appropriation claim by actress Shirley Booth. The magazine had run a photo of Booth at a Caribbean resort as part of a travel story. It later republished the photo as part of its advertising for the magazine. Booth sued, but a New York court ruled in 1962 that the later use of the photo to promote the magazine was not appropriation as long as its purpose was to illustrate the content and quality of the magazine.[30]

INTENTIONAL INFLICTION OF EMOTIONAL DISTRESS

In the 1980s, plaintiffs who wanted to sue magazines over what they published changed strategies because libel and privacy became more complex and harder to prove. One alternative was to sue for "intentional infliction of emotional distress," meaning the plaintiff alleged that the magazine's conduct was so outrageous that it was outside any bounds of decency and that it was intolerable in civilized society. Many of these cases were brought against television news organizations, but two cases against *Hustler* illustrate how intentional infliction of emotional distress works. They also stand for another important principle: Few if any magazines have ever lost a case for intentional infliction of emotional distress.

In the 1986 case of *Ault v. Hustler*,[31] an anti-pornography activist, Peggy Ault, sued *Hustler* after being named the magazine's "Asshole of the Month." She sued *Hustler* for libel, invasion of privacy, and intentional infliction of emotional distress. The federal district court in Oregon, where she brought the suit, dismissed the claim, saying intentional infliction of emotional distress was just an attempt to sue *Hustler* for the libel twice by using another name for the offense. Some humiliation is sure to accompany the damage to reputation that is the basis of libel, but the humiliation and emotional distress cannot be separated from the libel to be the foundation of a different cause of action, the court ruled.

The U.S. Supreme Court resolved a similar case against *Hustler* in 1988 when the Reverend Jerry Falwell sued over a parody meant to portray him as a hypocrite.[32] *Hustler* ran a piece in the November 1983 issue patterned after a popular ad campaign of the period in which celebrities described the "first time" they tasted Campari Liqueur. The Campari ads always played on the sexual connotation of the "first time" theme.

Under the headline "Jerry Falwell talks about his first time," *Hustler* ran the televangelist's picture and a made-up interview in which he described his first sexual experience as a drunken encounter with his mother in an outhouse. The interview also said he always got drunk before he preached a sermon. At the bottom of the page was a tiny footnote: "Ad parody—not to be taken seriously." It was typical *Hustler* fare: cheap, raunchy, and exaggerated to the point of being incredible. It wasn't libelous, because it was such an unbelievable insult; it wasn't an invasion of privacy because it was so obviously false that it was not revealing a private fact or putting Falwell in a false light before the public. But the parody certainly was outrageous, so it made a good foundation for an action for Falwell's suit based on intentional infliction of emotional distress.

The high court readily agreed with Falwell that the parody was repugnant. But the Supreme Court also pointed out that the ad parody contained important political opinions that deserved constitutional protection. Obviously, it was not meant to describe actual events in Falwell's life, but it was intended to criticize his political ideas, which he actively promoted through the 1980s, especially his attacks on pornography and lax sexual mores.

The Supreme Court said *Hustler*'s ad parody, as tasteless as it was, was akin to the blistering humor of American political cartoons dating back to colonial days. The *Hustler* ad, like Thomas Nast's famous cartoons chastising the Tweed Ring in New York, was using outrageous language to skewer a prominent political figure. Punishing a publisher for running an outrageous cartoon or comment runs the risk of punishing the publisher just because the words or images shock the audience, the Court said. If the First Amendment protects anything, the justices said, it must protect unpopular opinions and statements from the people who would silence them because they disagree with them.

The Court's solution to the First Amendment problem presented by Falwell's suit for intentional infliction of emotional distress was to apply the *New York Times v. Sullivan* rule for actual malice. After *Hustler v. Falwell*, public figures and public officials cannot win a suit for intentional infliction of emotional distress unless they also show that the publication was made with the publisher's knowledge that it was false or with reckless disregard for truth of the matter.

THIRD-PARTY LIABILITY

Occasionally, plaintiffs have sued magazines over advertising and editorial content they claim caused people to do something harmful. These cases are called third-party liability cases because the magazine didn't actually do the harm itself, but it is blamed for being a key player in causing the injury. These cases fall into two categories: incitement cases and negligence cases.

Incitement

An example of an **incitement** case is *Herceg v. Hustler*,[33] in which a woman sued the magazine over an August 1981 article about "autoerotic asphyxia," a dangerous practice of masturbating while "hanging" oneself. Supposedly orgasm is enhanced by cutting off the oxygen supply to the brain at the moment of orgasm. Diane Herceg asserted in the lawsuit that her 14-year-old son died when he tried the practice after reading the *Hustler* article. In short, she claimed the article incited her son to try the life-threatening practice, so the magazine was responsible for his death.

The federal district court jury decided in Herceg's favor, but a federal appellate court reversed. While it is true the boy might never have tried autoerotic asphyxia if he had not read the *Hustler* article, that still does not follow the very narrow rules laid out in earlier Supreme Court cases for punishing speech because it "incites" action. Under the First Amendment, statements can be punished for incitement only if they are aimed at provoking or causing "imminent lawless action." In the *Hustler* case, the court of appeals said a speaker in front of an angry crowd can be punished for whipping the crowd into a riot, but the editor of a magazine meant to be read in the solitude of one's home cannot be sued for incitement. The article, which even included a warning against trying autoerotic asphyxia, was not *advocating* any action, the court said. And it was not discussing an illegal practice or act. Therefore, there was no "incitement" and there was no "imminent lawless action." The boy might have found out about autoerotic asphyxia from the article, but the decision to try it was his own, as painful as that may have been for his mother to understand.

Negligence

The legal principles drawn from the negligence cases against magazines are not so clear cut, although it is safe to say that magazines cannot be successfully sued for negligence over most standard editorial or advertising content. In one case that illustrates the point, a young woman in California bought Playtex tampons after seeing them advertised in *Seventeen*. After using one, she became violently ill with toxic shock syndrome. She later sued *Seventeen*, claiming the magazine was negligent in running the ad. The California court ruled against her in 1987.[34] In a similar case, the New Jersey court ruled in 1974 that *Popular Mechanics* was not negligent in running an advertisement for fireworks, even when the fireworks injured a child who was watching

Poisonous or Precious: Parodies Pay Off

The editors at *Reader's Digest* weren't upset when *Mad* magazine published its parody, "Reader's Disgust," with a table of contents that promised a two-page condensation of the *Encyclopedia Britannica*. "It really began to dawn on us that we weren't just any magazine," wrote the editors in the 75th anniversary issue of *Reader's Digest*. "Reach a certain level of acceptance and you're in for a lot of ribbing. Actually, we enjoy the jokes—whether it's a parody from *National Lampoon*, or that episode of 'The Simpsons' where Homer gets so head-over-heels smitten with the 'Reading Digest.'"[1]

If imitation is the sincerest form of flattery, then parodies are the most amusing. *Harvard Lampoon* (this publication does magazine parodies, while *National Lampoon*, a separate title, runs comical and satirical articles) and *Mad* have been tickling reader funny bones for decades.

Harvard Lampoon produced the earliest magazine parodies, which were locally distributed as undergraduate humor publications on the Harvard University campus and on Cambridge, Massachusetts, newsstands. Before *Harvard Lampoon* became a national phenomenon, spoofs were published of *Saturday Evening Post* in 1912, *Popular Mechanics* in 1920, *Town & Country* in 1923, and *Vogue* in 1938, among others. The 1939 parody of *The New Yorker* was the first time the *Lampoon* successfully imitated an entire magazine format, including advertising layouts.

Other parodies followed, of *Newsweek* in 1956 and *Saturday Review* in 1960. But these were not nationally distributed. Finally, in 1961, *Harvard Lampoon* went national when *Mademoiselle*'s editors requested its own parody; the entire July issue was turned over to *Lampoon*'s editors. The issue "set some kind of circulation record of this usually doldrum month in the publishing business," and *Mademoiselle*'s editors asked for a repeat performance in 1962.[2]

By 1966, *Harvard Lampoon* was producing nationally distributed magazines under its own auspices. The entire run of 450,000 *Playboy* parodies sold out within three weeks in 1966. A 1968 *Time* parody, with the cover line "Does Sex Sell Magazines?" and hilarious letters to the editor from Jacqueline Onassis and Timothy Leary (just about anything is possible in a parody), had more than half a million readers. However, the hottest seller so far is *Harvard Lampoon*'s 1973 takeoff on

them being blown up.[35] In both these cases, the courts said it would simply be too onerous a task to require magazines to investigate the safety and suitability of every product they advertise.

ENDORSEMENT. When a magazine endorses a product, however, it takes on extra responsibility—and courts can find more easily that it breached its duty to its readers. In Hanberry *v.* Hearst Corporation in 1969,[36] *Good Housekeeping* was held liable for injuries a reader suffered when she slipped and fell while wearing new shoes that bore the magazine's "Consumer's Guaranty Seal." The seal carried the promise, "If the product or performance is defective, *Good Housekeeping* guarantees replacement or refund to consumer." The seal is *Good Housekeeping*'s strategy for making the magazine a better vehicle for advertisers because readers could be confident about a product's quality. That endorsement of the shoes made the difference between liability in this case and no liability in the fireworks and the toxic shock cases.

ADVERTISING. Two cases involving classified ads in *Soldier of Fortune* are more complicated because federal appeals courts decided similar cases differently. Both cases arose out of classified ads for "personal services" in a magazine that focuses on military, paramilitary, and mercenary subjects. In both cases, a murder victim's survivors sued *Soldier of Fortune*, alleging that the magazine negligently contributed to the murders by publishing the ad that brought together the murderer and the person who contracted the murder.

In *Eimann v. Soldier of Fortune*,[37] the mother and son of the murder victim sued the magazine, saying the victim's husband contracted her murder after reading this ad that ran in the September, October, and November 1984 issues: "EX–MARINES—67–69 'Nam Vets, Ex-DI, weapons specialist—jungle warfare, pilot, M.E., high risk assignments, U.S. or overseas." The man who placed the ad was convicted of murdering the woman at her husband's behest, but he testified at *Soldier of Fortune*'s negligence trial that he

Cosmopolitan, complete with a nude centerfold of Henry Kissinger; that parody sold 1.2 million copies.[3]

Harvard Lampoon's outrageous parodies are clearly identified as such on the covers, which have an amazing technical resemblance to the original magazine. Everything is made to look like the real publication—layout, typography, artwork, content, and even sentence structure. There are real ads as well as bogus ones throughout the parody, too.

Mad's parodies, on the other hand, tend to be cover treatments only. Its March 1987 takeoff on *Time*'s "man of the year" cover used the same typeface and red border, but with *Mad*'s name for the logo. The "head of the year" was television superstar Alfred E. Headroom (Alfred E. Neuman with slicked back blond hair and sunglasses), for an additional jibe at the TV show "Max Headroom."

In recent years, however, there have been some new kids on the parody block who spoof recent magazine successes that have distinctive visual and verbal styles. Jim Downey and Tom Connor have co-authored *Is Martha Stuart Living?* (in 1994) and *Martha Stuart's Better Than You at Entertaining* (in 1996), two wildly popular parodies of *Martha Stewart Living.* These best-selling spoofs are so realistic in their mimicking of the *Martha Stewart Living* formula that an article on how to make water from scratch seems downright reasonable and one on building and decorating a coffin both possible and plausible.

Downey and Connor also did a send-up of *Wired* under the title *re>WIRED* in 1996. With the same fluorescent colors and digitally enhanced image manipulation found in the original, the parody trumpeted "How to Pick Up NetChicks" by Bill Gates IV on the cover.

How have magazine editors and publishers reacted to these precious parodies? Martha Stewart, who poked fun at her image in an American Express television ad by advising viewers to recycle their old cards as swimming pool tiles, called the parodies "the highest form of flattery."[4] *Playboy* publisher Hugh Hefner, however, had the last word with his telegram to *Harvard Lampoon:* "*Playboy* is delighted with its treatment at the hands of the venerable *Harvard Lampoon.* In fact, if a better parody of *Playboy* is ever created—we reserve the right to do it ourselves."[5]

1 The Editors, "How a Little Magazine Went Around the World," *Reader's Digest* (75th Anniversary Issue, 1997): 20.
2 Martin Kaplan, ed. *The* Harvard Lampoon *Centennial Celebration 1876–1973* (Boston: Little, Brown and Company, 1973): 24.
3 Lambeth Hochwald, "Ha-Ha's in La-La Land," *Folio:* (January 15, 1995): 43.
4 Doreen Carvajal, "What Is a Book Publisher to Do When a Parody Hits Home?" *The New York Times* (February 12, 1996): C1.
5 Kaplan, 32.

and a partner originally ran the ad trying to recruit other Vietnam veterans for work as bodyguards and security agents for business executives. He testified that "Ex–DI" meant ex-drill instructor, "M.E." meant multi-engine planes, and "high risk assignments" was intended to refer to work as a bodyguard or security specialist.

Eimann presented evidence at the trial that as many as nine *Soldier of Fortune* classified ads had been tied to criminal activity over the previous two years, and in some of those cases, police investigators had contacted the magazine's employees for help in identifying the people who placed the ads. She argued that with such a history the magazine should have known its ads were dangerous, so it should be held responsible for negligently contributing to her daughter's murder. The trial court in Houston agreed with her and awarded her $9.4 million.

The Fifth U.S. Circuit Court of Appeals, which sits in New Orleans and hears cases from Louisiana, Mississippi, and Texas, overturned the District Court's judgment in 1989, ruling that the wording of the ad was too ambiguous for the magazine to foresee it could lead to murder. "Given the pervasiveness of advertising in our society and the important role it plays, we decline to impose on publishers the obligation to reject all ambiguous advertisements for products or services that might pose a threat of harm," the judges wrote in their opinion. "The burden on a publisher to avoid liability from suits of this type is too great: he must reject *all* such advertisements."

Three years later, in 1992, the 11th U.S. Circuit Court of Appeals in Atlanta decided Braun *v.* *Soldier of Fortune*[38] with similar facts but a different result—it upheld a $4 million judgment against the magazine. In the Braun case, Michael and Ian Braun, the sons of the murder victim, sued *Soldier of Fortune,* alleging that their father's business partner found a hit man through a classified ad in the magazine. The ad, placed by a man named Michael Savage, said: "GUN FOR HIRE: 37-year-old professional mercenary desires jobs. Vietnam Veteran. Discreet and very private. Body guard, courier, and other special skills. All jobs considered."

While on its face, the ad in the Braun case appears very similar to the ad in the Eimann case, the 11th Circuit Court of Appeals emphasized the differences in the wording to support its ruling that *Soldier of Fortune* negligently contributed to the death in this second case. While the ad in the Eimann case was ambiguous, as the Fifth Circuit pointed out, the 11th Circuit said Savage's ad was explicit enough for any publisher to foresee that it could lead to illegal and harmful activities. The warning signs the court singled out in the ad itself were the phrases "gun for hire" and "professional mercenary," the emphasis on privacy and discretion, the reference to "other special skills" after mentioning legitimate jobs of bodyguard and courier, and the open-ended lure that "all jobs" would be considered. "The ad's combination of sinister terms makes it apparent that there was a substantial danger of harm to the public," the court wrote. A reasonable publisher, then, would understand that Savage's ad presented a clearly identifiable threat to public safety, the court said. Because the magazine had not recognized such a threat, it negligently contributed to the elder Braun's death.

After Eimann and Braun, it won't be easy for magazine editors and publishers to know precisely when an ad crosses the line—there is not a bright line dividing acceptable ads from unacceptable ads. The principle, however, is helpful: Ambiguously worded ads from which physical harm results are not likely to support a ruling of negligence against the magazine. But an ad whose message, intent, or implication is more obvious could support a court's finding that the magazine negligently contributed to the harm.

The risk, of course, is that magazine editors and publishers may tend to overcompensate or self-censor in order to avoid even the hint of negligence. In the discussion of libel and privacy, that tendency was called the chilling effect. But magazines are not just business enterprises; they also are vehicles for public information and the exchange of ideas and opinions. To uphold that objective, editors and publishers will need to balance their legal concerns against their journalistic principles in making decisions about which ads to run and which ads to reject.

COPYRIGHT

Copyright may be the legal issue that magazine editors and writers confront most frequently—not in the context of a courtroom battle, but in making sure, day in and day out, that their magazines have full rights to the articles, photos, and other content they publish. They also need to ensure that their rights to the content of their own magazines are respected by other publishers.

The purpose of **copyright** is to protect the intellectual and creative work of authors, artists, composers, performers, photographers, illustrators, playwrights, choreographers, architects, and other "creators." Protecting their work means others cannot claim it as their own, so credit is given where it is due. Also, copyright protection encourages people to pursue creative efforts by guaranteeing them control over how their work will be used. With creative people thus protected, the law reasons, all society stands to benefit. Copyright lasts for the life of the author plus 70 years.[39]

The federal copyright statute says that copyright protects "original works of authorship fixed in any tangible medium of expression, now known or later developed, from which they can be perceived, reproduced, or otherwise communicated."[40] In that melange of legalese are hidden the basic components of copyright that editors and writers need to know.

Original Works

"Original works" means that the creation must have a minimum level of intellectual effort. The alphabetized listing of names in a phone book is not original enough to merit copyright protection, the U.S. Supreme Court ruled in 1991.[41]

Lists, nevertheless, can be problematic. In 1980, a court ruled that *Newsweek* did not violate author Lawrence Suid's copyright of his book *Guts & Glory—Great American War Movies* by arranging quotations about John Wayne in the same order Suid arranged them in his book and taking the same excerpts from John Wayne's letters that Suid quoted in his book. Suid was not claiming a copyright in the quotations themselves, which came from sources he interviewed for the book, or in the letters. Copyright law would never have supported such a claim because the letters and the quotations were created by someone else, and those creators would hold those copyrights. But Suid was claiming that his very act of selecting particular quotations and excerpts and arranging them in a particular order in the book amounted to original, creative work that was stolen by *Newsweek*. The Washington, D.C., federal court disagreed, ruling in *Newsweek*'s favor that the magazine could draw on Suid's research, even citing the same sources he used in his book, without using or compromising the originality of his work.[42] His original work lay in the way he wrote the book, not in the way he chose or used his sources' words.

Generally, almost any freelance article that reflects the writer's creative effort to present research would have enough originality under the law to qualify for copyright protection. The use of type, illustrations, graphics, and photos that go into a magazine's page design for an article is also original work and thus deserving of copyright protection.

It is important to understand that "originality" applies to an article itself, not to the facts discussed in the article. If a magazine publishes an article about winter care for gardens just a month after a competing magazine does, it is not necessarily a copyright infringement. Facts, knowledge, and information about taking care of a garden plot in winter cannot be copyrighted; copyright protects the particular presentation of those facts—the wording of the article, a particular illustration, photo, or graphic, even the unique design of the whole package—but not the idea of an article about that topic.

Tangible Medium

The copyright statute's phrase "fixed in a tangible medium" is the key for knowing when copyright protection begins for a work. An original work is fixed in a tangible medium as soon as it is written on a piece of paper, drawn on a sketch pad, recorded on an audio or video tape, saved on a disk or in the memory of a computer, or posted onto an Internet Web site.

The familiar copyright symbol, ©, does not have to be displayed for a work to be copyrighted. As the statute says, the author's or creator's right is recognized by the law as soon as the work is "fixed in a tangible medium." Nevertheless, giving proper notice of the copyright and registering the copyright with the federal government are important for editors. Copyright registration informs readers that they should have the magazine's permission before making copies of the work and gives copyright holders greater rights if they have to sue a copier for infringement.

A proper copyright notice includes the circled C, ©, the word *copyright*, or the abbreviation *copr.*, along with the year of publication and the name of the copyright owner. For an article, proper notice might read "© 2001 Desmond Jones." For an entire issue of a magazine, it might read "© 2002 Meredith Corp." for *Better Homes and Gardens* or another publication owned by Meredith. For an issue of *Sports Illustrated for Kids* published in 2001, proper notice would be "© 2001 Time Inc." because Time Inc. is the parent company for *Sports Illustrated for Kids*. Proper notice for *NBA Inside Stuff*, a specialty magazine published by Time Inc., was "© 1998 NBA Properties Inc." Even though Time Inc. published the magazine, it did so under contract with the NBA, and the NBA kept all rights. Unfortunately, the magazine folded as a result of the 1998 NBA strike.

Ownership

The matter of resolving who owns the copyright is important. The statute grants rights in the copy to the author. But the author for purposes of the law is not always the writer who prepared the copy, as the *NBA Inside Stuff* copyright notice implied. To be sure, freelance writers and photographers own the copyright to their original works, and because of that they can sign over publication rights to a magazine to publish the work.

Work prepared under contract, though, is what the copyright statute calls a work for hire. A writer employed by Time Inc. to prepare articles for *Sports Illustrated for Kids* does not own the copyright to her articles; they would be works for hire written under the terms of her employment contract, so Time Inc. would hold the copyright. A freelance writer who accepts a specific assignment from a magazine and signs a work for hire agreement with the editor does not retain the copyright to the article. Editors should use explicit, written work for hire agreements with all freelancers, and freelancers should require them of all editors they work for, because it is in everyone's best interest to have the question of authorship answered clearly before the work begins.

THE NAME GAME

The title of a magazine is one of its most valuable, though intangible, assets. Titles of magazines are trademarked, not copyrighted. While copyright protects original artistic or literary works, a trademark protects the product's identifying name, slogan, design, or symbol. The U.S. Patent and Trademark Office handles trademarks, although a product does not have to be registered to be legally valid. It can achieve trademark status through common law, which recognizes usage over time. But whenever there is potential for confusion over two product names, lawyers get involved.

Selecting the right name for a magazine can be a time-consuming process. According to accounts about the November 1936 start-up of *Life* magazine, *Dime* was the first of the many possible titles considered. Others on the list included *Show-Book of the World, Rehearsal, Album, Eye, Candid, Go, News Focus, Spectator, Nuze-Vuze, Picture, Promenade, See, Quest, Snap, Scan, Vista, Flash, World, Witness,* and *Wide Awake. Life* was suggested as a name early on, but the title belonged to a 54-year-old humor magazine with a dwindling circulation.

Although more than 200 possible names were bandied about, *Life* kept rising to the top. Finally, less than one month before the premiere of Henry Luce's new picture magazine, Time Inc. acquired the name and assets of the old *Life* for $92,000. The humor magazine's staff members were given Time Inc. jobs as part of the deal.[1]

Today's start-ups are a bit more complicated when it comes to naming a magazine. With so many brand extensions and franchises crowding the market, a name check requires extensive computer database searches and legal research through trademark registers. Two recent situations illustrate the problems that can occur in the magazine name game.

When Steven Brill, founder of *The American Lawyer,* announced in 1997 that he was starting a media watchdog magazine called *Content,* he immediately hit a brick wall. A Savannah, Georgia-based arts quarterly titled *Contents* had been publishing since 1993. Known in film and fashion circles for its elegant photo layouts—made more impressive by its oversized format—*Contents* had a national circulation of 50,000. Brill's lawyers contacted *Contents* founder and creative director Joseph Alfieris to reach an amicable settlement; Brill gave Alfieris a six-figure sum in exchange for not suing.[2] Brill further distanced his

The Internet and CD-ROM technology have created new controversies over copyright ownership and works for hire. Freelance writers who sold rights in an article for publication in a magazine have been in conflict with magazines that want to reuse the articles on Web sites or in CD-ROM anthologies. In the first case of its kind decided in American courts in 1997, a federal judge in New York rejected claims by freelance writers that publishers who bought their works were authorized to use them in print publications only. Publishers are not restricted to print, the original form for running the freelancers' work, when they are simply publishing a collection of the articles they already published, such as in a year-end CD-ROM anthology. The judge acknowledged that freelance writers may lose income from rewriting and reselling their work. But the loss comes from the change in technology, not from any publisher's action that violates the copyright statute.[43] The legalities of copyright and new technology will continue to develop, but in the meantime writers and the editors who buy their works should negotiate carefully and clearly to make sure all are in agreement on the terms for reuse of freelance articles.

Fair Use

Magazine editors must expect that their copyrighted works will be used by readers, just as editors will use the copyrighted works of others in their magazines. The law protects the fair use of copyrighted materials as a way of ensuring that the creative work can be distributed widely for society's benefit. For the use of a copyrighted work to be fair, however, the copyright statute says the new work must be original itself, not relying on the creativity of the original but rather transforming the original by making it a portion of a new creative work.

To be **fair use**, a new work also should take just a limited portion of the copyrighted work. For example, a magazine's review of a new book of poetry can quote a small passage to illustrate the reviewer's point that the poems are articulate and insightful (or wooden and hackneyed, as the case may be). But the review cannot quote several entire poems because that would eliminate magazine from *Contents* by titling it *Brill's Content* when the premiere issue hit the newsstands in August 1998.

Polo Ralph Lauren, the product line of designer Ralph Lauren, went to court in 1998 to get an injunction against the use of the name Polo by the U.S. Polo Association's official magazine, *Polo,* which had covered the sport since 1974. The problem was that the magazine had been revamped in late 1997 from a narrow sporting publication to an upscale lifestyle magazine that also covered the sport of polo. The changes, according to Polo Ralph Lauren, would cause people to view it as a product of the luxury designer, and that was an infringement on the company's name.

"We're not a company that takes legal action lightly," Polo Ralph Lauren spokesman Hamilton South says. "We're a company that vigorously defends trademarks."[3]

Trademark lawyer Michael Bednarek of Kilpatrick Stockton in Washington, D.C., says the Polo case involves the "anti-dilution" law, which protects a trademark against any similar mark, even when it's on a totally different product, if it "may tarnish the image."[4]

A federal judge ruled the magazine could keep the *Polo* name, as long as it distanced itself from the designer's product. Disclaimers now appear on *Polo*'s cover, masthead, and table of contents as part of a preliminary injunction granted to Polo Ralph Lauren until the case goes to trial.

AUGUST 1998 (PREMIERE ISSUE): Founder Steven Brill intended to call his publication *Content* but discovered a Georgia-based arts quarterly titled *Contents*; the solution was to use the name *Brill's Content* to clearly distinguish the media watchdog magazine.

1 Loudon Wainwright, *The Great American Magazine: An Inside History of* Life. (New York: Alfred A, Knopf, 1986).

2 Karen Hudes, "New Titles Play the Name Game," *Folio:* (January 1, 1998): 15.

3 "Magazine Keeps Name, for Now," *Dallas Morning News* (July 7, 1998): 7D.

4 Hudes, 15.

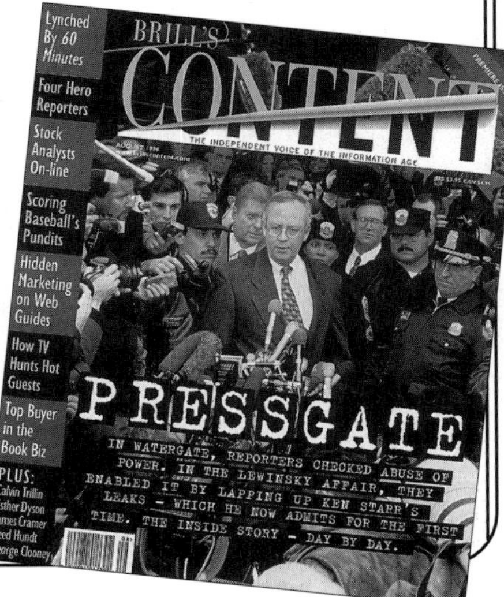

the market for the book. A reader would not buy the poet's book if he could buy the magazine and read all the articles, plus get most of the poems from the new book. The poet's publisher, as the copyright owner, has lost all control over the original work, so the magazine's use of the poems is unfair.

Fair use allows a writer to quote a copyrighted work as a source in an article, and it permits editors to use copyrighted works as sources in reviews or commentaries. It also permits readers to photocopy an entire article if their only purpose is to keep it for their personal use, such as filing away the article about winter care of garden plots for future use every winter.

Fair use does not allow editors to publish without permission significant portions of an article that belonged to a freelancer or that was published by another magazine. It would not allow a subscriber to make several copies of the main articles from a magazine to pass out to friends who just want to avoid buying the magazine themselves.[44] And it will not allow advertisers to copy a favorable review from a magazine for use in advertisements. For example, in 1987, a federal court ruled that a manufacturing company violated the copyright of *Consumer Reports* by quoting from a favorable review of a vacuum cleaner.[45] Similarly, a federal court ruled in 1952 that the Vogue School of Fashion Modeling in New York was not fairly using the cover of *Vogue* magazine when the school duplicated it for an advertisement.[46]

The fine line between fair use and infringement was illustrated by the U.S. Supreme Court in a 1985 case between *The Nation* and Harper & Row, the book publishing company.[47] In that case, *The Nation* ran a short excerpt from President Gerald Ford's book *A Time to Heal,* which Ford had written under a contract with Harper & Row. Shortly before the book was to be published, Harper & Row signed a deal with *Time* for $25,000 under which *Time* would have exclusive first publication rights for an excerpt in which Ford explained his decision to pardon President Richard Nixon of crimes growing out of the Watergate political scandal.

Just before *Time*'s exclusive was to run, *The Nation* obtained a copy of the unpublished manuscript from a secret source. *The Nation* rushed to put together an article, including about 300 words taken directly from the Ford manuscript, under the title "The Ford Memoirs—Behind the Nixon Pardon." After *The Nation* article ran in the April 13, 1979, issue, *Time* canceled its contract with Harper & Row, and the publishing house sued *The Nation* for copyright infringement. The federal district court sided with Harper & Row, but the court of appeals ruled for *The Nation,* saying the newsworthiness of the article made the publication a fair use of the Ford manuscript. The Supreme Court reversed the court of appeals and restored the district court's finding of infringement. The Supreme Court ruled that *The Nation*'s use of the excerpt was not a fair use under the copyright statute.

In evaluating whether *The Nation*'s use of the manuscript was fair or not, the Supreme Court followed the four considerations laid out by the copyright statute for determining fair use of a copyrighted work:

1. The purpose and character of the use,
2. The nature of the copyrighted work,
3. The amount and significance of the copyrighted work used, and
4. The effect that the use has on the market for the copyrighted work.

Regarding the purpose and character of the use, the Court noted that news reporting is specifically listed in the copyright statute as a fair use. But *The Nation*'s purpose was to beat *Time* and Harper & Row to the first publication of the Ford memoirs, thus undermining the copyright owner's right to control the manuscript's first publication. That made *The Nation*'s article more commercial than news, the Court reasoned. So for the first consideration, *The Nation*'s use tended toward not being fair.

Carol Burnett's successful libel lawsuit against *National Enquirer* for falsely reporting that she was drunk and quarreled with former Secretary of State Henry Kissinger in a Washington, D.C., restaurant resulted in a $1.6 million award in 1981 to the comedienne. Burnett proved the article was published with the knowledge that it was false or with reckless disregard for the truth. Although the appeals court slashed the size of the award, Burnett eventually settled for an undisclosed sum in 1984, which she used to establish the Carol Burnett Fund for Responsible Journalism to foster research, teaching, and public discussion of journalism ethics at the University of Hawaii in Honolulu.

Considering the nature of the copyrighted work, the Court focused on the fact that the manuscript was yet unpublished. The copyright statute grants wider protection to copyright owners of unpublished work to ensure they have control over when and in what form it is first published. At the same time, however, there is greater claim to fair use of factual or historical works, such as the Ford manuscript, than for works of fiction. So while this was a close call, the evidence tended to go against a finding of fair use.

The matter of amount and significance of the portion used raises questions of both quantity and quality. While the Court acknowledged that the amount was minimal—300 words from a whole book—the significance was substantial. Ford's account of pardoning Nixon was the most important part of the whole work from Harper & Row's and *Time*'s perspectives. So, in balancing amount and significance, this, too, was a close call, but the Court found it weighing against fair use also.

Finally, on the factor the statute calls the most important issue for evaluating fair use, the effect on the potential market for the work, the Court found it an easy call. "Rarely will a case of copyright infringement present such clear-cut evidence of actual damage," the Court said.[48] *Time*'s canceled contract proved the harm to Harper & Row by *The Nation*'s publication, so the final consideration clearly weighed against declaring *The Nation* article a fair use of the copyrighted memoir.

ACCESS TO INFORMATION

Information is at the foundation of good magazine journalism, and government at all levels is a trove of information. But while the First Amendment guarantees the right of magazines to publish information they have, it does not guarantee their right to access to information.

Generally, court decisions have recognized that journalists' constitutional rights of access to information are no greater than the rights of the general public. Whether it is government documents, public meetings, or crime scenes, magazine writers can expect to be treated as any other person seeking access. Chief Justice Warren Burger summarized the law this way: "There is an undoubted right to gather news from any source by means within the law, . . . but that affords no basis for the claim that the First Amendment compels others—private persons or governments—to supply information."[49] Trespass laws; restrictions on access to government property such as military bases, jails, and prisons; and police orders blocking admission to the scenes of accidents or disasters all apply to journalists just as they apply to ordinary citizens.

Fair Access

A corollary to this principle, however, can work to a magazine reporter's advantage; that is, the First Amendment requires that journalists be treated fairly in decisions granting or denying access. For example, *Sports Illustrated* assigned reporter Melissa Ludtke to cover the 1977 World Series between the New York Yankees and the Los Angeles Dodgers. But when she tried to get into the Yankee clubhouse to interview players after a game, she was denied access because of a rule in the major leagues at the time that female reporters would not be allowed into locker rooms for post-game interviews. She and *Sports Illustrated* sued Bowie Kuhn, the commissioner of major league baseball, and a federal court ruled she must be given access.[50]

In another case, however, a denial of access was permitted under the First Amendment. *The Nation*'s White House correspondent was denied a press pass that was essential for covering the White House. The Secret Service, however, refused to give a reason for its decision, insisting that its policy was never to explain why it denied press pass requests. A federal appellate court ruled the First Amendment dictated that the Secret Service must at least give an explanation for the denial and give the applicant, Robert Sherrill, a chance to respond to the decision. The Secret Service complied, explaining that Sherrill's previous conviction for physically assaulting the press secretary of the governor of Florida motivated its decision. His application was still denied.[51]

A special First Amendment right of access is found only in the court system, where the Supreme Court has ruled broadly that the First Amendment does guarantee journalists access to nearly all stages of criminal prosecutions—trials,[52] jury selection,[53] and pretrial hearings.[54]

Freedom of Information Act

Because the First Amendment generally does not guarantee journalists access to government information, Congress and the state legislatures have responded with freedom of information statutes to designate many government records as being open to the public. The federal Freedom of Information (FOI) Act was passed by Congress in 1966 to establish a basic assumption that federal records are open to the public, and a closure of records must be justifiable under the law. It applies only to the executive branch of the federal government and covers paper and computer records held by federal agencies.

The exemptions in the law that allow some records to remain closed are typical of freedom of information laws at all levels. In the federal law, the exemptions are:

1. *National Security*—Information that could damage the national interest if released can be withheld.
2. *Agency Rules and Practices*—Records of little or no public concern do not have to be released when they deal solely with internal personnel rules and practices, such as parking, filing procedures, sick leave, or use of the cafeteria. The point is to spare agencies from maintaining such records in a condition suitable for public inspection.
3. *Statutory Exemptions*—The so-called "catch-all" exemption allows Congress to declare in other laws that information is exempted from the FOI Act.
4. *Confidential Business Information*—Trade secrets and confidential commercial information required by law to be submitted to the government can be withheld to prevent industrial espionage.
5. *Agency Memos*—The "executive privilege" exemption protects working drafts of documents from being released so government executives can have the benefit of frank and open comments and recommendations from staff members that otherwise might be

watered down if they were to be read by the public before a final decision were made.

6. *Personnel, Medical, and Similar Files*—Government records about individuals can be withheld from the public if releasing them would create an invasion of personal privacy.
7. *Law Enforcement Investigations*—Information compiled for law enforcement purposes can be kept closed if releasing it would compromise an ongoing investigation. Examples of such records include the identity of confidential informants, protected law enforcement techniques or practices, and information that must be kept secret to protect a defendant's right to a fair trial.
8. *Banking Reports*—Like trade secrets, information that federally regulated financial institutions must file by law is exempted.
9. *Oil, Gas, and Water Well Information*—Geological data about wells are exempted to prevent land speculators from easily getting information that was expensive for drilling and extraction companies to develop.

The most common way to use the FOI Act to get a document is to write a letter to the Freedom of Information officer at the agency that possesses it. The letter should emphasize that the request is being made under the FOI Act and should describe the document in as much detail as possible. It also helps to state forthrightly that the request is being made for journalistic purposes so a quick response is important. Federal agencies are required under the law to acknowledge requests within 10 days, although it usually takes much longer for them to produce the documents. Good samples of FOI request letters can be found from organizations that support freedom of information causes, such as the Reporters Committee for Freedom of the Press in Arlington, Virginia, and the Society of Professional Journalists Project Sunshine in Greencastle, Indiana, to list just two. Most states also have local FOI organizations that can lend a hand with FOI requests or problems.

State open records laws and their exemptions are comparable to the federal law in their structure and content, though they can differ widely from state to state. There is no substitute for reading the law in a particular state to be familiar with the exemptions it allows. In every state, it is as important to know what records are exempted under the law as to know what is covered. Many state statutes have exemptions comparable to the federal exemptions. Law-enforcement information and personal privacy in medical or personnel records are the most common exceptions, but state laws tend to allow many other exemptions as well, often running to more than 20.

Sunshine Laws

State open meetings laws are also an important access tool for magazine journalists covering public affairs. All 50 states have laws, often called sunshine laws, requiring that meetings of public bodies such as city councils or state boards be open to the public. Strong state sunshine laws explicitly state which groups are covered by the law, require public notice before a meeting is held, and prohibit public officials from conducting business at informal or social gatherings. They typically allow for meetings to be closed when a body is discussing real estate transactions, lawsuits, or personnel issues, but the strong statutes require that the final vote on all decisions be taken in open session. Help with open meeting complaints can usually be obtained from state attorneys general's offices and from state freedom of information organizations.

OBSCENITY

Sex and sexuality are common topics for magazines of all kinds. From the cover of *Cosmopolitan* to the *Sports Illustrated* swimsuit issue to the titillation and teasing of some teen publications, an undercurrent of sex permeates many magazines. The law of obscenity in no way affects such magazine content.

As a legal concept, **obscenity** refers to a narrow category of hard-core pornography that is beyond the scope of First Amendment protection because it is so sexually explicit that it does not contribute to the exchange of ideas and information that the First Amendment protects. Obscenity does not include the material published in the most commonly circulated sex magazines, such as *Playboy, Penthouse, Hustler,* and the like.

Unlike most of the other legal issues discussed in this chapter, obscenity is usually a criminal matter. In other words, publishers, producers, and distributors of obscene materials are prosecuted for violating criminal laws. For that reason, defining obscenity—what materials will be subject to criminal prosecution—has been an important First Amendment challenge for the U.S. Supreme Court. If obscenity is not defined clearly and carefully by the Court, police and prosecutors might take constitutionally protected publications and ideas out of circulation.

The Supreme Court's test for obscenity has three prongs:

1. Applying a contemporary community standard, the average person would find that the work as a whole appeals to a prurient interest in sex.
2. The pornography must depict in a "patently offensive" way some sexual conduct that is specifically defined by an applicable state statute.
3. The work as a whole must lack any serious literary, artistic, political, or scientific value.

All three of the factors must be present to find a work to be obscene.[55]

Such a test does not cover written descriptions of sex or sexual topics, photos or drawings of mere nudity, or the come-hither pandering of mainstream magazine advertising. Four-letter words in an article cannot come under the label of obscenity. For most editors and writers working in the mainstream of American magazine journalism, then, the law of obscenity will not cramp their style, even if they are developing or publishing sexually oriented content in their magazines.

The Constitution does permit the regulation of nonobscene, sexually explicit magazines in some ways, the Supreme Court has ruled. For example, cities can have zoning laws that restrict the locations of businesses that sell pornographic magazines, either to confine them to one part of town, to diffuse them throughout town so they are not concentrated, or to keep them from locating close to schools, churches, parks, or residences.[56] Cities and states can also require that pornographic magazines displayed in stores appear behind an opaque cover or inside a sealed wrapper.[57] Such laws protect minors and unwilling consumers from being exposed to pornography, but they do not unconstitutionally deprive adults of access to the magazines or restrict the free expression rights of publishers. Similarly, the Supreme Court has upheld a federal law that prohibited the sale of sexually explicit magazines on military bases. Postal regulations also prohibit mailing nonobscene sexual materials to the homes of people who do not want to receive them.

American magazines operate in a legal atmosphere meant to guarantee tremendous freedom, because freedom is assumed to inspire greater creativity and more open social discussion. Generally speaking, legal limitations on the editorial or advertising content of magazines violate the free press and free speech clauses of the First Amendment. But that broad freedom brings tremendous responsibility for editors and publishers. Editors and publishers must make careful ethical decisions about editorial and advertising content because not everything protected by the First Amendment is responsible journalism. Editors also must recognize where the fuzzy line lies between ethics and law, so they know when they are crossing over into a zone where they risk legal punishment for a misstep.

There's no point in becoming paranoid about all the legal risks and ethical responsibilities involved in publishing a magazine. With just a bit of his tongue in cheek, Edward L. Smith, who practices publishing law in New York City, points out, "To eliminate totally the legal risks associated with accuracy and factuality, a magazine would be limited to writing about dead people or printing nothing."[58]

The American Society of Journalists and Authors (ASJA) drew up the first writer's contract in 1976. ASJA now has a Web site, "ASJA Contracts Watch," at <http://www.asja.org/cwpage.htm> for news about contracts, copyright law, and other related issues.

FOR ADDITIONAL READING

Adler, Renata. *Reckless Disregard.* New York: Alfred A. Knopf, 1986.

Friendly, Fred. *Minnesota Rag.* New York: Random House, 1981.

Goldstein, Paul. *Copyright's Highway.* New York: Hill and Wang, 1994.

Lewis, Anthony. *Make No Law.* New York: Random House, 1991.

Merrill, John C. *The Dialectic in Journalism: Toward a Responsible Use of Press Freedom.* Baton Rouge: Louisiana State University Press, 1989.

Powe, Lucas A. *The Fourth Estate and the Constitution: Freedom of the Press in America.* Berkeley: University of California Press, 1991.

Smolla, Rodney A. *Jerry Falwell v. Larry Flynt: The First Amendment on Trial.* New York: St. Martin's Press, 1988.

———. *Suing the Press.* New York: Oxford University Press, 1986.

Strong, William S. *The Copyright Book: A Practical Guide.* Cambridge, MA: MIT Press, 1993.

ENDNOTES

1 *Breard v. Alexandria*, 341 U.S. 622 (1951), at 645.

2 481 U.S. 221 (1987).

3 *Bantam Books, Inc. v. Sullivan*, 372 U.S. 58 (1963).

4 *New York Times v. United States* (The Pentagon Papers case), 403 U.S. 713 (1971).

5 *United States v. Progressive, Inc.*, 467 F. Supp. 990 (W.D. Wis. 1979) dismissed, 610 F. 2d, 819, (7th Cir. 1979).

6 *Procter & Gamble Company v. Bankers Trust Company*, 78 F.3d 219 (6th Cir. 1996).

7 78 F.3d, at 227.

8 *Goldwater v. Ginzburg*, 414 F. 2d 324 (2d Cir. 1969).

9 *Montandon v. Triangle Publications, Inc.*, 45 Cal. App. 3d 938 (1975).

10 *Kaplan v. Newsweek, Inc.*, 776 F.2d 1053 (9th Cir. 1985).

11 *Granger v. Time Inc.*, 568 P. 2d 535 (1977).

12 376 U.S. 254 (1964). After the Sullivan case the Court decided several cases to clarify, expand, and adapt the basic principle introduced in Sullivan. These included *Garrison v. Louisiana*, 379 U.S. 64 (1964); *Rosenblatt v. Baer*, 383 U.S. 75 (1966); *Curtis Publishing Co. v. Butts*, 388 U.S. 130 (1967); St. *Amant v. Thompson*, 390 U.S. 727 (1968); *Rosenbloom v. Metromedia*, 403 U.S. 29 (1971); *Monitor Patriot v. Roy*, 401 U.S. 265 (1971); *Ocala Star-Banner Co. v. Damron*, 401 U.S. 295 (1971); and *Gertz v. Robert Welch*, 418 U.S. 323 (1974).

13 418 U.S. 323 (1974).

14 383 U.S. 75 (1966).

15 *Time Inc. v. Firestone*, 424 U.S. 448 (1976).

16 *Wolston v. Reader's Digest Ass'n*, 443 U.S. 157 (1979).

17 *Curtis Publishing Co. v. Butts*, 388 U.S. 130 (1967).

18 *Goldwater v. Ginzburg*, 414 F. 2d 324 (2d Cir. 1969).

19 *Masson v. New Yorker Magazine, Inc.*, 501 U.S. 496 (1991).

20 H. Wat Hopkins, "Negligence Ten Years After *Gertz v. Welch*," *Journalism Monographs*, no. 93 (August 1985): 19.

21 *Keeton v. Hustler*, 465 U.S. 770 (1984).

22 *Barber v. Time Inc.*, 159 S.W.2d 291 (Mo. 1942).

23 *Virgil v. Sports Illustrated, Inc.*, 424 F. Sup. 1286 (S.D. Cal. 1976).

24 *Sidis v. F-R Publishing Corp.*, 113 F.2d 806 (1940).

25 *Dietemann v. Time Inc.*, 449 F.2d 245 (9th Cir. 1971).

26 449 F.2d, at 249.

27 *Time Inc. v. Hill*, 385 U.S. 374 (1967).

28 *Pring v. Penthouse Int'l, Ltd.*, 695 F.2d 438 (10th Cir. 1982).

29 *Murray v. New York Magazine*, 267 N.E.2d 256 (N.Y. 1971).

30 *Booth v. Curtis Publishing Co.*, 223 N.Y.S.2d 737 (N.Y. 1962).

31 13 Media L. Rptr. 1657 (D. Or. 1986).

32 *Hustler Magazine, Inc. v. Falwell*, 485 U.S. 46 (1988).

33 814 F.2d 1017 (5th Cir. 1987).

34 *Walters v. Seventeen Magazine*, 241 Cal.Rptr. 101 (Cal.App. 4 Dist. 1987).

35 *Yuhas v. Mudge*, 322 A.2d 824 (N.J. App. 1974).

36 81 Cal.Rptr. 519 (Cal.App. 4 Dist. 1969).

37 880 F.2d 830 (5th Cir. 1989).

38 968 F.2d 1110 (11th Cir. 1992).

39 "Legislation Extending Copyright Terms, Limiting Music Licensing Signed into Law," *United States Law Week*, 67: 18 (November 17, 1998): 2278.

40 17 U.S.C.A. §102 (West 1996).

41 *Feist Publications, Inc. v. Tel. Serv. Co.*, 499 U.S. 340 (1991).

42 *Suid v. Newsweek Magazine*, 503 F.Supp. 146 (1980).

43 *Tasini v. New York Times Co.*, DC SNY, No. 93 Civ. 8678 (SS), 8/13/97.

44 See *American Geophysical Union, Inc. v. Texaco, Inc.*, 60 F.3d 913 (2d Cir. 1994) in which a federal appeals court ruled that it was not fair use for Texaco to copy and distribute articles from scientific journals to its scientists for their research files to avoid buying a subscription to each journal for each researcher.

45 *Consumers Union of United States, Inc. v. New Regina Corp.*, 664 F. Supp. 753 (S.D.N.Y. 1987).

46 *Condé Nast Publications, Inc. v. Vogue School of Fashion Modeling, Inc.*, 105 F. Supp. 325 (S.D.N.Y. 1952).

47 *Harper & Row, Publishers, Inc. v. Nation Enterprises, Inc.*, 471 U.S. 539 (1985).

48 471 U.S., at 567.

49 *Houchins v. KQED, Inc.*, 438 U.S. 1 (1978), in which the Supreme Court upheld restrictions that denied a television station access to an area in a county jail in California where an inmate had committed suicide.

50 *Ludtke v. Kuhn*, 461 F.Supp. 86 (S.D.N.Y. 1978).

51 *Sherrill v. Knight*, 569 F.2d 124 (D.C. Cir. 1978)

52 *Richmond Newspapers, Inc. v. Virginia*, 448 U.S. 555 (1980).

53 *Press-Enterprise Co. v. Riverside County Superior Court* (Press-Enterprise I), 464 U.S. 501 (1984).

54 *Press-Enterprise Co. v. Riverside County Superior Court* (Press-Enterprise II), 478 U.S. 1 (1986).

55 *Miller v. California*, 413 U.S. 15 (1973).

56 *City of Renton v. Playtime Theaters, Inc.*, 475 U.S. 41.

57 *M.S. News Co. v. Casado*, 721 F. 2d 1281 (10th Cir. 1983), Upper Midwest Booksellers Ass'n *v.* City of Minneapolis, 780 F.2d 1389 (8th Cir. 1985).

58 Abbe Wichman, "Who's Responsible for Fact Checking?" *Folio:* (November 1989): 171.

C H A P T E R 12

Magazines *for the* Twenty-First Century

Ethics and the Culture of Commerce

Playboy magazine and the television show "Baywatch" are a team. Playboy's Playmates appear as characters on "Baywatch," and the magazine shows us the skinny on the series regulars. It's a marriage of commercial enterprises, turning the readers of the magazine into viewers of the show, and vice versa. Publishers, producers, and advertisers reap the benefits of an enlarged audience. What does this mean to American culture? The union of Playboy and "Baywatch" is good business, but is what's good for business automatically good for the country as a whole? How does the character of contemporary magazines affect the American character? And what can the magazine professionals of today and tomorrow do to create a magazine culture of which they can be proud? Today's magazines face a series of challenges unique to this time in history, many of them ethical. The ways in which professionals respond to these challenges will determine the face of the magazine of the twenty-first century. Proactive magazine staffs think about potential problems ahead of time and implement strategies to avoid and resolve conflicts. Codes of ethics have traditionally provided staffs with a well-defined response to ethical questions. The American Society of Magazine Editors, the American Business Press, and the Society of Professional Journalists are just a few of the organizations offering ethical guides for consumer, business, and organization magazines. However, magazine staffs continue to be beset with new problems caused by technological and cultural change. Advertising-editorial conflicts; mergers and acquisitions; new media opportunities; content decisions; and the "dumbing down" of editorial content present today's magazine staffs with decisions that will alter the ways in which magazines do business in the future.

Much is wrong with American magazines. Much, however, is also right with them. The future of the medium will be shaped by our defenses against the pitfalls we face and our ability to embrace the opportunities we're given.

ADVERTISING-EDITORIAL CONFLICTS

Some of the most contentious conflicts in the magazine publishing world have erupted between the advertising sales staff, with its emphasis on serving the needs of advertisers, and the editorial staff, with its emphasis on serving the needs of readers. Most magazines walk this line responsibly, recognizing that what advertisers want are loyal readers, because a quality magazine that serves readers also serves advertisers.

Undue advertiser influence not only hurts the magazine, it also hurts the advertiser, according to many industry professionals. It is a lose-lose situation, says Marcy O'Koon, executive editor of *Arthritis Today:* "The more independent we are, the better our magazine will be. The better and more valued our magazine is, the more advertisers will seek us out. We see our editorial independence as a way of creating mutual benefits for our advertising sales reps and our readers."[1]

Occasionally, though, the line between advertising and editorial blurs when advertisers expect to influence editorial content. Some advertisers ask for pre-notification, complementary copy, or placement adjacent to specific articles. Sometimes an advertiser sponsors an entire issue. Occasionally, an advertiser may request cover treatment, a situation that creates all sorts of difficulties for editors concerned about the magazine's integrity. **Bingo cards**—cards readers can use to request information on advertised products—may help assuage advertiser concern, but they're not necessarily representative of reader interest.

Clear Ad-Edit Distinction

Most magazines separate their advertising and editorial staffs, with the editorial staff planning and developing the magazine, then giving the sales people the information they need to sell the magazine. If a running magazine is planning a special series on buying running shoes, for example, planning for the issue is done by the editorial staff. The editors, in turn, give information on the series to the advertising salespeople who can then increase efforts to get advertising from shoe manufacturers. The division is clear: The magazine's content is determined by the editors. Magazine staffs often plan editorial content more than a year in advance and give advertisers—as part of a media kit—an editorial calendar, which lists major stories and themes for an entire year's issues. In that way, advertising follows—and supplements—editorial content.

James McGraw, a trade magazine pioneer and one of the founders of McGraw-Hill, believed a quality magazine was one that reported aggressively. Especially important, he said, was that the publication not depend on "write ups from advertisers." A business publication, he wrote in *Electrical World* in 1924, should not be influenced by advertisers, but must "be its own master" and "have no other guides for its opinions and policies but truth and the sound interests of the field it serves."[2]

Alvaro Saralegui, general manager of *Sports Illustrated* in 1997, offered a simple formula: "The way we all believe it works is, you put out a great magazine, you get terrific readers and that will attract great advertisers."[3]

Not so simple, said some major advertisers in 1997. Titleist and Foot-Joy Worldwide canceled nearly $1.5 million in ads in *Sports Illustrated*'s *Golf Plus* supplement in reaction to an April 7, 1997, story on the Nabisco Dinah Shore golf tournament in Palm Springs. The tournament had become, according to the magazine, a "spring break" for some 20,000 lesbians. Wally Uihlein, chairman and chief executive officer of Titleist and Foot-Joy Worldwide, the largest advertiser in *Golf Plus,* called the story "symptomatic of a condescending attitude toward women in golf in general." Managing editor Bill Colson suggested Uihlein respond in a readers' column in the magazine. Uihlein did, but also canceled the ads.

Advertiser Prenotification

One of the world's largest advertising agencies went a step beyond this and required prior notice from magazines that plan to publish controversial content. PentaCom, a division of BBDO Worldwide, and Chrysler Corporation's advertising agency, sent more than 100 magazines a letter in January 1996 that stated: "In an effort to avoid potential conflicts, it is required that Chrysler Corporation be alerted in advance of any and all editorial content that encompasses sexual, political, social issues or any editorial that might be construed as provocative or offensive. Each and every issue that carries Chrysler advertising requires a written summary outlining major theme/articles appearing in upcoming issues. These summaries are to be forwarded to PentaCom prior to closing in order to give Chrysler ample time to review and reschedule if desired."[4]

***M**ovieline* made history in 1996 when it became the first entertainment magazine to devote an entire issue—from front to back—to the black presence in Hollywood.

This request went far beyond the type of broad content overview offered in editorial calendars and was a blatant effort at censorship by advertisers, who didn't want to know just *what* magazines were covering, but wanted instead to know *how* it was being covered. Colgate-Palmolive provided guidelines to its advertising agencies requiring them to avoid magazine issues with "offensive" sexual content or material the company "considers antisocial or in bad taste." And the Ford Motor Company pulled ads from *The New Yorker* when that magazine didn't tell it about an article containing a four-letter word. *The New Yorker* responded by devising a system to warn some 50 "sensitive advertisers" that the magazine was planning potentially offensive content.[5]

The American Society of Magazine Editors (ASME) responded to the controversy with a position statement issued June 23, 1997:

> *The ASME board of directors is deeply concerned about this early-warning trend. Specifically, the ASME board worries that some advertisers may mistake an early warning as an open invitation to pressure the publisher or editor to alter, or even kill, the article in question. We believe publishers should—and will—refuse to bow to such pressure. Furthermore, we believe editors should—and will—follow ASME's explicit principle of editorial independence, which at its core states: "The chief editor of any magazine must have final authority over the editorial content, words and pictures, that appear in the publication."*[6]

American Society of Magazine Editors Guidelines for Editors and Publishers

The following guidelines for advertising pages and advertising sections are published by the American Society of Magazine Editors (ASME).

GUIDELINES FOR EDITORIAL AND ADVERTISING PAGES

1. Any page of advertising that contains text or design elements that have an editorial appearance must be clearly or conspicuously identified with the words "advertising" or "advertisement" horizontally at or near the center of the top of the page in type at least equal in size and weight to the publication's normal editorial body type face. The word "advertorial" should not be used.
2. The layout, design and type face of advertising pages should be distinctly different from the publication's normal layout, design and type faces.
3. At no time should a magazine's name, logo or editorial staff be used in a way that suggests editorial endorsement of any advertiser. Specifically:
   (a) No advertisement may be promoted on the cover of the magazine or included in the editorial table of contents.
   (b) The publication's name or logo should not appear on any advertising pages except when advertising the magazine's own products and services.

   Exception: The magazine's name or logo may be used to label its own multi-advertiser sections (e.g., classified ad pages, seasonal gift guides), merchandising joint promotions, and advertiser contests, but those pages must carry the words "advertising," "advertisement," or "promotion" as detailed in Guideline 1.
4. Advertising pages should not be placed adjacent to related editorial material in a manner that implies editorial endorsement of the advertised product or services. No advertising copy should state or imply advertiser control or improper involvement in the preparation of editorial materials in an issue. Similarly, an advertiser's name or logo may not be used on any editorial pages to suggest advertising sponsorship of those pages, nor shall any editorial page be labeled as "sponsored" or "brought to you" by an advertiser. If an advertiser or any other outside organization underwrites a contest featured on editorial pages, the editorial copy must not suggest an endorsement of that advertiser's products or services. The contest must remain under the sole control of the editors and the sponsoring organization may not participate in the contest judging or any aspect of the editorial presentation.
5. In order for the publication's chief editor to have the opportunity to monitor compliance with the guidelines, advertising pages should be made available to the editor in ample time for review and to recommend any necessary changes.

GUIDELINES FOR SPECIAL ADVERTISING SECTIONS

A special advertising section is a set of advertising pages unified by a theme, accompanied by editorial-like text or by editorial material from another magazine that supports the theme. Such a section consists of two or more pages, often including a cover, that is paid for by one or more advertisers.

1. Each text page of special advertising must be clearly and conspicuously identified as a message paid for by advertisers.
2. In order to identify special advertising sections clearly and conspicuously:
   (a) The words "advertising," "advertisement," "special advertising section," or "special advertising supplement" should appear horizontally at or near the center of the top of every page of such sections containing text, in type at least equal in size and weight to the publication's normal editorial body type face. The word "advertorial" should not be used.

ASME and the Magazine Publishers of America (MPA) issued a joint statement urging members to refuse to "submit table of contents, text or photos from upcoming issues to advertisers for prior review."[7]

Chrysler responded to the ASME and MPA criticism by backing off from requiring prior review, at the same time suggesting they would

(b) The layout, design and type, and literary style of such sections should be distinctly different from the publication's normal layout, design, type faces and literary style. The content of a special advertising section should be sufficiently distinct from the content of the issue in which it appears to prevent reader confusion between editorial pages and special advertising pages.

(c) If the sponsor or organizer of the section is not the publisher, the sponsor should be clearly identified.

3. Special advertising sections should not be slugged on the publication's cover or included in the editorial table of contents. The publication's name or logo should not appear as any part of the headlines or text of such sections, except in connection with the magazine's own products and services.
   Exception: The magazine's name or logo may be used to label its own multi-advertiser sections (e.g., classified ad pages, seasonal gift guides), merchandising joint promotions, and advertiser contests, but those pages must carry the words "advertising," "advertisement," or "promotion," as detailed in Guideline 2(a) and Guideline 2(b).
4. Advertising sections should not be placed adjacent to editorial material in a manner that implies editorial endorsement of the advertised product or services. Similarly, an advertiser's name or logo may not be used on any editorial pages to suggest advertising sponsorship of those pages, nor shall any editorial page be labeled as "sponsored" or "brought to you" by an advertiser.
5. The editors' names and titles should not appear on, or be associated with, special advertising sections, nor should the names and titles of any other editorial staff members of the publication or regular contributors to it appear or be associated with special advertising sections.
6. Editors and other editorial staff members should not prepare advertising sections for their own publications, for other publications in their field, or for advertisers in the fields they cover. No editorial staff members should work on custom publishing projects prepared by the publisher for one or more advertisers. Moreover, custom publishing projects must be sufficiently distinct from the graphics and content of the core magazine, as outlined in Guideline 2(b).
7. In order for the publication's chief editor to have the opportunity to monitor compliance with these guidelines, material for special advertising sections should be made available to the editor in ample time for review and to recommend necessary changes. Monitoring would include reading the text of special advertising sections before publication for problems of fact, interpretation and taste, and for compliance with any relevant laws.
8. In order to avoid potential conflicts or overlaps with editorial content, publishers should notify editors well in advance of their plans to run special advertising sections.
9. The size and number of special advertising sections within a single issue should not be out of balance with the size and the nature of the magazine.

ASME GUIDELINES FOR NEW MEDIA

The same ASME principles that mandate distinct treatment of editorial content, advertisements, and special advertising sections ("advertorials") in print publications also apply to electronic editorial products bearing the names of print magazine or offering themselves as electronic magazines. The dynamic technology of electronic pages and hypertext links create high potential for reader confusion. Permitting such confusion betrays reader trust and undermines the credibility not only of the offending online publication or editorial product, but also of the publisher itself. Therefore, it is the responsibility of each online publication to make clear to its users which online content is editorial and which is advertising and to prevent any juxtaposition that gives the impression that editorial material was created for, or influenced by, advertisers.

ASME is hereby calling on editors, publishers and advertisers to follow this set of standards.

1. The home page of a publication's web site (or other electronic venue) shall identify the publication by displaying its name and logo prominently in order to make clear who controls the content of the site.
2. On all online pages, there shall be a clear distinction made through words, design, placement, or any

place less advertising in magazines. Chrysler spokesman Michael Aberlich said the company responded to industry criticism: "We've said before that if the industry acted together we would abide by it." Nevertheless, he added, Chrysler would "become a lot more conservative" about choosing magazines and it may reduce its total magazine spending. That other effective method between editorial and advertising content.

3. In the case of special advertising sections ("advertorials"), or in any other case where there is significant danger that advertising, including "advertorials," will be mistaken for true, independently produced editorial content, the advertising in question shall carry the words "Special Advertising Section" or "Advertisement" from (company name) prominently at the top of each page or each body of material within a page, in type at least equal in size and weight to the publication's normal editorial body type face. The word "advertorial" should not be used.
4. Publications shall display their logos in conjunction with the logo of another company only in custom publishing arrangements where the publication solely controls the site's content and in no way endorses the advertiser's products or services.
5. Links that appear within the editorial content of a site shall be under the sole control of the editors. No publication may sell outright or make a condition of any advertising sale, either explicitly or by implication, a link from its editorial content to any other site.
6. Neither links nor other references to special advertising sections, or "advertorials," shall appear in the table of contents, directory of contents, or in any listing of editorial content of an online publication. However, a reference to a special advertising section or "advertorial" may be placed outside editorial areas and displayed in a design different from the publication's editorial design.
7. Editors shall not create content for special advertising sections or other advertisements.
8. Publications shall require that search engines and other applications be presented under the publication's brand and made accessible through the publication's Web sites, perform their operations free of influence from advertising or other commercial considerations.

Alterations that give greater prominence to an advertiser's site or link would constitute a betrayal of reader trust and are therefore prohibited.

SINGLE-SPONSOR ISSUES

If a magazine or special issue is supported by a single advertiser, the advertiser's support of the issue should be fully disclosed to readers in a publisher's or editor's letter. The letter should also make clear that the advertiser had no influence over the editorial content.

STANDARD FOR EDITORIAL INDEPENDENCE

ASME unveiled the following standard for editorial independence in October 1996, in an effort to affirm the highest standards in magazine journalism, and to underscore magazine editors' traditional independence from untoward commercial or other extra-journalistic pressures.

The chief editor of any magazine must have final authority over the editorial content, words and pictures, that appear in the publication. When an ASME member brings a possible violation of this principle to the attention of the ASME board, an Editorial Independence Committee appointed by the ASME board shall be empowered to investigate the circumstances of the breach and make a report to the board. In instances of egregious violations, the committee may recommend that ASME suspend the offending magazine from participation in the National Magazine Awards program.

JOINT MPA/ASME STANDARD FOR PRIOR REVIEW

In September 1997, Magazine Publishers of America joined with ASME in issuing a joint statement establishing a policy about prior notification of editorial content. This statement was an effort to underscore the importance of editorial credibility and provide an industry standard.

STATEMENT

As editors and publishers, we strongly believe that editorial integrity and credibility are the magazine industry's most important assets. As a result, we believe that magazines should not submit table of contents, text or photos from upcoming issues to advertisers for prior review. We are confident that editors and publishers can inform advertisers about a publication's editorial environment or direction without engaging in practices that may at the very least create the appearance of censorship and ultimately could undermine editorial independence.

Courtesy the American Society of Magazine Editors

could be a big bite out of the magazine pie: in 1996, the year before the conflict erupted, Chrysler spent about $270 million advertising in 350 titles.[8]

Complementary Editorial

Some advertisers believe that if they place an ad in a magazine they deserve a positive mention in the magazine's editorial sections. In the

"Magazine Voices" segment of this book, Robin Morgan, former editor of *Ms.*, explains how that magazine fought the battle with advertisers who simply expected all women's magazines to offer complementary editorial to advertisers. When *Ms.* refused to play the game, advertisers avoided the magazine.

Gloria Steinem painted a bleak picture of advertiser influence on women's magazines in "Sex, Lies and Advertising," published in the first ad-free issue of *Ms.* Manufacturers of food, beauty, and fashion products, she says, expect a "supportive editorial atmosphere" that includes "articles that praise food/fashion/beauty subjects to 'support' and 'complement' food/fashion/beauty ads." Steinem lists the food products the magazine tried unsuccessfully to woo: General Mills, Pillsbury, Carnation, DelMonte, Dole, Kraft, Stouffer, Hormel, and Nabisco. *Ms.*, however, ran no recipes, so these advertisers refused to see the magazine as a legitimate advertising buy, even though the readers clearly ate food. *Ms.* was fighting deeply held advertising industry beliefs of the relationship between editorial and advertising in a women's magazine:

> *Food advertisers have always demanded that women's magazines publish recipes and articles on entertaining (preferably ones that name their products) in return for their ads; clothing advertisers expect to be surrounded by fashion spreads (especially ones that credit their designers); and shampoo, fragrance, and beauty products in general usually insist on positive editorial coverage of beauty subjects, plus photo credits besides.*[9]

Complementary editorial is an issue that affects all magazines at one time or another. *Consumers Digest* has been criticized by competitor *Consumer Reports* for blurring the line between editorial and advertising. *Consumers Digest*—not associated with *Consumer Reports* in any way—has been offering a "Best Buy" rating, mimicking *Consumer Reports*'s rating of the same name. A *Consumers Digest* "Best Buy" often goes to products advertised within the magazine. The Dodge Neon, for example, not recommended by *Consumer Reports*, earned a "*Consumers Digest* Best Buy." Buyers who don't read closely may mistake that for a "*Consumer Reports* Best Buy," which has to be earned through scientific testing. *Consumer Reports* has trademarked its rating as a "CR Best Buy," but the confusion remains.[10] The primary issue is, of course, whether the rating comes along with an advertising buy.

Adjacencies

Occasionally an ad appears next to an article about the product: A window manufacturer advertises its new porch windows right next to an article on the resurgence of porches. Sometimes the editor did not know that the manufacturer would be promoting porch-related products and is honestly chagrined when the ad comes in. If it comes early enough, it can be moved to a less obvious page, or the editorial can be changed. If it comes in late, though, the editor is stuck.

Sometimes editors suspect that the ad sales representative knew about the content in advance, which is why the ad is late. In that case, the problem happens only once, if the editor and publisher are committed to editorial integrity.

In some cases, though, the adjacency is planned and paid for. A 1997 start-up, *Notorious*, caused waves in the magazine community by selling 10 pages of ads per issue to the alcohol advertiser International Distillers and Vintners, with the understanding that IDV would be its only liquor advertiser and the ads would be placed adjacent to related editorial. The editor of the magazine—which focuses on "sex, love, and romance"—said *Notorious* was "doing what every magazine in America is doing."[11]

Betsy Carter, former vice president of the American Society of Magazine Editors, agrees that adjacencies are far more common than critics suggest. "Look at fashion magazines or beauty magazines or the women's magazines. It happens all the time," she says.[12]

Like many magazines, *Better Homes and Gardens* allows advertisers to make general requests for placement next to editorial content—food advertising next to food editorial, home design products next to design editorial. Some advertisers, however, may get more demanding and ask to be next to a specific article—a food advertiser may request placement, for example, next to a story on tuna sandwiches. Managing editor Lamont Olson says the magazine avoids any appearance of "advertising-editorial collusion" through regular communication between the advertising and editorial staffs to avoid surprises. The staff may change the article if the adjacency places the publication's integrity at risk and if the ad can't be placed elsewhere.

Entire Issue Sponsorship

Single-advertiser magazine issues have been around for several years. For example, *Newsweek* produced a special issue about children in 1996 in which the only advertiser was Johnson & Johnson, the eighth largest advertiser in consumer magazines. *Time* has produced special issues in 1991 and 1996 on heroes in medicine and the frontiers of medicine, respectively, that had pharmaceutical giant and advertising leader Glaxo-Wellcome as the sole advertiser. Chrysler sponsored a special *Time* issue on multiculturalism in 1993.

However, the line between advertising and editorial priorities did not seem blurred until *Time* decided to schedule a sole advertiser for a regularly scheduled—as opposed to additional—issue of the magazine. The first regular issue of *Time* in 1999, dated January 11, had "The Future of Medicine" as its cover story. It had one advertiser: Pfizer, the third largest pharmaceutical advertiser in the country. That was a first in the magazine industry. While few magazine editors or critics believe that Pfizer shaped the editorial content of the issue, they were troubled about what may be a trend toward having big advertisers sponsor magazine issues on topics of interest to them.

APRIL/MAY 1998: *Notorious* caused waves in the magazine community when it sold ads to International Distillers and Vintners with the understanding that the company would be the only liquor advertiser and that the ads would be placed adjacent to related editorial.

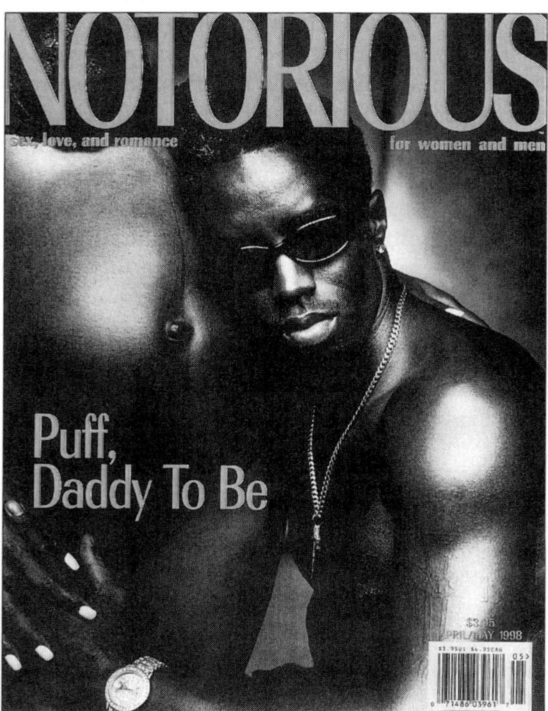

Jacqueline Leo, president of the American Society of Magazine Editors in 1998, said she was concerned that the arrangement sends the wrong signal to advertisers: "First, what happens to the other advertisers? You're eliminating a lot of other people who may have wanted to be in that issue for whatever reason."[13]

A different spin on the advertising-editorial relationship occurred in 1976 when an advertiser tried to underwrite a series of magazine articles, much as is done in television where a sole advertiser may sponsor a television program. But the brouhaha that occurred was so loud that only one underwritten article appeared.

The Xerox Corporation paid for a story written by Pulitzer Prize-winning author Harrison Salisbury in the February 1976 issue of *Esquire*. Although *Esquire* selected the author and the topic, Xerox paid Salisbury $40,000 plus $15,000 in expenses to write "Travels through America," a thoughtful essay run in conjunction with the bicentennial fervor sweeping the country. Although Xerox had no editorial control over the article, *Esquire* reaped a one-year, $115,000 advertising deal from Xerox. Author and essayist E. B. White criticized the arrangement, saying the project was "charting a clear course for the erosion of the free press in America."[14]

Advertisers on the Cover

Martha Stewart Living published a special issue in the fall of 1998 titled "Clotheskeeping" that was devoted to choosing and maintaining classic clothing. There was only one advertiser: Gap, filling 33 pages of the issue. Where the problem occurred for magazine ethicists was the magazine's use of Gap shirts on the cover, along with some from Barneys and Agnes B. Can you do this kind of advertising promotion, even with a special issue, and still maintain editorial integrity?

Allen Adamson, managing director at Landor Associates, a brand consulting firm that is part of Young & Rubicam advertising company, says, "Any illusion that this is not a promotional slash infomercial use is a fallacy." However, Suzanne

Sobel, publisher of *Martha Stewart Living,* does not see a problem: "We really handled this so it would not appear infomercialized. There was no collusion whatsoever. We didn't see the ads prior to them delivering them, and they didn't see the editorial. But we do have the same taste."[15]

The matter is not always clear cut. Advertisers regularly provide the props for specialized consumer and trade magazine covers—such as appliances or home products for shelter magazines; stereo systems for music magazines; clothing for fashion magazines—with the brand names of some products clearly visible. As long as the products used serve the magazine's editorial and design purpose and the advertiser does not pay for placement, most editors see this as serving both the readers and advertisers. Critics, however, see this as being dangerously close to the ethical line.

What happens, though, when the ad on an inside page is visible through the cover? Is it technically an ad? This tricky situation faced Patti Adcroft, *Omni* editor-in-chief in 1990, and caused her to resign in protest. The magazine's November 1990 cover, she said, contained an advertisement for Motorola. The pure black cover featured only the logo, price, date, and an oval hole that opened onto page 3—a hologram of a Motorola mobile cellular phone, part of a Motorola ad. Publisher Robert Guccione disagreed that the cover was an ad. Guccione, Adcroft, and managing editor Steve Fox could reach no agreement, so Adcroft and Fox resigned. Adcroft told *The New York Times,* "I felt that an advertisement on the cover of a magazine hurts the credibility of the magazine and was an infringement on editorial territory."[16]

The Nation hopes subscribers will remember it in their wills. In 1997, *The Nation* mailed a fundraising brochure titled "The Legacy Group" to select subscribers asking them to be part of "a new group of readers and friends now being formed to insure *The Nation*'s future well into the next century." While gifts to the magazine itself are not tax deductible, gifts to the Nation Institute, a nonprofit branch that holds seminars and conducts research, are. Donors can bequeath money from their securities, retirement plans, or life insurance—or create a life income bequest allowing interest, dividends, or other income from assets to be paid to a beneficiary during that individual's lifetime, after which the assets would be transferred to *The Nation.*

Bingo!

Most trade magazines and some association and consumer magazines include "bingo" cards at the back of the book. These cards list all advertisers in the magazine and give the reader the chance to express interest in that advertiser by marking a box in front of the advertiser's name. Advertisers are usually listed in categories—plumbing supplies, paper companies, accounting firms, and so on—and are numbered within the categories. Each advertiser, then, has one box to mark; each box has a letter and a number—A1, B6—hence the name, bingo.

Bingo cards can demonstrate to advertisers that readers are aware and interested in their products. They can also be the basis for databanks of consumer names that the magazine can sell as lists, and they can provide advertisers with opportunities for direct mail solicitations.

Aimee Kalnoskas, editor of *Wireless Design and Development,* suggests the use of bingo cards to provide solid evidence to advertisers of reader interest. She says she worries that "publishers want to flatter advertisers," losing sight of readers and causing reader response to the magazine to dwindle and advertising to suffer. Bingo cards can give editors important ammunition to counter such attempts.[17]

The downside to bingo cards is that they are not a true picture of actual reader interest. Some readers will eagerly respond; other won't respond at all. Those who do not respond might love the product—they may have already gone out and bought it based on the magazine's information—but they are not interested in telling anybody about it. The cards only represent the responses of a self-selected group, and it is virtually impossible to tell how representative that response is to the response of the audience as a whole.

MERGERS AND ACQUISITIONS

America's trend toward giant corporations seriously affects the quality of the magazine environment. The advertising-editorial conflict is exacerbated when the same large corporations own different product

AMERICAN BUSINESS PRESS EDITORIAL CODE OF ETHICS

Editors, reporters and writers employed by American Business Press (ABP) publications adhere to the highest standards of journalistic practice. In doing so, they pledge to:

- Maintain honesty, integrity, accuracy, thoroughness and fairness in the reporting and editing of articles, headlines, and graphics.
- Avoid all conflicts of interest as well as any appearances of such conflicts.
- Make a clear distinction between editorial and advertising. Editors have an obligation to readers to make clear what content has been paid for, what is sponsored and what is independent material. All paid content that may be confused with independent editorial material must be labeled as advertising.
- Maintain an appropriate professional distance from the direct preparation of special advertising sections or other advertisements.
- Show the distinction between news stories and editorials, columns and other opinion pieces.
- Accept as their primary responsibility the selection of editorial content based on readers' needs and interests.

AMERICAN BUSINESS PRESS GUIDE TO PREFERRED PRACTICES

Conflicts of Interest

- Editors, their spouses or minor children should not invest in companies and/or industries they personally cover (this does not preclude investments in pension or 401k plans that hold shares in a manner not directly controlled by the editor). Investments on the basis of "insider information" is a violation of securities laws.
- If a conflict arises in an investment held by an editor before his/her employment, or because of a merger or acquisition, he or she should immediately bring the conflict to the attention of his/her supervisor.

Gifts

- Editors should not accept any gifts or favors, except those of nominal value, from companies or

categories, some of which magazines seek, others of which they avoid. Editorial decisions can be influenced by corporate conflicts of interest because of corporation ownership of magazines as well as the products or services those magazines cover.

Corporate Conflicts of Interest

Time Warner owns 50 record labels including Warner, Atlantic, and Elektra. It also owns Warner Brothers film studios and television networks, including Home Box Office, Court TV, and Comedy Central. Then there are the magazines, such as *Time, People, Fortune,* and *Money.* So, what happens if *People* editors want to pan an Elektra recording, or *Time* wants to critique the making of a Warner Brothers film, or *Fortune* wants to analyze the economics of the entertainment industry?

Fairness and Accuracy in Reporting (FAIR), a media watchdog group, reported that writer and analyst Graef Crystal lost his job at *Fortune* in the early 1990s after writing about the compensation packages of Time Warner executives.[18] More common, however, are "sins of omission," when magazines choose to sidestep an issue entirely to avoid treading on corporate toes.

Time has traditionally had a clear separation of advertising and editorial, which has served the news magazine and its publishing brothers and sisters well. Since the Time Warner merger, Time Inc. magazines have worked toward an editorial balance, occasionally criticizing Warner executives and products, occasionally speaking positively about both. In all cases, when referring to various subsidiaries of Time Warner, the magazines make their interrelationship clear. *Entertainment Weekly* ran an article critical of Warner music executive Michael Fuchs in May 1995. Months earlier, it fended off corporate requests for special treatment of two other Warner music execs, Robert Morgardo and Doug Morris, who were fighting for placement atop the magazine's list of the entertainment industry's associations they cover, their public relations representatives or any other person or organization related to companies they cover. The editor's supervisor should determine what is of "nominal value."

- Editors may accept occasional meals and refreshments in the course of business dealings.

Outside Activities

- Editors should not accept freelance work from companies, associations or any other entity they cover.
- Because editors are expected to speak as authorities within their markets, they may accept invitations to appear on television, radio and other electronic media and may accept payment upon approval of magazine management.
- Editors should not accept payment of any kind for making speeches, judging contests or making appearances on broadcast media or at functions held by companies or associations they cover.
- Reimbursement of reasonable expenses incurred in connection with such speeches may be accepted. Editors may also accept "speaker gifts" of nominal value for participation in such events.
- Editors may accept fees for speeches given on their own time if there is no conflict with their editorial duties.

Travel

- Editors should not accept payment of travel and hotel expenses incurred in the course of performing editorial duties from any source other than their employers.
- In cases of group press affairs, presentations and other events involving representatives from several publications, editors may accept transportation and accommodations arranged by the information source. However, it is highly recommended that publications reimburse information sources for all of these expenses.

Relationship with Advertisers

- Selection of editorial topics, treatment of issues, interpretation and other editorial decisions should not be determined by advertisers, advertising agencies or the advertising departments of publications.
- Editors should not permit advertisers to review articles prior to publication.
- Advertisers and potential advertisers should never receive favorable editorial treatment because of their economic value to the publication. Similarly, non-advertisers should not receive unfavorable editorial treatment or be excluded from articles because they do not advertise.

Electronic Publishing

- The same principles and practices of print publishing should also apply to electronic publishing.

Courtesy the American Business Press

power players. The executives' attempts at editorial influence was business as usual for the magazine, said managing editor James Seymore: "People were trying to manipulate us, but they do that all the time."[19]

When media mogul Rupert Murdoch owned *TV Guide,* that magazine faced pressure to avoid negative stories about Murdoch's Fox network shows, such as the death of Chevy Chase's late night show after a dismal six-week run. The magazine relegated it to a tiny news brief. And Fox clearly benefited from the magazine's decision to run the network's program lists.

Advertisers Owning Advertisers

When a magazine chooses to avoid cigarette advertising, it may offend the owner of Kraft Foods. Why? Because Philip Morris, which owns numerous cigarette brands, also owns Kraft, as well as Miller Brewing. So the magazine that wants cheese or salad dressing advertising but wants to avoid beer advertising has to deal with the same corporation to woo one while rejecting the other.

Or how about the magazine that publishes an article that finds fault with the artificial ingredients in no-fat potato chips, including Pringle's? The writers do a good job, preparing an accurate, balanced, and fair report. Oops! Watch out for Procter & Gamble, manufacturer and distributor of Pringle's, in addition to Tide, Ivory Soap, Crisco, Duncan Hines, Charmin, Pampers, Folgers, and a laundry list of major consumer goods. That article could cost the magazine some of its largest advertisers.

Procter & Gamble spent $363 million in American magazines in 1997; Philip Morris spent $345 million. Those are big worms dangling on the advertisers' hooks. In the 1980s, when *Ms.* was still trying to win advertisers to its side, Procter & Gamble refused to be in any issue of the magazine that included material on "gun control, abortion, the occult, cults, or the disparagement of religion" as well as those covering sex

Society of Professional Journalists Code of Ethics

PREAMBLE

Members of the Society of Professional Journalists believe that public enlightenment is the forerunner of justice and the foundation of democracy. The duty of the journalist is to further those ends by seeking truth and providing a fair and comprehensive account of events and issues. Conscientious journalists from all media and specialties strive to serve the public with thoroughness and honesty. Professional integrity is the cornerstone of a journalist's credibility. Members of the Society share a dedication to ethical behavior and adopt this code to declare the Society's principles and standards of practice.

SEEK TRUTH AND REPORT IT

Journalists should be honest, fair and courageous in gathering, reporting and interpreting information.

Journalists should:

- Test the accuracy of information from all sources and exercise care to avoid inadvertent error. Deliberate distortion is never permissible.
- Diligently seek out subjects of news stories to give them the opportunity to respond to allegations of wrongdoing.
- Identify sources whenever feasible. The public is entitled to as much information as possible on sources' reliability.
- Always question sources' motives before promising anonymity. Clarify conditions attached to any promise made in exchange for information. Keep promises.
- Make certain that headlines, news teasers and promotional material, photos, videos, audio, graphics, sound bites and quotations do not misrepresent. They should not oversimplify or highlight incidents out of context.
- Never distort the content of news photos or video. Image enhancement for technical clarity is always permissible. Label montages and photo illustrations.
- Avoid misleading re-enactments or staged news events. If re-enactment is necessary to tell a story, label it.
- Avoid undercover or other surreptitious methods of gathering information except when traditional open methods will not yield information vital to the public. Use of such methods should be explained as part of the story.
- Never plagiarize.
- Tell the story of the diversity and magnitude of the human experience boldly, even when it is unpopular to do so.
- Examine their own cultural values and avoid imposing those values on others.
- Avoid stereotyping by race, gender, age, religion, ethnicity, geography, sexual orientation, disability, physical appearance or social status.
- Support the open exchange of views, even views they find repugnant.
- Give voice to the voiceless; official and unofficial sources of information can be equally valid.

or drugs. Those guidelines virtually eliminated *Ms.* as a Procter & Gamble buy.[20] And when *Ms.* ran afoul of Clairol's executives for running an article about congressional hearings on the toxicity of hair dyes, it also lost ads from parent company Bristol-Myers, which owned Windex, Drano, and Bufferin.

Imagine the editor facing her boss, the publisher, and explaining the loss of $150,000 for one page of advertising. What will she do to make it up? Multiply that loss by 12 issues and that editor is looking at losses in the millions of dollars. Any editor would shudder at that potential.

The confident editor, backed by a supportive publisher and a magazine with high reader and advertiser appeal, can take the high road and argue that serving readers is the best way to serve advertisers. What happens, though, when the publisher is not supportive or when the magazine is having trouble selling ad pages? The publisher might be willing to live with the prospect of offending one advertiser. Offending a huge corporation full of major advertisers is another, and far more ominous, matter.

A magazine that has trouble filling its ad pages probably has problems beyond advertiser influence. In this case, it is especially important to reassess and define the magazine's direction, and educate the ad sales staff on that direction.

- ▶ Distinguish between advocacy and news reporting. Analysis and commentary should be labeled and not misrepresent fact or context.
- ▶ Distinguish news from advertising and shun hybrids that blur the lines between the two.
- ▶ Recognize a special obligation to ensure that the public's business is conducted in the open and that government records are open to inspection.

MINIMIZE HARM

Ethical journalists treat sources, subjects and colleagues as human beings deserving of respect.

Journalists should:

- ▶ Show compassion for those who may be affected adversely by news coverage. Use special sensitivity when dealing with children and inexperienced sources or subjects.
- ▶ Be sensitive when seeking or using interviews or photographs of those affected by tragedy or grief.
- ▶ Recognize that gathering and reporting information may cause harm or discomfort. Pursuit of the news is not a license for arrogance.
- ▶ Recognize that private people have a greater right to control information about themselves than do public officials and others who seek power, influence or attention. Only an overriding public need can justify intrusion into anyone's privacy.
- ▶ Show good taste. Avoid pandering to lurid curiosity.
- ▶ Be cautious about identifying juvenile suspects or victims of sex crimes.
- ▶ Be judicious about naming criminal suspects before the formal filing of charges.
- ▶ Balance a criminal suspect's fair trial rights with the public's right to be informed.

ACT INDEPENDENTLY

Journalists should be free of obligation to any interest other than the public's right to know.

Journalists should:

- ▶ Avoid conflicts of interest, real or perceived.
- ▶ Remain free of associations and activities that may compromise integrity or damage credibility.
- ▶ Refuse gifts, favors, fees, free travel and special treatment and shun secondary employment, political involvement, public office and service in community organizations if they compromise journalistic integrity.
- ▶ Disclose unavoidable conflicts.
- ▶ Be vigilant and courageous about holding those with power accountable.
- ▶ Deny favored treatment to advertisers and special interests and resist their pressure to influence news coverage.
- ▶ Be wary of sources offering information for favors or money; avoid bidding for news.

BE ACCOUNTABLE

Journalists are accountable to their readers, listeners, viewers and each other.

Journalists should:

- ▶ Clarify and explain news coverage and invite dialogue with the public over journalistic conduct.
- ▶ Encourage the public to voice grievances against the news media.
- ▶ Admit mistakes and correct them promptly.
- ▶ Expose unethical practices of journalists and the news media.
- ▶ Abide by the same high standards to which they hold others.

Courtesy the Society of Professional Journalists

Kathie Robinson, editorial director of *NFPA*, the magazine of the National Fire Protection Association, acknowledges that "mergers and acquisitions are cutting into the number of separate advertisers we previously had. Our advertisers are extremely loyal, but a highly competitive market is becoming even more so. We try to give our ad reps everything we can to help them out."[21]

NFPA's editorial staff meets with the ad staff weekly to share information, and the two staffs work together to create a strong media kit and a solid editorial calendar, to which they adhere. The editorial staff listens to ideas from the ad staff, but makes final editorial decisions without advertiser input.

NEW MEDIA OPPORTUNITIES

Most consumer and trade magazines have on-line editions. Many of them are on-line to woo subscribers to the print version and to offer an ongoing sense of connection to the magazine. The beauty of on-line communication is also its curse: It's quick. This means that the user gets immediate information and the on-line communicator gets immediate distribution to the audience. It also means a mushrooming of errors of judgment as well as of fact. Problems unique to on-line publishing include polling errors and audience misrepresentation.

RESEARCH IN BRIEF

Editors Talk about Publishing On-line

Thousands of magazines covering a wide range of topics have gone on-line during the past five years. In 1996, Kathleen Endres, a professor in the School of Communication at the University of Akron, surveyed 123 on-line magazine editors to find out the kinds of publications being produced and their content.[1] With an average time on-line of 2.5 years, the largest group of responding editors were at consumer magazines (37 percent), followed by specialized interest publications (26 percent), specialized business magazines (25 percent), and "other" (11 percent). These last editors were individuals who put out personalized on-line magazines without a print counterpart. Endres found that arts and entertainment was the top content for magazines on-line, followed by computer and Internet and hobby and games in a tie for second place, with lifestyles and culture and science and nature in another tie for third place.

More than two-thirds of the on-line magazines had a print counterpart, although about half of the editors viewed the on-line version as an editorial entity distinct from the print one. Endres suggests this difference may be a result of the special characteristics of the on-line medium, which allows for frequent updates. Although 45 percent of the on-line editors said they had no way of gauging their readership, about 27 percent thought on-line readers were the same as the print magazines' and 27 percent said they were different. Only 8 percent of the on-line magazines required browsers to register.

Two-thirds of the on-line editors said their publications carried advertising, a contrast to a similar study done by Endres and Richard Caplan almost three years earlier in which only a minority carried advertising.[2] However, Endres points out, "This does not necessarily mean that the on-line publications are profitable; it only indicates that advertisers are more likely to venture on-line to present their messages to readers." The editorial department was the key factor, for more than 68 percent of the time, in determining whether a publication went on-line.

Endres says the main problem on-line editors have to grapple with is staff, because "the success or failure of getting—and keeping—a publication on-line often depends on one individual." Less than one-third of the on-line magazines surveyed had more than a single person working full-time on the on-line publication.

Endres admits that her study is not the definitive statement about on-line publications because the field is evolving too quickly. She suspects that as more journalism programs offer the technical and managerial skills needed to get a publication on-line, the content and degree of sophistication of the product will change.

[1] Kathleen Endres, "'Zine But Not Heard? Editors Talk About Publishing On-line" (paper presented at the annual meeting of the Association for Education in Journalism and Mass Communication, Baltimore, MD, August 1998).

[2] Kathleen Endres and Richard Caplan, "The Magazine in Cyberspace: A 'Site' to Be 'Zine'" (paper presented at the annual meeting of the Association for Education in Journalism and Mass Communication, Anaheim, CA, August 1996).

Spamming

Unique to on-line communication, spamming is an odd grassroots campaign in which like-minded people take over a poll and skew the results beyond recognition. In 1998 *People* magazine ran an on-line poll asking for votes for the "50 most beautiful people in the world." The magazine received more than 250,000 votes for Hank, the Angry, Drunken Dwarf. Hank—who would have beat out Leonardo DiCaprio if *People* editors had not rejected the votes—is Hank Nasiff, who is known for his unruly behavior and who was discovered by radio shock jock Howard Stern. What happened? Net users banned together and spammed *People*. Several voted multiple times.

Editor & Publisher offers these suggestions for on-line polling:

- Write a script that identifies user IDs. If someone with a particular user ID has voted once, they can't vote again.
- If that seems impractical, then just monitor the results as you go along. If it appears that someone is spamming the poll, then throw out the offending responses.
- Ask people to sign in with their e-mail addresses. This encourages accountability. People believe that you are paying attention. It also helps to post a notice that only one response will be counted.
- Write even-handed questions that won't inflame the respondents or bias their answers. This is particularly tricky with controversial subjects such as gun control and abortion.[22]

Audience Misrepresentation

Even when legitimate, on-line polling is far from representative of the attitudes of the public at large. On-line users are typically younger and more likely to be male than the general public. One survey indicated that a large proportion of on-line voters admitted to lying—14 percent say they falsify information 25 percent of the time.[23]

How do on-line magazines define their audiences? *Thrive,* an on-line publication created by Time Inc. and America Online, advertises 1,200,000 users. Given the ease with which these statistics can be manipulated, and the glee with which folks in cyberspace engage in such manipulation, the validity of any on-line audience might be questionable. However, researchers at print publications recognize that respondents can lie, so the legitimacy of audience statistics might be an issue there as well.

It is possible to go around the world with *The New Yorker* on the Crystal Symphony cruise ship. The 99-day, around-the-world cruise features lectures from the magazine's editors, critics, cartoonists, and writers.

CONTENT DECISIONS

Editorial decisions on content don't exist in a vacuum. Public relations professionals make a career out of getting magazines to print positive articles about their clients' products and services. Magazines of all types are wary about public relations influence in the form of gifts and junkets.

Decisions about illustrative content have broad social influence. The images within magazines are the bricks and mortar of our symbolic architecture. The impact of images, particularly magazine covers, as cultural artifacts can be significant; digital manipulation to "improve" the cover's visual content can skew the impact of those images.

New Product Releases

Most editors of consumer and trade publications, and many association editors, receive a stack of news releases daily. Bright and shiny new products—lamps, stereos, CDs, books, computer software—shout for attention. News releases can be important sources of information, but they can also turn into free advertising. This is another tightrope act for the editor—which news releases should be run and which should be tossed? The easy answer is, of course, to run those products that have the most reader appeal and that fill the needs of the audience.

When Pella Corporation reintroduced its Rolscreen—a window screen that rolls up and down like a window shade—after it had been off the market for more than a decade, it papered the magazine industry with news releases about the product. The corporation succeeded in getting mentions in more than 20 consumer and trade magazines on home building, decorating, and technology. Some magazines ran brief articles at the front of the book, in new product information departments; others incorporated the screen into larger articles on windows, screens, and product reintroductions. Clearly, editors of the various magazines customized the material for their audiences. It is also clear, however, that the primary reason many of the articles existed was the information from Pella Corporation.

A troubling aspect of this type of information in magazines is that new product departments can look more like advertising than editorial, even though editors write the copy, magazine designers create the page, and manufacturers are credited as being the source of the information.

In addition, editors can get caught in the middle when a major advertiser heavily promotes a new product that doesn't match reader need. Because readers take their magazines seriously, a mention of a new product reads like an endorsement. If the product isn't worth it, promoting it is a disservice to the audience. And any disservice to the audience turns readers off the magazine—advertising included.

Kathleen Edwards, vice president, member services, of the Printing Association of Florida, says editors must "present a balanced view—don't always feature the same companies. Showcase as many as you can, and rotate the companies featured in each issue. A careful balance will help eliminate the concern that any mention of products is unfair to those not included."[24]

Collectible Issues: Who's on First?

What makes a magazine collectible? Generally, the cover and story topic are most important, with date of issue being the second factor in a magazine's value. While the first issue is worth saving, older is not always better.

Nor are all magazines collectible. *Reader's Digest, Woman's Day, The New Yorker,* and *Saturday Evening Post* are not considered collectible, according to David K. Henkel, author of *Collectible Magazines: Identification & Price Guide.* Henkel says those magazine are "average" ones, which he defines as "any magazine that can be found in most households and that does not fall into a specific collecting category."[1]

Henkel cites *Life* and *National Geographic* as being popular "average" magazines to collect, primarily because of their photos. The most valuable *Life* is the premiere issue of November 23, 1936, with the Fort Peck Dam cover story shot by Margaret Bourke-White. It is worth up to $50 depending on the magazine's condition, which can range from poor (missing pages or pages written on) to fine (no fading of color photos, no stains or tears, tight spine, and a subscription label that doesn't affect the cover subject) to mint (nearly flawless, from a newsstand, no subscription label).

National Geographic is most collectible as a set, according to Henkel, who puts a value of $25,000 to $75,000 on a complete original set of everything published by the National Geographic Society since 1888. The most valuable single issue is the red-brick-colored cover dated Volume 1, Number 1, 1888: $5,000 to $13,000 depending on condition.

Henkel puts *TV Guide* in a category all by itself, saying, "To collectors this weekly chronicle of TV history is revered like bars of gold." Vintage *TV Guides,* he explains, "evoke happy feelings of the simpler days of youth for collectors who are willing to pay a price to recapture those fond memories." Plus, it offers information about television shows not found in reference books. Intended to be the "bible of television," *TV Guide* nevertheless had artistic aspirations with covers by Salvador Dali, Peter Max, Andy Warhol, Norman Rockwell, Charles Addams, and Al Hirschfeld.

The hottest *TV Guide* is not one with a cover drawn by a famous artist. As with most collectibles, it's the first one dated April 3–9, 1953, featuring a photograph of just-born Desi Arnaz Jr., with his famous mom, Lucille Ball, in the upper right hand corner; expect to pay $3,000 if you can find it in mint condition. *TV Guide* issues with Lucy, who appeared on 31 covers, are the most popular to collect, although the September 25, 1953, issue with George Reeves as Superman commands almost as much.[2]

Any magazine, regardless of its overall subject matter, may become a one-time collectible when it highlights a movie or television star on its cover. But, in general, collectible categories include the following:

Gifts and Junkets

Gifts and junkets are direct attempts to influence editorial content. A candymaker gives an elegant box of fudge to the staff of a drugstore trade magazine as a holiday gift. The staff munches on the goodies, gains weight, and remembers that manufacturer when planning an article on candy displays. Some magazines refuse to accept such gifts; others accept them but give them away to charities. Some accept them as a way of testing the product; others accept them because they get similar gifts from competitors, which dilutes their influence.

Junkets are free trips given to magazine staff members as a means of introducing them to a location, product, or event. Chambers of Commerce throughout the United States, as well as their international equivalents, pay travel costs to bring writers to a city or region. Once there, the writers get red carpet treatment, see the sites for free, and eat great food. They go back to their magazines thinking, "What a great place to visit," which can eventually lead to an article touting the location. Manufacturers of everything from floor tiles to medical equipment plan similar trips for specialty writers, bringing them to the plant for an in-depth view of production, while selling the writers on the quality of the product.

Junkets can provide magazine writers with excellent information, a significant benefit to staffs that are strapped for cash. Nevertheless, the information is one-sided; the competition may be equally good but less public relations-minded. The wise writer who goes on such trips is careful to do additional research once he is home to balance the

- *Adult magazines* featuring nudity and articles of a sexual nature. Titles here include *Ace, Adam, Bachelor, Casanova, Escapade, Gallery, Genesis, Hustler, Man, Rogue, Penthouse, Playboy, Satan,* and *Swank*. The first and second issues of *Playboy* are the most costly, at $1,000 to $2,000: the December 1953 cover with Marilyn Monroe and the January 1954 cover featuring Margie Harrison.
- *Detective, romance, and true story magazines,* which tend to be collected for their intriguing cover artwork and photography prior to 1950. Titles here include *Crime Detective, Master Detective, Real Detective, Living Romances, True Pictorial Stories, Confessions, Secrets, Man's Adventure,* and *True*.
- *Entertainment and movie/TV magazines* featuring gossip, stories, interviews, and photos of celebrities of film and television. The celebrity on the cover is what drives this market, which ranges from *Modern Screen, Motion Picture,* and *Movie Classic* of the 1920s and 1930s to *Photoplay, Screen Romances,* and *Screen Album* of the 1940s and 1950s, to recent issues of *People* and *US*. The most collectible star? Marilyn Monroe.
- *Monster magazines* specializing in monster, horror, or science fiction themes, with the purest form of monster magazines being those dedicated solely to monster and horror movies and TV shows. The granddaddy of monster magazines is *Famous Monsters of Filmland,* published in 1958. It's worth $200 to $400 now. Other monster titles include *Castle of Frankenstein, Horror Monsters,* and *Monster Times,* while the science fiction category has *Starlog, Starburst,* and *Fantastic Films*. Some, like *Fangoria, Filmfax,* and *Cinefantastique,* include both genres.
- *Rock-and-roll and teen magazines* featuring stories, photos, and posters of fans' favorite rock performers. Magazines with posters intact are most valuable, up to $100, if they feature Jim Morrison, Buddy Holly, or Jimi Hendrix. Issues of *Circus, Creem, Hit Parader, Spin,* and *Tiger Beat* are popular to collect.

Henkel doesn't include *Time* in his book, but New York City magazine dealer Mike Gallagher says *Time* is worth collecting. Gallagher puts a value of $1,000 on the first issue of March 23, 1923, featuring Joseph G. Cannon, the legendary Speaker of the United States House of Representatives. Three *Time* issues are valued at $500 each: March 23, 1930, with Chicago gangster Al Capone; August 31, 1925, with U. S. Amateur and U. S. Open golf champion Bobby Jones (identified as Robert T. Jones Jr. on the cover); and July 13, 1936, with New York Yankees slugger Joe DiMaggio. *Time*'s first Man of the Year cover of aviator Charles Lindbergh on January 2, 1928, fetches $200, the same as Vivien Leigh shown as Scarlett O'Hara in *Gone With the Wind* on December 25, 1939.[3]

[1] David K. Henkel, *Collectible Magazines: Identification & Price Guide* (New York: Avon Books, 1993): 4.
[2] Ibid., B3.
[3] "Old News Is Expensive News," *Time* (March 9, 1998): 192.

junket information with material available through old-fashioned reporting.

Most codes of ethics dealing with gifts and junkets are unequivocal and recommend against acceptance.

Printed Images

Magazine photos can hit readers' hot buttons, often for good reason. Both women and men wear skimpy clothing in ads that use explicit sex to sell products. In most cases, however, staffs have more latitude with news photos than with feature or advertising photos. Most readers will forgive an explicit news photo if it does a good job of explaining an issue. However, readers may say even some news photos go too far, being unnecessarily graphic.

In some notable instances, the photo cannot even get past the employees of the printing plant. *Editor & Publisher*'s printer refused to print an October 11, 1997, issue containing a story about a banned sex tabloid because of employee complaints: The article was illustrated with tabloid covers featuring topless women. The magazine tried to find another printer. After three tries, publisher Chris Phillips found a plant willing to print the image, but it was too late. The magazine was past deadline.

Phillips compensated by running a blank rectangle where the image would have been; inside the rectangle, the magazine added an explanation of why the image was missing. Phillips addressed the issue in his letter to readers, asking if it is more important for printers to "placate

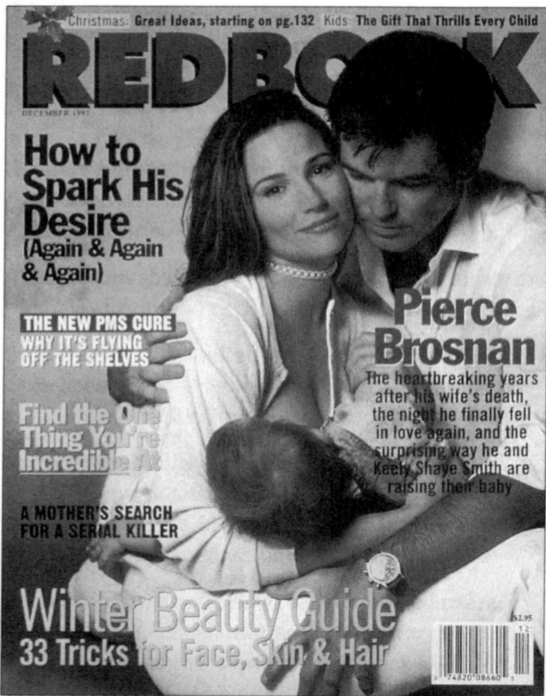

DECEMBER 1997: This *Redbook* cover was published in two versions, one for subscribers and one for the newsstands. This newsstand version showed Keely Shaye Smith breast-feeding their son Dylan Thomas as actor Pierce Brosnan looked on; home subscribers received a cover with all three looking directly at the camera.

their employees" than to "refuse to censor material protected by the First Amendment?"[25]

Teri Schrettenbrunner, spokeswoman for *E&P*'s printer, Cadmus Journal Services, says the issue was simple: "We have an obligation to ensure that our employees can come to work and feel comfortable. We also have a reputation that we're proud of for standing by our ethical standards."[26]

The now-defunct *Might* also lost a printer in 1996 over a cover story about AIDS that offended some employees. And *Pop Smear* magazine, with a "Porn Reviews" column that is billed as the "most intelligent review of porn today" was turned down by 20 printers in 1996 before it was accepted by Kingston Press of Sussex, Wisconsin, recommended by *Hustler*.

Creation of Cultural Images

"Your cover defines you in popular perception," says former *People* managing editor and former *Time* editor James Gaines.[27] Because of this, people remember cover images. Consequently, the choice of who or what to feature on the cover is not only an editorial one, but it can also be viewed as a social indicator of where any individual or group in society is today in terms of importance and value.

What sells on the cover? Sex, but it sells better on the newsstands than it does to subscribers. Newsstand magazine buyers are impulsive and a provocative cover line or a revealing image is often all it takes to catch a passerby. That is why editors will produce two covers of the same issue—one for the coffee table and one for the street. While that may be a smart business decision, it has a cultural effect. It is the newsstand version that tends to be held up as a reflection of where society is at any point.

Take the November 1998 issue of *Men's Health*. The newsstand version shouts "Put More X in your Sex." The home version, and the one that would be used to solicit new advertisers, has two headlines in the same space: "No More Backaches" and "Natural Sex Boosters." The same cover image is on both versions, and the story, "Put More X in Your Sex," about herbal supplements that may boost the sex drive, appears in both editions.

"We know that the newsstand buyers tend to be younger and more impulsive," says editorial director Mike Lafavore. "They want big muscles and they want to be sexy. The subscriber, on the other hand, tends to be older by five or six or more years and is interested in issues like stress reduction, nutrition and weight loss."[28]

Look at the December 1997 issue of *Redbook* with actor Pierce Brosnan, his companion Keely Shaye Smith, and their young son, Dylan Thomas. The feature story inside describes Brosnan's quest to find love following the cancer death of his wife, Cassandra Harris. The subscriber version has the elegant trio looking tastefully out at the reader; the newsstand version shows Smith breast-feeding Dylan as Brosnan looks on. Both editions have the same cover lines, although "How to Spark His Desire (Again & Again & Again)" and "Find the One Thing You're Incredible At" seem a bit racier on the newsstand cover.

In explaining her decision to run a split cover, then-editor Kate Wilson pointed out that the average age of subscribers is late thirties to early forties, while the average newsstand buyer tends to be in her twenties or early thirties. "I didn't want to force it on people who might be uncomfortable with it," White said.[29]

Digital Manipulation

A darker complexion for the O. J. Simpson mug shot on the June 27, 1994, cover of *Time,* straighter and whiter teeth for septuplet parent Bobbi McCaughey on the December 2, 1997, cover of *Newsweek:* These two examples of photo manipulation via digital computer techniques created an uproar in media circles. What are the ethical ramifications of digital manipulation? After all, it is impossible to tell when a digitized photograph has been manipulated—except by comparing it to the chemical original—or if it is the real person or scene.

Time and *Newsweek* both used the same Los Angeles Police Department's booking shot of O. J. Simpson as the cover for their respective June 27 issues. *Newsweek*'s credit line read "Photo by Los Angeles Police Department." *Time*'s credit line read "Photo Illustration for *Time* by Matt Mahurin." *Time*'s version had been altered, leaving Simpson with darker skin and heavier facial stubble; *Time* also reduced the size of the numbers and letters across Simpson's chest. Would the typical reader recognize that "photo illustration" meant the original image had been altered? Was that enough of a disclaimer?

Apparently not. Side by side on the newsstands, readers could see the difference between *Newsweek*'s straight news cover and *Time*'s alteration. The president of the National Press Photographers Association called the *Time* cover "an abomination to the impact of the original truthful looking photo." Journalists charged that *Time* "had darkened Simpson's face in a racist and legally prejudicial attempt to make him look more sinister and guilty, to portray him as 'some kind of animal,' as the N.A.A.C.P.'s Benjamin Chavis put it." One week later, *Time*'s managing editor, James R. Gaines, publicly apologized for the unintended effects of the Simpson photo manipulation. Gaines said the photo was not meant to be racist; rather, the digital manipulation was intended to shape the mug shot's "cold specificity" into "an icon of tragedy" to go with "the simple, nonjudgmental headline 'An American Tragedy.'"[30]

In 1997 *Newsweek* and *Time* both ran cover shots of Bobbi McCaughey and her husband, arguably the most famous parents in America following the birth of their seven babies. Once again, two images were side by side on the newsstands and readers and media critics immediately noticed the differences in the photos. *Time*'s cover showed Bobbi with teeth that were not straight and not white. *Newsweek*'s cover had a different dental bite: small, white, and even teeth.

According to the Gallup Poll, liberals believe news magazines have a conservative bias, while conservatives believe the magazines have a liberal bias.

"The photo we decided to use had a considerable shadow over her mouth," Richard M. Smith, *Newsweek*'s president and editor-in-chief, said. "The editors decided to lighten and improve the picture. In the process of doing that, the technical people went too far. The mistake was in guessing what was in the shadow and changing it." He said the *Newsweek* picture was not altered "to harm Mrs. McCaughey or deceive the reader," adding that the mistake was not similar to what *Time* did with the Simpson photo.[31] But isn't digital manipulation still misleading, whether it is a small portion of the photo or the entire image?

"There is never an instance where it is morally justifiable to alter a news photo," Tom Bentkowski, director of design for *Life,* said in 1989. "There is a grave responsibility to the reader. We should put out magazines that readers should never have to question. I think there is zero tolerance for making photos that never existed."[32]

What about removing indistinguishable blobs or background telephone wires, touching up varying sky tones, or removing a just-popped-up pimple on a senator's face? Most magazine editors say they won't change a news photo that is supposed to depict reality, but they agree that feature photos are more prone to manipulation. It is the difference between the unposed reality of photojournalism and the entertainment value and aesthetic sensibilities of the final page layout.

Shiela Reaves, a journalism professor at the University of Wisconsin at Madison, calls magazine art directors and photo editors "ethical relativists" for indicating that there is a photo hierarchy "that allows feature photos and cover illustrations to be taken less seriously than news photos." She asks, "Do readers really understand an implicit hierarchy; news photographs are not touched, feature photographs may be retouched, and illustrations are usually retouched? Would readers agree with the underlying premises, or would they believe they are being deceived?"[33]

RESEARCH IN BRIEF

Readers Don't Care About Bad Journalism

Letters to the editor are designed to offer feedback from the magazine's readers to the editors. A look at the letters in most magazines reveals a preponderance of congratulatory and positive comments reflecting agreement with previous articles; occasionally a negative observation or angry remark is made. Some topics set readers off more than others. *Time*'s 1973 *Last Tango in Paris* cover story, about the erotic movie starring Marlon Brandon, generated the most reader mail ever received by the magazine—12,191 mostly angry letters. The second highest number of letters—5,180—came in response to *Time*'s selection of Iran's Ayatullah Khomeini as 1980 "Man of the Year."[1]

What do letters to the editor say about reader reactions to whether magazines are doing a good job of upholding journalistic standards and ethics? Brian Thornton, a professor in the Department of Mass Communications at Midwestern State University in Wichita Falls, Texas, studied magazine letters to the editor to learn more about the ongoing conversation about journalistic standards conducted by magazine readers, and how that conversation has changed over time.

"People hate journalism and journalists nowadays," said Thornton, pointing to public opinion surveys, articles in reporting trade magazines that discuss the animosity between reporters and readers, and cover stories in consumer magazines such as *The Atlantic* explaining "Why Americans Hate the Media." He reasoned that "this glut of articles about Americans' rampant dislike of the press might lead one to believe this anger would find its way into letters to the editors in today's magazines. And it would seem that if letters to the editor in popular magazines from the beginning of this century were compared to modern letters, there would be much more comment in this era about how the media need to get their ethical house in order."[2]

Thornton found that only a handful of researchers have even studied letters to the editor, although they play an important role as a magazine department and they offer content information about readers' likes and dislikes to editors. So he set out to study all letters to the editor published between 1982 and 1992 in 10 magazines (*The Atlantic, Forbes, Harper's, Life, The Nation, The New Republic, Newsweek, The Progressive, Time,* and *U.S. News & World Report*) and compare them to letters to the editor published between 1902 and 1912 in 10 popular magazines then (*Arena, Collier's, Cosmopolitan, Everybody's, Harper's Weekly, The Independent, Ladies' Home Journal, McClure's, Munsey's,* and *World's Work*). That meant a total of 43,976 letters to the editor to read, with 41,822 of them appearing from 1982 through 1992.

He discovered only 3.5 percent of the letters from 1982 through 1992 discussed magazine journalistic standards or such qualities as truthfulness, honesty, and accuracy. In sharp contrast, 30 percent of the letters from the muckraking period between 1902 and 1912 debated journalistic standards and qualities.

Thornton said the implications of his findings pose important questions: Why has the number of letters to the editor about magazine journalistic standards declined? Does it mean that today's readers are uninterested in the good and bad qualities of journalism? Why do they say they are angry about the way journalists go about their business, but comment only on the accuracy of an article without engaging in a comment about journalistic standards? What has caused this indifference or alienation, which is in great contrast to the letters of the muckraking period, which nevertheless show an affection for the press amidst the criticisms?

Thornton continues to study letters to the editor as a way of examining the voice of magazine readers and as a historical record reflecting their attitudes toward societal change. He hopes the research "may contribute to a deeper understanding of muckraking, audience reaction then and now, and the discussion of journalistic standards among today's journalistic audience."

[1] "Dear Idiots," *Time* (March 9, 1998): 182.

[2] Brian Thornton, "The Shrinking Debate Over Journalistic Standards: Where Have All the Letters (to the Editor) Gone?" (paper presented at the annual meeting of the Association for Education in Journalism and Mass Communication, Anaheim, CA, August 1996).

When celebrities are used on covers, do readers understand that changes have been made to create a cultural symbol rather than to depict a regular, flesh and blood individual? Do readers agree that if an image is designated a "photo illustration," then anything can and probably will be done to alter it to create the right look? Does the public perceive the difference between a satirical photo composition, such as the October 1990 *Texas Monthly* cover of Texas

TABLE 12.1

Cover Hits and Misses at *Time*

Five Most Popular Newsstand Issues[1]

DATE	COPIES SOLD	COVER SUBJECT
September 15, 1997	1,183,758	Princess Diana: "Commemorative Issue"
September 8, 1997	802,838	Princess Diana: "Diana, Princess of Wales 1961–1997"
August 19, 1974	564,723	President Gerald R. Ford: "The Healing Begins" (following resignation of Richard Nixon)
December 22, 1980	531,340	John Lennon: "When the Music Died" (death of Lennon)
March 19, 1984	500,290	Michael Jackson: "Why He's a Thriller: Inside His World"

Five Least Popular Newsstand Issues Since 1980[2]

DATE	COPIES SOLD	COVER SUBJECT
October 10, 1994	100,827	Choreographer Bill T. Jones: "Black Renaissance"
August 22, 1994	101,125	Baseball umpire (generic drawing): "Stree-rike!" (baseball strike)
May 17, 1993	102,193	President Bill Clinton on left with worried President Lyndon Johnson in background: "Anguish over Bosnia: Will It Be Clinton's Vietnam?"
March 4, 1996	108,900	Nuclear engineer George Galatis: "Blowing the Whistle on Nuclear Safety"
June 10, 1996	109,300	Israeli Prime Minister Benjamin Netanyahu: "Can He Make Peace?"

[1] "Hits," *Time* (March 9, 1998): 177.
[2] "Misses," *Time* (March 9, 1998): 177.

gubernatorial candidates Clayton Williams and Ann Richards apparently dancing together (done via computer transplants), and a celebrity feature cover, such as Tori Spelling's digital makeover in the August 1994 issue of *Details* that removed blemishes, increased her cleavage, decreased her waist, and lengthened her legs? Do we want to run the risk of readers losing faith with the graphic images that accompany magazine editorial copy?

Tom Wheeler and Tim Gleason, two journalism professors at the University of Oregon, suggest that the term "photofiction" should be applied "to any photo that has been manipulated enough during processing to change readers' perceptions of its meaning—whether material elements in the photo are altered, added, removed within the frame or rearranged, and regardless of the method employed."[34] This would make it clear when photos have been altered and throw out such nuances as "news" versus "features" and "scenic" versus "portrait," or "photo" versus "photo illustration." By eliminating such distinctions, the credibility of legitimate documentary photography would be protected.

Digital photography is here to stay. It is up to magazine editors and art directors to adopt strict standards for applying the technology so that readers are not misled and photo credibility is not eroded.

"DUMBING DOWN" EDITORIAL CONTENT

Do magazines give their readers the opportunity to use all their wonderful brain cells? Or do they let their audience drift into an unthinking apathy? The truth, as usual, lies somewhere in the middle.

Some critics suggest that the media in general "dumb down" their content, reaching the lowest common intellectual denominator. Because of their ability to target precise audiences, magazines are both more guilty and less guilty of allowing their readers to think too little. Some magazines are great users of brain power, while others encourage a culture of easy-think. Too often, though, the magazines that sell well are those with cotton-candy content, suggesting that magazine audiences are more easily lured to

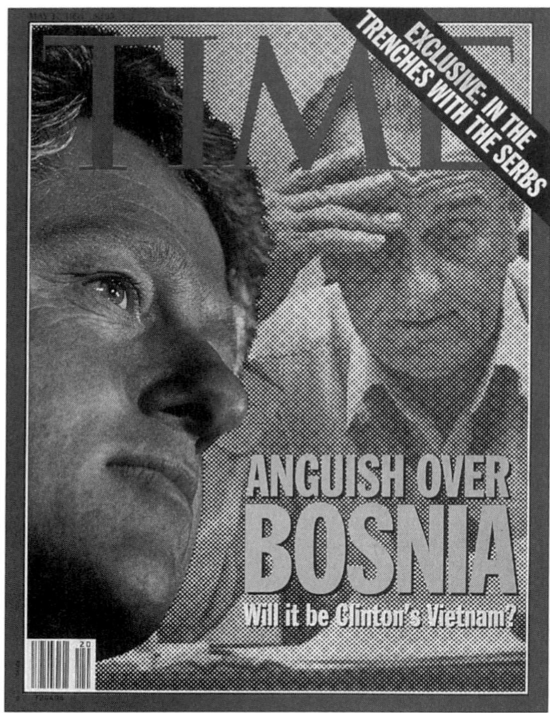

MAY 17, 1993: This *Time* cover story about Bosnia was the third least popular newsstand issue since 1980; the most popular was the September 15, 1997, commemorative issue about Diana, Princess of Wales.

brainless material than to thoughtful prose. Should magazines encourage their readers to put their brain power on hold?

The very existence of *People*'s "50 Most Beautiful People" list symbolizes one significant segment of American culture. It emphasizes the cosmetic, celebrates physical looks over substance, and presents the country with a definition of contemporary beauty: thin, sexy, and young. But can we blame *People*? We go to the movies, watch the TV shows, and buy the CDs that make these people celebrities. We are, after all, a celebrity culture. And nobody demonstrated that better than the late Diana, Princess of Wales, whose death brought the issue of paparazzi photographs into the national discussion.

Thoughtless Content and Audience Appeal

Time magazine's best-selling cover of all time deals with an issue of significant national importance, right? Sure, if the late Princess Diana is that issue. The two top-selling issues (see chart on page 317) had cover images of the former Princess of Wales. What didn't sell? Five of the least popular *Time* covers since 1980 featured the renaissance in black culture, the 1994 baseball strike, Bosnia, nuclear safety, and Israeli Prime Minister Benjamin Netanyahu. All of those topics were significant concerns for national and international readers, yet they did not attract newsstand buyers. Did subscribers ignore the cover stories also and turn instead to the cinema, books, or science departments?

Norman Pearlstine, editor-in-chief of Time Inc., admits that readers are less interested in international news and even hard national news. "There's always been a balance between educating your reader and serving your reader, but we're not getting a lot of demand for international coverage these days in broad consumer publications. You obviously balance telling them what you think they ought to read with giving them what they want to read, and that balance has clearly shifted away from international news in the last decade."[35]

But Ray Cave, former managing editor of *Time,* points out that it is a cop-out simply to say people aren't interested in substantive international and national news. "The general public has never been interested in it. But we delivered it, like it or not. By so doing, we piqued public interest in the very matters that must, to some degree, interest the citizens of a democracy."[36]

Interestingly, Time Inc.'s hottest magazine these days is *In Style,* which, for all practical purposes, is a homage to celebrities: movie stars, pop singers, sitcom stars, and talk show hosts. Popular with both advertisers and readers—it has grown from its 1994 circulation launch base of 500,000 to more than 1.1 million by the end of 1998—*In Style* doesn't offer self-help and never hints at imperfection. Instead, the magazine stresses the bond that readers feel with movie stars. "If you put 20 models in a row, and 20 movie stars in a row, your reader will more closely identify with the movie star. They have more variety, and they exude more personalities. Readers think they know their personalities. If I say *Ally McBeal,* you think: 'I know her; I know what she's about; I know what her life might be like.' You can't say the same thing about Kate Moss," says managing editor Martha Nelson.[37]

This kind of accessible escapism permeates the many magazine covers and content. At the time of her death, Princess Diana had been on the cover of *People* 43 times, *Time* eight times, and *Life* seven times.

Thoughtful Content

Magazines do deal with issues of major importance and stories that are not pretty. *Glamour's* August 1998 issue included an unvarnished look at such sexually transmitted, non-AIDS related, diseases (STDs) as gonorrhea and herpes. Along with the personal stories of 10 women, who were photographed and identified, the article detailed the protective devices, symptoms, diagnosis, and prognosis of STDs and how they affect relationships, health, and the ability to bear children. The younger fashion and lifestyle service magazines, such as *Glamour, Mademoiselle,* and *Vogue,* have published more articles about abortion than have the traditional women's Seven Sisters magazines of *McCall's, Good Housekeeping, Ladies' Home Journal, Family Circle, Woman's Day, Redbook,* and *Better Homes and Gardens.*

Teen magazines, likewise, are trying to deal with significant issues, to make readers think about divorce, AIDS, teen pregnancy, and self-mutilation. There has even been a movement away from articles that define teens by who they are dating and how they look. *Jump* and *Girl,* launched in 1997 and 1998 respectively, talk about the advantages of not having a boyfriend and being comfortable with the body you have. *Teen People,* launched in 1998, also follows that attitude, but as a general interest magazine for all teens, not just girls. All three run photos of teens with believable dimensions rather than waif models because they want to emphasize realistic images. All three reject the conventional attitude that teens don't have a serious thought in their heads.

At the other end of the spectrum are two magazines that reach neglected markets: baby boomer women (someone turns 50 every eight seconds) and full-figured women. *More* promotes itself as an alternative to traditional women's magazines and as a matter of editorial policy will not allow a model under the age of 40 to appear on its pages. Rejecting articles about tighter tushes in 10 days, *More* discusses hormone replacement therapy, cashing in on retirement nest eggs, and starting fulfilling second careers. *Mode* writes for women who do not wear a skimpy size 4 body thong, but require sizes 12, 14, 16, and beyond for their professional and personal clothing look. These women don't crave anorexic thinness—perfection to some—so much as they want to look real and maybe even gorgeous in their clothes. *Mode* was named 1997 launch of the year by *Advertising Age* for its acknowledgment that full-figured women wanted a top caliber magazine just for them.

Even men's service magazines such as *Men's Health* and *Men's Journal* say it's okay to have insecurities and to have to work at making yourself more attractive (messages that women's magazines, regardless of targeted age group, have been presenting for decades). There are articles about face peels, collagen injections, eyelid lifts, chin tucks, and, yes, liposuction—for men who are closer in age and attitude to the baby boomer's forties and fifties than to Madison Avenue's beloved Generation X group. *Men's Health* has carried its message around the world, with six editions outside the United States: in Germany, Russia, the United Kingdom, Australia, South Africa, and Latin America.

This dose of reality seems to reflect a shifting away from pie-in-the-sky fantasies of physical perfection. *Mamm,* for women with cancer, *Poz* for HIV-positive individuals, and *We,* for people with disabilities, all stress the reality of dealing with the hand life has dealt you. In *We,* models are in wheelchairs or posing with their seeing-eye dog companions while articles warn about the perils to the immune system when total paralysis occurs. All three originated as consumer publications, unlike *Arthritis Today* and *Diabetes Forecast,* which originated as magazines for association members or medical professionals.

Christine Miller, executive vice president of marketing for the Magazine Publishers of America, says the magazine industry has long depicted aging, chronic illness, and weight problems as negative, if discussed at all. "Reality is always portrayed as negative, and it's not. So there's a hole in the marketplace for living these things. Their only option has been negative, so these magazines fill a huge market need," Miller says.[38]

Amelia Earhart was the first celebrity editor at *Cosmopolitan,* which named her to the newly created position of aviation editor in 1929. Flying was the hot media topic after Earhart became the first woman to fly across the Atlantic Ocean in 1928. She was the celebrity of the day, generating coast-to-coast media buzz. She was chic, daring, boyishly slender, and ultrafashionable, starting a fashion craze with her trademark slacks and aviator scarf. Few readers knew that Earhart was self-conscious about her thick ankles, which is why the *Cosmopolitan* girl to end all *Cosmopolitan* girls wore pants all the time.

RESEARCH IN BRIEF

The Magazine Editor as Author, Auteur, Celebrity, and Manager

The late twentieth-century magazine editor has become like a film director in his shaping and controlling of the final product, argues Lee Jolliffe, a professor in the School of Journalism and Mass Communication at Drake University. This is in addition to the three other roles traditionally played by the editor—as author, celebrity, and manager—in the top job at a magazine.[1]

Historically, the editor has been viewed as the central force who provides the final personality of the magazine. Jolliffe points to such recent famous editors as Henry Luce, DeWitt Wallace, William Shawn, and Malcolm Forbes as individuals who have been closely identified by readers and the public at large with a particular magazine. Media scholars and magazine editors themselves, she says, comment that "Luce was *Time* magazine" or that John Mack Carter was "Mr. *Good Housekeeping.*" Sarah Josepha Hale, Louisa May Alcott, and Edward Bok were earlier editors who also were writers. They deliberately embedded their views and experiences into their magazines. The author role, Jolliffe writes, is a romantic one, revolving around a "gifted individual who brings inspiration and education to a work of art." Indeed, some editors have even been "romanticized in our research literature as creative geniuses," she says.

The celebrity role results from the fame that comes to successful editors, fame that usually is conferred upon them by the media rather than sought after by the editor. In this position, the editor is a public figure who "becomes the quintessential representation of the magazine, perhaps even of the audience's dream-self." Readers may admire the flamboyance of celebrity editors, and be seduced by their superstar status in popular society. Primarily a twentieth-century phenomenon, the editor as celebrity can function as a profit center for the magazine that promotes the publicity value of the name. Tina Brown, former editor of *The New Yorker,* is certainly the most well-known celebrity editor of the late twentieth century.

Jolliffe places the manager role in conjunction with a magazine's financial success. Managerial editors

But advertisers are wary of reality and typically do not flock to magazines for older women, overweight women, or disabled people. *Lear's* tried to reach the mature woman, but folded in 1994 after eight years, while *Mirabella,* which originally targeted older women, has repositioned itself as a general interest women's magazine. *More,* with one of the fastest-growing audiences in the United States, has successfully attracted such heavyweight advertisers as Clinique, L'Oreal, Chrysler, and Mercury Grand Marquis. Although *Mode* has large-size apparel retailers and even designer labels with plus-size collections like Elisabeth by Liz Claiborne as advertisers, editors have not been able to attract high-end cosmetic lines like Estée Lauder.

Mamm, Poz, and *We* attract pharmaceutical and vitamin ads, but have failed to reach automobile and cosmetics companies. "Why wouldn't you want to buy a lipstick if you have cancer?" asked Sean Strub, publisher of *Mamm.* "We're really very angry about it."

Roberta Garfinkle, senior vice president and director of print media at McCann-Erickson advertising agency, says, "I don't think it has anything to do with what the advertising community is ready for. It's an issue of, 'How ready is the culture of magazine readers to accept reality and get away from fantasy?'"[39]

The Celebrity Culture

Magazine observers say the celebrity culture dates back to the Watergate affair, which changed journalism in more ways than we realize. The modern era of the journalist as celebrity began as a result of Bob Woodward and Carl Bernstein's investigative reporting of President Richard Nixon that led to his resignation in 1974. The movie, *All the President's Men,* featuring Robert Redford and Dustin Hoffman playing Woodward and Bernstein, respectively, launched the public's fascination with the journalist as celebrity. And if movie stars could play reporters and editors on screen (Jason Robards Jr. portrayed Ben Bradlee, the *Washington Post* executive editor who gave so much leeway to Woodward and Bernstein), why couldn't movie stars actually be magazine editors as well?

CELEBRITY EDITORS. The celebrity editor has been around for a long time—Edward are sensible, competent, and businesslike, she says, and "are conscious of the bottom line, attentive to audience and advertiser needs, and carry out functions typical of managers in other industries." Although perhaps lacking the inspired genius qualities of the author as editor, the managerial editor is more than an anonymous technician. The manager as editor is first and foremost a professional and functions much as do managers in other industries. Consequently, he is concerned with the bottom line as well as efficient use of human resources in producing a magazine.

Finally, the auteur as editor puts her "signature" on the magazine, much as such film directors as Brian de Palma, Woody Allen, or Steven Spielberg do with their movies. Just as film critics can identify directors who are auteurs by their cinematic style that transcends the work of actors, scriptwriters, producers and cinematographers, Jolliffe says certain magazine editors can be identified by their ability to direct a huge collaborative work and rise above writers, photographers, and designers. "Auteurs can be viewed as imprinters of myth, image, and personal symbolism onto a collage of texts and pictures created by others." Rather than reflecting an ongoing personality, as the editor as author does, the editor as auteur offers a continuing artistic vision filled with personal idiosyncrasies.

These four personas seldom exist in a single individual. As deconstructed by Jolliffe, the author, auteur, celebrity, and manager roles of editors offer a way of understanding a magazine's evolution and place in the industry and in society through the individual at the top of the creative masthead.

[1] Lee Jolliffe, "Four Constructs of the Magazine Editor: Author, Auteur, Celebrity, and Manager" (paper presented at the annual meeting of the Association for Education in Journalism and Mass Communication, Atlanta, GA, August 1994.)

Bok, editor of *Ladies' Home Journal* from 1889 to 1919 made it a point, he wrote in his Pulitzer Prize-winning third-person autobiography, "to project his personality through the printed page and to convince the public that he was not an oracle removed from the people, but a real human being who could talk and not merely write on paper." Prior to Bok, editors used the indefinite and lofty "we" for their editorial comments. Bok, who used the first person singular and talked directly to readers, understood that the "American public loved a personality and was always ready to recognize and follow a leader, provided, of course, that the qualities of leadership were demonstrated."[40]

In recent years, Tina Brown, former editor of *The New Yorker,* and Helen Gurley Brown, former editor of *Cosmopolitan,* were celebrities in their own right—capable of creating media buzz and reader interest when they were away from the office. John F. Kennedy Jr. is a celebrity on the strength of his name alone; his *George* magazine derives a lot of its pizzazz from his participation. Publicist Don Klores, whose New York City public relations firm represents *New York* magazine and *Esquire,* among others, says celebrity editors who are invited to upscale functions and who host elaborate parties themselves make things easier all around: "It makes ad sales easier, it's easier to get people to say, 'Yes, I'll do that interview.'"[41]

Magazines such as *People* and *Vanity Fair* write about celebrity editors and journalists, and their names appear on society pages and in gossip columns. The editor as celebrity has led some critics to wonder if ugly—or nonphotogenic—people need not apply for the top editor-in-chief slot at magazines. Elizabeth Crow, the editor-in-chief of *Seventeen,* observes that "non-photogenic editors, editors who are severely overweight, might be a problem in some marketers' eyes."[42]

Folio:'s November 15, 1997, article asking "Is There a Place for the Shy or Homely Editor?" received a blistering reply from Lucy T. Avera, associate publisher and editor of *Asphalt Contractor,* who wrote, "On a personal level, as the overweight female associate publisher/editor of a trade book representing a $15 billion industry dominated by men, I think the fact that you

Henry Luce went postal with his own stamp issued by the U.S. Postal Service on April 3, 1998, his 100th birthday. That makes the founder of *Time, Fortune, Life,* and *Sports Illustrated* as much of a collectible as the early issues of his magazines.

consider an editor's attractiveness a factor in his or her ability to perform specific job duties is discriminatory, shallow, and insulting."[43] Avera continued, "For *Folio:* to plant such a discriminatory seed by making physical and personal attributes (or lack thereof) an issue is a disservice to our industry."

Barbara Love, editor of the "*Folio:* Plus" column where the article ran, responded simply that the item reflects reality today, adding, "Of course attractiveness should not be a factor in hiring an editor, nor should it be a factor in judging editors already in place. The item was intended to convey what is (at some titles) and not what should be."[44]

The editor as celebrity certainly isn't the biggest problem facing the magazine industry today. Journalism reformer James Fallows, former editor of *U. S. News & World Report,* says, "I don't think I'd put celebrity journalism on the top five list of major problems for journalism right now. By definition, it only affects an elite. But it is a problem because it aggravates other sources of people being mad at us—and therefore not listening to what we say or do."[45]

MOVIE STARS AS MAGAZINE EDITORS. The synergy between celebrities and magazines seems to be at an all-time high, with an increasing number of movie stars serving as guest editors for a single issue or as ongoing contributing editors. The January 1999 issue of *Marie Claire* saw Susan Sarandon overseeing the editorial content, which included fashion, beauty, and health features as well as design and layout. "Susan has a great sense of style, a sense of humor and a sense of justice. Her intelligence and integrity make her the ideal guest editor," says *Marie Claire*'s editor-in-chief Glenda Bailey. The equally stylish and intelligent Gwyneth Paltrow edited the January 1998 issue of *Marie Claire.*[46]

Almost the entire September 1998 issue of *Jane* was done by such celebrities as George Clooney, David Cassidy, Halle Berry, Yasmine Bleeth, Mariah Carey, Mark Wahlberg, Naomi Campbell, Maxwell, Vivica Fox, R.E.M., and Ben Stiller, who interviewed his *There's Something About Mary* co-star Cameron Diaz.

It is not just women's magazines that make use of guest editors. Sean Penn has been a contributing editor for *Interview* for several years and Roseanne helped with *The New Yorker*'s February 26 and March 4, 1996, combined issue focusing on women. Since February 1998, *Civilization,* which is published under a licensing agreement with the Library of Congress, has turned each issue over to a guest editor "chosen not only for their excellence in their own areas of expertise, but also for their broad critical understanding of the larger world."[47] The feature well is thematically orchestrated by the guest editor, resulting in a "specific (and ever-changing) signature that it didn't have before," says editorial director Nelson W. Aldrich Jr. To date, guest editors have included filmmaker Martin Scorcese, Czech Republic President Vaclav Havel, cartoonist Jules Feiffer, designer Bill Blass, and *Paris Review* founding editor George Plimpton.

CELEBRITIES WHO START MAGAZINES. Adding to the celebrity culture are the handful of celebrities who start their own magazines. In 1997, comedian Milton Berle launched *Milton,* a glossy quarterly about gambling, smoking, and drinking. Berle, who is 89 years old, is not involved in the day-to-day operations of the magazine; his wife Lorna (she married Berle seven years ago and is considerably younger) and her daughter Susan Moll serve as executive editor and editor-in-chief.

Are magazines launched by celebrities merely vanity presses? John F. Kennedy Jr., whose *George* has been a newsstand presence since September 1995, disproves the tendency to associate fluff with fame. *George,* with its circulation of 424,994 at the end of 1997, is considerably ahead of its competitors, which include established political magazines such as *The New Republic* (95,260) and *National Review* (165,226). Of course, perhaps the reason for *George*'s success lies in its editorial profile, which stresses that the magazine focuses on the personalities who shape public affairs and "cover the points where politics and popular culture converge" as it "demythifies the political process." Compare that to the straightforward wording of *The New Republic*'s editorial profile as a "journal of opinion with an emphasis on politics and domestic and international affairs."

THE BENUMBED AUDIENCE. Monica Lewinsky earned her reputation by having an affair with the president of the United States. This also earned her a sultry photo shoot in the July 1998 issue of *Vanity Fair.* In the opening two-page spread, the reader is treated to a shot that is reminiscent of early Marilyn Monroe in a carefree sprawl on a grassy hill, down to the plaid shirt and rolled-up blue jeans. "Who's That Girl?" asks writer Christopher Hitchens, while the story's subhead states: "Monica Lewinsky permits Herb Ritts to remove her first veil," as if she's Salome.

There are four more full-page photos—one showing her in front of a flag and another peering out behind a fan of hot pink feathers—accompanied by hyperbolic prose:

> *She has graduated, furthermore, into that pantheon of women who, it seems, shook enough men enough to shake history. Helen of Troy, Theodora of Byzantium, Cleopatra, Lady Macbeth, Sally Hemings, Wallis Simpson, Christine Keeler, Donna Rice, Camilla Parker-Bowles . . . they have nothing in common with each other, but everything in common with an ancient narrative that everybody, however coy or hypocritical, is encoded to understand.*

Vanity Fair's story, which was headlined above the logo as "Monica in Malibu: The Exclusive Photos by Herb Ritts," is the kind of pandering to public interest that increases magazine sales. Certainly the cover line attracted a different political reader from those drawn to the cover photo of Ron and Nancy Reagan for a "special report" about the former president and his wife. The story of the relationship between Lewinsky and President Bill Clinton resulted in high newsstand sales for news magazines in particular. In the first half of 1998, the top newsstand issues for *Newsweek* and *U.S. News & World Report* featured the duo; the topic was *Time*'s number two seller, behind a cover story on Michael Jordan.[48]

PAPARAZZI. Following the death of Princess Diana after a car race with paparazzi, the "mainstream" magazines were indignant: The paparazzi, they said, sullied the reputation of legitimate photographers and journalists. They pointed the finger at the tabloids—*The National Enquirer, The Star,* and *The Globe*—for printing paparazzi photographs.

The evidence doesn't support their outrage. Not only have mainstream magazines such as *Time, Newsweek,* and *The New Yorker* printed paparazzi images, they also have used the covers of the tabloids to illustrate their articles, so they could criticize the content at the same time they distributed it.

Still, the magazines distanced themselves from paparazzi. On September 1, 1997, immediately after Diana's death, Katharine Graham, part-owner of the Washington Post Company, which publishes *Newsweek,* told the "Today" show: "They're out to make a buck with their camera, and they have no attachments. They want to sell it to the press. But most of the press either can't afford to or doesn't want to buy them. I think if you start saying 'paparazzi' and calling them the press, we're making a bad mistake here."

Interestingly, the next issue of *Newsweek* was already in production. It featured two pages of photographs of Princess Diana and her boyfriend, "Dodi" Fayed. One of the photographs was taken the night the couple died, and it was a view through the window of their car. Not only did *Newsweek* use paparazzi photographs, it used photographs from the notorious paparazzi who swarmed around Diana right before her death.[49]

Even *The New Yorker* published dubious photographs: a close-up of the mangled car in which the couple died for an article by Salman Rushdie on the dangers of celebrity. At the time, *The New Yorker* was headed by Tina Brown, who left the job within the year to head for Hollywood.

"We're all journalists now because we have access to the press through the Internet," says Michael Godwin of the Electronic Frontier Foundation.

Most celebrity editors and writers are competent, respected journalists who paid their dues long before they reached superstar status. Professor John Lavine of Northwestern University's Medill School of Journalism points out, "Simply the fact that someone has become well-known isn't unto itself either wrong or bad. What we want to make judgments about is what kind of journalists are they? How credible are they? How much energy do they put into maintaining their credibility and caring about the public's confidence?"[50] Historian Daniel Boorstin offers a reasonable context for the celebrity journalism factor: "Journalists are the creators of well-knownness. In the process of creating well-knownness for others, it's not surprising that some of them become celebrities too. It's inevitable."[51]

THE FACE IN THE MIRROR

Magazine coverage of Princess Diana has contained a good amount of irony. The August 25, 1997, issue of *People* snippily talked about Diana's "cause du jour," as though she were just a silly rich woman looking for an issue to make her important. Two weeks later, after her death, the magazine's September 15, 1997, issue heralded her "boundless compassion." On August 4, 1997, *People* printed a headline calling Camilla Parker-Bowles "Queen of His Heart," the "his" being Prince Charles. On September 15, 1997, the magazine called the recently deceased Diana "Queen of Hearts."

When Diana was still virtually a newlywed, *Time*'s February 28, 1983, issue contained a cover article on "Royalty vs. the Press," which warned that "royal-watchers routinely engage in round-the-clock stakeouts, read lips with binoculars, suborn servants, chase their prey at crazy speeds in high-powered cars. There has been so much of this mad motoring that the wonder is that no member of the royal family or the public has been killed."

When talking about audiences, it is important to remember our own behavior not only as professionals but as readers. No matter what our position within magazines, we are all audience members. By our choices of magazines to buy and read, we are making cultural decisions. If we buy thoughtful content, in essence we are voting for that content. When we go the dummy route, that's one more vote for mindless content.

Gloria Steinem makes a plea for improved content in women's magazines, but her words could apply to magazines for all audiences:

> *Even as I write this, I get a call from a writer for* Elle, *who is doing a whole article on where women part their hair. Why, she wants to know, do I part mine in the middle?*
>
> *It's all so familiar. A writer trying to make something of a nothing assignment; an editor laboring to think of new ways to attract ads; readers assuming that other women must want this ridiculous stuff; more women suffering for lack of information, insight, creativity, and laughter that could be on these same pages.*
>
> *I ask you: Can't we do better than this?*[51]

FOR ADDITIONAL READING

Burlingame, Roger. *Endless Frontiers, The Story of McGraw-Hill.* New York: McGraw-Hill, 1959.

Duncombe, Stephen. *Notes from the Underground: Zines and the Politics of Alternative Culture.* New York: Verso, 1997.

Friedman, R. Seth. *The Factsheet Five Zine Reader: The Best Writing from the Underground World of Zines.* New York: Three Rivers Press, 1997.

Gorham, Joan, ed. *Mass Media 97/98.* Guilford, CT: Dushkin/McGraw-Hill, 1997.

Henkel, David K. *Collectible Magazines: Identification & Price Guide.* New York: Avon Books, 1993.

Lynch, Dianne. *Virtual Ethics: Debating Media Values in a Digital Age.* Boulder, CO.: Coursewise Publishing, 1999.

McGuire, Mary, Linda Stilborne, Melinda McAdams, and Laurel Hyatt. *The Internet Handbook for Writers, Researchers and Journalists.* New York: Guilford Press, 1998.

Shuping, Frances, ed. *A Guide to Periodicals Publishing for Associations.* Washington, D.C.: American Society of Association Executives, 1995.

Solomon, Norman and Jeff Cohen. *Wizards of Media Oz.* New York: FAIR, 1997.

END NOTES

[1] Anne Graham, "Peace Overtakes the Ad/Edit Conflict," *Folio:* (July 1998): 89.

[2] Roger Burlingame, *Endless Frontiers, The Story of McGraw-Hill* (New York: McGraw-Hill, 1959): 122.

[3] Constance L. Hays, "Titleist Withdraws Advertising in Dispute with *Sports Illustrated*," *The New York Times* (April 28, 1997): D10.

[4] G. Bruce Knecht, "Magazine Advertisers Demand Prior Notice of 'Offensive' Articles," *The Wall Street Journal* (April 30, 1997): A1.

[5] Ibid., A1.

[6] "ASME Expresses Deep Concern About Advertiser 'Early Warnings,'" News Release, June 23, 1997.

[7] Bruce Knecht, "Chrysler Drops Its Demand for Early Look at Magazines, *The Wall Street Journal* (October 15, 1997): B1.

[8] Ibid., B1.

[9] Gloria Steinem, "Sex, Lies and Advertising," *Ms.* (July/August 1990): 19.

[10] Rhoda Karpatkin, "What's a Best Buy?" *Consumer Reports* (July 1996): 5.

[11] Jeff Garigliano, "*Notorious* Lives Up to Its Name," *Folio:* (October 1, 1997): 20.

[12] Ibid., 20.

[13] Alex Kuczynski, "*Time* Magazine's One-Advertiser Issues Become an Issue for Debate," *The New York Times* (November 16, 1998): C1.

[14] "25 Good Ideas—and a Few Really Bad Ones," *Folio:* (April 1, 1997): 48.

[15] Alex Kuczynski, "Advice About Clothing and a Snug Fit for the Ads," *The New York Times* (October 19, 1998): C4.

[16] Richard D. Hylton, "2 Top Editors Leave *Omni* to Protest Ad on Cover," *The New York Times* (October 14,1990): 1N.

[17] Aimee Kalnoskas, "Communication in the Public Interest: Can Magazines Stand the Heat from Advertisers?" (panel presented at the annual meeting of the Association for Education in Journalism and Mass Communication, Baltimore, August 1998).

[18] "Where's the Power: Newsroom or Boardroom?" *Extra the Magazine of FAIR* (July/August 1998): 23.

[19] Marc Gunther, "All in the Family," *American Journalism Review* (October 1995): 36–41. Reprinted in *Mass Media 97/98*, Joan Gorham, ed. (Guilford, CT: Dushkin/McGraw-Hill, 1997): 62.

[20] Steinem, 26.

[21] Graham, 89.

[22] Ibid., 89.

[23] Jennie L. Phipps, "Angry Dwarves and other Polling Mishaps," *Editor & Publisher mediainfo.com* (July 1998): 25.

[24] Kathleen Edwards, "The Written Word: Editing for Your Reader," *A Guide to Periodicals Publishing for Associations*, ed. Frances Shuping (Washington, DC: American Society of Association Executives, 1995): 34.

[25] Steve Wilson, "When Printers Just Say No," *Folio*: (December 1, 1997): 15.

[26] Ibid., 15.

[27] Jill L. Sherer, "Celebrities Sell Magazines—Sometimes," *Advertising Age* (May 24, 1989): 84.

[28] Alex Kuczynski, "*Men's Health*: Versions 1 and 2," *The New York Times* (November 2, 1998): C7.

[29] "Breast-feeding Mom Might Land *Redbook* Next to *Penthouse*," *Des Moines Register* (November 16, 1997): 1E.

[30] James R. Gaines, "To Our Readers," *Time* (July 4, 1994): 4.

[31] Kenneth N. Gilpin, "Doctoring of Photos, Round 2," *The New York Times* (November 26, 1997): A14.

[32] Shiela Reaves, "Digital Alteration of Photographs in Consumer Magazines," *Journal of Media Ethics,* 6: 3 (1991): 176.

[33] Ibid., 181.

[34] Tom Wheeler and Tim Gleason, "Digital Photography and the Ethics of Photofiction: Four Tests for Assessing the Reader's Qualified Expectation of Reality" (paper presented at the annual meeting of the Association for Education in Journalism and Mass Communication, Atlanta, August 1994).

[35] Neil Hickey, "Money Lust," *Columbia Journalism Review* (July/August 1998): 32.

[36] Ibid., 33.

[37] Alex Kuczynski, "Time Inc.'s Softest Sell," *The New York Times* (November 30, 1998): C8.

[38] Alex Kuczynski, "Some Consumer Magazines Are Getting Real," *The New York Times* (November 19, 1998): C6.

[39] Ibid., C6.

[40] Edward Bok, *The Americanization of Edward Bok* (New York: Scribner's, 1920): 163.

[41] Robin Pogrebin, "Magazines Work to Make Headlines with Their Headlines," *The New York Times* (July 6, 1998): C1.

[42] "*Folio:* Roundtable—The Editor as Market Authority," January 1, 1998, (http://www.mediacentral.com/Magazines/folio 98/199801roundtable.htm).

[43] "Letters," *Folio:* (February 1, 1998): 18.

[44] Ibid., 18.

[45] Alicia C. Shepard, "Celebrity Journalists," *American Journalism Review* (September 1997): 28.

[46] "Star Track," *San Antonio Express-News* (August 1, 1998): 4D.

[47] Nelson W. Aldrich Jr., "Tacked to the Masthead," *Civilization* (August/September 1998): 13.

[48] Dylan Loeb McClain, "Hate That Story, Love That Story," *The New York Times* (October 9, 1998): C7.

[49] "Diana Mania," *Extra! Update* (October 1997): 1.

[50] Shepard, 31.

[51] Ibid., 28.

[52] Steinem, 27.

Magazine Voices

Between 1991 and 1995, Drake University, with funds from Meredith Corporation, invited prominent magazine professionals to campus to present their perspectives on the industry. Excerpts from the resulting Meredith Lectures appear on the following pages.

THE AD-FREE MAGAZINE: IT JUST FEELS LIKE JOURNALISM

Robin Morgan

Robin Morgan is an award-winning poet, novelist, political theorist, feminist activist, journalist, and editor. She has published 16 books, including five of poetry, two of fiction, and the classic anthologies *Sisterhood Is Powerful* and *Sisterhood Is Global.* A founder and leader of contemporary U.S. feminism, she has also been active in the international women's movement for more than two decades, serving on multiple boards and as founder of The Sisterhood Is Global Institute. In 1990, Morgan became editor-in-chief of *Ms.,* relaunching the discontinued magazine as an international, award-winning bimonthly free of advertising. She resigned in 1993 to become consulting editor and to have more time to write. She is a recipient of the National Endowment for the Arts Prize in poetry, the Front Page Award for Distinguished Journalism, the Feminist Majority Foundation Woman of the Year Award, and numerous other honors. She presented this speech in April 1992, when she was editor-in-chief of *Ms.*

Ms. was born in 1972, founded by a group of women including Pat Carbine and Gloria Steinem, who had been active in the magazine world. It never occurred to that first group to try the magazine without advertising because they wanted very much to create a mainstream feminist magazine.

They convinced Clay Felker, at that time owner and publisher of *New York* magazine, to print a small premiere issue of *Ms.* inside of an issue of *New York* magazine. Since *New York* magazine took ads, *Ms.* took ads. That pilot issue was an amazing success, and a year later the full-fledged magazine itself was born. The first issue sold out overnight and they went back to press and it sold out again overnight, and then it was off and running. Clearly it never lacked for readers, and for the next 18 years it would never lack for readers. But then there was the advertising problem.

When *Ms.* broke the first story on the toxic shock syndrome from tampons, all the tampon manufacturers pulled their ads. Well, they couldn't keep them pulled, because within three weeks this was a national story—everybody had this story—so advertisers couldn't selectively punish *Ms.* On the other hand, sometimes the punishment indeed goes on. In 1980, I did an exclusive interview with four Soviet feminist dissidents. These were women who had been forced out of the Soviet Union into exile for having published an underground feminist journal. They were all in their late twenties and early thirties. We ran it as a cover story, and it won three journalistic awards. It was a beautiful cover and it was a story we were very proud of. Well, Revlon got upset because the four women on the cover—who had these terrific, wonderful, strong faces—weren't wearing makeup, and they pulled their ads, and they never came back.

In addition, there was the whole idea of selling the advertising community that feminists were people; that feminists in fact liked children, often had children, often were married people, or some wished to be or some had been, or some might be again; that feminists in fact did not live on air, but often ate things and frequently cooked the things that they ate; that feminists were able to do more than boil water; that feminists drove cars sometimes; that feminists had stereo sets—you name it. The sales force at *Ms.*, which trained under Pat Carbine's infinitely patient and intrepid aegis, really educated the advertising world. The *Ms.* sales force was going out to try to say, "Actually women are consumers, they do buy, and they like to be treated with respect." Some of those *Ms.* saleswomen went on to become quite extraordinary, such as Cathy Black [now president of Hearst Magazines] who is now the publisher of *USA Today.*

Ms. was the first to demand that ads be integrated. This shocked the advertising world. Oh, definitely they had African-American models, but those were for *Essence* or for *Ebony*. What do you mean they should be in *Ms.*? Wasn't *Ms.* a white magazine? "Well, actually no," the sales force tried to explain. "*Ms.* is a magazine for all women." So, it was the first magazine to demand, and in many cases to be able to get, advertisers to explore mixed-race ads. Same in terms of age. The early sales force at *Ms.* had many extraordinary firsts. They had a number of remarkable triumphs. Sometimes they were able to get advertisers to change copy. Sometimes they weren't.

I remember one case in particular. There was a new woman in the *Ms.* ad department, and she was so happy that she'd finally got this account—a liquor manufacturer who had just put forth a new line of canned, ready-mixed drinks called the Club Line. And then the make-ready [pre-press proof] came in and we're riffling through the magazine saying "Oh this turned out nice, this turned out nice," and I see this ad for the first time, and on the surface of it it looks like a terrific ad. It shows a gray-haired woman, and she's not glamorous; she's in coveralls, and she's clearly doing some sort of construction work—she's got nails sticking out of the coverall pocket and a hammer in one hand and her hair is kind of tussled. She looks like a real person, and she has one of these cans in her hand and she's tossing it up, and that's all terrific. But the legend emblazoned across the top is "Hit me again, hit me with a Club."

I ran down the hall to Suzanne Levine who was then our editor-in-chief and who now is the editor of the *Columbia Journalism Review* and showed it to her, and at this point Gloria Steinem came in from somewhere, and we all hyperventilated a lot.

Somehow we had missed seeing the actual ad. The last we heard was that the account had come in but the ad had gotten somehow directly to the art department and had gone off to the printer. We called the printer, but we couldn't pull the ad. We were on press and rolling and we could not afford the hundreds of thousands of dollars it would cost us to stop. We quickly devised a blow-in card, but it was too late to put it in—we couldn't afford what it would cost to put it in so late. There was nothing, in other words, to be done.

So we stopped up our ears and waited, and the letters came, because *Ms.* readers have always been extraordinary. I like to think of them as reading the magazine in one hand, with a pen poised in the other. Mailbags of letters came in. We sent them all over to the advertising agency, and by the next issue we were able to run not only an apology from the magazine, but also an apology from the liquor manufacturer, who had taken the entire account away from the agency. It was around a $2 million account.

There were those moments of triumph, but by and large I think what gave Gloria and Pat and that original founding group apoplexy over those 20 years was that fight to get the advertising community to take women as consumers seriously, and then to get them to honor the line that supposedly exists between editorial and advertising because the other women's magazines were not trying that hard anymore, erosion having tired them all out. To make a long story short, by 1987, although the readers had never flagged, the magazine was tired of the fight with advertisers.

By late 1987, the original group sold the magazine to Fairfax Limited, an Australian-based multi-magazine corporation. Then followed what we in our more charitable moments term the Australian period. They were well-meaning, good people with, I think, a profound ignorance of the U.S. women's movement and the assumption that if they could only make *Ms.* jazzy and corporate and appeal to the high-level ranking corporate woman—who of course was off there reading *The Wall Street Journal*—that all would be well. The magazine at first had an enormous amount of capital, for *Ms.,* and at first its subscriptions and its circulation shot way up, close to 500,000, the highest it had ever been.

However, once the first issues were published, an interesting thing happened: Readers tired of it very fast, and advertisers—who at first thought, "Ah! Well now this *Ms.* has finally come to its senses and it's going to be decent and womanly and polite and not crazy and radical"—still didn't come on board. The curse was still there. The myth of feminism, the stench of feminism was still hovering over this magazine even though you would not necessarily have known it from reading its pages: fashion coverage, a wine column, and an amazing piece on why liposuction was a feminist act. I have a very inclusive vision of feminism. I am not interested in a narrow-minded feminism, but that one was a stretch for me.

For the first time, the magazine was in trouble with advertisers *and* with readers, and the figures plummeted. I'm beginning to sound like the "Perils of Pauline," but it was like that there for a while. So, while *Ms.* was lying bound on the railroad tracks going, "Ohhh, ohhhh, ohhhh," Lang Communications bought it—in 1989. Dale Lang thought he would be acquiring a good subscriber's list for his other magazines, *Working Mother* and *Working Woman*. Lang suspended *Ms.* from the October 1989 issue on because he didn't know what to with it. It really did seem as if *Ms.*'s time had come and gone, and maybe the most graceful thing to do would be for it to fold its tent and go away.

When the October issue didn't appear readers started writing. Hundreds of thousands of letters came in to him saying, "Look, we have not liked the way the magazine has been going in the past three to five years, we have not been happy with it one bit, but we want our *Ms.* We do not intend for it to die. It's a feminist institution. It means something to us." Well, that really startled all of Lang Communications, and then at the same point some of the old original group mustered themselves and dusted themselves off and came back in and said, "All right, what if we were to resurrect it as a newsletter? What if we were to resurrect it as a quarterly journal?" All of these ideas were being tossed around.

I was asked to come on as editor-in-chief. I made what I thought was a perfectly safe list of absolutely outrageous demands that would permit me to go on with my book writing and my organizing and my traveling and real life. I said, "I will come back this time and run the magazine, but on the following grounds: It must be completely free of all advertising. It must be editorially autonomous from Lang Communications—in other words, no one at Lang sees this magazine until it's in the mail to subscribers. I want to make it international; I want to have a minimum of six pages of international news in each issue plus at least one major feature. I want to do in-depth investigative journalism, and I want to name names (because now I could if I didn't have advertisers). I want to bring back world class fiction and poetry. I would suggest not a quarterly but six issues a year, but each to be a double issue of 100 pages of solid copy and art. Those are my terms." To my absolute horror, they met them, and I have not had a chance to wash my hair since.

That was in December of 1989, and my hair is now very dirty. I still have clothes at the cleaners; I haven't had a chance to pick them up.

The truth is that 600 pages of pure copy a year is put out by 13 women, which is maybe a magical number for a coven, but makes for a very tired editorial staff. And, I would add, that's including editorial copy, research, art, and production. So, none of us have washed our hair, come to think of it, since January of 1990. In any event, we are now quite a wonderful mix of lesbian and straight and as old as mid-sixties and as young as early twenties, or younger if you count the interns. We have two African-American women, one Native American woman, two Asian-American women, one Latino, a whole big potpourri of Eastern European women, and European American women ancestries.

We begin now to reflect the women's movement, and that shows in the pages. I'm very proud that in the past two-and-a-half years we've published Toni Morrison, Alice Walker, and Margaret Atwood. The magazine has won more awards in the last two-and-a-half years than it did in the previous 18, ranging from the American Library Association to five Utne awards in one year. We've already had seven design awards this year and the awards have only started coming out a month ago.

And *Ms.* is more commercially successful than all the years when it took advertising. So, as of July of 1991, we were already at 200,000 subscribers, and we sell an average of 50,000 to 70,000 copies on newsstands. We are upping the print run on every issue. When this first liberated *Ms.* came out in July of 1990, history repeated itself. We printed a first run of 60,000, and it sold out overnight. We went back to press and we doubled the print run, and it sold out overnight. So then the second issue sold out within four days, and the third issue did, and then we began upping the print run. We have virtually 100 percent pay up on subscriptions, and we were well on our way and self-supporting by the second issue.

The quality of writers and artists that we've been able to publish is the source of my deepest pride. It's a very simple recipe, ultimately. When you have freedom of the press, you get the best damned writers and artists you can. You respect them, and you respect your readers, and then you sit back and shut up and let them talk to each other.

And I have to tell you it just feels like journalism.

REDEFINING THE AMERICAN FAMILY: THE MAGAZINE AS HISTORY BOOK

Jean LemMon

Jean LemMon was named editor-in-chief of *Better Homes and Gardens* in May 1993, taking the helm of one of America's best-read magazines, with a circulation of 7.6 million and readership of more than 35 million. A professionally trained designer and writer, LemMon began her editing career at Meredith Corporation in 1961 when she joined the *Better Homes and Gardens* furnishings and design department. She served both as a staff member and as a freelance writer, designer, and editor of Meredith Publications. In 1986 she was named editor-in-chief of *Country Home,* which grew to a circulation of 1 million under her stewardship. The first female editor-in-chief of *Better Homes and Gardens,* LemMon is a graduate of the University of Minnesota and is the winner of four national awards for outstanding journalism in the field of interior design. This lecture was presented in April 1995.

The American family is continually redefining itself in response to various influences which include politics, economics, technology, and fashion. And as families change, magazines change. It's been our job to help readers deal with those family changes by giving them ideas and information relative to their homes, children, and shifting lifestyles. In helping readers throughout the decades, we have automatically become, in retrospect, the historian of American family culture.

Let me set the stage for you. It's the 1920s. These are the years of short-skirted, short-haired flappers, speakeasies, bathtub gin, gun molls, and gangland killings. Into this insanely irresponsible, madcap world, *Fruit Garden and Home* was born. The magazine was launched in July 1922, and in August 1924, it changed its name to *Better Homes and Gardens.*

There were still plenty of people, particularly in rural areas, who lived lives dedicated to creating better environments for their families, whom they considered infinitely more important than the craziness of the time. This has been the case throughout the decades. The family core we edit to has always been strong, and while not involved in fringe movements, has always been influenced by the world around it.

Naturally, a magazine called *Fruit Garden and Home* might be expected to include titles like these: "How Our Small Fruits Are Propagated" and "Pests of the Poultry Yard," but it also included a regular feature, "Music for Every Home," and titles such as "Budgeting for Home Furnishing" and "The Normal Baby."

Family has always been our focus as you can see in these early pages: "Better Fathers and Mothers" from 1926 and "Just Imagine the Fun of It!"—a piece on how to build a backyard play area. During the '20s all editorial material was in black and white. And if you read the antiquated copy, you'd know those writers could have done nicely with one-third the amount of words.

For our '20s readers, life centered around home, and we helped them decorate those homes with stories like: "More Color in the Bedroom" and "Getting Beauty into the Home." But just imagine the challenge of doing an editorial piece about color and publishing it in black and white.

In October 1929, the stock market crashed and the Great Depression had begun, setting up economic conditions that affected how most people lived. For some, the '30s meant poverty and homelessness; for others they meant radio dramas in comfortable living rooms. On *BH&G*'s pages, money was an issue—obviously. A 1934 baking powder ad talks about not being able to afford baking failures, while a Nash ad, even though it depicts the luxury of car ownership, positions the ad from an economic standpoint: "Daddy, are we richer than we used to be?"

In the late '20s and '30s, when cars became more available to more people, we saw the earliest interest in suburban living, with homeowners being able to drive into the city to their jobs. And we created stories—this time in color—on new color schemes for those suburban houses and on practical furniture at moderate cost.

In the '30s, marriage roles were certainly traditional, but we started to see the emergence of the male cook, and *BH&G* featured a men's cooking contest. The magazine also showcased the newly popular frozen desserts in a contest entered by 7,826 readers. By the end of the decade, we were running four pages of color per issue—three advertising pages and one editorial.

Kids have always been the mainstay of *BH&G*. In the '30s, many families were struggling to make ends meet, yet our readers—who numbered in the millions by then—were concerned about sending their children to nursery school and furnishing their homes, albeit practically and inexpensively, to suit the needs of their children. *BH&G* helped show them how.

The '40s started well; then we were plunged into war with all the sacrifices that meant; then we cruised to the close of the decade in better shape, economically and emotionally, than we'd been in years.

It started like this: Editorials to "Bored Wives" and ads that stated, "I wish I could afford a maid for you, honey." The December 1941 issue (which was prepared long before December 7 and Pearl Harbor) showed a lavish Christmas with the whole family intact. Only weeks later that great American scene would be shattered.

Following America's entry into World War II, editorial pages were filled with features like "Wartime Living," "Watch Out for War Nerves," and "Dad's Game Room Solved Their Fuel Problem." During the war years, we helped readers grow their own food, preserve it, and do without rationed meat by substituting soybeans—and not only substituting, but growing them as well. We also encouraged readers to produce their own milk, eggs, and meat with a backyard barnyard.

It was in 1944, with the war nearing its end, that *BH&G* gave the world a brave, new concept—the family room. Our editors felt that with families being reunited after the war's separation, they needed a place to re-bond and that the living room at the front of the house (usually reserved for company) wasn't going to get the job done. So they created a very informal room at the back of the house where family members could relax, play together, work together, and generally become family again. It's a concept that took hold because it fit the way Americans wanted to live.

Postwar issues helped families get back in the swing of things with articles like a refresher course in broiling a steak. And after years of radio production being dedicated to the war effort, *BH&G* was able to feature articles like this one in the December 1945 issue: "Radios Are Back—With New Faces and New Performance." In 1947, *BH&G* brought readers this revelation: "Television Receivers—They're Really Here!"

There's one other '40s trend I should mention because *BH&G* was responsible for launching it: the barbecue. Our food editor discovered this form of outdoor cooking in California and, on the pages of the magazine, introduced it to a country ready for informal cooking and entertainment.

The baby boom was starting in the '40s and *BH&G* was there to help families with stories such as: "A New American Comes Home." The subhead read, "Is a member of Uncle Sam's biggest baby crop headed your way? Here are things you'll want to know and have ready for the small stranger."

As this war-torn decade closed and we headed into the suburbs, we saw a shifting of the traditional attitude about homemaking. It may be best expressed by a 1949 article that set the pace for what was ahead: "Dogs, Kids, Husbands—How to Furnish a House So They Can't Hurt It!"

People were looking for clean air, space, grass, and good schools. There was a suburban building boom, the do-it-yourself mentality came into being, and during the '50s, 11 million more kids were born. There were new foods, new appliances, and new attitudes. There were long commutes from the suburbs to work and, for the first time, there was a thriving business for baby-sitters because families no longer lived close to the grandparents. There were cocktail parties in the suburbs and outdoor living continued to gain in popularity. In the '50s, the sale of lawn and porch furniture soared from $53 million in 1950 to $145 million in 1960.

Better Homes and Gardens grew fat—literally—on all this domesticity. In April 1956, we printed a 378-page issue—by then, largely four-color—and our circulation was over 4 million.

We presented the typical home of the '50s as "a home that can be a comfort, not a constant care." Fifties families wanted convenience for their new way of life. We offered a glimpse at the first microwaves, and what was then very advanced, home sound—"Putting Hi-Fi in Your Home." At about the same time, *BH&G* did our first feature on solar energy.

Family travel was mostly by car or by rail in the '50s, and as people traveled more, they were exposed to different foods in different places. So it was during this time that we addressed that interest in restaurants by starting a regular feature: "Famous Foods from Famous Places." At home, the barbecue was still going strong—the natural result of informal suburban living. This kind of living spawned a new food trend—the salad. In 1957, we ran a story spotlighting new, cool foods.

As a magazine reflecting the American family, we'd come a long way. These titles tell the story: In the early '50s, we did features like "Know What to Look for in Your Sitter" and "Three Ways to Help Your Baby Burp." As the decade closed, *BH&G* was doing articles such as "Are You a Candidate for a Heart Attack?" and "The Slavery of Sex Freedom." By the way, *BH&G* did not advocate sexual freedom.

By the end of the decade, the suburban living that had seemed so compelling had become a confining world of look-alike houses and constant cocktail parties. Families once again sought clean air and privacy. Camping was the answer! And as the decade flopped over into the '60s, we saw articles like this on the pages of *BH&G*: "Fresh Air, Fresh Fish and a Man's Touch."

The '60s: John F. Kennedy and Camelot. Assassinations. Black ghettos burning. Vietnam and draft dodging. Yet through all the struggles, 100 million Americans escaped the craziness and lived pretty much as they always had.

The peace sign was big in the '60s. But when *BH&G* talked about living in peace, it was putting the parents' quarters at one end of the house and the kids' rooms at the other. We also addressed a growing situation: kids with ideas of their own and the tension between generations.

In the '60s there was an awakening to color in everything, the wilder the better. Plastics were new and hot, and we showed readers what they might expect in home furnishings. There were new small appliances, too. A story from our foods department featured the new "automatic" electric griddle and push-button rotisserie—evidence of the quickening pace of family living and the search for convenience.

In the '60s, folks were getting together for a new kind of at-home entertaining. The fondue pot came into existence, and we pictured a typical '60s weekend night with everyone cooking their own food.

There was another condition existing in the American family of the early '60s that I am less thrilled to report. The early '60s were, as were the years that preceded them, traditional and male-dominated. Look at the February 1962 cover blurb: "How to Please Your Husband." And inside: "What Makes a Man Feel at Home?" Or this from 1963: "What the Men Are Having for Lunch." That was a food story meant to help us poor home-bound women learn about all the fabulous restaurants our businessmen husbands were enjoying. But there was hope. In a 1960s piece on "The New Baby Comes Home," dad's just as involved as mom.

In the 1960s, our circulation was at 6,750,000, and we were doing some spectacular things in editorial production, with double-gate folds and half-page inserts that showed changes in room designs.

In the '70s, the women's movement exploded and, in 1976, we ran a cover with a man at work in the dining room and the woman reading in the living room. The '70s also brought other issues that hadn't been faced before—such as energy and conservation, and *BH&G* addressed them with stories on underground housing and others titled "Is a Car Pool for You?" and "An Around the House Guide to Energy-Saving."

More women than ever before joined the workplace and prompted these stories: "Meals in a Hurry," "A Flexible Work Plan for Married Women," and "Would Looking Younger Help You Land That Job?"

Calorie-cutting was part of the '70s, too, and we ran calorie-conscious food articles that featured microwave cooking for families with limited time to spend in the kitchen.

In the '70s, women became involved in the home in ways they hadn't been before, and we saw articles like "Installing a Skylight," with couples working together on a do-it-yourself project.

In the middle of this decade, in the middle of all this sexual equality and advancing technology, something interesting happened. Our country's bicentennial! Suddenly America was intrigued with its own heritage and that intrigue affected how we lived and how we edited this magazine. Articles like these showed up: "Building on the Past," and "Folks Who Still Cook the Old Fashioned Way."

Country decorating became a runaway winner and there was a solid return to nostalgia among some Americans. However, many of them were gearing up for what Tom Wolfe labeled the "Me Decade"—a time of wanting and having and self-centeredness. In keeping with the bigger, better mind-set of the '80s, we ran the story: "Move-Up Houses—Ready for a Bigger, Better House?" We also did building stories titled, "Marble Tile—A Touch of the Taj Mahal" and "Master Suite Plus Home Gym." We showed not just a bigger, better kitchen, but one designed for two cooks. It was an '80s trend: multiple cooks, usually a "Him and Her" duet.

There was an emphasis on foreign foods in the '80s, as well as awareness of the links food and nutrition have with good health. There was also this approach: "Garden Fresh Cuisine." Only in the '80s would we refer to food as "cuisine," but the "garden fresh" was also part of the '80s. After years of canning and marveling over frozen foods, now "fresh" was best. Herbs were suddenly more important, in cooking and in landscaping. We pictured a whole yard given over to herbs—the hot, healthy interest of the '80s.

In decorating, the '80s brought a return to romance and softness as Americans looked for an escape from the stress of the high-tech world around them. For the first time an awareness was developing that we were all getting older. Articles in *BH&G* hit that new problem head-on: "Care for Mom and Dad" and "Those Little Aches and Pains."

So as we came into the '90s, we were looking at an American family quite different in structure than it was 70 years ago—different in taste, different in attitude and expectations. The only way in which it was not different was that it still devoted its energy and resources to creating the best environment and best standard of living possible for its children.

Today, we're concerned about being good parents and good citizens, about taking care of our health and our environment. We're concerned about eating right and saving money, while we express our design individuality in a way that wasn't possible years ago. We celebrate our heritage while we want comfort for today's living. We want to be able to get away and enjoy life, and most of all we want to do it with our families.

See, some things never change—in society or in *Better Homes and Gardens.* This magazine has not edited to fads. We've not pandered to the sensational. We've gone along, very successfully, for 73 years, helping readers achieve better homes, better gardens, and better lives with their families.

And we've seen plenty of changes.The magazine we published in 1922 bears little resemblance, physically, to the latest issue of *Better Homes and Gardens.* There is, however, one thing all *Better Homes and Gardens* issues have in common: They are the standard-bearer for what's most important to our readers—their homes and families. And because of that, we are, automatically, a chronicle of how the American family lives. I'm sure we always will be.

I have no intention of being this magazine's editor when it celebrates its centennial in 2022. But when it does, it wouldn't surprise me if that editor is still plugging in stories on the hot new colors, latest child-raising techniques, and current food fancies. And it wouldn't surprise me if she, or he, turns to the food editor and says, "Isn't it about time to do another story on barbecues?"

THE ALTERNATIVE MAGAZINE: BUILDING COMMUNITY

Jay Walljasper

Jay Walljasper was editor of *Utne Reader* when he gave this speech in 1994. During his leadership from 1980, when the magazine was founded, until 1995, *Utne Reader* was nominated for the National Magazine Award in the general excellence category for 1994, 1991, and 1987. Today, Walljasper is an editor-at-large for *Utne Reader* and a regular contributor to *The Nation.* His freelance articles have appeared in *Mother Jones, Tikkun, Europe, Midwest Living, Social Policy, TWA Ambassador,* and *New Age Journal,* as well as the *Chicago Tribune, Philadelphia Inquirer, Minneapolis Star Tribune,* and *Chicago Sun-Times.* Walljasper is editor of the book *Good Life: Mastering the Art of Everyday Living.*

The history of American alternative journalism goes back to the American Revolution when Thomas Paine wrote a pamphlet called *Common Sense,* which laid out the case for the independence of the 13 colonies from Great Britain. The abolitionist movement to get rid of slavery had a driving press, and Frederick Douglass published much of his work there. *The Nation,* one of the premier alternative magazines in the country, was started after the Civil War by people who had been involved with the abolition movement and asked, "Where are we going to go next?" In the late nineteenth century, a labor press was born at the same time as labor unions, which had such radical ideas as banning child labor and establishing the eight-hour workday. Anytime there's a great outpouring of people's passions and beliefs, it's inevitably going to find its way into print and become another component of the alternative press. Almost always, mainstream newspapers of the time initially won't be charitable to new views and ideas, so people use alternative publications to get their point of view out.

Today's alternative press owes a great debt of gratitude to *The Masses,* a magazine established in 1911. I like to call it the great-grandfather of the alternative press. I recently looked at some old copies of *The Masses,* and it was fascinating to see the alternative ideas that were happening in the years before World War I. The writers were discussing education reform, feminism, and new ideas in psychotherapy. *The Masses* was shut down by the government during World War I because it was thought to be seditious and not supporting the war effort enough. The magazine was not permitted to use the mail, which ultimately killed it.

Having credited *The Masses* as the great-grandfather of the alternative press, I would say the grandfather is George Seldes. Seldes was a newspaper reporter who founded *In Fact,* which was a little newsletter that carried no ads. Seldes broke an extremely important story that no other publication touched for decades afterwards: the link between smoking and lung cancer. He did that in the 1940s and the story went absolutely nowhere because cigarette companies advertised heavily in magazines, on radio, and in newspapers.

Another great forerunner of the alternative press was I. F. Stone. In the tradition of George Seldes, Stone published a newsletter called *I. F. Stone's Weekly* during the 1950s when radical ideas were not welcome in the United States. Yet Stone published stories about wrongdoing in the federal government in his newsletter each week. He didn't have a squadron of reporters or researchers, either. What Stone did as a journalist was to go through government documents—stuff that was the public record that any reporter or individual in America could look at—and he turned up revelations about corporate malfeasance and government corruption.

The alternative press as we know it today began in 1955, when *Village Voice* was started in New York City. The story of *Village Voice* speaks a lot about alternative journalism's role in building community. *Village Voice* was established by people living in Greenwich Village who were disgruntled with their local neighborhood newspaper which was called *The Villager.* These people, among them novelist Norman Mailer, were trying to reform the local branch of the Democratic Party. They were angry that *The Villager* never reported on their meetings and never talked about what they were doing.

So in the great tradition of American alternative journalism, they started their own newspaper so their community would have a voice. *Village Voice* turned out to be an incredibly influential publication in American history because it changed the shape of journalism in many ways. For example, newspapers at this time often had jazz critics, and they certainly had classical music critics. But rock 'n' roll was perceived as meaningless teen heartthrob music. *Village Voice* was the first publication to take rock 'n' roll seriously, pioneering rock criticism long before *Rolling Stone.*

In 1964, *Los Angeles Free Press,* which journalism historians credit as the first underground newspaper, was started. It came out of this same context of a community of people being tired of the coverage they saw in their local media and creating a new publication to do something about it.

Within a few years, it seemed that every city in the country had underground newspapers. These publications took off so quickly because mainstream newspaper journalists, and to some extent magazine journalists, too, were not dealing with a lot of things that were happening in American culture. Many people's strong feelings of outrage about the Vietnam War, racism, and environmental destruction were being minimized or ignored. Mainstream journalists didn't take rock 'n' roll seriously, they took a dim view of the drug culture, and they were frightened by the new experimentation in lifestyles and sexuality. Underground newspapers walked in and filled the void. They really did speak to and speak for a community.

By the 1970s, most of these papers were making quite a bit of money. They began calling themselves "alternative" publications as opposed to "underground," which had evoked romantic notions of being beyond the reaches of the law. Today's alternative publications offer different perspectives on politics, culture, and community issues in city after city across America. There's the gay community press, the alternative health press, the environmental press, the African-American press in inner cities, and other alternative ethnic publications.

There's a richness to this country, but sometimes it gets reduced in the media to oversimplifications about "what Americans think" or "what Americans do." What thrills me about alternative journalism is the recognition of our culture's diversity and that we don't speak with a single voice. There are a number of points of view on any subject. There's not just one single truth. To know the way it is, we need to take a lot of testimony from lots of different kinds of people.

Alternative journalism tends to reject the notion of objectivity. Objectivity is a concept that journalism borrowed from the physical sciences. It means a reporter can discern the truth by viewing a situation in a detached, clinical manner. While this may work in physics, in journalism it's impossible. No reporter can be truly objective. As human beings, we're shaped by innumerable forces in the world. Those forces tend to influence how we filter the news. It's dishonest to pretend there are no biases, when in fact every reporter has them.

I make a distinction between the facts and objectivity. Objectivity is more a state of mind. The facts are tangible things that we can talk about. The alternative press relies upon the facts just as much as the mainstream press does, but if we offer our own opinions on a subject, we admit it rather than hiding behind the cloak of objectivity. Every word you choose when you're writing a story gives you the opportunity to bring your point of view to it. What the alternative press says is we call them as we see them; we're not playing any word games.

So, is the alternative press impartial? No, it's probably not. But we offer something more important: a sense of passion. At *Utne Reader* we do something different from a lot of other alternative publications. It's been the thing that's kept me there for 10 years, because it's really a gas putting the magazine together. What we delight in doing at *Utne Reader* is mixing things up a little bit. We'll run a story, and then we'll run another story that may totally disagree with the first story. In fact, we may even hire someone to write a story that disagrees with the first story, and we may put in another story that brings in the third point of view or fourth point of view. We defy the notion that there are only two sides to every story. We assume there are at least 11, but it's probably more like 174. What we look for are the points of views that don't get presented in the mainstream media.

The process of putting together *Utne Reader* is pretty simple. About 2,000 publications come into our office each month. It's our job to sift through these different publications. If you want to see the diversity of American life, you should be looking at all the publications I look through. We get pacifist journals from the desert of Arizona. We get gay publications from Oregon. We get publications about psychobotany, which is the study of plants you can eat and have hallucinations with. We get a lot of church publications. As we look through these different publications, what we're really looking for are the stories that we're not seeing in *The New York Times,* not seeing on CNN. We want the important news behind the headlines, the news that didn't make it into the mainstream media.

I don't think the editors at *The New York Times* or *The Washington Post* are sitting on top of these incredible stories and refusing to print them. It's not that things are being suppressed in the media, because I really believe we have freedom of the press in the United States. But I think so many people in the media professions come from the same background; they've shared the same experiences. They have similar points of view. It's like group think. That's why important news sometimes gets overlooked.

I don't believe there's a great battle going on between the alternative press and the mainstream press. I think they complement each other. You shouldn't cancel your subscription to *Des Moines Register* and read only *Utne Reader. Utne Reader* makes a great complement to that, and to all the magazines you're getting like *Time, Newsweek,* or *Life.*

There's a little identity crisis happening in the alternative press right now. Perhaps it's one of the perils of success. I'm a devoted reader of *Time, Newsweek, The New York Times,* and other major publications because I need to know what they're writing about so I know that we're not saying the same thing. That's getting increasingly problematic. This wasn't the case 10 years ago when we had a wide-open field. At that time, the American media had veered quite a bit to the right during the Reagan years from where they had been during the Watergate years. There was a lot that wasn't being reported. But now, more and more of the writers that we've been reprinting in *Utne Reader* are in *Newsweek* or *Time.* That makes me happy because I think the alternative press has had a great influence on American culture. But we can't keep doing the kind of stuff we've been doing at *Utne Reader,* because *Time* and *Newsweek* are doing it in part.

My solution to this problem facing the alternative press is the idea of community. We want to re-instill the notion of community in American life. A magazine is sometimes a community in and of itself. If you read personal ads in the newspapers, you'll notice people convey a sense of who they are by saying "I'm a *Spin* magazine kind of person," or "I love *The New York Review of Books.*"

We write a lot about community in our magazine, but it isn't always a community that is the subject of the article. We have coverage about how to save the public schools, because that's one of the basic things that ties a community together. We write about the need for new transportation policies, because we can't have a cohesive community if the only time people see each other is through windshields. We try to foster community with our promotion of salons where people meet face to face and talk about what's on their minds. We promote the notion of the urban village. We try to re-create what was good about the simpler world that we used to live in, and hopefully not repeat what was bad about it.

In his book *Moral Fragments and Moral Community,* Larry Rassmussen, a Lutheran pastor and theologian at the Union Theological Seminary in New York City, discusses what he calls the elements of community. These elements also make a good list for the elements of a successful magazine, showing the tie between community and magazine.

The first element is historicity, or a sense of historical continuity. The most important thing for a magazine to have is a clear identity from issue to issue. *Newsweek* has to have a different identity from *Time,* because if they're interchangeable, why do you care whether you pick up one or the other? Each magazine has to carve out its own identity. That's a function of community.

Another element is mutuality, which means open-ended obligation. There's an obligation in putting out *Utne Reader.* It's an obligation to publish a magazine that people find interesting.

On the crassest level you pay money and you get a magazine, but there's an exchange about ideas and sensibilities involved which is central to magazines.

Rassmussen identifies plurality as another element to community. This equals the fact that there isn't just one single voice on a magazine. There's usually a community of people who put out a magazine.

An additional element in community is autonomy. A magazine has to have its own independent voice.

Participation is important for communities and magazines both. It's been proven in survey after survey that one of the most highly read sections of any publication is the letters, because people can participate that way in magazines.

Finally, integration is an element of community; integration is balance. That's important in a magazine as well. A magazine that just makes the same point over and over again, doesn't have that much to offer.

When I worked at *Better Homes and Gardens*, the job I always wanted was to write the last page. I wanted to be Burton Hillis, the man next door, because he writes about community. His column has a great small-town quality, with stories, jokes, and wisdom about a group of people who live together in a community. What keeps me interested in journalism is that notion of reaching people as part of a far-flung community. When you're thinking about a career in journalism, you might not be thinking about the idea of community, but it's something that's part of the job.

THE EVOLVING MAGAZINE: INFLUENCE OF CELEBRITY JOURNALISM

James A. Autry

While editor of *Better Homes and Gardens* from 1970 to 1981, James A. Autry was instrumental in shaping the field of service journalism. When he gave this speech in 1991, Autry was president of the Magazine Group and a senior vice president at Meredith Corporation. Since his retirement from Meredith, Autry has achieved fame as an award-winning author and poet. His book, *Love and Profit: The Art of Caring Leadership,* won the prestigious Johnson, Smith & Knisely Award as the book which had the most impact on executive thinking in 1992. His most recent book, *Confessions of an Accidental Businessman,* was a finalist in the 1996 Global Business Book Awards.

Prior to World War II, there was a general sense that anything not involved with news and news features was not journalism. News and features pretty much drove magazines. But as people's information needs began to shift and become more intense, magazines were driven by an emerging emphasis on different kinds of journalism, which was, in turn, driven by emerging information and subject needs of readers.

In the late 1960s, we saw a new form introduced. It became known as New Journalism. (A humor columnist at the *Kansas City Star* named Bill Vaughn referred to New Journalism as the "self-interview.") New Journalism was not very well accepted at first in the journalism establishment. But with people like Tom Wolfe as a leading exponent of New Journalism, it became an electrifying form for a lot of people who were looking to get away from the old objectivity of reporting and to become "activist journalists." This sort of activist journalism, or New Journalism, put the reporter in the middle of the story and made the reporter's involvement part of the story. New Journalism, I think, brought a big change in journalism as we think of it both in magazines and newspapers.

In the 1970s, Watergate brought us a huge re-emphasis on investigative reporting. During the 1970s, every journalism graduate wanted to be an investigative reporter. The most intense interest was in ferreting out corruption in high places. Writing obituaries or doing the police beat just didn't seem like real journalism. And forget any notion of home-building or remodeling or travel writing being regarded as journalism!

It was during this period that some of us in the business began to articulate what we called service journalism. I remember doing what I called my service journalism manifesto. I guess the simplest way to define service journalism is as information people can act upon. It's really action journalism, but the subjects can be as seemingly trivial as recipes or as serious as some of the major social issues of the day.

Service journalism began to get a little panache of its own and to be talked about a lot. As other magazines and editors picked it up, service journalism began to inform the way magazines were done. Then in 1974, Time Inc. established *People* magazine. Dick Stolley, the founding managing editor of *People,* coined the phrase "celebrity journalism." So along with news, features, New Journalism, and service journalism, celebrity journalism began to inform the making of magazines during the 1970s. Those things came together with niche marketing and very highly selective, special interest magazines.

Then an interesting thing began to happen. Let's say there was a special interest magazine on growing roses. Now what do you need to grow roses? You need to know how to do it, right? First there's the inspiration, these beautiful pictures of roses. You think, "I can have that." You don't think about the weeds, all the blight, and all the stuff you have to do. But you need that inspiration and you need the information. Inspiration and information cover it. But what began to happen—and I call this to your attention as one of the most interesting phenomenons that's happened in journalism—was that celebrity journalism began to invade all of this. It began to invade fashion, news, sports, service—everything—so that you didn't just have a rose magazine about growing roses, you had "Charlton Heston Shows You How to Grow Roses." This has happened throughout journalism.

Look at television, look at cable, and see to what extent celebrity journalism has invaded every kind of journalism. We have a new tabloid mentality that knocks me out. Look at the magazines that have started up to do nothing but celebrity journalism: *People, US, Vanity Fair, Entertainment Weekly.* Then consider other magazines like *Ladies' Home Journal.* We have to find "who's hot." Is it going to be Elizabeth Taylor? Is it going to be Princess Di? Kevin Costner? All this has to do with selling magazines. Interestingly enough, very little of *Ladies' Home Journal* has to do with anything other than service, advice about personal issues, relationships and parenting, as well as the fashions and foods and other things that go into service magazines. But we're always going to have at least one feature on a celebrity and that celebrity probably is going to be on the cover. Because that magazine is competing on the newsstand with all the other magazines that have celebrities on the cover.

It's maddening, but look at the successful magazines today and how many of them are driven by celebrities. Let me stretch this a bit further and ask, "What's the big news in sports?" Is it who's playing and who's winning, who's warming up, how's the team been going, and who's being traded? No, it's contracts and how much money is going into the new sports celebrity contracts. These people are superstars. I can tell you that years ago nobody cared very much about the home life or the sex life of a heavyweight champion of the world. These days they do. That's the celebrity aspect.

In the fashion field, who used to know the fashion models? The whole point of finding a fashion model in the old days was that she would be someone to put the clothes on so you could see the clothes. Have you watched what's happened to photography in fashion magazines? You can't see the clothes. It's very much evolved into a sort of photojournalistic style of covering fashion.

Well, in my days, the whole notion of photojournalism was to tell the story with a picture. Now more often than not, the photographer is also a celebrity. We have what's his name to shoot what's her name. Is anybody asking the questions: "Can you see the clothes? How much does the dress cost?" Believe me, folks, they're losing the connection. But that's the celebrity aspect of fashion. Now we even know who the models are and all about their night life.

I do see celebrity journalism as beginning to wane—still driving a lot of journalism, but beginning to wane. What seems to be happening is that celebrity journalism is getting boring. The excitement is hard to maintain. Real people are becoming more interested once again in real people.

There's going to be some fallout. I think service is going to re-emerge because the essential role of magazines is, first, information, informed a little bit by entertainment, but not the other way around. If it goes too much the other way around, then magazines are nothing but extensions of television, which has been part of the problem I'm talking about. Magazines have been trying to edit to the interests that television whets. But what interests does television whet? The lowest common denominator interests. It is a downhill march for magazines.

So, I predict that the influence of celebrity journalism on service magazines is going to wane and that there will be a new emphasis on service and a return to the "simple life." I think you'll see a re-emergence of a need for basic information, home, and family. I also think you'll find that time and money and special interests—the readers' time and money and special interests—will be what informs the magazines and how they're edited.

Actual malice Knowingly publishing something false or with a reckless disregard for the truth.

Adjacency An advertisement placed on the page next to an article about a similar subject.

Advertorial An advertising tool that combines articles and advertising in a magazine supplement sponsored entirely by the advertiser.

Advocacy journalism Taking an editorial stand on issues.

Agenda setting The theory that the media do not tell us how to think, they tell us what to think about.

Ancillary products Products to which magazines lend their names for increasing profits. Most of these products are marketing related, created to expand the profitability and advertising reach of the original brand.

Appropriation The unauthorized use of a person's name, picture, or voice to endorse a commercial product or service.

Bingo card A card that lists all advertisers in the magazine and gives the reader the chance to express interest in that advertiser by marking a box in front of the advertiser's name.

Bleed A graphic element that extends past the edge of the page.

Blueline A page proof that shows all type and art and is produced on light-sensitive paper in blue ink.

Break-of-the-book The determination of which article or advertisement goes on what page; also occasionally called the ladder or map.

Business plan A document that offers a clear statement of economic strategies and tactics; usually includes background statements on editorial philosophy, formula, and audience.

Byline Identification of the author of the article.

CPM (Cost per thousand) The cost for an advertiser to reach one thousand readers.

CPP (Cost per point) Method of determining the cost of an advertising page to reach a specific market segment.

CTP (Computer-to-plate) Technology that eliminates the film stage in magazine production.

Calender A process of smoothing stock by compression; also the machine that performs the smoothing.

Camera-ready pages Computer-generated pages that contain all finished art and type and are sent to the printing plant for production.

Circulation promotion A strategy to build circulation by promoting a magazine to readers.

Color separation A color graphic that has been scanned and separated into the four process colors.

Composite Final page of film, including all text and art.

Continuous tone Any art that includes gray tones, including photographs, paintings, and watercolors.

Contract proof A printing proof that shows the accuracy of color reproduction; it gets its name from the fact that it is actually a contract between the magazine and the printer that the final printed color will match the contract proof.

Controlled circulation Form of subscription in which readers who possess specific occupational characteristics receive the magazine free, because these readers have high appeal to advertisers.

Copyright Protects intellectual and creative work—written and artistic—by ensuring that the rights to that work are respected by publishers and other users. The federal copyright statute says that copyright protects "original works of authorship fixed in any tangible medium of expression, now known or later developed, from which they can be perceived, reproduced, or otherwise communicated."

Cover line A short title or teaser that appears on the cover of a magazine.

Cropping The figurative cutting away of portions of a photo to enhance or refine the photo's message.

Cutline Words that provide information about an image or its context; also called a caption.

Cylinder Metal plate that contains all the magazine's material being printed by the rotogravure process.

Demographics Easily quantified audience characteristics such as age, income, or geographic location.

Dingbat Small design device at the end of each article.

Dull coat A paper treated to hold ink well but be less reflective than high gloss; often chosen for magazines with photos and large blocks of type.

Duotint Black-and-white photograph over which spot color has been added as a solid block.

Duotone Black-and-white photograph that is printed twice, once usually in black, and once in a second color.

Editorial formula The practical application of the editorial philosophy, detailing the specific content of the magazine, how much emphasis will be given to each area, the editorial/advertising ratio, and the number and names of continuing departments.

Editorial philosophy A magazine's highly specific focus, giving the publication its identity and personality and covering such issues as what areas of interest the magazine covers, how it approaches those interests, and what voice it uses.

Fair comment and criticism Public expression of opinions about public events and issues to allow freedom of discussion.

Fair use Using a limited portion of a copyrighted work in another work or photocopying an entire copyrighted work for personal use.

False light Invasion of privacy by publishing offensive statements or photos out of context.

Font The name of an individual typeface.

Gatefold A fold-out sheet.

Grid Magazine design format that establishes margins, number of columns per page, widths of columns, cutline and photo placement, title placement, and the use and placement of white space, or air, in a layout.

Gravure See **Rotogravure.**

Halftone Printing term for black-and-white photograph that has been scanned for reproduction.

High gloss A paper that has been coated and calendered to be highly reflective and shiny; often used for pages with photos.

Imposition The placement of pages on a signature.

Incitement Statements aimed at provoking or causing "imminent lawless" action

Infographics Charts, diagrams, and graphs that convey statistical data.

Initial cap The first letter of a word used in a large size to make it stand out.

Insert An advertisement created and produced by the advertiser; it comes to the magazine already printed and is then bound into the magazine.

Intrusion Invasion of privacy by entering a place not open to the public, such as a person's home.

Iris print A proof used early in the proofing process to check placement and design issues.

Kerning Reduction or enlargement of space between letters within a line of type.

Kicker A subtitle that appears above the title.

Leading (pronounced *ledding*) The amount of space between lines of type.

Legibility The ability of a typeface to jump off the page at a quick glance and into the reader's consciousness.

Libel Publishing a false statement about a specific person that injures that person's reputation.

Line art Art created in solid color, with no gray tones.

List kit Promotional kit that includes a list of subscribers to a publication for sale to other publishers and marketers.

Logo The design of the magazine's name.

Masthead The list inside the magazine of staff members.

Match print A contract proof that is an accurate representation of color; usually given for art only.

Matte coat The least polished of the coated stocks, it has the least reflectivity but holds type well.

Media kit A magazine promotional tool that usually consists of the most recent issue, information about the audience, positive articles about the magazine in other publications, and an advertising rate card.

Moiré pattern A wavy, shadowy pattern imprinted in an image from improper printing methods.

Monowell Editorial material placed together, usually in the center of the magazine, with all ads either in the front or back of the book.

Multi-well Editorial material placed in wells throughout the magazine with advertising between wells.

Negligence Publishing an article without the professional care, fairness, and accuracy usually used for that type of story.

Obscenity Hard-core pornography that is so sexually explicit that it does not contribute to the exchange of ideas and information and thus does not fall under First Amendment protection.

Offset Printing process that gets its name from a rubber plate onto which the image is transferred—or offset—from the metal image plate; the paper comes into direct contact with the offset plate.

Operating profit The revenue remaining after expenses have been deducted from income.

Outsert A preprinted publication that contains advertising and may also include editorial material. It is not bound into the magazine and is mailed to subscribers with the magazine, with the two being connected by a shrink wrap.

Pass-along readership The additional readers of a magazine beyond the original buyer.

Perfect binding A binding process in which the pages that form each signature are stacked on top of one another, the edges glued and a cover attached.

Pica Unit of measurement that indicates width and depth of columns, photos, and page space. There are 12 points in one pica; 6 picas equal one inch.

Plates Metal sheets that contain all the magazine material being printed by the offset process.

Point Unit of measurement used to indicate size of type. There are 72 points in one inch.

Prior restraint When a government official reviews articles before publication and has wide discretion in deciding what may or may not be published.

Private facts Invasion of privacy by publishing true facts about a person that are highly offensive to an average person and not legitimately newsworthy.

Privilege Admittedly libelous statement that is allowed to go unpunished because it is from an official source, such as a government document or testimony given under oath, and reported in a fair and balanced article.

Process color The four colors— magenta (red), cyan (blue), yellow, and black—used to print full-color, or four-color, art.

Prototype A professional-quality mock magazine that may or may not include actual articles, but does include representative cover lines, titles, and pull-quotes.

Psychographics Audience characteristics such as values, attitudes, and beliefs.

Pull-quote Words pulled from an article that are used as a design element to break up large blocks of type.

Rate base Audited circulation on which magazine advertising rates are based.

Readership Total circulation plus pass-along readership.

Reverse type White type on a black or color background or on a graphic element such as a photograph.

Right to privacy Right of people to be left alone or to control the way they are portrayed to others.

Rotogravure Also called gravure, this printing process moves with high speed and precision and uses highly fluid ink.

Saddle-stitch binding A binding process in which magazine pages are stapled in the middle so that the sheets of printed pages that form a signature are placed within one another.

Sans serif Typefaces, such as Helvetica, Futura, and Avant Garde, that are geometric in appearance, and as the name implies, lack serifs.

Screen Process that is used to turn continuous tones into halftones, traditionally measured by lines per inch, with most magazines using at least a 133-line screen. Also refers to blocks of color added to a page at less than full strength.

Sell-through rate The number of copies of a magazine the publisher provides to newsstands to be sold divided by the number of copies actually sold.

Separations See **Color Separation**

Serif A typeface which has delicate vertical and horizontal lines, or "feet," at the end of letter strokes that serve as a guideline for the eye; these finishing strokes are the serifs.

Sheet-fed press Printing press that takes one sheet at a time.

Signature Sheet of multiple pages in which magazines are printed, usually in multiples of four.

Spot color A color added to a page for special effect, such as highlighting a word, sentence, or image.

Stock Printing industry term for paper.

Style Typeface options, such as boldface or italics, within a font.

Subhead Words used as organizational cues between paragraphs to break up large blocks of text.

Subtitle Information that immediately follows the title before the start of an article.

Super calendered Paper with less coating and finish than coated stocks, but more than uncoated stocks.

Tracking Adjustments in the amount of space between words on a page, making them tighter or looser overall.

Transparencies Slides; usually used for art reproduction instead of printed photographs.

Typography The typeface(s) used in text, titles, and cutlines; the overall effect conveys the magazine's character.

UV coating A coating added to a printed product and dried with ultraviolet light.

Varnish A slick coating printed atop a finished sheet to prevent ink from running or for special effects.

Web press A printing press that uses a continuous roll of paper.

Wells Blocks of editorial material unbroken by advertising.

X-height Measurement of a lowercase x.

ACKNOWLEDGMENTS

Chapter 1
p. 5, © The New Yorker Collection. 1947 Charles Addams from cartoonbank.com. All Rights Reserved. p. 9, Courtesy *Premiere*. p. 11, Courtesy *New York Magazine*. p. 12, Courtesy *Catholic Rural Life*. p. 14, Courtesy, *Religious Conference Manager*. p. 15, Courtesy *Modern Maturity*/Sygma. p. 17, Courtesy Polly Flug/*Family Ties*. p. 18, Crayola, Chevron, and Crayola Kids are registered trademarks; Rainbow/swash is a trademark of Binney & Smith, used with permission. p. 22, Printed with permission of Black Collegiate Services, Inc.

Chapter 2
p. 27, Courtesy *AutoWeek*. p. 30, Courtesy *Folio:*. p. 39, André Da Miano/*Life* Magazine © Time Inc.

Chapter 3
p. 44, Courtesy American Antiquarian Society. p. 49, Courtesy American Antiquarian Society. p. 51, Courtesy American Antiquarian Society. p. 53, Courtesy American Antiquarian Society. p. 58, Courtesy *Scientific American*. p. 60, Courtesy American Antiquarian Society. p. 63, Courtesy *Reader's Digest*. p. 64, Courtesy American Antiquarian Society. p. 66, Courtesy National Geographic Society.

Chapter 4
p. 78, Courtesy *Aviation Week & Space Technology*/World Wide Photos. p. 79, Courtesy Culver. p. 81, Reprinted by permission from *Outside Magazine*. Copyright 1996, Mariah Publications Corporation. p. 84, Courtesy of Tom Rockwell. p. 88, Liberation Publications Inc., Courtesy *The Advocate*. p. 91, Cover Photography by Jack Ward. © 1996 by the Condé Nast Publications Inc. Courtesy *Glamour*. p. 94, Courtesy *Esquire*. p. 98, Courtesy *Condé Nast Traveler*, September 1987, Copyright Condé Nast Publications Inc. Photograph by Christopher Buckley. p. 100, *People en Español* is a registered trademark of Time Inc., used with permission. p. 101, Courtesy *A. Magazine: Inside Asian America*.

Chapter 5
p. 108, Courtesy *Harper's Magazine*. p. 113, Courtesy *Poz*. p. 117, Courtesy *Mode*. p. 122, Courtesy *Fly Rod & Reel*. p. 125, Reprinted with permission from *Pharmaceutical & Medical Packaging News*, "Cover," October 1998. Copyright © 1998 Cannon Communications LLC. Photography by Roni Ramos. p. 126, Courtesy *Mother Earth News*. p. 131. Courtesy *Mother Earth News*.

Chapter 6
p. 136, Courtesy *Vibe*. p. 140, Courtesy *Keyboard*. p. 142, Courtesy *The New Republic*. P. 149, Courtesy *Harper's Magazine*. p. 145, Courtesy Better Homes and Gardens ® *Family Money*.

Chapter 7
p. 168, Courtesy Condé Nast Publications. p. 174, Courtesy Hearst Communications Inc. p. 177, Courtesy Reiman Publications. p. 179 Courtesy Meredith. p. 180, Courtesy Time Inc. p. 182 (from left), Photo by Mark Seliger. From *Rolling Stone*, January 21, 1999. By Straight Arrow Publishers Company, L.P. 1999. All Rights Reserved. Reprinted by permission. Photo by Marc Baptiste (Drew Barrymore), inset photo by Steve Granitz/Retna (Tom Cruise). From *US* Magazine, November 1998. US Magazine Company, L.P. 1998. All Rights Reserved. Reprinted by permission. Photo by Lee Cohen. From *Men's Journal*, December 1998/January 1999. Men's Journal Company, L.P. 1998. All Rights Reserved. Reprinted by permission.

Chapter 8
p. 192, Courtesy *Sunset*. p. 195, "How Iraq Reverse-Engineered the Bomb" by Glenn Zorpette © 1992 *IEEE Spectrum*. p. 197, Courtesy Playboy Enterprises Inc./Magnum. p. 198, Courtesy *Entertainment Weekly*. p. 199, Courtesy *Sales & Marketing Management*.

Chapter 9
p. 219, Courtesy Better Homes and Gardens *Window and Wall Ideas*. p. 221, Courtesy *Raygun*. p. 224, Courtesy Will Hopkins, Hopkins/Baumann. p. 239, Courtesy *Wood*. p. 243, Courtesy *Print*: Designer, Robert Newman; Art Director, Andrew P. Kner; Associate Art Director, Michele L. Trombley. p. 245, Courtesy *Icon*.

Chapter 10
p. 250, Courtesy *Chronicle*. p. 251, Courtesy *Country Living Gardener*. p. 254, *Rolling Stone*, November 9, 1967, by Straight Arrow Publishers, Inc. 1967. All Rights Reserved. Reprinted by permission. p. 260, Courtesy *Prevention*. p. 261, Courtesy *Car Stereo Review*.

Chapter 11
p. 271, Courtesy *The Progressive*. p. 279, Reprinted from *The Saturday Evening Post* © 1963. p. 291, Courtesy *Brill's Content*.

Chapter 12

p. 302, Courtesy *Notorious*. p. 312, Courtesy *Redbook*. p. 316, © 1993 Time Inc.

Color Sections

Courtesy *Sierra*; Courtesy *Outdoor Life*; Reprinted by permission of *Men's Health* Magazine. Copyright 1997 Rodale Press, Inc. All rights reserved; Courtesy of Playboy Enterprise, Inc.; Reprinted by permission of *Ms.* Magazine. © 1997; Courtesy *Cosmopolitan*; Courtesy *Tricycle: The Buddhist Review*; Courtesy *Today's Christian Woman*; Courtesy *High Times*; Courtesy *Utne Reader*; Courtesy *Latina* Magazine. Photo by Albert Sanchez for *Latina* Magazine; Michael Nichols/NGS Image Collection; Courtesy *Better Homes and Gardens.*

Courtesy *Ladies Home Journal*/Photo by Robert Bean; Courtesy American Antiquarian Society; Tom Rockwell/The Curtis Publishing Company; *Vogue* Cover by Salvador Dali, June 1, 1939. Courtesy *Vogue*, © 1995; Courtesy *Harper's Bazaar*, © 1968 Time; David Deahl/*Life* Magazine © Time Inc.; Photo by Annie Leibovitz. From *Rolling Stone*, January 22, 1981 by Straight Arrow Publishers, Inc. 1981. All Rights Reserved. Reprinted by permission; *Vanity Fair* Cover by Milton Glaser, March 1983. Courtesy *Vanity Fair*, © 1983; Courtesy *I.D. Magazine.*

Literary Credits

p. 329, "The Ad-Free Magazine: It Just Feels Like Journalism" by Robin Morgan, an abridgement of her original speech, "Women and *Ms.* Making the Connections," 1992 Meredith Magazine Lectureship. Copyright © 1992 by Robin Morgan. By permission of Edite Kroll Literary Agency Inc. p. 333, "Redefining the American Family: The Magazine as History Book" by Jean LemMon. Reprinted by permission. p. 337, "The Alternative Magazine: Building Community" by Jay Walljasper. Reprinted by permission. p. 341, "The Evolving Magazine: Influence of Celebrity Journalism" by James A. Autry. Reprinted by permission.

INDEX

A

B

F

G

H

I

J

K

L

M

Q

R

S

T